ALAN J. FLETCHER

Drama, Performance, and Polity in Pre-Cromwellian Ireland

UNIVERSITY OF TORONTO PRESS
Toronto Buffalo

© University of Toronto Press Incorporated 2000
Toronto Buffalo
Printed in Canada

ISBN 0-8020-4377-1 (cloth)

Printed on acid-free paper

STUDIES IN EARLY ENGLISH DRAMA 6
General Editor: J.A.B. Somerset

Canadian Cataloguing in Publication Data

Fletcher, Alan J.
  Drama, performance and polity in pre-Cromwellian Ireland

  (Studies in early English drama ; 6)
  Includes bibliographical references and index.
  ISBN 0-8020-4377-1

  1. Theater – Ireland – History.   2. Irish drama – History and criticism.
  3. Theater – Ireland – Dublin – History.   I. Title.   II. Series.

  PN2602.D8F53 1999   792'.09415   C99-930368-6

University of Toronto Press acknowledges the financial assistance to its publishing
program of the Canada Council for the Arts and the Ontario Arts Council.

University of Toronto Press acknowledges the financial support for its publishing
activities of the Government of Canada through the Book Publishing Industry
Development Program (BPIDP).

Contents

vi   Contents

Illustrations

Preface

The earth for this study was tilled more years ago than I now care to remember, when as an undergraduate I attended Peter Meredith's dazzling lectures on medieval drama. Its seed was planted a few years later in 1980, by Alexandra F. Johnston. What they were both (unknowingly) responsible for outcrops in the following pages and I hope they will be pleased to acknowledge it. In due course when the material upon which this study has been largely based is published, it will be appropriate for me to recite a litany of thanks to the many others who have helped along the way by their contributions. However large or small, all these have been invaluable. In the meanwhile, I would like to mention by name three constant companions, each a *fer léiginn* in his own right, from whose advice and encouragement I have always benefited: Alan Harrison, whose enthusiasm for and singular understanding of native Gaelic traditions of performance in ancient and modern Ireland have ever been refreshing and informative; Seán Donnelly – what he may have forgotten about the history of the performing arts in Ireland throughout the centuries is probably more than I am ever likely to know; and Howard Clarke, whom I have repeatedly pestered with historical queries, yet never did I receive the reproach deserved for having encroached so much upon his time. Borrowing the words of Nowadays in the play, I might truthfully say of all these people that 'All þe bokys in þe worlde, yf þei hade be wndon, kowde not a cownselde ws bett.'

More hours than I also now care to count were spent gathering material for this study in archives throughout Ireland and abroad. Especially I would like to thank the many librarians and archivists in whose company those uncounted hours have been spent, and from whom I have received unflagging courtesy. Though I mention one by name here, the Dublin City Archivist, Mary Clark, who has probably sorted out more documents on my behalf than anyone else, I am well aware of numerous others waiting in the wings for their acknowledgment in a forthcoming volume. My thanks are due also to University College Dublin for granting the sabbatical leave without which the study could not have been completed; I am also indebted to Andrew MacKriell for so carefully setting the music and text of Appendix I, to Stephen Hannon for drawing the maps of Dublin, Kilkenny, and Limerick, to Elizabeth Baldwin for double-checking most of my transcriptions, and to Audrey Douglas for checking WRO, MS 865/502 for me. With unfailing good humour, Kristen Pederson and Barbara Porter of the University of Toronto Press have borne the weight of seeing this book into print, and Miriam Skey has been a meticulous copy-editor.

Confidence like that of one sixteenth-century author of a colophon to an Old Irish legal tract would be a fine thing: 'Finim don cairdirne so eir na teaglam .i. do nós adhbhuir na habhlainne' ('Here ends this tract, whose compilation has been like that of the ingredients for the host'; BL, MS Egerton 88, fol. 25v, col. b). While I would like to think that I have been as scrupulous, I am very conscious that evidence may yet come to light that may substantially modify the picture which this study draws. If the writing of it stimulates others to look for new evidence and to bring it forward, however, it will perhaps have served its turn.

Abbreviations

BL	London, British Library
Bodl.	Oxford, Bodleian Library
BR	Brussels, Bibliothèque royale Albert Ier
CAI	Cork, Cork Archives Institute
CARD	J.T. and R.M. Gilbert, eds. *Calendar of the Ancient Records of Dublin in the Possession of the Municipal Corporation*, 19 vols (Dublin, 1889–1944).
CHL	Derbyshire, Chatsworth House Library
CIH	D.A. Binchy, ed. *Corpus Iuris Hibernici*, 6 vols (Dublin, 1978).
co.	county
CUL	Cambridge, University Library
DCA	Dublin, Dublin City Archives
DCL	Dublin, Dublin City Library
DIL	*Contributions to a Dictionary of the Irish Language* (Dublin, 1913–76).
DNB	*Dictionary of National Biography*
EETS	Early English Text Society
EIS	William S. Clark, *The Early Irish Stage* (Oxford, 1955).
JCS	G.E. Bentley, *The Jacobean and Caroline Stage*, 7 vols (Oxford, 1941–68).
KAO	Maidstone, Kent Archives Office
KCA	Kilkenny, Kilkenny Corporation Archives
LPL	London, Lambeth Palace Library
MED	*Middle English Dictionary*, ed. H. Kurath et al. (Ann Arbor, Michigan, 1952–).
NA	Dublin, National Archives
NLI	Dublin, National Library of Ireland
NRO	Northampton, Northamptonshire Record Office
OED	*The Oxford English Dictionary (A New English Dictionary on Historical*

	Principles), 2nd ed., prepared by J.A. Simpson and E.S.C. Weiner (Oxford, 1989).
PRO	London, Public Record Office
PRONI	Belfast, Public Record Office of Northern Ireland
RCB	Dublin, Representative Church Body Library
RIA	Dublin, Royal Irish Academy
s.a.	*sub anno* (under year)
SCA	Sheffield, Sheffield City Archives
sd	stage direction
SPC	A. Gurr, *The Shakespearian Playing Companies* (Oxford, 1996).
STC	*A Short-Title Catalogue of Books Printed in England, Scotland and Ireland and of English Books Printed Abroad 1475–1640*, compiled by A.W. Pollard and G.R. Redgrave; revised and enlarged by W.A. Jackson and F.S. Ferguson, completed by Katharine F. Pantzer, 3 vols (Oxford, 1986).
TCD	Dublin, Trinity College
UUL	Uppsala, University Library
Wing	D. Wing, *Short-Title Catalogue of Books Printed in England, Scotland, Ireland, Wales, and British America and of English Books Printed in Other Countries*, 2nd ed., 3 vols (New York, 1972–88).
WRO	Trowbridge, Wiltshire Record Office

The following standard British palaeographical and codicological abbreviations are used:

MS	manuscript
fol.	folio
mb.	membrane
sig.	signature

A Note on Texts, Transcriptions, and Terminology

Because many of the documents on which this study depends are either unpublished or not conveniently available in print, it has been necessary to quote substantially from them in the course of the discussion. Quotations in Irish, French, and Latin are followed by English translations; quotations in English are selectively glossed whenever obscure lexis might hinder the reader.

Almost all source documents quoted in the main body of the discussion (and some quoted in the notes) have either been transcribed for the first time or, even if a printed edition already exists, afresh. In latter cases, as well as citing the shelfmark of the manuscript transcribed, the notes refer to a printed edition of the corresponding passage. A foliation, pagination, or numeration in square brackets has been allocated to any manuscript whose leaves or membranes have either not, or only very inadequately, been counted.

Principles of transcription are conservative. Manuscript lineation is not observed, but line breaks in some early printed texts are indicated by a vertical bar, |, inserted at the point at which the line break occurs. A diagonal stroke, /, is used to mark ends of lines of English verse (these cases should be readily distinguishable from those where the stroke is used to transcribe a virgule or some other punctuation mark). No attempt has been made to alter original punctuation, word division, capitalization or spelling, though most abbreviations have been silently expanded. Abbreviations for sums of money (ie, 'li,' 's,' 'd') have been retained but lowered to the line when superscript in the manuscript. Very occasionally, marks of ambiguous orthographical value accompany letters. When they do, their presence is signalled by a single inverted comma set after the letter to which they are attached. Abbreviations in English, Irish, or French with counterparts in the standard Latin repertoire are expanded, as appropriate, according to their usual Latin orthographic values. A few abbreviations peculiar to Irish are expanded according to their traditional Irish orthographic values where these are unambiguous. In cases when their orthographic values may vary according to the grammatical status of the word they accompany or according to the scribe's preferred spelling if he ever writes the letter or letters for which they stand out in full, then they are accordingly expanded. A superscript dot over a consonant indicating lenition is expanded as an h, except in a few names of texts where it is retained (for example, *Míadślechta*). The initial letter of a word between two dots has been expanded to the word's full form and the dots omitted (for example, *ní .h.* to *ní annsa*), always according to the scribe's preferred spelling when writing the word in full, if ascertainable. Abbreviations of a few common words have been left intact, including, for example, abbreviations for measures and sums. Some other common abbreviations are also left unaltered, like the ampersand. Left intact in Irish texts are the following 'Tironian' signs: 7 (= Latin *et*, Irish *ocus*); .i. (= Latin *id est*, Irish *ed ón*); ɬ (= Latin *vel*, Irish *nó/no/ná*, according to function). Superscript letters have been lowered to the line except when they occur with numerals (for example, vij[th]). 'Xp' and 'xp,' the Greek opening letters of the *nomen sacrum*, have been transliterated as 'Chr' or 'chr' when occurring in Latin documents, and as 'Cr' or 'cr' in vernacular ones. 'I' and 'J' have been uniformly transcribed as 'I,' and 'ff' (for 'F') retained. A cedilla on ȩ, found occasionally in early texts to mark an æ vowel ligature, is retained. The hair line often placed on i to distinguish it from neighbouring minims is only indicated as í when the vowel is historically long; otherwise no length marks are supplied other than those indicated in the manuscript.

Superscript circles, ° °, enclose text that has been subsequently added in a hand (or hands) other than that of the main entry. Caret marks are indicated by the sign ∧, followed by the matter for insertion, set in its appropriate place in the text. If this matter was originally written interlinearly above the line, it is enclosed in half square brackets thus, ⌈ ⌉, and if below the line, in half square brackets, ⌊ ⌋. In quotations from source texts, full square brackets, [ ], enclose scribal deletions (in translations they enclose words not actually present in the source text but supplied to complete modern sense). Within square brackets, dots (to a maximum of three) estimate the number of characters deleted and now illegible. Angle brackets, < >, enclose conjectural restorations of text illegible for some other reason or lost on account of manuscript damage. Within angle brackets, dots (to a maximum of three) estimate the number of characters illegible or lost. Places where space has been left for words to be added later are indicated as '*(blank)*'. Rubricated words or letters, *litterae notabiliores*, letters written in display script or otherwise somehow distinguished from their surroundings, are printed bold. Otiose flourishes and line-fillers have been ignored.

Curled brackets, { }, enclose brief editorial explanations, normally of obscure lexis, or suggested emendations of simple scribal lapses like omission of a mark of abbreviation. They are introduced into quotations immediately following the text to which they pertain. Any longer explanations considered necessary have been re-legated to the notes. Folio, page, or membrane changes within a document are sig-nalled by an upright, |. Three dots within or immediately following a quotation indicate editorial omission of matter respectively from either within or immediately following that quotation. In some quotations from accounts in which each entry occupies a line or lines of its own, three dots immediately above or below an entry indicate other entries in the manuscript immediately above or below the one quoted.

Documents extant in more than one copy are not normally collated unless col-lation is of substantive interest for the discussion. Appendix I, a collated and emended text of the Dublin *Visitatio Sepulcri* play, has its own editorial policy which should be consulted separately.

This study uses three sets of terms conventional to Irish historiography to de-note three ethnic traditions in Ireland. Each had distinctive allegiances and politi-cal outlooks. The 'Old English' (used interchangeably here with 'Anglo-Irish') were those English who settled in Ireland following the Norman conquest of 1169. Their confessional sympathies were catholic, yet they were also traditionally loyal to the English throne, a combination requiring skilful negotiation in the years fol-lowing the Reformation. 'New English' is used of the protestant planters and administrators who entered Ireland in the wake of the Reformation. The native people of Ireland, indigenous before either of these immigrant groups arrived, are referred to as the Gaelic Irish.

DRAMA, PERFORMANCE, AND POLITY
IN PRE-CROMWELLIAN IRELAND

Prologue: Insubstantial Pageants

'But such as neither of themselves can sing, / Nor yet are sung of others for reward, / Die in obscure oblivion.'
Edmund Spenser, The Ruines of Time[1]

Ask that elusive being, the average man in the street, if he can name a famous historical playwright and theatre, and you may get the answer 'Shakespeare' (who has never been lost from sight, whether people have actually read or seen his plays or not) and perhaps 'The Globe' (especially since the latter has been reincarnated into popular consciousness recently on London's South Bank). Ask the same question of that even more elusive being, the average Irishman, and he may come up with 'Shakespeare,' or with 'Shaw,' 'Wilde,' 'Yeats,' 'Synge,' 'O'Casey,' or any of the other names of the Irish dramatic pantheon. And while he has probably heard mention of the Globe, it is likely to be the Abbey, Ireland's national theatre, that he will cite in answer to the second part of the question.

In so replying, he would have been displaying faithfully enough the contents of his colonial inheritance, weighing Shakespeare and more recent Irish playwrights in a similar set of scales, and being aware of the prestige of the Abbey, the self-appointed arbiter of canonical Irish theatre, as well as, and perhaps before, the prestige of any playhouse across the water in England. It would be a far rarer Irish bird who replied to your question with the name of Dublin's first playhouse following the Restoration, the Smock Alley Theatre, despite the successes of a modern theatre company in keeping this old name alive. And only the specialist is likely to have any space in the lumber room at the back of his mind for Ireland's first purpose-built public theatre in Werburgh Street, Dublin, which put on plays from the latter part of the 1630s. Yet Werburgh Street is where this study ends, merely a final point in a long history of drama and the performing arts that was already well in place before the theatre there opened its doors to the public.

Not just our putative average Irishman, then, but academic theatre historians too, while they may not be technically unaware of how far back traditions of performance in Ireland reach, have generally become disconnected from what was happening in the pre-Cromwellian era. There are several reasons why this should have come about. One of the most obvious is the lack of sources. It is indisputably true that over the years Irish records have suffered from a coalition of misfortunes. Most notorious was the fire at the Four Courts in Dublin in 1922, which made away with vast quantities of archival material, including one of the plays examined in chapter 2 of this study. And this was but one of the more spectacular cases of loss. Some records have suffered less famously, but no less detrimentally, from neglect, a neglect that in certain archives went unchecked until only very recently. Indeed, apart from the grounds of document loss, it seems otherwise difficult to explain why absolutely nothing is heard from some of the dramatists who settled in Ireland during the period under review. John Long, for example, who authored plays in Bath, came to Ireland as primate of Armagh in 1584; and some time in the early years of the next century, Robert Daborne, playwright and director, took holy orders, eventually becoming chancellor of Waterford, then dean of Lismore in 1621. After these men had entered the service of the church in Ireland, the rest seems to have been silence.[2] Yet although document destruction and loss have been a constant impediment to understanding, more in fact has survived than has been realized, both in terms of antiquarian transcriptions of missing originals and in manuscript sources never before examined.

Another substantial reason why some theatre historians have given the early history of performance in Ireland such comparatively short shrift is that many pertinent sources have been a closed book to them. Their lack of familiarity with Irish, and Irish in its earlier phases at that, has taken its toll. One of the important tasks of this study has therefore been to call attention to this rich body of evidence which hitherto has tended to remain the strict preserve of the Celticist.

While loss of sources, insufficient research, and lack of linguistic skill rank foremost among the reasons for the atrophy in understanding, subtler reasons have also been contributory. If we were to put the man in the street back in the dock again and this time quiz him about what he thought the word 'drama' meant, one of his answers might well be, 'What you see in a theatre.' His answer would be a fair one, and in it he would show that he had something in common with certain academic theatre historians for whom there must be plays (of however many acts), play texts, props or no props, theatrical trumpery and devices, or none at all, a proscenium, or no proscenium – in short, for whom all such paradigmatic variables are tacitly assumed to constitute the familiar syntax of regular theatre. Remove enough of those variables, those present (or absent) conventions, and drama itself vanishes. Yet when those conventions are sought for in an earlier age, disappointingly few may come to light, and not only for the reasons already rehearsed, but also for the fact that earlier cultures were often more oral than literate, and consequently less liable to leave behind tangible traces.

But apart from all this, it is also unduly limiting and inappropriate to define drama simply in terms of the outward and visible signs of classical theatre, for this may be to mistake the substance for its shadow. The definition of drama serving this study will include not only theatricality, that is, the sort of phenomenon spoken of above, where the subject actor is normally inscribed in a symbolic structure and code, and his or her identity subordinated to the bodying forth of some given role in a given narrative; it will also include performance, where subservience to narrative is not necessarily an issue, and where no intelligible meaning need be presented at all. While theatricality is a signifying practice, performance may simply draw attention to the signs that a signifying practice manipulates. Performance may highlight the nuts and bolts out of which theatricality, to be sure, may be constructed, but which on their own account may have little or no decidable meaning. 'Drama' for the purposes of this study, then, is seen as a continuum in which theatricality and performance are subsumed.[3]

The widening of drama's catchment area in this way allows the study to include varieties of performance that some theatre historians have felt needed to be discussed, but about which they have often sounded sheepishly apologetic when they did.[4] Such performances may be included here, conversely, without a qualm. For example, when Sir Henry Sidney entered Limerick in 1567, he came in his formal role as Lord Deputy of Ireland. The ceremonial stage on which he played out this role, this drama of his performative self, was Limerick city, not a theatre in any conventional sense but a place whose identity its inhabitants doubtless routinely took for granted. It was not normally necessary for them to be consciously aware of what Limerick *meant*. But for the duration of the civic entry the city became an existential space, its quotidian reality being temporarily exchanged for an identity that was theatrical. For a while Limerick too became a role that could be performed. Thus what Sidney did there, and the attendant pageantry prepared to greet his coming, become matters of interest which fall within this study's terms of reference. To take an example even further down the path away from theatricality conceived in a narrow modern sense and towards pure performance, those early Irish *drúith* ('buffoons') who twisted and contorted their faces in public to earn a living, making a performance event out of their bodies and bodily parts, also become eligible for attention. Their performances did not, as far as we know, serve the ends of any intelligible theatrical narrative but were offered for enjoyment in and of themselves. Thus they merit attention, falling as they do within the dramatic continuum where performance and theatricality associate. In the pages that follow much will therefore be said about performers for whom dramatic ability, in the modern sense, was just one in a range of skills that they would have to master. Once more radical criteria of definition are adopted, then drama and the performing arts in pre-Cromwellian Ireland ought no longer to seem quite the desert, relieved by the occasional oasis, that they have hitherto in critical writing.

The scheme of the study, distributed over seven chapters, is largely determined by the sources that have survived, and since source survival has been a random affair, there is some risk that randomness might afflict the shape of the discussion. To an extent this is unavoidable. In being obliged to follow where the sources lead, we may sometimes find ourselves on a meandering path. But I have tried to limit any appearance of randomness by binding the study together with chronological, geographical, and thematic threads, and by endeavouring always to bear in mind certain key issues: who were the performers? what did they do and in what circumstances? whenever actual play texts survive, how were these plays presented? and what function had drama and the performing arts in the larger social process? These questions may help to lend a potentially centrifugal discussion a centre of gravity.

The first chapter investigates the evidence from Gaelic Ireland and includes some of the earliest material with which this study deals. European historians of drama and the performing arts have not generally appreciated how early some of the Gaelic evidence is – it begins substantially in the seventh century – and it is also comparatively detailed. It is broadly true to say that the Gaelic material affords very early snapshots of varieties of performance which may be seen elsewhere in Europe but only at a much later date. Also the taxonomy of medieval Irish performers and performance attested in the Gaelic evidence is extraordinarily rich and detailed. Important as the *drúith* were, both in Ireland and abroad,[5] many other names are used to identify the professional entertainers who inhabit early Gaelic sources and it will be informative to attempt to uncover their historical basis. The field of Gaelic texts is a wide one, document losses notwithstanding, and the texts themselves belong to diverse genres of the sort that historians have traditionally been very wary of: homilies, saints' lives, sagas, poetry, and the like. The social fabric of Gaelic Ireland is seldom accessed through the sorts of documents that have been the historian's usual refuge, like books of accounts, court proceedings, quitclaims, deeds, or leases. Even those Gaelic documents that purport to have a purchase on historical reality, the various sets of Irish annals, for example, may weave into their historical narrative the legendary stuff of saga without distinguishing, or having indeed ever been capable of distinguishing, where the actual ended and the fabulous began. Similarly, saints whom we know to have been historical are shown in their Lives to have had regular commerce with a supernatural world in which we are no longer inclined to believe, a world ever likely to interrupt reality as we know it and rewrite its norms. Even the remarkable corpus of early Irish law has also been treated with some scepticism, though recently some scholars have tended to counter the prevailing distrustful view with vindications of the laws' historicity.[6]

Although the nature of the Gaelic evidence poses problems, therefore, these may not be insuperable. We can take heart from a simple reflection. Even the most overtly fantastical of texts is not so utterly fantastical that it does not connect at some point with the real world; if it did not, it would not even be fantastical but would collapse utterly into meaninglessness. So it is entirely plausible that prior historical realities may underlie even the most apparently unpromising of texts. An episode concerning professional entertainers in a saga narrative, for example, may point in the direction of what such people really did, just as their appearance in saints' lives, irrespective of the miraculous contexts in which they usually appear there, may be similarly suggestive. Often the last thing on the agenda of the Gaelic texts in which performing artists appear was plain historical reportage, and performing artists and their ways are not likely to be reported neutrally in literature of this sort. But by networking texts that might otherwise be discounted as fictions with ones whose purchase on historical reality is less readily contradicted, a reasonable hypothesis can be ventured about the reality which must lie somewhere behind representation.

What many Gaelic texts are liable to witness to, therefore, is historical performers or performances skewed in some way to fit the texts' larger interests. The skew in itself may have historical interest in being in turn the product of history: the motives driving the way a writer represented or invented reality may also be informative to identify, in that they may tell us much not only about the writer but also about how others sharing his social background may have viewed what was represented. Thus two related but potentially separable things are to be encountered in these texts, reality and its representation. Both may be of interest to the theatre historian. The proposed networking of sources may offer a useful means of distinguishing the two. Concrete illustrations of networking in action will appear in chapter 1.

The remaining chapters need relatively little explanation of how the sources upon which they depend have been used to answer the key questions of this study. Moving on from the wide geographical and chronological sweep of chapter 1, chapter 2 will focus more narrowly on medieval Dublin, from where two actual play texts have survived, plus much other external evidence of early drama and performance. This chapter will also lay the foundation for the investigation of civic drama that largely preoccupies chapter 3, which shifts to Dublin in the Renaissance. A point of contrast and comparison is provided in chapter 4, for though it remains in the province of Leinster, it passes from Dublin to sixteenth-century Kilkenny. The investigation of the Kilkenny evidence will also extend into the seventeenth century. Chapter 5, the shortest of the seven, is chronologically similar, for it covers sixteenth- and seventeenth-century manifestations of civic entries designed to fête visiting dignitaries, and Kilkenny will feature here once again. However, the chapter will also travel outside Leinster and into the province of Munster to take account of similar entries organized there. Fundamental aspects of the patronage of drama and the performing arts in Ireland are dealt with in chapter 6. Like the material investigated in chapter 1, that on which chapter 6 rests is nationwide, deriving from each of the four Irish provinces, and some of the themes from chapter 1 here find their extension into the sixteenth and seventeenth century. The seventh and final chapter returns once more to Dublin at the close of the period under review. This chapter reconsiders the evidence for the Werburgh Street Theatre, the plays put on there, its players, and its playwrights. In finishing here, the movement of the study, if it may be characterized in general terms, will be seen to have been from one end of the dramatic spectrum to the other, from performance towards theatricality.

In sum, the essential aim of this study will be to provide a survey, not to argue any single thesis, and to try to rescue from obscure oblivion some awareness of what has gone, by comparing in a way not attempted before the evidence from all the cultural factions that jostled for place on the island of Ireland. The net result, if it cannot finally escape accusations of eclecticism, nevertheless testifies in that very eclecticism, I believe, to the sheer vitality of drama and the performing arts in pre-Cromwellian Ireland that lacunae in the evidence, abetted by unwitting academic conspiracies, have done so much to obscure.

1

Drama and the Performing Arts of Gaelic Ireland

A NATIVE GAELIC TRADITION?

It is fair to say that the general opinion on whether Ireland ever had a native dramatic tradition is slowly shifting. Historians of Irish culture from the eighteenth to the nineteenth century had categorical views on the matter: 'Though many Irish tales are highly dramatic, the Irish never developed Drama in the proper sense of the word,' said P.W. Joyce, and he went on to assert that 'There was no Irish theatre, and no open-air acting.'[1] In some quarters, views as stringent and unequivocal as Joyce's still command respect.[2]

By the 1950s, however, the prevailing orthodoxy began to be gently questioned. William S. Clark, for example, drew attention to the kinds of social context in which 'tentative dramatic elements' might be reasonably expected,[3] and more recently, some critics have been inclined to deduce the existence of early native Irish varieties of drama either from what they think may be its reflex in later folk traditions or, more persuasively, from their comparison of what such folk traditions seem to imply about their origins with evidence derived from early documents. In the first category, Máire MacNeill has conjectured an ancient seasonal drama behind the August Lughnasa festivals,[4] while in the second, Alan Harrison's investigation of the *crosáin* and their buffoonery has presented them as a species of actor practising characteristic roles and skills.[5] This chapter, which will begin by drawing mainly on sources from the Old to the end of the Classical Irish periods (that is, from the seventh century to about 1650), will seek to challenge the traditional view further, and to suggest that a native Irish dramatic tradition did indeed exist, as a phase or aspect of a greater continuum which constituted the Gaelic performing arts. The chapter will also seek to show how early Gaelic society hosted activity falling well within the scope of the working definition proposed for drama in the Introduction, and then proceed to review corroborative evidence for that activity as it appears in a substantial corpus of non-native sources. The task ahead, then, is to make the dry bones live once more: how are we to gain access to any such Gaelic drama, or failing that and at the very least, in what contexts may we reasonably assume that it flourished?

'Áes cíuil ocus airfidid oilcena' ('Musicians and minstrels besides')

Uraicecht Becc (the 'Small Primer')[6]

Deemed worthy of inclusion in the miscellany of maxims, sage counsels, and assorted bits of wisdom that its putative author, King Cormac Mac Airt, assembled for his son, Cairbre, was a set of instructions about how to run an alehouse properly.[7] The house was to be well lit, everyone in it had to be cheerful, and its stewards needed to be attentive and to serve generously. But it was not merely to be a watering hole. There also had to be:

mesrugud senma sceluccad ngoirit ... taoi fri comhod
coicerta {*read* cocetla} mbindi.[8]

[Music in moderation, short story-telling ...
silence during a recital(?), harmonious choruses.]

Entertainment of wider girth than plain belly cheer ought to be found there. Cormac's instructions suggest one of the trails worth following in the search for drama and its affiliated performing arts: accounts of festive gatherings like fairs and feasts need winnowing for mention of any entertainment that was put on at them. When the purveyors of that entertainment are named as belonging to a particular *class* of entertainer, such as the *fuirseóir* ('clown') or the *clesamnach* ('juggler,' 'trickster,' 'acrobat'), for example, then by networking evidence from various sources it should be possible to establish a profile of the sort of performance that might be expected from anyone who belonged to that class. This fuller profile should help to elucidate the likely meaning of writers who for the most part were content simply to mention the class to which an entertainer belonged without saying anything further about what he or she did. Presumably, elaboration was unnecessary when they could rely on their original readers' familiarity with the diverse actual entertainments that came within an entertainer's purview. That familiarity was enough to flesh out the briefest mention with meaning. To make a study such as this in any exhaustive way would, of course, be a vast undertaking, and so what this chapter proposes is a representative survey. It will take as its point of departure the famous diagram of the *Tech Midchúarda*, the medieval banqueting hall of Tara, pictured in its earliest version in the Book of Leinster (see fig. 1).[9] Many groups on this ground plan can be

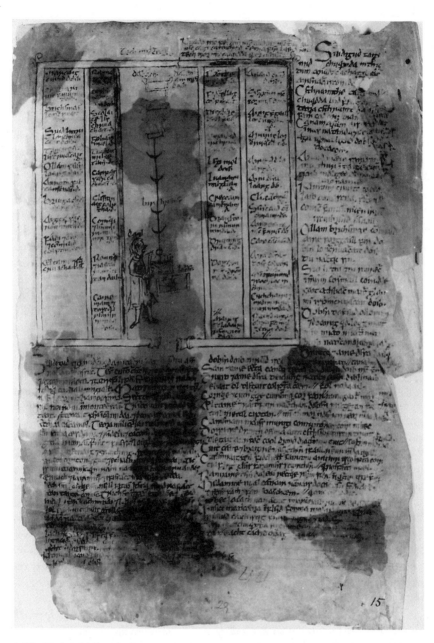

1 The Tech Midchúarda diagram, TCD, MS 1339 (H.2.18; Book of Leinster), fol. 15, cols a–b.

classified as entertainers of one kind or another, and for our present purposes it will be important to understand as nearly as possible how they went about their work. In order to do this, the activities must also be taken into account of some of their performing colleagues who are not in fact mentioned on the plan, entertainers of still other classes with whom those in Tara's banqueting hall consorted closely in other sources. In this way, the question of a native Gaelic tradition in drama, and of the sort of drama it is likely to have been, can at least begin to be broached.

The Book of Leinster plan, copied around the mid-twelfth century, is a pre-scription of seating etiquette on occasions of feasting (see fig. 1). The different orders of society are allocated set positions in the hall and served with meat portions answering their status. Thus, for example, the élite *ollam filed* ('professor of poetry') feasts on thigh steaks, while the *mairig* (?'tramps') and *cladiri* ('vagabonds') must content themselves with a fatty portion, the 'thick part of the shoulder' (*remur nimda*). About ten of the social orders are members of the entertainer class most likely to create a festive context conducive to dramatic activity: the *cruittiri* ('harpers'), who sit in the far-left rank near the top between the *marcaig* ('horse-men') and the *brithemain* ('judges'); the *cuslennaig* ('players on the *cuisle*'; that is, a form of pipe), who sit near the top of the near-left rank, between the *rannairi* ('dis-pensers,' 'carvers') and the *scolaige* ('scholars'); the *clessanaig* ('jugglers,' 'tricksters,' 'acrobats'), who sit further down the same rank next to the *cornairi* ('horn-blowers,' 'trumpeters') and the *bunniri* ('players on the *buinne*,' that is, another form of pipe); the *bragetori* ('farters'), who sit far down the near-right rank, next to the *druth ríg* ('royal jester,' 'king's jester'); the *senchaid* ('reciter of lore'),[10] who sits about mid-way down the far-right rank; and lastly, in the same rank a little further down from him, the *maccfurmid* ('poet of the sixth grade') and *fochloc* ('poet of the lowest grade').[11] The seating plan discloses its compiler's particular view of the relative sta-tus of the entertainer classes and of the nature of the association between them. This view was not, moreover, merely idiosyncratic, for parallels to it can be found in other texts.[12] For the most part there is an evident correspondence between what cuts of meat particular groups may expect, according to where each group sits, so that, for example, harpers, sitting second from the top in the far-left rank and 'champions' (*seguinni*), sitting second from the top in the far-right rank will receive 'pork back' (*muc formuin*), and players on the *cuisle*, sitting second from the top in the near-left rank, and 'chess players' (*fidchellaig*),[13] sitting second from the top in the near-right rank, will both have 'shank' (*colptha*). There is a clear tendency for the fat-eating lower social orders to sit either at the bottom or towards the bottom of the ranks.

The first of the entertainer groups, the *cruittiri*, are out in a class of their own.[14] Sitting near the top on the far left and eating, if not quite the choicest of cuts, by no means the lowliest, they keep no company with entertainers of any other order.

No doubt their placing and fare were meant to reflect the pre-eminence traditionally accorded to harpers in the Gaelic musical hierarchy; as one Old Irish maxim
uncompromisingly put it, *cáid cac ceól co cruit* ('all music is pure until compared with
the harp').[15] By the sixteenth and seventeenth centuries, pre-eminence was turning
into poetic apotheosis, as named harpers were increasingly allowed to share the
limelight with chieftains as appropriate subjects for praise poetry.[16] The privileges
of harpers were codified repeatedly throughout almost the entire period under
review here. As early as *c* 800, along with young landowners, doctors, and queens,
harpers were permitted the distinction of being allowed to keep lap dogs.[17] At the
latter end of the period, in Meredith Hanmer's notes (which he compiled probably
a few years before his death in 1604), harpers were assigned the udders of the animal to eat, a portion evidently considered worthy of their profession.[18] Yet the view
that their instrument was of exalted status, a view that one might suspect professional harpers would have actively encouraged,[19] did not prevent the harp from
becoming associated with performers of lower social standing in other contexts
where its idealization was less of an issue. Annalistic literature, a genre perhaps less
preoccupied than some with the burden of singing the harp's praises, provides good
examples of such association. A story in the *Cath Almaine* (the 'Battle of Almu'),
much of which was probably composed during the tenth century,[20] but narrating
events held by the annals to have taken place in the year 721, illustrates this in the
course of relating how taste in entertainment may be diagnostic of morals, a ven-
erable biblical theme.[21] The story tells how Fergal mac Máele Dúin, king of Tara,
visited his two sons secretly during the course of the same night to test them both.
The elder son was known by the company he kept, as was the younger:

Rá frithaighid iad iar ttain, 7 ra báil don athair andearbadh maille, 7 tainicc a ndeireadh
oidhche do cum an taighe iraibhe an mac bá sine, 7 ra bhaoí acc cloisteacht frisin teach sin;
as dígáir tra, salach ra bhás san taigh sin. Rá bhattur fuirseoiri, 7 cainteadha 7 eachlacha, 7
oblóiri, 7 bachlaigh ag beceadhoig, 7 acc buireadhaigh ann. Dream ag ól, 7 dream na ccodladh,
7 dream og sgeathraigh, dream occ cusleannaigh, dream oc featchuisigh. Timpanaigh 7
crvithiri og seanmaimh; dream og imarbhaghadh 7 oc reasbagaibh. Ad chuala Feargal amlaidh
sin iad. agas tainig iar sin dinnsoiccidh an taighe dherrid i rabha an mac assóo, 7 rá bhaoi ag
cloisteacht risan teach sin, 7 ní chuala nach ní ann acht lp. 6l acht atluccadh bvidhe do Dhia
gach ní fuarattar, 7 cruitireacht ciúin bind, 7 duana molta an coimdheadh ga ngabail, ...[22]

[Then they were entertained; and their father wished to test them both, so he came in the
last part of the night to the house in which the elder son was staying, and he was listening
at that house: it was very foul indeed inside that house. There were clowns and satirists and
whores and jugglers and oafs, roaring and bellowing there. Some were drinking, some sleep-
ing, some vomiting, some piping, some whistling. Drummers and harpers were playing; a

group was boasting and arguing. Fergal heard them thus. And he came then to visit the secluded house where the younger son was staying; and he listened at that house, and he heard nothing there but thanksgiving to God for all that they had received, and sweet, quiet harp playing, and the singing of praise songs to the Lord.]

Although a qualitative difference in its playing distinguishes the harping in the two households, it is nevertheless interesting that there is room for harping in both. Harpers contributed to the strenuous, giddy atmosphere in the house of the elder son, just as harp music, whose acoustic (and moral) contrast is implied in the adjective *binn* ('sweet'), was heard in the more demure house of the younger son as an accompaniment to pious songs. The possibility of association in practice, regardless of any dissociation in theory, between harpers and other kinds of entertainers also seems implied in a passage in the Annals of Clonmacnoise. The Irish original of the translated annals does not survive, but one imagines some form of the word *cruittiri* lying behind the 'harpers' mentioned in this excerpt for the year 1351, in which William Ó Ceallaigh invited a plentiful assortment of entertainers to his house at Christmastide:

William o'Donogh Moyneagh o'Kelly, Inuited all ye Irish Poets, Brehons, bards, harpers, gamesters or Common kearoghs {< *cerrbhach*, 'gambler'}, Iesters, & others of theire kind of Ireland to his house upon Christmas this yeare. where euery one of them was well vsed, Dureing Christmas holy Dayes, & gaue [them] contentment to each of them at the tyme of theire Departure, soe as euery one was well pleased, and extolled William for his bounty.[23]

Here harpers jostle shoulder to shoulder in the same sentence between 'bards' and 'Gamesters or common kearoghs' (for some, these latter were a particularly detested class, as we shall later see), but all equally enjoy the seasonal goodwill of Ó Ceallaigh and his Christmas hospitality. In some sources, the *cruitire* even left his exclusive province of harping to tell stories, thus entering the province of the *scélaige* ('storyteller').[24] Such is the role of *scelaigi is chruittiri* ('storyteller and harper') that Gilla Mo Dutu Úa Casaide, author in 1147 of the poem *Ádam óenathair na ndóene* ('Adam the first father of the folk'), conceived for the legendary hero Feidlimid.[25] And in the *Vita Sancti Ciarani de Saigir*, composed between *c* 1185 and *c* 1230, we hear not only of the soporific qualities of harpers' music, but also of the narratives that the harpers of King Oengus performed before him: 'acta heroum in carmine cytarizantes cantabant' ('they used to sing to the sound of the harp of the deeds of heroes in poetic measures').[26] A final example, though this time from the sixteenth century, illustrating how harping may have been considered as simply one ingredient among many which together created a convivial atmosphere, is found in the famous picture of a Gaelic chieftain banqueting in John Derricke's *The Image of Irelande* (see fig. 2). Here, allowances have to be made for a picture which betrays a certain lack

2 A Gaelic chieftain's feast, from John Derricke, *The Image of Irelande.*

of sympathy for and understanding of Gaelic culture,[27] as well as for artistic licence which, *Guernica*-like, may cause to be depicted simultaneously events which originally may have occurred separately. Nevertheless the artist, whether or not he was aware of the connotations of musical pre-eminence distinguishing the harper's art in Gaelic society, for all practical purposes presented him as a member of the generic entertainer class. Immediately behind the harper and the character with arms spread wide whom the harper seems to be accompanying are two fellows whose hitched-up shirts and dropped breeches show off their bare backsides to the banqueters. The explanation of what these men were up to is not necessarily so readily apparent as it may at first sight seem. A scene of public defecation, if that is what it was really intended to be, would certainly have handed Derricke's English readers a convenient epitome of Irish lack of couth. During this period they were being fed a diet of (largely negative) Irish stereotypes, and a particularly pungent one may have seemed reassuringly familiar. That absent civility, so often regretted in the Irish by the sixteenth-century English authors who wrote for this market, would thus have been graphically illustrated in one of its grosser aspects, and Irish harping would have been tainted by association. But the men in Derricke's woodcut do not adopt the hunkering position described by Captain Josias Bodley only a few years later, nor is excrement depicted.[28] If xenophobia haunts the woodcut, it may be that it does so rather more subtly. It is not utterly beyond possibility that the bare-bottomed posturers are meant to be entertainers, this time dealers in low humour, of whom gentle society should doubtless not approve, but for rather different reasons: 'Aspice spectator sic me docuere parentes' ('See, viewer, thus did my parents teach me') declares one of them in a self-justification that becomes a self-discommendation.[29]

Music, a likely part of any festive occasion as in King Cormac's alehouse, had its various practitioners, and of these the *Tech Midchúarda* plan shows a small sample. Players on the *cuisle* are required to sit towards the top of the near-left rank and then lower down the same rank, horn-blowers (*cornairi*) and *buinne*-players (*bunniri*). These two groups are paired together, possibly suggesting that their function and status were perceived to be similar.[30] Whether or not any social separateness was implied by the seating arrangements on the plan, *cuisle*-players often associated closely at least with *cornairi* (*bunniri* are less commonly heard of) in other sources,[31] and indeed, *cuisleandchu 7 cornaire 7 cruitire* ('*cuisle*-players, and horn-blowers and harpers') were all three in association in one annal entry.[32] Whatever their theoretical social distinctions, several different kinds of musicians, including the prestigious harper, were lumped together as purveyors of the same basic commodity, minstrelsy, in an eleventh-century poem composed about the fair of Carmun, a fair held every third year on the August Lughnasa festival:

IS iat a áda olla. stuic. cruitti. cuirn chroes tolla‽
cúisig timpaig. cen tríamna. filid 7 fenchlíara.[33]

[These are [the Fair's] great prerequisites: trumpets, harps, hollow-throated horns,
pipers, tireless players on the *timpán*, poets, and sprawling bands of musicians.]

A little later, the list continues with:

Pipai. fidli. fir cengail. cnamfhir 7 cuslennaig‽
sluág etig engach egair. béccaig 7 buridaig.[34]

[Pipes, rebecs, gleemen, bones-players and *cuisle*-players,
an ugly, noisy, profane crowd, roarers, and bellowers.]

Furthermore, the music mentioned here seems to provide an accompaniment to others
who, from their description ('an ugly, noisy, profane crowd, roarers, and bellowers'), were scarcely on this occasion musicians themselves, but who may have been
performers of another type, just as the performers on the Derricke woodcut may
have been exhibiting various performance skills: certain of the groups on the *Tech
Midchúarda* plan, in view of the behaviour which other literary sources attribute to
them, may have been the kind to have comprised these roaring boys loose at the fair
of Carmun, and it is through them that we come the closest we can to traces of a
variety of Gaelic performing art that could appropriately be called dramatic.

The *druth ríg* ('royal jester,' 'king's jester') and the *braigetori* ('farters') sit side by
side at the lower end of the near-right rank. A third group, the *clessanaig* ('jugglers,'
'tricksters,' 'acrobats'), is set next to the horn-blowers and *buinne*-players in the
near-left rank. These three groups of entertainers, *druth ríg, braigetori,* and *clessanaig,*
though here kept distinct (*druth ríg* and *braigetori* on one side and *clessanaig* on the
other), practised arts which sometimes overlapped, and of the three, it is the profession of the *drúth* that documents most commonly mention and amply describe.

The *drúth*, a professional jester or buffoon,[35] seems in some of his incarnations
to have enjoyed a heightened status, as indeed on the *Tech Midchúarda* plan where
he is a *druth ríg*, a royal or a king's jester.[36] But even the position of *druth ríg* speaks
more of a general prizing of the *drúth*'s skills and of his institutional entrenchment
within Gaelic culture than it does of his actual social standing.[37] According to the
early Irish laws, this was in fact very low. The laws mention the *drúth* many times,
indirectly testifying once more to his indispensability, but always fixing him well
down the social scale. Certainly, he was to be properly maintained, and failure to
do so might be punishable by a fine adjusted to suit the circumstances. The Old Irish

law text *Di Chetharslicht Athgabála* ('On the Four Divisions of Distraint') framed the following legislation:

Cuic bai smacht nemdenma gaire in druith co norbo 7 co nobloirecht. is aire is bec in smacht[38]

[Five cows is the fine for neglecting to provide for the maintenance of a *drúth* with land and with juggling ability, [and his having these] is the reason why the fine is small.]

Nevertheless, by virtue of his profession he could expect no *díre* ('honour-price') for any injury that he suffered (the *díre* was a monetary valuation of a person's status calculated according to his circumstances at any given time).[39] The Old Irish law tract *Míadslechta* ('Rank Sections') says:

Reimm dno .i. fuirseoir ł druth nach fer dobeir remmad fo corp 7 a enech ni dligh dire uair teit asa richt ar belvib sluagh 7 sochaidhe// [40]

[A contortionist, then, that is, a clown, or a *drúth*; any man who brings contortion upon his body and his face is not entitled to an honour-price, because he goes out of his shape in front of crowds and hosts.]

The *drúth*'s entitlement to receive a *díre* was extrinsic and solely dependent upon the status of the person by whom he was retained. The law tract *Uraicecht Becc* (the 'Small Primer'), in a complex passage of Old Irish legal prose (with later glosses), makes this quite clear:

aes ciuil .i. cronanaig 7 airfidid .i. fedanaig oilcena .i. uili cena .i. monaig .i. bid ar monaib a neach isna hænaigib ocus araid .i. doniad in arugecht .i. in indus cedna na gilli urraith luamain .i. luamairet na hetair 7 comail .i. doniad in cerd comaind 7 daime .i. marbaid na sitcaire 7 creccoire .i. doniad crecad glas arna roscaib 7 cleasamnaig .i. cuirid na goo clis a nairde 7 fuirseoire .i. donia {read doniad} in fuirseoracht asa mbelaib 7 bruigedoire . {read bruigedoire .i.} doniad in bruigedoracht asa tonaib 7 fodana olceana .i. drochdana uili cena is a hincaib oga mbiad .i. is a caich aga mbi hincaib an siat ata eneclann doib is as direnaiter .i. is as sin erniter eneclann doib nis ta saire cena fo leith.[41]

[Musicians, that is, crooners, and minstrels, that is, pipers besides, that is, all besides, that is tricksters (?trick riders), that is, who are wont to be on the backs (?) of their horses at the fairs, and charioteers, that is, who drive the chariots, that is, in the same way, the *gillai urraith*, steersmen, that is, they steer the boats, and conjurers (?), that is, who practice magic, and bands (?), that is, they kill the denizens of the fairy mound, and *creccairi*, that is, they perform the green *crecad* on eyes, and jugglers, that is, they raise up their false tricks,

and clowns, that is, they perform the clowning from their mouths, **and farters,** that is, they perform the farting from their rears, **and [the practitioners of] minor crafts besides,** that is, all evil crafts besides, **it is on the basis of the honour of those with whom they are,** that is, it is according to the honour of whomever they are with that they have an honour-price, **that penalties are paid to them,** that is, it is on that basis that honour-price is paid to them in compensation. **Otherwise they have no franchise apart.]**[42]

The *drúth*, indispensable even if lightweight in social status, might master many skills, and in practising them he might move nimbly between various categories of the Gaelic entertainer class, donning different hats to suit the circumstances. Thus Tulchinne in the eighth-century tale of the *Togail Bruidne Da Derga* (the 'Destruction of Da Derga's Hostel'), while *rígdrúth* to King Conaire, was also his *clesamnach* ('juggler,' 'trickster,' 'acrobat'), another of the seemingly separate entertainer grades met with on the *Tech Midchúarda* plan. There is good reason to believe that the account of Tulchinne's feats of juggling, though clearly embroidered, is an idealized evocation of actual performance practice; without question it gives a vivid impression of a medieval juggler in action, and is probably the earliest and most developed account of its kind from anywhere in the British Isles:

.ix. claidib ina láim 7 noí scéith airgdidi 7 .ix. nubla óir. Focheird cech ai dib in nardae 7 ní thuit ní díb for lár 7 ní bí acht óen dib fora bois 7 is cumma 7 timthirecht bech illó ánli cach ae sech araile súas[43]

[[There were] nine swords in his hand, and nine silver shields, and nine balls of gold. He throws every one of them up [into the air], and none of them falls to the ground, and there is only one of them on his palm at a time; and each whizzing upwards past the other is like the buzzing of bees on a beautiful day.]

That his activity was not entirely detached from reality can be proved from an article in another Old Irish law tract, the *Bretha Étgid* ('Judgments of Inadvertence'). The article takes for granted the actuality of juggling with spears (or swords, or knives) and balls, for it sets up a system of compensations for any injury accidentally met with while watching a juggler's performance. The juggler, someone who 'multiplies the juggling spears in the air, or juggling balls in the air,' is classed as having two sorts of jugglery, one 'dangerous' and the other comparatively 'safe': 'IS ed is clesa aicbeili ann cach cles arnabia rind no faebur. IS ed is clesa nemaicbeile ann cach clesarna bia rind na faebur.'[44] ('"Dangerous feats" are all the feats using [spear-]point or [sword-]edge; feats which are "not dangerous" are all those which do not use [spear-]point or [sword-]edge.') Frequent association of the *clesamnach* with various kinds of musician, as for example in the texts *Críth Gablach* or the quotations from

Old Irish law tracts contained in TCD, MS 1337 (H. 3. 18), may also suggest that the performance of a *clesamnach* could take place to musical accompaniment.[45] Further, it seems that the feat-performing that the root etymology of his name implies evidently extended beyond the specific skill of juggling to include simple trickery, sleight of hand, and feats of illusion.[46] In this regard, English and Continental analogues are of interest, and establish a European context for the *clesamnach* and his range of skills. At the English court in the later fourteenth century, it was the task of the *tregetour*, as he was sometimes known, to provide spectacular diversions and illusions at feasts.[47] At the French court in 1378, the work of a *tregetour*, or his French confrère, was to be seen on vivid display at a banquet presided over by King Charles V: the siege of Jerusalem, plus a pageant ship that floated through the banqueting hall, was presented as the spectators dined.[48] To be sure, there were no Gaelic courts of similiar scale, but when a comparable sort of diversion at the court of the Great Khan was rendered from English into Irish in 1475, the word that came to the translator's mind for those responsible for having engineered it was *clesamnaigh* (*clesuidhi* here):

Tigcit clesvidhi ina fíadnaisi 7 doníad innshamail greine 7 esca lan do dellrad do denum umhla dósan mar grein 7 mur esgca.[49]

[Jugglers come before him and cause the likeness of a sun and moon full of radiance to do him reverence as a sun and as a moon.]

A text like this perhaps suggests that we might think of the *clesamnach* as having sometimes functioned as a kind of Gaelic revels master, whose job could include the presentation of mimetic games.[50] In the story of *Cetharnach Uí Dhomnaill* ('O'Donnell's Kern'), composed probably in the sixteenth century and perhaps some time after the death of Black Hugh O'Donnell in 1537, the conjuring skill and arts of illusion of the *clesamnach* are fully to the fore. A magical kern comes before Tadhg Ó Ceallaigh and declares his trade: 'clesaidhe maith me' ('I'm a good juggler/trickster/acrobat!'), and goes on to say that for five marks he will perform a trick for everyone. One of these tricks is to make one of his ears wag while the other stays still. Ó Ceallaigh agrees, and the kern simply takes hold of one ear and waggles it about. Expectation had far outstripped performance, and hence the joke. Five marks made it an expensive feat for what it was, but Ó Ceallaigh was amused, and the kern followed up by producing a *pièce de resistance* before mysteriously vanishing away. This was a spectacular variation on the Indian rope trick, and this time Ó Ceallaigh got his money's worth:

Tug an clesaidhe ceirtle síoda amach as a mhála cleasaighecht 7 tug urchar a nairde dho go

ndeachaidh a neal an æoir, 7 tug gearfhiadh amach as an mhala cheadna 7 dimthigh an
gearfhiadh na rith suas air an tsnaithe 7 tug cu bheag 7 do leig a ndiaigh an ghearfhiadh i 7
do bhí si taffann go binn ar a lorg, tug giolla beag amach as an mhala ciadhna 7 dubhairt leis
dul suas air ₍ₐ₎[a] tsnaithe andiaigh na con 7 an ghearfhiadh,, tug oigbhean alainn inniolta amach
as mhala eile bhi aige ogus dubairt leithe an giolla 7 chu do leanmhainn 7 an gearfhiadh do
chaomhnadh gan masladh on ccoin, do rith an rigbhean na ndiaigh go luath 7 dob aoibhinn
le taodhg o ceallaidh beith ag amharc na ndiaigh & ag eisteacht le seastain na sealga go
ndeachadar suas san neal as aithne go lear, Do bhadar seal fada na ttost iar sin, go ndubhairt
an cleasaidhe, is eagal liom, ar se go bhfuil droch char ga dheanamh an sud shuas, 7 ma ta
ni rachaidh gan dioghal,, cred sin air taodhg o ceallaidh: ata air an cleasaidhe go mbiodh
an chu ag ithe an ghearfiadh 7 an giolla dol chum na mna,,, bu dual sin fein air taodhg,,,
tairngios an tsnaithe iar sin agus |fol. 73v| fuair an giolla idir dhá chois na mná, 7 an chú ag
crinn chnama an ghearfhiadh,,[51]

[The juggler took a ball of silk out of his conjuring bag and threw it upwards so that it went
into a cloud in the air. He took a hare out of the same bag, and the hare went running up the
thread; and he took out a little dog, and let it go after the hare, and it was barking sweetly
in pursuit. Then he took a small youth out of the same bag and told him to go up the thread
after the hound and the hare. From another bag that he had he took a beautiful, neat young
woman, and told her to follow after the youth and the dog and to protect the hare from
harm by the hound. The young woman quickly ran up after it. And Tadhg Ó Ceallaigh
enjoyed looking at them and listening to the noise of the hunt, until they finally went up
into the cloud completely out of sight. They were silent for a long time, until the juggler
said: 'I'm afraid there's mischief going on up there, and if there is it won't go unpunished.'
'What's that?' asked Tadhg Ó Ceallaigh. 'The dog will be eating the hare,' said the juggler,
'and the youth making love to the woman.' 'That would be natural,' said Tadhg. He pulled
down the thread and found the youth between the woman's legs and the hound gnawing the
hare's bones.]

That the profession of *drúth* might in practice border upon, and sometimes
indeed completely overlap, that of other Gaelic entertainers is also indicated by the
relative flexibility in the way the various terms for members of the entertainer class
were used. Since in some sources the *drúth* is spoken of in the same breath as other
performers, and in such a way as to suggest that all the terms used signify something
in common (for example, the *drúth* may be classed with the *réim* ('contortionist'),
the *oblóir* ('juggler'?), the *fuirseóir* ('clown'), the *clesamnach* ('juggler,' 'trickster,' 'acrobat'), the *braigetóir* ('farter'), and so on), it seems reasonable to consider descriptions
of the performance of any of these entertainer classes as affording valid access to the
drúth's range of behaviour and performance skills.

In the course of his performance, the *drúth*, like some of the other entertainer classes, could well prove noisy. Noise is attributed to him in several sources.[52] The Old Irish law tract *Bretha Crólige* ('Judgments of Blood-Lying'), for example, warns that the *drúth* should not be let into a sick man's bedroom, implying that a loud and boisterous *drúth* would be the last thing the bedridden man would want to put up with,[53] and the *Di Chetharslicht Athgabála* speaks also of the physician allowing neither *druith na cainti* ('fools nor satirists') into the sick man's house.[54] In a Middle Irish poem on the *Tech Midchúarda* preserved in the Book of Leinster and the Yellow Book of Lecan, the *druith delma aitt* ('fool strange of sound') is listed among other menials and entertainers.[55] Possibly the strange sound, in the context here of the *drúth*, may have been interpreted as farting, one of the specialized meanings, in fact, of the noun *deilm* ('din,' 'rumbling'). Alternatively, it may have referred to some specific and practised vocal art with which the *drúth* was particularly associated, and this suggestion would find support in a famous story in the *Cath Almaine*. The story explains the origin of the *géim drúith* (the 'jester's shout/roar'), which from the time it was first heard, the story says, remained amongst the *drúith* of Ireland. Supposedly in the year 722, the *rígdrúth* Úa Maglćine, after being taken captive at the battle of Almu, was forced to make the jester's shout:

Ra gabhadh annsain an druth hua maighleine, 7 do radadh fair geim druith do dhénamh, 7 do rigne, bá már, 7 bá binn an gheimsin, go mair geim ui Magleine ósin ale oc drvthaibh eirenn. Ra gadadh achenn [iarrain] iarttain dfergal, 7 ra gadadh a cenn don drvth. Ra baoi mac alla gheimi an drvith sin ai ₍ᶠeˡor go cenn tri la 7 tri noidhche. As de asmberar geim ui maigleine og tafan na fer san monaidh.[56]

[The fool Úa Maiglćine was taken captive there, and he was asked to give a fool's shout, and he did; that shout was great and melodious, so that the shout of Úa Maiglćine has remained from that time with the fools of Ireland. Afterwards Fergal's head was cut off, and the fool's head was cut off. The echo of the fool's shout was in the air for three days and three nights. This is the origin of the saying, 'the shout of Úa Maiglćine pursuing the men in the bog.']

Even if the figment of some storyteller, Úa Maiglćine's shout is said to have been the archetype for shouting jesters ever since, and in adding this detail the storyteller might well have been accounting for a real-life practice in his own day, inventing for it the kind of historical basis on which storytellers were fond of setting aspects of their narrative which were already familiar to their audiences in real life.

The *drúth* might also include capering and dancing in his repertoire. The way in which the late-tenth century poem *Saltair na Rann* (the 'Verse Psalter') hibernicizes the account of King David dancing before the ark of the Lord is revealing: in order to translate the idea suggested by 2 Kings 6:14 that *David saltabat totis viribus ante Dominum* ('David danced with all his might before the Lord'), the Irish text says that he behaved *amal druth icfurseoracht*, 'like a *drúth* clowning.'[57] Thus the *fuirseóracht* of the *drúth* might include the performance art of dancing, or perhaps rather acrobatic tumbling, leaping, and cavorting – whatever precisely the king of Israel was conceived as doing when early Irish audiences imagined him *saltans* with all his might before the Lord.[58] His likening to Gaelic society's jesters doubtless gave the simile some social punch.[59] Kings tend to do things superlatively, and not least King David, whom audiences were momentarily allowed to imagine as the *drúth par excellence*, putting on a right royal performance. The physical exertion that *drúith* or their like might display when they were *ag fuirseóracht* is also well exemplified in *Tromdámh Guaire* ('Guaire's Burdensome Poetic Band'), a tale composed possibly in the late-twelfth or early-thirteenth century about events held to have taken place in seventh-century Ireland. Here, by cunningly turning their tiring physical activity against them, a troublesome troupe of entertainers that had come visiting was effectively shown the door, yet this was conveniently contrived without infringing on the laws of hospitality. Marbhán their host repeatedly invited them to perform a particularly exhausting form of the *crónán*, the *crónán snagach* (the 'base/hoarse crónán'), *ar daigh gu mbrisdi a cinn 7 a cosa 7 a mvinil* ('in the hope that they might break their heads and their feet and their necks') as a result.[60] The ploy succeeded handsomely; the physical exertions of one of the performers were so great that his eyeball started from its orbit.

The words *fuirseóir*[61] and *réim*, observed earlier in the company of other words for entertainers whose activity was similar to that of the *drúth*, colour in the picture already drawn of juggling, feats of illusion, shouting, gambolling, and acrobatics with further details, such as the ability of the *drúth* to perform physical contortions (a near cousin to acrobatics) and to pull comical faces. The *Míadšlechta*, in a passage already cited, seems to equate the *réim, fuirseóir*, and *drúth*, and draws attention to the contorting and girning that they appear to share in common. Similarly, the late Old Irish *Sanas Cormaic* ('Cormac's Glossary') defined a *réim* as:

Remm nomen do fuirseoir fobith cach riastardæ dobeir for a agaid [62]

[*Réim*, [that is] the name for a clown, because of every contortion which he brings on his face.]

And the *Uraicecht Becc* called *fuirseóiri* those who *donia* {read *doniad*} *in fuirseoracht asa mbelaib* ('who perform the clowning out of their mouths')[63] although this instance is perhaps ambiguous, since it may refer to vocal buffoonery and jokes as much as to the mops and mows of comic facial distortion. Less ambiguous seems the sinister case of the *drúth* Mac Glass in the late Old Irish story of *Fingal Rónáin* (the 'Kinslaying of Rónán'). Towards the end of this tragic tale of a repulsed woman's vengeance, her spite brings down not only its direct object, Rónán's son Mael Fhothartaig, but also indirectly Mael Fhothartaig's fool, Mac Glass. Mac Glass was *occlessaib for lár in taige* ('juggling on the floor of the house'), innocently enough, when a warrior of Rónán dealt Mael Fhothartaig the blow from which he was later to die. The fool sprang away, but the warrior hurled a spear at him which ripped out his innards. Mael Fhothartaig, still alive at that point, was able to witness the spectacle:

Nobered immorro in fiach a inathar on drúth for irdrochiut. no fhencad a beolu. no thibtís ind athig. mebul la mælfothartaig. IS and asbertsom. A mic glais timthais tinathar inniut. cid na fetarsu náire athig ocgáire immut.[64]

[A raven was taking the fool's entrails out of him on the steps. He was contorting his mouth. The churls were laughing. Mael Fhothartaig was ashamed. Then he said, 'O Mac Glass, put your bowels back in. Why have you no shame? Churls are laughing at you.']

The skewered fool, this time contorting his face in deadly earnest rather than in sport, was ironically still able to cause amusement, and this extraordinary scene at once attests, while grimly twisting, the face-pulling aspect of *drúth* performance.[65]

The *drúth*, as the etymology of his name implies, would also have dealt in lewd horseplay and scurrilous jesting.[66] In one of his more specialized manifestations on the *Tech Midchúarda* plan, that of the *braigetóir* ('farter'), he has made of farting an entertainment art, and although this accomplishment was prized in entertainers throughout these islands during the Middle Ages, it is only from Ireland that substantial early evidence survives for specialists in it.[67] At least one categorical description exists of what the *braigetóir* did, for a gloss in the *Uraicecht Becc* speaks of 'bruigedoire . {*read* bruigedoire .i.} doniad in bruigedoracht asa tonaib' ('Farters, [that is], those who perform the farting from their rears').[68] Although those who rejoiced in the name *braigetóir* were no doubt so egregious in that skill that they derived their name from it, *braigetóracht* ('farting') might take its place in the line-up for an evening's entertainment, and again be but one of an entertainer's sundry turns.[69] A medley of talents, including farting, was displayed by Mac Con Glinne as he sported at Dún Coba in the household of Píchan, son of Maelfind the king of Iveagh:

fororbairt fuirseoracht fon samail sin don tslog do lár in rigthige .i. ní narba comadais dia persaind cáintecht 7 bragitoracht 7 duana la filidecht do gabail coro hasblad he na tanic riam ł iarum bid errdarcu i cerdu cáintechta.[70]

[In this way he began clowning for the host from the floor of the royal house (that is, something not fit for his person), and satirizing and farting and singing songs; and it has been said that never before, nor since, has there come anyone more renowned in the practice/arts of satire.]

This excerpt from the late-eleventh century tale *Aislinge Meic Con Glinne* (the 'Vision of Mac Con Glinne') lists four aspects to Mac Con Glinne's entertainment, of which farting is the third; first comes the all-embracing *fuirseoracht*, a word denoting clowning in general, then more particularly *cáintecht* ('satirizing'), *bragitoracht*, and finally *duana la filidecht* ('the recitation/singing of poems'). Apparently the art of satire was Mac Con Glinne's forté (*coro hasblad he na tanic riam ı iarum bid errdarcu i cerdu cáintechta*), if *i cerdu cáintechta* ('in the practice/arts of satire') is not in fact another way, like *fuirseoracht*, of describing his multifold art generally.

The well-established practice of satire in early Gaelic society is frequently associated with the *drúth* and with other species of Gaelic entertainer like the *braigetóir*, which suggests not only satire's heavy investment in scurrility (something that surviving literary sources spectacularly confirm),[71] but also that its delivery might often have been something of a performance, a more highly wrought and energetic affair than mere recitation.[72] Entertainers might also turn satirist if their skills and requests were spurned, as will be seen further below. The *Tech Midchúarda* plan seats together two sorts of satirist, the *maccfurmid* and the *fochloc*, low down the far-right rank. The *maccfurmid* composed *sétnad* and *sainemain* verse, and was second lowest in the poetic hierarchy of the *filid* ('poets'),[73] while the *fochloc* was a poet of the lowest grade who composed the *dían* metre.[74] Both of these were evidently in theory metrical specialists, even if they shared some of the satirist's broader characteristics. Turning for a moment to the Yellow Book of Lecan version of the *Tech Midchúarda* plan, we find the satirical roles of the *fochloc* and *maccfurmid* subsumed in the word most commonly used to signify a satirist of any kind, the *cáinte*.[75] Unfortunately, no accounts survive of the sort of performance that a *cáinte* in full flow was capable of, although perhaps there is a glimpse of it in Mac Con Glinne's sport and in the description of the grave-side chanting of the *crosáin* at nightfall in the twelfth-century tale of the *Sénadh Saigri* (the 'Enchantment/Blessing of Seirkieran') that will be discussed below.[76] Three things that the sources tend to agree on were his petulance, importunacy, and appetite. Like the *drúth*, he could serve the clerical writer as an icon of anger, greed, and lust, yet his presentation as a walking collaboration of guts and genitals, testy into the bargain, might at once serve to celebrate the great instinctual urges as to parody them.[77] His disruptive conduct may have been as much an avocation as an occupational hazard, a socially necessary way of life as much as a habit forced upon him by penury and the prospect of an uncertain future.

The *cáinti* were as well established in society as many other entertainers, no matter how much clerical authors might complain about how better off society would be without them, or even warn that their coming amongst men could be a sign of the approaching Day of Doom.[78] The satire of the *cáinti* was, in fact, an indispensable instrument of social control in Gaelic society, whatever scurrilous offence it might give to the clergy, and at its best was a means whereby people might be shamed into observing custom and the law.[79] Satirical verse was, after all, only the inevitable inverse of praise poetry, whose role in cementing the bonds of early Irish society needs no illustration here.[80] Further, the satirist's lampoons were credited with the power of causing physical injury and in extreme cases mortality: the early-eleventh-century poet Cúán Ó Lothcháin, for example, had alledgedly been able to rhyme his murderers into a state of fatal putrefaction within moments of his death.[81] The fame of poetic miracles like these lasted at least into the sixteenth and seventeenth centuries, becoming known also to outsiders like Sir Philip Sidney and James Shirley.[82] Lampoons were a veritable verbal arsenal, sticks and stones to break the bones, that a chief might even find advantageous against an enemy as he went into battle. In a society in which public reputation, even more than in our own, was decisive in determining a person's acceptability and perceived worth, the *cáinte* might well be as feared as valued, a maker (or more usually, breaker) of reputations, and it is not surprising to find laws framed to attempt to regulate his activity.[83] Unwelcome or not, there was no removing him.

The last of those persons on the *Tech Midchúarda* plan who would have culti-vated skills cognate to those of the actor was the *senchaid* (the 'reciter of lore,' 'his-torian'), to whom this chapter will return before it is out.[84] Any reciter or storyteller hoping to hold the attention of his audience must in some measure have *performed* his narrative, not merely related it, and to this extent he practiced a dramatic art.[85] No doubt story-tellers worth their salt would not have been content with a mono-chrome delivery, but would have energized it dramatically, especially since those who on one occasion were capable of the *drúth*'s skills might on another practice the art of storytelling: the *rígdrúth* Úa Magléine told stories, for example.[86] Once again we should bear in mind the fact that most of the words for the different sorts of entertainer that have been surveyed here are, in effect, simply convenient dis-criminations made within a broader continuum of entertainment activity, and that aspects of one sort of performing art might be called on to enrich another. Of the ancient quality of the *senchaid*'s performance nothing can now be said, apart per-haps from what its modern descendants suggest it may have been like,[87] and of this Tadhg Ó Murchú has given clear testimony. Describing the impressive performance of a Kerry storyteller in the 1930s, he noted how the storyteller was a man whom the narrative much moved, and how 'he uses a great deal of gesticulation, and by the movement of his body, hands and head, tries to convey hate and anger, fear and humour, *like an actor in a play.*'[88] Conservatism of tradition is a safe pledge that the quality of this Kerryman's performance would have shown lineaments of a descent from earlier times.[89]

So far, we have been distilling evidence for what Gaelic entertainers and performing artists did: they might make strange and comical noises, pull faces, contort their bodies, do acrobatics, gambol, juggle, jest, fart, satirize, recite poems, tell stories, ask riddles, and perform conjuring tricks and feats of illusion;[90] perhaps like their Norse counterparts, the *trúðar*, they even performed occasionally with animals.[91] Very often all this took place in a festive context where music featured. But there is evidence of another sort which gives at least some of them a close resemblance to those bands of professional entertainers and actors who are known to have toured elsewhere in these islands from at least the fifteenth century on:[92] some Gaelic performing artists dressed in distinctive sorts of costumes and were organized into bands, some of which were indeed touring troupes. The professional minstrel class in Ireland was evidently of many complexions;[93] it was composed not only of men maintained in the aristocratic households, but also of men who, either individually or in groups, took their entertainment wherever they could find patronage for it. Sometimes annal entries witness to such patronage directly.[94] A selection of the plentiful evidence for the itinerant entertainer will be considered presently, but first we might begin with some descriptions of the sorts of outfit that Gaelic entertainers seem to have worn.

Use of distinctive costume would have served many purposes. To onlookers it would have signalled an entertainer's social role and function, and some touch of the freakish about it would have helped to heighten the sense of comic occasion in which the entertainer was most usually wont to live, move, and have his being.[95] Costume would also have been a means of defining his institutional status. Then, as now, costume might express a social stance or position, and in the entertainer's case, its unconventionality no doubt proclaimed him as being in society but not entirely of it, and like Lear's all-licensed fool, as being at liberty to wander about in it with comparative ease, overstepping the social bounds which normally restrained society's more regular and workaday subscribers.[96] As will be seen, city waits and retained minstrels in the walled towns of Ireland would also wear distinctive livery, though since in their case it was normally prescribed in detail by their employers (that is, by civic authorities or private individuals), their institutional status, by contrast, was regulated with a degree of civic or private supervision and standardization that the Gaelic entertainer, at least in this respect, was free of.

The picture of the king's fool Róimid[97] in the late Middle Irish tale of the *Mesca Ulad* (the 'Intoxication of the Ulstermen'), though no doubt in some measure a decorated literary fiction, has certain features which suggest that in essence it was not utterly fantastic, but dependent upon a recognizably real phenomenon within the Gaelic society of its time:

Unsea riu anair anectair ar crom deróil Atcondarcsa and budin da dæscarslúag oenfher eturru. Súasmæl dubrintach fair mocolshúli móra oengela ina chind. Aged ethiopacda slemangorm aci. Bratt ríbáin i forcipul immi. frithchuman umaidi ina brutt uasa braini. sithbacc creduma ina láim. Clucin ceolbind ina chomaitecht. Bertaid a echlasc bar in slúag co tárcend suba 7 sogra dond ardríg 7 dond tshluág uili.[98]

['Here before them, to the east, outside,' said Crom Deróil, 'I saw that band of rabble. One man among them had a close-cropped, black and bristly head of hair; the eyes in his head were big, bulging and pure white. He had a smooth and black face like an Ethiopian. A striped cloak was wrapped about him; a brazen pin above on the front of his cloak; a long bronze crook in his hand, and a sweetly melodious little bell beside him. He brandishes his horse-switch before the host, so that it gives delight and joy to the high king and to all the host.']

The author of *Mesca Ulad* headed his list of the details which made Róimid so conspicuous with that of his dark face. So dark was it that the whites of his eyes shone out by contrast, and he looked like an Ethiopian (*Aged ethiopacda slemangorm aci*). *Mesca Ulad* gives a particularly early account of what looks to have been that deliberate strategy for outlandishness long adopted by entertainers, face-blackening.[99] Similar blackenings associated with entertainers elsewhere in early Gaelic sources suggest that the *Mesca Ulad* account should not be dismissed as being merely an imaginative concoction, utterly without purchase on reality. The *Sénadh Saigri*, for example, talks about the infestation of 'nine shaggy jet-black *crosáin*' around the grave of Donnchadh the Fat in the following terms:

Bá gilithir snechta a súile 7 a fiacla 7 bá duibidhtir gual cach bald eile díb.[100]

[Their eyes and teeth were whiter than snow and every other part of them was blacker than coal.]

Here the blackening shows not just in their faces, though it is upon the impression their faces make that this text, like the *Mesca Ulad*, once again focuses.[101] Since the earliest times, then, face-blackening seems to have been an option available to certain members of the Gaelic entertainer class.[102]

The mantle hanging in folds, fastened at the chest by a brass clasp, may have marked Róimid out as being distinctively dressed, though just how distinctively cannot now be told. The little bell at his side certainly sounds very particular, and puts him early in the long tradition of medieval jesters who are known to have used bells and who would have jingled their way through their routines.[103] Mac Con Glinne mentioned earlier was dressed curiously and distinctively when he performed before

Pichán;[104] the *crosáin* in an Old Irish poem on the honorific food portions seem to
have worn bizarre headgear;[105] and the fool Glasdámh in the Middle Irish *Bórama*
(the 'Tribute paid in Cattle'), as a last act of self-immolating loyalty, offered his
cloak and hood to Cummascach his prince so that the prince might disguise himself when his enemies had fired the house but had agreed to let Glasdámh escape
unharmed.[106] Had cloak and hood not been perceived as distinctively those of a fool,
the disguise would have failed. On the other hand, the fool's costume might resemble in some measure that of the royal personage by whom he was retained. In some
texts, he wore a *mind* ('diadem'), a reminiscence perhaps of the ancient motif of the
fool as the king's alter-ego, though the *mind* might still be distinctively that of a
fool and not an exact replica of that worn by the king himself.[107] Sometimes, however, the fool's *mind* caused him to be mistaken for royalty.[108]

Entertainers' livery is mentioned too in the Middle Irish *Immram Curaig Ua Corra*
(the 'Voyage of the Uí Chorra'), and here it is also described as being the communal
property of entertainers who are organized into what appears to have been a touring troupe.[109] Before one of the *crosáin* who made up this troupe was allowed to go
off to join a band of pilgrims, his fellows demanded back from him his *crosán* costume:

IN tan tra ba mithig leo dul anacurach adconncatar buigin secha 7 ba hi buidin boi and cliar
crosan Adconncatar na crosain in curach ga chur amach arin muir Cuich na daine cuires in
curach aran fairrgi ar siat Adubert fuirseoir na clére Aithnimse iat ar se Trí meic conaill dirg
í corra fhind di connachtaib .i. na foglaidi 7 na dibergaid ac dula da noilithri 7 do iarraid an
coimgidh ar muir 7 ar mor 7 ar morfhairgi Acht cheana ar in fuirseoir tar mu breithir ní mo
rancatar a les dul diarraid nimhe indusa Tar mu brethir ar taisech na clere is fada cu ragasa
dot oilitri Ní hamair dogentar ar in fuirseoir ach rachatsa leo sut dom ailithre anossa can
fuirech AS briathar duinn arna crosain nach béra arnétaigini lat uair ní let fein a fuil détach
umut Ni headh sin nom fastfasa acaibsi ar se. [110]

[Moreover, at the time when they should go into their boat they saw a group going by, and
this group was a troupe of *crosáin*. The *crosáin* saw the boat being launched onto the sea.
'Who are the people launching this boat onto the sea?' they said. The clown of the troupe
said, 'I recognize them. They are the three sons of Conall Dearg, descendants of Corra Finn
of the Connachtmen, that is, the robbers and plunderers, and they are going on a pilgrimage
seeking the Almighty on the sea and mighty ocean. Nevertheless,' said the clown, 'by my
word, they do not need more than I to go seeking heaven.' 'By my word,' said the leader of
the troupe, 'it will be long before you make a pilgrimage.' 'Don't say [that], it shall be done,'
said the clown. 'I shall go and make my pilgrimage now without delay.' 'We have [your]
word,' said the *crosáin*, 'you won't take our clothes with you because what you are wearing is
not your own.' 'That will not keep me with you,' he said.]

And so they sent him away to the pilgrims stark naked. The other *crosáin* seem to have been on a journey somewhere themselves, though the story does not say where.

Signs of the existence of itinerant entertainers, like the ones in this story, and of their organization into troupes, are scattered but persistent in Gaelic records and appear from the earliest times unto well into the sixteenth century.[111] Sometimes the entertainers are mobile necessarily because on a royal progress, and so, for example, in the late Middle Irish story of the *Aided Guill Maic Carbada ocus Aided Gairb Glinne Rige* (the 'Violent Deaths of Goll Son of Carbad and Garb Son of Glenn Rige'), the men of Ulster set out for a feast attended by a *fiallach ciuil 7 airfitid* (a 'troupe of musicians and minstrels').[112] At other times – and these are more interesting because they suggest their profession was well-defined and autonomous enough to allow them to travel on their own – they moved about the country either singly or in a troupe. Evidently such troupes were common enough to warrant a word to describe them: *clíar* is often used in this capacity.[113] These troupes comprised any number of up to ten or more members, and were probably organized into some sort of hierarchy.[114] The *áes n-imthechta nó taistil sliged* ('travelling folk or folk of the journeying way'),[115] as they were often styled, travelled wherever they might find an audience, and after the English settlement of Ireland in the late twelfth century, this included audiences within the English Pale, as the next chapter will reveal. The extraordinary travelling feats of the kern in the sixteenth-century story of *Cetharnach Uí Dhomnaill*, feats made possible by magic, might perhaps be regarded as a fairy-tale extension of a real-life peripatetic tendency.[116] Liminal characters like him would always be prone to footloose wandering in any age: one of the reasons why Ulster mumming was dealt a heavy blow in recent times was that from the beginning of the northern troubles in the early 1970s, the Royal Ulster Constabulary was disinclined to issue licenses to mumming troupes liable to rove without restraint back and forth across the border with the Republic.[117] Before the dawning of the age of police forces and partition, church legislations, which from the earliest times tried to set some bounds to the wanderings of entertainers, betray how deeply entrenched this peripatetic tendency was. A series of clerical injunctions for the proper observation of the sabbath, known as the *Cáin Domnaig*, and which the Annals of Ulster mention as having come to Ireland in the year 886, attempted to restrict Sunday wanderings:

Druith 7 cainti 7 gobainn ni imtiagat ann. an dobertha doib isin tshollomain doberar doib áig {*read* día} luain.[118]

[Jesters and smiths and satirists do not journey on that day; that which would be given them on the festival [of Sunday], is given on Monday.]

In many other places too the church shows itself to have found roving troupes vex-
ing. Various saints were harrassed by petulant entertainer bands who demanded food
of them.[119] A graphic encounter in the twelfth-century *Vita Sancti Flannani* between St Flannán and a band of 'nine jesters, men with particularly ugly faces and
horrible costumes' illustrates well what appears to have been a literary topos of fairly
standard formula:[120]

ecce nouem iaculatores uiri ˄⌈valde⌉ deformes uultu & habitu horribiles instinctu diabolico
inducti. & ut ita dicam appetitu canino superati: a beato uiro nouem nigros arietes mutillatos:
deum ac sanctum attemptantes. Ioculatoria uociferatione & incompatienti petitione omnes
insimul clamantes sibi dari postulabant dicentes. Sancte flannane uir nobilissime satis fac
petitioni nostre. Alioquin omni tempore uite nostre te uituperando diffamabimus & toti regie
tue genelogie diutinam obproprij |fol. 173v, col. b| contumeliam inferemus.[121]

[Behold, nine jesters, men with particularly ugly faces and horrible costumes, led on by a
devilish instinct and overpowered, so to speak, with a dog-like appetite, clamouring all
together with jesting shout and impatient demand, putting God and the saint to the test,
kept demanding of the blessed man nine black de-horned rams, and saying, 'Holy Flannán,
most noble man, grant our request. Otherwise, every day of our lives we will go about
defaming you with our reproaches and inflicting enduring scandalous insult on all your royal
ancestry.']

In some cases, although the jesters got what they demanded, they also suffered
unpleasant side effects. In this story, as they seized their unappetizing dinners they
were promptly turned to stone; and there they still stand for all to see and wonder
at, says the solemn hagiographer. The band of *aos cíuil* ('minstrels') who insulted
St Coemgen when he was unable to give them the food they asked for got off lightly
by comparison. In their case, it was only their harps that were petrified.[122]
    No less than St Patrick himself, according to the early-tenth century redaction of
the *Bethu Phátraic* (the 'Life of Patrick'), was nearly discountenanced by a hungry *cléir
aesa ceirdd* ('band of men of art') who approached him one day and asked for something to eat. The clear implication is that were he not to have provided their fare, he
would have been satirized.[123] As Providence would have it, a boy and his mother carrying a cooked ram on her back happened to pass by, and the ram was obtained for
Patrick who handed it over to the band. They were at once swallowed up by the earth,
presumably in return for their affrontery. The Latin life upon which the *Bethu Phátraic*
was based spoke of the band as having comprised a *praeco [cum comitibus suis]*,[124]
who also died on receiving the ram, though less picturesquely.[125] If the patron saint
of Ireland was not immune, nor was it likely that anyone else would be. St Columb
Cille was approached by *daine eladhna* ('people of art,' 'poets') who demanded a gift

on the spot, failing which satire would be visited upon him. The saint's consternation at having no gift to hand caused alarming physical symptoms which, as it proved, saved the day. Smoke rose from his head, and when he brushed away the sweat that poured down his face, he discovered that it had conveniently turned into a piece of gold that he could pay the *daine eladhna* off with and so save his reputation.[126] St Fintán too was able to fob off a troupe of *histriones* and *mimi* with a fish which, though resistant to all attempts to cut it up, they declared was better than nothing, and carried it away with them.[127] Female saints were no more exempt, for St Lasair too was plagued by similar demands, though embarrassing her seems to have been an easier offence to get away with. The *da nénbhar deicsibh 7 dáes ealadhna* ('two enneads of poets and men of learning') who got food from her did so with impunity. Nevertheless the author of the late Middle Irish *Beatha Lasrach* (the 'Life of Lasair') left his readers in little doubt about his distaste for this *dáimh doiligh dicheillidh* ('harsh, insensate band'), and these *daimhe doirbhe drochráitige* ('peevish and evil-speaking folk') were thus firmly put in their place by naked authorial contempt, even if not this time by divine intervention.[128] All these episodes were contrived to redound to the honour of the saints in question: Flannán, Patrick, Columb Cille, and Lasair were seen publicly to discharge the Gaelic obligations of hospitality and thus to avoid the reproach of satire. To this extent, it seems not particularly important that it took itinerant bands of entertainers to precipitate their hospitality; any catalyst, in principle, would have done. But it is significant nevertheless that entertainers so frequently *were* chosen to be that catalyst, and possibly this is because they were exactly the kind of folk liable to tour around and visit unexpectedly, and then demand gifts and privileges of hosting.[129] That this might really be their disposition, and not merely a characteristic foisted upon them by a hostile hagiographical genre, can be quickly established. An unpublished record of a Munster court case of 12 June 1315 shows how, rather than depart empty-handed, a spurned minstrel might descend to actual robbery. A certain Muriartagh O Coyqnan [*sic*] was accused of being a common robber and incendiary in co. Cork, and 'of being in the habit of coming to the houses of the liege men of the country as a minstrel to ask for alms, and if they were refused him, of endeavouring to rob them.' Witnesses testified that although they did not believe Muriartagh was an incendiary, 'he as an actor commonly begs hospitality (*curialitates*) from the liege men of the country.'[130] Judging by his name, Muriartagh was a native Gael. He was evidently in the habit of repeating the demands of the entertainer that were routine in his own culture also in the culture of the Anglo-Normans. And again a record of 8 October 1537 shows that something similar was still going on in the county of Kilkenny:

ther ar emonges the inhabytauntes of this countrey many harpers, rymers, and messingers, whiche comen at ther pleasures to any inhabytaunt, and wille have mete, drynke, and dyverse greate rewardes ayenst the voluntarye wylles of the same inhabytauntes, of an evyll custome. Wherefor they desyre that it may be ordeyned that suche harpers, rymers, and messyngers maye not take suche exaccions of the said inhabytauntes, nor the said rymers to make any rymes of them, uppon certeyn paynes to be lymytid.[131]

And as late as 1582 in Connacht, a set of orders issued for that province required 'that every body shall be an Officer for takinge of whores and Arlotts, vagabonds, sturdy beggars, harpers, carrowes {< *cerrbhach*, 'gambler'}, and other naughty members that slander Gentlemen when they deny them of anything they demand; and them to send to Her Majesty's gaol to be punished according to the lawes provided for such persons.'[132] The relationship between the traditional Irish obligation of hospitality and the peripatetic entertainer may well have been symbiotic: each would have fostered the other. The power that Gaelic entertainers had to influence (in these cases probably by reinforcing) early Irish social structures is impressive. Anyone acting as host to a touring band would no doubt have been just as anxious to secure their good report as to avoid their public scorn.

The official clerical attitude to entertainers, strolling or otherwise, had long been one of disapproval, in spite of occasional hints that some clerics harboured them.[133] In a list of penitential commutations, for example, dating probably to about the year 800, *druidechta 7 caintechta* ('druidic practices and satirizing') are put on a par with murder, incest, heresy, and the like, and are classed amongst the gravest of sins for which no remission of the penance due for them is possible.[134] It is not surprising that the early Irish laws also catch something of this attitude, since the very act of commiting them to the written page would have brought them within the sphere of clerical influence and letters. According to the Old Irish law tract known as the *Córus Béscnai* (the 'Regulation of Proper Behaviour'), a *fled domonda* (a 'devil's feast'), that is, a banquet held *do macaib bais 7 droch dainib* ('for sons of death and wicked men'), is something held *do druthaib 7 caintib 7 oblairaib 7 bruidiraib 7 fuirseoraib 7 merlechaib 7 geintaib 7 merdrechaib 7 drochdainaib arcena*[135] ('for *drúith* and satirists and jugglers and farters and clowns and robbers and heathens and whores, and other wicked people'). And one of the early Middle Irish homilies in the *Leabhar Breac* contemptuously lumps together *furseori 7 dáine dóescaire* ('clowns and scurrilous folk').[136] Disapproval might also slip in in parenthesis. The author of the *Aislinge Meic Con Glinne* adds that Mac Con Glinne's clowning was 'a thing not fit for his person' (*ní narba comadais dia persaind*) almost as an aside, and as if to advertise that he was quite aware of the official party line on *mimis, joculatoribus, et histrionibus*.[137] In practice, however, there must have been much tolerance of the entertainer, if not frank enjoyment of his performances. The arrival of the friars in Ireland in the 1220s was no doubt welcomed by any who found their taste for entertainment awkwardly at odds with their ecclesiastically formed consciences.

The friars, 'God's jesters,' as St Francis put it,[138] became well known for their talents in music, song, and poetry, and in attempting to reconcile secular pastime with pious profit, they would have helped absolve the natural human delight in entertainment from possible moral impeachment. They wandered freely around Ireland, and as they were bearers of news and God's blessing, the doors of many a household must have been willingly opened to them;[139] to some they may even have seemed like a sanitized version of the secular Gaelic entertainer, and it is not hard to imagine certain friars self-consciously conforming to that role; after all, they had St Francis himself as their authority in this respect.[140] Whatever the exact secret of their success, exceedingly popular they surely became, for by the end of the thirteenth century their orders had firmly established themselves *inter Hibernicos* as well as *inter Anglicos*.[141] Yet even if indigenous Gaelic entertainers of the more purely secular sort did have some of their thunder stolen by the mendicants, they would not have been left quite shiftless, and presumably because they were free to deal in forms of entertainment that even the *joculatores Dei* could not meddle with. The clerical ban on involvement in scurrilities still held, and friars could only go so far in catering to popular appetites for diversion.

The entertainment business in Gaelic Ireland was not altogether a male monopoly, even though the balance of the evidence for it weighs far more towards male than female involvement.[142] The few glimpses afforded of female performing artists suggest that the sort of entertainment they offered, though possibly reduced in scope, did not markedly differ from that of their male counterparts. Considering they had the difference of sex to capitalize on, this may seem a little curious: it may be that gaps in record survival have robbed our picture of completeness, and to be sure, entertainment from women must have had a gendered piquancy peculiar to itself. Yet extant evidence speaks mostly of the existence of the *bancháinte* ('she-satirist'), who would seem simply to have been a female version of the satirist (*cáinte*), unless there is more in a name than we can now tell. One text on the Fifteen Signs before Doomsday, probably composed sometime after 1200, lumps satirists and she-satirists together: 'Uch cuirfiter déinleith an uair sin ... na drvithi 7 na cainti 7 na crosanaigh ... na cainti na banchainti ... 7 lucht gach vilc ele' ('Oh, then will be cast on one side ... the unchaste folk and the satirists and the *crosán* ... the satirists, the she-satirists ... and every other evil person').[143] And a detailed account of *bancháinte* behaviour which features in the story of the early Middle Irish *Genemain Áeda Sláne* (the 'Birth of Áedh Sláine') shows them possessed of the similar sort of greed, petulance, and taste for mischief that male *cáinti* often displayed.[144] The story, from the late-eleventh-century manuscript *Lebor na hUidre* (the 'Book of the Dun Cow'), tells of the uneasy relationship between the two queens of King Dermot, son of Fergus Cerrbeol. One of them, Mughain, was jealous of the other, Mairenn. Because Mairenn was bald and hid the defect under an elaborate gold headdress, Mughain decided to embarrass her publicly by hiring a *banchάinte* to snatch the headdress off. The *banchάinte* first demanded gifts, and when Mairenn said that she could not grant them, the *banchάinte* went to work, tearing away the headdress:

Tanic trá in banchάinti co airm i mbuí mairend 7 boí oc tothlugud neich furri. Asbert in rígan ná baí acci. Bíaid ocut so or si oc tarraing in catbairr orda día cind.[145]

[So the she-satirist then came to the place where Mairenn was and started demanding something from her. The queen declared that she did not have it. 'Have this, then,' said the she-satirist, and she snatched the gold headdress from her head.]

The episode ended happily for Mairenn, for by the help of God and St Ciarán, in the intervening seconds before anyone had a chance to register that she was bald, curling golden locks sprouted from her head, thus saving her from disgrace.

Records are on the whole silent about the participation of women in the other more specialized aspects of the *drúth*'s performance such as were surveyed earlier,[146] let alone about any varieties of entertainment reserved exclusively for female entertainers. It may be that the energies of professional female performers were largely invested in the practice of satire, and hence the emphasis in that direction in surviving texts. Yet just as satire in some cases seems to have been simply a phase or aspect of the wider performance continuum, a case made *ex silencio* that female performances were in the main limited to satire may be unfounded, especially if the role of the *banchάinte* was at all *closely* analogous to that of the male *cáinte*. For example, given the disposition of the latter sometimes to cut capers, one might wonder whether there were not also dancing girls to be met with, not that they need necessarily have been full-time professionals, but at least girls available to exercise their dancing or acrobatic skills for a reward. If there were, early Gaelic treatments of the story of St John the Baptist may have served as a caution against the dark and dangerous eroticism liable to inhere in any such female performance, and of its potentially destructive consequences for its male consumers. Yet from the medieval Gaelic point of view, perhaps what the daughter of Herodias did was conceived not quite in the way it is today, as a lithe, exotic dance trimmed to tantalize a revelling king, but rather as something much more robust and bracing, a minstrel act undertaken on the promise of a reward, rash though that promise was. A Middle Irish homily in the *Leabhar Breac* describes what Salvisa (as the Irish source names her) did.[147] Entertainment ran in the family: her sister, Neptis, was talented *ocambrán 7 ocluindiucc 7 oc fethcusib 7 cíuil examail ar chena* ('in song and in melody and in piping and all kinds of music'), though whether she joined Salvisa in a sisterly combo is not clear.[148] It was Salvisa's *clesaigecht 7 lemenda 7 fri hopairecht* ('juggling/acrobatics and leaping and activity') that stirred up King Herod, and all of these words dilate upon the Vulgate's solitary word for what she did, *saltavit*, in Matthew 14:6 and Mark 6:22. *Saltavit* was also the word used of King David's dancing, as was seen, but this had been a performance which by contrast bore the seal of divine approval. *Opairecht* in the homily is difficult to define, the neutral sense 'activity' at which the editors of the *Dictionary of the Irish Language* arrive no doubt being thrust upon them for want of attestations of the word. *Clesaigect* and *lemenda*, on the other hand, seem clear enough. With the first term, we are returned to the familiar lexicon of entertainment, and are presented with a woman who was, in effect, a *clesamnach*. And as if to emphasize the impressiveness of the acrobatic dimension of her act, she was also said to be good at leaping (*lemenda*). In short, there is nothing intrinsically new in all this, in performance terms at any rate, apart perhaps from the fact that it was a woman who did it. But was even this entirely new? There are reasons to doubt that it was other than those previously hinted at in the context of the *bancháinte*. Leaving aside the fact that female dancers or acrobats were historical realities across the water in England (and as has been seen, cultural contact with England implies cultural exchange), they make a fleeting appearance early in the seventeenth century in Fynes Moryson's *Itinerary*: 'the wemen of some partes of Mounster, as they weare Turkish heades and are thought to haue come first out of those partes, so the {*read* they} haue pleasant tunes of Moresco Danses.'[149] By the later seventeenth century, troupes of *banraingceóiridhe* ('female dancers') are encountered in the *Párliament na mBan* (the 'Parliament of Women') who also seem historical realities, whose gyrations were able to whip up physical frenzies that precipitated thousands *go hifrionn dubh* ('into black hell').[150] And as a final point of comparison between female and male performers in Gaelic society, there is much evidence that the women, like the men, might be itinerant too: the *mná siubhail* ('walking women') often mentioned by English writers of the sixteenth century possibly come into this class.[151]

In sum, then, the Gaelic entertainer was already well established in society in the earliest documents, and he was versatile, capable of moving amphibiously between one social context and the next where his varied skills might be required, providing whatever entertainment suited the moment and the tastes of his patrons.[152] Not only might he be called on to buoy up levity on occasions, as at banquets,[153] but sometimes to lighten the gravity of an occasion, as at a wake, or to incite courage, as on the eve of a battle.[154] As regards performers at wakes, the evidence is plentiful, and dates from near both ends of the period under review. The *vita* of St Mochulla, for example, composed probably in the second half of the twelfth century, mentions a *concentus cornionum atque tubicenum* (a 'harmonious music of horns and trumpets') at funeral obsequies,[155] and in 1618, at a provincial synod in Armagh presided over by David Rothe, Catholic bishop of Ossory, it was decreed that wake excesses at which might be found *quorumdam nebulonum et joculatorum nequitiam … inhonestæ cantiones, lascivæ gesticulationes* ('wickedness of certain fools and jesters ... immodest songs, lascivious gestures') must be avoided at all costs.[156] The signs are that some of the Gaelic entertainer's skills were dramatic in a way that would satisfy modern definitions of that word, although he could hardly have conceived of himself as an actor in any limited modern sense; acting skill was for him simply one field in the wider province of entertainment that he inhabited generally. Even entertainment itself might be but one among other provinces; there is reason to believe that certain entertainers doubled as domestic servants, for example.[157] In several respects, then, he would have already resembled his English counterparts, with whom, as will be seen, he would eventually compete for trade after the English had come with entertainers of their own to settle in Ireland. Hierarchies within his profession, and his joining with colleagues to form distinctively costumed touring bands, would have brought his conduct and way of life further into line with English entertainers. It seems likely that when entertainers from both traditions were brought together in the households of the great Anglo-Irish lords, as chapter 6 will further explore,[158] the common ground they already shared in the performing arts would have expedited their comparison and exchange of performance skills.

In such circumstances, hybrid forms of entertainment would have evolved of a distinctively Anglo-Irish kind. Evidence of this evolution, though scattered, is telling. For example, perhaps a passing reference in Geoffrey Keating's famous history of Ireland, the *Foras Feasa ar Éirinn* (the 'Basis of Knowledge about Ireland'), points obliquely to a blending of performance traditions that by the seventeenth century was widespread in Ireland. His work, completed between 1633 and 1638, and therefore coming towards the end of the period with which we are here concerned, uses an interesting simile to disparage the historian Edmund Campion whom Keating accused of having an unjustifiably low opinion of Irish credulity. Keating claimed that Campion, to support his case, had related how a cleric had actually talked money out of some Irishfolk with a tale of how St Peter once upon a time wielded his heavenly keys and hit St Patrick over the head with them for having presumed to urge that the soul of an Irish mercenary soldier be admitted into heaven. 'My answer to him [Campion] here,' said Keating, is that *cosmhala é re cluithcheoir do bhiadh ag reic sceul sgigeamhail ar scafoll ioná re stáraidhe* ('he is like a player who would be reciting jeering stories on a scaffold rather than an historian').[159] Campion is reprimanded for his mischievousness by the application of a simile that turns him into a mountebank. Perhaps Keating's main experience of mountebanks had been in France where he had been educated, but if they were utterly unknown in Ireland, his insult would have lost most of its point.[160] There may be an overlooked clue that Ireland had acquired a mountebank tradition of its own by the seventeenth century, one either purely native or, more likely, cross-bred on Continental European lines.

Not only, then, would Gaelic entertainers be liable to encounter their English counterparts on Irish soil after the Norman invasion of 1169, but, given the habit of some of them to wander in search of patrons, that encounter might have been with entertainers in other Celtic kingdoms, if not further afield.[161] For example, at some stage a pinch of Welsh seasoning may have been added to the native Gaelic melting pot, for there is a little evidence for early contact between Irish and Welsh entertainers. Irish entertainers were certainly known about in medieval Wales; the fact that the Welsh word *croessan* ('buffoon,' 'jester'), to take but one salient case, was a direct borrowing from Irish *crosán* suggests that *crosáin*, or at the very least their reputations, had travelled eastwards across the Irish sea.[162] Any such travelling *crosáin* would have entered a culture which hosted parallel performing arts. When a late-medieval Welsh text described how the *clerwr* typically behaved (like the Irish *crosán*, the Welsh *clerwr* was another variety of low-class buffoon), it made him sound very much like a Welsh cousin of the *cáinte* and his ilk:

Ar y clerwr y perthyn dynwared, ymsennv, ymwaradwydhaw, ymserthv, ac ymdhybhalv; a hynny ar gerdh chwithic dhigribh, i beri chwerthin.[163]

[To the *clerwr* pertains: imitating, taunting, disparaging, vilifying, and mocking in imaginative language, and that in an amusing, perverse poem, to cause laughter.]

And here *dynwared* ('imitating'), the essential skill of any actor, heads the list of the abilities of a *clerwr*. Gruffud ap Cynan, to whom the Welsh text was attributed and who lived *c* 1055–1137, was born in Ireland of an Irish mother, and as the annalist Tadeus Dowling recounted it in his *Annales Hiberniae*, Gruffud *duxit secum ex hibernia lyras, tympanas cruttas cytharas Cytharizantes*[164] ('he [Gruffud ap Cynan] took with him from Ireland lyres, *timpáns*, harps, and harpers'). Conditions were right for a degree of cultural exchange, and for an influence that could have been reciprocal, not just one-way traffic.

But it was not only professional entertainers who might participate in the elements of play-acting, for in certain kinds of social context, ordinary Irish country folk joined them by becoming nonce players themselves, just as in Kilkenny and Dublin, ordinary townsfolk were found 'playing' on the feast of Corpus Christi and on certain other occasions. It is to these contexts, the seed bed also for a non-professional, 'lay' variety of native Gaelic drama, a drama popular in the strict sense, that we will now turn.

'You'd hear the penny poets singing in an August fair.'
(J.M. Synge, *The Playboy of the Western World*)[165]

One of Nathaniel Hawthorne's attacks on the repressiveness of New England Puritanism is couched within a lyrically confectioned description of a folk wedding around a maypole.[166] The Puritans, 'dismal wretches, who said their prayers before daylight,' have spied on the proceedings in order to overthrow them, and eventually hack down the maypole and with it the way of life that it stands for.

The sort of rosy distortion at work in Hawthorne's account of the wedding revellers and their kind, 'wandering players, whose theatres had been the halls of noblemen,' has, on reflection, a lot in common with its ostensible opposite, the antipathy often expressed against such celebration in the period under review here. Illiterate folk culture, which *de facto* cannot write any manifesto of its own in which it may represent itself to posterity, may soon fall a prey to the party interests of the literate who report it, and often its very documentation, whether by the ill or the well disposed, is likely to stand as *prima facie* proof of some sort of radical alienation from it on the part of the documentor. Yet this documentation, circumspectly used, may yield insights, in spite of identifiable biases. Indeed, since it is normally all that there is to go on, it seems prudent to make some attempt to come to terms with it.

From early Gaelic Ireland there survives no description as elaborate as that which Hawthorne invents for comparable sorts of folk custom. The folk gatherings that took place at *oenaige* ('fairs,' 'assemblies'), seasonal festivities, and wakes, and which, as will be seen, were likely *foci* for dramatic activity, are usually to be glimpsed fleetingly in the sources. When a cleric alludes to them, scant allusion and ample censure seem the order of the day.[167] This looks to have been a clerical policy, for any more detailed description of goings-on considered scandalous might prove unproductively enticing to those who were supposed to be being warned off them. Even the (rather fewer) friendly descriptions of folk gatherings may look meagre from the modern point of view, though this time probably because authors could assume their audience's prior familiarity with activities which thus needed mentioning only in passing and in the briefest of terms. Hence for one reason or another, some of the important folk contexts in which the Gaelic entertainer functioned are largely obscured, though as we will see, perhaps not utterly. Now we will move on to consider some of those fitfully-glimpsed contexts in which not only professional performers may have been active, but also amateur ones. One of the key activities for investigation in this regard will be the playing of games, or *cluichí*, as they are often called in Irish. *Cluichí* seem to have been a factor common to folk gatherings of many different types. The explanation in the *Sanas Cormaic* of the *Lughnasad* (the ancient August assemblies originally commemorating the god Lugh) virtually equates games with fairs: *Cluiche no aonach, is dó is ainm násad* ('a game or a fair, for that reason is its name *násad* [i.e., an assembly of festive or commemorative nature]').[168] Understanding what a *cluiche* could entail may shed additional light upon the early Gaelic perception of the nature and function of the activity that we now tend more stringently to quarantine as 'drama.'

Aristocratic banquetings provided the occasions on which most of the professional entertainment surveyed earlier in this chapter took place. Only one example was given of attendance of professional performers at the larger and more public open-air assembly known as the *oenach* (plural, *oenaige*).[169] Though professionals gravitated towards gatherings like these (an English tract of 1623, for example, speaks of 'bardes Caroughes {< *cerrbhach*, 'gambler'} rymers Irish Harpers pipers & others of their kinde' assembling at christenings, marriages, funerals, and other solemn occasions),[170] they would not have been the sole purveyors of entertainment, for *oenaige*, seasonal festivities, and wakes, which unlike private household banquets would admit a wider wedge of the population, seem typically to have featured communal *cluichí* in the course of their proceedings. Before looking at the *cluichí* in more detail, it might first be said that an *oenach* was another of those occasions whose circumstances were already peculiarly conducive to fostering the kind of activity from which play-acting draws its being. The early Irish laws made it clear that each king throughout Ireland was bound to convene an *oenach* for his tribe at regular intervals, and the site of the *oenach*, normally an ancient burial ground, might even be adapted for the purposes of the meeting by the building of appropriate earth works. The raising of *forad* and *fert* mounds,[171] for example, apart from whatever ritual or social significance they doubtless had, would also have served the purely practical turn of giving a good vantage point to those who occupied them, and thus the *oenach* site was, in the most essential sense, a θέατρον, a place for viewing. Indeed, when a glossator at work in the early-ninth-century Book of Armagh writes the gloss *in oinach* against the *in theatrum* of Acts 19:29 ('Et impleta est civitas confusione, et impetum fecerunt uno animo in theatrum' 'And the city was filled with confusion, and they rushed together into the theatre'), and when he adds on the word *theatrum* a further gloss 'uel teathrum .i. spectaculum' ('or theatre, that is, a spectacle'),[172] he seems to imply precisely this, that the *oenach* was a place for viewing things, a *theatrum* in which no less than *spectacula* were presented. Contests of various sorts were prominent at *oenaige*, according to a glossator of the early-fifteenth century *Leabhar Breac*.[173] But since contests are only *cluichí* in a specialized form, they too, like *cluichí*, require a spectating audience.[174] In this sense, the views of the two glossators, though separated by some five or six hundred years, are quite consistent with each other.

References to *cluichí* at *oenaige* abound, although only rarely is their content described. The *oenach* of Carmun, for example, mentioned earlier as a venue for Gaelic entertainers, had its *cluichí*.[175] The more famous *oenach* of Tailtiu too, according to one of the poems of the *dindshenchas* tradition ('history of notable places' or literally, 'hill lore'), provided a forum for the playing of *cluichí*. The poem, attributed to the famous Cúán Ó Lothcháin in 1006, explains that this *oenach* originated with the legendary lady Tailtiu who, after felling a wood single-handed and reclaiming its land for a meadow, was mortally weakened by her exertion. Nevertheless before she died, she was able to tell the men of Ireland that they should play a 'mourning game' (a *cluiche caíntech*) to commemorate and lament her passing:

Im kalaind Auguist atbath,
día lúain, Loga Lugnasad;
imman lecht ón lúan ille
prím-óenach hÉrend áine.[176]

[About the Calends of August she died, on a Monday, on the
Lugnasad of Lugh; round her grave from that Monday forth
is held the chief *oenach* of noble Ireland.]

'The chief *oenach* of noble Ireland' is thus explained as being descended from Tailtiu's funeral rites, rites which included *cluichí*. Here the association of the *oenach* originally with funeral rites is significant, and hints at another social context and venue in which game-playing featured, the wake and the graveyard. A strong connection evidently existed in Gaelic tradition between assembly places for the *oenach* and burial grounds,[177] and it makes an interesting comparison to observe that when in 1367 Archbishop Thomas Minot banned *ludos teatrales & ludibriorum spectacula* ('theatrical games and spectacles of wantonness') from churchyards in the Dublin province,[178] he was attacking an activity which, even if it may have been imported in the first place from England, would have been encouraged by meeting with its like when transplanted to Irish soil. Wakes and graveyards are, in the anthropological sense, liminal occasions and places, thresholds of commerce between the living and the dead that are liable to attract and be negotiated by ritual forms of behaviour. It should be recalled that the nine shaggy jet-black *crosáin* who erupted into the narrative of the *Sénadh Saigri*, that *locus classicus* of *crosán* behaviour, assembled at nightfall around the grave of the dead king, Donnchadh the Fat. Though *cluichí* were absent from what the *crosáin* did on that occasion (or at least from as much as we are told of it), the essential point is that they were said to be involved at a time of death and at a graveside: and the *crosáin*, of course, were performers who kept company with such professional *drúith* and their kind as were discussed earlier.[179]

Like the *cluichí* played at *oenaige*, so too those played at wakes are mentioned with similar frequency and brevity in early sources. In the late Middle Irish story of the *Tochmarc Luaine ocus Aided Athairne* (the 'Wooing of Luaine and Violent Death of Athirne'), for example, the hapless Luaine, target of a satire virulent enough to kill her, has a mourning game played after her death:

Do-ronnad nuallguba dermáir ós cind na hingine and sin, 7 ro hagad a cepóc 7 a cluithi caíntech 7 ro sáigid a lia.[180]

[A mighty lamentation was then made about the young girl, and her death-chant and her mourning game were performed, and her gravestone was planted.]

Or again the late Old Irish *Orgain Dind Ríg* (the 'Destruction of Dind Ríg') may be compared, when Cobthach arranges his funeral rites in advance:

'Tairsiu imbárach,' or Cobthach, 'cor' altar mo fhert-sa latt, [7 coro clantar mo lia, 7 coro hagthar m'oenach ngubae, 7 coro ferthar mo hilach adnaccuil], ar atbélsa ar lúath.'[181]

['Come tomorrow,' said Cobthach, 'that my grave may be built by you, and that my grave-stone may be set up, and that my mourning assembly may be held, and that my funeral cry may be poured forth, for I shall die shortly.']

The editors of the *Dictionary of the Irish Language* were confident enough to assume that Cobthach's *oenach ngubae* (strictly, 'mourning assembly') signified 'funeral games,'[182] possibly because they had in mind the common currency of *cluichí* at any *oenach*, and the fact that *cluichí* and funeral rites associated closely.

What the nature of these *cluichí* may have been is an important question, but one that may only be broached obliquely. Often when they are given any further definition at all, they prove to have been contests of one kind or another, and in some cases they were probably horse-races.[183] But for the most part they are not so defined. The word *cluichí* remains open-ended, signifying 'games' generally, and is used by writers without further explanation. Had Luke Gernon, author of *A Discourse of Ireland*, been clearer about what he had in mind when he referred to the 'antickes at theyr buryalls,' that is, at burials among the native Irish, we might now be better placed to understand more about the nature of *cluichí*: it is teasing to recall that in 1620 when he wrote his *Discourse*, the noun 'antik' in English usage very commonly meant a grotesque pageant or theatrical representation.[184] As it is, there seems only one way that the disadvantaged modern reader can approach the possible referents behind the early *cluichí*, and that is by drawing analogies with festival and wake *cluchí* that until quite recently were played widely throughout Ireland.[185] Analogies, of course, cannot be pressed too far, for it is impossible to prove the lineal descent of modern games from those played in earlier times. It is never-theless a safe conclusion that the modern games provided a means of addressing social needs that would have been equally as urgent in Gaelic society. Moreover, since the modern games characteristically occurred in exactly the same sort of social context as was afforded by the early Gaelic *oenach* or *oenach ngubae*, it becomes a matter of some interest to observe that very many of the modern *cluichí* had action that was strongly mimetic, so much so, indeed, that *cluichí* of this sort were identified by one modern commentator as having formed a distinctive and well established game genre, the *cluichí aithrise* ('imitative games').[186]

The wake game of *An Muilleoir Bodhar* ('The Deaf Miller'), to choose but one example of this genre, entailed impersonation of characters in a rudimentary plot, and was, in effect, a short play.[187] In this game, someone playing the deaf miller would sit in the middle of the floor mixing soot and water in a dish with a stick. He continued his mock milling, talking to himself, until eventually his 'mill-hand' entered carrying another player, a 'sack of corn,' on his back, and told the miller that the corn in the sack was for grinding. The miller pretended not to hear, and ordered the mill-hand to stack the sack up behind him. Later, having stacked up five or six such sacks, the mill-hand shouted that the mill was ablaze, upon which the miller threw his sooty water backwards over his shoulder onto the heaped-up players. However unsophisticated all this may sound, as a game *An Muilleoir Bodhar* had undisputable dramatic vigour. This was precisely the energy that one nineteenth-century Irish country man thought so singularly lacking in stage plays, pale imitations by comparison. Lady Wilde reported his reaction on seeing his first Dublin play, put on in one of the city's theatres: 'I have now seen the great English actors, and heard plays in the English tongue, but poor and dull they seemed to me after the acting of our own people at the wakes and fairs; for it is a truth, the English cannot make us weep and laugh as I have seen the crowds with us when the players played and the poets recited their stories.'[188] Evidently, acting in the Dublin theatre had suggested to him a comparison with things he had seen performed at wakes and fairs; he did not say whether these wake and fair performances were 'plays' or 'games' (though he implied they were dramatically mimetic in some way when he spoke of 'the acting of our own people ... when the players played' in them). In fact, it may be that for him the distinction between a 'play' and a 'game' was not a very substantial one. This opens an interesting possibility that deserves further illustration, and from a period closer to that with which we are primarily concerned.

Some time between 1621, the year of its publication in Flanders, and 1636, an English version of the rule of St Clare came itself to be translated into Irish by Fathers Aodh Ó Raghailligh and Séamus Ó Siaghail.[189] The particular word they chose by which to translate the English word 'playes' in the following injunction to the sisters is noteworthy:

Furthermore, we ordaine, that all the Sisters present and to come, do alwayes, and in all places abstaine from all secular, & vaine pastimes, and from all worldly vaine playes of what thing, or in what sort soeuer they be.

Tuilledh ele, ordoighem don uile Shíar dá ffhuil 7 da mbía, iad féen do chongbháil gach amm, 7 in gach áit ón uile chaithemh aimsire sáoghalta, 7 díomháoinech, 7 óna huile chluichthibh díomháoine domhanda gíbé ní nó modh ar bioth ma mbíd.[190]

It is improbable that the English word 'playes' in this context was intended to refer exclusively to dramatic performances; it seems more likely that something less specific, 'games' in general, was what was intended. If so, 'playes' would simply be a variation on the word 'pastimes' mentioned earlier in the same sentence.[191] But on the safe assumption that Ó Raghailligh and Ó Siaghail were competent translators of English, their choice of the Irish word *cluichthibh* to render 'playes' is noteworthy. In the early-seventeenth century, the word 'playe,' without respect to any restrictions on its meaning that its context here might impose, denoted a wider range of activity than it generally does today. It might mean, for example, 'plays' in the modern, narrowly theatrical sense, or 'games' and even 'sports' or 'contests.' Consequently, it looks as if at some level there may have been no conceptual difference between 'play' as 'drama' and 'play' as 'game'; or to put it another way, that the activities of 'drama' and 'game' were perceived to have had enough in common for them to share one word, 'play.'

This perception of the fundamental similarity between drama and simple recreation is a far cry from certain serious-minded modern views which prefer to find in drama some lofty purpose, however that may be conceived, and which are therefore prone to regard simple entertainment as a trivialization. Yet a perception of drama in which 'a play is play,' as Peter Brook put it, was a longstanding one in these islands at least from medieval times.[192] Therefore, Ó Raghailligh and Ó Siaghail's choice of *cluichthibh* to translate 'playes' may imply that *cluichthibh* may similarly have been a hold-all word, and that in Ireland no less than in England, the same word could serve various ends. If this particular Irish word for 'games' was capable of containing, and therefore concealing, senses that today would be more stringently distinguished as 'plays' or 'drama,' another reason emerges to explain why any native dramatic tradition would be hard to detect from our modern vantage point. We may simply be approaching the Irish word from too limited a present-day comprehension of what activities *cluichí*, 'games,' could have embraced, not to mention our approaching it from some refined reluctance to admit that 'games' is a word compatible with our dignified notions of what theatre proper ought to be about.

It is entirely likely, then, that certain *cluichí* may have been dramatic in nature, but any drama they contained, as the word *cluichí* implies, would have been perceived as a drama of 'sport' or 'game.' The implications of this are important to grasp. A drama of 'sport' or 'game' does not imply one which entails an all-round lack of seriousness, even though the final product, as in the game of *An Muilleoir*

Bodhar, might be hilarious entertainment; the game played today by a team of professional footballers, for instance, is taken very seriously, and is the result of weeks of dedicated, strenuous effort. Games succeed in entertaining only if in some sense they are played seriously and their rules carefully followed. Like any other game, dramatic *cluichí* equally would have been undertaken in a certain spirit of earnest, called for not only by the inner requirements that shape any game, the rules which structure it, but also by the context in which the *cluichí* occurred. Rites of passage, certain seasons of the year, and fairs might demand *cluichí*, and also perhaps *cluichí* that were peculiar to the occasion, just as storytelling, for example, seems to have been thought appropriate to specific times of the year and reserved for them.[193]

Any drama of 'sport' or 'game' played under the general aegis of *cluichí* further suggests a drama that would have been perceived essentially as a *pretence*. Its mimesis was probably achieved by declaredly unreal means and with few concessions to illusionism, just as in another modern wake game, *Na Beacha ag Cruinniú Meala* ('The Bees Gathering Honey'), onlookers were required to pretend that the boys who buzzed in a ring around another boy, and who held water in their mouths, ready to spit it onto him, were bees returning with honey to a hive.[194] The distance here between signifiers and signified would have been interpreted as the sort of comic rift appropriate to 'game'; a make-believe is often the more enjoyable for the postures it makes against the very reality that it proffers to mimic. Such a drama too is easily manufactured from very few means (elaborate props and scenes, for example, are neither needed nor desired), and consequently as drama it is economical, practical and, even more so than is usually the case, ephemeral. In these respects it would have resembled a veritable Poor Theatre, to use Grotowski's phrase.[195]

Where a variety of circumstantial evidence exists for believing that certain of the early *cluichí* may have had dramatic status, it seems perverse to deny that they could have contributed anything to a native Gaelic dramatic tradition, despite the absence of categorical proof that they ever did. But this survey has argued not merely from circumstantial evidence; earlier, a case was made for the cultivation of dramatic skills amongst members of a well established, professional class of performing artists. These entertainers, as will be seen in the next chapter, were sometimes welcomed within the Pale where they vied successfully with their English and Anglo-Irish colleagues. Certain English expatriates in Ireland would formerly have been accustomed to seeing dramatic shows and pastimes. In some cases, these people would even have seen shows of great sophistication presented at the London court.[196] If Gaelic entertainers ever performed in front of these English men and women, and evidence survives to prove that indeed they did, it makes no sense to suppose that they would have been incapable of catering to their tastes. Adaptability, rather, is the condition that one fourteenth-century Gaelic poet archly advertises, if here only within the practice (and thus performance) of poetry:

Dá chineadh dá gcumthar dán
i gcrích Éireann na n-uarán,
na Gaoidhilse ag boing re bladh,
is Goill bhraoininnse Breatan.

I ndán na nGall gealltar linn
Gaoidhil d'ionnarba a hÉirinn;
Goill do shraoineadh tar sáil sair
i ndán na nGaoidheal gealltair.[197]

[There are two races to whom poetry is sung in the land of
Ireland of the springs – the Gaels, known to fame, and
the Galls of the dewy isle of Britain. In poetry for the Galls
we promise that the Gaels shall be expelled from Ireland;
in poetry for the Gaels we promise that the Galls shall
be driven eastwards over the sea.]

In keeping customers satisfied, it would have paid to be flexible, and the signs are
that dramatic skills were already to hand in the native Gaelic tradition, making flexibility in this area too a relatively simple matter. Probably it was less a question of
the Gaelic entertainer aping something new after the English fashion, as has generally been thought, than of his tailoring similar long-standing skills from his native
tradition to the requirements of whomever he was performing in front of, whether
that was native Gael or newcomer Gall.

A GREAT CLOUD OF (HOSTILE) WITNESSES

The seduction of English audiences, who since Richard de Clare's landing in 1169
were now beginning to arrive in Ireland in quantity, seems to have proved a relatively easy thing for Gaelic entertainers to contrive. Early signs of weakness were
shown by Giraldus Cambrensis who, though very little in Ireland suited his taste,
made a notable exception in the case of Irish music. His initiation into this, or at
least its reputation, may already have occurred in his native Wales, and so disposed
him favourably for his eventual encounter with it on its home ground.[198] Unlike the
tarda & morosa ... modulatio ('slow and mournful ... modulation') that the British
were accustomed to hearing from their musicians, Irish music, as played on harp and
timpán, had a sonority (*sonoritas*) that was *uelox & preceps. Suauis tamen & iocunda*
('swift and dashing, yet sweet and pleasing').[199] Whether later writers were intimi-
dated by, or simply deferential to, the *auctoritas* surrounding Giraldus's *Topographia
Hibernica*, they respectfully recycled its opinions, and hence helped to further the

reputation of Irish music abroad. If Giraldus, who was not to spend long in Ireland, could be won over, how much more so those colonists who stayed and were acculturated? It would be a sturdy man who chose to swim against the tide of high opinion prevailing in his host culture about the merits of native Irish music. Homegrown dissenters to the received view, like the sixteenth-century Dubliner Richard Stanihurst, were therefore not surprisingly few and far between. His scathing account of a harper in action says as much about the security of his Old English identity as it does about his personal musical likes and dislikes; evidently, this identity was robust enough in other respects not to feel that it was obliged to rehearse traditional pieties about Irish musicianship in order to flag an Irish loyalty, and Stanihurst was comfortable enough with himself to be able to afford the following unflattering sketch: 'when the harper twangeth or singeth a song, all the company must be whist, or else he chafeth like a cutpurse, by reason his harmony is not had in better price.'[200] In any event, his heretical opinion was the exception to prove the rule, and not long afterwards was trounced by Philip O'Sullivan Beare in the *Zoilomastix*. O'Sullivan Beare addressed Stanihurst not as a credible historian but as a benighted iconoclast of Irish culture, emphasizing his rooted antipathy to the very society that he presumed to describe.[201]

Some Gaelic performing artists, and notably (though not exclusively) harpers, were being perceived as pillars of the Gaelic social order, and this not only by the Irish natives. The powerful institutional entrenchment of the Gaelic performing arts, which until now this chapter has chiefly illustrated from native sources, is witnessed yet again refracted through the stern reactions that those arts and their practitioners were able to provoke from the people whose job it was to govern the island and reduce it to order. The heightened English awareness of the seditious, oppositional role of Gaelic entertainers may be an indication that Gaelic society, at this date largely factional and lacking in such national political institutions as might confer upon it a sense of nation-wide solidarity, was tending to rely on its ritual specialists – storytellers, harpers, and performers of various sorts – to head its political and military response to the English colonial presence.[202] Possibly the earliest example of this sort of testimony is to be found in the *Breviat* of Patrick Finglas. Finglas held various judicial offices in Ireland from 1509 until his death in 1537, including from 1523 to 1524 that of chief baron of the Treasury.[203] His *Breviat*, written between 1509 and 1534 (probably towards the latter end of that time span),[204] decrees:

that noe Irish mynistrells Rymouers, Shannaghes {< *senchaide*, 'reciters of lore'}, ne Bardes messengers come to desire anie goodes of anie man dwellinge within the English pall {'Pale'} vpon payne of forefeiture of all their goodes, and their bodyes to be imprisoned at the Kings will/.[205]

Almost contemporary were two other testimonies to English apprehensiveness, the letter of Robert Crowley to Secretary Thomas Cromwell of July 1537, and in the same year, *The Justice Luttrels Booke*. Both are particularly telling documents, identifying as they do a theme in English criticism of Irish minstrels that would swell to a burden as time went by. The relevant excerpt from Crowley's letter runs as follows:

Harpers Rymors Irishe Cronyclers Bardes and Isshallyn {< *aos ealaíon*, 'people of art,' 'minstrels'} comonly goo with praisses to gentilmen in the english pale praysing in Rymes otherwise callid danes {< *dán*, 'poetry'} their extorcious Roboryes and abvses as valiauntnes/. whiche reioysith therin in that their evell doinges./ And procure a talent of Irishe disposicion and conuersacion in theme/ whiche is likewise convenyent to bee expellid/.[206]

This complaint reveals precisely the sort of impish policy that the Gaelic poet had recommended as far back as the fourteenth century, a trimming of the performance to suit the tastes of the audience. To judge by Crowley's assessment, this policy had actual subscribers. What is more, his concerns show how right the English administration was to be fearful when Gaelic entertainment might offer not merely gratification for the nonce, but in due time might also accomplish a more challenging and dangerous form of cultural seduction: entertainers helped to win the English over to an Irish way of life. The performing arts in Ireland, which as we have seen might affirm in their audiences a sense of their Gaelic cultural identity as much as they might merely provide entertainment, could pose a material threat to English cultural dominance or 'civility,' as it was usually called by its proponents. A steady stream of complaint that flowed from the walled towns and colonial centres from the fourteenth century onwards was, by the sixteenth century, in full spate, and the volume of this complaint seems to have been directly proportional to the attendant sixteenth-century English anxiety to secure Irish interests once and for all. The documents that English settlers left, hostile witnesses though they be, usefully corroborate some of the things already observed from native sources concerning the Gaelic entertainer classes, while adding details either sparsely represented in the Gaelic sources or even not represented there at all. A unique survival preserved among the Carew Papers in Lambeth Palace Library may serve as a convenient entrée to this wealth of English material, and through it two related matters of interest may be broached: first, the question of which Gaelic performing artists came to loom largest in the English consciousness, and second, what exactly the English imagined them as doing and in what circumstances.

On 7 November 1584, instructions were drafted for the earl of Desmond to 'diligently enquire and true presentment make of all such persons within this Realme of Ireland as Carry the names of Poetes, Cronyclers or Rymers, declaringe their names, dwellinge places, the Countyes they dwell in,' as well as to 'sett downe whom they appertayne vnto or serve, Or of whom for the most part they depend and followe, And who be their cheif mainteyn<ers> and vpholders.'[207] Though this inquest was stated to apply to 'this Realme of Ireland,' in practice it centred on the province of Munster, Desmond's home territory, and only a portion of it at that. The earl had been in rebellion between 1579 and 1583, and the instructions were part of a programme of repressive measures adopted by the English administration to help subdue a fractious province. Though the list declared 'Poetes, Cronyclers or Rymers' to be the agents of sedition that needed to be identified and routed, in fact it went a little further, for names of bards, she-bards, and harpers were also included on it. In all, an impressive tally of some seventy-three or more persons mounts up and, in some cases, their locations, specific professions and employers were also recorded.[208] Those who were poets, bards, and rhymers can, with some qualification, be set aside for present purposes: English sources were not altogether consistent in what they imagined these words to have referred to in a Gaelic context,[209] and while it is doubtless true that some poets, bards, and rhymers would have performed their own verse,[210] the mere mention of them cannot in itself be taken to imply as much. Indeed, there is evidence to suggest that at least by the late twelfth or early thirteenth century, those who composed verse were not necessarily also those who recited it: recitation was sometimes performed by a specialist *reccaire* ('reciter'), as was seen earlier.[211] And by the sixteenth century, such evidence is even clearer. Thomas Smyth, whose observations of 1561 will later be revisited, noted that the 'Rymer' who composed the verse was only one part of a quartet (the other three being the 'Rakry,' the harper, and the bard, the latter 'a kinde of folise fellowe'), and that while these other three saw his composition into effect, the 'Rymer' preened himself on a back seat: 'Nowe comes the rymer· that made the Ryme with is Rakry the Rakry· is he that shall vtter· the Ryme and the Rymer· him selfe sittes by with the captin verie proudlye/ he bringes with him· also his harper; who please {'plays'} all the while that the Raker singes the Ryme/ also he hath is barde which is a kinde of folise fellowe/.'[212] Two texts from the native tradition confirm the fundamental accuracy of Smyth's account. One, the anonymous poem *Maithim d'urra dána acht Dia* ('I desire only God for chief of my poetry'), preserved in the seventeenth-century poetic anthology known as the Book of the O'Connor Don, includes the verse: 'Budh í as bhuidhean damh ler ndán / dá mhac [an] muirear [dom] riar; / beirthear leam gomadh é m'iul / mo thriur i gceann an té as triar' ('Two youths, my ministering family, shall form my poetic band; may the three of us be brought by me to the One in Three and may He also be my guide').[213] Here, the poetic band comprised a trio, the poet himself and two others, one of whom we later hear was a *reacaire*.[214] The other text, a report on the mission to Scotland which the Irish Franciscan Cornelius Ward and his confrères undertook in the latter part of 1624, relates how Ward, now arrived in Muckairn on the Scottish mainland, set about converting the laird Campbell of Calder. Ward smuggled himself into Calder's presence *simulandi me esse poetam Hybernum (hos inibi in maximo honore haberi solere novi) cumque unum poema encomiasticum in domini illius laudem composuerim, mox cum uno cytharoeda, et cantore (ut moris erat) ingredior, et honorificentissime excipior* ('pretending that I was an Irish poet – I knew it was the custom there to hold these in the greatest esteem – and when I composed a laudatory poem in that laird's praise, I straightway went in, with a harper and, as was customary, a singer, and was most honourably received').[215] The ruse of inventing a poetic band (another trio, it will be noticed) turned upon Ward feigning himself a professional poet, another man a harper, and another a *cantor*, the latter perhaps the Latin equivalent in this context of the *reccaire*. Edmund Spenser too in his 1596 treatise *A View of the Present State of Ireland* noted that 'There is amongst the[re] Irishe a Certaine kynde of people called the bardes, ... theire vearses are taken vpp with a generall applause, and vsuallie sounge at all feasts metinges ... *by certaine other persons whose proper function that is*, which also receyve for the same greate rewardes, and reputacon {*read* reputacion} besides.'[216] Although Spenser did not mention Smyth's 'Rakry' (< *reccaire*) by name, he evidently had the office of someone similar in mind. But before taking final leave of poets, bards, and rhymers, we might pause briefly to reflect on how much they had insinuated themselves into the heart of upper-class Anglo-Irish society; on the strength of the Desmond inquest alone, it can be seen that Lord Barrymore, Lord Roche, and the late earl of Desmond had all kept rhymers.[217] The Gaelic lords had their poets, as is well known; some of the Anglo-Irish ones, no less like them in this respect, evidently had them too, and for similar purposes.[218] The nuclear organization of the poetic class, and the social entrenchment that this implies, is also glimpsed in the list's notice of at least one bardic school in the lordship of Mac Carthaigh Mór in co. Kerry. It mentions: 'Okyll in mc Cartye more is contrey a rymer and one that kepes ma<n>y rymers & bardes togither calling them be the name of okyll is scoule {'Ó Cuil's school'} / Cwnely okylle brother to the syd {*read* sayd} okill, a rimer.'[219] A certain 'Okyll' (< Ó Cuil), had gathered many under his tutelage, and the cohesion of his school may have been strengthened by familial ties: his brother 'Cwnely' (< Cuanla) was in the same profession. Harpers similarly might cluster in families; also included on the list are three harpers who all appear to have been related to each other.[220]

Let us now turn to the remaining *bête noire* at the head of the Desmond list, the chroniclers, to see who these may have been and, through comparison with other sources, what they did. The English word *chronicler* (as for example in Robert Crowley's letter cited above) would appear most nearly to answer to the interlinked Gaelic professions of *scélaige* and *senchaid*, aspects of whose activity, as was earlier illustrated, would have taken place within the sphere of the performing arts. These men, the custodians of the history of the tribe, buttressed the sense of regional

Gaelic identities by invoking the precedents of tradition and keeping past custom before the mind.[221] Along with the efforts of the poets, bards, and rhymers, theirs too acted as a social gelling agent. Public recitation of tales, lore, and genealogies was part of their brief. On an island so manifestly inhabited by competing ideologies and agendas, a state of affairs especially noticeable after the arrival of the New English planters in the years following the Reformation, it is thus not surprising to find *scélaigi* and *senchaide* targeted by hostile witnesses: tradition-bearers are usually among the first to fall in a putsch or invasion. To discover in more detail what they did, it is necessary to consult a range of sources. *Scélaigi* had of course earned a reputation with the Old English administration long before the sixteenth century, for they had already been named in that hapless attempt to stem the waxing tide of Gaelicization, the Kilkenny Statute of 1366. In company with *Tympanors fferdanes … Bablers, Rymors, Clercz* and *autres minstrells Irrois* ('*timpán*-players, poets … bablers, rhymers, clerics' and 'other Irish minstrels'), the *Skelaghes* (< *scélaigi*) were being harboured by the English and given gifts.[222] Their reception, as already noted in the case of other entertainers in other circumstances, was helping steadily to undermine Englishness. The sixteenth century saw several attempts to describe them and, since description then was rarely impartial, to stigmatize them in the same breath. Of the *senchaid* and what he was thought to do, Thomas Smyth has afforded one of the most sustained explanations in this period, though the earliest explanation appeared in Finglas's *Breviat* and the parliamentary ordinances of 1534 discussed above. Smyth is possibly to be identified with the Dublin alderman and apothecary of the same name who eventually became sheriff in 1576 and then mayor in 1591. His tract *Information for Ireland* is situated within a genre of jaundiced English writings about the nature of Irish society which were characteristic of his century, yet which, for all their disaffection, might sometimes be fundamentally well informed.[223] Smyth certainly seems to have been in touch with authentic traditions. About the *senchaid* he had this to say:

The secounde· sourte is the shankee; which is to saye in Englishe they {read the} petigrer they haue also great plaintye of cattell; where· withall they do sucker the rebells./ They make the ignraunt men of the country to belyue that the {read they} be discended of Alixander the great, or of Darrius, or of Ceasar· or of some other notable prince which makes the ignraunt peple to rune madde, and carithe not· what they do; the which is verye hurtfull to the realme[224]

For Smyth, the 'Shankee' (< *senchaid*) was the 'petigrer,' a word not recorded by the *OED* but which is evidently an agentive noun formed upon the word 'pedigree' and meaning something like 'genealogist.' The next significant appearance of the *historicus*, as his Latin incarnation styles him, is in William Camden's *Britannia*. Camden's informant, one William Good, a Limerick priest and schoolmaster active about

1566, must have been sufficiently close to Gaelic culture to be able to describe it to Camden in terms that were accurate enough:

Habent etiam hi magnates suos Historicos qui res gestas describunt, Medicos, Poetas, quos Bardos vocant, & Citharoedos, quibus singulis sua prædia assignati sunt, & singuli sunt vnoquoque territorio è certis & singulis familijs, scilicet Breahani, vnius stirpis & nominis, Historici alterius, & sic de cæteris, qui suos liberos, siue cognatos in sua quilibet {read qualibet} arte erudiunt, & semper successores habent.[225]

[These lords also have their chroniclers who will relate deeds done, doctors, poets (whom they call bards), and harpers, to each of whom are assigned their lands, and some individuals are from one territory and from certain particular families, namely the brehons, of one family and name, the chroniclers of another, and similarly with the rest, who instruct their children or relatives in every art, and always have successors.]

Here the 'chroniclers,' like doctors, poets (*quos Bardos vocant*), harpers, and brehon lawyers, are said to form part of the entourage of Gaelic lords, and in 1571, Edmund Campion noted that: 'One office in the house of great men is a tale-teller, who bringeth his Lord on sleepe, with tales vaine and frivolous, whereunto the number give sooth and credence.'[226] Richard Stanihurst probably got the same idea from him (the two men knew each other), for he repeated it almost verbatim in *A playne and perfect description of Irelande*, published in 1577 as a section of Raphael Holinshed's *Chronicles*.[227] Whatever the case, both Stanihurst and Camden sustain William Good's observation that taletellers consorted with lords, while adding the detail about bedtime reading: the job of lulling people asleep, traditionally one of the harper's accomplishments, is here adopted by the taleteller.[228]

One significant group of performers that the Munster inquest did not uncover, or at any rate not explicitly, was that of the gamblers. They feature in several English documents, and interestingly, it is substantially only here, not in the native Irish records, that they are represented. Today, a liaison between professional gambling and the performing arts may not seem immediately self-evident, though brief reflection should rectify this: the paraphernalia that accompany investing stakes in predicting the future – which dog will outstrip the others in their race after a stuffed mechanical hare, or which six of a jumble of parti-coloured ping-pong balls will fall before any of the rest out of a drum – are the stuff out of which performances are made. (And many modern wrestling matches, so carefully scripted and choreographed as they have become, might be considered theatrical productions in their own right: here, even the pretence of an uncertain outcome must also be performed.) The fact that the events gambled on and which the trappings surround are, in the main, inherently trivial, is altogether to the point. Again we find ourselves returned to the province of game and, as was seen earlier, that necessarily also means to the province of play in the dramatic sense in the period under review. How Irish gamblers could present themselves dramatically will shortly become quite clear, but first, it may be informative to weigh some of the extensive evidence for their existence and way of life.

Their earliest mention in extant English sources is in the 1366 Kilkenny Statute, where they appear in the list of proscribed Gaelic entertainers noted earlier. After this the English records fall silent until the sixteenth century, when evidence for gamblers becomes extensive. Thomas Smyth, in his *Information for Ireland* of 1561, says of the *carruage*,[229] as he has anglicized him:

he is muche like the habram mane {'Abraham man,' 'beggar'}/ and comenlye he goithe nakid/ and carise disses and cardes with him and he will playe the heare of· his head·/ and his eares·/ and thies be mantained by the rymers.[230]

This description anticipates the content and tone of descriptions written throughout the rest of the century and into the next. The carruage or carrowe was already at large in Ireland for several years before 1561, of course, and thus it may well be that the vagaries of record survival are partly responsible for bringing him so copiously to light only from the sixteenth century; in Irish he had already appeared as early as 1486 in the Annals of Connacht, where the death notice of Ruaidrí Mac Diarmata, a chieftain of Moylurg, proclaimed Ruaidrí to be a *congbala cliar 7 cerrbach* (a 'supporter of minstrel bands and gamblers').[231] After Smyth, the carrowe next appears in English records in 1563 in a set of orders to be observed by the earl of Desmond.[232] Next he appears twice in 1576, first in a set of ordinances issued by the Lord Deputy, Sir Henry Sidney,[233] and again in some sessions pertaining to co. Cork which were heard before Sir William Drury in October of 1576. The sessions complaint was to the effect that the gentry of that county were generally neglecting their duties, and were not even managing 'to kepp the stocks in places appointed for to punyshe stowt beggers, Idell vacabounds, naked hasards, shamelesse flatringe slaves, (as to saie) Bards, Owlers, and manye such lick, whereby the foresaid lordes maie be lawfully suspected that they will soner nourishe mantaine and defende such rather then to see them punyshed accordinge to their desarts.'[234] Carrowes, though not mentioned in the sessions complaint by name, feature nevertheless in the guise of *hazards* (that is, dice-players), men on record in these islands from the late thirteenth century.[235] Naked they were, like the carruage of Smyth's account, probably because the chances of losing their bets had conspicuously got the better of some of them. According to the English sources, gamblers sometimes played away everything they owned, including not only the shirts off their backs. One year later, Richard Stanihurst gave an extended description of them, and introduced startling details which would be elaborated by subsequent writers. In Stanihurst, as in Smyth and Drury, gamblers were classed as members of the wider wastrel collective, and moreover in Stanihurst's account, they proved how drastically true the maxim might be that *súil le cúiteamh a chailleas an cearrbhach* ('expecting to recoup is the gambler's downfall'):

There is among them a brotherhood of Karrowes, that profer to play at chartes {'cards'} all ye yere long, and make it their onely occupation. They play away mantle and all to the bare skin, and then trusse themselues in strawe or in leaues; they wayte for passengers in the high way, inuite them to game vpon the grene, & aske them no more but companions to holde them sporte. For default of other stuffe, they paune theyr glibs, the nailes of their fingers and toes, their dimissaries, which they leese {'lose'} or redeeme at the curtesie of the wynner.[236]

Here the gamblers were card-players, as they were in Smyth. The 1580s saw at least four different documents citing them,[237] and two more in 1596: Edmund Spenser's *View of the State of Ireland* and the letter of William Lyon, bishop of Cork, to the Lord Chamberlain. Lyon's letter is worth quoting, for it not only associates carrowes with other familiar offending minstrels, but it also tells us a little about the occasions when they they were wont to come into their own:

Item that some streight order may be taken for idle persons as caroughes, hazardes, Rimers, bardes, & harpers which runne about the countrey not onely eating the laboures of the poore, but bring newes & intelligenses to the rebells agaynst her Majestie, and bruite false tales amongst her subjectes which breedeth great mischief: And also the Rithmers doo make songes in comendacions & prayses of the treasons, rebellions, spoylinges & prayeinges, & theveinges made, to the greate encoraging of such a people as this is not well stayed vnd_∧[r] governement.

Item that all Lordes & gentlemen be commaunded, that they keepe noe idle men but such as are officers in their houses, for the Lordes & gentlemen vse to take quiddyes {< *cuid oidhche*, 'evening portions,' 'night suppers'} & night suppers vpon their tenantes, & vpon others which are not their tenantes which is a greate nourisher & maynteyner of vagabundes & idle persons. ffor when they goe to those quiddyes & night suppers, then those bardes caroughes Rithmers, hazardes & harpers flock after them in great multitudes, to the mayntenaunce of idlenesse & great grevaunce & impoverishinge of her Majesties subjectes as they daylie complayne of the same. Yt were good if order were taken that these quiddyes, night suppers, coyne, {< *coinnmed*, 'quartering'} & livery, if they be lawfull to be taken were turned into certeyne rent, for then they would not maynteine soe many, if they were maynteyned vpon their owne charges as they doe now vpon other mens costes. And the Shriffes of the countyes are in fault for these idle men, for neyther they nor their officers will apprehend any of these idle persons, because they shall gett nothing' by the[y]m, for they will not serve but for profit, they serve themselves but not her Maiestie: ...[238]

It is clear from all these cases that the word carrowe by the last quarter of the sixteenth century, and probably in fact much earlier, had established itself securely in Hiberno-English usage to describe this reprobate class of gamblers.[239] For Spenser, carrowes were men who played at both cards and dice. Rather more practically minded than their wayside-loitering colleagues who simply waited to pounce on the unsuspecting passer-by, these took the initiative, seeking out gentlemen whose moral backbone they might painlessly remove.[240] Nothing is said of their costume, or lack of it, though this theme, by now perhaps a topos, returns forcefully in the *Itinerary* of Fynes Moryson, written in the early years of the seventeenth century and owing nothing directly, as far as we can tell, to Stanihurst's influential account:

Agayne the Irish in generall more specially the meere Irish, being sloathfull and giuen to nothing more then base Idlenes, they nourished a third generation of vipers vulgarly called Carowes, professing (forsooth) the noble science of playing at Cards and dice, which so infected the publique meetings of the people, and the priuate houses of lordes, as no aduenture was too hard in shifting for meanes to mantayne these sports. And indeed the wilde Irish doe madly affect them, so as they will not ∧⌈oly⌉ {*read* only} play and leese their mony and mouable goods, but also [mitigate] ∧⌈ingage⌉ their lands, yea their owne persons to be ledd as Prisoners by the winner, till he be paid the mony, for which they are ingaged. It is a shame to speake but I heard by credible relation, that some were found so impudent, as they had suffered themselues to be ledd as Captiues tyed by the parts of their body which I will not name, till they had mony to redeeme themselues.[241]

When nothing was left, they suffered themselves to be tethered by the genitals and so lead about, an outlandish eventuality not registered even by Stanihurst, unless *double-entendre* was lurking in the *dimissaries* that he spoke of.[242] The carrowes continued strong into the next century, appearing in 1610 in Barnaby Rich's *A New Description of Ireland*,[243] fleetingly in Sir Parr Lane's poem *News from the Holy Isle* of *c* 1621,[244] and finally in the *Advertisements for Ireland* of 1623.[245]

The brotherhood of carrowes, as both Stanihurst and Rich called it, may have operated either on an individual basis or in groups; on this question the English documents are not on the whole very helpful.[246] If in groups, then presumably each group had internal rules and conventions, however informal, by which its activity was regulated, and its constitution as a distinct group would have made it comparable to those other groups of banded entertainers discussed earlier. Stanihurst and Rich were also both in agreement that carrowes covered their nakedness, which to both authors was a direct consequence of their gambling debts, with straw and leaves (Stanihurst) or simply straw (Rich). If we picture for a moment a group of straw-clad carrowes, ready with their dice or cards to start gaming with whoever was willing to engage them, then an interesting possibility emerges: perhaps the dressing in straw and leaves was not necessarily an expediency forced upon them, rationalized as such though it was by both our commentators, but a form of distinctive *costume*. (The persistence to this day of the Ulster strawboys shows that the practice of using straw for devising antic costumes has a long Irish history.[247]) This suggestion gains some weight from comparison of a unique and remarkable text which documents certain events that occurred in Ulster in 1602. Captain Josias Bodley, brother of the more famous Thomas who gave his name to the eponymous library in Oxford, recorded his Christmastide entertainment, which took place possibly at Downpatrick, but in any case somewhere in the barony of Lecale, co. Down. His account repays close attention:

Et jam iterum ad Lecalium nostrum, ubi inter alia, quæ ad hillaritatem conferebant, venerunt vna nocte post Cænam Maschari quidam ex Nobilibus Hibernicis, numero quatuor (si recte memini) Illi primum miserunt ad Nos literas Fustianas secundum antiquam phrasim, post nostras cordiales commendationes &cetera dicentes, se fuisse certos Aduenas nuper arriuatos in illis partibus, & valde cupidos preterire vnam, vel alteram horam Nobiscum, & post concessam veniam isto ordine ingrediuntur. Primo puer cum tæda accensa, tunc duo pulsantes tympana, tunc ipsi Maschari duo, & duo, tunc altera tæda. Vnus ex Mascaris portabat sordidum emunctorium cum decem Libris intus, non ex Bullione, sed ex noua pecunia nuper impressa, quæ habet Lyram ab vno latere, & Insignia Regalia ab altero. Induebantur Canisijs {*read* Camisijs} cum multis folijs Hæderæ hic, & illic sparsim consutis, & super Facies suas habebant Maschas ex pelle Cuniculi cum foraminibus ad videndum extra, & Nasi erant facti ex papyro, Galeri vero alti, et pyramidales (more persico) etiam ex papyro ornati cum dictis Folijs. Dicam breui, ludimus Tesseris; nunc Tympana ex illorum partibus, nunc Tuba ex nostris sonabat.[248]

[And now back to our Lecale, where, amongst the various things which roused our mirth, there came one night after dinner certain maskers, Irish noblemen, four in number, if I remember rightly. First they sent us preposterous letters (according to the old expression) which, after cordially greeting us, announced that they were certain forreigners, recently arrived in those parts, and that they were very keen on spending an hour or two with us. And after getting permission, they enter in this order. First, a boy with a lighted torch, then two [men] beating drums, then the masquers themselves, two by two, then another torch. One of the masquers carried a dirty handkerchief with ten pounds in it, not in bullion, but in the new currency recently minted, which has a harp on one side and the royal arms on the other. They were dressed in shirts with ivy leaves sown on, thickly in some places, and thinly in others, and over their faces they had masks made out of rabbit skin, with holes to see out of, and their noses were made of paper, with high, conical helmets (in the Persian manner), also made from paper and decorated with the same leaves. Let me be brief: we play at dice, now with drum rolls from their side, now with trumpet flourishes from ours.]

The scene is set after supper, when Bodley and his friends were ready for recreation. The masquers, as he calls them, were in fact Irish nobles, not low-class carrowes, to be sure, but for the rest, the salient features of their performance beg comparison with the carrowes as already glimpsed in the earlier English documents. There were four in all, so evidently they operated as a group on this occasion. They assumed a fictitious identity (as characters in a game or play often do), announcing it in letters sent in to the company in advance: they were 'certain forreigners, recently arrived in those parts' (*certos Aduenas nuper arriuatos in illis partibus*). When they entered, they did so dramatically, preceeded first by a boy with a blazing torch and then by two drummers. They themselves entered in two pairs, and finally there came another torchbearer. The appearance of these 'forreigners' seems especially to have struck Bodley, for he recorded it carefully: shirts with ivy leaves sown on, rabbit-skin masks with paper noses, and headdresses which were conical paper affairs similarly covered with ivy leaves. The action at the centre of this garnish was a game of dice, punctuated with drum rolls and trumpet flourishes.

It may be suspected that the evening's entertainment was a hybrid of English and Irish forms. Elements of the upper-class English pastime of masking are clearly apparent in it, especially in the way in which it was stage-managed. In substance the entertainment had already been anticipated long before in fourteenth-century England when a group of mummers played dice, tactfully loaded to allow their royal contestant to win, with the young prince Richard.[249] The arrangement depicted in a sixteenth-century English illumination of masquers entering a hall similarly shows them entering in pairs, the front two carrying torches and the back two musical instruments, which makes the choreography of the scene very like that of its Irish cousin and unlike only in terms of its relative economy, with four persons in the English example as opposed to eight in the Irish one.[250] Irish input into the Lecale performance might be suspected in the way in which the masquers dressed: their conical headdresses seem to foreshadow those still worn by the Ulster strawboys for mummings. The masque genre had already been imported into Ireland some years before its appearance in Lecale, as will later be seen in chapter 6, and acquaintance with the genre might have been expected in men who, by virtue of their social position *ex Nobilibus Hibernicis*, would thus be more likely to have encountered it. Yet dressed in leaves and playing dice, they are also reminiscent of the Gaelic carrowes, albeit ones elevated to the masquer's level.[251] For all the paraphernalia of their pretence, their gambling stakes remained real enough: when eventually the masquers were quite cleaned out, they returned home in the early hours dispirited, 'like a dog that has been hit with a cudgel or a stone, running off with its tail between its legs,' as Bodley put it.[252]

This account of what a selection of hostile witnesses had to say about Gaelic performing artists can now be brought to a close with some consideration, as promised earlier, of the circumstances in which the English were particularly aware of their various performances having taken place. First, it might be useful to summarise those circumstances, many of which have already been alluded to in this chapter, which Gaelic evidence shows were liable to attract entertainers. They may be generally categorized as occasions of public or private celebration, whatever serious business they also saw transacted. There were public fairs and assemblies, like the *oenaige* previously discussed. There were ordinary times of recreation within aristocratic households and times of greater importance on festive high days; the former afforded a steady opportunity to entertainers to ply their trade throughout the year and the latter a special showcase for their wares. Of feasts it might be said that there were various sorts.[253] Some were private functions, some were offered ostentatiously by lords to an invited group of outsiders, and some were exacted by lords from their clients. Feasting by invitation, which chapter 6 will consider in more detail, and guesting by exaction, were often seasonal affairs. The rhythm of everyone's life, whether of the aristocrat or the menial, was determined by an annual agricultural cycle. From the start of Samhain (1 November), the longer nights focused attention on matters domestic as people congregated indoors in larger numbers. One of the two great Christian feasts, of course, fell during this period, and the English were fully aware of how this was one of the times of year when entertainers were liable to roam. For example, orders were passed for Connacht and Thomond, as well as for Munster, in the Dublin parliament of 12 July 1541 to head such entertainers off. These orders were intimately related to a similiar set passed for Dublin whose text, somewhat less corrupt than that of the provincial ones, may be given here in illustration: 'Item similiter constitutum est quod nulli mimj histriones aut ceteri Munerum exquisitores in solemnitatibus natalis domini aut pasche aut alio quocumque tempore decetero admittantur nec aliquid minus {*read* munus} eis tribuantur {*read* tribuatur} sub pena perdicionis vnius auris' ('Item. It is similarly decided that no *mimi, histriones,* or other seekers after rewards be admitted on the solemnities of the birth of Our Lord or Easter or any other time whatsoever, and that no reward be given them, on pain of the loss of an ear').[254] This dark time of the year was the season associated with storytelling.[255] From January to Shrovetide ran the period associated with feasting and guesting, *cáe,* when nobles might billet their servants upon their clients or make a circuit of those clients and call for hospitality for themselves and their retinues.[256] Then there were the extraordinary occasions for entertainment which fell outside the predictable calendar of events, like funerals or eves of battle. English sources of the sixteenth and seventeenth centuries were aware of many of these occasions, and particularly of the occasions of exacted hospitality which occurred during the cuddy or coshery, as Bishop Lyon's letter quoted above, for example, makes clear.[257] They also noted the presence of entertainers at weddings and christenings, occasions about which the Gaelic sources, oddly enough, are themselves less forthcoming.[258]

In sum, then, the English were right to fear the corrosive potential of the Gaelic performing arts. The ethnic cleanliness of the colony was being muddied, and reiterated English misgivings, traditional though they may in part have been, nevertheless seem a reliable gauge of the sturdiness of those performing arts throughout the sixteenth and well into the early seventeenth century.

CODA

As noted at the outset, the swathe of evidence gathered into this survey has wide chronological limits. Texts have ranged between the seventh and the seventeenth century, and within this period relatively few may be dated with precision. This is especially true of the earliest texts, whose composition dates are to be estimated only on linguistic grounds. Also, comparatively little evidence concerns any historically actual performing artist, let alone any determinable place of performance. Named performers in Gaelic sources are often fictional or legendary, and the sites of their performance vague, exotic, or fabulous. Generalities have unavoidably been thrust upon this chapter. But distressing as these may seem to historians for whom times, places, and persons are the *sine qua non* of adequate history, certain interprovincial and transhistorical trends have persisted in weaving the seemingly disparate evidence together. Not only is this remarkable in itself, but whenever these trends can be corroborated from sources whose purchase on historical reality is less open to doubt, then there should be less reason to be anxious about the historical reality of the sorts of performers and performances described here. So while detailed regional and chronological differences and varieties cannot now be traced in any satisfactory way, more important seem the continuities that can.

Although this chapter has primarily been organized on a thematic rather than consecutively chronological basis, perhaps a brief chronology may be permitted by way of conclusion and as a preface to the chapters ahead in which chronology will be more important. The evidence for the Gaelic performing arts corresponds to three main phases of Irish history. First, there is the phase lasting until the beginning of the Norman invasion and settlement in 1169, which is roughly coextensive with the Old and Middle Irish periods. Next comes a shorter phase, running from the late twelfth century until the Reformation, which saw the establishment of the Old English colony. And finally follows the shortest phase, though in terms of the retrenchment of Gaelic culture the most urgent, from after the Reformation until the end of the period under review. Increasingly from the late twelfth century, then, the island of Ireland is revealed as the site of competing cultures. Those moments of interface when they touched, when each sought to define itself in reaction to the other, expressing identity through difference, were highly productive of the textual evidence that has been drawn upon in this chapter. Interestingly, the status and function of the performing artist were often key issues of these moments of self-definition. But even before the new pluralism of the late twelfth century had begun to express itself, Gaelic society was already internally contradictory in its view of some of the performing artists to whom it played host. They might be perceived at once as central and marginal, as was earlier illustrated. A paradigm of this para-doxical view is the definition of the *réim* ('contortionist') already considered. The *réim* could not expect an honour-price, according to the Old Irish *Míadšlechta*, 'because he goes out of his shape in front of crowds and hosts' (*uair teit asa richt ar belvib sluagh 7 sochaidhe*). What is being said in this text, a law tract anxious to define and thus stabilize a social structure, hedging it around with penalties and sanctions, is that society cannot bestow unequivocal approval on what amounts to a public display of the dissolution of personal integrity and the collapse of identity. The *réim* had a proper 'shape' (*richt*) that he wilfully abandoned. When fixity was the name of the social game, normative texts like *Míadšlechta* would understand-ably be inclined to extol the self-presence of personal identity as a socially cohesive good. Yet the *réim* and his kind, though in society, were not fully of it either, and the law tract strove to set limits to the unstable place which they occupied.[259] It was not only the legal system that tried to do this. As the old maxim had it, *ubi stabilitas, ibi religio*: the church too tried to construct walls of definition and containment around the volatile performing artist. There is a sense, then, in which some perform-ing artists were already thought of as existing in terms of sets of oppositions within Gaelic society even before the deepening complexity of Irish culture that followed in the wake of the twelfth century. And as the pressure on that culture from its competitors mounted – a fate that was to take its toll most noticeably towards the end of the period under review – then those same performers came to be perceived very clearly for what they had ever been, the inalienable, if alternative, voice of a culture.

2

Early Dublin Drama

It is time now to pass from Gaelic Ireland into the heart of the English Pale, although even here, as will be seen, Gaelic Ireland would not be entirely lost from view. On the contrary, Pale dwellers were sharply aware that theirs was an enclave, a wedge carved out of wider dominions whose inhabitants were rarely content with the terms of their 'pacification.'

In the same year that King Henry VIII acceded to the English throne, the cathedral church of St Patrick in Dublin perhaps did as it had been doing for many years when it paid a group of players for some show *cum Angelo magno & paruo ac dracone* ('with the big angel and the little one and the dragon'). Their payment looks to have been quite routine, and nothing in the layout or wording of the entry in the accounts in which it appears would suggest there was anything extraordinary about it. Dramas of various kinds had already been performed in Dublin for a good two hundred years before this. Some would be swept away in the age of change that Henry's accession heralded and other, newer dramatic forms would emerge to cater for newer Renaissance tastes. No less important, they would cater for newer Renaissance power struggles, as the next chapter will show. But for all the changes wrought in the history of Dublin drama during the sixteenth century, there seem comparatively few points at which a radical break was made with past tradition. Varieties of drama would persist throughout the sixteenth century which showed their essential kinship with much earlier forms. The final impression left by a study of the history of drama and the performing arts in Dublin (as indeed by their histories in many other towns in these islands) is one of a tenacious, if evolving, continuity rather than one of rapid revolution.

The founding years, if we may so call them, of Dublin drama yield two pieces of hard evidence of a kind unmatched in the sixteenth century, for two actual play texts survive from this period, one complete and the other fragmentary.[1] Yet at the same time as they strongly suggest theatrical activity in Dublin in the medieval period, they presage its elusiveness for a modern theatre historian.[2] Both play texts have something of the incidental about them. The first piece of evidence, the complete play, exists in two parchment liturgical manuscripts whose primary function was to facilitate the divine office, while the second, the incomplete play, was hastily and untidily copied on the back of an account roll, destroyed in the explosion and fire at the Dublin Four Courts in 1922, of the Priory of Holy Trinity.[3] The way in which the play on the account roll survived makes its preservation look like an afterthought, as if it were something to be jotted down in a spare moment and in a spare space. Evidently theatre, or a knowledge of theatre, existed in medieval Dublin; this at least the play texts imply. Perhaps theatre actually throve, but looking for such a theatre as this that leaves only oblique and incidental traces of itself may prove to be a little like playing a game of hunt the thimble.

CHURCH DRAMA

The complete play, an enactment of the visit to Christ's tomb by the three Marys on Easter Sunday morning, is the Latin liturgical drama generally known as the Dublin *Visitatio Sepulcri*, preserved in two manuscripts which were copied certainly after 1352 and probably *c* 1400: Dublin, Marsh's Library, MS Z.4.2.20, and Oxford, Bodleian Library, MS Rawlinson liturg. D. 4 (hereafter M and R respectively).[4] Many portions of the play's dialogue can be heard elsewhere in other church dramas from England and the Continent, but its particular amalgam of those portions is unique, and conceivably it was manufactured in Dublin out of imported parts, perhaps in the late thirteenth or early fourteenth century.[5] Its great interest lies not merely in the fact that it is the earliest play from Ireland fully extant, but also that the circumstances of its medieval performance can be almost exactly reconstructed. Its stage directions, or perhaps more appropriately, its rubrics, are unusually detailed,[6] and though they leave some room for interpretation, in most respects they are perfectly clear, specifying in detail what all of the actors, apart from the angel, had to wear and even, to an extent, the direction and manner in which they were to move as they performed their parts. The play's text and music are also intact. The main ingredients are therefore to hand for an interesting experiment in practical theatre, the play's faithful reconstruction according to its medieval requirements. Since no liturgical drama from anywhere in the British Isles is as clearly recoverable as is the Dublin *Visitatio Sepulcri* play, a careful analysis of its performance is fully warranted. Such analysis will be given to it in the pages immediately following. However, since the requisite detail will inevitably tarry this study's narrative, readers eager to reconnect with it may prefer to skip to page 75, glancing as they do at figs 5 and 6 where the results of the analysis are pictorially summarized.

Before embarking on the reconstruction, though, it should first be said that there is no unequivocal proof that the Dublin *Visitatio* was ever actually performed, and that strictly speaking, any reconstruction would be of its potential as a performance rather than of some decayed historical actuality; as is often the case with liturgical plays, no external records survive which unambiguously refer to it having taken place, nor is there anything in the manuscripts themselves to force this conclusion. Even the spottling of the play's opening in M with wax (on fols 58v–9) means no more necessarily than that at some stage the manuscript was open at these pages and that a candle was burning nearby which somehow managed to spill upon them. To go further than this and envisage a choir member using it either during or in preparation for a play performance might be to conceive a beguiling fiction. Yet it would be taking scepticism too far to insist on the lack of proof positive, and for three good reasons. Both manuscripts, thoroughly practical books designed to facilitate the liturgy, show clear signs of extensive use through their wear. Second, the elaborate Easter liturgy, in which the *Visitatio* features, was of especial concern to the compilers of the manuscripts. M contains two versions of a ritual that often attended *Visitatio* dramas, the *Elevatio crucis et hostie.*[7] The second of these two *Elevatio* versions, on fols 138v–40, was copied, less carefully than the bulk of the text, towards the end of the manuscript and evidently after most of the text had already been completed. Its late insertion implies that even if an afterthought, it was one of consequence. This ritual (an abbreviated version of that also appearing in R on fols 127v–30) was sufficiently important to one of the M scribes to warrant him including it after the manuscript had been largely completed. Had it not been a ritual connected with Easter, the principal feast of the church calendar, then perhaps he would not have troubled to make good its earlier omission. If the fact that he did so suggests the relative importance that the *Elevatio* portion of the Easter ceremonies held, it may therefore point toward the play (for the play is the *Elevatio*'s natural extension) having been performed rather than to the contrary.[8] And third, we know for a fact that some sort of drama of the Resurrection, the very topic which the *Visitatio* presents, was staged in the cathedral church of the Holy Trinity (commonly called Christ Church) as late as 1542. The significance of this and the Christ Church connection will become apparent during the discussion.

THE DUBLIN *VISITATIO SEPULCRI*: RECONSTRUCTING A PERFORMANCE

If an attempt is to be made to make the play come alive again, first we need to know more about the place in which its performance may have originally occurred. Since every performance space inevitably impinges upon the drama played within it and shapes that drama's character – for example, a roomy venue will lend itself readily to a more 'epic' and diffused treatment of the action than a small one which will beg conversely for an action focused and detailed – the size and physical disposition of any original performance space in which the Dublin *Visitatio* may have been presented are important to ascertain. In the case of many early dramas, it is often no longer possible to do so, but the Dublin *Visitatio* is one of the exceptions. The fact that we know where both of the Dublin *Visitatio* manuscripts were owned may offer an important clue to understanding the performance space available to the play and the theatrical dynamic that this was likely to have imposed. In the fifteenth century, both M and R were in the possession, and presumably the use, of the church of St John the Evangelist which originally stood a few yards to the northeast of Christ Church Cathedral (see fig. 3). Although the church was demolished in 1884, John Rocque's map of Dublin, printed in 1756, shows it to have been of rectangular shape, with no pronounced distinction between nave and chancel, and measuring approximately 90′ x 40′ on the outside.[9] The medieval church had already been rebuilt in the early-sixteenth century and again between 1680 and 1682, and it is this late-seventeenth-century stage of rebuilding that the Rocque map must reflect.[10] Yet while the fabric of the church may have changed over the years, successive rebuildings seem not to have greatly altered the late medieval church's internal dimensions. These, to judge by those of the Georgian church, were approximately 70′ x 35′.

In order to understand how this performance space would have been arranged for a performance of the *Visitatio*, the fuller rubrics of the longer *Elevatio* ritual repay attention because they supplement and clarify what can be inferred from the play's own rubrics, especially in helping to determine the question of the nature and location of the focal point of the play's action, the Easter Sepulchre.[11] This must have been located towards the east end of the church and somewhere within the choir.[12] The *Visitatio* rubrics agree with this. It is the destination of the three Marys at the beginning of the play, and from the rubrics it is clear that they are steadily making their way towards the choir. Furthermore, because of this the number of possible locations for the Sepulchre is much reduced. It cannot easily have been located in the middle of the choir at point a (see fig. 4) without producing a ludicrous effect, since in this case the three Marys, who are supposed to be 'seeking Jesus' (*querentes Ihesum*), would have to have walked around and past it, for they walk the full length of the choir before stopping in front of the step to the altar, and still they have not arrived at the Sepulchre (see the discussion below). Its position there would have also inhibited processions through the choir.[13] Nor can it have been located at the high altar itself at point b (see fig. 4). The Sepulchre and altar were evidently quite separate. This can be inferred both from the structure that the Sepulchre must have had, which will be considered presently, and the fact that after

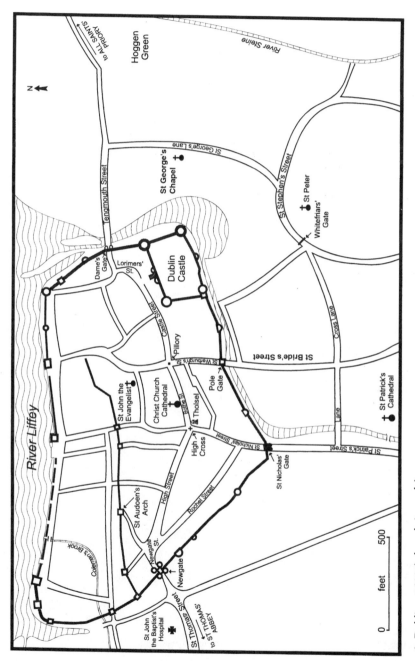

3 Dublin *c* 1500 (selected sites only).

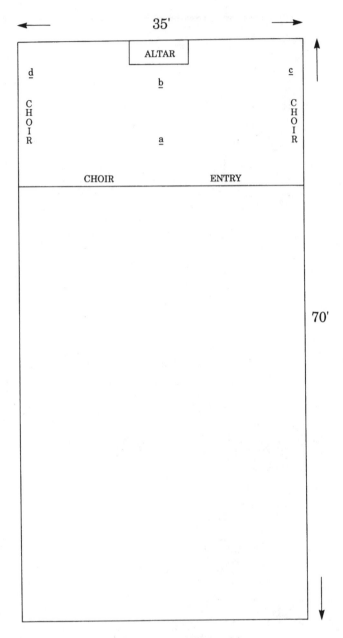

4 The Dublin *Visitatio Sepulcri* play, location of the Sepulchre.

the host had been taken out of the Sepulchre during the *Elevatio* it was then placed on the altar in a pyx, before being removed to a tabernacle.[14] Two possible locations for the Sepulchre remain within the choir, either to the south or north of the altar, that is, in the vicinity either of points c̲ or d̲ (see fig. 4). Of the two, there is a good reason for believing that it was located somewhere around point d̲ on the north side, and this is because in these islands at this date there was a powerful tradition for locating the Easter Sepulchre on the north side of the church.[15] The nature of the structure required for representing the Sepulchre also eliminates, as has been said, the possibility of point b̲, for a good impression, even if only in general terms, can be formed of what it looked like. A rubric from the longer *Elevatio* and another from the *Visitatio* show that it had a 'gate' or 'way in' (*ostium*) and some means of showing if this 'way in' were open or closed.[16] Moreover, it had to be a structure of sufficient size to accommodate the three Marys inside it, since one of the *Visitatio* rubrics specifies that 'they enter it, bowing, and looking about on all sides within.'[17] Also, the directions specified in this rubric would have been pointless if after the Marys had entered they were at once lost from sight. Therefore the structure representing the Sepulchre could not have been visually impervious, and was, presumably, put in position temporarily for the ceremonies of Maundy Thursday until Easter. Something like a booth, hung about with curtains at a height of some 3′ or 4′ from the ground so that people inside would be visible from about the waist upwards, might have given sufficient illusion of solidity and served the turn well enough. A drape across the front of it which could easily be drawn might have stood for its entrance.[18] Also, the structure was not merely an empty enclosure. According to the longer *Elevatio*, lights were kept burning within it,[19] and when after vespers on Good Friday the host and a cross were deposited in it, it is scarcely likely that they were merely laid on the ground. Rather, some sort of receptacle would probably have been placed within the Sepulchre ready to contain them.[20] If there already existed a suitable minor altar along the northern wall of the church, and this seems in fact to have been the case, then no doubt it would have served as an altar of repose with the Sepulchre erected around it and the receptacle placed upon it.[21] Such an altar would also have provided a good resting place for the Sepulchre lights, well out of the way of the voluminously dressed Marys moving around on the inside.

The Dublin *Visitatio* is unusual by the standards of the majority of medieval *Visitatio* plays in possessing rubrics whose comparative richness allows the reconstruction of much of its action. It would probably be quite wrong to imagine the rubrics having been written specifically with the physical circumstances of St John the Evangelist's in mind, for even if both manuscripts were manufactured in Dublin for that church's use, a degree of vagueness in the rubrics would have been a practical advantage were the play to be adapted for use in other Dublin churches whose internal layout and dimensions may have been quite different.[22] So while they are rich, the rubrics are general enough to allow the play to have been accommodated just as easily, for example, had there been any need, within the nearby Christ Church Cathedral, where a somewhat different set of physical circumstances would have obtained. Indeed, the two manuscripts might even have come originally to St John's as cathedral hand-me-downs. Although, therefore, there is a sense in which it would be fair to reconstruct the play's action in correspondingly general terms, the fact remains that it was St John's that owned both manuscripts in the later fifteenth century, and so it is with the layout of that church in mind that this discussion shall proceed.

The play starts with each of the three Marys entering in turn from some unspecified place in the church, and each moves, as the rubric states quite clearly, 'ad ingressum chori uersus sepulcrum' ('to [or possibly 'towards'] the entry of the choir, towards the Sepulchre').[23] This rubric cannot possibly be interpreted to mean that they have gone beyond the choir entry and towards the Sepulchre already, because a subsequent rubric will instruct them to proceed *adhuc paululum*, 'a little further in this direction.'[24] A short pause is left between their respective entrances. Where they have come from precisely is not apparent, but it seems likely that each starts to proceed from a different point somewhere at the west end of the church.[25] Their first stop en route to the Sepulchre would appear to be at the 'entry of the choir' (*ingressum chori*), where each Mary has presumably arrived by the time she has sung her opening lament. It is not known whether St John's had a choir screen, though screens had certainly become fashionable in these islands by this date.[26] If it had, then the entry to the choir would have been comparatively narrow, and its width whatever the width of the opening in the screen may have been. Alternatively, without a screen, the choir entry would have been much wider – simply that point in the church at which the nave ended and the choir stalls began.[27] Whichever the case, the Marys, when they have arrived here at the choir entry, presumably keep some little distance between themselves, since a subsequent rubric is going to require them physically to 'join together' (*se coniungant*),[28] and this makes no sense or is at the very least redundant if the Marys have already been standing close together, even though each has entered *consimili modo*, 'in exactly the same way.'[29]

The second phase in the action will be their progress from here at the choir entry to the Sepulchre. When the rubric directs the first Mary to sing *adhuc paululum procedendo*, the *adhuc*, 'to this place,' presumably refers to the Sepulchre, the goal of all the Marys' movement, and the *paululum procedendo*, 'proceeding a very small extent,' must mean that the first Mary has now gone a little beyond the choir entry into the choir itself.[30] It seems fair to assume, given the initial parallelism between the three Marys in the first phase of the action (their entrance *consimili modo*), that here in the second phase the second and third Marys move once again in a similar way when 'proceeding a very small extent to this place' (*adhuc paululum procedendo*), although no rubric specifically calls for them to do so. However, perhaps equally the absence of any rubric calling for a short interval to be left between the three sections of this second set of Marian laments may mean that, once begun, the sections should follow more closely on one another.[31] The next rubric locates them quite unequivocally. After their second set of laments, they are instructed to join together and proceed *ad gradum chori ante altare*, 'to the step of the choir in front of the altar,' singing in unison.[32] Now they are standing together at the east end of the church. From here they will proceed to a place 'near to' (*prope*) the Sepuchre, where the first and second Marys will sing in turn of their intention to anoint Christ's body, and the third to question who will roll the stone of the tomb away. After a dramatic anticipatory pause, an angel appears 'next to' (*iuxta*) the Sepulchre, and the famous *Quem queritis* dialogue begins.[33] After this, upon being invited to see the place where Christ had been laid, the Marys enter the Sepulchre, bowing, and looking all around it. Then moving away a little out of the Sepulchre, they sing that Christ is risen. As they sing this, they are approximately facing in a westerly direction away from the angel, for the next rubric requires that they 'turn back to the angel' (*reuertant ad angelum*) as he sings his instruction that they are to announce the Resurrection to the disciples.[34] It seems likely that at this point the angel retires out of sight again, since he will not be required when the Sepulchre is next visited, this time by the apostles Peter and John.

The third phase of the action begins with the entry of the apostles, who in the meanwhile have come to the entry of the choir, as had the Marys earlier, and presumably like the Marys they have come from some westerly point of the nave. The Marys now prepare to return. Turning back from the tomb and making their way as if to leave the choir together, they each intone their share of the *Victime paschali* sequence. Assuming that they retrace their steps exactly as they had come in, they would move away from the Sepulchre to the step of the choir in front of the altar, and then down into the middle of the choir where the apostles meet up with them. The rubric instructing the apostles to meet the Marys *in medio chori* must mean almost precisely that, 'in the middle of the choir' in the fullest sense, that is, at some distance down the choir away from the mid-point before the altar step.[35] It is unlikely simply to mean that they meet at any mid-point of the choir, and certainly it cannot mean the Marys' earlier mid-point position before the altar step, though that position could indeed be described as a 'middle' in the sense that it would have been located at approximately the middle of the width of the church, assuming that the altar in St John's was sited centrally. Any possible ambiguity which *in medio chori* might contain seems resolvable by considering the available space for the Marys and the quantity of text they are to sing while crossing it. It appears that they proceed away from the Sepulchre as they sing.[36] The middle of St John's, looking east-west down the church, would have been at any point approximately 17′ out from both the north and south walls. Since the Marys are already outside the Sepulchre before they start the third phase of the action (their return from the Sepulchre) there is not much space left for them to cross during the time it would take to sing the lines of text allocated to them. Allowing a conservative 5′ for the distance the Sepulchre would have covered in projecting from the north wall, and an equally conservative 2′ for the physical space inevitably occupied by each Mary when at rest, only about 10′ remain before they reach this mid-point.[37] Since it would be unsatisfactory from the dramatic point of view to overcome the problem by having them sing very quickly while at the same time taking tiny steps, or ponderous and inappropriately slow ones at this joyous moment (after all, the news of the empty tomb will cause the apostles to *run* to it) it would be solved by giving them the extra distance to cross that would be available were *in medio chori* to be literally interpreted. Hence, at least under the constraints that the setting of St John's would have imposed, it must have meant quite literally 'in the middle of the choir.' After their dialogue with the apostles, the Marys proceed to the choir entry as the apostles run to the Sepulchre. Seeing that it is empty, the apostles turn back to sing to the choir that a single Mary is more to be believed than a host of lying Jews. The choir members then sing the final stanza of the *Victime paschali*, the *executor officij* begins the *Te Deum*, and the six characters of the play 'return' (*recedant*).[38] What this means is not entirely clear. Presumably they all leave the choir, which has become the principal 'theatre' area for the play and which will recover its primary liturgical status once the play's characters no longer function within it; cessation of 'play' would conveniently be marked simply by the physical exit of the characters from the choir. Westwards and out of the choir has already been the trend of the three Marys' movement before the play's final rubric; perhaps it is reasonable to assume that they are returning to the same unspecified point of entry towards the west of the nave from which they originally came. Similarly too may the apostles have returned and, to judge by the way the final rubric lumps all the characters together, this exit would appear to have included the angel.

Two diagrams (see figs 5 and 6) may summarize and present more clearly this suggested reconstruction of the play's three phases of movement. The length to which the choir extends down the church is hypothetical, as are the size of the high altar and the Sepulchre itself. Otherwise the plan is drawn to scale. The reconstruction should also be understood to be hypothetical in such points of detail as the exact positioning of the Marys, apostles, and angel when each comes to rest (represented by circled letters on the diagrams) and the exact direction in which each person walks (for example, when the two outer Marys join together with the one in the middle and proceed to the choir step before the altar, ⓒ, they might have converged more gradually and diagonally, rather than have taken the sharp right-angled turn implied in fig. 5). The blank circles in both diagrams mark hypothetical points of departure. For greater clarity, the paths of the Marys are indicated by broken lines, and those of the apostles and angel by continuous ones.

A question worth asking to help complete the picture of this play's movements, and which has already been raised once as having some practical consequence, is the extent to which movement and song are consecutive (whether movement precedes song or vice versa) or simultaneous. The Latin of the rubrics in this respect is less than clear. The first rubric (Appendix I, lines 1–6) admits two possible interpretations. Either the first Mary's song follows on after her movement to the entry of the choir, or her song and movement are simultaneous. Whichever of these two it may have been, the pattern would have been repeated for the entry of the second and third Marys, for they enter *consimili modo*.[39] The rubric introducing the second phase of the action, the movement of the Marys into the choir and eventually to the Sepulchre, is similarly ambiguous. It is once again impossible to tell from the gerund construction (*procedendo*) whether movement and song are consecutive or coextensive, but as before, whichever it may have been, it would, presumably, have been repeated for each Mary.[40] The point at which the Marys are instructed to join together and proceed to the step of the choir in front of the altar appears less problematic. The use of the present participle, that they proceed *simul dicentes*, implies that words and movement are definitely coinciding.[41] Next, the three of them proceed near to the Sepulchre. Once again, it is not absolutely clear whether words and movement are consecutive or simultaneous, but the ambiguity is possibly resolved by a consideration of the space the Marys have to cross and the time they would need to cross it. The Marys at this stage are standing before the altar, and have an estimated 10′ to cover before they arrive at the Sepulchre. The quantity of text that each is given to sing, when added all together, would involve the Marys in a problem similar to that discussed earlier – if they are to sing and move simultaneously the unsatisfactory solution is to sing comparatively quickly while taking tiny steps at the same time. Therefore it would seem more likely that here movement and song were consecutive.[42] The dialogue between the angel and the Marys at the Sepulchre appears to have been largely a static one, with the actors simply singing back and forth to each other. The Marys move again after the angel invites them to see the place where Christ was laid.[43] At this point, when they enter the Sepulchre, bow, and look all around inside, the movement must occur, at least to some extent, independent of any song, since it would be meaningless to have the Marys enter the Sepulchre singing *Alleluya resurrexit dominus* even before they have bowed and looked around. Rather, it appears that they sing of the Resurrection either immediately after they have looked around and as they come out of the Sepulchre (they are instructed to leave it at the end of the rubric, Appendix I, lines 46–7) or that they come out, stand at a short distance from it and then sing, which is perhaps the more likely possibility of the two. In either case, we are presented with movement that is

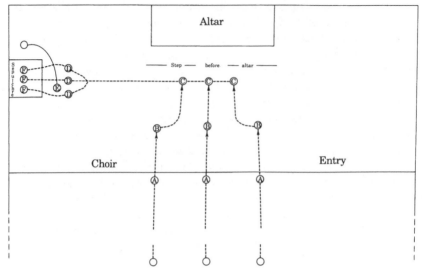

5 The Dublin *Visitatio Sepulcri* play, phases 1 and 2.

not entirely covered by any song. The Marys sing of the Resurrection, looking westwards down the choir, as has been mentioned, then turn around to face the angel,
who presumably has not left his place by the Sepulchre, as he tells them to let the
disciples know what has happened. The apostles Peter and John, who have come to
the entry of the choir while this has been going on, meet up in the middle of the
choir with the Marys who are returning from the Sepulchre and who, as was argued,
are singing the *Victime paschali* as they return. There is no song as the Marys, after
their dialogue with Peter and John, proceed together to the entry of the choir while
Peter and John run to the Sepulchre.[44] The apostles turn westwards to face the choir as
they sing that they have been told the truth, and the singing of the *Te Deum* covers
the withdrawal of the six actors.

   It is clear from all this that there is roughly an equal balance between those times

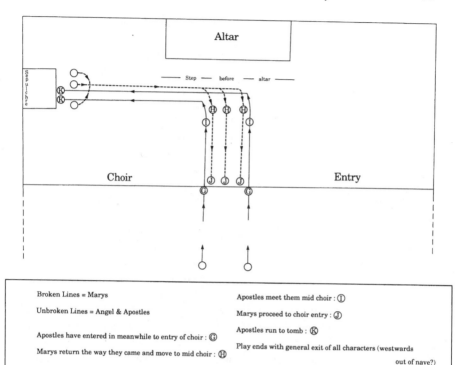

6 The Dublin *Visitatio Sepulcri* play, phase 3.

not where, either evidently or by deduction, movement and song are coextensive and those where they are sequential.[45] However, this discussion so far has rested upon an implicit definition of 'movement' as the distance covered by an actor passing from one place to another. If this definition of movement is broadened, as it no doubt should be, to include *gesture*, then we must conclude that the play shows a distinct tendency (though it can be put no more strongly than that) to require actors to sing and move simultaneously, since the three Marys, when they meet Peter and John in the middle of the choir, sing of the Sepulchre *quasi monstrando*, and this must mean that they make some physical gesture of indication in its direction.[46] However, it might be too crudely inductive to argue from this a case that in the equivocal instances, for example the first entrance of the Marys, song and movement would necessarily have been made to coincide.[47]

Some mention should be made of the actors' smaller movements and gestures which comprise, as it were, the finer detail of the play. Even these are not wholly irrecoverable, although they are by their nature likely to prove to be one of the play's most elusive aspects. That movements were used to some extent to express meaning is made clear in at least one rubric (Appendix I, lines 44–7). When the Marys have actually entered the Sepulchre, they are seen *inclinantes se & prospicientes undique* (Appendix I, lines 44–5), and this action of bowing or bending down and looking around everywhere is evidently meant to communicate to onlookers their search for Christ's body.[48] Other movements and gestures remain as interesting but unknowable possibilities. When the Marys first entered, did they literally move *quasi … querentes ihesum*, and show in some way by their movements and bearing that they were actively searching?[49] And were movements also intended to convey mood? When, for example, the Marys sing *quasi lamentando* (Appendix I, line 6), was their grief communicated by vocal expression, by particular gestures, or even by a mixture of both? Presumably, when the Marys, on witnessing the tomb empty, sing *alta uoce quasi gaudendo & admirantes* (Appendix I, lines 45–6), the rubric primarily aims to instruct in musical dynamics. Nevertheless, it might have been very hard to stop the extra effort required to sing *alta uoce* from showing in some physical movement, even if this were unconscious, and therefore in this case the coinciding of vocal with some degree of physical expression would doubtless have occurred automatically.[50] Again, the Marys sing to the apostles about the Sepulchre *quasi monstrando*, and on balance it would seem to mean, as was suggested, that they point to it in some way, since it is hard to conceive how one could interpret *quasi monstrando* as a meaningful instruction in purely musical terms. No doubt the dimension of gesture in the play was originally somewhat richer than can now be perceived with any measure of certainty.[51]

COSTUMES AND PROPS

The play rubrics give costuming directions in considerable detail, and mention some of the props that were used. The Marys wore surplices beneath their silk copes (possibly these are choir copes),[52] and they had their heads covered. Their head coverings could have been achieved in a variety of ways, but on the whole it is more likely to have been a known liturgical garment (an amice, for example) than any less usual covering got up specially for the occasion.[53] The colour of their copes is unspecified, and so we cannot tell whether the Marys were differentiated in this respect.[54] Each carried a pyx (often at this date these lidded boxes were circular in shape and readily portable) to represent her jar of spices.[55]

The one character whose costume is not mentioned at all is the angel, and the only available way of forming some impression of what he would have worn is to investigate his costuming in other Easter plays. However, because angels in liturgical drama seem to have been presented with some variety and inventiveness – a *Visitatio* from Narbonne, for example, goes as far as giving each of its two Sepulchre angels a pair of wings[56] – it is difficult to arrive at a reliable consensus much beyond suggesting that his basic costume is likely to have been an alb.[57]

The description of the two apostles is the fullest. Both had on plain albs without apparels, and they each wore on top a tunicle, Peter a red one and John a white.[58] Furthermore, both held their own differentiating attributes. John had a palm branch, while Peter held his familiar keys. The instruction calling for them to be *nudis pedibus* possibly has its source in a contemporary iconographical convention requiring the apostles to be depicted barefooted. As the roughly contemporary vernacular text *Dives and Pauper* put it, 'Comounly alle apostelys been peyntyd barefoot in tokene of innocence and of penaunce.'[59] It may be that here the presentation of Peter and John followed suit, signalling their apostolic status, and at the same time emphasising how highly emblematic their presentation was, something which their respective attributes of keys and palm branch also suggest.

Apart from that of the angel, costume in the Dublin play, in comparison to that of most other Easter liturgical dramas, is quite elaborately recorded, and the props required were all basic. The play would have needed little, if anything, extra for its production than a well-equipped church could have provided, and any lack at St John's could no doubt have been repaired from the resources of the neighbouring cathedral of Christ Church, from which St John's was served.

'THE PLAY'S THE THING'

The method of presenting the Dublin *Visitatio*, then, although shadowy in point of fine detail, is broadly recoverable. The reconstruction traced above allows both certainties and uncertainties their place together in the reader's mind, and that is doubtless the most circumspect way of proceeding, even if the final impression it leaves is less than full-blooded. Yet for all its appropriate caution, a theoretical outline evoked in words and schematic diagrams remains a sterile substitute for an experience of the *Visitatio* as performed drama. Were a modern reconstructed performance conducted entirely within the terms that have been discussed, it would arguably be just one more of the possible manifestations of the play for which its manuscripts provide the blueprint.[60] Such a performance may yield valid insights into the general working of the medieval play which would be hard to arrive at solely through staging it in a theatre of the mind.

In this regard, some strong impressions arising from recent productions may be worth reporting.[61] One of the most striking impressions that the play leaves with modern observers is of its pervasive symmetry and of the patterning which binds its structure together. Symmetry is displayed in the play's melodic rhymes, its voice dynamics, and its even distribution of the vocal parts, as well as in the matching of its movements, gestures, costumes, and words. Order, balance, and proportion, glimpsed so often behind such differing guises as these, seem to constitute a deliberate strategy. While the narrative content of the play celebrates the Resurrection, the Resurrection message of Christ's triumph over the chaos of death is equally consolidated at a metaphorical level in the content's ordered and symmetrical orchestration. If it is true that the content and form of a work of art are inseparable, if the medium is commensurate with the message, then hardly might an observer be more conscious of the importance of pure form than in this play where the insistence on symmetrical ordering in itself seems resonant with meaning. There is nothing self-effacing about the play's symmetries; on the contrary, they are foregrounded in a way that modern taste, educated by and large on the submergence of such structural artifice for the sake of realistic and representational effect, is not normally accustomed to. So celebration of Resurrection is one with celebration of structure, and the play operates through, not in spite of, intense stylization.

This impression left by the formal weight of the play seemed to find its corollary in the way in which the attitude of the various cast members who performed it gradually altered towards what they saw themselves as doing. It was difficult at first for them to realise that there was to be little scope for virtuoso display and that the play largely required the subordination of their own individualities and idiosyncracies in the service of a more evenly distributed, corporate act. Yet once acquiescent to the play's pervading balance and symmetry, whose effect was to equalize rather than differentiate, cast members commented on the unexpected ease and confidence that they were deriving from the play; somehow the weight of the responsibility for representation as such was being lifted from their shoulders, and this they found to be surprisingly welcome. The structure of the play, of which they were simply the constituent parts, was assuming the responsibility for them. This altering of their reaction could be regarded as the testimony of the actors' experience to the heavy functional load that the play's observers saw in its insistence upon structure.

In sum, the play in performance is a brief presentation of the transforming discovery of the Resurrection, made moving not by virtue of any sense of personal identification with the characters (something virtually impossible) but rather by an appreciation of their symmetrically proportioned pointing, like icons in human shape, away from themselves and towards the central Christian mystery expressed by the empty tomb. The Sepulchre, the only localized place in the play, orientates absolutely all the actors and is the sole object of their movement. They exist exclusively in relation to it: their movement is towards it, around it, or away from it. Here is the structural centre of the play, and yet the Sepulchre, as the angel declares, is empty, for just as the actors point to it so also through its emptiness it too points metaphorically beyond itself to the risen Christ who is now to be sought elsewhere.

Like its English and Continental relatives, the Dublin *Visitatio* shows itself to be very much the child of its parent, the Latin liturgy. Essentially its action is one of restrained liturgical formality, replaced only momentarily by action of a more illusionistic sort. (The best example of this is when the apostles Peter and John, though in themselves little other than human icons, distinguished as they are only by the colour of their costumes and their respective attributes of keys and palm branch, break with formality and actually *run* towards the Sepulchre to see if what they have been told of Christ's Resurrection is true.)[62] Yet these occasional gestures towards realism are contained carefully. A framework of regimented symmetry surrounds them, and they are hemmed about also by the measure necessarily imposed by chanted dialogue.[63] Similarly, the play is itself bordered and contained within the larger framework of regular liturgical worship.

The Dublin *Visitatio* was not, therefore, autonomous drama, but like the drama of other liturgical plays, bound strictly to its context. It would also have been performed only once a year, in the early hours of Easter Sunday morning, after the first nocturn of Matins, in a church artificially lit.[64] Its actors would have been well suited for their task, since they would have been professionally acquainted with the conduct of the liturgy and its procedures. They were most probably the Augustinian canons of the adjacent Christ Church Cathedral. By an order of Archbishop Luke, given *c* 1230, the Christ Church canons had been required to serve at St John's in person, and not depute its cure to a vicar deputy.[65] It may also not be entirely fortuitous that the Dublin *Visitatio* appeared when and where it did. The manuscripts are very close in date to the time when the prior of Christ Church was one Stephen de Derby (the latest reference known to him is in a St John's deed of 1379).[66] During his priorate there seems to have been something of a small renaissance in the cathedral, and it is tempting to regard the appearance of a liturgy enhanced by drama as one of the signs of this artistic ferment.[67]

BEYOND ST JOHN THE EVANGELIST

Whether the *Visitatio* was the only liturgical play to be performed in medieval Dublin cannot be told. It is the only one whose text has survived, but it is hard to imagine the greater cathedrals of the city allowing themselves to be outshone by any example set by the lesser church of St John the Evangelist.[68] In fact, it can be shown that Dublin's premier cathedral of Christ Church, standing so close by and staffed by the same order of canons, even if it did not use the same play, to which it would have had ready access, also had a dramatic tradition. A unique piece of evidence establishes play performance, probably of the liturgical kind, within the cathedral.

As late as 1542, in the very year of its reformation, an Easter play of the Resurrection, the very topic enacted in the *Visitatio*, was still to be found there: a sum of 6d was laid out towards the cost of putting it on.[69] Moreover, there is clear evidence that plays of some sort, even if this time they may not have been strictly liturgical, were also performed a short distance down the hill from Christ Church, either in or around the cathedral church of St Patrick (plotted in fig. 3).

Though founded by Archbishop John Comyn in 1191, it is not until some three centuries later, in 1509, that the first unequivocal record of drama at St Patrick's, the one with which this chapter began, comes to light.[70] A memorandum for that year, found in canon John Andowe's accounts as proctor of the cathedral, reads as follows:

Et de – iij s. j d. solutis Thome Mayowe ludenti cum vij luminibus in festo Natalis domini & purificacionis hoc Anno ... Et de – iiij s. vij d. solutis ludentibus cum Angelo Magno & paruo ac dracone in festo pentecostes Et de – iiij s. ij d. solutis pro victualibus eisdem ludentibus in diebus eiusdem festi hoc Anno [71]

[And for three shillings and one penny to Thomas Mayowe for playing, with seven lights on the feast of the Lord's Nativity and the Purification in this year ... And for three shillings and sevenpence paid to the players with the great angel and the little one and with the dragon on the feast of Pentecost. And for three shillings and twopence paid for food for the same players on the days of the same feast in this year.]

The memorandum admits several interpretations. Was the first payment, made to one Thomas Mayowe 'ludenti,' for a one-man performance or for his services as impresario?[72] It is also not entirely clear whether the 'seven lights' mentioned were directly connected with Mayowe's efforts, since the accounts elsewhere note seven lights as an expense in preparation for Christmas, but do not mention any accompanying dramatic activity.[73] The second and third payments in Andowe's accounts, when taken together, help explain each other, and are perhaps further clarified in the light of another much later cathedral account of 1555. The second payment is to persons playing 'with the big angel and the little one and with the dragon' at the feast of Pentecost. It is not clear whether angels and dragon were part of the same performance, or in different ones; perhaps the latter, because the players presumably played more than once (they were paid *in diebus eiusdem festi*) and it seems less likely that they played the same piece repeatedly over a number of days. Some clues to the nature of the 'great and little' angels may be afforded by an entry in the 1555 proctors' accounts of Gilbert Corey and Nicholas Miaghe:

Et de iij s. solutis pro paruis cordulis occupatis circa spiritum sanctum in festo penthecostes

... de iij s. vj d. solut {*read* solutis} pro fabricacione angeli thurificantis in festo penthecostes de i<ij s.> iij d. pro cordis dicti angeli ...[74]

[And for three shillings paid for little threads employed about the Holy Spirit on the feast of Pentecost; ... for three shillings and sixpence paid for manufacturing a censing angel on the feast of Pentecost; for three shillings and threepence for the strings of the said angel; ...]

The first payment *pro paruis cordulis* ('for little threads')[75] which are *occupatis circa spiritum sanctum* ('employed about the Holy Spirit') at the feast of Pentecost, the second payment, *pro fabricacione angeli thurificantis* ('for manufacturing a censing angel') for the same feast, and the third, *pro cordis dicti angeli* ('for the strings of the said angel'), all strongly suggest two things. Either they were payments for items used in a Pentecost tableau (a decorative addition to the cathedral or its precincts during the feast, or to the Pentecost liturgy itself),[76] or they were payments for props used in a Pentecost play. It is impossible to decide which, because we simply do not know exactly how the items were to be used. But on balance the evidence seems to tilt towards a play. While a tableau seems suggested by the fact that no payments to actors are mentioned, if the actors were cathedral staff, they may not have been paid for something routinely undertaken in the line of duty. Considering also that the 1509 plays at Pentecost establish a precedent for Whitsuntide drama, the possibility that the items paid for in 1555 were play props seems even more likely. Threads and strings (which often feature, incidentally, in play production accounts elsewhere)[77] suggest that the items were made to move in some way, such as a 'Holy Spirit' (an animated dove or descent of tongues of fire?) and a 'censing angel' (presumably it swung a thurible?). Any play needing props like these would obviously have been on a religious theme, and its performance at Pentecost, along with the use of some contrivance for an animated 'Holy Spirit,' hints that it would have dramatized the descent of the Spirit to the apostles, with a colourful, if apocryphal, censing angel included.[78] Whatever the nature of this performance, if it be interpreted as a later reflex of the 1509 play, also mounted at Whitsuntide, then it is likely that the 'great and little' angels of 1509, which sound as if they are spoken of as being somehow *distinct* from the actors (the payment was 'to the players *with* the great angel and the little one'), were theatrical puppets, incorporated into an otherwise live play.[79]

These plays at St Patrick's cannot easily be interpreted as ones of the more strictly liturgical sort, as was the St John's *Visitatio Sepulcri* play.[80] The 1509 Whitsuntide play, with its great and little angels, seems to have been a much more energetic piece of theatre, not to mention the dragon that may or may not have been part of it. Although by the sixteenth century the Pentecost liturgy in some churches in the British Isles had become mimetically enriched, to the extent of incorporating such devices as an artificial dove on cords (a feature reminiscent of the St Patrick's 'Holy

Spirit' of 1555), there is practically no evidence for the effectual dramatization of the Pentecost story within the context of the liturgy proper,[81] and the 1509 payment *ludentibus* ('to the players') suggests that we are dealing not with a liturgy that was simply mimetically enriched but with a fully fledged drama of some sort.[82] The cathedral authorities, then, showed a commitment to drama, and acted as its patron, if not its instigator. All this is not to say that St Patrick's did not have liturgical drama too, of course, but clear evidence of it is lacking. Circumstantial evidence is promising, however. Apart from its predisposition to support drama, witnessed at Pentecost, the building of St Patrick's within the liberty of St Sepulchre may have urged the appropriateness of performing Easter Sepulchre drama there.[83] And an Easter drama would have kept the cathedral abreast of its rival Christ Church up the hill. Also, the archiepiscopal palace of St Sepulchre, which stood not far from St Patrick's, would have maintained via its dedication a measure of awareness of the significance of the Holy Sepulchre amongst the inhabitants of the medieval city, and at St Patrick's in particular.[84] In fact, a thirteenth-century seal matrix surviving from the manor of St Sepulchre depicts a scene which, though hitherto unremarked, depicts the visit of the three Marys to the Sepulchre (see fig. 7). The angel greeting them is visible on the right, while the Marys are assembled in a group on the left.[85]

This survey of early Dublin church drama has a relatively modest centre of gravity, for the evidence around which it turns is not vast. Yet enough significant evidence has survived to demonstrate that Dublin hosted a greater dramatic richness on the ecclesiastical front than the rather homogenous title 'Church Drama' begins to suggest. We have moved from the *terra firma* of a specific play text out into a *terra incognita* of references in accounts to plays which, though church based in as much as they were church sponsored, seem in other respects to have been quite unlike the solemn liturgical play of St John's. The complexity of the church's involvement in Dublin theatricals will be seen to ramify as we turn to our second surviving play text, and in doing so the category 'Church Drama,' whose usefulness is already showing signs of strain, must now yield to a somewhat different one.

CLERICAL AND LAY DRAMA

The elegant parish clerk Absolon, whom Chaucer, in *The Miller's Tale*, presented as an earnest young man of exquisite and fastidious taste, seems to have ranked his services to the church and to the stage on a par; he might, as occasion required, act as clerk in minor orders or as King Herod on the 'scaffold hye,' and discharge both roles equally well. For all Absolon's rich particularity within Chaucer's fiction, his ludicrously incompatible mix of spiritual and secular aspirations, he nevertheless displays, however wryly, something of that general commerce between clerical and

7 Thirteenth-century seal of the manor of St Sepulchre, Dublin.

lay culture which would have been a real enough feature of medieval life. Such commerce was as much an aspect of life in Dublin as in Chaucer's fictionalized Oxford, and similarly drama was one of the sites in which it expressed itself. A new category, whose appropriateness will become clear as the discussion proceeds, is needed for the second extant piece of medieval Dublin drama, the Hiberno-English play of *The Pride of Life*.

When the fourteenth-century Latin accounts of the Priory of Holy Trinity, Dublin, perished in the Four Courts fire of 1922, so too did *The Pride of Life*, a play that two scribes had interpolated into the accounts sometime in the first half of the fifteenth century. Their interpolation preserved a play which has proved unique in these islands, one whose cultural significance to medieval Dublin, and indeed to the British Isles generally, it is hard to exaggerate. Yet *prima facie*, the circumstances of their committing it to parchment seem unpromising, suggesting that it was originally copied as a mere afterthought, untidily stuffed into the spare spaces of a roll that was already in large part used up. Nor does the very appearance of the scribes' handwriting do anything to help. It is undistinguished enough, even when all due allowance has been made for its cramping in the limited available space. The reproduction of part of the roll by its first editor, James Mills, allows us to judge for ourselves just how accurate his view was that the interloping text had a 'rather crowded' look about it.[86] Beneath the relatively neat mid-fourteenth-century Anglicana hand of the accounts proper can be seen squeezed into four columns a portion of *The Pride of Life*'s text. Unquestionably, its two scribes were exceedingly indifferent. The palsied and unpractised appearance of the hand of one of them, that responsible for column 2, lead Mills to conjecture someone either infirm or who had not been used to writing, and the verdict delivered by a more recent editor, Norman Davis, on this scribe's colleague, the copyist of columns 1, 3, and 4, was succinct: 'incompetent.'[87] Thus *The Pride of Life* comes to our attention under a cloud.

But was its entry on the account roll really an afterthought, and are the apparent careless circumstances of its survival testimony to a relative textual unimportance in its own day? Before too hastily returning a 'guilty' verdict and closing the case, it is worth pausing to reflect again on these circumstances, while also bringing into view the wider context of the copying of Middle English texts. First, there are the evident scribal infelicities, and the question of incompetence. Mills made an interesting point when he observed that the scribe of columns 1, 3, and 4 may not have been accustomed to writing English.[88] Since this observation, it has become increasingly clear that what might at first sight look like incompetence or slovenliness in the copying of English texts, especially ones of the early Middle English period, may not in fact be a function of wilful inattention or irresoluteness at all but of lack of familiarity with writing the vernacular.[89] Yet to a modern observer, this incompetence might without proper reason be interpreted as scribal nonchalance, that somehow the matter copied was not to be taken too seriously. Second, what attitude to the text on the part of its copyists (and readers) are we entitled to infer from the fact that its physical appearance is so cramped, a text seemingly entered as an afterthought in a spare moment and in a spare space? The text is cramped, yes, but unavoidably so; this is often likely to be the fate of texts inserted later into documents which had an anterior purpose, whether those texts were entered as marginalia, glosses, or appended in whatever other way. The point to grasp, however, is that such insertion was an entirely common practice, and that we should therefore not allow a text's inevitable appearance of untidiness automatically to damage our impression of the seriousness with which it may have been regarded or of the value attached to it in its day. Scribes had every reason to be economical. Parchment cost money, so why bother to purchase more when unfilled membranes were still to hand? Thus the subsequent insertion of a vernacular item into a pre-existing Latin document need not imply that that item be at once dismissed as an ephemeral whimsy before the nature of the Latin document in question, as well as of the item interpolated, have been given careful consideration. Its insertion there may, on the contrary, have been a provident means of ensuring its survival to posterity.

This is a case that can with justice be made for *The Pride of Life*. The Augustinian canons, whose affairs the accounts record, had evolved careful policies for the preservation of their muniments.[90] These were not normally left randomly about, and we should imagine that the play's two copyists were persons who would have had access to the priory archive. Application of Ockham's razor should therefore incline us to believe that the two copyists were themselves none other than members of the Augustinian order.[91] The way in which they copied and preserved their text implies a certain attitude on their part towards it. We may presume that originally they copied it in full. (Membranes already missing from the roll before its destruction doubtless once contained the remainder of the play.)[92] It was probably not, then, copied by them for any one individual actor to learn his part from. This seems to have been the purpose, incidentally, of a single actor's part which was copied in the fifteenth century onto a late-thirteenth-century assize roll for Norfolk and Suffolk, and whose circumstances of survival therefore make an interesting comparison with those of *The Pride of Life*.[93] Rather, the copy of *The Pride of Life* seems to have been intended for more general consultation, whether as much for edifying reading as for the purposes of actually producing its text as a play.[94] It is clear that the two scribes wanted to record it, and to be sure they did so in a thoroughly pragmatic and undistinguished way. But by copying it amongst the priory accounts, they safeguarded it against prompt disposal.[95]

Was *The Pride of Life* ever actually performed in Dublin, or was it only ever an élite, literary event, something read but not seen and heard? The answer must be quite simply that we do not know. Yet having said that, we might invoke once more the context in which the play was preserved and, as will shortly be argued, authored, to see whether any case at all can be made for its performance, if only a case built on circumstantial evidence.

Curiously, it has never been recognized that *The Pride of Life* shares an intimate connection with the Dublin *Visitatio Sepulcri.* Like the *Visitatio, The Pride of Life* may also be a fourteenth-century composition; it shares with the *Visitatio* similar Augustinian auspices. Both plays emanated from the same Augustinian centre and, along with the evidence of the Hoggen Green Christmastide plays of 1528 which will be discussed in the next chapter, they point to a lively participation generally by the canons regular of St Augustine in the city's early theatrical life. Since, therefore, Dublin's Augustinian canons were demonstrably active in promoting drama on various fronts, there is room to suggest that, like the *Visitatio Sepulcri* and the Christmastide plays of 1528, *The Pride of Life* constituted yet another item in the canons' varied repertoire. Furthermore, a case can be made for believing that *The Pride of Life* was composed in Dublin, not imported from England, and by an author familiar with the temporal interests of Dublin's Augustinian canons.

In this regard, it is important to digress for a moment to consider a place name mentioned in the play which has hitherto resisted every attempt at identification, for its identification may indeed prove a key to the play's provenance. The King of Life promises his messenger Solas that 'Þou schal haue for þi gode wil / To þin auauncemente, / Þe castel of Gailispire on þe Hil, / And þe erldom of Kente.'[96] The problem has been the location of 'Gailispire on þe Hil.' Though Mills was quite right to observe that Gailispire was an English name, it is English only in the sense that its etymological components appear to stem from Germanic, rather than Celtic, roots.[97] Moreover, since no place name in England makes a convincing candidate for association with Gailispire, the possibility is open that Gailispire was a name given to an Irish place by the Anglo-Normans or conceivably, before them, by the Hiberno-Norse.[98] In fact, a good case can be made for identifying Gailispire with one such Irish candidate, and that candidate becomes all the more persuasive for being not only topographically consistent with a place which the play describes as being situated 'on þe Hil,' but also for the connection with the Augustinian canons of Dublin that this place once had and for the proximity to it of a medieval manor house which at least by the sixteenth century was being referred to as a castle. The present-day townland of Giltspur, in the barony of Rathdown, co. Wicklow, is the candidate deserving consideration.

Price, in his study of the place names of co. Wicklow, believed that in the twelfth or thirteenth century, Giltspur 'was given some such name as 'the gilt spur land.'[99] It got this name, he thought, from the fact that in a deed of 1196–9, Richard de Felda and his heirs had agreed to pay annually to the owners of Giltspur, Diarmait Mac Gilla Mo Cholmóc and his heirs, a pair of gilt spurs in return for a carucate of land in Kilruddery.[100] This suggestion looks suspiciously like folk etymology. Furthermore, it does not account for the fact that at least by the eighteenth century, Giltspur was also referred to as 'Gilsper Hill' and 'Gillspur Hill,' both without the medial -t-.[101] These eighteenth-century forms without medial -t- would be consistent with an early etymon comprised of the Old Norse place-name element *gil* ('narrow valley' or 'ravine'), plus a second element whose original vowel is now obscured, since in falling in an unstressed, word-final position, it would have been liable to variant spellings in its later reflexes: the Old English and Old Norse word *spor* ('track') seems a likely option, and is again a common enough place name element. Thus Giltspur may originally have referred to the 'track of the narrow valley,' rather than any pair of gilt spurs that Diarmait and his heirs might have expected to receive annually from the de Felda family. But just how exact a fit would the 'Gailispire on þe Hil' mentioned in the play be with this proposed etymology? Although 'Gailispire on þe Hil' certainly bears a striking resemblance to the eighteenth-century appellations 'Gilsper Hill' and 'Gillspur Hill,' the -ai- spelling of its first element, 'Gaili-' or 'Gailis-,' still needs to be reckoned with, since the medial -ai- might suggest derivation from some diphthongal etymon. As it happens, there is no difficulty about this. The Old Norse *geil*, a word cognate with *gil* and of similar meaning, would easily be accommodated within the Middle English reflex 'Gaili-' / 'Gailis-.' The -ai- spelling in Gailispire could thus be explained quite straightforwardly as reflecting a common variant of the same etymon.[102]

In addition there are, as mentioned, corroborative cultural and topographical reasons for believing that Giltspur may have been the place intended. As is well known, the Augustinian canons had secured a firm foothold in medieval Dublin, where they inhabited two other important houses apart from that of the Priory of Holy Trinity.[103] One of these, the Abbey of St Thomas the Martyr, or Thomas Court as it came to be more familiarly known, had acquired land in Kilruddery, the townland adjacent to Giltspur, from Richard de Felda. Thus the temporal interests of Dublin's Augustinian canons were stongly represented in this area from the very early days of the Anglo-Norman settlement. Merely half a mile east-northeast of Giltspur stands Kilruddery House, which though today a building dating from the 1820s, either stands on or in the vicinity of an earlier medieval manor house.[104] The medieval manor house here would make a prime candidate for association with 'Þe castel of Gailispire on þe Hil': by the thirteenth century, its estate included a *molendinum, gardinum, et boscum, necnon muros et fossata curie* ('mill, orchard and wood, and sev-

eral walls and embankments of the manor house'); and by the sixteenth century, it
was indeed being referred to as a castle.[105] Also, the nearby presence of the valley of
the Dargle river, which runs to the west of Giltspur, about a mile-and-a-half away
from Kilruddery House, would fully justify the use of the qualifying phrase 'on þe
Hil,' as well as the meaning implicit anyway in the etymology for Gailispire proposed above. This onomastic detour can be brought to a close with the conclusion
that a place name in north co. Wicklow should be considered a strong contender
for identifying 'Gailispire on þe Hil.'

To return to the question of performance, references in *The Pride of Life* indicate that, like the 1528 Christmastide plays, it too was intended for playing out of
doors.[106] This being so, *The Pride of Life* would necessarily have been a far more
boisterous, flamboyant production than the ritualistic *Visitatio Sepulcri:* for example, it would not have troubled to convey fine shades of expression through subtle
intonations of the voice, since besides the fact that outdoor performance makes this
sort of delivery virtually impossible, the declamatory style in which it is written also
works against it. In fact, the play's bold style may be counted amongst the symptoms
of outdoor performance.[107] If its prologue is trustworthy, it was also a more truly
popular play in the inclusiveness of an outdoor audience which its author conceived
as comprising men and women, rich and poor, clerics and laity.[108] Wider reception
was automatically ensured, of course, by its composition in English rather than in
priestly Latin.[109] Hence the theological and social antidote which, as will be argued,
it would propose for current historical anxieties had the potential in such a performance to reach the widest possible tranche of Dublin's population.

An outdoor audience of the kind envisioned also posed its own practical problems
for the playwright, but some of them he had anticipated and tried to tackle. He
foresaw an audience that would be mobile – people are referred to as standing[110] –
and no doubt it would also have been vocal, so its attention had to be caught. He
therefore devised an arresting prologue, addressed to all conditions of folk, that would
still the unwelcome movement of their limbs and tongues before he proceeded to
summarize for them the play's plot. Much later, when the play was well under way,
the playwright was still careful to maintain the rapport earlier established between
actors and audience, and this he did to such an extent as to blur occasionally the
distinction between who was actor and who spectator. For example, a play character
might address members of the audience directly as if they too were play characters,
rather in the way a modern pantomime dame enrols her audience in the make-
believe presented on stage. Thus the playwright could turn to purely practical advantage an engaging technique of audience involvement which at once made his
drama more entertaining: the audience, offered a role to play imaginatively, were
treated more like participants than mere spectators. If they responded to his tactics,
they would co-operate more fully in his play, painlessly digest its messages, and

become as tractable as a playwright writing for an open-air, take-it-or-leave-it kind of theatre could wish.[111]

The approximate size of *The Pride of Life*'s cast can be inferred from the prologue's description of the plot.[112] Two Kings (the King of Life and King of Death), two knights (Strength and Health), a Bishop, a Queen (wife to the King of Life), the messenger Solas, the Virgin Mary, at least two devils, the body and the soul of the King of Life and Christ comprise the *dramatis personae*, and total thirteen roles. Some of these could have been doubled (for example, in the missing section of the play where the body and soul of the King of Life were in debate, it would have been unnecessary to introduce an additional actor to play the King's body; the King himself would most naturally have suited this role, with some appropriate costume change, for example from regalia to winding sheet, to signify his *post-mortem* status). A cast of six actors, the same number in fact as played the *Visitatio Sepulcri*, could have played this play with ease.[113]

Its stage directions are few, but a couple of telling ones, together with deductions that can be made about the nature of the dynamics of the action, suggest how the playing place for *The Pride of Life* would have had to have been arranged. At one point the King of Life withdraws to sleep, tells his knight Sir Strength to 'Draw þe cord,' and then there follows the stage direction: 'Et tunc clauso tentorio dicet Regina secrete nuncio' ('And then *having closed the tent*, let the Queen say privately to the messenger').[114] A *tentorium*, some sort of curtained structure, probably a booth rather than a 'tent' in the modern sense, is called for to conceal the King from sight.[115] The messenger, sent on a private errand by the Queen to fetch the Bishop to reprimand her erring husband, leaves her declaring: 'I am Solas, I most singe / Oueral qwher I go.'[116] He sings (a Latin stage direction, 'Et cantat,' reinforces this) and makes his way to the Bishop. Apart from the fact that the messenger's singing makes an appropriate attribute of one who rejoices under the name of 'Solas,' his song is functional and this not merely in a decorative way. The use of music, here also to cover a journey from one place to another, is commonly met with at breaks in the action in other contemporary plays, but most noticeably in ones employing the method of production known to theatre historians as place-and-scaffold theatre.[117] The messenger's music as he proceeds helps to put the earlier events played at one locale into the background, to hold the attention of the audience and to prepare it for the transition to a new locale and new stage business. The messenger arrives at the new locale, the scaffold, presumably, where the Bishop is installed upon a throne (like the King of Life earlier) and wearing a mitre. It is clear that the locales housing King and Bishop would have stood at some unspecified distance from each other, and that at least that of the King of Life had its *tentorium* into which an actor could disappear. The arrangement of the Bishop's locale may have been similar. The use of the word *platea* in another stage direction (if this is what the manuscript indeed originally read) is also significant.[118] It is a commonplace in the terminology of place-and-scaffold theatre, where it normally designates the 'place,' that is, the undifferentiated playing space at ground level between the different locales (these latter often being raised on scaffolds, as the *tentorium* of the King of Life may also have been).[119] Therefore, all the signs are that the Dublin *Pride of Life* was written not only for presentation outdoors, but also in a place-and-scaffold type of theatre.[120]

Even if questions any more detailed than those already asked about the nature of the play's staging have to be satisfied with general answers, such answers can still give a sharper focus to our notional picture of how *The Pride of Life* may have been staged. For example, how many scaffolds are likely to have been used? As noted earlier, its text appears to call for at least two, one for the King of Life and one for the Bishop. As far as we know, these were identified as particular settings (King's palace, Bishop's palace) by only the vaguest of representational touches: a throne was set on each scaffold. In which case, in a highly economical production of *The Pride of Life*, these two scaffolds alone could have been made to double (one of them to treble) in order to accommodate the five different narrative settings that the play seems to require,[121] as and when each setting became necessary. Alternatively, it is conceivable that up to three further scaffolds were employed in addition to the two essential ones, making a maximum total of five scaffolds. Of course, any increase above two scaffolds would proportionally decrease the necessity for scaffold doubling (and trebling), while there would at the same time have been a correspondingly increased opportunity to mark out a scaffold definitively as representing a particular setting (King's palace, Bishop's palace, heaven, hell, or wherever) by means of additional touches of appropriate set detail. We might best summarize this discussion of a reconstructed staging of *The Pride of Life* in an artist's impression. A notional three-scaffold production is pictured in fig. 8.[122]

It has been seen how any production of this play, even a relatively economical one, would have required a considerable investment of time and expense. Who could its actors and stage hands have been, and when and where in Dublin might it have been performed? Given the Augustinian auspices of its manuscript, there is likely to have been some sort of clerical input into its production, as has been argued, but it is not possible to tell what precise form this took, whether the canons were involved in its organization at a remove, as its financial backers, for example, or whether some of them even acted in it.[123] Dublin laity would presumably have been required to organize certain aspects of the play's production, if only to attend to practicalities like setting up the requisite number of scaffolds.[124] Conceivably, Dublin laity may also have provided the actors. For example, in any production of *The Pride of Life* after 1418, the year in which the Tailors guild was formally established in the city, the canons could have sought first among its guild members for likely candidates to involve in the play which they had preserved on their account roll.[125] With the

8 Reconstruction of the staging of *The Pride of Life*.

establishment of the Tailors guild chapel in the church of St John the Evangelist, which as has already been noted was in the canons' cure and also home to both of the extant *Visitatio* manuscripts, tailors and canons would have come into close regular contact.[126] Furthermore, other evidence suggests that the Tailors were also acquiring the right sort of experience for mounting dramatic performances of the outdoor kind such as *The Pride of Life* must have been. 1498 sees them for the first time on record as participants in the Dublin Corpus Christi pageant procession, but they had already been taking part in the procession for several years before this date.[127] In any event, whoever may have made up *The Pride of Life's* cast, all would probably have been men, with a boy (or boys) playing the roles of the Queen and the Virgin.[128] The place in Dublin where they played it would have had to accommodate the substantial concourse of people envisioned in the play's prologue, and an audience sufficiently large to make a performance worthwhile. The venue must have been spacious enough to avoid obstruction to any city traffic (assuming, that is, that no arrangements had been made to re-route the flow of people during the performance). There would have been a greater premium on space within the city walls, but even here the play could have been staged in a few locations.[129] Outside the walls there would have been less difficulty, and we will see in the next chapter both how the Hoggen Green came to establish itself as an important dramatic venue, and how the Christ Church canons made use of it for play production.

   The Pride of Life could have been mounted whenever in the year its producers wished. Unlike the Easter *Visitatio*, which was strictly bound to an annual liturgical occasion, it was suitable for performance at any time. There is nothing distinctly seasonal about it, and its atemporal theme, the unequal struggle of life and death, would have made it perennially relevant. The only restriction upon it may have been that as outdoor theatre, it would more likely have been played when there were better chances of clement weather, though it must be admitted that such considerations did not inhibit the Hoggen Green Christmastide plays of 1528, as the next chapter will reveal.

CIVIC DRAMA

The important contributions made by the church to dramatic activity in Dublin, which were to continue until well into the sixteenth century, were matched during the course of the fifteenth by contributions from the civic sector. The records suggest not so much a faltering of such church drama as has been reviewed as an increasingly sturdy participation in drama and general public ceremonial by the laity. It is true that any church dramas which implied or openly supported the doctrine of the transubstantiated host would have smacked too much of heresy for a Reformation palate, and in due course would doubtless have been suppressed, leaving the field increasingly open to colonization by lay dramas which avoided tendentious issues in theology. But a generation before this, on the eve of the Reformation (and in the case of Christ Church, Reformation reforms were being implemented even as late as the early 1540s), there is nothing to indicate that dramas held under church auspices were ailing.[130] Rather, there is evidence that church and state were continuing to collaborate fruitfully in organizing dramatic presentations, though the involvement of the civic body, growing steadily more conspicuous as the fifteenth century wore on, threatened to overshadow that of the church.[131]

The people ideally placed to handle the mounting of public displays were the members of Dublin's religious and trade guilds, and like many of their English contemporaries, Dublin guild members too involved themselves in the pageantry of Corpus Christi. Dublin's unique Corpus Christi pageant lists of 1498, preserved in the Great Chain Book of the corporation, require careful attention, especially since they offer the only extant account of the composition of the medieval pageant procession. The Chain Book, originally kept for reference purposes in the corporation's guildhall or Tholsel, as it was commonly known, contains two lists, the first essentially similar to the second except for its slightly fuller detail.[132] Both were drawn up in 1498. They specify those crafts which the city ordered to take part in the Corpus Christi procession. The format of each list is basically the same. To the left appears the name of the guild, and to the right a brief description of the pageant allocated to it (see fig. 9). The first list runs as follows:

Corpus christi day a pagent

the pagentes of corpus christi day made by an olde law & confermed by a semble {'assembly'} befor Thomas Collier maire of þe Citte of diuelin & Iuries {'aldermen'} ₐ⌈baliffes⌉ & communes þe iiij[th] friday next after Midsomer þe xiij yere of þe reigne of kyng henri þe vij th

Gloueres. Adam & Eve with an angill followyng berryng a swerde ⌈peyn xl s.⌉   5
¶ Corvisers {'Shoemakers'} Caym & Abell with an avter & þer ofference peyn xl s.
¶ Maryners vynters shipcarpynderis & samoun takers Noe with his shipp apparalid acordyng peyn. xl. s.
¶ Weuers Abraham ysaak with þer avter ₐ⌈& a alambe⌉ & þer offerance peyn. xl s.
¶ Smythis Shermen bakers sclateris {'slaters'} Cokis & masonys. pharo with his hoste peyn xl s.   10
¶ Skynners house carpynders & tanners & browderes {'embroiderers'}. for þe body of þe camell & oure lady & hir chile {'child'} well apereled with Ioseph to lede þe camell & Moyses with þe children of Israell and þe portours to berr þe camell peyn .xl. s.
<The > steynours & peyntours to peynt þe hede of þe camell .xl s.
¶ <Goldsm>ythis þe iij kynges of Collyne {'Collogne'} ridyng worshupfully with þer   15
offerance with a sterr afor them peyn .xl. s.

9 The Dublin Chain Book, DCA, C1/2/1, fols. 56v–7.

¶ hopers þe sheperdis with an angill syngyng gloria in Ex<cel>sis deo peyn .xl. s.
<¶> Corpus christi yild Criste in his passioun with iij maries & angelis berring
serges {'tapers'} of wex in þer hand xl. s.
¶ Taylours pilate with his fellaship & his lady & his knyghtes well beseyne   20
{'apparelled'}. peyn xl s.
<¶> Barbours An<na> & Caiphas well araied acordyng xl s.
¶ Conpteours {?'(city) auditors'} Arthure with knightes peyn xl s.
¶ ffisshers þe xij apostelis peyn xl s.

fol. 57

¶ Marchauntes þe prophetes peyn .xl. s.   25
¶ Bouchers ∧⌐vj⌐ Tormentours with þer garmentes well & clenly peyntid xl s.
¶ þe maire of þe bulring & bachelers of þe same þe ix worthies ridyng worshupfully
with ther followers acordyng peyn. xl s.
The hagardmen {'stack-yard men'} & þe husbandmen to berr þe dragoun & to repaire
þe dragoun a Seint Georges day & corpus christi day peyn [.xl. s.] °xl s. xl s.° ¹³³   30

It appears from this list that any failure to meet its requirements was punishable by
a forty-shilling fine.¹³⁴ Prospects of fines no doubt also helped to concentrate the minds
of the guildsmen and to curb any tendency on their part to deviate from the prescribed subject matter. An item in the Dublin Assembly Rolls for 1504 orders the
Corpus Christi guild, the only purely religious guild mentioned in the Chain Book
pageant lists, to adhere to its traditional pageant, which the lists had stipulated as
Christ's Passion:

Item. It is ordinet and grauntit by þe seyd Semble {'assembly'} that þe mayster and wardynes
of Corpus Christi yeld schall bere no pagyentes vn Corpus Christi day <bot> scwch {'such'}
pagyentes as þei dide of old tyme.¹³⁵

The ordinance conceivably represents the official response to some petition of the guild,
now lost, for permission to alter its pageant in some way. Alternatively, it might represent steps taken against the guild for having been too cavalier in its approach to its
allocated subject matter, perhaps even to the extent of presenting a pageant on a different topic. Whatever the case, the civic authorities were evidently monitoring very
carefully what the guild was doing.
      In 1498, at least sixteen pageants threaded the Dublin streets on Corpus Christi,
with the spectacular addition, no doubt to remind onlookers about who was ultimately running the festivities, of the Dublin dragon. This beast, the emblem of the
corporation, came into its own during the city's St George's Day celebrations, but

was also carted out on Corpus Christi. The date of the first Corpus Christi pageant procession in Dublin is unknown. The 1498 lists speak of its pageants as having been made 'by an olde law,' and the earliest known reference to a procession, which already must have been of considerable size, appears in an Assembly Roll entry of 1466:

> Item hit is ordeynet & graunt by the Seide Semble {'assembly'} that ffro thens forward suche persones as will cum to the Citte in the ffestes of Corpus Christi Seint George Seint Patrik for procession and pylgrymage and hors for Rydyng at Corperaunt {'Shrove Tuesday'} be fre with oute enny Wexacion cummyng Goyng and abydyng a day befor and a day after so that thei bryng no man his horse of the Citte °with them the wiche was stoll° {?'provided that they bring no man's horse with them from the city, which was stolen'}.[136]

There is no clear indication here that actual pageants featured in the 1466 procession, but its size, which seems to have motivated this piece of legislation by the authorities to regulate the flow of people during the feast, circumstantially suggests that they may well have done. The 1466 decree envisaged crowds out and about on Corpus Christi, St George's Day, St Patrick's Day, and Shrove Tuesday ('Corperaunt'). An entertaining pageant procession may have been just the thing to lure people onto the streets in such numbers as to oblige legislation for crowd control and freedom of passage. Whatever the date of the first actual pageant procession, one had established itself at least by the second half of the fifteenth century, and a significant attempt was made in 1498 to define and regulate it. In subsequent years, the Chain Book was to become the standard source of reference for prescribing the sequence that the guilds had to observe in processions. Appeals made to it, as well as the very fact of its codification of processional protocol, show the civic authorities to have been anxious to draw their cordon of control around a large-scale public enterprise which could ill afford any proneness to vary at random.[137]

It seems most likely, then, that there was a time before 1498 when the Dublin Corpus Christi procession was a somewhat different affair, probably both in the content of its pageants and their order of precedence. How different it is not possible to say, whether there were fewer, more or alternative pageants.[138] As is the nature of things, some variation was likely from one year to the next, for the fluctuating fortunes of each participating guild may have affected the quality of the pageant that it was able to present.[139] Unfortunately, insufficient evidence inhibits our tracing this aspect of guild involvement in their pageants. One of the most damaging record losses has been that of most of the Dublin guild muniments. Only three sets of documents have survived which bear directly upon guild pageant production, and even then they are all of the sixteenth century: the Account Book of the Tailors guild, the Account Book of the guild of Carpenters, Millers, Masons, and Heliers, and the Treasurer's Book of Dublin Corporation, which includes matter relevant to the guild of St George.[140] Though the information contained in these records may hint at the shape of things in an earlier age, it can do no more than that. Neither can anything secure be inferred from the date of a guild's founding charter, where it is known, about the date after which that guild might be presumed to have been able to join in the procession. The Butchers guild, for example, which was given responsibility for a striking pageant in the 1498 list, did not receive its charter until a good seventy years later, in 1569; before then, it evidently existed less formally.[141]

However, most of the guilds that appear in the 1498 list had in fact already been granted charters conferring their powers and allowing their free hand in the appointment of guild wardens and masters.[142] Each guild, certainly each chartered one, had a formal administrative machinery that could be set in motion once the pageants were being prepared. It has been seen how the civic authorities kept a vigilant eye on the pageants when they passed their ordinance curbing the Corpus Christi guild in 1504. Evidently Dublin's civic authority forged links of surveillance and general control between itself and the administration of each participating guild.

The precise nature of the liaison between civic authority and guilds when preparing for Dublin's days of public pageantry is unknown; regretably, there is no way of closing the gap in our understanding caused by too little evidence. Comparison of what went on in other cities in Great Britain might suggest the sort of procedures adopted in Dublin, however, and some evidence from Dublin in 1649, though to be sure it falls a little after the official terminus of this study, may also suggest what was done in an earlier period. As regards procedures in other cities, Chester, on the face of it, would seem the most natural candidate for comparison, for not only did it support an elaborate Corpus Christi procession of its own, but by the late fifteenth century, commerce and trade between Chester and Dublin were well established, and Dublin attracted settlers from in and around Chester.[143] These people, accustomed in Chester to witness a Corpus Christi feast enhanced in some years with an impressive pageant procession, may have expected celebrations of a similar order in their adoptive city. Moreover, the civic ceremonies of the Shrove Tuesday bearing of balls and the Black Monday progress were shared by both cities, making comparison between them all the more interesting.[144] Yet though the city of Chester, like Dublin, also supervised carefully the pageant presentations of its own guilds, it does not provide the clearest model in this respect. For this, we must turn to another English city with which Dublin had some cultural affiliation, and that is York. Of the British towns and cities from which pageant lists survive, none, not even Chester, has lists quite so strikingly comparable to Dublin's as those contained in York Corporation's A/Y Memorandum Book.[145] If for no other reason than this, comparison with York seems worth pursuing.

First, both the Dublin and the York Books are civic documents. Both contain two pageant lists. In both, the first list is somewhat fuller than the second, since the first describes the content of each particular pageant in more detail.[146] Even the layout of the lists in both Books is remarkably similar. For example, the first list in both Dublin and York has a heading announcing the list, the name of the current mayor, and the date when the list was drawn up. Beneath the heading, the name of each participating guild is written in the left margin, preceded by the same deictic mark, a *capitulum* (ℭ). To the right of the guild name is a short description of the content of its pageant.

The function of the first list, or the *Ordo paginarum* as it is normally called, in the A/Y Memorandum Book of York, seems clear enough: drafted in 1415, it provided an official description of the order and general content of the guilds' pageants. A yearly reference was made to it in Lent by the common clerk of the city when he copied down a prescriptive description of each individual pageant and had this delivered to the guildsmen concerned.[147] The function of the second list is much less clear. Its comparative brevity suggests it may have been some sort of quick checklist, but the occasion of its use is uncertain.[148]

Possibly York's practice in some respects paralleled that of Dublin. There would seem little point in Dublin's civic authorities preserving an official list of Corpus Christi pageants if that list's information was not also to be shared in some way with each participating guild. An efficient method of communicating to each guild the prescribed content of its pageant, as well as usefully reminding it that the civic authorities were keeping open a watchful eye, would have been to follow some procedure after the manner of York. And as has been seen, the various striking similarities between both cities' lists make plausible the suggestion that their communication procedures may have been broadly comparable. This conclusion seems supported by the survival of a Dublin writ of 3 September 1649.[149] This writ was signed by the mayor and dispatched to the guild of Goldsmiths, requiring it to be ready on Christ Church meadow at 4:00 a.m. in the morning of 10 September to ride the city franchises. The franchise riding will be considered later, but for the present suffice it to say that the procedure of issuing a writ from corporation to guild to summon it to a civic procession was similar to the procedure adopted in York, albeit at an earlier date. The Dublin writ of 1649 may have had long-standing precedents. It would be wrong, of course, to press the comparison on points of detail. For example, it is not known whether the Dublin authorities may have notified the guilds of forthcoming Corpus Christi processions on a regular yearly basis, as the York authorities intended for their own guilds from 1415. Dublin may have been more like Chester in this respect, where the Corpus Christi pageant procession and play may well not have been an annual event.[150]

For all the points of similarity between the Dublin and York lists, there are informative points of dissimilarity which are of equal interest. Several of the pageant descriptions in the first list of the A/Y Memorandum Book, while they concentrate on naming characters appearing within each pageant, also give some sense of a particular pageant's narrative content. It seems that the descriptions were indeed describing *plays*. Thus, for example, the description of the Coopers' pageant of the Fall, of 'Adam and Eve and the tree between them; the serpent deceiving them with apples; God speaking to them and cursing the serpent, and an angel with a sword expelling them from paradise,'[151] gives some sense of a sequence of events as well as merely naming the characters involved. Compare the Chain Book account of the equivalent Dublin pageant, presented by the Glovers, from the first pageant list: 'Adam & Eve with an angill followyng berryng a swerde.' If this Dublin description can at all be interpreted as suggesting consecutive narrative events, it does so in a much less obvious way than does the York description. Its style is in fact typical of every one of the Dublin pageant descriptions in both of the Chain Book lists, even of the first, which is slightly fuller than the second. Conceivably, the difference between York and Dublin here was simply one of conciseness; Dublin may have implied the same kind of thing as York but in fewer words. Yet it is harder to believe that than to believe that an actual qualitative difference is registering here about the way the pageants of York and Dublin were perceived by the compilers of the two sets of lists. In the case of York, an awareness of the pageants as plays seems to have coloured the descriptions of several of them, while in Dublin, no such awareness has shown through. The Dublin pageant lists seem to envisage no more than a procession of pageants.

Even though this may be so, it does not necessarily follow that these same pageants, or certain of them at least, were never involved in some sort of dramatic production at any time on Corpus Christi. Granted, it seems unlikely that the pageants, as the lists reveal them, did much more than move through the streets as dumb tableaux during the actual Dublin Corpus Christi procession.[152] But this does not exclude the possibility that plays were performed from the pageants outside the context of the procession itself. This is what seems to have happened, for example, in the early years of the Chester cycle, when it was still being mounted at Corpus Christi;[153] the play was acted in one place, at St John's outside the east wall of the city, after the liturgical procession had ended.[154]

The idea, therefore, that Dublin saw a dramatic presentation from pageant wagons on Corpus Christi is not ruled out by the fact that the Chain Book lists appear to cater for a procession only. The idea remains tenable, but in need of support. In this respect it is unfortunate that an early historian of the Irish stage, Joseph Walker, gave no source for his assertion that the Dublin Corpus Christi pageants 'moved in solemn procession to St. George's Chapel, the scene of their dramatic exhibitions.'[155] His statement would at least square with what is implied by the Chain Book lists, in so far as if the Dublin pageants were ever fully dramatic at any point during the day's proceedings, they were probably not so during the procession itself. As was seen, regulation of a procession was the prime concern of whoever had the Chain Book lists drawn up; it may have been beyond the lists' remit to prescribe arrangements for anything more than that, much less for anything taking place beyond the city walls and, moreover, after the actual procession had ended. Yet how may Walker's claim be supported? Only one clue has survived, but it suggests that at least certain of the Dublin pageants did indeed feature in a dramatic production of some sort on Corpus Christi. The Account Book of the Tailors guild records several payments incurred by the guild for the festivities of Corpus Christi and Midsummer. In the Chain Book lists, the Tailors in 1498 were responsible for the pageant of Pilate, Pilate's wife, and their company. In 1554 and 1556, the Tailors were still producing what appears to have been essentially the same pageant. The phrasing of certain entries for those respective years is noteworthy: 'Item paid to Stewen Casse for playnge pilote a corpus criste day ii^S. irishe' and 'paied to Stephan Casse for plainge on corpus Cristy daie ii^S.'[156] The word 'playing' in both entries suggests something more demonstrative than merely going in a procession in the guise of Pilate. It is a word commonly met with in sixteenth-century play accounts, including, for example, those from Kilkenny, the only Irish town where it is known beyond a shadow of doubt that Corpus Christi plays were acted.[157] 'Playing' usually seems to have meant that the person or persons so described behaved as would an actor in a traditional modern sense: it signified role impersonation through word and gesture. However, although this was its frequent meaning, in certain contexts it might include other possibilities: subtract dialogue from a performance and the result is a mime or dumb-show, but still in the sixteenth century such a mime might be referred to as a *play* presented by *players*;[158] go a step further and subtract gesture as well, and a motionless, picture-like mimesis results, a *tableau vivant* where role impersonation is conveyed by little more than the actors' very appearance.[159] This sort of performance stands at the opposite end of the dramatic spectrum to full-blown impersonation through word and gesture, yet a person involved in such a static performance might still in a minimal sense be deemed to be 'playing': at least the element of counterfeit remains. The sixteenth century had evolved no elaborate taxonomy of drama, though presumably such dramatic terminology as there was was perfectly, if pragmatically, serviceable.[160] So although it is a little difficult to know where precisely on the dramatic spectrum the Tailors' Corpus Christi 'playing' should be located, the least likely of all possibilities would be that it designated merely a silent and unmoving *tableau vivant*; on balance, it points rather to some greater degree of dramatic animation.

At this stage it may be helpful to review briefly the opinions on the question of whether medieval Dublin saw Corpus Christi drama or not before proceeding any further. In the earliest criticism, there was a general assumption that it did.[161] This assumption held sway until Chambers checked it with his influential verdict in 1903 that if it did, the Dublin Chain Book lists could not be cited as supporting evidence because they appeared to bear witness to nothing more than a procession of pageants.[162] Since Chambers, most critics have not wished to rule out entirely the possibility of a Dublin Corpus Christi drama, but all have been hard pressed to argue for it on any grounds other than conjecture and inference. Chambers's interpretation of the Chain Book lists was surely correct, though as argued, it should not foreclose the possibility that Corpus Christi drama was performed in Dublin outside the procession proper. And indeed the morsels of information just reviewed, though not wholly unproblematic, point in this direction, however faintly: on the one hand, the assertion of the eighteenth-century antiquary Joseph Walker, that the pageant wagons were taken outside the city walls, drawn up by St George's Chapel, and plays acted from them; and on the other, the two sixteenth-century Tailors guild payments to Stephen Casse for 'playing' on Corpus Christi day.

If a variety of Corpus Christi drama ever were performed in Dublin, the Chain Book lists presumably give some idea about what this putative play or play cycle dramatized. Seeking its shape in them is not ideal, for as was seen, detailing the contents of any play cycle as such was evidently beyond their brief. In fact, if each of the sixteen listed pageants had a play associated with it, not to mention the seventeenth, the pageant of the Dublin dragon, which brought up the honourable rear, a 'cycle' would result so extraordinary by comparison with the play cycles of other cities in the British Isles as to be unthinkable. The first five pageants would follow each other perfectly well, since they would dramatize a chronological group of popular Old Testament episodes commonly presented in Corpus Christi play cycles. The sixth, however, would be curious. Part of it, 'Moses and the children of Israel,' fits in neatly enough with the narrative events of the fifth pageant of Pharaoh and his host, but the lists' descriptions of it focus less upon Moses and the Israelites than upon a fabulous camel which carried upon its back the Virgin and the Christ child, and which was tractably led along by Joseph.[163] No doubt it added spectacular impact to the appearance of the Holy Family to have them transported by a fabricated dromedary, but this part of the pageant can scarcely have lent itself to dramatization without upsetting the chronological order that the previous pageants had observed so far and without also fancifully embroidering a portion of gospel narrative not normally lending itself to such treatment.[164] How the camel came in seems explicable; it looks like an exotic metamorphosis of the traditional ass upon which Mary rode in her flight to Egypt. But even if it was, dramatizing the flight to Egypt precisely at this point would still have destroyed chronology, since properly the episode could not occur until after the Nativity, and the two succeeding pageants, the seventh and eighth, deal respectively with Nativity events (the Epiphany and the annunciation to the shepherds, in that order).[165] The ninth, tenth, and eleventh pageants, in being concerned with Passiontide narrative, are all related thematically, but they

also appear to have lost some of their strict chronological consecutiveness. The
ninth pageant expressly presented 'Christ in his Passion,' and the presence in it of
the three Marys suggests that it was a pageant either of the Crucifixion or of the
events immediately leading up to it, on the road to Calvary. However, this preceded
the tenth pageant of Pilate and Pilate's wife; the appearance of Pilate's wife evokes
the episode well before the Crucifixion where Pilate's wife, troubled by dreams, in
effect counsels her husband not to allow Christ to be put to death. The lady vanishes after she has told her fears, not to reappear after the Crucifixion has been executed. The sequence of pageants clearly did not constitute a strict chronological
narrative. It is not possible to tell whether Annas and Caiaphas, who appear in
pageant eleven, were also chronologically displaced, since they are reported in the
gospels to be actively in league both before and after the Crucifixion happens. The
next pageant, the twelfth, was certainly disruptive in introducing the procession's
first major break with sacred history. It presented King Arthur and his knights.
After this non-biblical twelfth pageant, it becomes well nigh impossible to locate
those of the remaining pageants which may be biblically inspired anywhere precisely on the sacred time scale; indeed, perhaps no attempt should be made to do
so. It is as if the liberal, but essentially intelligible, chronology of the first eleven
pageants is now quite abandoned.[166] The thirteenth pageant of the twelve apostles
sounds to have been no more than that, not locating the apostles in any of their
familiar narrative contexts, such as the Last Supper or Pentecost.[167] The fourteenth
pageant of the prophets is vaguer still, while the fifteenth, a pageant of the 'tor-
mentors,' poses a problem of knowing exactly who its grisly crew were intended to
represent.[168] The sixteenth pageant is the second unbiblical one, and features the Nine
Worthies,[169] while the seventeenth, again unbiblical, features the Dublin dragon.[170]

It seems clear that if there ever were a traditional Corpus Christi play cycle in
Dublin, not all of these pageants can have taken part in it. The likely candidates for
association with any such cycle are those which self-evidently presented sacred history, pageants one to five, that part of the sixth dealing with Moses and the children
of Israel, and pageants seven to eleven. This would amount to about two-thirds of
the procession pageants reappearing for an actual performance, and probably after
the procession itself was over. In comprising many of the popular Corpus Christi
episodes, this putative play would have had much in common with those produced
in other medieval British cities.[171] Its scale would have been more modest than only
that of the most ambitious of them.[172] Interestingly, there is no scope to infer from
the Chain Book lists that it would have featured a Doomsday pageant, the episode
which often brought in a cycle's conclusion. This would not be entirely unprece-
dented, nevertheless. A list of the pageants of the city of Norwich, written c 1530
into the city's Old Free Book, also stops short of a Doomsday pageant.[173] Norwich
undisputably had a play cycle, whose earliest performances may have taken place

on Corpus Christi; by 1527 the cycle had been shifted to Whit Monday.[174] Also, in years when it is known which pageants were played, no Doomsday appeared among them.[175] This does not necessarily mean that Doomsday never featured in any of the productions of the Norwich cycle, because the incomplete state of the city's records forestalls so definite a conclusion. But what is irreducibly true is that a play cycle which did not contain Doomsday could be performed. If Doomsday had equally been dispensed with in Dublin, the resultant cycle would certainly be unusual, but not altogether unparalleled.[176]

In sum, discussion of the putative Dublin cycle has shaded steadily from certainty into uncertainty. It is a fact that there was a Corpus Christi pageant procession in medieval Dublin, and that it lived on into the sixteenth century; it is possible that some of these pageants were involved in a Corpus Christi play, performed outside the city walls after the procession had ended; and it is advanced speculation to deduce the contents of such a play from the pageants listed in the Chain Book. The loss of the bulk of the guild accounts means that our understanding of what may actually have occurred in Dublin must always acknowledge the degree to which the few seeds of fact from which it stems have had to be irrigated by fancy.

THE PAGEANTS AND THEIR ROUTE

If Dublin Corpus Christi drama is an elusive quarry, tracking the route of the pageants offers more promise. The first eyewitness accounts of large-scale civic pageantry in Dublin are late, and describe the procession known as the riding of the franchises. The custom of marking the bounds of the mayor's jurisdiction by a procession had established itself in medieval times, but although a formal civic affair which even employed city musicians, it seems that in its earliest days it was relatively unadventurous. Certainly it had no pageants.[177] With the eventual demise of the procession on Corpus Christi, which had occurred by late in the third quarter of the sixteenth century,[178] and of other kindred processions, like those to St George's Chapel on 23 April, also probably ceasing at about the same time, as the next chapter will show, the city pageants were in danger of becoming redundant.[179] This eventuality appears to have been avoided by their absorption into the riding of the franchises, thereby helping to inject into the riding a new and apparently needed lease of life.[180]

The late franchise riding descriptions show how elaborate an enterprise the early riding was destined to become. The riding also became internationally famous, and attracted people from considerable distances to come to see it.[181] Most of its participating trade guilds processed with their pageant wagons. These often served as imaginative advertisements for the wares of each particular trade. Eye-witness accounts are generally in agreement about what the wagons were like. When his book *Irish Varieties* was published in 1836, J.D. Herbert, speaking of the franchise pageantry which to his knowledge had been in existence at least sixty years prior to his first actual recollection of it, said that every trade had its own 'fancy car and platform.'[182] John O'Keeffe, whose memories of the riding also reached back into the eighteenth century, gives a vivid description of how as a boy he watched the procession go by from what must have been an upper window of a house in Thomas Street.[183] He variously described the wagons as 'carriage' (the term which he favoured), 'high phaeton,' 'pageant,' and 'vehicle.'[184] Two other writers, Jonah Barrington and J.E. Walsh, give the picture sharper focus. Walsh said that each pageant, or 'vehicle,' as he prefered to call it, was horse-drawn.[185] This detail is found also in Barrington, whose account of the wagons is perhaps the most spacious and evocative. He was another who had seen the franchise riding in its eighteenth-century heyday, and remembered how as a child it 'made such a strong impression on my mind that it never could be obliterated.'[186] He went on to recall the pageant wagons as follows: 'Every corporation had an immense carriage, with a great platform and high canopy; the whole radiant with gilding, ribbons, and draperies, and drawn by six or eight horses equally decked and caparisoned.'[187] All four writers agree on the basic structure of the pageant wagons: they had wheels; they were either square or rectangular; and they had a deck or platform on which people and objects were mounted.

It is worthwhile dwelling on these eighteenth-century wagons because there is reason to believe that in these fundamental respects, what the antiquarians so vividly recollected would have been reminiscent of most (though as will be seen not quite all) of the Corpus Christi pageants of 1498.[188] Allowances have to be made for their size, because for reasons that will soon become clear, the eighteenth-century wagons may have been larger than their medieval ancestors. A pageant wagon which was so ambitious as to simulate a smithy in full swing, or to house a real printing press from which broadsheets were struck off and thrown to the spectating crowds, cannot but have been substantial and, presumably, most conveniently towed by horse power.[189] The scenes presented on the medieval pageant wagons, conversely, were rather more modest, and it is less clear that these wagons were drawn by horses. The nearest we can come to them is in three sets of sixteenth-century records, in details concerning the Tailors' pageant of Pilate and Pilate's wife, the pageant camel of the Carpenters, Millers, Masons, and Heliers, and the corporation's pageant featuring St George's dragon.

In 1567, the Tailors paid a painter 'for tremynge of the pagantte.' The way in which this is phrased suggests that the 'pagantte' was an actual construction, quite independent of the players who were to accompany it, in this case the 'Emperor' and the 'Empres.'[190] The word 'pagantte' denotes something very specific which the painter could 'trem'; the 'tremynge' presumably included painting, since that was the profession of the man whom the Tailors hired, and it sounds as if he may have been treating the 'pagantte' to a general refurbishing job.[191] In the 1567 record a 'pagantte' was evidently not being constructed from scratch, but undergoing routine maintenance.[192] The best conjecture as to what the Tailors' 'pagantte' looked like would be that it was a wheeled wagon with a flat deck, an earlier example, in fact, of the kind of thing most of the Dublin trade guilds were towing in the later and rather more spectacular franchise ridings that we have just been considering.[193] Taking a further step back from 1567, the 1498 Tailors' pageant was probably also housed on a wagon, as were many of the other guild pageants mentioned in the Chain Book lists.[194] But it is interesting that two of the medieval Dublin pageants are spoken of as being *carried* – the camel that the porters have to 'berr' and the dragon that the hagardmen and husbandmen have to 'berr' as well. The verb 'berr,' used in both cases, suggests that the manner of propelling these two pageants had something in common which was not shared by the rest, else why bother to specify it?[195] (It is also interesting that both these pageants, by virtue of their subject matter, would have been disqualified from appearing in any putative Dublin play cycle, assuming of course that this would have been a cycle in the traditional sense.) And indeed, sixteenth-century accounts concerning the construction of camel and dragon support this. They indicate that they were probably not housed on a wagon at all.[196] So the 1498 pageant procession was probably a mixed affair. Most of its pageants could have been housed on wagons, but at least two, the camel and the dragon, were presented differently in that they were carried in some way. What the evidence seems to suggest for Dublin in 1498 in this respect finds an analogue in several later pictures of public pageantry presented abroad, and perhaps most impressively in Denis van Alsloot's famous painting of Isabella's Triumph, the Ommeganck staged in Brussels in 1615.[197] Here can be seen an example of that combination of wheeled pageant wagons with pageants borne on foot which, save in magnitude and early baroque splendour, also may have happened on the streets of Dublin in an earlier age.[198] The Brussels Ommeganck even provides as magnificent specimens of pageant camel and dragon as could be wished for (see figs 10 and 11), though in Dublin's case it is more likely that the dragon was carried by one man, and hence closer in its construction to the dragon of Norwich, whose eighteenth-century offspring still survives (see fig. 12).[199]

The dimensions of the Dublin pageant wagons would have been intimately related to the particular route which the Corpus Christi procession took. While the portable camel and dragon were probably not as bulky as the wagons, and would therefore have negotiated a narrow medieval street with comparative ease, strict limits would have been imposed on the wagons' size by street widths and heights of gate arches. The questions naturally arise, therefore, of which route the procession took, and of how much room a wagon would have had to manoeuvre along it. To some extent the second question determines the first, for a route leading down exceptionally narrow streets would be automatically ruled out. Although there is no

10 Pageant camels from Denis von Alsloot's painting of Isabella's Triumph, Brussels, 1615.

11 St George and the dragon from Denis van Alsloot's painting of Isabella's Triumph, Brussels, 1615.

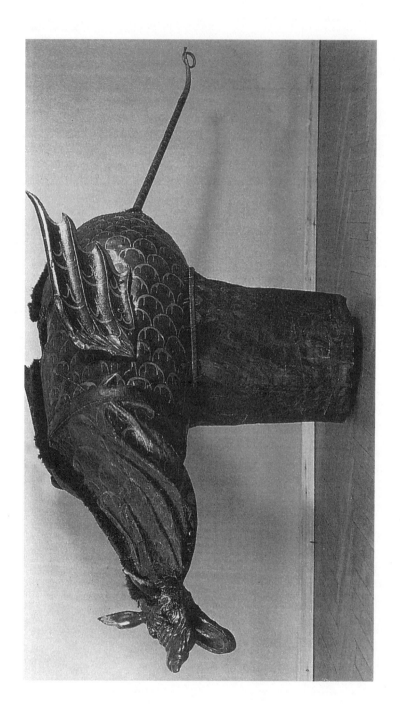

12 The Norwich Snapdragon, 1795.

surviving account of the actual route of the medieval Corpus Christi pageant procession, by keeping in mind the practicalities entailed in having to manoeuvre a
pageant wagon around it may be possible to reconstruct what the probable route
was.[200]

We have Walker's word for it that the pageants 'moved in solemn procession' to
St George's Chapel. This, then, can be assumed as their final destination (though
the possibility of an alternative final destination on the Hoggen Green, not far from
St George's Chapel and therefore not materially upsetting the conclusions drawn
here, will be examined in the next chapter).[201] The pageants' initial assembly point
and their subsequent route would have been determined by available space and the
lie of the land. Their assembly point would have to have been roomy enough for
people and pageants to foregather in and prepare to move off. It could have been
either inside or outside the city walls, though somewhere outside the walls would
probably have offered more manoeuvering space.[202] Its location would also have
affected the route the pageants were to take. It must be assumed too that this route
proceeded, for at least some of its length, intramurally. The whole rationale of a
processional festival such as this demands that at some stage it pass through the city
itself, not merely skirt it;[203] civic pride would scarcely have been adequately aired in
a procession that only wound through the suburbs.

For convenience's sake, an assembly point can be conjectured in the vicinity of
St John the Baptist's Hospital outside the city walls, a little to the west of the Newgate (see fig. 3), and this with some reason, when it is recalled that the 1649 assembly point for the franchise riding had been Christ Church meadow, a nearby area of
open ground where now stand Stevens's Hospital and the Guinness brewery. A
venue here would have been spacious, and its proximity to the Newgate entrance
would have readied the procession to sweep through those principal and ancient streets
which formed the medieval city's spine.[204] Now whatever the point of departure,
given that part of the procession's route is virtually certain to have been intramural,
and that its eventual destination was to be the extramural chapel of St George, one
particular route commends itself for three reasons: first, it was in fact the most economical and direct route to that destination; second, it presented the procession
with the fewest obstacles to negotiate en route; and third, it took fullest advantage
of ensuring that the procession was an intramural, fully civic event for as long as
possible before finally moving outside the walls.

Assuming that the procession entered Newgate Street (today called the Cornmarket) through the Newgate arch, it is likely that eventually it passed by the High
Cross (streets and landmarks named here are indicated on fig. 3). The High Cross,
situated at the junction of High Street with Bothe Street (today called Christ Church
Place), was a focal point of the medieval city.[205] It was also very close to the Tholsel,
the seat of the organizers of the procession itself, Dublin Corporation.[206] The Tholsel

would no doubt have afforded a good view of the passing procession to those fortunate enough to be able to watch it from the building's upper stories.[207] From Newgate Street there were two possible routes to the High Cross, either straight down
High Street or, alternatively, down Rochel Street (today called Back Lane) and then
turning left up St Nicholas's Street. The High Street route would have been the better
of the two, because the street proceeded directly to the cross, was a major thorough-
fare and thus able to accommodate more comfortably the procession and its spectators, and also avoided the effort of a brief uphill incline otherwise met with if the
procession travelled down Rochel Street and then up St Nicholas's Street.[208] Having
now arrived at the High Cross, the procession had three possible exit points en
route to St George's Chapel. Two were on the south side of the city wall, either through
St Nicholas's Gate or through Pole Gate, and the third was on the east side, through
Dame's Gate. Tracing the route through each of these gates in turn makes clear which
would have been the most appropriate for the procession to take.

Were a procession to make its way from the High Cross to St George's Chapel
exiting by St Nicholas's Gate and then taking the shortest route there, it would first
have had to move down St Nicholas's Street, out through the gate and onto St Patrick's
Street, then turn sharply left down a lane (in the region of what is now Bull Alley
Street) which led out into St Bride's Street (now called Bride Street). From here it
would have crossed St Bride's Street and proceeded along Cross Lane (now called
Golden Lane), presumably passing through the extramural arch of Whitefriars' Gate
and into St Stephen's Street. Skirting the church of St Peter on the right hand side,
it would then have turned left into St George's Lane (now called South Great George's
Street), eventually arriving at the chapel. This route would have been well over half
a mile,[209] would have required the pageants to negotiate Whitefriars' Gate,[210] and
would result in the bulk of the procession taking place in the suburbs outside the
city walls (it is traced by dots in fig. 13a).

The second exit point via Pole Gate would have required the procession at the
High Cross first to move down Bothe Street to where the public pillory stood, then
turn right down St Werburgh's Street and out through Pole Gate onto St Bride's
Street. Passing down here it would eventually have taken a left turn into Cross Lane,
and from this point its route would have been similar to that of the first mooted
procession. The distance covered by this route would have been a little less than
that of the first one, but it would still have been fractionally over half a mile, the
pageants would have faced a similar negotiation of Whitefriars' Gate, and though
slightly more of the procession would have been intramural, most of it would nevertheless have been outside in the suburbs (the route is traced by dashes in fig. 13a).

The last and final possibility, an exit through Dame's Gate, would have produced a very different result. From the High Cross, the procession would have moved
down Bothe Street, Christ Church Cathedral being on the left, past the pillory,

then into Castle Street. With Dublin Castle on the right, the procession would next have turned left into Lorimers' Street (now called Cork Hill) and proceeded down this until it met with the right-hand turning towards Dame's Gate. Passing through the gate, over the dam, and into Tengmouth Street (now called Dame Street), it would then have eventually turned right into St George's Lane and come to the chapel a little way down, possibly on the right hand side (the route is traced by a line in fig. 13b).[211] Such a route would have been shorter than the first two, taking a little under half a mile. Differences in route length ranging from just over to just under half a mile may seem slight, but they may have been appreciable to the steerers of the pageant wagons, especially if manpower rather than horsepower had been drafted to propel them.[212] This route presented no extramural gates to negotiate, and this time, since just over half of the length of the procession would have lain within the walls, it would have allowed greater scope for civic display and would, moreover, have conducted the procession past some of Dublin's most prestigious sites, both secular and spiritual, before arriving at its destination.[213]

This hypothesis could be checked were the widths of the medieval streets ascertainable, for forbiddingly narrow streets would deter certain routes. Although the first map of Dublin with substantially reliable street dimensions, that by John Rocque, shows a city whose contours had been significantly altered by post-medieval development, it was executed just three years before the Wide Streets Act took effect, and it is striking how much narrower the old established streets tend to be in comparison with the newer ones of the Georgian city's expansion. This comparative narrowness presumably gives some impression of what the late-medieval street widths were like, even if the widths in Rocque could not be expected to reflect precisely what the medieval widths were. Ideally, it would be necessary to know the construction date of the buildings facing each other on Rocque's map which between them prescribed a street's width, for if they were medieval, then necessarily the street width was too.[214] In the circumstances, then, an approximation of medieval street widths is the most that can be hoped for. That granted, it is worth noting that the street widths that Rocque recorded along the third hypothetical pageant route proposed here are not so narrow as to have impeded any procession, but the same cannot be said of the first two routes. The first of these, already discounted on other grounds, seems also to be discounted by three awkwardly narrow widths shown on Rocque's map; first, the opening into St Nicholas's Street from the junction of High Street with Bothe Street appears to have been scarcely more than 8′ wide; second, although St Nicholas's Street widens to an ample 33′ part way down, it narrows sharply again to about 8′ before becoming St Patrick's Street; and third, another narrow 8′ appears to have been the width of the opening into Bull Alley. These widths of 8′ may not have been utterly impossible for a pageant wagon, but they would barely have left room for it to manoeuvre in, assuming, of course, that the wagons

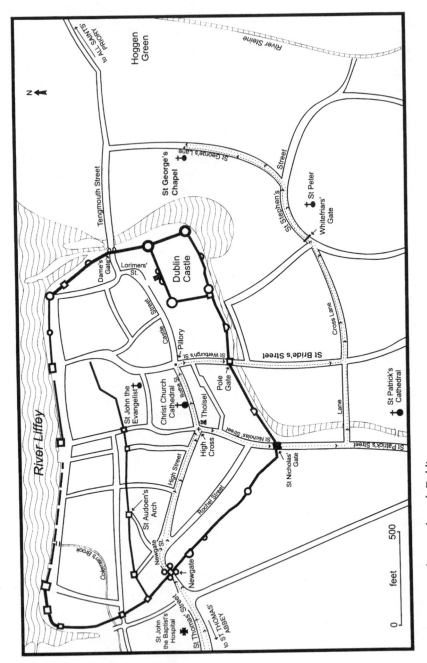

13a Processional routes through Dublin.

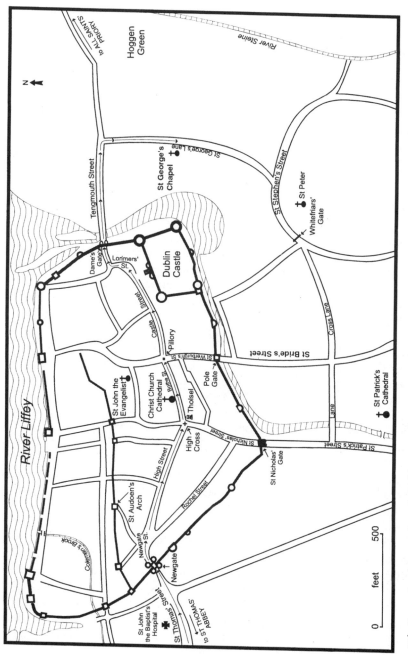

13b Processional routes through Dublin.

were not of diminutive size. True, the second hypothetical pageant route is less cramped than the first, but even it is not quite as comfortable as the third route lying through the city and out at Dame's Gate.[215] Thus even when due allowances have been made, Rocque's street dimensions may hint that the third route was the one that the pageants were likely to have followed.

Assuming, therefore, that the Corpus Christi procession took what might be called the 'city' route to St George's Chapel, one particular width is especially important to discover, because it would effectively have determined the width limit of a medieval Dublin pageant wagon. What was the width of the aperture in Dame's Gate itself? Unfortunately, the gate is long since demolished. It may be of some comparative interest to know that the aperture of the only surviving city gate, St Audoen's Arch, measures 10' 6", but this may not advance matters, because if other Dublin gates varied from this by even a few inches, the range of possibilities for a wagon's dimensions would alter significantly. Furthermore, St Audoen's Arch is an intramural gate and therefore not necessarily representative. Sir John Perrot's survey of the city walls, commissioned in 1585, is also of no practical help. Though several of the principal gates are described and their measurements given, Dame's Gate receives no more than a perfunctory notice.[216] Neither do illustrations help. One of the earliest gate illustrations, in John Derricke's *Image of Irelande*, may be notional rather than accurate.[217]

However, a key to the problem may lie late in the seventeenth century, in the Dublin Assembly Rolls. In 1699, two citizens, Thomas Pooley and Marmaduke Coghill, presented the corporation with a petition. Because 'the steepnesse and narrownesse of the passage through the said Gate' (that is, Dame's Gate) was daily causing 'great inconvenience to all persons that passe that way with coaches and carriages since the great increase of the citty, which is now much greater in the suborbs than within the walls,' an alteration was proposed that the gate be 'raised, beautified and enlarged fourteen foot six inches in the narrowest part, fit for two coaches.'[218] As it stood in 1699, the gate's 'narrowest part, *which is not now nine foot,*'[219] could not cope with a flow of city traffic that had grown far heavier over the years and that was now making impossible demands on a medieval gateway. Assuming that Pooley and Coghill were satisfactory surveyors, a pageant wagon exiting via this gate could not therefore have been any more than 8' wide.

It is interesting at this juncture to compare the known dimensions of Restoration pageant wagons used in the city of London for royal entries and the Lord Mayor's Show, since these have also been argued to reflect the dimensions of their medieval forerunners: a width of 8' is frequently called for. The length of the London wagons could vary between 13' and 15'.[220] So it seems quite possible that the width of a medieval Dublin pageant wagon would not in fact have been much less than that of a pageant wagon from Restoration London. Indeed, precisely because the dimensions of the Restoration London wagons may resemble those of their medieval predecessors, the size of the pageant wagons of both medieval cities, Dublin and London, would seem to have been approximately the same.

The height of the Dublin wagons, conversely, is less readily estimated because no headway dimensions are known for those gates through which the wagons may have passed. The headway of Dame's Gate, like that of all the other principal gates, cannot have been less than about 8′, the approximate distance between the top of the head of a man mounted on horseback and the ground. However, allowing the deck of a wagon an elevation of about 4′ from the ground, an 8′ headway would have been too low for an average-sized man standing on the wagon deck to pass underneath without ducking. At its apex, the headway of the St Audoen's Arch today is about 20′, and given the tendency of floor levels to rise over the course of time, its medieval headway was probably higher. A headway to the Dame's Gate even roughly comparable would have allowed not only a man standing upright on a wagon deck to pass underneath comfortably, but also for the construction of the familiar frame and canopy on the wagon deck in the fashion of other cities in the British Isles. Even allowing for a portcullis on the Dame's Gate which might have diminished its headway somewhat, only about 12′ to 13′ would have been needed to accommodate a canopied pageant. This would not seem to make excessive demands of Dublin gate headways, given the present height of St Audoen's Arch.

PROFESSIONAL ENTERTAINMENT

The late-medieval pageant procession through Dublin's streets on Corpus Christi, which concluded outside the city walls at a venue in which the citizens may have witnessed some sort of dramatic display, was a large-scale civic enterprise. Essentially a corporate affair, it doubtless recruited any players that it required from among ordinary townsfolk, presumably after they had shown proof of perfomance flair.[221] For the most part, then, its players in their everyday professional lives were probably tradesmen. Yet the city was not without its professionals in the performing arts too, and these may have been recruited to add their distinctive leaven to the occasion, especially if dedicated performance skills, more specialized than tradesmen would have been able to cultivate, were called for.

Throughout these islands generally in the Middle Ages, the prospect of drama is always imminent wherever there is evidence of the activity of paid entertainers. For them, as for their Gaelic counterparts surveyed in the previous chapter, dramatic skill is likely to have been only one shade within the wide spectrum of entertainment; a versatile entertainer would have been able to draw upon acting ability as he equally might upon skills like story telling (which as has been seen in the Gaelic context was a potentially dramatic form in its own right), musicianship, feats of legerdemain, tumbling and so on. It is true that to describe medieval entertainers in terms of such broad versatility is to paint a generic picture, when in reality there also existed specialists, performers whose skills excelled in particular domains. Thus, for example, Matilda Makejoy, a *saltatrix* ('dancer,' 'acrobat') at the court of Edward I, is only ever so described; dancing (perhaps with its associated skills) seems to have been her singular forte.[222] Earlier still, an entertainer at the court of Henry II, Roland le Fartere of Suffolk, regaled the king annually at Christmas with his *saltum et siffletum et bumbulum* ('leap and whistle and fart'), the latter feat inviting comparison with the stock-in-trade of the medieval Irish *braigetóiri* also unearthed in the previous chapter.[223] Although one imagines that Roland's repertoire would have seemed somewhat starved if this was its full extent, no matter how superbly he may have executed it, and that he may have had other tricks up his sleeve for whiling away the time, specialization still seems the keynote. So specialists existed, as did jacks of all trades; the latter, of course, being the more marketable.

Examples like these point to another fertile field in which to look for the growth of professional entertainment and hence of dramatic skills – the court and the aristocratic households. This is not simply because it is to these more privileged echelons of society that surviving documents tend to give access – though that is a consideration – but because in society's upper levels resources existed to keep entertainers on as retained men who, even if not necessarily employed as entertainers full-time, would at least have counted provision of entertainment among their other household duties. As well as these, another class of entertainer existed, people who took their talents wherever they could find a paying audience. Sometimes their patronage came from the court, sometimes from any level of society having the means. Hence members of this other class would have been characterized by their itinerancy.[224]

That both the Gaelic chieftains and the Anglo-Irish lords paid entertainers is amply documented, and some of this documentation was discussed in the previous chapter, but now attention must be confined to performances taking place in and around Dublin, and to determining, if possible, whether they were ever dramatic in nature. A tradition exists that when Henry II spent Christmas in Dublin in 1171 – history does not relate whether Roland of Suffolk was with him to perform his annual Christmas star turn – he was entertained by play performances, but the tradition is unsubstantiated, and two of the particular sorts of play that he reputedly saw, 'the Sport and the mirth, the continuall musick, *the Masking, mumming* and strange shews' (my emphasis), sound unlikely at that date.[225] In fact, the two genuinely early accounts of his festivities are silent about dramatic entertainment; one concentrated on the unstinted banquet fare and the cooked crane that the Irish lords, against their better judgment, forced themselves to eat for the sake of politeness, and the other on the construction in Dublin of a temporary royal palace for the occasion, engineered in the Irish manner.[226] The first noticeable signs of the consolidation of the right sort of context for the aristocratic sponsorship of drama in Dublin come later, as late in fact as 1361. In this year Edward III dispatched to Ireland his son Lionel, duke of Clarence, in response to mounting pressure to safeguard his loyal but beleaguered Anglo-Irish subjects. Clarence took up residence in Dublin Castle, and evidently he was not expecting to spend all his time campaigning in the field. Various improvements were made to the quality of life available at the castle. Its gardens were extended and provision made for the holding of tournaments in the grounds. The works undertaken 'for sports and his other pleasures' raised the aristocratic tone of his Dublin residence and were conducive to an atmosphere in which entertainments of the dramatic kind might be expected to flourish;[227] Clarence after all had been accustomed to the sophistication of London, where already for many years dramatic games and pastimes had formed an important part of court culture.[228] Moreover, he retained a personal troupe of *histriones* ('entertainers,' 'actors'). We learn of the presence of three of them with a servant in Cambridge only a year later.[229] It is unknown why they were not with Clarence in Dublin at that time, but it is difficult to believe that they were to be forever left behind as excess baggage, especially when Clarence had evidently taken such pains to maintain a stylish household. If the revitalized Dublin Castle sports and pleasures were a replica, even in small, of what he had been accustomed to elsewhere, then drama would have featured among them. But of this there is no direct proof, only the right sort of context.

Of course, he might have recruited a new troupe from personnel on the ground in Dublin. Individual entertainers resident in the city are mentioned sporadically in the records from the late-twelfth century onwards.[230] And a petition in the Patent and Close Rolls proves that, if not before, certainly by 1436, an organized band of entertainers had indeed established itself, perhaps in the form of some sort of minstrel guild.[231] The petition also reintroduces the entertainers of Gaelic Ireland, itinerants who moved back and forth between the Pale and the vaster Gaelic hinterland:

Rex William Lawles marescallum Anglicorum ligeorum mimorum Hibernie (recitatur quod Hibernici mimi, ut clarsaghours, tympanours, crowthores, kerraghers, rymours, skelaghes, bardes & alii veniunt inter Anglicos Hibernie, exercentes minstralcias & artes suas, postmodumque vadunt ad Hibernicos inimicos et deveniunt inductores ipsorum super eosdem ligeos Regis, contra formam statutorum Kylkenny 40 E. III) assignavit ad dictos clarsaghours, &cetera, capiendum &cetera. Dublin, I Aprilis.[232]

[The king has assigned William Lawless, marshal of the liege English entertainers of Ireland (it is reported that Irish entertainers, like harpers, *timpán*-players, fiddlers, gamblers, rimers, storytellers, bards, and others come among the English of Ireland practising their minstrelsy and arts, and after a while return to the Irish enemies and become their inciters against the

same liege men of the king, contrary to the form of the Kilkenny Statutes of 40 Edward III)
to seize the said harpers, et cetera, et cetera. Dublin, 1 April.]

One William Lawless, 'marshall of the liege English entertainers of Ireland,' was
here authorized to apprehend any members of the wide Gaelic minstrel class who
came among the English performing 'their minstrelsy and arts.' The Kilkenny
Statute of 1366 was invoked, and the Irish entertainers arraigned as being the
means whereby Irish enemies were led against the English; the implication seems
to be that by returning among the Irish and stirring up anti-English feeling, these
entertainers became agents of sedition. The accusation probably held water, but one
suspects that it was also couched in this way to appeal to English insecurities so that
the English *mimi* could seize a legal weapon to protect their vested professional
interests with; they most likely regarded Irish competition inside the Pale as poach-
ing from a preserve over which they had a prior claim. Whatever the case, William
Lawless was leader of an English troupe of entertainers, and his position over them
as 'marshal' possibly suggests that within the English Pale they had an officially recognized status.[233] If they were retained, as seems conceivable, it is not known whether
by Dublin Castle, a likely patron, or by some other body with comparable resources,
though of such bodies there cannot have been many. Dublin Corporation, which as
will be seen in chapter 3 maintained the city waits, seems the only other likely candidate. Assuming that protectionism partly motivates the wording of the petition,
then the English *mimi* would have been especially jealous of competition if, conversely, they were *not* retained and relied solely upon getting an income wherever
they could (and it may be significant that they are described as the liege entertainers
'of Ireland,' as if they were not bound to any one institution, patron or household).[234]
For all their protests, it looks as if by 1436 the waxing tide of Irish entertainers was
one they were hard pressed to turn back. Already some fifty years earlier, on 25 October 1375, parliament had been successfully petitioned to allow one Dowenald
O'Moghane, *ministrallus Hibernicus*, to exercise his art within the Pale, the Kilkenny
Statute of 1366 notwithstanding, during his good behaviour:

Rex (recitatur quod in statuto apud Kilkenny anno 40 edito contineatur quod nulli
ministralli Hibernici inter Anglicos ejusdem terre moram trahant, nec aliqui Anglici ipsos
recipiant, sub certa pena ibi specificata); quia tamen coram Willelmo de Wyndesore
gubernatore Hibernie & consiliario Regis, in parliamento apud Kilkenny in octabis Sancti
Michaelis proximis preteritis tento, per diversos fidedignos testificatum extitit & recordatum,
quod Dowenald O Moghane, ministrallus Hibernicus, inter Anglicos moram trahens, ad
fidem, pacem & obedienciam Regis continue steterit, diversa mala Hibernicis inimicis Regis
perpetrando, per quod ad eosdem Hibernicos accedere non audet, proinde concessit ei quod
inter Anglicos moram trahere possit continuam, & quod Anglici ipsum in domos suas recipere

& retinere valeant, prout sibi placuerit, dicto statuto non obstante, quamdiu idem Dowenald erga Regem & pacem bene se gesserit. Kilkenny, 25 Octobris.[235]

[The king (it is related that in the Kilkenny Statute given in the fortieth year [of his reign] it is included that no Irish minstrels stay amongst the English of the same land, nor that any English men receive them, on certain penalty specified there); because, however, it is testified and recorded by various trustworthy men in the presence of William of Windsor, governor of Ireland and counsellor of the king, in a parliament held at Kilkenny within the octave of [the feast of] St Michael last past, that Dowenald O Moghane, an Irish minstrel, remained continually in the king's faith, peace and obedience, doing various injuries to the king's Irish enemies, on account of which he does not dare go back to them, [the parliament] has accordingly granted him permanent stay amongst the English, and granted that English men may receive and retain him in their households, as long as it pleases them, the aforesaid Statute notwithstanding, as long as the same Dowenald behaves well towards the king and the peace. Kilkenny, 25 October [1375].]

This was a dangerous precedent for William Lawless and his associates. Evidently there came other minstrels after O Moghane, unofficially, disgruntling with their flying performances fully paid-up members of society who believed the job of providing entertainment was rightfully theirs.

The 1436 entry is also interesting for the way it illustrates the English perception, at this date, of what some of the species were that made up the class of Gaelic *mimus* and which were examined in the previous chapter at greater length. At least in this context, the word *mimus* cannot be interpreted to mean 'actor' in any narrow modern (or indeed classical) sense, for if actual dramatic skill was something the *mimus* drew on from time to time, it was not to the fore in any of the entertainer categories listed here, apart perhaps from in that of the *skelaghes* (<*scélaige*, 'storyteller'). Evidently *mimus* in the 1436 petition had a hold-all meaning. It might also be argued that the English encounter with the various types of Irish *mimi* that the petition reflects was an encounter with types of entertainment considered to have a distinctively Gaelic flavour. A good case for this can be made on various linguistic grounds. Since two of the seven sorts of *mimus* listed, the *kerraghers* (<*cerrbach*, 'gambler') and *skelaghes* ('storytellers'), are anglicized forms of Irish words,[236] there would have been no need to coin two words from Irish if English ones adequately approximate to *kerragher* and *skelagh* already existed.[237] Of the remaining five, *bardes* here antedates by about twenty-five years the earliest example of the word's first recorded appearance in the *OED*, as does *crowthores* ('fiddlers'). Both ultimately are words of Celtic derivation.[238] Similarly the word *clarsaghours* ('harpers') comes from the Celtic, and its use here, antedating the first *OED* example this time by over eighty years, may suggest that its route into English was first through Irish rather than through any other Celtic language.[239] The root of the word *tympanours* had entered the English language already in the Old English period from Latin, but *tympanours* here would doubtless have been understood rather to refer to the strong native Irish tradition of *timpán* playing, celebrated both in Irish sources and well known beyond Ireland at about the same date as the 1436 entry was made. As John of Trevisa put it, 'Irische men beeþ connyng in tweie manere instrumentis of musyk, in harpe and tymbre þat is i-armed wiþ wire and wiþ strenges of bras. In þe whiche instrumentis, þey ʳþeiˈ pleye hastiliche and swiftliche, þey makeþ wel mery armonye and melody wiþ wel þicke tunes, werbeles, and nootes.'[240] Only one word out of the seven listed in the 1436 petition, *rymours*, is decisively not of Celtic derivation, though perhaps tainted by association with the other six, it too may have been understood to refer to some characteristically Irish class of poet entertainer.[241]

In practice Gaelic performing artists were opening doors which in legal theory ought to have remained shut. At the level of entertainment, as at so many others, there was evidently a significant, if not unfailingly amicable, commerce between the Irish and English communities.[242] One imagines that outside Dublin in the provincial Anglo-Irish households, opportunities for traditions to mix and produce hybrid varieties of entertainment would have been greater still, when even within the heart of the Pale, not every Englishman found the pastime peddled by the likes of those who so antagonized William Lawless to be uncongenial.

THE FORM AND PRESSURE OF THE TIMES (*c* 1350–1509)

Dublin between *c* 1350 and 1509 saw periods of upheaval as well as of relative tranquility, and it may be interesting finally to examine the ways in which its drama, responsive to the age, showed the times their form and pressure. The varieties of drama reviewed earlier were very much the product of specialized sets of social circumstances. Only a particular sort of liturgy, for example, would sustain the *Visitatio Sepulcri*, just as it was a particular kind of guild network that produced Dublin's Corpus Christi pageants. Indeed, such productions, like any dependent for their existence upon some specific and highly organized social context, might both be enabled by the resources of that context to become ambitious enterprises and also profoundly expressive of it. The Corpus Christi montage especially, as will be seen in more detail in the next chapter, must among its other social consequences have given a public voice to implicit institutional values. In short, the greater the institutionalization of drama, with all the opportunities for dramatic elaboration that that might bring, the greater would be drama's sensitivity to any changes in the social fabric enfolding it.

However, as a preface to a consideration of the relations between Dublin's early dramas and the historical contexts shaping them, one final dramatic species needs considering which, on the contrary, was far less likely to mutate beyond recognition or collapse as a result of economic or ideological convulsions within society. Moreover, the same reasons for this resilience make it even more difficult to detect than the drama fostered by the institutions. For want of a better term, it might be called the drama of the folk. It was a dramatic species which inhabited the margins of 'official' society, society as constructed by the literate producers of the documents through which the whole must now perforce be studied. It could flourish anywhere, in city or countryside; certainly, it required no underpinning of elaborate urban resources. An unwritten drama, it can only be glimpsed obliquely in reactions to it, and perhaps also in its echo in some 'official' dramatic writing. The traces it leaves of itself, necessarily indirect, nevertheless argue for its once sturdy existence.

An early instance of some variety of folk drama at large within the Dublin Pale seems to be indicated in the seventh of a group of Constitutions issued by Archbishop Thomas Minot from Kilkenny in 1367:

Constitucio ne mercata in ecclesijs vel earum acriis seu cimiterijs teneantur ˏ⌈nec⌉ **negociaciones seculares excerceantur.** ... Et quia in cimiterijs dedicatis multa sanctorum & saluandorum corpora tumulantur quibus debetur omnis honor & reuerencia sacerdotibus parochianis nostrarum diocesis & prouincie districte precipimus vt in ecclesijs suis denuncient publice ne quisquam choreas luctas vel alios ludos in honestos in ecclesijs vel cimiterijs excercere presumant precipue in vigilijs & festis sanctorum cum huiusmodi ludos teatrales & ludibriorum spectacula per que ecclesie coinquinantur predicti sacerdotes sub pena suspencionis eos moneant & precipiant eisdem quod ab huiusmodi penitus abstineant & desistant pena excommunicacionis maioris Alloquin {*read* Alioquin} nomina loci ordinario vel. ipsius Officiali seu commissario denuncient vt per ipsos contrafacientes pro suis demeritis canonice puniantur. ...[243]

[A constitution that transactions be not held in churches or their lands or cemeteries, nor that secular trades be conducted. ... And because many bodies of saints and of the saved, to which all honour and reverence are due, are buried in dedicated cemeteries, we strictly instruct parish priests of our diocese and province to give official notice publicly in their churches that none should presume to hold dances, contests [wrestling matches?], or other base plays/ games in churches or cemeteries, especially on vigils and feasts of saints, with theatrical plays/ games and spectacles of wantonness, through which churches are polluted; that the aforementioned priests, on pain of suspension, warn those [so doing] and advise them that they utterly abstain and desist from [pursuits] of this kind, on pain of the greater excommunication. Otherwise let them give official notice of their names to the ordinary of the place or his official or commissary, so that they may punish those behaving contrarily according to their demerits.]

This seventh Constitution, a prohibition of carryings-on considered scandalous, has

the tone typical of the strictures which entrenched popular customs of any sort,
viewed by unsympathetic clerical eyes, could provoke at any time, especially whenever such customs encroached onto the church's domain. Much earlier, in the mid-
thirteenth century, ecclesiastical legislation in the *Crede Mihi* had already warned
Dublin clergy of the risk of bloodshed at similar profitless pastimes,[244] though in
the Kilkenny Constitution of 1367, wording has become a little more specific: among
the abuses targeted were *ludos teatrales & ludibriorum spectacula* ('theatrical
plays/games and spectacles of wantonness'). An antic drama of some sort was keeping bad company with dances, contests (wrestling matches?), and other base plays/
games all of which the archbishop sought to ban beyond the pale of church and
churchyard. It is difficult to tell much about this drama, except that its manifestations were not confined to the city – the Constitutions were issued for the whole
Dublin province – and it was festive in a way the archbishop found disgraceful. His
perspective as hostile outsider doubtless blurred his view of the festivities. Their
coincidence with 'vigils and feasts of the saints' was no adequate palliative; as far as
he was concerned, any respectability foisted upon them through that association would
have been quite transparent.

  But it is unlikely that these were celebrations that he and his colleagues would
have succeeded in putting down, since the impetus behind them was exceptionally
strong. Folk dramas often address fundamental and perennial human needs, from
providing pure entertainment to articulating some reassuring communal myth. Many,
for example, attempt to objectify people's intuitive awareness of the seasonal rhythm
of birth, growth, and decay, for by means of drama, the stages that life passes
through from cradle to grave can be tangibly embodied and thus more readily ap-
prehended and assented to. Furthermore, repetition of the life narrative in such
dramas might be felt as harnessing the forces upon which the continuity of society
depends: the old was bound to pass away, but continuity might be safeguarded by
rehearsing the arrival of the new.[245] Therefore, as well as reconciling people to the
inevitable trajectory of life, such dramas may serve as a sort of sympathetic magic
to ensure the return of life and fertility after the time of death and barrenness.
These are rationalizations, of course, of some of the fundamental appeal of many
folk dramas and of their hopeful message. It is unlikely that their actual performers
either today or in times past ever conceptualized what they were doing in terms so
detached. At most they may have expected performances to bring 'good luck,' and
their neglect, 'bad.'[246] So these folk dramas, largely independent of historically contingent social structures and hence proof against institutional change, were tenacious for other reasons. The human needs that they addressed were basic, and they
could be put together quickly from simple means. Folk dramas would therefore
have stayed buoyant and, once in place, have been driven by the added impetus of
tradition. They are glimpsed briefly in their own right in the Kilkenny Constitution

of 1367, and are perhaps more subtly refracted in the official dramatic product that is *The Pride of Life*, for its plot is reminiscent of precisely the sort of ancient life narrative that many folk dramas dealt with.[247]

Not very long before 1367 and Archbishop Minot's decree, a major social upheaval had come in the form of the Black Death, the plague which had racked the Continent and was now at last taking its toll in Ireland. As might be expected, it had been particularly epidemic in the walled towns. Even if the figure of 14,000 dead that the annalist John Clyn, who may himself have fallen its victim, reported for Dublin between August and Christmas 1348 is inflated, it is none the less real as a measure of the fear that the plague years instilled, nor would that fear be easily allayed once the worst ravages had passed.[248] Mid-century anxieties were not to be forgotten by those fortunate enough to survive the first pandemic. Throughout the rest of the century and well into the next, their descendants had fresh reminders of life's uncertainty, for even if on a smaller scale, there were to be recurring plague outbreaks in Dublin.[249] It would have seemed to some that the old propitious rituals of the sort enshrined in some of the folk dramas had lost their luck; at any rate, God was angry.

The linguistic dating that Norman Davis has advanced for the composition of *The Pride of Life*, any time from *c* 1350, and the possibility of its actual composition in Dublin, are therefore most suggestive for any attempt to grasp the original social valence of the play and the likely nature of its early reception. The nearer it originated to the mid-fourteenth century, the nearer was it located to a period of social turbulence.[250] In such a context, the first part of *The Pride of Life*, which is preoccupied with the dominion of death, would have chimed precisely with the contemporary experience. The King of Life's contest with the King of Death was a reminder, were one needed, of how much a lost cause it was bound to be. If before the plague years people had tended to live less mindful of their end, now confrontations with death would be brutal and repeated, and social consciousness of death's imminence would be heightened reciprocally. The play's preoccupation with the dominion of death may thus be regarded as the incarnation in a dramatic guise of such a consciousness. And not only itself a product of that consciousness, the play's preoccupation would in turn have kept that consciousness alive amongst those who copied, read, and perhaps even saw it acted. But the play had more in hand than simply to remind people of what they already knew but might well have preferred to forget. The routine human absurdity of people who make plans and live heedless of death is absorbed into *The Pride of Life* not only as an absurdity which the times (and the play which reflects them) have utterly exposed, but it is also focused as an absurdity with spiritually dangerous consequences. It might be observed, of course, that even had no plague come to whet audience awareness, the sheer bravado of the King of Life in flouting the representatives of common sense (the Queen, his wife) and moral authority (the Bishop) should have been sufficient warning of his approaching overthrow: hubris has a long history, and pride would have gone before a fall at the best of times. Yet since a more urgent sense of mortality must be assumed in those who experienced *The Pride of Life*, as it must also in the playwright himself, we should consider whether the play's strategies had some contribution to make to the general project of social engineering that had largely fallen to the church's lot during the years of massive mortality. It was important for society to retrieve a means of making sense of death, for death's threat might be alleviated if its damage, irreparable though that might be within the created order of this world, could somehow be limited within the uncreated order of the next, where Providence ruled. Contemporaries were historically well equipped to condemn the aspiration of the King of Life while at once recognizing how they shared in the absurd confidence lying behind it. Thus he was a figure whom they might both identify with and judge. However, *The Pride of Life*, being also the product of a clerical culture, would not merely allude to these real historical anxieties; it would also seek out a unique way in which to negotiate them.

When at last the King of Life was overwhelmed, the playwright would proceed to make the dominion of death intelligible, and thus humanly bearable, by imposing a theological rationality upon it. In the end, the soul of the King would be saved from the worst *post-mortem* consequences, regenerated in response to the Virgin's intercession. It seems that here too the way in which the play's Christian optimism was acted out could have struck another familiar chord in its contemporary audience, since it resembles the life narrative that some folk dramas are notable for. In *The Pride of Life* too, death is finally succeeded by a rebirth in which the long-term continuity of the community is affirmed and celebrated. The play's essential action, revolving around a protagonist, an antagonist, their combat, the protagonist's overthrow, and his eventual regeneration by a wonder-working agency, duplicates the action of the hero-combat dramas of folk tradition.[251] It is possible that the assimilation of this formula within the *The Pride of Life* testifies obliquely to the currency in Ireland of such dramas.[252] Thus in an urban, clerical play, the ancient, regenerative associations of dramas of this sort may have been recuperated and baptized to promote Christian ends.

A private reading of *The Pride of Life*, and even more so a public performance, whatever its value for reader or spectator as pure entertainment, should additionally and more importantly be imagined to have been a source of comfort to a community oppressively aware of the threat of looming dissolution. A drama that gave flesh and blood, however briefly, to Christian faith in the operation of a regenerating Providence beyond death would have been as much humanly reassuring as it was morally bracing and didactically informative of the theological brief that the church held for society. One cultural response by the church to the social needs wrought by the Black Death, therefore, seems to have been its invention of a new, complex dramatic species of which *The Pride of Life* represents the first extant example. Theatre historians would assign it to the genre that they have called the morality play. They would also maintain that morality plays are characteristically so preoccupied with diagnosing the state of the soul and dispensing spiritual medication through allegories that they tend to float free from anchorage in historical time and to lack historical referentiality.[253] Certainly, their setting is normally timeless and placeless, a disembodied landscape usually inhabited by abstract personifications. But the way in which they can sometimes bite into their historical moment should not be lost sight of, and *The Pride of Life* may present another case in point. Not only understandable in general terms as the product of peculiar historical circumstances, it may also allude to its particular historical moment directly. If the reference to 'Gailispire on þe Hil,' as argued earlier, was topical, so too may have been the other half of the domain, 'þe erldom of Kente,' that the King of Life promised as a reward to his servant Solas. Around the year 1400, any reference in Dublin to the earldom of Kent would have had a sinister ring, appropriate enough from the mouth of the pomping King of Life, and a sign of how hollow his promised largesse was. Thomas Holland, duke of Surrey and third earl of Kent (1374–1400), would have been well known in Dublin. Richard II had appointed him king's lieutenant in Ireland on 26 July 1398 for a three-year term. He had returned to England with the king after the Irish campaign in the summer of 1399, and his fate was linked to Richard's.[254] Stripped of his dukedom on 6 November 1399, the earl of Kent, as he now was, began conspiring against the new king, Henry IV. On 7 January 1400 he was captured and beheaded by the men of Cirencester. He was then only twenty-five years old – a neat object lesson to swell that favourite medieval theme of how death spares no estate, but visits in various guises, calling too upon the young and the powerful. Of course, if the play's reference was intended to be topical, this would bear upon the date of its composition. Some time in 1400 would then be likely, or in however long a period after that the memory of the violent end of Thomas Holland would have lingered in the mind.

The politically troublous years between the Black Death and Bolingbroke's deposition of Richard II in the autumn of 1399 were also close to the production of the two processional manuscripts belonging to the church of St John the Evangelist. Performance of the *Visitatio* drama, hermetically sealed within liturgy, would necessarily have been less perturbed by the troubles of society at large and also less obviously a response to them; liturgical celebration would only be disturbed in the most turbulent of times. In this respect it would act as a fixed point in an otherwise uncertain world, and any plays it hosted only collude with the timeless and dehistoricized aesthetic of the liturgy. The *Visitatio* was also a comparatively small-scale, annual affair, requiring nothing more to produce than clerics alone would have been able to provide. Late-fourteenth-century secular society, by contrast, may have been too distracted with matters of national security to spare much thought for organizing city-wide dramatic performances, even if less ambitious performances of various sorts may have been available within private households.

It was also during this period that the Crown made several grants of money and resources to Ireland in the hope of securing order and recovering lands and revenues which were being lost through the insurgency of Gaelic and Anglo-Irish enemies. None of these investments was to show any lasting return, however. The dispatch of Lionel, duke of Clarence, to Ireland in 1361, which, as was seen, may have boosted the aristocratic entertainments on offer in Dublin Castle, was a case in point. His father, Edward III, had sent him in answer to a plea for assistance from the Irish Council which had met the previous year in Kilkenny. The council's fear for social and political stability had been particularly aggravated by the depletions caused by plague. Now even more than before it might be difficult to resist attack. Lionel was prompt to lead campaigns into Leinster and Munster, but in the long term these were to achieve little, and after his wife's death in 1364, he pulled out and returned to England. Not long afterwards, a fresh outbreak of war between England and France relegated Irish issues down the list of English priorities. The governance of Ireland was evidently not an attractive office, and the unsatisfactorily rapid turnover in its personnel can hardly have done anything for governmental coherence and continuity. In 1392, the citizens of Dublin wrote to Richard II to ask him to take Irish affairs in hand as a matter of urgency. When at last a truce had been concluded with the French and when there was peace with Scotland and at home, Richard felt secure enough to visit Ireland personally in 1394. To help regain control over those areas which had fallen back into Gaelic hands or the hands of Anglo-Irish rebels, absentees from Ireland were ordered to return and defend their lands. Richard also determined to rid Leinster of its Gaelic lords. Whatever the theoretical worth of these plans, in practice they foundered, and when the king returned to England in 1395 the work he had done in Ireland was already starting to unravel. His second visit in 1399 to salvage the settlement he had worked for was to be his last, and it was to be the last whole-scale English intervention in Irish affairs for many years to come. Left now largely to their own devices, Dubliners and the colony would have to shift for themselves.

What had changed, therefore, to encourage the development of such elaborate civic performances as Dublin was witnessing by late in the next century? One obvious explanation, in view of the possible inhibiting effect that the earlier social and political unrest might have had, is that eventually Dublin came to enjoy sufficient domestic stability to allow a complex civic enterprise like the Corpus Christi pageantry of 1498 to take root. Yet if relative stability may have been the precondition of its growth, it also required nurturing in a particular organizational context, and this, as documents show, was afforded by the Dublin guild system. It is noticeable that not until the fifteenth century is much heard about the existence of differentiated Dublin trade guilds, founded in their own right with masters and wardens: thirteenth- and fourteenth-century civic records speak only of Dublin's ancient parent guild, the Guild Merchant, to which various trades of the city belonged in common.[255]

Even so, suggesting why historical circumstances may have been right for the growth of large-scale civic pageantry still avoids the more difficult question of why precisely Dubliners should have wanted to present it. To this question a host of answers seems possible, some of which might equally explain the motivation of other cities in these islands where Corpus Christi was celebrated with similar energy.[256] However, two possible reasons might be ventured here as particularly relevant in medieval Dublin's case. In the first half of the fifteenth century, the concept of the English Pale in Ireland was hardening into a physical reality.[257] Dubliners, long aware of a surrounding Gaelic world which pressed in upon their borders and liberties, may have experienced the need to find ways to objectify, affirm, and rally their sense of civic identity. As was seen, circumstances in the latter part of the four- teenth century do not appear to have been conducive to addressing this need with much effectiveness, but in time, Corpus Christi celebrations would offer a perfect opportunity. And perhaps it was Corpus Christi more than any other feast which became the pre-eminent occasion for Dublin pageantry because Dubliners knew of the precedent set for Corpus Christi celebration by other cities in these islands, notably by the cities of Chester and York with which Dublin had cultural connec- tions. A Dublin celebration of Corpus Christi similar to those cities would have had the further advantage of expressing cultural solidarity with England.[258]

We arrive once more at the point from which we began, the 1509 Pentecost per- formances at St Patrick's Cathedral, better prepared to see, from having explored Dublin's early investment in drama and the performing arts, what the sixteenth century would build on, what modify, and what overturn. Drama and the perform- ing arts, on the eve of the Reformation, were poised to move in any of several pos- sible directions, but centre stage would be the drama of the city.

3

Dublin Drama in the Sixteenth Century

ALL THE CITY'S A STAGE

Cities have long relied on artists of sundry sorts to stage-manage and celebrate their corporate image. Sometimes those artists have taken the liberty to invent the image on their own account, presenting it as they see it without having to heed restraints and obligations that a formal artistic commission will normally impose. Thus on occasions, from the point of view of the establishment, an independent presentation may seem askew, offering an unflattering image or worse, a threatening one. Dublin's colourful history in the annals of civic self-representation is seen perhaps most famously this century in James Joyce's treatment of the civic image, invented in a series of snapshots in *Dubliners*, and later even endowed with a mythology in *Ulysses*. Standing as he did a little aloof from the civic rank and file, viewing his chosen subject from the armchair distance of self-conscious artistic endeavour, it is not surprising that in his day the image which he projected caused some official offence: *Ulysses* was first published in Paris, not Dublin. Now, in changed times, Joyce's once offensive avant-garde has been domesticated and architecturally collected into the city's very fabric. His mythology has been annexed at several turns in the city streets by brass plaques which proclaim portions of the text of *Ulysses* in front of landmarks to which the text refers. Hence Joyce's former distance has been effaced and his presentation aggregated into the general project of self-labelling administered, in this case, by Dublin Corporation.

Dublin in the sixteenth century was at least no different in experiencing a need to seek out and project a corporate image, gathering into the general portfolio of its own self-interest attempts at self-representation. Of course, some of the impulses driving that need, being historically contigent, were necessarily somewhat different. Then, as now, the city had its literary celebrators, like the chronicler Richard Stanihurst, whose account of the Renaissance city, published in 1577 as a section of

Raphael Holinshed's *Chronicles of England, Scotlande, and Irelande*, bristles with an evident civic pride. But equally then, as now, the efforts of literary pundits were rather less likely to impinge on the general mentality than were the media of mass public display and ceremony. The impact of these, not fettered to the ability to read books, let alone to afford them, would have been freely and widely available, as they still are each year in Dublin on St Patrick's Day, to cite one salient case. The city's large-scale sixteenth-century self-representations operated in a very particular political environment and were, if anything, expressions in support of, not in opposition to, that environment's interests.[1] They could never be considered as adversarial in the ways that some artists now choose to conceive and politicize the social function of what they do. If they were adversarial, it was only in that they contested the interests of any other parties which sought to encroach upon their own. And the dramatic fabric available at the close of the fifteenth century from which sixteenth-century Dublin might sew and tailor its self-representation was a rich one, as we have already seen in the previous chapter. As it happens, no play texts have survived from sixteenth-century Dublin, and in that respect, the medieval city enjoys an advantage. What does survive, however, is plentiful evidence for the staging of plays and pageants, mainly at the city's behest, and in more abundance than before.

EXTRAMURAL AND INTRAMURAL

But before examining some of the more theatrical means by which Dublin put itself on display, its sixteenth-century deployments of what was essentially a medieval legacy, I should first describe the city's broader geopolitical situation, since this was the ever-present backdrop against which civic self-representation was presented and understood. This situation may also help to explain some of the reasons why the need for self-representation may have been so pressingly felt, a pressure evident in the repeated legislations enforcing civic display.

Dublin was not only the colonial capital of the English government in Ireland, but also a city with a strong mercantile community whose agenda in the sixteenth century was not always coextensive with that of the English government. Most of the country outside the English Pale, except for that in the control of the various walled towns of Ireland, or of the Anglo-Irish aristocracy, was in the hands of native Gaelic overlords who had either more, or less, cordial relations with the English administration. Some overlords were in open revolt. Not far to the south of Dublin, the hills of Wicklow harboured native Gaelic families like the O'Tooles and the O'Byrnes, clans who for the larger part were hostile to the English presence, and who made no secret of their attitude by conducting periodic raids from their fastnesses into the Dublin suburbs.[2] In the sixteenth century, some decay was noted in this part of the city to the south of the walls, and Dubliners embayed themselves within the walls for added protection.[3] The *Dublin Chronicle*, as I will call it, an unpublished document which survives in various sixteenth- and seventeenth-century redactions, records hostings by the citizens against the Wicklow marauders, and against tribes further afield, such as the O'Mores of co. Laois and the O'Connors of co. Offaly.[4] These hostings were ongoing necessities, also inherited from the previous century. The Dublin Franchise Roll records occasions in 1478 and 1480 when quarterly meetings of the city council had to be suspended while its personnel were assisting in campaigns against Irish enemies.[5] In such a context, Dublin never entirely lost a sense of being an embattled city: some of the arguments advanced in pleas to the Crown for financial support are as much evidence of a siege mentality as they were the understandable response of a city calling for material assistance with its (intermittent but repeated) war effort. However, relations with surrounding Gaelic communities were not inevitably fraught, and what is more, an avoidance of hostility, whenever possible, could only be to the city's mercantile advantage. Standing as it did on the fertile estuary of the river Liffey, Dublin was supported by a thriving agrarian economy and was served with a port. Notwithstanding the inconveniences caused to shipping by the proneness of the river to silt up, Dublin traded successfully, especially in goods to and from Chester and Liverpool, the nearest English ports across the Irish Sea. Dublin also had extensive trade connections with its hinterland and further afield, as for example with northeast co. Kildare, and with some of the areas where a Gaelic writ was more respected than an English one. In spite of a reluctance widespread in Dublin's ruling class to have any truck with the Irish natives, social and commercial liaisons with them had developed progressively and naturally, so much so that according to the chronicler Richard Stanihurst, Dubliners could speak both English and Irish.[6] While he might muse about the last surviving Anglo-Irish member of the Pale forbidding his daughter to marry any Gaelic person, no matter how noble by Gaelic standards that person may have been, it is nevertheless clear that some of the 'meere Irish' were entering Dublin, and not always to the dismay of the city authorities, no matter what the professed attitudes were.[7] Indeed, the reason why Dubliners had both English and Irish was *propter cottidiana commercia, quæ cum vicinis Hibernis habent* ('on account of the daily transactions that they have with [their] Irish neighbours').[8] So Dublin's perception of the surrounding Gaelic Irish was a complex and contradictory thing, often antipathetic, to be sure, but also sometimes tolerant since, through trade, relations with them might be profitable, and in some cases, even familial. And this ambivalent perception necessarily coloured the sense of what it meant to be a sixteenth-century citizen of Dublin, an identity which the civic display staged by Dublin Corporation would somehow have to negotiate, reconcile, and shore up, just as much as the corporation would strive to shore up the city walls themselves, those perennial objects of urban concern during the period.

But civic identity was already a complex matter even before it had peered out over the city walls at the wider Gaelic world against which it sought to define itself.

Dublin's prosperity was founded largely on agriculture. From the late twelfth and early thirteenth centuries, Dublin merchants who traded on that agricultural base had worked steadily to consolidate their interests, hedging them about with hard-won legal defences. By the mid-sixteenth century, they had secured for the city a formidable autonomy from governmental interference, and had thus effectively turned themselves into the city's principal power brokers. Their wealth gave them access to influential circles, and there the influence that they courted, sometimes directly by marriage alliances, helped to buttress their position further.[9] This position was no less than their insinuation into the heart of the city's council and thus into the centre of the machinery of urban legislative power. Their increasing infiltration of the civic assembly, and the confluence of mercantile and municipal interest that this entailed, can be charted quite clearly.

Dublin's civic power and independence, growing throughout the later Middle Ages, was endorsed ever more resoundingly in the sixteenth century, the century in which the litany of the city's privileges would be writ large. In 1534, the corporation had refused to meet the demand of the earl of Kildare, Thomas Fitzgerald, for access to Dublin Castle. Fitzgerald had fallen into rebellion, and finding himself rebuffed by the city, laid siege to it. Many Dubliners lost their lives in its defence. After Fitzgerald's eventual overthrow, Henry VIII promised to reward the citizens' loyalty, and this came in 1539 with the granting to the city's use of the property and lucrative revenues of the dissolved priory of All Hallows, plus some remission of the 200 marks payable by the city in fee-farm rent. Civic repairs were to be paid for out of these new sources of income. A few years later, in 1548, Dublin was awarded the accolade of incorporation as a county borough, and henceforward members of the corporation would benefit from a heightened authority and prestige.[10]

The composition of the corporation which ran Dublin's affairs had already by the fourteenth century assumed the formal shape that it was to retain throughout the sixteenth.[11] Twenty-four *jurés* or aldermen comprised the highest administrative group. They served for life. Each year, they elected the senior of their number as mayor, and were themselves elected to the bench by co-option.[12] Beneath the aldermen, there were forty-eight *demi-jurés*, and beneath them, the ninety-six 'numbers,' men elected from the city's various trade guilds. In substance, however, this formal composition was to change dramatically between the medieval and Renaissance periods. In the fourteenth century, it seems that although there was even then a pecking order to the threefold council body (the aldermen carried most clout), authority was rather more evenly distributed through it than it was by the end of the sixteenth century. In about the year 1500, a list of the twenty-four and the forty-eight was drawn up (no mention is made of the ninety-six).[13] The composition of the forty-eight on the eve of the sixteenth century still testified to the survival of substantial guild representation in the corporation's structure: of the forty-five members whose names were listed, the trades of thirteen are known, and of these, less than half were merchants.[14] By about 1600, conversely, of the forty-eight whose occupations are ascertainable, most were merchants, while of about a third of the ninety-six 'numbers' whose trade is known, three quarters were merchants.[15] Evidently, the civic administration was experiencing a creeping takeover by the merchant class. One of the means by which this takeover was achieved was articulated bluntly in an ordinance of 1574 which decreed, with breath-taking class confidence, that members of guilds other than the Trinity guild (that is, the Merchants guild) could serve among the forty-eight or the ninety-six only if no other more suitable member of the Trinity guild had put himself forward.[16]

Thus when sixteenth-century Dublin put itself on public display, that display was organized in the context of a merchant class, ensconced in key positions of civic power and jealously guarding the civic priviliges that it had in no small part helped to win. If the merchants were equating the security of their interests with the general weal of the city, then not surprisingly, public displays would body forth this equation. And this is what we find: the ruling oligarchy watched with equal concern over public displays, and to a great extent controlled their means.

THE CIVIC CALENDAR

Dublin's civic calendar included a busy schedule of public events and rituals whose clockwork reliability no doubt helped to structure the year and thus also to lend definition to individual citizens' sense of civic identity. Salient and regular occasions for civic display in sixteenth-century Dublin were: musters, of which four were chief, Easter Monday (or Black Monday as it is normally called),[17] May Day, Midsummer Eve, and St Peter's Eve; station days; guild observances on their patron saint's eve; the Shrove Tuesday bearing of balls ceremony; franchise ridings; St George's Day; St Patrick's Day; and Corpus Christi. (Intermittent occasions of display were also afforded by civic receptions, parliaments, marriage festivities, and funerals.) The corporation monitored lapses, as for example when the Butchers were reproved in 1563 for having failed to keep their light in the fleshambles on Midsummer Eve for the last four or five years, and likewise the Fishmongers, for neglecting their light and fire in Fish Street on St Peter's Eve. Both were ordered to reinstate these 'auncyent laudable usages,' upon pain of a twenty-mark fine.[18] Punishment for failures or derelictions was, of course, no new thing, as the forty-shilling penalities stipulated in the 1498 Corpus Christi pageant lists of the Chain Book have already shown. The most important civic ceremony, from a narrowly territorial point of view, was that of the riding of the franchises. This was a public perambulation of the city limits within which the mayor's authority was acknowledged as binding, and it provided a useful rehearsal and reminder of the civic status quo when other franchises or liberties also existed within the city, as for example those under the jurisdiction of the archbishop of Dublin.[19] Instituted in the medieval period, the riding seems to have fallen into abeyance after about 1525. Civic records next speak of it on 10 August 1568, then in 1574, and 1583, and when next heard of in 1584, its former neglect was mentioned as a cause for alarm: it was feared that its lapse might have entailed the lapse of the civic priviliges which it protected by their public acclamation.[20] Perhaps its revival was stimulated in an atmosphere of renewed anxiety about anticipated encroachments on the corporation's prerogatives after a period of relative complacency.[21] There may have been grounds for some urban smugness before 1584 and during the middle of the century: not only had Dublin's autonomy been formidably strengthened by its 1548 charter of incorporation, it must also be remembered that the franchise riding, though an imposing civic ceremony, was expensive, at best sporadic, and its specific object, however important, was limited, being simply the publicizing and delimiting of jurisdictions.[22] Other ceremonies, annually observed, helped to endow sixteenth-century Dublin with the additionally potent advantage of a mythology, and possibly their sway into the third quarter of the sixteenth century may have acted as a partial disincentive to the franchise riding, or at least, may have lessened the felt need for franchise display, since these ceremonies also embodied, if less formally, some of the same aspirations that the franchise riding cherished. When these ceremonies themselves decayed, as evidence suggests they were doing by the time that the franchise riding was resumed in the late 1560s, they left a rift open in the civic calendar which the riding might usefully fill.

Apart from franchise ridings, the Dublin Assembly Rolls, which contain the decisions and minutes of the civic assembly, make it clear that at least by 1466, three major days each year featured processions through the city: Corpus Christi (that international celebration of the institution of the Mass and its theology); St George's Day (by this date, patron saint of England and also patron of the corporation's own guild of St George); and St Patrick's Day (patron of Ireland).[23] These three festivals together encode in brief the complex nature of Dublin's identity (an identity that we have already begun inferring from other historical evidence). That identity was international,[24] loyal to its English cultural origins,[25] and yet also in some sense inalienably Irish and independent.[26] By the later sixteenth century, the mutual compatability of these components of civic identity would come under strain, and civic independence would seek new ways of voicing itself. Of the nature of the civic ceremony on St Patrick's Day little evidence remains. It can be presumed that some activity would have focused on St Patrick's Cathedral, but nothing is known for certain. We are better served by Corpus Christi and St George's Day. In 1498, on the eve of the century of concern here, the list of Corpus Christi pageants reviewed in the previous chapter was formally entered in the Great Chain Book of Dublin Corporation. This list needs to be revisited if we are to understand better how Dublin went about representing itself, and the reader might find it convenient to refer back to the list (pp. 91–3 above) during this discussion.

The 1498 document began solemnly: the list was issued under the full authority of the mayor and the whole assembly, the *jurés* (the twenty-four aldermen) and the commons (the combined chambers of the forty-eight and ninety-six). As such, the procession prescribed in it somehow spoke for the whole civic body, or at least, for the larger, enfranchised part of it. Striking is the extent to which the trade guilds were given pageant responsibilities. They assumed the bulk of the procession. (In some cases, there was an appropriateness between a trade and the topic presented, a feature familiar from comparable English pageant lists.)[27] Four pageants had no trade guild affiliation, however. One was organized by a religious guild, the guild of Corpus Christi. This guild played the Passion, a subject not only thematically, but also physically, central to the procession; it is worth observing how its pageant came at the mid-point of the list. Two other pageants had no guild auspices of any kind but were the responsibilities of civic institutions. One of these, on the subject of the Nine Worthies, was presented by the Mayor of the Bullring. He was an official charged with governing the youth of the city, a master of their ceremonies who took his name from the iron bullring set in the Cornmarket at which bulls were baited.[28] His was the penultimate pageant. The other pageant was presented by the 'Conpteours' (probably the city auditors or accountants) on the subject of King Arthur and his knights. Finally, the dragon was carried (and repaired) by the haggardmen and husbandmen, with the additional note that it should also be carried by them on St George's Day, a festival to which we shall return. The dragon, in the position of honour bringing up the rear of the procession, was the emblem of the guild of St George, and this guild, as noted, was none other than that of Dublin Corporation. The influential merchants had just one pageant assigned, that of the prophets, though to be sure, it came close to the end of the procession. So the list specified the ingredients for a celebration of civic identity, seemingly egalitarian in the generosity of its breadth and inclusiveness, and put on for the benefit of everyone in the city, including, presumably, those citizens enfranchised but not necessarily guild affiliated, and for yet others without any formal civic status at all. Yet we know that whatever the appearance of catholicity engineered in this procession, the corporation with its dragon, plus the related civic institution of the Mayor of the Bullring, had the last word, bringing up the honourable rear, and ultimately in charge was the corporation itself, the focus, as was seen, of the confederacy of mercantile and municipal interest. So while an egalitarian appearance might seem to be served by this procession, its 'political unconscious' is apparent, because the real axis of power in the city, known from other historical sources to be swinging towards the merchants, has centred itself in the display within pageants set in key positions.

Corpus Christi continued to be observed in Dublin at least until 1565, when Sir Nicholas Arnold, Lord Justice, reminded the mayor to ban its observance among the city's 'arthyffyeares' (presumably, its tradesmen).[29] In fact, the feast may have survived as late as 1569, since a corporation memorandum of this year still adverts respectfully to the authority of the Corpus Christi list in the Chain Book.[30] It is unclear whether the procession was held annually until the 1560s, but sporadic evidence suggests that at least early in the century it was. After all, the observance of Corpus Christi in Dublin during this period was supported not only by its intrinsic importance and stature as a liturgical feast, but also by its appropriation by the city fathers in a special way. Following the profanation of St Patrick's Cathedral, which had occurred during civil strife in 1512, a penance had been imposed upon the mayor of Dublin for him to perform on the city's behalf. Henceforth he was to go barefoot before the host in the Corpus Christi procession.[31] A regulation of 1504, noticed in the previous chapter, reveals that the corporation was already vigilantly supervising the procession's content: the Corpus Christi guild was itself being brought to book for allowing the subject matter of its pageant to diverge from the Passion narrative prescribed in the Chain Book list. In 1541, when the parliament held in Dublin coincided with Corpus Christi, the *Dublin Chronicle* notes that the pageant of the Nine Worthies was performed, and that the Irish lords used the occasion of the procession to ride about in their parliament robes.[32] Apart from these fitfull references, it might also be noted that the Corpus Christi guild, like the other religious guilds of Dublin, would survive the Reformation.[33] It was not to suffer the same fate as its English counterparts. So the ostensible rationale for the Corpus Christi procession, embodied by the Corpus Christi guild, would have lived on for a long time. Indeed, in the very year when Sir Nicholas Arnold sought to visit his reformed zeal on the feast and ban its observance, the guild was further endowed by Christ Church Cathedral with a fee-farm lease of a property in St Michael's Lane.[34]

We have seen how the distribution of civic power was given a harmonious and democratic gloss on the feast of Corpus Christi, though it was also not too hard to gaze beneath this surface to a submerged political actuality. Through a celebratory procession, this actuality was publicly parading, reconciling and justifying itself. But in addition to its endorsement of the status quo, for that is an aim which most varieties of civic display might share in common, Corpus Christi pageantry allowed the city to absorb a mythology and articulate its civic structures in an allegorical guise: here transmuted, they would catch the reflected glory of a biblical world and its respectability, and through pageants like the Nine Worthies and King Arthur, they would also partake of the legends and ethos of Christian chivalry. Their valorization by these processes, thus contrived, must have been both efficient and beguiling.

PLAYS ON THE HOGGEN GREEN

Where did the procession process to? The case for St George's Chapel was reviewed in the previous chapter, but we should recall that the evidence for that venue was not entirely watertight. Another venue in which we know for certain that pageants, indeed plays, were presented, if not at Corpus Christi then at other times of the year, was the Hoggen Green. (Its location was not so utterly remote from St George's Chapel that, were it ever to be finally demonstrated that the Corpus Christi pageants actually ended up there, it would materially upset the previous chapter's conclusions about the nature and significance of the pageant route.) The Hoggen Green was a civic rallying place a little to the east of the city walls, in the area of what is now College Green (see fig. 3). It had a long tradition of multiple civic use. As early as 1328, it had seen the judicial burning of one Adam Douffe, a notorious blasphemer who counted among his many crimes his assertion that the Virgin Mary 'was but a harlot.'[35] Other public examples of the cautionary kind would follow in the fifteenth century.[36] More routine, if less spectacular, was its use for archery practice, for it was here that the city butts had been set up, and it made a convenient mustering ground for military drills.[37] No less important was it as a venue for civic receptions: when, for example, Sir Henry Sidney was received into Dublin on 16 January 1566, the mayor and aldermen, doubtless robed in their traditional scarlet gowns of office, came out to meet him there.[38] (John Derricke's *Image of Irelande* depicts a similar sort of reception before the city gates which is conceivably taking place either in or adjacent to Hoggen Green; see fig. 14.)[39] Thus Hoggen Green hosted displays of various hues which were of considerable civic importance, and to these should be added its established use as a venue for theatrically conceived ventures of the kind under review.[40] In 1506, the Passion of Christ was performed here, though we are not told by whom:

Nycolas harbard maior the xxjte yer of kinge henre the vijth Iohn blanchfel and patrick harbartt balyfes This yer the pasyon of Cryste wasse pleytt {'played'} on the hogen gren [41]

And on 20 July 1523, the life of St Laurence was also played here:

then deyde mawde darssey wyff to christoffer Wssher and one {'on'} blake mondaie followinge it raynede so sore that ye maior with his bretherne and comens coude nott goo to the wode but they all tarryede in Chrychyrche {'Christ Church'} in the witsontyde after was a greatte

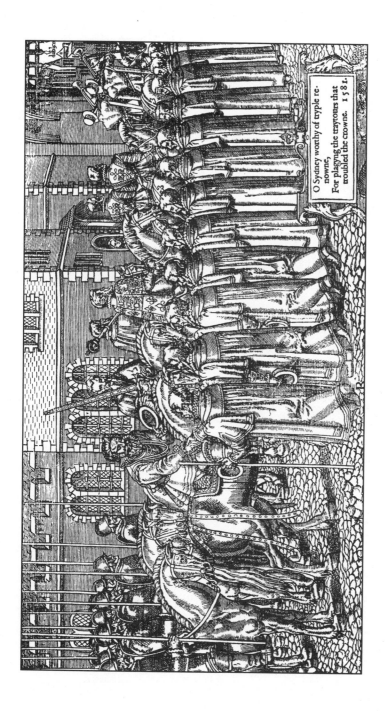

O Sydney worthy of tryple renowne,
For plaging the traytours that troubled the crowne. 1581.

14 Sir Henry Sidney's civic entry into Dublin, from John Derricke, *The Image of Irelande*.

flode and on saincte margett is tyme folowinge wase the lyff of saincte larens playyde one the hoggen gren[42]

The source for our knowing about these plays is in both cases the *Dublin Chronicle*, that sixteenth-century witness to Dublin's need to locate itself in the august field of annalistic discourse. Whatever their original auspices, the commemoration of these plays was evidently a matter of civic consequence, concern, and record.[43]

An elaborate show of which more substantial notice has survived took place on the Hoggen Green in 1528. Its plays were put on to entertain Thomas Fitzgerald, 'Earl of Kildare':

Thomas fitz Gerrald Earl of Kildare, Lord Lieutenant of Ireland Anno .one thousand, fiue hundred, twenty Eight, was invited to a new play euery day in Christmas time, Alexander Vsher being then Maior, and ffrancis Herbert, and John Squire Bayliffs; wherein the Taylors acted the part of Adam, and Eue; the Shoomakers represented the Story of Crispin, and Crispiana. The Vintners acted Bacchus, and his story; The Carpenters presented the story of Joseph, and Mary. Vulcan, and what related to him, was acted by the Smiths; The Comody of Cæres, the Goddess of Corne, was acted by the Bakers: Their Stage was putt vp on Haggin-Green, now called the Colledg Green, on this stage the Priors of Saint Johns of Hierusalem, of the blessed Trinity, and of Allhallowes, caused two playes to be acted; the one representing the Passion of our Sauiour, the other the seueral deaths which the Apostles suffered.[44]

This Christmastide mixture of entertainment and edification lasted for several days.[45] Six plays, three sacred and three secular, were put on by the guildsmen. There was also a notable degree of church involvement in their enterprise. The participation of the priors of St John of Jerusalem, of Holy Trinity, and of All Hallows in producing two other plays testifies to the kind of collaboration between secular and spiritual institutions that was argued in the previous chapter for the production of *The Pride of Life*: it should be noted too that the Augustinian canons of Holy Trinity, under whose aegis *The Pride of Life* (and *Visitatio Sepulcri*) fell, were once again to the fore here in the sixteenth century. Some episodes in the 1528 show overlap with ones featured in the Corpus Christi procession, though only in one case did those responsible, the Carpenters, offer an episode akin to their Corpus Christi pageant. For the rest, three trades (Vintners, Smiths, and Bakers) introduced neo-classical topics which, even if as before cognate to the professional concerns of their craft, now also catered to the modern tastes of newer, Renaissance enthusiasms.[46] All the Hoggen Green plays, and certainly those of 1528 when 'Their Stage was putt vp' there, look to have been stationary, place-and-scaffold performances of the sort also proposed in the previous chapter for *The Pride of Life*. In many respects, the 1528 event seems to continue medieval traditions of production, subject matter, and undoubtedly venue.

IRELAND, HARRY, AND ST GEORGE

Whether the Corpus Christi pageants processed to the Hoggen Green or to St George's Chapel is immaterial from the point of view of the social significance of the intramural part of the processional route, for this would have been the same in both cases: both green and chapel lay practically next to each other a little to the east of the city walls, and hence any procession originating within or passing through the city was likely to have reached either of these places by taking the same route, exiting via Dame's Gate.[47] No less in Dublin than anywhere else, processions were an important component of civic display generally, and their route is not an incidental issue if we wish to understand as nearly as possible their social and political function. The other of the 1466 processional days for which extensive evidence survives, the feast of St George, affords another interesting case study, and here, conversely, we know where the destination of the St George procession was to have been: it was St George's Chapel in St George's Lane.[48] The Chain Book formerly contained yet another list, apart from the Corpus Christi ones, in which the organization of the pageantry of St George's Day was described in some detail. Though now missing, the list's content can be supplied from an antiquarian transcript made in the seventeenth century when it was still in place. In the transcript it is undated, but since the list was evidently drafted before the chapel's demolition – the list assigns an important role to the chapel in the celebrations – and on the strength of its reference to the city *bailiffs*, its *terminus ante quem* can be established. The date of the chapel's final demolition is a little difficult to determine, but it probably occurred sometime between the Michaelmasses of 1563 and 1564. The chapel's days were numbered, ironically enough, from 10 May 1555, when alderman Robert Cusack was ordered by the Dublin Civic Assembly to 'builde and erecte' it – it was evidently at that time in disrepair – using for the purpose stone allocated from the now dissolved priory of All Hallows.[49] Instead, he seems to have recycled the chapel's timber and stones to build a civic oven in which he had a personal interest.[50] In spite of this depredation, something was still left of the chapel in 1557, for in that year funds were found for repairing its roof and fabric.[51] However, accounts falling between the Michaelmasses of 1563 and 1564 in the corporation Treasurer's Book speak of the freight of St George's timber in terms which suggest that the chapel's timber was being carried away somewhere,[52] and an act of the corporation for 19 January 1565 in which the chapel grounds were leased for fifty-one years, 'with proviso if the churche shalbe buylded againe that then the sayd lese shalbe voyde,' sounds quite unambiguous about the chapel's condition.[53] We also have Stanihurst's word for it, published in 1577 but written a good few years earlier, that by his day the chapel had been dismantled 'and the stones thereof by consent of the assembly turned to a common Ouen, conuerting the auncient monument of a doughty, aduenturous, and holy knight, to the coalerake sweeping of a pufloafe baker.'[54] So the list was certainly drafted before 1563–4, and this date can probably be further narrowed to sometime before 1548, for this was the year in which the city bailiffs were upgraded to city sheriffs in Dublin's charter of incorporation issued by Edward VI. The St George pageant list, conversely, was still referring to them as bailiffs.[55]

Let us first look carefully at the content and organization of this pageant, before proceeding to consider its political thrust and the social significance of its likely processional route. The list ran as follows:

The Pageant of St Georges day to be ordered & kept as hereafter followeth.

The Major of the yeare before to finde the Emperour & Empress with their followers well apparelled that is to say the Emperor with 2 Doctors & the Empress with 2 Knights & 2 Maydens to beare the traynes of their Gownes well apparelled. And St Georg to pay their wages.

Item mr Mayor for the time being to find St Georg a Horsback & the wardens to pay 3^s 4^d for his wages that day And the bailives for the time being to find 4 Horses with men upon them well apparelled, to beare the poleaxe, the Standard, and the Emperor & St Georges swordes

Item the elder mr of ye yeald to find a Mayd well aparelled to lead the Dragon. And the clerk of the market to find a good Line for the Dragon.

Item the Elder warden to find St Geo. with 4 Trumpettors & St George to pay their wages.

Item the yonger warden to finde the King of Dele & the Queene of Dele & 2 Knights to lead the Queene of Dele, with 2 Maydens to beare the trayne of her goune, |fol. 149v| all wholy in black apparell, and to have St Georges chappell well hanged & apparelled to every purpose with cushins .... russhes & other neccessaries belonging for said St Georges day[56]

St George, that most English member of the Church Triumphant, began his Dublin acculturation from as early as the late twelfth century, when a chapel dedicated to him was built in St George's Lane.[57] Its position outside the city walls would have left it vulnerable to attacks from Irish enemies. These seem to have taken their toll, for when in 1426 Henry VI issued letters patent for the establishment of a fraternity or guild of St George on the chapel's premises, it evidently needed renovation; doubtless the presence of an active St George's guild would help to keep it in good repair.[58] The guild was adopted as that of the Dublin Civic Assembly, and its officers selected from outgoing assembly members. The mayor of the previous year supplied the guild master, and the two outgoing bailiffs (sheriffs after 1548) supplied its two wardens.[59] Apart from at those times when it was pressed into assisting with military campaigns, as in the late fifteenth century, for example, the guild's functions seem to have been largely of a ceremonial sort, and already by 1466, as we saw, St George's feast had been enrolled as one of the three great days of civic procession when the guild would have come into its own.

The rich detail of the list gives a good impression of the nature of the pageant's narrative and personnel. The mayor of the year before, that is, the current guild master, was to find people to play the parts of the Emperor, the Empress, and their six attendants. Their wages were to be paid by the person chosen to play St George. He would be selected by the current mayor and paid 3s 4d for his efforts by the guild wardens. It was perhaps from this stipend that St George paid for Emperor, Empress and their six attendants, as well as for his four attendant trumpetors; these latter were to be selected by the elder guild warden. No other details are given about who was responsible for paying whom, but we are told that the bailiffs provided four men and horses who attended St George and the Emperor, the elder guild master a maiden who led the dragon, and the clerk of the market a line (possibly the leash by which the maiden led the dragon along). It was the job of the younger warden to select the King and Queen of Dele plus their four attendants, and to ensure that St George's Chapel was appropriately decked for the occasion with hangings, cushions, and rushes.

The pageant required sixteen persons, plus four horsemen, four trumpeters, and a dragon. This impressive crew processed to the chapel, perhaps with pauses for mimetic action en route, after which a liturgy of St George would have been offered up.[60] Although it is not known for sure that the pageant characters engaged in a fully fledged play at some point during the day's proceedings, it is worth noting that the presence of several of them seems to have been dictated rather more by the need to present a St George narrative than the desire merely to pad out a procession's panoply. The narrative significance of the characters would have been made conveniently explicit by enacting it in a play. And the fact that the corporation sustained repeated costs, recorded in the Treasurer's Book, for mending the dragon may also be telling; repeated dragon repairs could be explained by the beast's involvement in some sort of mimetic fight with St George liable to damage it. Perhaps the contemporary St George play of the city of York may serve as a model for what happened in Dublin, for in several of its particulars it invites direct comparison with the Dublin event.[61]

From the point of view of the pageant's political investment, what stands out is its complex network of apportioned responsibilities, the effect of which would have been to cement relations between key corporation officials and St George guild members, uniting them all in a common, self-validating enterprise. The guild had no very extensive practical role that we know of apart from occasional military involvement, and though guild accounts, from which the nature of its involvement in the community might be more clearly determined, do not survive, it is not likely that it ever did have a role, or at least, not as had the trade guilds.[62] Its ceremonial role, conversely, seems to have been paramount. Once again, this time on St George's Day, the corporation by means of the guild's agency displayed itself in transfigured terms, glowing with the mythic lustre of Christian chivalry. And on this occasion that lustre was unalloyed: no other pageants were present to offer the least distraction from it as they might on Corpus Christi, despite the careful manipulation of that feast's celebrations to the greater glory of God and the Dublin Civic Assembly. But the St George pageant had further political inflections quite unlike those noted in the Corpus Christi procession, or at least, ones given much sharper emphasis, that are noteworthy. Central elements in it were reminiscent of existing ceremonials *shared by city and state*. In Dublin at this date, a sword might be borne before the mayor (the mayor, we recall, was specifically responsible for finding St George, who in the pageant also had a sword borne before him) and before the Lord Deputy (the other pageant persona dignified with a sword bearer was the Emperor): thus by a metonymy for St George one might read 'mayor' and for Emperor, 'Lord Deputy.'[63] Hence the corporation could be said to consort with the state government in this pageant, and through a theatrical metaphor to establish a parity that was at once an independence. Further, the pageant mythically twinned the interests of the government with those of the corporation. The government would do well to remember that St George was a God-sent, liberating dragon slayer: throughout the sixteenth century (and indeed from the fifteenth, when the guild of St George was directly called upon), the English administration had depended on the military muscle flexed by the mayor of Dublin and his aldermen to fight off attacks against the Pale. When for example in 1517 the Lord Deputy the earl of Kildare campaigned successfully against the O'Tooles, the head of Shane O'Toole was struck off and sent to the mayor 'for a present.'[64] We are not told what he did with it, but doubtless he set it on a spike for all to appreciate. Again in 1539, the mayor combined forces with the Lord Deputy and the mayor of Drogheda to rout O'Neill, who with O'Donnell had burned the towns of Ardee and Navan within the Pale.[65] The *Dublin Chronicle* was proud to recall such military involvements, and noticed the governmental recognition that might consequently be bestowed on mayors by their knighting at the Lord Deputy's hands.[66] St George pageants, in this context, were unifying rituals that helped to both express and consolidate a political reality in which playing together wove the threads of staying together into a public tapestry.

We may return, then, to the earlier question about the significance of the route that the procession took. At this juncture, we may also reconnect with the question of the significance of the route of the Corpus Christi procession, for while both processions were intramural, both were likely to have shared a common course. Like the James Joyce plaques that today gloss particular city landmarks, so these sixteenth-century processions would have glossed the civic, governmental, and ecclesiastical centres lying along the route by which they passed, endowing them with meaning, as they in turn drew meaning from them. An excellent case of this close ceremonial symbiosis between processions and buildings is expressed in a letter of 23 January 1538 sent from the mayor and aldermen of Dublin to Thomas Cromwell petitioning for the preservation of Christ Church Cathedral against dissolution on grounds that were as much civic as spiritual. It was emphasized that the building stood 'in the middes of the said Cittie & Chambre in like maner as paules Chirch is in london,' and that since it was 'the verie station place wher as ... the congregacions of the said Citie in processions & station daies and at all other tymes necessarie assemblith,' its suppression would dishearten Dublin, creating 'a fowle waste & deformitie of the said Citie and a great comforte & encoraginge of our Soueraine Lords the kynges Irish enymyes.'[67] Nor should the fact be neglected that the fashionable quarters of the city in which the aldermen had their mansions were also contiguous with the processional route. It was usual too for buildings to be decorated both within and without on ceremonial occasions.[68] In this way, architecture itself might participate in pageantry, echoing an assent from the institution decorated to the day's event. Thus civic spaces and places also became dramatic participants: all the city's a stage indeed, where at the corporation's expense wine might flow at sites once routinely familiar but which had now been transformed by the drinkable signs of beneficent civic paternalism.[69] While Corpus Christi and St George's Day were different occasions with differing emphases, the processions on both rehearsed the various aspects of one englobing project: their civic celebration at once affirmed civic power, articulated civic identity, and facilitated the internal stability of the civic status quo. In this latter regard, it should be remembered that there were always potential, internal civic tensions that these processions might in their way help to contain. Dublin's ceremonial was, after all, compulsory, for it was perceived that derelictions 'if they be not reformed will give boldness to outhers to disorder themselfs in higher poincts.'[70] The awareness of possible internal dissent was never altogether forgotten, and by such means as the enforcement of rigorous processional protocols and the prescription of modes of personal dress on ceremonial days, oppositions might be controlled, if not neutralized.[71] And civic ceremonial took charge over the most basic of life's rituals, as in the public acclamation of the marriage of any citizen which had taken place during the year at the Shrove Tuesday ball bearing ceremony.[72] Those grimmer pageants of determination, the heads which were spiked over the city gates as minatory trophies of city and state, might have a message for the people of Dublin as well as for their Gaelic enemies beyond the Pale.

THREE BRIEF LIVES: RICHARD STANTON, GEORGE SPRINGHAM, AND STEPHEN CASSE

It is easy to lose sight of the individuals who constituted the generalities that we invoke whenever we speak of 'city' and 'state,' yet these are the broad concepts that have hitherto tended to preoccupy this discussion of drama and pageantry in sixteenth-century Dublin. Often for want of evidence this may be inevitable, so that we find ourselves obliged to speak of the workings of conglomerate corporations or administrations rather than of the particular men and women who made those workings possible. But occasionally precious indications survive of how Dublin drama and pageantry touched the lives of individual citizens. In this regard, I want to consider the careers of Richard Stanton, George Springham, and Stephen Casse, for an understanding of how these three men participated in their city's life, as well as in its drama and pageantry, will test and extend the conclusions already drawn about what stakes were played for on Dublin's great processional days. Stanton, and even more so Springham and Casse, exist for us now only in official documents, and thus mediated, we should not expect to feel much of the grain of their personalities. Yet their lives in brief still have an important tale to tell.

Richard Stanton is the best known of the three, in that unlike the other two, he also earned a place for himself in the annals of Dublin. He first appears in the Assembly Rolls in a list of corporation officials which was drawn up on 30 September 1530. Here he is referred to as 'Keeper of the gaol.'[73] This was doubtless the city jail at the Newgate where in the regnal year 23 Henry VIII (22 April 1531 – 21 April 1532) he also took a delivery of irons.[74] He served here as city jailer until 1533 when he was replaced by a certain John Freu.[75] Stanton must have been at least a young adult by 1530, and given the nature of his prison employment, one imagines that he was a sturdy one, too. Although he handed over office to Freu in 1533, he evidently retained some connection with the jail, for when next heard of, in Holinshed's *Chronicles*, he is still referred to as jailer of the Newgate, and this in 1534, in a memorable context. Earlier that year, the Lord Deputy, Sir Gerald Fitzgerald, ninth earl of Kildare, had been summoned to London, and had left his son Thomas, Lord Offaly, as vice-deputy. Thomas had subsequently fallen into rebellion, and by August 1534 was besieging Dublin. It was probably in this month that Stanton, 'commonly called Dicke,' became the city's darling in an act of valour. Not only had he displayed outstanding markmanship in shooting dead one of the rebels, but he had sortied outside the city gate to strip the body of its clothes and weapons, and had brought them inside the city. For this deed he became the only citizen to be singled out by name for honourable mention in Holinshed's *Chronicles* for defending the city while it was under siege.[76] After this adventure, he reappears in civic documents towards the end of the siege period, on 2 October 1534, and now as one of the serjeants of the mayor, in the same list in which Stephen Casse makes his début as a common serjeant.[77] (Since Stanton, Casse, and Springham, as we shall see, moved in similar circles, the men doubtless all knew each other.) Stanton's office as serjeant to the mayor was normally also combined with that of water bailiff, and he is first mentioned in both capacities in 1536.[78] He was still holding both offices in 1541, but it appears that between these dates he may also have resumed his job as jailer, for in 1541 he was ordered by the council, beginning from Michaelmas of that year, to occupy either the office of mace-bearer (his position as serjeant of the mayor) or jailer, but not both simultaneously.[79] Evidently he chose to remain as mace-bearer, because in 1542 he was referred to as holder of that office.[80] From 1546 to 1552, he served as serjeant and water bailiff.[81] His last year on record as being in active service was 1553, when he was again listed as water bailiff.[82] In the following year of 1554, we hear for the first time of George Springham, in a memorandum in which he and Stanton were directly associated. Springham, evidently a relatively young man, was appointed on 26 October 1554 to the office of serjeant that Stanton had formerly held, and henceforth Stanton, now of pensionable age, could look forward to a life annuity of £6 13s 4d.[83] Springham's career seems to have mirrored Stanton's in that Springham, by contrast, began as serjeant of the mayor and then exchanged that position for city jailer. In 1555, still as mayor's serjeant, he is on record in the Treasurer's Book as having been given 21s for the livery of David Wycombe.[84] (Wycombe, as we learn from a subsequent set of accounts, was warden of the beggars and *custos* of the swine, offices often paired and answerable, it appears, to the mayor's serjeant.)[85] Evidently by 7 May 1557 Springham had married, for at this date he and his wife Anstace took out a sixty-one-year lease on a house and garden in St Bride's parish from the dean and chapter of Christ Church.[86] His career as jailer was combined at this date with other, more military commitments: in a set of accounts for February 1558 he is noted as having acted as captain of a ship rigged and manned to repel pirates, and as having been empowered to impress soldiers for the purpose.[87] This seems to have been a temporary arrangement, for in 1562 he was in his wonted post as city jailer, taking a delivery of bolts, shackles, and irons.[88] A probable military venture supervened again in 1563, when he was paid 'for seruing in the North' in the stead of Walter Rochford.[89] He may have changed residence in 1564. On 6 July in that year, he took out a sixty-one-year lease, again from the dean and chapter of Christ Church, on a property in Oxmantown Green, and on a messuage and garden in Fisher Lane, Oxmantown.[90] Given that his predecessor, Richard Stanton, had in 1541 been obliged to resign one or other of his offices of mayor's serjeant or city jailer, it may be that Springham, who is next heard of officiating as one of the two mace-bearers at the solemn civic funeral of Mayor Robert Cusack on 22 September 1564, had resigned as city jailer and resumed a post as mayor's serjeant.[91] He evidently still held this office in 1567–8, when he appears in a set of accounts as waterbailiff.[92] This is the last we hear of him.

Our last potted biography is of Stephen Casse, a man who first appears, as was noted, in a document of 2 October 1534 as a common serjeant. His official duties, by contrast, seem never to have varied, and he held on tenaciously to this office in 1536–7, 1539–42, 1546–50, and 1552–4.[93] In a set of accounts in the Treasurer's Book, running between 29 September 1548 and 5 November 1549, he was paid 4s 3d for, appropriately enough, mending his mace.[94] (Possibly he occupied the office of common serjeant during the years between his known periods of tenure, but if so, the records are silent.) This tenancy of the same office spans some twenty years. If he was a young man when first heard of in 1534, he must have been in middle age twenty years later. In 1559, one Thomas Lynam was appointed to the office of one of the common serjeants, 'with all comodities and profits belongyng therunto, in as large manner as Stephen Casse had the same.'[95] We do not know when he died (as similarly with Stanton and Springham), but a deed of 25 March 1586 mentions the grant of a house in Fishamble Street, which had formerly been demised to Stephen Casse, deceased.[96] It would seem, then, that he had lived in the heart of the city. Unlike Stanton and Springham, whose stipends derived from corporation sources, Casse made his living elsewhere. He may have been a tailor by profession, for the other documents in which he features are the accounts of the Tailors guild, where he is paid for his pageant appearances. It is not likely that the master and wardens of the Tailors guild would have recruited someone from outside their trade to perform in their pageantry, but one of their number who already held civic office would present a natural choice.

We may now superimpose what is known of the pageant involvement of these three men upon their careers and see what the resulting picture has to reveal. Stanton appears only once in connection with civic pageantry, but he took an important role on that occasion. He rode as St George on the Triumph of the Peace, an extraordinary celebration organized sometime during 1545–6.[97] This was at a time well into his civic career when he was locally famous for his courageous defence of the city and was serving as serjeant to the mayor. George Springham similarly appears only once by name in a pageant role, in a set of accounts running between 14 April 1566 and 29 September 1567, but it looks to be precisely the same role as Stanton played, St George.[98] By that time he too had been in military service on the city's behalf. It begins to look as if there may have been a traditional connection between the office of mayor's serjeant and the role of St George. Bearers of that office were, after all, liable to do military service and their achievements in that capacity might be appropriately crowned by pageantry, rather as laureate Roman generals might expect to be fêted in civic triumphs. There also seems nothing inherently difficult in reading a general inference into what this equation of the office of mayor's serjeant and the role of St George suggests: perhaps particular civic officers were regarded as appropriate candidates for undertaking particular roles in the

St George's Day pageant. At any rate, if as seems the case there was a traditional link between mayor's serjeant and St George, then one way of regarding the role might be as an extension into pageant dimensions not only of personal achievement on behalf of the city, but also of the power and civic discipline embodied in the mayor's serjeant's office. In the cases of Stanton and Springham, we can justifiably surmise that both would have brought to the role of their respective St Georges a certain physical robustness and sense of male well-being that would have entirely suited the champion of Christendom. Casse, though he would evidently have known these men, never aspired to play St George, as far as we know, but then he also seems never to have trodden any of the higher rungs of the civic ladder. He came into his own playing Pilate within the pageant organized by the Tailors in 1554–5 and in 1556.[99] His pageant involvement occurs at about a ten-year midpoint between that of Stanton (1545–6) and of Springham (1566–7). So as we have already seen and will see again in a moment in the case of the brethren of the bullring, it appears that not only were particular pageants associated with specific social groups within the city, but that specific individuals may have been associated with particular roles within those pageants. This seems at least to have been true of those pageants closest to the corporation's heart. The involvements of Stanton, Springham and Casse illustrate how finely tuned the correspondences between pageant performance and civic practice might be.

THE BRETHREN OF THE BULLRING

The rapport between civic interest and pageant performance which our close-up of the St George ceremonies has revealed to have been even more subtle than we may at first have suspected was also but an element, if perhaps one of the most salient, within the general ceremonial enterprise undertaken by the corporation. The peripheries of civic life were also places which the corporate centre tried to patrol and bring under its central control. Close to the honourable rear of the Corpus Christi procession, it will be recalled, and immediately next to the George-and-Dragon pageant which occupied the final place of honour, was the pageant of the Nine Worthies. The Dublin Civic Assembly seems to have delegated the training and formation of the youth of the city to another civic official who, like the mayor himself, was also annually elected, and styled the Mayor of the Bullring. He was accompanied by two sheriffs, and so in all its salient, formal respects, his office was a facsimile in small of that of the mayor proper. The function of the Mayor of the Bullring was not only to channel exuberant youthful energies in ways which were socially constructive (he officiated especially at military musters, for example, and was charged with prosecuting keepers of bawdy houses, a pursuit which offered a lucrative source of income to his office), but as the historian Richard Stanihurst colourfully described it, it also fell to him to manage ceremonies of particular concern to the young men of Dublin in which their civic rites of passage were performed.[100] Through his offices, the city's youth was inducted into the value system of the civic patriciate, a patriciate in which some of them would themselves play leading parts in the fulness of time. That induction might incidentally be fun to participate in, but at the end of the day its brief, succinctly captured in the motto that the city still uses, was a clear one: *Obedientia civium urbis felicitas*.[101] An important entrée to this value system was again via pageantry. From at least 1498 and its appearance in the Chain Book lists, the Mayor of the Bullring had been entrusted with responsibility for presenting the pageant of the Nine Worthies.[102] Whatever other reasons may have singled out those who played the Worthies for attention, one imagines that these young men would also have been picked from amongst the most physically imposing youth of Dublin (good grounds for assuming sturdy physique have already been inferred in the case of the two St Georges considered earlier). Doubtless the Worthies were all appropriately accoutred, too; by 1563, for example, their armorial bearings had all been carefully formulated in Gerard Legh's popular *Accedens of Armourye*. It seems likely that the Dublin Worthies pageant, at least in some of its incarnations subsequent to 1498, featured dialogue and set speeches, and it is not beyond possibility that these were once contained in a version of the acts of the Nine Worthies 'in ould English verse' that is now missing from London, British Library, MS Additional 33991, one of the compilations of the seventeenth-century Dublin antiquarian, Sir James Ware.[103] If Shakespeare's aborted presentation of the Worthies in *Love's Labours Lost* testifies to his comic irreverence towards the pageant, it also testifies to its institutional longevity in these islands. Perhaps too as an institution it creaked with venerability and was thus prone to parody: pageants of the Nine Worthies, like those in Dublin, had been played from at least the fifteenth century, and also, as in Dublin, they were often mobilized on civic occasions.[104]

After their 1498 appearance, the Worthies are mentioned in civic documents on another four occasions which cluster between 1541 and 1561. It is not necessarily to be inferred from this that a twenty-year period in the middle of the sixteenth century was the Worthies' heyday in Dublin, for incomplete record survival might be responsible for creating a lopsided impression. What may safely be inferred, however, is that since the pageant flourished through the reigns of at least five English monarchs with radically different confessional allegiances (from Henry VII to Elizabeth I), it evidently contained nothing offensive to the religious sensibilities of any party such as might bring it into disrepute and threaten its survival. It had nothing to fear in this respect. If the silence after 1561 is anything to judge by, then perhaps by that date the Worthies seemed part of a fatigued tradition, though that could hardly be maintained of their sponsoring office of the Mayor of the Bullring, for the last mention of this in corporation documents before the Commonwealth set in occurs in a series of accounts in the Treasurer's Book, dated between 20 April 1606 and 5 April 1607.[105] Nevertheless, a by-law passed on 27 October 1554 hints at a corporation now anticipating resistance, for whatever reason, to putting the pageant on: neglect of its performance would incur a fine of ten pounds payable to the city treasury, and a fine of six shillings and eight pence payable to the Mayor of the Bullring from any young man refusing to play his part once he had been selected.[106] Even more punitive was the fine laid on Mayors and Sheriffs of the Bullring generally negligent of their office, for on 16 July 1557 it was decreed that lapses on the part of the Mayor of the Bullring might incur a twenty-pound fine, and on the part of the Sheriffs, a ten-pound fine, in each case payable again to the city treasury.[107] Perhaps any neglect that befell either the pageant or the office was the result of the prospect of costs that participants in them might have to sustain out of their own pockets. Certainly in the case of the mayoralty proper, an incumbent's expenses could quickly mount up to a damaging liability which, civic grants notwithstanding, would be liable to fray his patience with the discharge of the costlier responsibilities of his office.

It suited the corporation to have some pageant at its beck and call, and in the Worthies it had one to hand which it could requisition whenever it needed bailing out of any potential ceremonial deficit. Evidently the Nine Worthies fitted the bill very well. Three of the occasions known about between 1541–61 on which the Worthies were played are informative. The first, in 1541, coincided with the Dublin parliament of that year, which in turn coincided with Corpus Christi (16 June). This was a feast at which the Worthies would have been presented in any event as part of a pageant series, but we are not told about any of the other pageants, only about the Worthies.[108] In the 1541 celebration at which the interests of the state, in the persons of the dignitaries who joined the Corpus Christi procession clad in their parliamentary robes, were more than usually prominent, the Worthies seem to have been reckoned sufficiently impressive to keep the corporation's end up. On the second occasion known about, in 1556–7, the Worthies appear also to have been accompanied by mounted trumpeters, whom the mayor provided with horses and rewarded to the tune of 20s sterling.[109] The Worthies were also treated to a civic dinner. It is not known for what occasion their performance in 1556–7 was staged – possibly it was for Corpus Christi again, for during Mary's reign the Catholic theology of this feast would have not seemed untoward – but like the 1541 performance, it took place outdoors. The 1561 performance, conversely, seems to have been part of an indoor banquet entertainment organized by the mayor for the new Lord Lieutenant, Sir Thomas Radcliffe, third earl of Sussex, though in falling on 5 June of that year, the performance again coincided with the feast of Corpus Christi. The venue for it is not specified, but it was likely to have been the Tholsel. This was the traditional focus for the round of civic hospitality, and the setting for many a civic dinner in the sixteenth century offered by the corporation to state officials.[110] In 1561 the city waits also played their music, possibly as an accompaniment to the Worthies and certainly to accompany the departing notables on their way back to their lodging in Thomas Court. Once again on this occasion, as in 1541, the civic authorities found the Worthies a convenient and appropriate entertainment to put on before the Crown's representative. So it would seem that the corporation found in the Worthies a versatile answer to its requirements: the young men of the city, the next generation of Dublin's civic aspiration and its hope for the future, paraded and performed at the behest of their elders before the powers that be of the state. Their performance in the Worthies added another distinctive strand to the tapestry of Dublin's pageantry. It was a strand in a general texture, to be sure, along with the pageants surveyed earlier, but like them, its public articulation of that part of the polity that it represented was in certain respects a unique one.

THE CITY MUSIC

The essential seriousness with which Dublin undertook its dramatic pageantry is underscored by its investment in another performance art which, as we have seen also in Gaelic Ireland, was ever likely to feature when drama or its kindred performances were being presented. Music attended the Worthies, for example, as it did St George: in both cases, it was the big, brass-band sound, resonant with royal overtones, that was heard.[111] The corporation financed music on two main fronts. On the one hand, it retained civic trumpeters and drummers whose performances were less of a purely musical than of a ceremonial nature. These men heralded public proclamations, for example, accompanied the mayor on progresses, assisted at musters or sounded for funerals. On the other hand, the corporation also retained the city waits, musicians who might be enlisted to play on similar ceremonial occasions, to be sure, but whose accomplishments might suit other kinds of event, like the Tholsel banquets, which were regular expressions of civic hospitality.[112] Stanihurst noted various mayors well known for having kept 'woorshipfull portes,' among whom was the same Robert Cusack seen earlier converting the fabric of St George's Chapel into an oven. Stanihurst went as far as to claim that hospitality in Dublin was a civic addiction.[113] Musicians would have had ample opportunity for employment in so convivial a context as this, if Stanihurst is to be believed. There may be a fine line to be drawn between the two categories of performer that I have distinguished, for it is entirely conceivable that a ceremonial trumpeter might take his turn as a wait, or vice versa, but for present purposes, my concern will principally be with those men whom the records term waits, musicians, or minstrels.

It would be misleading to speak of the Dublin waits as if they operated in a musical vacuum. This was certainly not the case, for Dublin was of sufficient size and means to be a centre for various sorts of musical skill. The two cathedrals, for example, had already by the fifteenth century established lively traditions of choral music, and the aristocratic households were also retaining musicians, as a later chapter will more fully reveal.[114] The point made earlier should also be recalled that itinerant musicians had long been entering Dublin from beyond the Pale. These various forms of musical activity within the city by no means occurred without their practitioners' awareness of each other, or without occasional mutual co-operation between them, the converse of the antagonism that records suggest more usually marred their relations. Thus, for example, the singing men of Christ Church might be invited to appear out of their regular liturgical context in order to 'sing in the said Courte after theire wonted manner,' or the cleric Walter Kennedy might be admitted to the franchises of the city on condition that he with his singing boys attend upon the mayor on ceremonial occasions.[115] Similarly, the city waits might be licensed to perform for local magnates like the earl of Kildare, or the retained musicians of those magnates might supply music that ordinarily the waits might have been expected to supply, as when the Tailors guild hired Lord Howth's musicians to play for some event when the Dublin waits, that day attending on the mayor, had been unavailable, or when the corporation paid the Lord Deputy's musicians 'for a play.'[116]

In appointing a band of waits, Dublin behaved like other cities of the British Isles and the Continent.[117] Waits first appear on record in Dublin in a civic edict of 4 October 1465, when two of them were appointed, John Colleron and Robert Hanwood:

Item hyt graunt by the Sayd Semble {'assembly'} that Iohn Colleron & Robert hanwod schall be waytys within the Sayd Citte takyng for þer wagis as otherys hath don be for in the Sayd offyce that ys to sey iiij d. of euery hall & ij d. of euery schope wyth in the sayd Citte & þer fyndynges {'maintenance'} on þe Iures {'aldermen'} & euery of þem a liuere {'livery'} gown of Mayre & Baylyfys[118]

It is, however, quite clear from this entry that their office had existed much earlier in the city. The provision towards their wages of 4d levied on every hall and of 2d on every shop compares exactly with a provision made some ten years earlier, on 23 April 1456, for the city 'pyperys,' and this exact correspondence in the terms of payment suggests that the 'pyperys' of the earlier edict were indeed musicians, not merely civic plumbers. Though not designated as waits as such, the 1456 'pyperys' were also paid for 'hare {'their'} wachyng abowt þe town' and for 'þe making of þe pypys of þe sayd Cytte for A yere.'[119] It therefore seems that pipes of some sort (perhaps shawms?) constituted the earliest recorded instruments played by the Dublin waits. In view of this, the first Dublin piper on record, 'Willielmus le pipere,' who appeared in the roll of the Dublin Guild Merchant for 1246–7, may conceivably have been a civic employee functioning in a similar capacity.[120] The fact that part of the job of the 1456 'pyperys' entailed 'wachyng' around the city connects the Dublin waits of this date with the earlier function of waits in these islands as watchmen, a function that seems steadily to have decreased as their more purely musical duties took over.[121] Part of the waits' brief in a later edict of 24 October 1466 also required them to 'wache';[122] by the sixteenth century, 'wachyng' is seldom mentioned amongst the waits' duties, though it may be that this aspect had been implicit in the circuit of the city that from at least 20 January 1570 the waits were required to make on three days each week.[123] The 1465 edict is also of interest for its prescription of the responsibility of the aldermen ('Iures') for the waits' maintenance, and for the fact that both Colleron and Hanwood were to be provided with a livery gown at the expense of the mayor and bailiffs. Provision of their upkeep and apparel was thus carefully enjoined upon the central personnel of the corporation, and this arrangement serves as an index of the institutional importance of the waits and of the centrality of their office in helping to bear up the pomp and circumstance of civic authority.[124] Livery payments run throughout the sixteenth and seventeenth centuries with great regularity in the Treasurer's Book and the Assembly Rolls.[125] In addition, the waits' provision with a livery would have set a distinctive seal on what they did. It should be recalled that the wearing of a livery at this date conferred an important social passport upon its wearer. The nature of the waits' medieval livery is unspecified, though conceivably it resembled its sixteenth-century counterpart, about which rather more is known. By 1570, their livery coat was officially required to bear 'a cognisaunce of this Cittie,' and by 1599, not only was the city's badge to appear on the livery cloak, but the material from which it was made had to be of blue watchet cloth.[126] (A legislation of 1624 was at pains to preserve the distinctiveness of the civic colours by requiring that members of the Tailors guild add their own arms to their livery which was 'onelie white and watchett with a redd cross, without any difference whereby it might be discearned or known from the city cullors.')[127] Possibly these requirements were formalizations of earlier practice, but what is clear is that the liveried uniformity of the Dublin waits, at least by the sixteenth century if not before, would have proclaimed the corporate ownership of their musical activity at the same time as it also conferred upon them their coveted civic status. That the corporation considered itself their principal proprietor is also clear not only from its decrees concerning their livery, but also from its repeated statements about their attendance on the mayor's pleasure. Absenteeism amongst waits was likely, considering that their musical skills were saleable and evidently in demand. It has already been observed that the earl of Kildare showed interest in them, and that on at least two occasions the Tailors would have hired them for their own festivities had they not already been attending the mayor or otherwise going about their civic duty. Since they might be enticed away from the corporation by other potential patrons, their wearing of livery might also have served as a useful personal reminder of the civic hand that chiefly fed them, and of what their prior responsibilities in that direction were. Yet they might also act as ambassadors of the corporation's prestige, and the corporation seems to have recognized the demand they were in and to have responded to it most reasonably by granting them leave to depart the city subject to the mayor's prior approval.

As was seen, Dublin waits are first on record from 1465, when two men were appointed, though the arrangements to pay the 1456 'pyperys' in a similar manner suggests that city waits existed by at least the mid-fifteenth century. It may be that a two-man band was a normal size at that date. What relation, if any, William Lawless and his *mimi* may have had in 1436 to the corporation is unknown, but his petition reveals that a number of minstrels, presumably more than two, were already organized into some sort of professional body before the Dublin waits were first officially heard of.[128] Perhaps it would be appropriate to imagine an earlier period in the city's history in which there existed an organized minstrel troupe that might serve the needs of various patrons, but that as time went by, the corporation came more exclusively to retain musicians of its own. Even after the Dublin waits first appeared, the need for a minstrel troupe of the sort suggested by the 1436 document would not necessarily have vanished, and such a state of affairs is perhaps hinted at behind a much later appointment, on 16 July 1591, of Edward Gore and his associate musicians as Dublin waits: these men had evidently already been active as a musical band before their appointment attached them to the corporation.

If the earliest waits were only two in number, this small complement did not last very long into the next century. Payments in 1549 and 1550 to the fiddler Patrick Cawyll and to one Bullock, a taborer, may be amongst the last of this kind.[129] There would soon be four of them, a figure which can be deduced from the yardage of livery cloth that the waits were often assigned.[130] Four waits are also explicitly mentioned in a payment for liveries made to Thomas Quycke in the financial year ending 29 September 1568.[131] Quycke himself seems to have been a drummer or taborer (a percussionist was commonly a member of such a musical band), and may have been the senior wait in whom the responsibility for distributing the corporation's payment was vested.[132] A tradition of waits in Dublin may have been unbroken at least from the time of their earliest recorded appearance until the seventeenth century, even if the quality and number of the band may have fluctuated, and even if its members were not always referred to specifically as waits but as 'minstrels' or 'musicians.' Lack of evidence for 'waits' as such after 1465 does not necessarily mean that their office fell into decay but perhaps rather that records of it have not survived; when in a set of accounts dated between 29 September 1545 and 4 November

1546 the 'mynstrals of the Cittie' were paid 40s for their liveries, it is most likely that these minstrels were waits in function, even though not in name.[133]

As for the musical forces which they employed, scattered pieces of evidence refer to pipes of some sort, fiddles, hautboys, and tabors, as well as human voices and the requirement, from the sixteenth century on, to 'keepe alwayes a good singinge boy from time to time.'[134] Such forces compare with those deployed by the waits of English cities.[135] Trumpets occur only in references to the corporation's ceremonial (largely outdoor) music.[136] This is not surprising, since brass fanfare instruments would not have been suited to sustained playing at more intimate gatherings like dinners, though as has been noted, there may have been some commerce between those who played them and the waits proper. In fact, an excellent example of the concerted mixing of instruments of ceremony with those more usually associated with the dining hall is afforded in a Gaelic context in which is described that typically English phenomenon, an egress of *æs ciuil na cathrach* ('city musicians') to meet an incoming dignitary. There were *orgán 7 gitart 7 galltrumpa 7 tabur 7 fhedan 7 cruiti 7 clairsigh 7 na huili archena* ('organs and gitterns and clarions and tabors and pipes and lutes and harps and all other sorts of instruments').[137] The text in which the description appears, although a fifteenth-century translation into Irish of a fictional Middle English text, a Romance of Sir Guy of Warwick, would nevertheless have introduced its Gaelic readers to the possibility of a mixed ensemble of city musicians who on occasion joined forces; indeed, Gaelic readers of literature of this sort could have encountered in reality the English *æs ciuil na cathrach* of the kind the Romance describes, whether in Dublin or in one of the other walled towns of Ireland.[138]

Harpers, those musicians with whom Gaelic Ireland abounded and who are prominent among the *æs ciuil na cathrach* of the Romance, are never explicitly mentioned in Dublin's records concerning waits, though from the earliest days of the city's Hiberno-English settlement, there is ample evidence that harpers were at large there and sometimes in volatile circumstances: in one late-thirteenth-century prosecution, a certain Roger le Harpour successfully sued Robert le Feure, whom he claimed had maliciously broken his harp by hurling a stone at it, damaging it to the tune of 2s,[139] and one sixteenth-century lawsuit even revolved around the murder of one harper by another.[140] Harpers might play in eminent and more tranquil contexts, as the reward of 3d 'to the little harper' (*parvo Cittheratori*) for his entertainment on 23 January 1338 in the chamber of the prior of Holy Trinity suggests.[141] Perhaps their absence from references to the waits is again to be attributed to lack of evidence, for it is interesting to note that James Hanwood, a harper who appears in a Dublin record of 11 May 1487, shared his surname with one of the two first recorded Dublin waits, Robert Hanwood, who had earlier been appointed to office on 4 October 1465.[142]

Whether Robert and James were actually related is unknown, but the possibility suggested by the shared surnames of these two fifteenth-century musicians, that professional music might run in families, is certainly proveable by the late sixteenth and early seventeenth century.[143] The Huggard family is a clear case in point. The first mention of William Huggard occurs in the Dublin Assembly Rolls on 12 October 1599 in an entry confirming that he and his fellow musicians should continue to enjoy the same stipend as was formerly levied for them on the citizens, provided that they observed certain conditions.[144] (The documentation of the earlier arrangement made for them has not survived.) Perhaps William had immediately succeeded Edward Gore, appointed with his fellow waits on 22 October 1591.[145] William was subsequently admitted to the city franchises by a special grace and on payment of a 20s fine to the Treasury on 21 October 1603.[146] His eldest son, John, was admitted to the franchises by virtue of his father's free status on 24 June 1607, and he took over the ensemble on 15 October 1632 after his father's death.[147] This would have been when he was about forty-five years old.[148] He was well situated to carry out his duties, since by 1626 he is also known to have been living in the city centre, in Fishamble Street, and he remained there, probably not far from the rest of the Huggard family, at least until 1646.[149] Another of William's sons, Nicholas, was admitted to the franchises on 20 January 1621 and again as a musician. Hence for a few years in the seventeenth century, it appears that the Dublin waits were largely recruited from the Huggard family.[150] In respect of the pursuit of music within families, official musicians within the Pale seem to have had something in common with their Gaelic colleagues without.

If, to judge by the waits' own complaints, there was plenty of professional music to be had in Dublin, the corporation could rely on recruiting around itself a musical establishment of quality. The waits got a good deal – regular liveried employment, an official musical monopoly,[151] licence to earn extra income, subject to the mayor's approval, from other patrons[152] – and so did the corporation, which could soon terminate employment if the waits' conduct or music failed to please; there would always be others eager to step into their shoes and don their privileges. Through this patronage the corporation's status, blazoned in so many ways by visual pageantry, would further have been bruited by accomplished concerted music. Power was to be heard as well as seen.

ORATIONS AND EXTRAORDINARY BESPEAKS

Since such a dendritic network of patronage and supervision has emerged from this analysis of the nature of the corporation's involvement with drama and the performing arts, the conclusion necessarily follows that they were central to bodying forth the whole idea of the corporation and of what it stood for. They provided the symbolic language through which the corporation might articulate itself. If Dublin acquired its grasp of this language largely in response to political circumstances, that grasp in time became a fluent and sophisticated one. Moreover, it was a language that entered into subtle dialogue with other interest groups both within the city and without: within, inside Dublin's own body politic, teaching the enfranchised the terms in which they ought properly to conceive of themselves and of the nature of their social role; and without, expressing the reconciliation and happy union of the city's authority with that of the state. One of the nodal occasions for express-ing the latter sort of liaison, a liaison already partly investigated in the context of St George's Day pageantry, was the open-air civic oration. This was a conspicuous and stage-managed public performance offered to mark joyful occasions of national importance in the life of the colony. The fact that the corporation chose to spend handsomely on orations is a basic proof of the earnest with which they were under-taken. And as a later chapter will show, other walled towns in Ireland at this date, like Limerick, Waterford, and Kilkenny, could present civic orations with all the full-blown colour of drama proper.

In sixteenth-century Dublin, it is less evident that the various civic orations on record were dramatic in any mimetic sense, but their attendant circumstances were no less comparable to those of other places in Ireland where orations of a dramatic kind are known indubitably to have been delivered. It is also hard to imagine the capital incapable of outflanking a Limerick or a Waterford, and therefore on circum-stantial grounds too, it seems unlikely that Dublin's civic orations would have come off without some benefit from the performing arts.

Orations often took place in the context of a solemn procession of the mayor, aldermen, and citizens to greet the honorand of the day, indeed in the sort of egress that was described in the Romance of Sir Guy of Warwick. In August 1534, it fell to the lot of the city recorder, Thomas Fitzsimon, to congratulate the newly arrived Lord Deputy, Sir William Skeffington, and the earl of Kildare, 'in a pithy oration.'[153] This civic egress with its accompanying oration, the first of its kind in Dublin on record, took place on the green of St Mary's Abbey, but no further detail of the cir-cumstances of the oration's delivery is known. The choice of venue was perhaps dic-tated by the landing of the Lord Deputy in a port on the north side of the city.[154] On the south side the Hoggen Green, traditionally the site of so many different sorts of display, as was earlier seen, also not surprisingly served as host to official welcoming parties, as when on 16 January 1566 the mayor and aldermen went out to meet Sir Henry Sidney, recently appointed Lord Deputy, as he rode in to Dublin.[155] The two orations whose circumstances are most clearly discernible in civic records fall at the end of the century. Sometime between the Michaelmasses of 1598 and 1599, Sir Robert Devereux, twentieth earl of Essex, was received into the city. Gun-powder was expended at his reception (probably on gun salutes), a trumpeter was hired to meet him, and four ells of sarsenet were purchased to make scarves for the 'leders' when the citizens greeted him.[156] A pew was made for the orator, George Lye, to stand in, and expenses were laid out on beautifying the place in which the oration was delivered. Where this was is not revealed, but evidently the locale was decorated, perhaps with bunting and foliage or the like. One of the most expensive items that the corporation had to find was the commission for the oration itself, for which Lye was paid a handsome £3 10s sterling. The second oration from this period, or rather orations, were those welcoming the Lord Deputy, Sir Charles Blount, Lord Mountjoy, after his victorious return from the siege of Kinsale.[157] They were delivered in a 'convenient place' at St Catherine's Church in St Thomas's Street, another extramural space though this time one to the west of the city walls, and a stage was repaired from which the two orators spoke. One of these was a certain Matthew Lye, whose surname perhaps relates him to the George Lye who had orated three years earlier at the Devereux reception. Like George before him, Matthew too was well paid (£3 sterling), as was his co-orator, a Mr Fyrewelthe. On this occasion the two orations were by far the most expensive item on the corporation's bill, exceeding even the 41s 8d spent by the citizens in gunpowder for an accompanying 'showe.'

If it was not just the midnight oil that the corporation was paying so generously for when it reimbursed Mr Fyrewelthe and the Lyes for composing their orations, then the orations themselves must have required something extra whose costs the orators' fee was partly intended to offset. Whether that extra something was an expenditure on the dramatic is not known. For example, if the orators were garbed in some distinctive manner, if they uttered their speeches in the guise of an adopted persona, costumes might have needed purchasing, and would have moved the event further in the direction of a dramatic spectacle.[158] But this is speculation. What at least seems more secure is the identification of the profession of one of the orators and his profession's liability to attract extraordinary bespeaks of the dramatic kind. Nothing has yet come to light about the professions of the Lyes and Mr Fyrewelthe, though the earliest of the named Dublin orators, Thomas Fitzsimon, was city recorder, the sort of literate professional whom one might well expect to find offered an oratorial commission. But another kind of professional liable to attract such commissions was the schoolmaster. Richard Stanihurst included in his list of Dublin schoolmasters one Michael Fitzsimon, a man who had written an *Orationem in aduentum comitis Essexiæ Dublinium*.[159] Though it is not clear that Fitzsimon had also personally delivered this speech, Renaissance schoolmasters, as is common knowledge, were often well versed in dramatic presentation, if for no other reason than that they might study classical dramas as part of the curriculum.[160] Some wrote plays themselves, and others encouraged their charges to take part in them as a form of moral recreation. In these circumstances, the corporation's reward to its schoolmaster, David Duke, for his efforts on 1 April 1583 should come as no surprise. The Treasurer's Book and other corporation documents make it clear that the corporation, assuming some of the educational responsibilities that before the Dissolution were likely to have fallen upon the religious houses, maintained a school and sponsored a schoolmaster there from at least the early 1560s.[161] In 1583 David Duke was appointed, and in the same year he was also paid the sum of 26s 8d by a warrant of the mayor and aldermen for his pains in playing an interlude on Black Monday (1 April in that year).[162] This, the earliest surviving reference to an interlude in Ireland, is tantalizing in its brevity. Did Duke himself play in the interlude, or did he produce it? Or did he do both? If he produced it, one is inclined to imagine that he would have cast some of his pupils in its roles. The first unambiguous record of the casting of children in dramatic roles in Ireland dates several years later, to the year 1620, but there is no reason to suppose that children could not have been used in 1583.[163] In various ways in the latter part of the sixteenth century, Dublin was consciously emulating London's example, and the drafting of schoolboys into plays would have been in keeping with what had already been for many years since the English capital's practice.[164] That Duke was involved in an *interlude* may also be suggestive of the circumstances of its performance. The interlude was often presented at mealtimes as an indoor sport.[165] One put on as here in the context of the Black Monday celebrations could well have been offered as an entertainment at a civic dinner in the Tholsel. This suggestion also takes some colour from the fact that the mayor and aldermen had a penchant for the private dramatic bespeak during this period; a few years later, in the summer of 1589, they rewarded the queen's players with £3 sterling (£4 Irish).[166] Judging by the reward that the troupe of the queen's players got, it might be that the (proportionally) rather larger sum voted to David Duke was not simply a personal gratuity, but also a fee intended to help meet his production costs.[167]

THESEUS What are they that do play it?
PHILOSTRATE Hard-handed men that work in Athens here,
Which never labour'd in their minds till now.
(William Shakespeare, *A Midsummer Night's Dream* V.i.71–3)[168]

As its unfolding would prove only too well, Theseus's curiosity about the men who were to present the interlude of *Pyramus and Thisbe* at his wedding banquet had been justly satisfied by Philostrate his revels' master. Whether the hard-handed men who also laboured in Dublin fared like the mechanicals who 'never labour'd in their minds till now' is quite another matter, however. It seems appropriate to return finally to them, since this chapter has by and large been preoccupied with the performance efforts of other parts of the community. Dublin may not have had any equivalents of Shakespeare's tinker and his bellows-mender that we know about, but it had its carpenters, joiners, weavers, and tailors, all of whom were active in play and pageant production, and doubtless more proficiently than any Quince, Snug, Bottom, or Starveling: the artisans of Dublin, those included in the Chain Book pageant lists, had already for many years been immersed in play and pageant production even before the lists were drafted. By the sixteenth century, therefore, they were hardly novices. The guild book of the Tailors and that of the Carpenters, Millers, Masons, and Heliers, afford a few further glimpses into the practical arrangements that Dublin's mechanicals were wont to make for pageant performance, and these deserve notice for the additional colour that they lend to the picture.

In 1498, the Carpenters were one of the groups responsible for the composite sixth pageant of the Corpus Christi procession discussed in the previous chapter. This pageant included, along with Joseph, Mary, and the baby Jesus, a camel. In the Christmastide show of 1528 on the Hoggen Green, the Carpenters were again presenting the story of Joseph and Mary. Whether their camel put in an appearance is not recorded, but like the corporation's dragon, it too seems to have secured a firm place for itself in Dublin's pageant tradition, and also like the dragon, its construction may have been from similar components. In a set of accounts dating between 22 April 1546 and 28 January 1547, a payment of 9d was made for timber for the 'Gamayll.'[169] Payments were also made for eight hoops at a penny a hoop and for 3d worth of nails. The three men who dressed the 'Gamayll' were also paid 20d in food, drink, and wages.[170] A good ten years later, in a set of accounts running between 17 November 1558 and 16 November 1559, the 'Gaymaylle' was dressed again, though on this occasion only 4d sterling was paid, and nails cost 2d sterling, as did hoops.[171] The use of hoops and nails in 'Gamayll' construction is directly comparable to the construction requirements for dragons, and perhaps not surprisingly when, as was seen in the previous chapter, these pageants seem to have been fundamentally similar in that they appear not to have been propelled like any of the rest, but to have been *carried* in some way. For example, in a set of dragon-building accounts which features in a longer account list in the Treasurer's Book and which was presented on 5 November 1560, a hooper was paid 10s 4d for mending the dragon, and this payment included the cost of its linen cloth and nails. A further payment for its subsequent painting was even more expensive, and came to 12s.[172] What appears to have been required for both camel and dragon was a wooden or wickerwork chassis with hoops, over which was nailed linen cloth, then the whole was painted and given its distinctive finishing touches. One, or perhaps two, porters would have animated each of these beasts.[173] Hence unlike the *ersatz* props got up by Shakespeare's crew, Dublin's mechanicals took the construction of their animal pageants seriously enough, and this doubtless applied too in the case of the construction of the pageant wagons themselves, the evidence for which was surveyed in the previous chapter. The painted wagon which in the mid-sixteenth century carried Stephen Casse in his role as Pilate (or Emperor, as players of this part also seem to have been called by this date) had paraded on it a correspondingly colourful cast. Several records between 1555 and 1569 in the Tailors guild account book itemize props and clothes whose quality and state of repair were being carefully monitored. Pilate (alias the Emperor) was often provided with gloves, as was his Lady Empress, though perhaps as favours rather than as parts of a pageant costume.[174] Twice his 'head' was painted.[175] This 'head' may have been some kind of headpiece which covered his head completely, or a wig, or a mask, or both: the exact meaning of the word is uncertain.[176] He was also provided with swords in 1560. The fact that these were plural may suggest that we have to deal here not simply with the inert symbols of his *imperium*, but with props actively manipulated at some stage during pageant performance; the fact that one of the swords is 'trimmed' in 1567 at the cost of 6d, and one 'mended' for the same price in 1569, seems also to imply as much. How they may have been used in the livelier way proposed is unknown, but a sword-juggling Pilate might not have been inconceivable, a character in the mould of the sword-juggling King Herod ingeniously conjectured to have performed in the city of Chester at about the same time.[177] To complete the picture, Pilate's 'head' was also crowned, as was that of his Empress.

It is unfortunate that more records of this order have not survived, for what few there are show promise of a once vivid theatricality that was doubtless not confined to the guilds of the Tailors and of the Carpenters, Millers, Masons, and Heliers. Equally on account of this loss, the nature of the collaboration between trades guilds and the corporation on pageant days has been robbed of definition. In the only surviving clue to the storage of costumes and props in Dublin from one year to the next, for example, the Tailors come again to the fore on 22 July 1558, when they were housing the corporation's own props for St George in their guild hall in Wine-tavern Street.[178] Their accommodation of the St George trappings also in some measure rendered them partners in pageantry and assenters to the agenda of civic display that was investigated earlier. It should come as no surprise, therefore, to find that 1569, the last year in which the Tailors' pageant gear is on record as being refurbished, coincides exactly with the last recorded mention of Corpus Christi in the corporation's documents.

CODA

Times change, and with them Dublin's political reality. The last quarter of the sixteenth century, a period marked by mounting tensions between city and government, had also seen the demise of St George and Corpus Christi from the city's records and account books. St George is last heard of in the Treasurer's Book in a set of accounts for 1566–7, and the celebrations on Corpus Christi in 1565, when they were being explicitly forbidden by the Lord Justice, Sir Nicholas Arnold.[179] This can hardly be coincidental, or indeed just a death following naturally upon the loss of St George's Chapel or the suppression of Corpus Christi as a liturgical feast. Dublin from 1568 was reinvesting in the franchise riding, less a spectacle of power sharing in the mode of St George pageantry than of naked claim staking. The 1584 legislation for the riding, whose wording, as we saw, betrayed the city's nervousness about losing its privileges if the riding lapsed, was framed when the repercussions of the Baltinglass rebellion were still being felt. Not fully four years earlier, in July 1580, James Eustace, Viscount Baltinglass, a staunch believer in papal supremacy, had led a military rising against the Protestant administration of Dublin. The severe measures adopted by the administration for putting the rebellion down left a legacy of bad feeling which served only to widen a rift that had already been steadily growing between municipality and government.[180] In so changed a climate, some of the older civic rituals were no longer appropriate; their optimistic message of collaboration was now a vainer hope than it may once have seemed.[181] The last celebrations of St George's Day for which evidence survives before the sixteenth century drew to a close appear to have been impressive ones. On 23 April 1578, the same day that he received his letter of final recall from Elizabeth I, Sir Henry Sidney rode in solemn procession in his Garter robes to Christ Church. The cathedral choir was hung about with blue broadcloth, on which were embossed 'the armes of the companyons of the most noble order of the garter all gorgiusly wrought in metall.'[182] Sidney had long been an observer of the feast, for his household accounts of 1568–70 detail payments to one 'Henry Dillon for making a Standard and gylding banqueting disshes against St Georges ffeast in Reward xiij s. iiij d.' and to 'Sundrie Trompetors at the said St georges feast in Rewarde xl s.'[183] Whatever the domestic dimension accompanying the 1578 observance, it was certainly also displayed sumptuously in the streets. The second extant account of St George's Day comes at the very end of the century. To hail the arrival in April 1599 of Sir Robert Devereux, earl of Essex, as Lord Lieutenant of Ireland, Dublin saw a 'magnificente and princelie celebracion of Sainct Georges feaste (with a multitude of Nobles and Gallantes of great esteeme …).'[184] On both of these occasions, however, the public St George's Day celebrations seem to have been instigated not by the corporation, but by the government.[185] It was pageantry of this quality whose nuances were so unerringly read by Fynes Moryson.[186] Reflecting on the celebrations of 1601, he said, 'no doubt, as there is a secret mystery of State in these solemne pomps; and as his Lordship therein, for his person and carriage, was most comely, and (if I may vse the word) Maiesticall; so the magnificence of this feast wrought in the hearts of those Rebels, and by their relation in the hearts of others after submitting … such an awfull respect to her Maiesty, and such feare tempred with loue to his Lordship, as much auailed to containe them in due obedience.'[187] Rebellion outside the city walls, in the lawless lands beyond the Pale, was nothing new, and doubtless it was this that Moryson chiefly had in mind, especially when Dublin Castle was at that time hosting those Irish chieftains who, following Lord Deputy Blount's winter campaign of 1600–1, were now suing for pardon and reinstatement. But at the time Moryson wrote, the awesomeness of state that so struck him was something that would not altogether be wasted on the citizens of Dublin either. If some of the heart had gone out of the playing together of corporation and government, their staying together would have to continue, however less cordially; too many vested interests were at stake on both sides to permit anything else.

4

Drama and the Performing Arts
in Old Kilkenny

'The best vplandish towne ... in Ireland.'

Richard Stanihurst, *A playne and perfect description of Irelande*

'Municipium est nitidum, elegans, copiosum, & inter mediterranea huius insulæ facilè primum.'
('A beautiful, elegant, abundantly furnished town, and easily chiefest amongst the inland towns of this island.')

William Camden, *Britannia*[1]

If Dublin's Corpus Christi pageantry was derelict by the end of the sixteenth century, there was one Irish town where it was still thriving. Remarkably, it also throve there until at least 1637, which probably makes it the longest lived of any of the Corpus Christi dramas known in the British Isles. Its longevity was nourished on an unusual cocktail of circumstances: the town's relative distance from Dublin, the centre of English reform and conformity, relieved it of the obligation of having to behave as a dedicated follower of the capital's fashion; it had its own particular agendas which drama and pageantry, as in Dublin, could eloquently help to express; and its sense of corporate identity, as also in Dublin, had become firmly wedded to those great moments of self-definition that its days of drama and pageantry afforded. The town of Kilkenny (from 1609, city), located about seventy miles southwest of Dublin, was to prove a serious rival to the capital in the extent of its investment in comparable forms of public display; after such displays in Dublin had become extinct, Kilkenny's would be left unchallenged.

While Richard Stanihurst's opinion of the town was high and vocal enough, that of William Camden, elegantly turned in Latin, was expressed with additional flourishes. Both men had independently made up their minds about Kilkenny's considerable merits. Stanihurst knew the place especially well since he had been sent there from Dublin in the 1550s in order to attend the celebrated grammar school run by Dr Peter White. Stanihurst was enthusiastic even without the benefit of having witnessed the ambitious building projects that characterized the town in the latter part of the century. Had he seen these, one suspects that his enthusiasm might have reached heights higher still. By about 1600, the bricks-and-mortar testimony to Kilkenny's accumulated prosperity had been rendered strikingly palpable in many pieces of civic architecture, not least in the mansions of the burgesses, some of which still stand in the centre of the modern city.

Kilkenny, situated on a bridging point on the river Nore and within the small fertile plain that lies at the centre of its county, enjoyed comparative affluence throughout Stanihurst's and Camden's time. It had long been the chief seat of the Butlers, earls of Ormond, whose castle stands to this day on a knoll on the city's western edge. The tenth earl, Sir Thomas Butler (1531–1614), or Tomás dubh ('Black Tom') as he was more familiarly known, was an especial favourite of Elizabeth I.[2] By all accounts a handsome man and endowed with nature's gifts, he had also benefited from the gifts of nurture, having received his education with Edward VI at the English court. He was also a cousin of the Boleyns. Not only was he therefore thoroughly at home in Protestant London, where he might bask in his queen's favour at first hand, but he was astute enough to make the most of the advantages that he enjoyed abroad for the undergirding of his interests at home in Ireland. Here he fostered relations with burgess agents in Kilkenny whose business activities had already been attracting wealth into the region. Consequently, the town's prosperity was further promoted by the earl's collaboration with a closely knit group of successful Anglo-Irish merchants who, like their earl, were for the most part loyal friends to the Crown, even if seldom like-minded in matters of confessional allegiance.[3] Although, to be sure, there would be various occasions in the sixteenth century when the county of Kilkenny would be obliged to pay a high price for its loyalty, Kilkenny town itself was usually left unscathed by any harrying. Its merchant families had established trade links within Ireland and abroad, especially with Bristol and Flanders, and as will be seen, it would be their finances, as much as their piety, that impelled Kilkenny's Corpus Christi and Midsummer drama: after the earl himself, it was one of their number who was perhaps to be counted the richest man in Kilkenny, and members of his family, no less than the families of the other burgesses, would play a substantial part in maintaining the town's old established dramatic traditions in a healthy condition long after they had vanished elsewhere.[4]

Well before the sixteenth century had come bringing with it a social and economic climate peculiarly congenial to drama and the performing arts, circumstances favourable to them had already been developing from medieval times. In the first place, Kilkenny had a long history of urban settlement, with all the potential resources of civic cooperation that that might put at the disposal of any incipient dramatic enterprise. An important ecclesiastical site was founded with a church of St Cainnech (or in Irish, a *cill Chainnig*, from which the modern place name derives) long before the Anglo-Normans invaded in the 1170s,[5] and after the invasion, the native Irish found themselves not so much expelled as assimilated into or at least accommodated near the society of the newcomers. Conspicuous among the outward and visible signs of this Hiberno-Norman rapprochement was the creation of an Irishtown with its own administrative system and corporation. The Irishtown was located beyond the Bregagh, a stream flowing into the Nore a little to the east of Kilkenny's walls (these were built in the first half of the thirteenth century), and it centred around the substantial, thirteenth-century cathedral that had been raised over an earlier Hiberno-Romanesque church of St Cainnech (see St Canice's Cathedral, fig. 15).[6] The Irishtown was in effect an acknowledgment of an earlier Irish status quo now brought within the pale of an Anglo-Norman administration. It was governed by a portreeve who acted under the supreme authority of the bishop of Ossory. The epicentre of the Anglo-Norman administration, on the other hand, was in the Englishtown or Hightown, that portion of Kilkenny to the west of the Bregagh and enclosed within the walls. The Hightown also had a corporation of its own. It was governed by a sovereign (mayor from 1609), annually elected on the Monday next after Midsummer from among a body of twelve councillors (aldermen from 1609).[7] These twelve councillors, the greater twelve, served for life. They are likely to have been selected from the merchants and legal men of the town. Under them was another group of councillors, the lesser twelve or the demi-councillors, who seem conversely to have been closely associated with the trades. Office amongst the lesser twelve went on election, possibly by the commons in the county hundred.[8]

Assimilation, of course, is likely to be a two-way business, and such proved the case in Kilkenny. Not only had Hightown and Irishtown to accommodate each other's jurisdictions (sometimes not without friction), but cheek-by-jowl existence with the 'wild Irish,' who were never very far away, was also liable to leave its mark on civic mores. By 1366, alarm at the rapid acculturation of the Anglo-Norman lords to a Gaelic life-style, and not only in Kilkenny but generally throughout the province, issued in the Statute of Kilkenny mentioned in earlier chapters and which, amongst other corrupting influences, identified Irish minstrels *cestascavoir Tympanors fferdanes, Skelaghes, Bablers, Rymors, Clercz ne nullez autres minstrells Irrois* ('that is to say, players of the *timpán*, poets, storytellers, babblers, rhymers, clerks, nor any other Irish minstrels') and tried to prevent them from coming amongst the English.[9] The statute, the Anglo-Normans' belated reaction to the unforeseen consequences of their tolerance, was directed here against entertainers and minstrels from the native Gaelic tradition, not against any ones who may have come over from England in Anglo-Norman entourages at the time of the invasion. As has

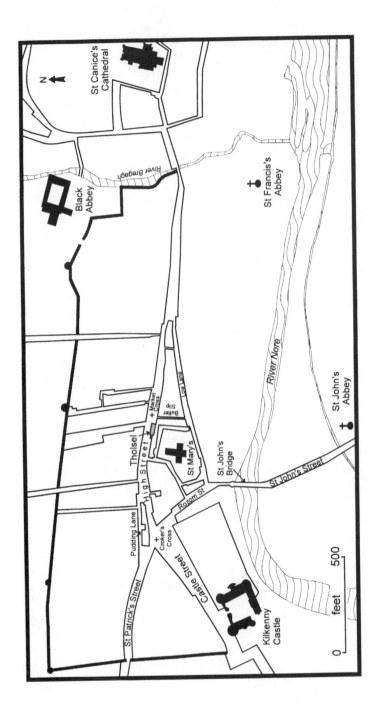

15 Kilkenny *c* 1600 (selected sites only).

been seen, Ireland had a highly developed and organized travelling minstrel class well before the Anglo-Normans ever set foot in the island. Judging by the statute, Gaelic minstrels were successfully competing for patronage within the walled towns (Dublin's state in this respect was considered in the previous chapter and a particularly well documented case of 1315 from co. Cork in chapter 1). From the earliest times in these islands, evidence has survived of commerce between entertainers of different ethnic traditions; it is likely that any entertainments introduced into Kilkenny by native Gaelic minstrels would have been compounded with entertainments imported by the Anglo-Norman settlers, and as in so many other walks of life, so too in the area of the performing arts there would doubtless have occurred a lively exchange of skills and expertise.

Kilkenny also soon became a home to those traditional patrons of sanitized forms of entertainment, the friars. They settled in Kilkenny early on and by the end of the thirteenth century were flourishing there.[10] In the early fourteenth century Richard Ledrede, Franciscan bishop of Ossory, proved a true son of his order when he devised pious Latin alternatives to the *cantilenis teatralibus turpibus & secularibus* ('theatrical, base, and secular songs') with which clerics of his cathedral were wont to 'pollute their throats and mouths.'[11] Whether his *contrafacta* caught on or not is unknown, but at any rate the disgraceful *cantilenae* were flourishing. Whether or not the friars ever sponsored religious drama in Kilkenny is also undisclosed, but they are not likely to have been adverse to any steps taken in that direction when dramatic representation was so much in keeping with the ethos of religious affectivity that pervaded their order.[12] As well as the high profile of the mendicants there, and the cultural implications of that, Kilkenny was becoming a noteworthy centre by virtue of royal visitations and the parliaments and synods which it was also hosting. For example, when Richard II made his visits to Kilkenny Castle in the 1390s, now the home of James Butler, third earl of Ormond (a fluent Irish speaker, incidentally, Kilkenny Statute notwithstanding), the occasions would presumably not have passed off without festivity of any kind.[13] Even if the earl could not come up with any suitably convivial pastimes (which seems highly improbable), evenings would not have been left altogether cheerless if Richard II's harper William Dodmore (alias William Blyndharpour) had anything to do with it.[14] The political power of the house of Ormond, though temporarily eclipsed during the mid-fifteenth century, shone out once more on the accession of Henry VII, for the Butlers had customarily supported the Lancastrian cause. From the late fifteenth century on, Kilkenny started to recover lost ground, and by the later sixteenth century, the time when Stanihurst and Camden knew it, the royal favour shielding it would deflect the worst effects of the depredations which followed in the wake of Elizabeth I's plans for the reconquest of Ireland.[15]

JOHN BALE AND THE ROMISH CATERPILLARS

The times, therefore, were propitious, and if it is not until the middle of the century that the first unequivocal records of dramatic activity appear, then the reason for that is most likely to be laid at the door of document loss. However, before we move on to consider more closely the remarkable circumstances of this apparent début, it should be appreciated that it occurred in the context of a community whose sense of identity, as has been mentioned, was also textured in terms both of its confessional sympathies and of its loyalties to the Crown. The early days of the Reformation in Ireland, presided over by the likes of such conservative Henricians as Archbishop George Browne of Dublin, were evidently not proving too disconcerting an upheaval: the liturgical reforms of the first Book of Common Prayer of 1549 had not been so strident that unreformed sensibilities would inevitably have been outraged by them, and it is clear that the order for Holy Communion in the first Prayer Book could be so conducted as to make celebrations appear very much in the spirit of the old Mass. This was the relatively tranquil accommodation that had been arrived at between old and new into which John Bale, armed with the new and sharper-edged 1552 version of the Book of Common Prayer, erupted as bishop of Ossory in 1553.

Born on 21 November 1495 at Cove, near Dunwich in Suffolk, Bale joined the Carmelites when he was twelve years old and eventually went up to Cambridge in 1514, still as a member of the order. But by about 1534, he had embraced the reformed faith, and zealously emulating the volte-face of his hero St Paul, he soon became a sedulous advocate of the new religion. His propaganda tactics were versatile and extended to plays. His early years in East Anglia had been spent in a part of England which by the late Middle Ages was rich in dramatic activity, and his inception in Cambridge would also have brought him into contact with that university's own lively traditions of dramatic presentation.[16] Throughout his formative years, therefore, drama had been an inevitable part of his element, nor did he shun it, as his later multiple involvements as actor, producer, and playwright would confirm. While still in England he came to lead a troupe of players patronized by Secretary Thomas Cromwell. It was variously spoken of as 'Bale and his fellows' or 'the Lord Cromwell's men,' and the thrust of its productions colluded with Cromwell's campaign for monastic suppression.[17] Most of Bale's plays, including the five surviving from a once ambitious repertoire of twenty-four pieces, were written in the 1530s, and through them Bale, ever the fifth-columnist with his inherited medieval theatrical traditions, denounced Rome and urged the Protestant cause.[18] The first known performance of three of these pieces, each still extant, took place in Kilkenny on Sunday 20 August 1553, 'to the small contentation of the prestes and other papistes there,' as he himself remarked.[19]

Bale had been prevailed on by the privy council the previous August to accept the see of Ossory in Ireland, then vacant for over two years. Regarding his appointment rather in the spirit of a neo-Pauline mission, he set sail for Waterford where he landed on 23 January 1553. The first conspicuous signs of antagonism between himself and the Irish clergy quickly followed. He contested the terms of the order for his consecration in Dublin at Archbishop Browne's hands, and would have none of the old rite, which the archbishop and his assistants favoured, insisting instead on being consecrated according to the new Edwardian Ordinal whereby he would be handed a Bible rather than the traditional accoutrements of episcopal office. Heedless of the embarrassment caused, he persisted until he got his way. After all, in Bale's view Browne was but a lukewarm man, a spiritual invertebrate and a woeful advertisement for the episcopacy. Since it was the job of this 'purely to preache the Gospell,' Browne was self-evidently a shirker, and infamous for his biennial sermons, one in summer and one in winter, that were now so threadbare that everyone knew exactly what he was going to say before he opened his mouth.[20] He fell before Bale's determination.

By Lent, Bale was in Kilkenny, and preaching there on Sundays in spite of a sickness that he had contracted. Predictably, conflict began to tarnish relations with his cathedral clergy, men more given to chanting, piping, and singing than Bale was, in church at any rate. It seems that they were turning out to be worthy successors to bishop Ledrede's clerics, even if their musical indulgences were liturgical rather than secular. They refused to use Bale's preferred 1552 Book of Common Prayer because, they said, they had not enough copies of it to go round, nor was it being used by the archbisop of Dublin (hardly an impediment, this, in Bale's view).[21] When on 6 July these recalcitrant priests heard of Edward VI's death, they congregated in the taverns about the town to celebrate the prospect of having their 'maskynge masses' back again.[22] On 27 July, Lady Jane Grey was proclaimed queen, with the customary celebrations, and very soon after on the proclamation of Queen Mary, on Sunday 20 August, the day of Bale's plays, festivities were widespread in Kilkenny, the diocese and beyond: 'erat congratulatio magna in Clero et populo, cum hymnis et canticis, cum tripudijs et triumphis per vicos et plateas ciuitatum et oppidum' ('there was a great rejoicing amongst the clergy and people, with hymns and songs, with dances and triumphs through the streets and places of cities and the town').[23] In the heat of the jubilation, Bale and his clergy clashed. They insisted that he vest in cope, crozier, and mitre for a procession to honour the day. He refused to wear traditional pontificals, and the result was an ungainly compromise in which he was left to process in his black gown, but with a priest going before carrying his mitre, and another carrying his crozier, thus making '.iij. procession pageauntes' out of one:

On the .xx. daye of August / was the ladye marye with vs at kylkennye proclamed Quene of Englande / Fraunce and Irelande / with the greatest solempnyte that there coulde be deuysed / of processions / musters and disgysinges / all the noble captaynes and gentilmen there about beinge present. What a do I had that daye with the prebendaryes and prestes abought wearinge the cope / croser / and myter in procession / it were to muche to write. I tolde them earnestly / whan they wolde haue compelled me therunto / that I was not Moyses minister but Christes / I desyred them that they wolde not compell me to his denyall / which is (S. Paule sayth) in ye repetinge of Moyses sacramentes & ceremoniall sohaddowes Gal. v. with yat I toke Christes testament in my hande / & went to ye market crosse / ye people in great nombre folowinge. There toke I the .xiij. chap. of S. Paule to ye Roma. declaringe to them breuely / what ye autoritie was of ye worldly powers & magistrates what reuerence & obedience were due to ye same. In ye meane tyme had the prelates goten .ij. disgysed prestes / one to beare the myter afore me / Ifol. 24vI and an other the croser / makinge .iij. procession pageauntes of one. The yonge men in the forenone played a Tragedye of Gods promises in the olde lawe at the market crosse / with organe plainges and songes very aptely. In the afternone agayne they played a Commedie of sanct Johan Baptistes preachinges / of Christes baptisynge and of his temptacion in the wildernesse / to the small contentacion of the prestes and other papistes there.[24]

Bale's abhorrence of ornate Roman liturgy is continually expressed in terms which betray his sensitivity to that liturgy's theatricality: although 'maskynge masses' and 'procession pageauntes' were things for reproof, and although to him a vested priest might appear 'disgysed / lyke one that wolde shewe some conueyaunce or iuglyng playe,'[25] he valued drama proper, especially when it could present a message as effectively as sermons could, if not more so. Preaching, as his words and actions show, was for him a crucial part of his vocation. Thus his play writing might be regarded as an inflation into dramatic proportions of the preacher's office. In this he perhaps shared more in common with his orthodox, medieval predecessors and mentors than he might have wished to acknowledge. But in addition to sharing their motives, though not of course their theology, it was also their legacy of medieval stagecraft that he strove to divert towards his own reformed ends.[26] In drawing heavily not only on this traditional stagecraft but on the aesthetic resources of the liturgy of the religious tradition that he had come to despise, Bale was attempting a delicate ambivalence that must, in practice, have been a difficult thing to maintain. Such was the way in which the proselyte preacher and dramatist strove to bite the hand that fed him. He evidently had few qualms about allowing his plays to employ the theatricality of the unreformed liturgy to underline doctrine of which he approved, flooding with old Catholic affect their new Protestant cognitive content.[27] Yet conversely, outside a strictly dramatic context and in its original place within church worship, such liturgy had become repellent to him.

God's Promises was performed by the 'yonge men' at the Market Cross in Kilkenny before noon on Sunday, 20 August 1553, making extensive use of religious music that in a liturgical setting Bale might otherwise have scorned but which here he thought appropriate enough. Bale had written this play perhaps about the time when he wrote its two companion pieces, *Johan Baptystes Preachynge* and *The Temptacyon of Our Lorde*, which date to *c* 1538, and which like *God's Promises* received their first recorded public airing in Kilkenny, after *God's Promises* on the same day in the afternoon. All three plays had appeared in print *c* 1547, and so it can be presumed that Bale would have had copies conveniently to hand from which his cast might learn their lines. The play of *God's Promises* foregrounds a structure which is highly formal and schematized. Its symmetrical construction may have been one of the qualities which in Bale's view qualified the play for the lofty distinction of being called a 'tragedy'; it certainly has no tragic trajectory in the conventional sense. *God's Promises* is divided into seven acts of almost perfectly corresponding shape: God (Pater Coelestis) enters into dialogue with, respectively in each act, Adam, Noah, Abraham, Moses, David, Isaiah, and finally John the Baptist, at the end of which dialogue each of these seven persons sings one of the seven Advent O-Antiphons, with an option for rendering it, as stage directions indicate, either in Latin or in English. Each antiphon was also accompanied *cum organis* ('with organs') and a chorus. A speech by Bale himself, promising what was to come, introduced the play, and another speech concluded it, summarizing what had been seen and distilling from the presentation various salutary morals. Fortified by their midday break, those in the audience whose patience had not been exhausted by fatigue or outrage may have been inclined to return for the two comedies, as Bale by contrast would call them, of *Johan Baptystes Preachynge* and *The Temptacyon of Our Lorde*, also carefully planned pieces but very unlike *God's Promises* in their structural impact. These have none of the conspicuous high symmetry of *God's Promises*, though informally they observe proportion by falling into discrete sections or narrative episodes of roughly equal length.[28] Nor are they as long, each being only about half the size of the morning's tragedy. There are also more characters on stage at any one time, especially in *Johan Baptystes Preachynge*. In the first section of this, John the Baptist addresses Turba Vulgaris, Publicanus, and Miles Armatus, each of whom confesses his faults, is baptized, and exits; the second section follows with a series of exchanges between John the Baptist and the unrepentant Pharisaeus and Sadducaeus, and their eventual exit; and the final section presents the baptism of Christ, in which the single piece of stage machinery explicitly mentioned in all three plays contrives the animated descent of the Holy Spirit in the form of a dove over Christ, while the voice of Pater Coelestis speaks from heaven. Like *God's Promises*, both *Johan Baptystes Preachynge* and *The Temptacyon of Our Lorde* begin and end with speeches delivered by Bale. These three plays, relative to some of Bale's other dramatic output, were fairly restrained, although sentiments of reformed theology ripple throughout each, and choice of costumes in *Johan Baptystes Preachynge* for the two villains of the peace, Phariseus and Sadducaeus, might have proved very provocative had they simulated the clothes worn by contemporary Roman clergy; without question, Bale's conclusion to *Johan Baptystes Preachynge* was incendiary enough: 'Beleve neyther Pope, nor prest of hys consent. / Folowe Christes Gospell, and therin fructyfye.'[29] And in *The Temptacyon of Our Lorde*, the polemical device of using the enemy's clothing against him is indeed put into effect, for Satan dons a monastic habit in order to disguise himself.[30] Moreover, when Christ puts Satan behind him, the angry archfiend protests that even if he has been routed here, he can at least expect to find an ally in the Vicar of Rome.[31] Small wonder, then, that Bale incensed some of the members of his Kilkenny audience.

In the light of what the texts of *God's Promises, Johan Baptystes Preachynge* and *The Temptacyon of Our Lorde* together require in production terms, and in view of the topography of Bale's production venue, the Market Cross in Kilkenny High Street, several conclusions can be drawn about the nature of the stagecraft employed for his Irish début. Apart from the role of presenter-preacher that he seems to have reserved to himself, all the other characters were played, he says, by the 'yonge men.' While it is not absolutely clear who these young men were, there is ample room for speculation.[32] Kilkenny, like Dublin, had an identifiable body of young men (often so described, incidentally, in civic documents) who were banded together and organized by a town official, the Lord of Bullring. His office seems to have had much in common with that of his counterpart in Dublin. The Kilkenny Lord of Bullring trained up the young men for military service and supervised musters. Another of his duties seems to have been the policing of the town against adultery and fornication, and it is likely that as in Dublin so in Kilkenny, his office derived some of its income from successful prosecutions in such cases. A by-law of 9 February 1609 ordered that he should receive fines arising from frays, bloodshed, battery, and raising the hue-and-cry.[33] He was very much the enforcer of civic discipline, and was elected from members of the Merchants guild who had not already undertaken the office.[34] He had an official gown, which he was obliged to wear on high feasts, station days, muster days, and for burials of members of the greater or lesser twelve.[35] Doubtless one of the principal focus points of his ceremonial activity was the town bullring itself, for whose baitings he was obliged to provide ropes and ties. Bullbaiting was taken very seriously in sixteenth-century Kilkenny; a full and carefully itemized set of accounts dated to December 1596 still survives for the construction of the civic bullring.[36] (Midsummer, a time of fairs and of plays discussed below, was also a time when bulls were baited.)[37] The Lord of Bullring was the young men's master of ceremonies, organizing them to participate in a variety of civic events; and as was seen at least in Dublin, these events

might extend to dramatic presentations. It seems possible that Bale's cast was recruited from amongst their ranks. And further evidence that there indeed already
existed an identifiable constituency of respectably Protestant 'yonge men' in the
town at this date, ones with whom Bale would have seen eye to eye, is forthcoming
during the uproar that arose some two weeks after the provocative trio of plays had
caused their annoyance. On 8 September, when Bale had to be rescued by the sovereign of Kilkenny leading a large Protestant militia from what may have been an
assassination bid near his residence at Freshford, about eight miles northwest of the
town, the 'yonge men' sang psalms and other Godly songs in thanksgiving after he
had been successfully delivered.[38]

Excluding Bale as presenter-preacher, *God's Promises* and *Johan Baptystes
Preachynge* had each eight roles, while *The Temptacyon of Our Lorde* had four. For
each play, Bale would have needed a minimum of four of his young men to make
up a cast. In *Johan Baptystes Preachynge* and *The Temptacyon of Our Lorde*, one of
this group was on stage all the time, and in *God's Promises*, it seems likely that the
same actor would have impersonated God throughout, despite gaps between the acts
that could have allowed for a fresh actor to resume the role had this have been thought
desirable. A maximum of four were on stage at any one time in *Johan Baptystes
Preachynge*, and exits of characters would have been sufficiently covered by dialogue
to have allowed for costume changes and role doubling by actors other than the one
playing John the Baptist, if doubling was thought expedient for this play too. Other
'yonge men,' whose disposition for singing was to be spontaneously demonstrated
at Bale's September rescue, could have made up the chorus for *God's Promises*, if the
whiff of sectarian vitriol had caused the vicars choral and stipendiaries of his cathedral to jib at taking part. Two of the more musically accomplished 'yonge men'
could have performed the two-part song of the angels that comes near the end of
The Temptacyon of Our Lorde.[39] The organs also played during *God's Promises* would
have presumably been of the portative kind, and are likely to have been readily
available since Kilkenny had been a home to organ builders from at least the late
fifteenth century.[40]

Since dramatic action centred around the Market Cross, the cross itself may
have been structurally incorporated into the play stage.[41] *God's Promises*, whose
action is otherwise unlocalized, refers to Moses speaking with God 'In thys hygh
mountayne,' and the elevation that here seems required for a modicum of verisimili-
tude, as well as for the facilitation generally of audience sight lines, would have
been aptly provided by the elevation that the cross already had to offer.[42] Many
other reasons made the Market Cross site a natural choice for Bale's display. The
cross was a focal point of the town, standing not far from the Tholsel which, at
that period, backed onto Pudding Lane a few yards down the street (see fig. 15). As
its name suggests, it also stood in the place where markets were regularly pitched.

The High Street was at its widest at the Market Cross, and thus this was the part of the street where the greatest number of people could have been accommodated. On either side of the street, and exactly opposite the cross, was a slip, a narrow passageway between the buildings. These slips, which would have made convenient tiring areas and points of exit and entrance, still survive, though the fourteenth-century Market Cross itself (see fig. 16) was dismantled in 1771. Today, the width of the High Street, measured exactly from where the apertures of the slips debouch upon the street, is 65′ 9″, and this dimension should give a good impression of the room for manoeuvre that Bale would have had at his disposal. The central part of his playing space would of course have been occupied by the Market Cross itself, which was a square construction on a base approximately 11′ x 11′, to judge by the dimensions given to it by John Rocque on his map of the city.[43]

In *God's Promises*, as was noted, the elevation provided by the Market Cross may have been used to suggest the high mountain on which Moses spoke with God; in *Johan Baptystes Preachynge*, it seems likely that it would also have been from the Market Cross, this time representing the altitude of heaven, that the voice of God was heard, and that from the cross the dove effigy would in some way have been made to descend. The stage mechanics of the descent are not known, but it would not have been a complex illusion to manufacture, and was in any case a common enough effect in contemporary stagecraft abroad, if not also in Ireland.[44] *The Temptacyon of Our Lorde* requires at least two high places, the pinnacle of the Temple in Jerusalem and the mountain from which Christ is invited to survey the kingdoms of the world. One of the reasons Christ gives to explain why it would have been perverse to cast himself down from the Temple heights, as Satan has prompted, is that it already had *gresynges* ('steps') up and down which a man could easily walk.[45] So too had Kilkenny's Market Cross, five in all to be exact, to judge by early depictions of it (see fig. 16).[46] Though steps could doubtless have been constructed for the occasion, here they would have come ready made, thus sparing some carpenter a chore and saving Bale's crew an expense.

These three plays were Bale's first and last dramatic fling in Kilkenny. His epilogue there is quickly told. After their production, his position in the town worsened rapidly. Emboldened by the accession of a Catholic queen, and in defiance and reaction to the régime for which Bale stood, the Kilkenny clergy took to the streets in a general procession 'most gorgiously' on 31 August while he was out of town. They flung up their caps and paraded their copes, candlesticks, holywater stoops, crosses, and censers, and sang the Latin litany. Matters finally came to a head with the events of 8 September. Although a holy day in the Roman calendar, being the Nativity of the Blessed Virgin Mary, Bale had let five of his household servants go out haymaking. They were ambushed and killed by men intending to surprise the bishop himself. Bale's rescue and removal to Kilkenny has been related, but the

16 The Market Cross, Kilkenny, reproduced from an engraving of 1853.

matter did not end there. Determined to provoke him further, Justice Howth required him to celebrate a requiem Mass for the recently departed soul of Edward VI such as Queen Mary had called for in England. Bale prevaricated, knowing that although Howth had originally appointed Saturday 10 September and the following Sunday for these exequies, they had in fact been deferred because festivities in Thomastown, a place about ten miles away to the south, had proved an irresistible alternative attraction. If so frivolous a reason could defer a king's requiem, Bale argued, the requiem they required of him could wait a little longer until he had consulted with the authorities in Dublin about how he should proceed. His account incidentally brings to light the only traces known of dramatic activity in the neighbouring town of Thomastown at this date:

If these youre suffrages be a waye for him {Edward VI} to heauen / & so that he can not go thydre without them / ye are muche to blame / that ye haue diffarred them so longe. Ye had (sayd I) a commaundement the last saterdaye / of the iustice hothe / to haue solempnised them yat nyght and the next daye after. But the deuyll which that daye daunsed at Thomas towne (for they had a procession with pageauntes) and the aqua vite & Kob {read Rob} Dauie withall / wolde not suffre ye than to do them. I desire yow / considering that the last sondaye ye differred them to se the deuill daunce at Thomas towne / that ye will also this sondaie differre them / tyll suche tyme as I sende to ye Quenes commissioners at Dublyne / to knowe how to be discharged of the othe which I made to ye Kynge and hys counsell for abolyshment of that popish masse.[47]

But the ruse was a desperate one, and Bale left Kilkenny later in September, never to return. For all his zeal, perhaps on account of it, there had been no lasting Protestant sea change in Kilkenny during his episcopate, as the despair of John Horsfall, one of his successors in the see of Ossory in the early seventeenth century, would testify. He lamented that the town was a spiritual sump and crawling with Romish caterpillars, a plaint with which Bale would have wholeheartedly sympathized.[48]

AFTER BALE

Bale's sojourn in Kilkenny had lasted only a matter of months. The bishop baiting had been a continual irritant, even if he had managed to construe it positively as another of his Pauline thorns in the flesh. When eventually his life had come under threat, however, and his position had become quite untenable, discretion prevailed. In retrospect, his period in office must have seemed a colourful aberrance in the life of the town, for soon after his departure the status quo there settled down again, and the old orthodoxies continued, disguised only as flimsily as they ever had been before. The feast of Corpus Christi itself, for example, which in Dublin in 1561 was coming under heavy pressure from the authorities, appears to have persisted relatively unruffled in Kilkenny at least as late as 1637, and probably well into the 1640s, when Kilkenny became the headquarters of the Catholic confederation.[49] It may be that the feast had been briefly in abeyance a little before 1591, for a corporation memorandum in this year decreed that the Corpus Christi fair should be reinstated, but even this possible hint of suspension is not entirely clear, because the memorandum speaks strictly of the fair and not of the liturgical feast: if the 1588 Midsummer performance of the Resurrection play in St Mary's Church is indicative of any disruption (as will be seen, Kilkenny's Resurrection play was more normally associated with Corpus Christi), then that disruption was shortlived. In any event, Corpus Christi, if not its fair, was certainly observed in 1590, the year before the corporation's decree was made.[50] Trimming and temporizing, then, seem to have been the order of the day, and why not, when they made for a life quiet and conducive to the pursuit of civic and private profit? More things were wanted for the social well being of Kilkenny than might ever be dreamed of in Bale's restless philosophy.

The prospect that Kilkenny's lost Corpus Christi play may one day turn up in some highly unlikely place is the sort of happy dream that Irish serendipity over the last few years tends to keep alive. When a holograph manuscript of a missing Haydn Mass can turn up in a farmer's attic in co. Antrim, or when treasure hunters unearth a companion piece to the Ardagh chalice in a peat bog in co. Tipperary, it would not seem too much to hope for that somewhere fate may also have spared the Kilkenny playbook. In fact in 1637 at least two such playbooks were in existence to take their chances through time; one came to Dublin and the other, presumably, stayed in Kilkenny.[51] The likely places in both these cities have now been searched out, and the unlikely places, by their nature, can never be.[52] But although no actual play text has as yet come to light, it is possible to form a good impression of what Kilkenny's Corpus Christi play was like, and consequently to appreciate how different in many of its respects drama in Kilkenny was to that once presented in the capital. It is from the year 1580 onwards that records of sufficient detail survive to give this impression some colour. Of the two main occasions for civic drama, Midsummer and Corpus Christi, the records for Corpus Christi are the more extensive, so we may conveniently begin with them.

By the year 1500, the general observance of the feast of Corpus Christi in Kilkenny was sufficiently large to make the corporation legislate for its proper ordering. (As was seen in chapter 2, comparable legislation had been passed in Dublin in 1466.) From 11:00 p.m. on Corpus Christi eve until 11:00 p.m. on the following Friday, freedom of passage was allowed to the populace, and this extended to the visitors who came into the town for the feast and fair.[53] Midsummer, the other occasion for civic drama, was also a time when a fair was held. This coincidence of play and fair is important to grasp for several reasons, not least amongst which is the festive and mercantile ambience that it establishes surrounding the dramatic event. Whatever the outlay on play production costs, some income would have accrued to the town from the extra trade which visitors to the fair brought with them. Although Corpus Christi, unlike Midsummer, would not be one of the three annual occasions officially recognized as fair days in Kilkenny's civic charter of 1609, it is nevertheless probable that the Corpus Christi fair continued, even if only informally and without statutory recognition.[54] There are several signs of corporate attentiveness to the convenience of visitors, amongst which were the arrangements made for providing overnight accommodation and the enforced clean-up of the town. In 1591, the sovereign offered a 40s annuity to anyone prepared to run an inn. In the interim, all victuallers and freemen were required to keep clean bedding for strangers, under penalty of a 40s fine for default.[55] And public cleanliness was in order. The interests of Corpus Christi tourism would ensure that Kilkenny became a tidy town, at least for the duration of the fair. Dung and filth had to be cleared from the streets, then as well as on other days when visitors were liable to drop in, including visitors as eminent as the Lord Deputy.[56] The first clear evidence of some sort of Corpus Christi drama does not appear until 1556, yet when it does it appears only as an *obiter dictum* and in a curious context: perhaps the incidental way in which it is reported suggests that John Bale had also been producing his plays partly as pious antidotes to a tradition that had already taken root no less in Kilkenny than in other places in these islands before he arrived, and that Protestant polemics apart, he was not doing anything newfangled in presenting drama in Kilkenny High Street. On Corpus Christi in 1556, Richard Cody, the town treasurer of Cashel, was finally able to steal back the body of Cashel's former archbishop, Edmund Butler, from its resting place in St Canice's Cathedral because the townsfolk were so absorbed watching the performance of the Corpus Christi play that there was no one around to notice the macabre theft going on:

Tandem Edmundus 5 Martij 1550 Stylo Anglicano naturæ cessit Kilkeniæ, & ibidem per annos quinque sepultus, clero cassellensi necquicquam contendente vt cadauer casseliam deferretur, Imo Richardus cody thesaurarius |p. 621| cassellensis occasionem quotannis cadaueris clam auferendi aucupabatur; qui conatus quinto tandem anno, ciuibus ad se ludis theatralibus in die corporis christi haberi solitis recreandos intentis ...[57]

[At length Edmund {Butler} succumbed to nature 5 March 1550, English Style, at Kilkenny, and for five years was buried there, while the clergy of Cashel argued in vain that his body be returned to Cashel. Indeed, Richard Cody, treasurer of Cashel, each year looked for his opportunity to make off with the body by stealth. He finally made his attempt in the fifth year, while the citizens were absorbed in the theatrical plays with which they were accustomed to recreate themselves on Corpus Christi day ...]

Whether at any earlier stage in its history the Kilkenny Corpus Christi play may have been undertaken as a collaborative venture between the trade guilds, as the Dublin Corpus Christi pageant procession partly was, is not known for certain, though on balance this would seem unlikely when one guild, that of the Merchants, always seems in the records to have held chief sway.[58] Its primacy among the guilds is likely to have exerted a centripetal force upon how the Corpus Christi enterprise was run, focusing this enterprise upon the Merchant guild. In effect, this is what came to pass, in the guise of a drama which, even more than in Dublin's case, was corporation sponsored. Even had the guilds ever once been corporately responsible, by 1580, when evidence starts to become abundant, the axis of responsibility had radically shifted, for what is patently clear is that by this date the Corpus Christi play was centred upon and being run by Kilkenny Corporation. The corporation in turn, as was noted, drew its membership largely from the established Kilkenny merchant oligarchy.[59] Hence the play, as well as providing the standard bill of fare of edification spiced with entertainment, would also have handed interested parties a way of celebrating the equation of civic prestige with their own standing and with that of the ruling mercantile families. In some ways, what was happening in Dublin seems comparable. But in Kilkenny, where less heed needed to be paid to the whims and orthodoxies of the English administration, pageantry was freer to express this sort of familial and civic aspiration without having to channel quite as much of its energy towards reminding the English administration of what the town's independent and abiding privileges were. In this regard, it is interesting to note that Kilkenny Corporation made no investment in the pageantry of the feast of St George comparable to Dublin's, where on St George's Day the powers of city and of state were held through pageantry in a mutually respecting equipoise, at least until the third quarter of the sixteenth century when St George pageantry organized by the corporation fell away there and a blunter form of territorial claim-staking won the field in the guise of franchise ridings.[60] One has only to consider how frequently the names of members of Kilkenny's ten ruling families, or 'tribes,' as they are known, occur in documents concerned with the play to begin to appreciate the play's local kudos and the stakes for which it was played (see table 1 below).[61] The *optimates* of Kilkenny and their relatives appear not merely as members of the corporation authorizing play payments but also as actual actors: the names Archdeacon, Archer, Cowley, Langton, Lawless, Raggett, Rothe, and Shee all appear, which makes an impressive tally of eight 'tribes' out of the ten.[62]

Further research may uncover additional information about the circumstances of the play's personnel, such as what their precise family connections were, what their occupations, where they lived or held property in Kilkenny, and even their approximate age at the time of their play involvement. This information will add finesse to the picture. In the meanwhile, it is worth observing some of its broader brushstrokes. The careers attached to certain of these names have an interesting bearing on our understanding of the social context which sustained the Kilkenny plays and which was in turn sustained by them. As has been seen, and as might indeed be expected, the names signal that members of the corporation were mainly recruited from the prominent members of the Kilkenny bourgeoisie. But more importantly for present purposes, they also signal that the corporation, via its constituent families, was deeply committed to the plays, even possessively committed. A play performance in St Mary's Church is highly suggestive in this regard. St Mary's was an ancient and substantial foundation, by now thoroughly identified with the fortunes of Kilkenny Corporation, under whose special care it was (its location is plotted in fig. 15). The town clock was maintained in its belfry, the corporation paid its clock-keeper his salary, its clergy theirs, and corporation meetings before the Reformation were also often held there.[63] Furthermore, it had been colonized by the Archers, Rothes, and Shees as their preferred burial place, those very families whose names, incidentally, occur with the most frequency in the list given below in table 1. Most of those who actually performed in the plays are more difficult to trace, sometimes even when their surnames suggest their affiliation to the ruling families. Adam Shee, who rode on Corpus Christi and on Midsummer Eve both in 1580 and in 1585, falls into this category, since by virtue of being a Shee he was probably well connected, but otherwise little is known of him.

However, the names suggest other possible professional involvements which are significant. What also seems clear from them is the extent of the clerical input into the plays, both in terms of production and acting. William Kelly, for example, who acted St Michael on an occasion in 1602 (probably in fact on Corpus Christi), may well have been the same 'William Kelly of Kilkenny, clerk' who is mentioned in a deed of 28 February 1601.[64] It is also interesting to note that a certain John Murphy heads the list of recusant priests identified by the Protestant bishop of Ossory, John Horsfall, as being active in the diocese in 1604; a John Murphy had taken a prominent role as Satan in 1602, probably in the Corpus Christi play, and again in some (unspecified) role in 1603.[65] John Kennedy, one of the setters-forth of the Marys, is also cited in a deed which suggests he may have had some ecclesiastical connection.[66] Similarly James Krininge, who set forth the Marys in 1585, signed his name and his profession as 'Clark' on the warrant for his payment, in acknowledgment of its receipt.[67] Even if 'clerk' might be thought ambiguous, for the word then could also simply mean an officer who had charge of records,[68] this ambiguity is cleared up by a warrant for payment which still survives in the Kilkenny Tholsel. Here, Arthur Shee, sovereign of Kilkenny, had directed Edmund Raggett, bailiff of St John's, to deliver to James Krininge, *organ clerk of St Mary's Church*, the sum of £3 sterling for a year's wages.[69] We might also note that by the 1630s, mention is being made of 'children' being instructed to participate in the Corpus Christi play,[70] and there may be some support for this in the list of personnel given in table 1: if John Purcell, actor of a Conqueror at Corpus Christi and Midsummer in 1637, is the same John Purcell whose father, Richard, died in 1635, John was only twelve years old when he played the part.[71]

TABLE 1: Personnel connected with Kilkenny's Corpus Christi and Midsummer Play,
29 May 1580 – 22 September 1639

Named personnel

John Rothe Fitz Jenkin	Town bailiff, 29 May 1580; 6 June 1580.
Adam Shee	Rider on Corpus Christi (2 June) and Midsummer Eve, 1580; again on Corpus Christi (10 June) and Midsummer Eve, 1585; again on Corpus Christi (2 June) and Midsummer, 1586.
Peter Shee	Superior of Kilkenny, 29 May 1580 (*); 6 June 1580.
Richard Nogell	Placer of the stations on Corpus Christi, 2 June 1580.
Edward Rothe	?Town bailiff, 6 June 1582.
David Savage	Rider on Corpus Christi, 14 June 1582; again on Corpus Christi (18 June) and Midsummer Eve, 1584.
Robert Rothe	Sovereign of Kilkenny, 6 June 1582.
Darby Brennan	?Town bailiff, 21 May, 18 June, and 8 August 1584; payer of John Trumpetor for his pains on Corpus Christi (18 June) 1584.
John Trumpetor	Trumpetor (presumably not a surname) on Corpus Christi (18 June) 1584.
Arthur Shee	Sovereign of Kilkenny, 21 May and 18 June 1584; Deputy sovereign, 7 and 9 June 1585; subscriber to a payment to John Davis, 4 June 1597; and to a payment to John Murphy, John Lawless, and actor of Belfiger, 20 June 1603.
Edmund Raggett	?Town bailiff, 1584 (precise date not specified).
William Courcy	Actor and player of a trumpeter's part on Corpus Christi (18 June) and Midsummer Eve, 1584; setter forth of the Corpus Christi play, 3 June 1602; also 23 June 1603; custodian of clothes and props for the 'comedy of the Resurrection' (probably the Corpus Christi play) for more than five years before 1603.
Thomas Pembroke Fitz David	Town bailiff, 7 June 1585.
Patrick Morgan	Freren bailiff, 9 June 1585 (**).
James Krininge	Clerk and setter forth of the Marys, probably on Corpus Christi, 10 June 1585
Piers Archdeacon	Subscriber to a payment to James Krininge, 9 June 1585.
Thomas Archer	Subscriber to a payment to James Krininge, 9 June 1585; sovereign of Kilkenny, 1 and 25 June 1588; again on 18 and 19 June 1593; and subscriber to a payment to John Davis, 4 June 1597; and to a payment to John Kennedy, 20 June 1603.

TABLE 1 (*cont.*)

Walter Archer	Subscriber to a payment to James Krininge, 9 June 1585; payer of John Murphy, 20 June 1603.
Edward Langton	Subscriber to a payment to James Krininge, 9 June 1585.
Richard Raggett	Sovereign of Kilkenny, 3 June 1585; authorizer of a payment to Adam Shee, 2 and 24 June 1586.
James Langton	Town bailiff, 3 June 1585.
John Busher	Setter forth of the Marys, probably on Corpus Christi, 10 June 1585; perhaps again on Corpus Christi, 6 June 1588; setter forth of the Resurrection play in St Mary's Church, Midsummer, 1588.
Redmond Savage	Town bailiff, 1 June 1588; again on 25 June 1588.
Robert Archer	Town bailiff, 18 June 1590.
Thomas Langton	Sovereign of Kilkenny, 18 June 1590.
John St Leger	Town bailiff, 18 and 19 June 1593 (†).
Thomas Lucas	Setter forth of the Marys, Corpus Christi, 14 June 1593; actor of Charlemagne, and paid half a Conqueror's wage for his effort, probably Midsummer, 1593 (†).
Robert Rothe	Subscriber to a payment to Thomas Lucas, 18 and 19 June 1593; and to a payment to John Kennedy, 2 June 1602.
Geoffrey Rothe	Subscriber to a payment to Thomas Lucas, 18 and 19 June 1593; and to a payment to John Davis, 4 June 1597.
Edward St Leger	Subscriber to a payment to Thomas Lucas, 18 and 19 June 1593.
John Davis	Actor of a Conqueror on Corpus Christi, 26 May 1597.
William Raggett	?Town bailiff, 4 June 1597.
John Mooney	Town bailiff, 17 June 1600.
Simon Archer	Actor of a Conqueror on Midsummer Eve, 1600.
Helias Shee	Sovereign of Kilkenny, 17 June 1600.
Richard Shee	Subscriber to a payment to Simon Archer, 17 June 1600; and to a payment to John Murphy, John Lawless, and an actor of Belfiger, 20 June 1603.
John Lawless	Brother of Philip immediately below and an actor of a Conqueror, probably Midsummer, 1600; standard bearer on Corpus Christi, 3 June 1602; actor in the Corpus Christi play, 23 June 1603.
Philip Lawless	Actor of a Conqueror, probably Midsummer, 1600; actor of Joshua, some time after 31 May 1602.

TABLE 1 (*cont.*)

Edward Raggett	Subscriber to a payment to Simon Archer, 17 June 1600.
William Keevan	Freren bailiff, 31 May and 2 June, 1602.
John Kennedy	Setter forth of the Marys, some time after 2 June 1602; again probably on Corpus Christi, 23 June 1603.
Patrick Archer	Superior of Kilkenny, 31 May and 2 June 1602.
Robert Rothe	Subscriber to a payment to John Kennedy, 2 June 1602.
John Rothe Fitz Piers	Subscriber to a payment to John Kennedy, 2 June 1602.
William White	Actor of Julius Caesar, probably on Corpus Christi, 3 June 1602.
Robert Rothe	Subscriber to a payment to John Lawless, William White, and Philip Lawless, 31 May 1602; and to a payment to William Kelly and John Murphy, 2 June 1602.
George Comerford	Subscriber to a payment to John Lawless, William White, and Philip Lawless, 31 May 1602.
William Kelly	Actor of St Michael, probably on Corpus Christi, 3 June 1602.
John Murphy	Actor of Satan, probably on Corpus Christi, 3 June 1602; actor in the Corpus Christi play, 23 June 1603.
Patrick Mooney	Freren bailiff, 20 June 1603.
Lucas Shee	Superior of Kilkenny, 20 June 1603.
R[ichard?] Shee Thomas Archer Nicholas Langton	Subscribers to a payment to John Kennedy, 20 June 1603.
Walter Archer Richard Shee	Payers of John Murphy, 20 June 1603.
James Brian	Payer of John Lawless, 20 June 1603.
R[ichard?] Shee P[atrick?] Archer Arthur Shee	Subscribers to a payment to John Murphy and John Lawless, 20 June 1603.
George Shee	Mayor of Kilkenny, 20 September 1603.
William Consey [*read* Courcy?]	Granted annual stipend 13 January 1631 for instructing the children for the Corpus Christi play.
Thomas Daniel	Actor of St Michael sometime in 1636; payment ordered on 4 June 1637 for his props for St Michael in the Corpus Christi play, 8 June 1637.
James Cowley	Mayor of Kilkenny, 30 May, 1 June, 4 June, 7–8 June, 10 June, 17 June, 8 July, and 26 September 1637.
Patrick Murphy	Subscriber to a payment to Thomas Daniel, 30 May 1637.

TABLE 1 (cont.)

John Purcell	Actor of a Conqueror on Corpus Christi (8 June) and Midsummer, 1637.
William Shee	Subscriber to a payment to John Purcell, 1 June 1637; also to a payment ordered to Thomas Daniel, 4 June 1637; treasurer, 8 July 1637; also subscriber to a payment to James Barry, 10 June 1637.
Henry Archer	Subscriber to a payment to John Purcell, 1 June 1637; also to payments ordered to Thomas Daniel, 4 June 1637; to Matthew Hickey, 7 June 1637; to William Lawless, 17 June 1637; and to John Palmer, 26 September 1637.
Robert Rothe	Subscriber to a payment ordered to Thomas Daniel, 4 June 1637.
Christopher Coyne	Copyist of a duplicate of the book of Corpus Christi plays, some time before 4 June 1637.
Richard Cowley	Subscriber to a payment to the Corpus Christi play musicians, 8 June 1637; also to John Palmer, 26 September, 1637.
Peter Rothe	Subscriber to a payment to Matthew Hickey, 7 June 1637; also to the Corpus Christi play musicians, 8 June 1637; also to John Palmer, 26 September 1637.
Matthew Hickey	Actor of two Conquerors on Corpus Christi (8 June) and Midsummer, 1637; and of a Conqueror on Corpus Christi (13 June) and Midsummer, 1639.
Mary Rothe	William Courcy's wife, paid 8 July 1637 for a breakfast given to the young men who acted in the Corpus Christi play, 8 June 1637.
Thomas Archer	Warrantor and subscriber to a payment to Mary Rothe, William Courcy's wife, 8 July 1637.
William Lawless	Actor of Godfrey and Hector on Corpus Christi (8 June) and Midsummer, 1637.
John Palmer	Paid 26 September 1637 for his 'paynes taken about Corpus Christi play,' 8 June 1637.
James Barry	Actor of a Conqueror on Corpus Christi (8 June) and Midsummer Eve, 1637.

Unnamed personnel

Eight pairs of gloves for the 'Maryes,' implying an eight-character play?	Players probably on Corpus Christi, 10 June 1585.
Christ Mary Mother John the Evangelist The 'other three Maryes' }	Players probably on Corpus Christi, 10 June 1585.

TABLE 1 *(cont.)*

Six pairs of gloves for the 'Maryes,' implying a six-character play?	Players probably on Corpus Christi, 6 June 1588.
St Michael ⎫ Devil ⎭	Players in the Resurrection on Corpus Christi, 18 June 1590.
The 'other Devill' ⎫ Christ ⎬ St Michael ⎭	Players who 'went in stations' on Corpus Christi, 18 June 1590.
The Marys	Players (number unspecified) on Corpus Christi, 14 June 1593.
The Marys	Players (number unspecified) probably on Corpus Christi, 3 June 1602.
'Him that plaies the Divell in Stacions'	Player who 'went in stations' probably on Corpus Christi, 3 June 1602.
The Marys	Players (number unspecified) probably on Corpus Christi, 23 June 1603.
'Him that plays [Belfiger] and goeth about in Stacions' (††)	Player who 'went in stations' on Corpus Christi, 23 June 1603.
'Young Men that acted uppon the Stage'	Players (number unspecified) on Corpus Christi, 8 June 1637.
Musicians	Performers (number unspecified) for the Corpus Christi play, 8 June 1637.

Notes

(*) Designation as 'Superior' in the records above is evidently an alternative to 'Sovereign,' the title adopted by the head of the corporation until 1609 when Kilkenny acquired city status in its Great Charter. At this date, 'sovereign' was replaced by 'mayor,' although 'mayor' was evidently being sometimes used in documents before 1609, as William Courcy's petition of 20 September 1603 illustrates.
(**) The Freren bailiff appears to have been an official responsible for administering church lands ceded to the corporation at the Reformation.
(†) 1593 is misprinted as 1598 in Watters, 'Notes of Particulars,' p. 239
(††) Watters, 'Notes of Particulars,' p. 240, reads 'Kelfiger,' but this is likely to be either a misprint or a misreading of the more probable name for a devil, 'Belfiger' (i.e., Belphegor).

Today, although the holdings in the city archives are a sad reflection of their former extent, a fresh search has revealed new documents which, together with the published nineteenth-century antiquarian transcriptions, shed further light on the organization, staging and content of the play.[72] It appears that Kilkenny's civic drama, whether on Corpus Christi or Midsummer, was intended to be presented annually, at least by the 1580s when records of it are thicker on the ground.[73] Only from 1610 does a record survive of a formal decree by the mayor and aldermen that Corpus Christi that year should be celebrated 'in decent and solemn manner as usual,' yet this unique survival can hardly witness to a once-off decree; similar decrees, the records of which have not survived, were no doubt also made in other years, 'as usual.' Whatever the exact terms of the 1610 decree, they were formulated according to advice received from the corporation. It seems that each year one, or perhaps two, individuals may have been appointed as chiefly responsible for producing the actual play, and that ultimately the corporation would shoulder all the expenditures that they incurred in its production, as well as pay them some reward for their labours.

The producers of the play are consistently referred to as being those by whom it was 'set forth' (once as 'set out'). This early instance of the standard phrasal verb 'to set forth,' witnessed by the *Oxford English Dictionary* only from the year 1613 for the sense appropriate to its use here, conveys the meaning 'to set forth publike playes and games.'[74] There are five people on record as setting forth the Marys: John Busher in 1585 (when he seems also to have been accompanied by James Krininge) and again in 1588; Thomas Lucas in 1593, who in addition acted a Conqueror and the part of Charlemagne; John Kennedy in 1602 and 1603 (when he also seems to have been accompanied by William Courcy); and William Courcy who, apart from (apparently) assisting John Kennedy in 1603, had complained in that year that while he had been paid for setting forth the Marys for the past five years, he had not been paid for so doing for several years before that, a statement which dates the (unpaid) period of his setting forth to a stretch of some years before 1599. It seems that at least in some years, play production may have been a shared responsibility. Perhaps it always was, but records have not survived to confirm this. There is information on all of these setters-forth in other Kilkenny documents. Though at least two people with the name of John Busher, a John the elder and a John the younger, feature frequently in the Corporation Book of the Irishtown, one of these seems a likely candidate for association with the man active here. The John Busher in question may have been the one prominent in the second half of the sixteenth century, who was voted into various positions of administrative responsibility in the corporation of the Irishtown between 1562 and 1586, including the office of portreeve itself in 1566.[75] His professional interests, to judge by the Corporation Book, were largely secular and commercial. The pursuits of his colleague of 1585, however, James Krininge, were by contrast chiefly vocational and artistic, since as has been noted, he was organ clerk of St Mary's Church. Thomas Lucas is heard of as a witness to a quitclaim of 15 June 1590, and as a lessor of a chamber and orchard in Greyfriars for sixty-one years from 1591.[76] He must have been a respected citizen, but no further information seems available on his profession. John Kennedy bore some responsibility as a setter forth with William Courcy in 1602 and 1603. We hear of a John Kennedy as witness to an indenture of 3 May 1590 in a context which, as already noted, suggests that he may have had some ecclesiastical connection.[77] William Courcy, his colleague in those years, may like some of the other personnel in table 1 have had a long-standing involvement with the play, though we do not know his regular profession, assuming also that he is not the same William 'Consey' of 1631 and the William Courcy of 1637, the latter being the husband of Mary Rothe. If, on the other hand, 'Consey' and Courcy of 1637 were in fact one and the same person, it may be that this 1630s Courcy was a schoolmaster, a profession appropriate enough for someone concerned with drama. It is also conceivable that the 1603 William Courcy was the same person as well.[78] In any event, this 1603 William Courcy, as setter forth, has left behind a document which is of great importance to the recuperation of our understanding of the Kilkenny Corpus Christi play, and it deserves reporting in full:

The humble petition   To the woorshipfull the mayour
of William Coursy   & aldermen of the Citty of
                             Kilkenny

Shewinge That where your suppliant was promised to haue asmuch this last yeare for settinge foorth of Corpus Christi play as he had any other yeare, whervppon your suppliant bestowed his labour & paynes in settinge foorth the same in the best manner he could the last Corpus Christi day, not doubtinge of performance of that promise, he hauinge had thirty shillings sterling the yeare before for the like service. And wheras your suppliant was allowed fifteene shillings sterling yeerly, for keepinge safe & preseruinge the cloaths & other ornaments belonginge to the comedy of the resurrecion, wherof your suppliant was payd for severall yeares, but for fiue yeares past your suppliant hath not beene paid therof, although he hath carfully kept & preserued the said cloathes & ornaments;
The premises considered, It may therfore please your woorships to take a course for satisfiing your suppliant aswell of the said 30s. for settinge foorth the said last Christi play, as of the areares of the said fifteene shillings for the said fiue yeare last past for keepinge the said ornaments, amountinge to 3l – 15s sterling. And your suppliant shall pray &c.

|dorse|

1603
The humble peticion of William Coursy

°20 September 1603

The maior and aldermen being so assembled together at the newe tholsell of the Citty of
kilkinny concluded and agreede that the peticioner shall haue for his paynis taken aboute
the sayd play of the Corporacion Revenews the some of twenty shillings Irishe

George Shee

maior Kilkenny° [79]

From this single document a small wealth of detail is deducible about the organization of the play at the turn of the sixteenth century. Courcy had been promised
as much income for setting forth the Corpus Christi play in 1603 as he had had in
previous years; in 1602 this had been 30s sterling. Hence the Corpus Christi play
by this time was an annual fixture, and some sort of contract, probably verbal, had
been entered into between the setter forth and the corporation. Courcy claimed
also to have been given a yearly allowance for looking after the clothes and 'ornaments' (props?) of the comedy of the Resurrection, but that for the last five years
this had not been paid. Either the comedy of the Resurrection was another way of
referring to the Corpus Christi play, or was a specific episode within it.[80] The setter
forth evidently had responsibility for properties, as might a modern stage manager.
As well as for the setters forth, some information is available too for the actors (in one
case, Thomas Lucas, a setter forth, also acted a Conqueror and the role of Charlemagne). It has already been noted that William Kelly, who acted St Michael in
1602, may be the same William Kelly of Kilkenny, clerk, who appears in a document of 28 February 1601, and similarly his partner in 1602, John Murphy, who
acted Satan, probably in the Corpus Christi play, and who acted again in some
(unspecified) role in 1603, may have been the recusant priest identified in 1604 by
Bishop John Horsfall.[81] Another actor, John Lawless, brother of Philip, and who
had been a Conqueror in 1600, a Corpus Christi standard bearer in 1602, and a
Corpus Christi actor in 1603, may on the other hand have been the same man
elected portreeve of the Irishtown on St Matthew's Day 1619, chosen because 'none
could be allowed to serve butt a conformable man.'[82] This last detail is of considerable interest. Protestant persuasion seems to have been a prerequisite for tenure of
the portreeve's office, at least in 1619. Yet unless Lawless had converted between
then and earlier in the century, when he seems to have been thoroughly involved
in various capacities in Corpus Christi drama, we are faced with the prospect of a
Protestant who did not cavil at participating in a feast packed with Catholic significance. Given Kilkenny's political circumstances sketched earlier, however, this is
not so hard to imagine: many of the Protestant stomachs there seem to have had
cast iron constitutions, proof against such strongly Catholic fare. Furthermore, the
civic and political significance of the Corpus Christi play may for some have outweighed any narrower considerations of sectarian doctrinal significance.

How those who set forth the play selected their cast is not clear, and while no evidence for formal auditions survives, it can be safely assumed that some sort of quality control was exercised, if only for the sake of ensuring an actor's audibility. The stone-flanked playing place at the Market Cross would of course have assisted by contributing a sympathetically resonant acoustic, and there is some indication that at least certain of the cast members would have been professionally accustomed to projecting their voices in public (the clerical members noted above, for example). There are some signs that the setters forth may have automatically inherited certain of their players, people who had become, as it were, traditional pieces of the play's furniture (compare the repeated play involvements over a number of years of Adam Shee and David Savage in table 1 above, to cite one salient case).[83] On the other hand, it may have been equally traditional to choose young men (sometimes even children) for the parts (note in this regard also in table 1 William Courcy's activity in the 1630s).[84] Not every last detail of expenditure, either directly or indirectly connected with the play, was accounted for by the setters forth themselves. For example, when in 1637 Mary Rothe prepared a breakfast for the young men who acted in the Corpus Christi play, her reimbursement for 20s sterling was ordered by Mayor James Cowley and by Thomas Archer. The chit they signed, dated 8 July 1637, acted as a warrant to the then receiver of the corporation revenues, William Shee, for Mary Rothe's payment, and a corresponding record survived until the nineteenth century, dated to the very same day, in which William Shee noted that she had been paid.[85] The setters forth, whoever they may have been in 1637,[86] seem to have been bypassed by this process, and no doubt in other respects they were freed from what otherwise would have been the tedious prospect of having to settle personally on the corporation's behalf every last item of play expense. The corporation was evidently being dealt with directly by various people, of whom the setters forth may only have been the principal ones, and in Mary Rothe's case, she wasted no time in claiming her money. The standard procedure adopted in Kilkenny was apparently to issue the payee with an endorsed warrant which he or she would then present to the official designated to make the payment. When the sum had been paid out, the official would make a note of it.[87] Presumably, some notional budget was agreed with the setters forth, at least verbally, as William Courcy's complaint of 1603 indeed suggests, but there is no surviving evidence of sums officially set aside for play production. All that remains is a series of warrants of expenses incurred, happily vouched for, and endorsed by corporation officials. That this relaxed arrangement proved not to be entirely satisfactory is shown not only by Courcy's complaint, but also by the fact that on 23 July 1610, the corporation earmarked a 20s salary for maintaining the apparel used at the Corpus Christi Day station, and the apparel of the Marys and players of the Resurrection.[88] It seems that in the early-seventeenth century, relatively casual methods of payment were being regularized and put onto a more formal basis.

The Corpus Christi play was usually staged in precisely the place where John Bale had performed his trilogy, near to the corporation offices at the Tholsel, about half way down High Street and around the medieval Market Cross. As Courcy's complaint also indicates, by about 1600 a new Tholsel had been built to replace the earlier one which backed onto Pudding Lane (the lane running parallel to High Street on the north side of High Street's western limit; see fig. 15). This new building was raised on the site where the city's present Tholsel stands, and was located virtually overlooking the Market Cross.[89] Thus after this date the play and its sponsors could hardly have been more conspicuously linked. The Corpus Christi play, like Bale's production, also appears to have been of the stationary, place-and-scaffold type, with players acting from one or more fixed stages. It was therefore not a pageant-wagon production of the sort that threaded through Dublin's streets, although a processional element, discussed below, was connected with it.[90] A record of 13 April 1632 implies the erection of what was probably some sort of fixed stage, perhaps on the south side of the Market Cross: 'The north side of the market cross granted to two persons for shops during the fair time of Corpus Christi, in regard their shops are stopt up by the stations and play of Corpus Christi day.'[91] (The south side of the Market Cross, in the immediate vicinity of the Tholsel, was a trading area of long standing where stalls were set up, and it therefore seems most likely that here is where the obstructed shops were to be found.)[92] The Market Cross itself in the centre of the street probably provided a second convenient scaffold location, if multiple locations were required for the Corpus Christi play. Seating may also have been set up somewhere in the vicinity, as a decree of 20 April 1610 suggests: carpenters were to be employed 'to make rails for keeping out horses and the mob, and for *placing strangers at the place where the interlude shall be plaid.*'[93] 'Strangers' is the term normally used in civic documents for visitors to Kilkenny, so by the early-seventeenth century, if not before, these could expect their interest in the play to be catered for, as well as their creature comforts. It may be that a number of seats were reserved for them to purchase. Certainly feast, fair, and concomitant play would have been well known locally and liable to attract many visitors from surrounding districts. The rails to keep out horses and mob were temporary barriers put in place for the duration of the play and were perhaps set up across either end of the High Street. Excellent views of the play from the upper storeys of the town houses lining the High Street, and especially from the new Tholsel, would also have been available to a privileged few.[94]

Actors could have had access to the playing area from either end of the High Street, but during a performance this may have meant negotiating a way through a crowd. Although provision for this could have been made, more convenient for such entrances and exits, as probably too in the case of John Bale's productions, would have been the narrow passageway known today as the Butter Slip which opens onto High Street exactly on the south side of the spot where the Market Cross originally stood. The slip would have been ideally placed for this purpose, and could have been kept free of spectators quite easily.[95]

If, as the records suggest, the Corpus Christi play was performed mainly in one locale, there nevertheless seems also to have been a separate, mobile performance presented either before or after the play and which is described as having gone 'in stations.'[96] This may have been the performance that the 'mob' excluded from the stationary performance would have had a better chance of seeing. Some sort of differentiation between this 'stations' performance and the stationary play proper is implied in the record of 13 April 1632 quoted above for the relocation of market stalls on the north side of the Market Cross. The stations are mentioned in the earliest of the extant records, when already they were being spoken of as if they were a traditional feature of the Corpus Christi celebrations: one Richard Nogell was paid 8d sterling on 6 June 1580 for 'placing the Stacions on Corpus Christi Daye last past according to the conclusion of the Counsell and the custome of the Town.'[97] The fact that the stations could be 'placed' suggests that they were physically marked out in some way, though whether with a scaffold stage or with something less substantial is not known. It is also not clear precisely where, or how many, they were, but it is interesting to compare the locations at which stages were placed in Kilkenny in 1637 to greet Sir Thomas Wentworth's triumphal entry (considered more closely in the next chapter), since station places and sites of civic display often prove to be resiliently traditional. On this occasion, stages were set up in St John's Street and at Croker's Cross (see fig. 15).[98] Since maintenance of the latter, like the Market Cross itself, was the responsibility of the masons of Kilkenny, it was thus also a site of civic concern.[99] Here, then, may have been two of the station places also referred to in the sixteenth century. The expression 'to go in stations' implies too that characters who did so moved between one station and the next, no doubt in some pre-determined sequence. Moreover, at least one of these stations, in the record of 13 April 1632 noted above, was either close to or actually coextensive with the place in the High Street where the play proper was acted. Most probably, then, the stations were identifiable locales arranged along some street route and which functioned as halting places where appointed characters would display themselves, and perhaps even present some narrative action, before moving on to the next. An excellent illustration of a qualitative distinction drawn between play and stations is to be found in a corporation chit dated 18 June 1590:

Robert Archer towne balife, you may not faile to pay unto St. Micchel & the Devill, that played the resurrection on Corpus Christi Day, the sum of Six Shillings Stg. and to the other Devill & Criste that went in Stacions eighteen pence, and to Michell that went in Stacions 9d. Stg. forwhich this shall be yo[r.] warrant, Dated the 18th of June 1590. You shall also pay to John hoyle for a Piece of Tymber for mending the Ducking Stole 15^d Stg. and to Daniell Kupp for making the same, and mending the Castelle Gate two Shillings Sterg. Total 11^s 7^d

Thomas Langton Souvraine.[100]

Payment for acting in the play is substantially greater than for 'going in stations'; St Michael and the Devil received 6s sterling for acting, while the 'other Devill' and Christ who 'went in Stacions' got 18d sterling, and Michael (probably St Michael again) got 9d sterling. If, as might be expected, payment was commensurate with effort, it looks as if whatever occurred at a station was a much less demanding business than acting in the play itself. The period of display at a station may therefore have been comparatively short; perhaps characters confined themselves to delivering a few lines, accompanying them, as suggested, with some suitable action and gestures.[101] This does not necessarily mean, however, that these short scenes were merely repeated identically from one station to the next. They may have been, but it is also equally conceivable that Kilkenny supported a variety of *processional play* somewhat in the manner of the late medieval English *Conversion of St Paul.* This unique dramatic survival from East Anglia distributes its narrative action among three stations. Its audience was invited to follow the action from one station to the next.[102] In Kilkenny's case, however, the narrative enacted at a station is unlikely to have been as comparably substantial, given the payment differential between play actors and stations actors noted in the chit of 18 June 1590.

As well as the stationary and the mobile dramatic presentations, it looks as if there was also a Corpus Christi procession of some kind – there are many payments to individuals for 'riding' on Corpus Christi[103] – though by the 1580s it is perhaps not likely that the host would have been carried about in it, even in a town as impervious to reform as Kilkenny evidently was. Even though the Protestant sensibilities of many there were skin-deep, Kilkenny must nevertheless have had a committed, Protestant enclave, and this in socially influential circles, as has been seen. Too ostentatious a public parade of the old theology may not have been easily tolerated. Perhaps the emphasis of the Corpus Christi procession had become largely secular, for were its Catholic significance muted in this way, while it might still have continued the commemoration of a Catholic feast, it would not have done so too nakedly and provocatively. Some sort of tactful adjustment in the direction of secularism would facilitate the reconciliation to the feast of 'conformable men' like John Lawless. It is at any rate clear that notwithstanding this possibility, Corpus Christi in Kilkenny continued to offer plenty of scope to those who wanted to turn it into a platform for Catholic triumphalism; no such secularizing dilution of the feast's Catholic significance registers in 1604 in the words of James White, vicar apostolic of Waterford and Lismore, when he visited Kilkenny to rededicate St Mary's Church, for so long the bastion and spiritual headquarters of the Protestant establisment, in the name of the Catholic faith. He went 'on the eve of the festival of Corpus Christi … from Waterford to Kilkenny, in order to celebrate that festival with all possible solemnity, because of the immense number of Catholics in the latter city, and the crowds that flocked thither from all parts of Ireland to reverence the wood of the Holy Cross that day.'[104] Though his reclamation was reversed shortly after, it is interesting to observe that he felt Corpus Christi was the right time to strike. Its procession offered him a public occasion for 'all possible solemnity' which he doubtless conducted in the fullest possible counter-reforming fashion. It is not clear precisely when on Corpus Christi the procession occurred, though in all likelihood it would have taken place before rather than after the play.[105] Nor is the processional route known. However, it would seem appropriate for it to have followed the route along which the stations had been placed, for some of its course at least.[106] The dramatic performance which went in stations would either have been integrated into the liturgical procession, or have taken place as a separate event, and if so, it probably duplicated some of the procession's route.

Much of the narrative of the Kilkenny Corpus Christi play is ascertainable. On 9 June 1585, James Krininge received 20s sterling 'for setting forth of the Maries' and 16d sterling 'for Six paire of Gloves for Criste, John Evangeliste, Mary Mother, and the other three Maryes.'[107] Corpus Christi seems the most likely occasion for this setting forth, since in 1585 the feast fell on 10 June, the very next day after Krininge's payment.[108] (The narrative of the Corpus Christi and Midsummer plays evidently had much in common, if it was not in fact identical.[109] If anything, it is the placing of the *stations* on Corpus Christi that seems to distinguish the arrangements made for that feast from those made for Midsummer.)[110] There is another warrant for a payment of a mark sterling to John Busher which is dated a few days earlier, on 3 June 1585.[111] Busher was also being paid for 'setting forth of the Maries,' and he received an additional 16d sterling, this time for eight pairs of gloves. Gloves cost 2d sterling a pair in 1585, as they did in Krininge's warrant of 9 June, but here eight pairs are mentioned, presumably implying at least eight characters in the 'Maries' play.[112] When in 1588 three years later John Busher appeared again, two payments were being ordered to him and, though both name the play differently, it seems to be the same play to which both refer. Busher was again responsible for putting on the 'Maryes,' as one warrant calls it, and as another calls it, the play of the Resurrection.[113] In 1588 the occasion is quite clear. This time it was not Corpus Christi but Midsummer, and we are told that the play had a Sepulchre (7d was paid for 'twoe pereles' for it)[114] and that it was acted in St Mary's Church.[115] The warrant of 18 June 1590, given above, adds the characters of St Michael and Satan to the cast list for the play of the Resurrection, which in this year was being presented again on Corpus Christi.

It is clear from all this that the Kilkenny Corpus Christi play (and the Mid-summer play too) was essentially a Passion play which included episodes on the Crucifixion, the Harrowing of Hell, and the Resurrection.[116] In Ireland by the six-teenth century (if not indeed before), it is clear that the Passion narrative was mat-ter enough to have plays devoted exclusively to it, as the Kilkenny play, in company with Dublin's 1506 play of the Passion of Christ on the Hoggen Green, demon-strate.[117] Perhaps the content of the Kilkenny play, farced as it evidently was with the apocryphal fireworks of the Harrowing of Hell, may even hint at that of the Dublin one of 1506. But in Kilkenny's case, such consistently single-minded choice of religious subject matter on the part of the corporation also suggests the central place occupied by the Passion narrative in the religious consciousness of Kilkenny citizens, whether they were Protestant or Catholic, as much as it embodies the cor-poration's veneration for the civic tradition that its drama represented. This unwaver-ing emphasis in the drama would have found its parallel in the preoccupation with Passion imagery in art, particularly in the plastic arts of tomb sculpture, that char-acterizes Kilkenny and its neighbouring counties during this period.[118]

The Passion play was not necessarily the only dramatic presentation on either Corpus Christi or Midsummer, for as in Dublin so in Kilkenny, a pageant of the Nine Worthies was also proving popular. It is true that unlike its Dublin counter-part which the Mayor of the Bullring organized, there is no evidence to suggest that the Kilkenny pageant was organized by the Lord of Bullring, or that its perfor-mance was perceived as the prerogative of the young men in the Lord of Bullring's charge. Yet absence of evidence does not amount to evidence of absence, and it has been seen that in 1637 on Corpus Christi at any rate, the 'young men' played upon the stage, which suggests that there could have been some traditional association between plays and the Kilkenny youth which went back at least as far as John Bale's days. The first extant mention of the Worthies dates to 1593, when one Thomas Lucas, who also set forth the Marys on Corpus Christi in that year, was paid 6s 8d 'for half a Conqueror's Wadge' and 3s 4d sterling 'for his paynes for rendering the part Charlemayne.'[119] The warrant, dated 18 and 19 June 1593, does not reveal whether his performance in the Nine Worthies pageant took place at Corpus Christi (on 14 June in that year, in which case his payment would have been ret-rospective), or whether it was forthcoming at Midsummer, which may be more likely. However, it is clear from seven warrants of 1637 that in some years both the Passion play and the Nine Worthies pageant might coincide on the same day. A payment of 6s 8d sterling was ordered on 4 June 1637 to one Thomas Daniel in exchange for the wings, coronet, and banner of St Michael in the Corpus Christi play,[120] and this, along with Mary Rothe's payment for her breakfast given to the Cor-pus Christi play actors in the same year, as well as a payment for the play's musi-cians, establishes that 1637 saw a Corpus Christi play performance.[121] But there must also have been a pageant of the Nine Worthies some time on the same day. John Purcell, Matthew Hickey, William Lawless and James Barry were all paid various amounts for acting in it.[122] Indeed, Hickey and Lawless doubled parts; Hickey played two Conquerors, and Lawless the parts both of Godfrey and Hector.[123] It is clear too that in 1637, if not in other years as well, two performances of the Worthies would follow each other with only a few days' interval, as on Corpus Christi (8 June) in 1637 and Midsummer (24 June) the same year. The Worthies pageant may have been presented in the same playing area as the Corpus Christi play, presumably with some interval between the two different performances when both occurred on the same day, or it may have gone in stations, or even both; there is no clear information on the matter. As well as its expression of local politics and theology, the sixteenth-century drama of Kilkenny Corporation evidently embodied the wider Anglo-Irish fascination with the Worthies. Dublin on the east coast had long been making them known, now Kilkenny in the southeast was, and though the context is not dramatic, on the west coast too a sixteenth-century Limerick gentleman might be found sedulously noting down the names of the Worthies in his diary.[124]

In sum, Kilkenny civic drama, documented only after Bale but probably in place already before he arrived, resembles that of Dublin only in superficial respects. Some of the subject matter dramatized was common to both places, and broadly speaking, issues of civic status common to both were negotiated publicly in dramatic terms. Yet far more striking are the differences, the ways in which the civic drama of both was supremely contingent upon two very different civic histories and struggles for corporate identity.

THE MULTITUDE OF JESUITS

How bedraggled Bale's hopes for Kilkenny were to seem by the early years of the seventeenth century is evident in the success there of a particularly tenacious and militant group of his spiritual opponents. When the Jesuits first obtruded into the English consciousness and language in the mid-sixteenth century, they came in a rash. Like many who had been demonized before them, they too were said to be both ubiquitous and subversive. The Protestant imagination, if anything even more defensive in Ireland than in England, was soon populated by these slippery agents of sedition, who though rife throughout the kingdom were yet cunningly able to cover their tracks and elude detention. Whatever the contrasting actuality of the Jesuits' presence and mission, it is curious that Kilkenny did not become one of their bases sooner; perhaps Kilkenny's tepid Reformation zeal meant that greater challenges elsewhere were likely to claim their prior attention. The first evidence for Jesuit activity in the city and its environs dates to the opening decades of the seventeenth century.[125] By 1618 they had established a Kilkenny residence and school, though precisely where is not known. The Kilkenny mission prospered. By the 1640s it was ripe for expansion, and the Jesuits were put in possession of the grounds of the dissolved Augustinian priory of St John's as a site for their college.

A history of the Irish mission compiled by William St Leger (1599–1665), a Jesuit who had joined the teaching staff in Kilkenny in 1629, overlaps with the very end of the period under review here.[126] St Leger, when commenting on the educational regime of the school, noted that *In scholis splendide, et concinne exhibebantur drammata, tragoediæ, aliæque scholasticæ exercitationes, summo concursu et applausu* ('dramas, tragedies, and other scholastic exercises were splendidly and beautifully mounted in the schools before great crowds and to much applause').[127] The essential accuracy of his observation is confirmed by the survival of a unique playbill dating from the period of the Kilkenny Confederation when the city had become the Catholic headquarters of Ireland.[128]

In 1644 the scholars of the Society of Jesus in Kilkenny produced the five-act *Titvs, or the Palme of Christian Covrage*. Its plot, which related the eventual triumph of the Christian courage of Titus over the ruthless efforts to deflect him from the true faith by the King of Bungo, was of more ancient ancestry than the immediate source of the play's inspiration might suggest. The immediate source was the *Histoire Ecclesiastique des Isles et Royaumes du Iapon* by François Solier, who wrote an account of the Jesuit mission to Japan in the 1580s. However, this account served simply as the play's point of departure.[129] Titus and his family have no named parallels in Solier's work, though they may be loosely based upon the family and character of a certain Don Paul, a persecuted christian in Japan whose wife voices the principle around which the play also revolves: 'Il vaut bien mieux … perdre les biens & la vie pour la confession de la foy, que les aduanturer apres pour quelque autre subiect' ('It is much more worthwhile to lose possessions and life for confessing the faith than for venturing them on account of whatever other cause').[130] In Solier's *Histoire*, refusal by the Christians to swear an oath which would in practice have required them to abjure their faith finally wins the day, though it does so less obviously through the magical power of Christian fortitude than through the expediency of political circumstances. In the play, by contrast, the accent is more emphatically upon the might of Christian fortitude to withstand oppression and pull a happy-ever-after ending out of the hat. In this respect, *Titvs* must therefore also be seen as the outcropping of a literary tradition of Christian self-vindication that reaches back long before the *Histoire*.

In 1644 in Kilkenny, however, this chestnut would have taken on fresh significance. Some two years earlier, and following the nationwide rebellion of 1641, the city had set itself up as the centre of the united opposition to the detested policies of the New English administration, a position that Kilkenny was to retain until it fell to Oliver Cromwell in 1649. The oath administered to confederate Catholics declared loyalty to King Charles and support for 'the free exercise of the Roman Catholic faith and religion throughout this land.'[131] The loyal Catholics, comparable in this regard to Titus in the play, had lost lands and liberties as a result of reformist oppression, but in their Kilkenny fastness in the early days of their confederation, it must have seemed that, for the present at least, their Christian courage, again like that of Titus, might yet win the day. Thus the production of the play could be regarded not merely as a typical gesture of Catholic propaganda, or as part of the humanistic ideals which tinged the Jesuits' educational program, where room seems often to have been made for drama: while it was both these things, in 1644 it was also a fillip to Kilkenny's morale at a time of open conflict.

The place in Kilkenny where *Titvs* was performed is unknown, though as has been seen, by 1644 the city had a tradition established for virtually a century of using its Market Cross as a theatrical venue. It might be supposed that the most effective forum for the sort of optimism that *Titvs* expressed would have been in some comparably central and spacious place. And the playbill mentions thirty or more characters taking part in the action, which amounts to a substantially larger cast than was needed for Bale's earlier endeavours. Of course, school plays by nature often try to involve as many school members as possible in their production, nor should it be supposed that *Titvs* was necessarily any different in this respect. Father St Leger noted that lodgings had been available at the school for some twenty to thirty or more pupils, and that was for boarders alone. It is clear that there would have been plenty of potential actors on hand to take the parts. In such circumstances, the practice of role doubling would have been unnecessary and indeed undesirable, if one of *Titvs*'s practial aims was indeed to rally morale. In which case, the more who acted, the merrier. The play text itself is lost, nor is it known who its author was, but were the truth known, it would come as no surprise if a Kilkenny Jesuit had had a hand in it.

CODA

There has been a strange symmetry to this account of drama and the performing arts in Kilkenny, for similarities have emerged where on the face of it none might have been expected. The account began and ended in a similar place, in two species of ideologically driven drama, dissimilar only in so far as they were the products of the warring forces of Reformation or of Counter-Reformation, and perhaps in the extent of the production resources at their disposal. They were similar too in their social consequences: Bale had naively misjudged the likelihood of his Protestant polemic sticking, while the anonymous author of *Titvs*, though waving the flag before the converted, could not have foreseen the eventual collapse less than five years hence of the society in Kilkenny that he stood for. Sandwiched between these committed playwrights, both ill-fated for different sets of reasons, came the more accommodating drama of civic aspiration, the Corpus Christi and Midsummer plays which, judging by their persistence, long managed to juggle successfully with the complex elements of Kilkenny's Anglo-Irish identity, elements upon which Kilkenny's prosperity had been founded.

At least two of these three dramatic camps had been pitched in the commercial and ceremonial centre of Kilkenny at the Market Cross in the High Street. Here was where drama's bid for the hearts and minds of the citizens would principally be played out. Corpus Christi and Midsummer, of course, had tended to exceed the bounds of a single site to become a Kilkenny-wide celebration, an event thus liable to appear far greater than the sum of individual partisan and factional parts. This was the drama of the united front where potential dissonances within the civic body could be harmonized and reconciled by art, and the colourful result even presented to greet representatives of the Crown on the occasion of their official visits, as the next chapter will reveal.

5

Provincial Pomps and Triumphs

'Is it not passing brave to be a King, / And ride in triumph through Persepolis?'

Christopher Marlowe, *Tamburlaine I*, Act II, sc. v[1]

Very few English kings, and no queens, were ever to ride in triumph through Ireland during the period covered by this study, even though their right to rule the island had been confirmed long since in the mid-twelfth-century Bull *Laudabiliter*. Their island was administered on their behalf. From 1172 onwards, chief governors were appointed as viceroys, their powers ceding to the monarch whenever the monarch might be present in person. Yet in the monarch's stead these men were the next best thing, and at least from the sixteenth century they might expect to be greeted with the sorts of dramatic civic displays that many an English town and city famously lavished on royal visitors.[2] From 1494, Ireland's chief governor, appointed directly by the Crown, was the Lord Deputy, and it is evidence for civic receptions laid on for two of these, one from the sixteenth and the other from the seventeenth century, that will be investigated here.[3]

The office of Lord Deputy came laden with ceremony. Investitures of Lords Deputy occurred far more often than coronations of kings and queens, and each afforded an opportunity for official civic rejoicing of the sort likely to express itself in public pageantry and drama, even if not on a coronation scale. Thus the public ceremonies of state were almost as regular a part of civic experience as those which marked other high days of the urban and ecclesiastical year. Dublin, being the Lord Deputy's base, saw most of this activity, in ceremonies centred on Christ Church Cathedral and Dublin Castle. A description of the civic entry of Sir Henry Sidney into Dublin on 26 October 1568 conveys a good basic impression of the ceremonial routine that one of these entries might entail:

Nota. that. on tewesday. beyng the .2.6. day of october anno .1.56.8. mr Robart Weston

esquier and Lorde chancelor of Ierlande. to gether wyth sir Wyllyam . fyzwyllyams. tresorer
forthe wars. Ierland. beyng the lordes Iusteces .dyd. mete. the honorable sir henry sydney.
apoyntted. agayne to be the Lorde Deputye. of all Ierland. ther mettyng was abowght
{'about'} the space. of .v. mylles. from the citey [of] at the wych mettyng ther was a very
gooly {read goodly} company abowght the nomber of vj^C. horses. in wych company cam the
seryfes {'sheriffs'} of the citey of Dublyn with agrete comppany of the citisens very well
apoyntted. also wyth ‸⌐owth⌐ the subberbes of the citey the maior of citey. wyth the aldermen.
dyd ‸⌐salute & wellcom⌐ the sayd sir henry sydney and the the lordes Iustyces and on the
bryge. of the sayd cite. there was dyvers Iustices and men of Law and burgesses of the citye
the wych also wecommed {read welcommed} the sayd sir henry sydney Kt and entryng Into
the citey. prosyded vnto the caste‸⌐ll⌐ and after hys entry inn to the sayd castell there was a
good pele of gon shotte bothe of the sayd citey and castell. wyth the sounde. of trumpette⌐s⌐
& of other musyke[4]

It often transpired that no sooner was the new Lord Deputy in office than his presence
was required in the provinces, whether for military campaigns or for more peaceful
embassies. In the latter context, provincial progresses brought the loyal towns and
cities of the colony into salutary contact, by proxy, with their monarch, and served
as a ritualized means of tying the colonial periphery more closely to its administrative centre. Civic receptions were likely to be organized to mark such occasions, signalling (though only *inter alia*) the organizers' loyal intentions to the Crown. Even
towns whose means were comparatively modest laid receptions on. The progresses
of Sir Henry Sidney, whose Irish career will be considered more extensively in the
next chapter, provide the earliest detailed evidence. Here civic receptions already appear
so well practised that, but for document loss, their history in Ireland would doubtless have registered well before Sidney encountered them.

About a year after his first taking the Lord Deputy's oath (20 January 1566),
Sidney went on a tour of Munster, supervising sessions of assize in its counties.[5] He
arrived in Waterford by boat on 25 February 1567 (see Appendix IIIa). Burgesses of
the city had arranged for a barge to be fitted with cushions and carpets, and decorated
'withe afayre pesee {'piece'} of tapsterye.' Probably so that it could be towed into
Waterford harbour, this barge was joined to a larger boat armed with cannon. In
the harbour Sidney was greeted with artillery peals from other boats and shouts,
and after mooring, was met at the quayside by the mayor, sheriffs, and aldermen.
A certain Nicholas White delivered an oration declaring the goodwill of the citizens
towards the queen, and towards Sidney as her Lord Deputy. Not surprisingly, White
spoke of both queen and Lord Deputy in association, for in terms of their formal,
political capacities, little meaningful distinction was to be drawn between them:
one was the authorized mouthpiece of the other's policies.[6] However, lest this civic
declaration of goodwill be construed as servile compliance, it was promptly followed

by reminders of the liberties granted to Waterford by past kings and princes, thus placing the current tally of civic privileges well beyond the reach of the powers that be. The speech drew a courteous acknowledgment from Sidney. Next he entered the city, where a pageant had been prepared within the gate. Anacoluthon has disrupted the source document at this point (Appendix IIIa, lines 21–3) so that, other than a person or persons 'verye properlye in the same verye well decked whoe wellcomed the said Lorde Depwetie withe a verye good oracione,' it is unknown what the pageant contained and depicted. Yet another oration was delivered en route to Sidney's lodging, to which the mayor, carrying the civic sword, conducted him, and with Ulster king of arms dressed in the queen's arms going before (compare the processional protocol shown in fig. 14, p. 135). Behind followed the aldermen. Sidney was also received by the bishop of Waterford, Patrick Walsh, and his clergy. Walsh was one of those who had succeeded in being all things to all men, having won the recognition of both Crown and papacy: for all that he wore a cope, he and his clergy, tactfully enough for any Protestant sensibility, went 'singinge the presescione {'procession'} in ingylshe {read inglyshe}.' The item of principal interest in this account, the pageant, should thus be seen as one strand in a sequence of ceremonial events which, while recognizing Sidney's authority, also defined and defended that of the city. The pageant was an important strand, of course, in that it would have been the first thing that Sidney saw on entering the city gates. Its drama would have amplified and consolidated the (doubtless political) import of its accompanying oration.

From Waterford Sidney continued his progress westwards into Munster. The next town in which he was treated to a civic reception on the grand scale, again with at least one pageant, was Limerick, where he arrived on 26 March 1567 (see Appendix IIIb). The men of Kilmallock, a town some eighteen miles to the south of Limerick through which Sidney had previously passed, had accompanied him Limerick-wards until a great escort of men came riding out from the city to meet him. He was received near the city by the mayor and aldermen, ordinance and artillery shots were fired, and he entered the 'base towne' (also called the Irishtown). Unlike his route through Waterford, that through Limerick can be traced (see fig. 17). Entering the Base Town, Sidney was greeted by a 'proper lade,' one Bartholomew White. Possibly this meeting occurred somewhere in the High Street, which connected with the Tide Bridge over the river Shannon. Over this bridge Sidney must then have passed to enter Limerick's larger quarter, the Hightown or Englishtown. Reconnecting with High Street on the northern side of the bridge, Sidney and his entourage steadily made their way towards St Mary's Cathedral. Sir Jacques Wingfield carried the sword of state before him, and as in Waterford, so here too Ulster king of arms, who probably rode by Wingfield's side, wore the coat of arms of England. The mayor, bearing his mace, rode with the queen's sarjeant of arms, and both

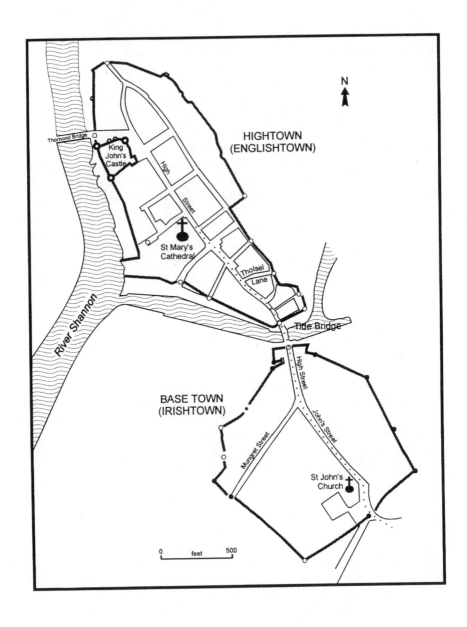

N

HIGHTOWN
(ENGLISHTOWN)

Thomond Bridge

King
John's
Castle

High
Street

St Mary's
Cathedral

Tholsel
Lane

River Shannon

Tide Bridge

BASE TOWN
(IRISHTOWN)

High Street

John's Street

Mungret Street

St John's
Church

0   feet   500

17 Limerick *c* 1600 (selected sites only).

went in front of Ulster king of arms and Sir Jacques Wingfield. At some point in the High Street en route to the cathedral, a pageant had been set up.[7] Its content, overtly political, depicted the state of Limerick, and a young man, Stephen White, dressed as a messenger of peace in a scarlet mantle and garlanded with bays, explained to Sidney the pageant's significance. The oration finished, he gave Sidney a written copy of it, with another book containing the complaints of the citizens. Sidney thanked the mayor and aldermen in the queen's name for their welcome, promising he would do his utmost on their behalf. The group then moved to the cathedral where the bishop of Limerick, Hugh Lacy (another of those recognized by Crown and papacy), received him in the churchyard, though this time 'with a pressione {'procession'} in Latine singing and the said bisshope was in his ponticalie {'pontificals'} after the popes fascion.' The theatrical pomp of Limerick's receptions would impress Sidney a second time, during a visit on 4 February 1576: 'I was received, with farre greater pompe, then either I my selfe have here tofore had, or sawe yelded to any other in this land.'[8] This was high praise because not long before, Kilkenny had entertained him 'with all shewes and tokens, of gladnes, and pompe, aswell vpon the water, as the land; presented with the best commoditie they had,'[9] and the memory would still have been fresh in his mind. What the 1576 reception comprised Sidney did not say. Orations probably featured again, for they continued to be the staple of such occasions throughout the sixteenth century and well into the next.[10]

It was oratory that loomed largest in Sir Thomas Wentworth's recollection of his various civic receptions in the summer of 1637. In a letter larded with irony, probably to tickle his own humour as much as that of his correspondent, Lord Conway and Killultagh, he broached the theme of how 'Oratory hath abundantly magnified it self' in the recent days of his progress through Munster (see Appendix IIIc). He began by listing the orations he had heard – one in Carlow, three in Kilkenny, two 'very deadly long ones' in Clonmel, and four in Limerick – before proceeding to sketch the pageantry presented in Limerick, from where his letter was addressed. Although Wentworth seems more interested in displaying the urbanity of his response to this provincial pomp than in documenting its content, some of this can still be recovered by reading between the lines. Part of the décor for the civic reception included that characteristically seventeenth-century ingredient, the triumphal arch with ornaments and inscriptions.[11] The Limerick pageant forms were heavily classical. Cupids, Apollo, ancient genii and laureate poets all featured, and the centrepiece that attracted Wentworth's closest attention, though again not without ironic inflection in the telling, was evidently a pageant machine presenting the seven planets. These were somehow set in circular motion, and an actor (or actors) in each planetary sphere sang Wentworth's praises. The sphere of the sun was also made to squirt 'sweet waters' (perfume?) onto Wentworth and his entourage. Even in Limerick, a relatively small city in the west of Ireland remote from the London court, it was possible for a pageant machine to be prepared pretending to the height of fashion. The Limerick device begs comparison with the engine that Inigo Jones had contrived only some six years earlier for the Whitehall performance of *Tempe Restord*, a masque in which to the sound of music: 'In the midst of the ayre the eight *Spheares* in rich habites were seated on a Cloud, which in a circular forme was on each side continued vnto the highest part of the Heaven, and seem'd to haue let them downe as in a Chaine.'[12] Yet setting aside pageant machinery with fashionably flattering cosmological themes, Limerick's civic entry in another respect was curiously old-fashioned, for it marks the last civic entry decorated with dramatic pageantry on record in the British Isles. The reign of Charles I was not notable for its elaborate civic receptions.[13] The last of the kind that the king was treated to happened in Edinburgh in 1633. But in Limerick in 1637 his deputy was received in his stead with all the old traditional pomp and circumstance, presented in an up-to-date guise. Part of the Limerick pageantry seems also to have included festal water transport, as it had done for Sidney in the previous century in both Kilkenny and Waterford. Another source describing Wentworth's reception relates that he was rowed to and from Bunratty, a town some eight miles to the west of the city along the coast, in the civic barge.[14]

Vivid though the pageantry of Limerick's civic entries was, there is no extant internal information about the minutiae of its organization. As in other Irish provincial towns and cities – save one – the pageantry of the civic entry is recorded only externally, via the random impressions of those before whom it was presented. The sole exception is from Kilkenny.[15] Here, internal evidence for the preparations made for a civic entry provides an especially valuable complement to the Limerick event, because the Kilkenny entry was laid on for the same Lord Deputy, Sir Thomas Wentworth, and during the same provincial tour in which he visited Limerick. Wentworth's impression of Kilkenny's reception of him is summarized in a letter to his wife of 16 August 1637: 'the town hath entertained us with the force of oratory and the fury of poetry.'[16] Though terse, the summary was just: oratory and poetry are both to the fore in the corporation accounts of expenditure for the occasion, as well as poetry in the guise of songs composed and sung by 'James Kyvan and the other chorister.'[17] Indeed, music was as important a component of Kilkenny's pageantry as it was of Limerick's. Wentworth seems to have visited Kilkenny twice within a short period, sandwiching his Limerick visit in between. It is unclear exactly when the two Kilkenny receptions were held, or what they precisely comprised, but their components seem on each occasion to have been broadly similar. Wentworth's itinerary went roughly as follows. He left Dublin 9 August 1637 to begin his progress.[18] He entered Kilkenny either on 10 August or very soon after, and by 13 August he had removed to Clonmel, some twenty-eight miles to the southwest.[19] By 19 August he had arrived in Limerick, some forty-six miles to the northwest of Clonmel, where he witnessed the cosmic pageantry described above. Here he stayed, spending time also at Bunratty, at least until 28 August.[20] His return home brought him back again via Kilkenny, sometime early in September, when the second civic reception took place.[21] As in Limerick, a triumphal arch was erected in Kilkenny, again 'at the Square at the Bridge' (that is, on the north side of St John's Bridge; see fig. 15, p. 164) where the earl of Ormond's musicians had been retained to play for him on his first entry.[22] This was probably the location of one of the three Kilkenny orations that he mentioned having heard in his letter to Lord Conway and Killultagh from Limerick on 21 August. The arch was of timber, painted and decorated with sallows, and it featured in both of Wentworth's Kilkenny visits.[23] Rushes had been strewn along St John's Street, and as he entered the city, he proceeded up Rozom Street (see fig. 15; modern Rose Inn Street), which had been cleaned for the occasion, and past Croker's Cross, where two stages had been erected.[24] (These may have been the sites of the two other orations mentioned in his letter to Lord Conway and Killultagh.) It is not known where Wentworth lodged, but since the earl of Ormond had vacated the castle during the visit and taken up residence with members of the Shee family, wealthy Kilkenny burghers, it is possible that Wentworth was given the run of the place.[25]

Wentworth's Kilkenny visits seem to have centred upon Hightown, and on a very particular section of it. No mention is made of pageants, triumphal arches, stages, nor any of the other traditional circumstances of the civic entry, at any place other than here, at the castle end of the city. Strangely, the commercial and civic centre of Kilkenny along High Street, where stood those sites anciently associated with the corporation, the Tholsel and Market Cross, seems to have been as much neglected as was Irishtown to the east of the city walls, and this even though it was the corporation that organized and financed Wentworth's reception. The apparent omission is conspicuous, especially in view of the long-standing importance of the Market Cross as a venue for plays and civic shows. It seems therefore as if the tone of Wentworth's visits was essentially more aristocratic, more distant, than had been that, for example, of Sidney's civic entries in the previous century, and in this aloofness the corporation was nevertheless acquiescent.

Yet if we look at the aggregated evidence for the pageantry presented to Sir Henry Sidney and Sir Thomas Wentworth, and which spans some seventy years (1567–1637), certain patterns emerge. In some respects, perhaps the most salient ones, the two Lords Deputy were treated to pageantry of broadly comparable dimensions, not only, as far as this can now be gauged, in terms of the pageantry's mechanics (orations, poetry, music at stations along a route), but also in terms of the interrelated questions of civic location and general political thrust (notwithstanding the fact that the particular nuances of that thrust, being historically contingent, were therefore rather different in either Lord Deputy's case). For both Lords Deputy, pageant preliminaries were presented at the thresholds of the city *before* any other pageants that may have been displayed once the party of dignitaries moved inside. In Sir Henry Sidney's case (and perhaps in Sir Thomas Wentworth's, though unequivocal evidence is wanting), the impending civic event was heralded by the large mounted escort that rode out to meet him. And while not a pageant in strictly formal terms, the contingent of men from the legal profession stationed on Dublin Bridge, which would have lent the site a distinctive appearance and presence, might be compared at least in terms of location with the pageant proper organized for Wentworth and stationed at the bridge in Kilkenny. Thus pageants, or pageant preliminaries, forcefully staked out the boundary and inception of the civic enterprise with all the dramatic power at their disposal. Contrast those discreeter roadside heralds of what lies ahead that are in use today: 'Welcome to Wherever,' perhaps tastefully enlivened with Wherever's heraldic device. The flagging of the sixteenth- and seventeenth-century Irish civic entries was far more imposing, and doubtless necessarily so, when they were negotiating the admission into the city's midst of powers that the city might need to reckon with.[26] Pageant preliminaries served not alone as escorts of the honorand; looked at from another point of view, they were also the outriders of inviolate civic privilege and authority.

The same perhaps might be said of the circumstances of many English triumphal entries,[27] but to explain the Irish experience simply by appealing to English pageant precedents would be to miss the political circumstances peculiar to Ireland in which Irish triumphal entries were played out and interpreted. For example, given the weight of Old English representation in the corporations of old towns and cities like Waterford, Limerick, and Kilkenny, it is reasonable to assume a greater degree of civic nervousness than is likely to have manifested itself in England at the prospect of welcoming the chief New English administrator. It is interesting that points of ingress, those traditionally vulnerable points in a city's defences (its bridges, gates, and apertures), were so often the sites chosen to be guarded, as it were, by pageantry. Lords Deputy might be welcome to enter, but the city's thresholds, potential breaches in its security and hence in its autonomy, had still to be negotiated on the city's terms. This was done by constructing gates and arches of another sort, ideological ones of pageantry, in those liminal places through which the powerful, if they were to gain admission at all, were also obliged to pass, and in the passing, might find themselves somehow brought to book.[28] We see this metaphor forcefully literalized when actual books recording the content of the event were handed to the Lord Deputy, as happened to Sidney in Limerick, and as may have happened to Wentworth in Kilkenny.[29] These books were palpable traces, civically sanctioned, of the evanescent words uttered, civic position statements whose public acceptance before so many witnesses, liable therefore to being construed as assent, might compromise the accepter. Thus much is implicit in the fact that when, for example, Elizabeth I was to be handed a book as part of the proceedings for her coronation triumph through London, she first ascertained what the book was before accepting it. Only when she knew that it was 'the Byble in Englishe' could she safely kiss it, clasp it to her bosom, and so turn her gesture of public acceptance into a *coup de théâtre* that delighted the spectating Londoners.[30] Interesting testimony to the public power latent even in small-scale civic entries is found in an entry not otherwise reviewed here: probably in Clonmel, co. Tipperary, on 25 May 1599, Sir Robert Devereux was moved publicly to contradict the import of one of the orations delivered in his honour.[31] The Irish civic entries for which we have evidence could be viewed less as a means of offering apotheosis to the honorand, after the manner of certain English entries taking place in more acquiescent political circumstances, than of inscribing him in a role that, in being a definition, was at once a limitation, of the extent of his power, the sugar of pageant flattery serving only to help that (potentially uncongenial) limitation slip down more easily.[32] Ireland, like England, had its pageantry of *laudando praecipere*, but perhaps one more urgent in the Irish context.[33] The semiotics of its performance were complex. Two theatres of self-representation, those of state power and civic authority, entered a dramatic dialogue at a symbolic level. Unlike dramas conceived in a traditional modern sense, these civic entries had no single audience: the city spectated itself and the Lord Deputy, while the Lord Deputy spectated himself and the city. In the process of self-representation, each necessarily made some claim to represent the other. Thus, to take an example, when Limerick put itself on display, it also preempted in some degree how Sir Henry Sidney exercised his power within it, just as the Lord Deputy's personal ceremony of state called forth and in some degree determined the response of the city and obliged it to measure the legitimate extent of its authority: the occasion of Sidney's visit caused Limerick to conceptualize and voice an identity for itself, via pageantry, in the symbolic order; only here could that identity be usefully intelligible to the citizens. Put another way, and more generally, pageantry reified symbolically the dominant strains of civic ideology, foregrounding them, and thus making them substantial, in civic consciousness. As seen in previous chapters, Ireland's formidable investment in the theatre of civic authority has emerged again here, though now it is a theatre accenting a united civic front in the face of an external force, when civic solidarity must supersede civic consensus.[34] The task of describing how formidable in the Irish context could be investments in the theatre of personal power lies largely ahead, when in a survey of aristocratic patronage of drama and the performing arts it will become clear how they satisfied far more than the basic human appetite for entertainment. No wonder in these circumstances that cities, especially provincial ones hopeful of gain and very fearful of what they might lose, might invest in pomps and pageants which spoke as much about their own interests, united for the nonce, as about those of the dignitaries whom they ostensibly fêted.

6

Patrons, Households, and Institutions

INTRODUCTION

'An múr 'na aonar anocht
'na gcluininn gáir chrot is chliar ...'[1]
['The walls where once we heard harps and bands of poets are lonely tonight.']

Since all elegies tend to commemorate the brightest fragments of former existence, it is not surprising that in Irish poetry, *ubi sunt* reminiscence should often make mention of life's convivial moments when social well-being found issue in music and feasting. Gaelic minstrels and performing artists, who were wont to inhabit and orchestrate such moments, came naturally to symbolize a whole way of life, society at its most sanguine best. More than merely provide entertainment, through their unique resources of display they also publicly acclaimed the values of their patrons. Not only, then, were the various minstrel classes and their performances likely to be evoked in elegies, but also in the praise poetry with which aristocratic patrons were frequently served. A patron might secure esteem and a healthy reputation for being endowed with all sorts of socially desirable qualities if he treated minstrels well.

Consequently, a rich vein of information on the performing arts is to be found running through a series of Irish texts composed between the thirteenth and the seventeenth centuries, many of which are eulogies in which may be described in some detail, even if only en passant, the circumstances of aristocratic Gaelic patronage and pastimes. While due allowance has to be made for the inclination of these texts towards hyperbole and for the fact that most of them were hardly disinterested, designed as they were to advance their composers, they may nevertheless yield valuable historical information if used circumspectly.[2] Evidence for aristocratic Gaelic patronage and pastimes, of course, is found well before the thirteenth century, as has already been seen, but it is only from the early Classical Irish period that the picture begins to assume a more personalized depth. This chapter will begin by considering how this material may shed further light on performance practice within the upper-class Gaelic households, before proceeding to broach the evidence for performance practice within the households of the Anglo-Irish and the New English lords. These three categories of convenience will then be merged in a consideration of the common role played by household servants and domestics as performers and purveyors of entertainment. Finally, moving outside the private households, the evidence for the more public patronage of performers and touring companies will be investigated. Prominent in this category will be corporate and institutional patronage.

GAELIC HOUSEHOLDS

Gaelic aristocrats retained musicians and performing artists, in the wide sense examined in chapter 1, in their entourages as a matter of course.[3] Their obituaries frequently noted their generosity *dfhiledhaib .7 doirfidechaibh .7 do aos gacha cerda* ('to poets and minstrels and folk of all arts'),[4] more as if this were a hallmark of aristocratic magnanimity than a purely practical device, which it undoubtedly also was, by which patrons might burnish their reputation. In other contexts, notably in praise poems, aristocratic households might be celebrated as centres of minstrel activity. For example, so great was the sound of music that wafted from the ramparts of the home of Toirdhealbhach Luineach Ó Néill at the Creeve, co. Antrim, claimed the poet Tadhg dall Ó hUiginn, that approaching it Tadhg would have had difficulty hearing what anyone said to him, even were that person standing at his shoulder.[5] And to illustrate how rooted in Gaelic poetry throughout Ireland the tradition was that every household worthy of the name should have its share of minstrels, a further example might be cited from a castle in a different Irish province. Cahir Castle in co. Tipperary, a residence of some of the more Gaelicized Butler lords, was said to have been *Longphort lionmhor domnaibh banda . bithe beilbhinn . lan do chrutibh tédoibh taighiuir . is aos leighinn* ('A princely dwelling populous with gentle ladies, demure, melodious-mouthed; full of harps with strings of sweetly mournful sounds; and men of learning').[6] The examples date to the sixteenth century, though the tradition is much older. However much a eulogistic topos it may have been, it was not necessarily the less historically true because of that. The Book of Magauran, the earliest *duanaire* ('poetic anthology') extant, contains various eulogies to members of the Mág Shamradáin family of co. Cavan from the late-thirteenth to the early-fourteenth centuries in which household music is given a prominent place. A poem addressed to Brian Mág Shamradáin (†1298) not only celebrates Brian and his accomplishments directly, but also indirectly pays him homage by praising his household in Tullyhaw, where might be found *Fir ig daghsenm uma uair ig dula ar carfe⌈d⌉m go ciuin ar nimadh anam in oil ri himad oir na crand ciuil* ('Musicians deftly playing on cold brass strings, steadily producing their notes, we [poets] striving [in recitation] during the banquet with the accompaniment of gold [(?)] harps').[7] Again in another poem from the same *duanaire*, addressed to Mághnus Mág Shamradáin (†1303) by the poet Raghnall Ó hUiginn, the harp is cast in one of its familiar roles, as princely soporific: 'Gan cruit nogan timpan tedbind ni thed na cholludh craebh liag dadha gormshuil mar blath mbhugha do mongdhuin snath uma iad' ('Liag's Branch [i.e., Mághnus Mág Shamradáin] never goes to sleep without [the music of] harp or sweet-stringed *timpán*; brass strings can make the eyelashes close over his two eyes, blue like hyacinths').[8]

So unerring might the timing and size be of the largesse shown towards the men of art that it could hardly have been better calculated to leave a lasting impression on them and on those who witnessed it. A tradition arose of the *gairm sgoile* (the 'invitation to a bardic assembly'), which an aristocratic patron might extend not just to a small group but to numerous men of art at one of the chief feasts of the year. It is possible that the first historical glimpse of a *gairm sgoile*, or of something very like one, comes to light in the context of a massacre. It occurred at Branganstown, co. Louth, on 9 June 1329, when the men of Ardee and the kern of John de Bermingham, first earl of Louth, set about each other. John was evidently a man who had acquired a taste for Irish culture, and though the precise reasons are unclear, he was hated by his co. Louth tenants. His affectation of Irish ways can have done little to endear him when to be Irish in this part of Ireland at this date, as has been pointed out, was to be regarded de facto as an enemy.[9] When the earl's home was sacked by the men of Louth, not only members of the family, but a famous harper, the blind Maelruanaigh Mac Cearbhaill, plus twenty or more other harpers, were also slaughtered. As the annalist John Clyn put it:

in vigilia pentestes {*read* pentecostes} et beati barnabe apostoli dominus Iohannes [Iohannes] de Brimegham comes de Lowht occiditur contra eum & conspiraverant omnes de comitatu suo nolentes eum regnare super eos; consilium fecerunt in unum et in multitudine magna armatorum congregati nulli de familia ejus parcentes eum cum 160. et amplius cum 2. fratribus ejus et de cognomine ipsius circa novem interfecerunt. In ista strage et eodem die Cam o'Kayrwill famosus ille timpanista et cytharista in arte sua fenix ea pollens prerogativa et virtute cum aliis tympanistis discipulis ejus circiter 20. ibidem occubuit. Iste ā *(blank)* vocatus cam .o.Kayrwyll quia luscus erat nec habebat oculos rectos sed oblique respiciens, et si non fuerat artis musice cordalis [aliis] primus inventor omnium tamen predecessorum et precedentium ipsum et contemporaneorum corrector, doctor et director extitit.[10]

[On the vigil of Pentecost and of the blessed Apostle Barnabas, the lord John de Bermingham, count of Louth, is killed. And all the men of his county conspired against him, not wishing him to rule over them. They made a plan together, and assembled with a great crowd of armed men. Sparing none of his household, they killed him, with one hundred and sixty others and more, including his two brothers and about nine bearing his surname. In that slaughter and on the same day, Cam Ó Cearbhaill, a famous player on the *timpán* and harper, that phoenix mighty in his art and of outstanding power, died with about twenty other *timpán* players, pupils of his. He was called Cam Ó Cearbhaill, however, because he was half blind, and his eyes were not set straight but squinting. And if he was not the first inventor of the art of stringed music, yet he stood out as the corrector, teacher and director of all who had gone before, who were now, or who were to follow after him.]

The question is, what were all those harpers doing there in the one household at the same time? It might also be noted that they were all in attendance just before the feast of Pentecost (11 June in that year). Perhaps this assembly of harpers is another piece of evidence that the earl had indeed gone native, and had issued a *gairm sgoile*. In any event, the first clear *gairm sgoile* on record, already noted in chapter 1 though in a different context, took place in 1351, when William Ó Ceallaigh invited 'all ye Irish Poets, Brehons, bards, harpers, gamesters or common kearoghs, Iesters & others of theire kind of Ireland to his house vpon Christmas this yeare.'[11] The site of the Ó Ceallaigh convention is uncertain, though evidently it took place at one of his residences somewhere in the west of Ireland.[12] In addition to its registering in various sets of annals – a sign that Ó Ceallaigh's strategy for publicizing himself had succeeded – one of the invited poets, Gofraidh Fionn Ó Dálaigh, earned his keep by commemorating the occasion in encomiastic verse. Although the actual event, and Ó Ceallaigh with it, were transmitted varnished for posterity with Ó Dálaigh's laudatory glaze, certain details of the arrangements made for the *gairm sgoile* may have been historically truthful enough.[13] Ó Dálaigh relates that a temporary wattle village was constructed for the visitors next to Ó Ceallaigh's castle, and was apparently also sectioned according to their profession. Thus poets had their quarter, and a 'street' (*sráid*) each was assigned to several of the sorts of entertainer discussed in chapter 1: to *lucht senma* ('people of instrumental music,' 'musicians'), *senchaide* ('reciters of lore'), *clíara* ('poetic bands'), and *clesaigi* ('jugglers').[14] The need to erect temporary quarters on such a scale suggests that the number of entertainers present must have been very large. Indeed, some eighty years later, at Killeigh within the Gaelic lordship of Ely O'Carroll (a region roughly coextensive with present-day north co. Tipperary and north-west co. Offaly), a *gairm sgoile* was issued for a convention in which some two thousand seven hundred were said to have participated. Margaret, daughter of Tadhg Ó Cearbhaill, hosted it, and the names of the guests were entered onto a roll by Gilla na naem Mac Aedhagáin, hereditary lawyer to Margaret's husband, Ó Conchobhair Failghe. The guests included 'gamsters and poore men ... with the arts of Dan {< *dán*, 'poetry'} or poetry, musick and Antiquitie,' and these received not only hospitality but gifts into the bargain.[15] Not surprising, then, that when Margaret died in 1451, these men of art lamented her passing and so helped to hand down her memory gilded to posterity.

The sheer size of these *gairm sgoile* enterprises (doubtless the phenomenally big ones were exceptions) would have furthered the desired end: maximum publicity for the host would be ensured thereby. However, as the Gaelic way of life came under increasing pressure from the new wave of English settlers during the sixteenth century, so inevitably did the large-scale practice of the *gairm sgoile*. By the middle of the century it had vanished from record.[16] To be sure, entertainers continued to serve up the traditional fare to their aristocratic Gaelic patrons, especially in those regions, like Ulster, that longest resisted English cultural influence, but they did so on a scale less triumphal than that of the *gairm sgoile* in its heyday. The sixteenth century would be marked by an inevitable retrenchment. Nevertheless, performing arts practised in the households of the Anglo-Irish lords make an interesting bridging point between those in the households of the Gaels and of the New English, because it is hard to resist the conclusion that among the Anglo-Irish too, and even among some of the New English, as will be seen later, patrons were as sensitive as the Gaels to the fame and good report, as well as to the sheer entertainment, that might accrue from maintaining performing artists conspicuously in their entourages.

ANGLO-IRISH HOUSEHOLDS IN THE SIXTEENTH AND SEVENTEENTH CENTURIES

The web of loyalties and interests in which the Anglo-Irish aristocracy was enmeshed was often of an exceedingly complex weave, and as a result this group is particularly intriguing to study. On the one hand the Anglo-Irish were usually conservative in confessional allegiance, which following the Reformation might precipitate difficulties for them with the English authorities, yet on the other hand many of them were traditionally faithful to the Crown. Such bifocal loyalties, uneasy bedfellows whenever the monarch was Protestant, were resolved by individuals with varying degrees of success. Some Anglo-Irish lords had a bumpy relationship with the English administration but still managed to stay within the terms of English authority; others fell into rebellion against it; and yet others managed to juggle artfully with the contradictions in which they so often found themselves placed.

In the latter category, the household of the Ormond Butlers is prominent. As was noted in chapter 4, the tenth earl, Sir Thomas Butler, had largely succeeded in being all things to all men. Thoroughly familiar from his childhood years with the London court, where eventually he came to enjoy Elizabeth I's favour, he might nevertheless be celebrated back at home in Gaelic praise poetry. An anonymous poem of *c* 1588 makes his household a kaleidoscope of conviviality:

Mná dhá ttochmarc ór dá bhronnadh seóid dá ttogha déigsidhibh
óig ag svirghe ól ar fhíontaibh ceol ar chaoine a caolghlacvibh
dán dá éisteacht dáimh dhá réighteach mná dhá mbréaga ar bhréag aireacht
agus raingce tímpcheall tínte ig bvidhin tsingmhi tréin nertmhvir[17]

[Women being wooed, gold bestowed, the choosing of gems
for poets, youths courting and the drinking of wine, sweet music
from narrowed hands, poetry being listened to, poets reciting,
women being seduced, a noble gathering and dancing round fires by
a strong, vigorous and graceful band.]

Dancing, incidentally, seems to have been a time-honoured Butler pastime: one Butler met his death while dancing on Shrove Tuesday evening in 1418, but no memory of his mishap seems to have daunted the dancers described by the anonymous Gaelic poet in the next century, or indeed John Butler in the next, who took the modish step of enrolling at a dancing school.[18] At his principal residence in Kilkenny Castle, Sir Thomas entertained guests with the sort of hospitality for which Anglo-Irish lords, as much as Gaelic ones, were happy to become famous. Over the Christmas period of 1575 he was visited by the writer and adventurer Thomas Churchyard. Only the year before, Churchyard had been commissioned by the city of Bristol to write the pageants for the civic reception there of Elizabeth I, and now he was serving in Ireland. He subsequently published a verse epistle, probably composed either during this time or early in 1576, which he addressed to Sir Henry Sidney, to whom he was well known and with whom he had recently been campaigning in Ulster.[19] Sidney was at that time spending Christmas in Cork, and Churchyard was anxious to explain that the reason he was not keeping him company there was because after his exertions he was resting up in Kilkenny at the earl of Ormond's house. The epistle refers frequently and incidentally to the performing arts, to the pastimes of masques, maypoles, and music, as though these were the common coin of aristocratic life even in Ireland, where military campaigns were ever liable to disrupt and consume the time. Nor is it likely, in the light of what the Gaelic poet said of it, that Churchyard would have missed in his host's residence in Kilkenny the Christmas conviviality of the restorative sort that he extolled: 'In sutche extreemes, fine Christmas games are good, / And Musicks sounde, reuiues the drouzie braine: / A tale well told, of merie Robbin Hood, / The wandryng harte, it shall bryng home againe.'[20] In fact, it is clear that Churchyard could at least have heard 'Musicks sounde' from the troupe of musicians that Ormond retained: just a few months before Churchyard's visit, Sir Walter Devereux, nineteenth earl of Essex, had rewarded them with 20s, and he had given twice as much again to Crues, Ormond's harper, a celebrity in English circles.[21] The Butler household was therefore characterized by its pluralist disposition towards the performing arts which would have made it a venue congenial to most tastes and cultural persuasions. This disposition might be regarded as a natural corollary of the pluralism of the Butler lords themselves. As well as the resort of musicians retained there on a more permanent basis, the household by the seventeenth century had also becòme a stopping-off place for visiting players and musicians.[22] A set of household accounts which survives from this period gives a good impression of the sort of wide-ranging patronage which the Butler lords exercised. The accounts date between 1630 and 1632, the last years in the life of the eleventh earl, Walter Butler, who had succeeded Sir Thomas in 1614. They include payments to musicians of various kinds (trumpeters, 'Musitioners,' drummers, fiddlers, hautboy players, and harpers),[23] and a payment for a play put on probably in Kilkenny Castle by actors on 29 January 1631: 'Laide oute for my Lord to the actors of the pley at the Castle the 29 of Ianuary 40s. of which my Lord deliuered me 20s.'[24] Either the actors in question were on tour, since as will be seen, by the late sixteenth and early seventeenth centuries the southern Irish provinces had become an attractive prospect for touring troupes, or they were local talent which, given Kilkenny's vigorous theatrical traditions, it is not hard to imagine being available.[25]

As well as the Butlers, the Desmond and Kildare branches of the Fitzgeralds provide further prime examples of the half way houses maintained by the Anglo-Irish lords. A confluence of ethnic traditions is witnessed on the so-called Dalway harp, an instrument manufactured for Sir John Fitz Edmond Fitzgerald of Cloyne, co. Cork, in 1621.[26] It is inscribed in Latin and Irish, and the long Irish inscription lists some of Sir John's chief household staff, including the harp's carpenter and the two musicians who had care of it, Giollapatrick and Dermot Mac Cridan. (It is likely that these latter two were members of the same family, judging by their shared surname.) Yet on the harp's forepillar, that part of the instrument that faced out towards the audience when it was being played, were also carved the arms of England surmounting the arms of Sir John himself.[27] Thus the harp provides a striking emblem of the cultural mixing characteristic of the Anglo-Irish tradition, manifested here specifically within the sphere of the performing arts. A similar mixing of traditions nearly a hundred years earlier is evidenced within the Kildare branch of the Fitzgerald family. A certain Owen Keynan of Cappervarget, near Rathangan, co. Kildare, is recorded as having received a pardon in 1541. The fiant in which he appears declared that he had been a servant of Gerald, late earl of Kildare (this was the ninth earl, who had died in the Tower of London on 2 September 1534). Keynan combined the roles so familiarly excoriated in English sources hostile to Gaelic performing artists: he was a harper, rhymer, poet, and bard, and like so many of his profession, he was blind.[28] Thus while he seems to have been a typical product of the native Gaelic tradition, he nevertheless found employment in the household of

Earl Gerald, a man who had once enjoyed the confidence of the Crown as Lord Deputy.[29] It is probable that Keynan would also have been known to Gerald's son and successor, the tenth earl, Thomas, the same man who had eventually turned rebel and besieged Dublin in 1534. Yet when the castle of Thomas in Maynooth, co. Kildare, was later captured in reprisal by Sir William Brereton, we learn that the earl had evidently also emulated the English and characteristically royal practice of maintaining a choral establishment in the castle chapel: upon the castle's surrender, most of the inmates were slaughtered, but two of the chapel's singing men had performed the song-motet *Dulcis amica* so beautifully that their lives were spared.[30] The capacity of the Fitzgerald household to absorb the performing arts of different ethnic traditions shows how cosmopolitan it had become by the early years of the sixteenth century.

NEW ENGLISH HOUSEHOLDS OF THE SIXTEENTH CENTURY

Important as the evidence for the Gaelic and Anglo-Irish households may be, it is outweighed in quantity and detail by that for the households of the New English. The members of this tightly knit group also patronized players and performing artists generously, and in ways differing fundamentally in certain respects from those of their Gaelic and Anglo-Irish contemporaries. All cultural persuasions appreciated the entertainment value of performance, but whereas public reputations, not to mention private vainglory, were also prime considerations for Gaelic (and probably for some Anglo-Irish) patrons, for the New English, these considerations were seldom likely to be ends in themselves. The reason for this was that at the end of the day, even the greatest of the New English was no greater than a plenipotentiary who derived his authority from the monarch. Thus for the New English, performance often functioned preeminently to uphold the panoply of the life of the state, whose representatives they were, and no more eloquently than when performance was centred on the persons of the various Lords Deputy, the monarch's representatives in Ireland. Performance was also often a token of English civility and a means whereby loyalty to a class and culture could be trumpeted amongst those who witnessed, patronized, or even participated in it directly. The socio-cultural affiliation of the New English emerges not only from the way in which they retained their own performing artists, but also from the way they reciprocally patronized those of their New English (and Anglo-Irish) associates. Hence the New English households, mutually connected as they often already were by ties of kinship and marriage, were further bonded in a close network of performance patronage. It is likely that this patronage was already established in the earliest of these households: for example, the 'iiij mynstrelles of yreland' who were retained by Sir Anthony St Leger (Lord Deputy for the first time between 7 July 1540 and 12 October 1543) evidently travelled outside Ireland, for they appeared in 1542–3 in Plymouth, where they were rewarded with 3s 4d for services rendered.[31] It is not until the second half of the sixteenth century, however, that clear evidence for the activity of performers on Irish soil comes to light. The households of Sidney, Fitzwilliam, Devereux, Perrot, Russell, and Blount will be examined next, in that order, and in the course of examination the complex network of patronage in which they all participated, and its importance, will become apparent.

The earliest and most copious of the extant sixteenth-century household records illustrate the patronage of Sir Henry Sidney (1529–86), thrice Lord Deputy of Ireland.[32] Those of his household accounts in which patronage evidence is contained and that can be dated with confidence are coextensive with all four periods of his Irish residence.[33] He first came to Ireland as vice-treasurer and member of the Irish council in May 1556 with his brother-in-law Sir Thomas Radcliffe, third earl of Sussex, after Radcliffe's appointment as Lord Deputy. The prospects of English preferment caused him to resign his vice-treasurership in March 1557 and return to England. However, those prospects dematerialized and by the end of July in that year he had returned to Ireland and resumed his office. During an absence of Radcliffe in England, Sidney was appointed Lord Justice in August 1558, and surrendered the sword of state to Radcliffe again on his return. Upon the death of Queen Mary, Sidney was once more entrusted with the sword during Radcliffe's absence, and confirmed in his office by Elizabeth I on her accession on 17 November 1558. Radcliffe returned to Ireland in the summer of 1559 and Sidney, who had in the meanwhile been appointed Lord President of the Welsh Marches, yielded to him the sword, turned his Irish vice-treasurership over to his brother-in-law, Sir William Fitzwilliam, and left for home. From 1562 Sidney was engaged on various foreign diplomatic missions, but returned to Ireland late in 1565, now as Lord Deputy, where he was sworn in in Dublin on 20 January 1566. The civic triumphs in Waterford and Limerick examined in the previous chapter date to this first period as Lord Deputy, when Sir Henry Sidney was on a progress in the south, organizing sessions of assize in the spring of 1567. This proved a relatively brief tenancy of the office, however, for early in October 1567 he went back to the court in London, where he was at first coolly received and his policies in Ireland criticized. He retired for a while to his family seat in Penshurst, but by the spring of 1568, he had reinstated himself at court, and was for the second time appointed Lord Deputy of Ireland. He was presented with the sword and sworn in in Dublin on 28 October 1568. But eventually disheartened by the attention that Elizabeth I was paying to the complaints made against him by her favourite, Sir Thomas Butler, tenth earl of Ormond, he left Dublin for England on 25 March 1571, having seen Sir John Perrot installed as Lord President of Munster and Sir William Fitzwilliam as Lord Justice. (Fitzwilliam was subsequently appointed Lord Deputy in December 1571.) The details of the final visit of Sidney to Ireland need not long detain us. After receiving the sword from Fitzwilliam in Drogheda in September 1575, Sidney set out at once to pacify Ulster, now in some chaos after the failed attempts at colonization by Sir Thomas Smith and the nineteenth earl of Essex, Sir Walter Devereux. Having achieved a temporary peace, he returned to Dublin, but promptly set out again for Kilkenny, where he was well entertained by his old critic, Sir Thomas Butler. Thence he travelled to Waterford, then to Cork (where as noted in a previous context he spent Christmas), and then to Limerick, where he was received with pomp early in February 1576. He left Limerick later that month, passed through Athlone, and was back in Dublin by mid-April 1576. At Christmastide in 1577, he was in Kilkenny again, negotiating terms of agreement between the president of Munster and Sir Gerald Fitz James Fitzgerald, fourteenth earl of Desmond. But Elizabeth was finding Sidney's administration too expensive, and he received his letter of final recall on St George's Day 1578.

Before the evidence for his performance patronage is meshed into this busy historical framework, one salient aspect of his character is worth observing, since it has a bearing on the matter in hand. Sidney seems to have been a bon viveur. As a (generally approving) description of him in the Book of Howth put it, he was 'a man of a comely and great stature, pleasant in nicking terms ... a lusty feeder and a surfeiter,' though on the latter attribute it entered the disclaimer that such indulgence 'was great pity in so goodly a personage.'[34] His was not a character that one imagines would have found the accomplishments of performers wasted endeavour, and a genial disposition is confirmed by the ample evidence for his performance patronage. From the first period of his Irish residence survive many details of payments for household and (possibly) civic music: a bagpiper at Mellifont, co. Louth, where the English administration maintained a residence, received 6d; minstrels at Swords and at Lusk, both in co. Dublin, received respectively 12d and 3s; musicians at Limerick (the city waits?) received 5s, as did musicians at 'Laughlin' (probably one of the modern Loughlinstowns),[35] and a harper at Lord Delvin's, co. Westmeath, received 2s.[36] Largesse given to the musicians of other magnates, or to those retained by corporations, might be perceived by its recipients as a seal of institutional approval, issuing as it did from the Lord Deputy, as well as remuneration for services rendered, and in this respect it also seems reasonable to regard Sidney's patronage as part of a larger social project. Patronage of performers was one of the public rituals of acceptance and accommodation, rituals which the more tactful representatives of New English authority in a colonized country were careful to develop and foster: Lord Delvin, who belonged to an old Anglo-Irish family, some of whose members in the sixteenth century were perfectly capable of writing Gaelic poetry,[37] saw his harper so recognized, as were the musicians at Limerick who, if in fact the city waits, would also have been the corporation's representatives, and thus by association the

corporation too would have been endorsed in the persons of its ceremonial employees.[38] Rewards of this kind, which might be termed the rewards of vertical patronage, were also doled out in a patronage that might be termed lateral when they were
offered to performers maintained by colleagues within the same New English ruling
class. For example, Sidney's brother-in-law, the Lord Deputy Sir Thomas Radcliffe,
also evidently kept a troupe of household musicians, since Sidney is on record as
having patronized them at least twice, to the sum of 8s 4d.[39] Lady Mary, Sidney's
wife, also rewarded performers during this period, and she is associated with music
in her own right as a lutenist and player on the virginals.[40]

In addition to music, provision was also made for players and, for the first time
in Irish records, for masking, that sixteenth-century courtly dramatic pastime par
excellence. To be exact, the players were sword players who performed at Lord Slane's
residence and who were rewarded with 5s for their pains.[41] It is not clear precisely
what they did in front of Sidney. In all likelihood it was a display of sword-dancing,
a mode of performance that other sources suggest had become a popular option on
convivial occasions in upper-class households, of whatever ethnicity, at least by c 1600.
Sidney conceivably saw something like the display described by Fynes Moryson
who, writing at the beginning of the seventeenth century, observed a relish for dancing among the Irish, and on many an occasion their 'Matachine daunse with naked
swordes.' Moryson's description seems to imply, moreover, that sword-dancing at
that time also had a characteristically Gaelic air:

They delight much in dansing, ʌ⌈vsing⌉ no Arte of slowe measures or lusty galliards, but only
Country [vsing] danses, whereof they haue some pleasant to beholde, as [Ballurdye],
Balrudry, and the and the Whipp of Duneboyne and the daunse a bout a fyer (Comonly in
the midst of a roome) holding whithes {'withies'} in their handes, and ʌ⌈by⌉ Certayne
straymes {movement of persons in the same direction?} drawing one another into the fyer
and also the Matachine daunse with naked swordes, which they make to Meete in diuers
comely postures, and this I haue seene them often daunse before the lord Deputy in the
houses of [diues] Irish lordes, and it seemed to me a dangerous sport, to see so many naked
swordes so neere the Lord Deputy and cheefe Commanders of the Army, in the handes of
the Irish kerne, who had ether lately beene or were not vnlike to proue Rebells./ [42]

It is incidentally interesting to compare the class auspices of the entertainment described here by Moryson – a presentation by lower-class performers (Irish kern) in
upper-class contexts (the houses of Irish lords) – with the class auspices much later
and in England of the Revesby Sword Play.[43] Sometimes sword-dancing even merged
with masking, as will be seen below in the context of the only masque text to have
survived from Ireland.[44] Whether the sword players who performed at Lord Slane's
could be classified as masquers is unclear, but there is no question about masques

being performed in Sir Henry Sidney's own household. What form his masques took is not known, but from the earliest days of his Irish residence they seem to have been a regular part of his household round. Sometime between 1556 and 1559, 45s were paid for making eleven visors, and 9s 4d for trimming (refurbishing?) existing masking apparel; the latter payment suggests a modicum of household thrift being exercised in this department.[45]

The second phase of Sidney's Irish residence was his first as Lord Deputy, when his earlier patronage towards performing artists was not only continued but also developed in further directions. As Lord Deputy he was now more of a cynosure and focus for ceremonial activity than ever before, and it is hard to determine at what precise point private household entertainment ended and public (ceremonial) pastime began – if indeed any useful distinction may be drawn between these two spheres. Will the Fool was maintained in Sidney's household, and appears for the first time during this second phase of his Irish residence in household accounts dating between 1566 and 1569.[46] Will is also, incidentally, the first professional fool on record in Ireland in the employ of a New English administrator, although as was seen in chapter 1, performers of his ilk had roamed Gaelic Ireland for hundreds of years, and Will's antics, 'counterfaiting a vaine gesture and a foolish countenance, singing the foote of many Songes as fools were wont,' would therefore not have seemed especially novel to Irish eyes.[47] Indeed, Sir Charles Blount (1563–1606), first earl of Devonshire and eighth Lord Mountjoy, would keep a fool of the Irish nation, as will be seen later. Sidney's fool, however, may have been an Englishman, to judge by a further payment in a set of domestic accounts which coincides with Sidney's final visit to Ireland and his third tour of duty as Lord Deputy. Between January and February 1576, three yards of motley were purchased to make a coat for someone named 'Sheyntton.'[48] Evidently Sheyntton was a fool, and it may be that Will the Fool of 1566–9 was the same Sheyntton the Fool of 1576. If so, it may also be that the place-name Sheinton in Shropshire supplied his patronymic. As Lord President of the Marches of Wales, a post which he held from 1559 and concurrently throughout his three stints as Lord Deputy, Sidney had acquired interests in Shropshire, establishing a residence at Ludlow Castle. His fool may have been a local man who had attached himself to the household and been exported to Ireland with his master. But whatever the fool's nationality, he became part of the domestic furniture, as his reappearance during Sidney's third and fourth phases of residence, his second and third times as Lord Deputy, indicates.[49]

It is also probable that like his brother-in-law Sussex before him, Sidney as Lord Deputy retained household minstrels, though strangely enough no evident payments to them have survived.[50] In fact, other than Radcliffe's minstrels, the only identifiable musical troupe in Sidney's household accounts is probably to be associated with the Dublin city waits of the late 1560s, primarily performers by appointment to the corporation, but secondarily also free-lancers to the gentry as the corporation deigned to give them leave.[51] This was the troupe headed by Mr Quycke, which was paid for its performances on at least two occasions.[52] Several other payments of this sort, further examples of Sidney's vertical patronage, are on record,[53] especially ones to singing men and boys, who were either secular performers or performers who, though for the nonce operating in a secular context, otherwise serviced the church's liturgy.[54] A good example of the latter sort is the payment, probably dating to about the time when Sidney received the sword of state on 28 October 1568, of 20s to the choristers of Christ Church, Dublin, for having presented him with songs and new verse.[55]

Wherever Sidney visited efforts seem to have been made to fête him with festive performances of one sort or another. Of course, in this there was nothing new. Such performances had a long history, no less in Ireland than anywhere else.[56] They might efficiently and formally signal the community's joy at (and hence assent to) the arrival in its midst of the embodiment, or proxy, of authority; the previous chapter illustrated some of the more elaborate instances in which this kind of formal joyous assent was expressed in centres other than Dublin. But what Sidney's accounts do interestingly demonstrate is the availability also in Ireland of some of the similar sorts of performance already familiar in England: for example, a bearward was paid 20s (where he exhibited his bear is not clear); a dancer with a hobbyhorse, which could also imply a morris side or a kindred group of performers, was rewarded with 5s at Carrickfergus, co. Antrim; and in Drogheda, co. Louth, a lord of misrule was given 10s.[57]

Vertical and lateral habits of performance patronage were thus firmly associated with Sidney, and hence with his office, by the time that he yielded the sword of state to another of his brothers-in-law, Sir William Fitzwilliam (1526–99), who succeeded him as Lord Deputy in 1571.[58] Next to Sidney's household accounts, those of Fitzwilliam rank as the second largest sixteenth-century collection able to cast light on patterns of Irish viceregal performance patronage. All the account documents save one were prepared during Fitzwilliam's second sojourn as Lord Deputy, between 1588 and 1594. The sole exception is a document belonging to the end of the period of his first term in office, between 1571 and 1575.[59] Since Fitzwilliam's fortunes and affairs were connected in so many ways with those of Sidney, his accounts make a useful complement to Sidney's, and illustrate broad continuities in the realm of the performing arts which united the two viceregal households.

When Fitzwilliam was first sent to Ireland in 1554 to investigate financial improprieties, he had already forged an Irish link seven years earlier through the acquisition of some land leases. By 1556 he had become a supporter of the party of the Lord Deputy, Sir Thomas Radcliffe, and in 1559 had succeeded Sidney as vice-treasurer, a post which he held until 1573. During absences of Radcliffe between

1560 and 1562, Fitzwilliam was appointed Lord Justice by Elizabeth I. Throughout the 1560s he made several visits to England, but returned to Ireland early in 1571, and was appointed Lord Justice again at the beginning of April on Sidney's departure. He was appointed Lord Deputy later in the year and took the oath on 13 January 1572. 1574 saw him on successful campaigns against the rebellious Gerald Fitz James Fitzgerald, fourteenth earl of Desmond, whom he obliged to submit to the Crown at Cork in September of the same year. However, the viceroyalty was a costly office, nor was Fitzwilliam in the best of health. His difficulties were compounded by a truculent Irish Council, by the siphoning away to the Ulster plantation of much needed resources, and by sundry quarrels, including ones with the nineteenth earl of Essex, Sir Walter Devereux, which helped him forfeit the queen's favour. When his wife, Lady Anne Fitzwilliam, concerned for her husband's health, went to England in 1575 seeking his recall, she found herself knocking at an open door. He was recalled and Sidney returned as Lord Deputy in September of that year for the third and final time. Fitzwilliam now remained in England for twelve years, mainly on his estates at Milton in Northamptonshire. But on 17 February 1588 he was once more appointed Lord Deputy, and returned to Dublin on 23 June to fill the post that Sir John Perrot had just vacated. This second and final tour of duty was no less troublous, and was now marked by quarrels with Sir Richard Bingham, Lord President of Connacht, whose own household arrangements will be considered later. Bingham's protestations of innocence at the charges alleged against him were heeded at court, and this lead to Fitzwilliam's reprimand by the queen. In 1594, now ailing and losing his sight, he went back to England, never to return, and was succeeded in office by Sir William Russell.

Vexatious and unhappy as it may have been, Fitzwilliam's prolonged immersion in the preoccupations and traditions of the ruling culture in Ireland left its mark: since he seems to have been far less a man for adopting new initiatives on the political front than for recycling past policies of his predecessors, it should come as no surprise to learn that neither did any radical departures distinguish his public and private patronage of the performing arts. It is true that there are a few additions and omissions that contrast with Sidney's household. Rewards for May games and observances are a notable addition during both his periods in office as Lord Deputy: a reward of 12d was given for a May game on 13 May 1575; the singing boys of Christ Church Cathedral, Dublin, received 10s on May Day in 1590; musicians at Grangegorman were paid 6s 8d for a performance in May 1591; and musicians at Sir William Sarsfield's house got 3s 4d, and the 'mayor of the May game' there 6s, sometime shortly after 12 May 1594.[60] Sidney's Dublin household, by contrast, had not been notable for its May Day observances, although his children at his Ludlow residence in Shropshire certainly enjoyed them.[61] And a conspicuous omission from Fitzwilliam's household accounts is any mention of his maintenance of a fool, though

Fitzwilliam was not otherwise averse to fools since he frequently rewarded a certain John, fool to Adam Loftus, chancellor of Ireland and nephew to the archbishop of Dublin, between 1591 and 1593; diligent reformer though the archbishop may have been, his nephew was plainly no precisian.[62] Music on Fitzwilliam's domestic front was again cast somewhat in the mould of Sidney's household: mistress Anne's virginals are mentioned being transported back and forth between Dublin and the viceregal residence in Kilmainham, for example, and so it appears that as before, the ladies were continuing to cultivate their household music.[63] One new musical accent in the household, however, is the emphasis on harping: by the time of his second period in office as Lord Deputy, Fitzwilliam was retaining a harper by the name of Plunkett, and other payments made during this period include various outlays on harp components and accessories.[64] Of course, the maintenance of a harper by a Lord Deputy was not in itself a new departure either, as will become clear, but harping is not heard of in Sidney's household, although he certainly patronized the harpers retained by others, as in the case of the harper at Lord Delvin's noted above.[65]

It may be that the minor apparent differences in performance patronage between the Fitzwilliam and Sidney households amount to little more than small variations in a fundamentally similar taste shared by both men; the overriding impression that their households leave is of the similarities and continuities existing between them. Thomas Quycke and his minstrels, the Dublin waits who had accommodated Sidney, reappear in the service of Fitzwilliam throughout 1574, and now on such a regular basis that one imagines that they may have been obliged to quit their corporation post.[66] Moreover, counting Quycke, there was at that time a total of six musicians in the Fitzwilliam consort, an impressive musical establishment and greater by two than when Quycke was receiving his livery from the corporation as a Dublin wait late in the 1560s.[67] Outside the confines of the Fitzwilliam household, vertical and lateral habits of patronage comparable to Sidney's also continued. The Drogheda waits, for the first (and only) time on record, were given 5s on 16 April 1591, and the Dublin waits 6s 8d for their attendance on New Year's Day in 1592, the latter occasion falling within the traditional festive season similarly honoured by Sidney and doubtless by many before him.[68] Also in Sidney's fashion, Fitzwilliam acknowledged through a series of rewards several other minstrels of members of the ruling class: during his first period in office as Lord Deputy, the musicians at Sir Christopher Barnewall's got 3s 4d, and during his second, Lord Slane's musicians got 10s, and those who performed at Sir William Sarsfield's got 3s 4d, probably in the latter case in connection with a May game there.[69]

While it is true that of the four remaining sixteenth-century households for which evidence of present concern survives, none rivals in quantity that surviving for the households of Sidney and Fitzwilliam, the households of Devereux, Perrot, Russell, and Blount nevertheless add important details to the general picture as it has been emerging here, and will be considered next. Following Fitzwilliam it is chronologically appropriate to start with Sir Walter Devereux (1541–76), nineteenth earl of Essex and second Viscount Hereford, since the Devereux evidence roughly coincides with Fitzwilliam's first period in office as Lord Deputy. Devereux is the odd man out among the patrons under review here in that he is the only one who was not a Lord Deputy. His involvement in Irish affairs was of a different order. He had been raised on the family estate in Wales and came to court on the accession of Elizabeth I. After performing various military services for her in England, he undertook in 1573 to colonize Ulster as a private adventurer and to bring it under English control, having been granted in return territory in co. Antrim on very favourable terms. Part of his expedition left England the same year, but storms scattered his ships and he landed himself with difficulty at Carrickfergus, co. Antrim. His best attempts to secure Ulster foundered; his soldiers were fractious and Lord Deputy Fitzwilliam, who had never approved Devereux's plans in the first place, refused to send help. Devereux appealed to the queen, who ordered Fitzwilliam to assist. When early in 1574 Devereux called upon Fitzwilliam for aid, the latter responded perfunctorily by dispatching only a small band of Palesmen, and even these deserted. With disease and famine rife in his Carrickfergus base, Devereux escaped to the Pale later in 1574 with what remained of his army. Fitzwilliam asked him to visit Gerald Fitz James Fitzgerald, fourteenth earl of Desmond, on a fact-finding mission in June of that year to see what he could ascertain of Desmond's designs. After this embassy, Devereux turned his attention to Ulster once again. The queen's Ulster policy was vacillating, however, and in May 1575, she finally wrote to him telling him that his enterprise was at an end. When in November 1575 the new Lord Deputy Sir Henry Sidney visited the region that Devereux had endeavoured to plant, he found it quite uninhabited. Devereux retired to his Welsh estate the same November, and although he still pressed ahead with his unfinished Irish business, being appointed earl marshal of Ireland by Elizabeth in 1576, his return was short-lived, for he was stricken by dysentry and died the same year.

Busy adventurer though he may have been, Devereux still had a household to maintain in Ireland befitting his state. Household accounts of interest here coincide with only a small portion of the very end of Devereux's Irish career. They run between April and October 1575, and thus fall within the penultimate year of his life and just before his departure from Ireland consequent on the queen's letter terminating his enterprise. One way in which he kept up aristocratic appearances was by retaining a band of musicians (a payment of 100s to them is recorded),[70] though the troupe of players that he is also known to have patronized, and who might have added a distinct lustre of their own to his household, was not with him during this period, but evidently on tour in England. (They appear in the Corporation Chamberlains' Accounts of the city of Gloucester at about this time, where the mayor ordered a reward paid to them of 13s.) [71] There were, however, various reasons why they may have found their patron's particular Irish circumstances in the mid-1570s uninviting, not least amongst which was the fact that precisely because Devereux was a mobile adventurer, he was in no position to maintain any household of the more stable sort such as Lords Deputy, by contrast, could expect to surround themselves with, and in whose more settled environment players might flourish. Nevertheless, musicians remained one of Devereux's essential staples, and perhaps because since music had the edge over drama in being the showier medium for fanfaring status, it could the less readily be missed from the household round. [72] But whatever the reason, the absence of his own players might be mitigated by extending patronage to players elsewhere, whenever opportunity arose. For example, some time between 3 April and 4 June 1575, he gave 5s to 'certaine boyes that played in enterlude,' and though it is not known who these boys were or where their interlude was played, it is possible that some school-produced drama had been made available to him, in the manner of the interlude organized by the Dublin-based schoolmaster and producer, David Duke, whose activities were considered earlier in chapter 3. [73] The £4 which Devereux gave to 'Iames the ffoole' ranks as too substantial a reward to have been a once-off payment, and therefore it appears that like some of the other New English administrators, Devereux also kept a fool with him in Ireland. [74] Therefore for someone who evidently valued dramatic performance, the evidence that can be assembled for his patronage of it in Ireland is modest enough, perhaps for the reasons earlier proposed as well as the besetting problem of losses of source documents. The vertical patronage characteristic of the Lords Deputy was also a habit that he cultivated, and payments that he made bring to light the existence of other retained musicians: the singing men at Mellifont, co. Louth, were given 10s, and the singing men at New Ross, co. Wexford, 5s; 3s went to a harper retained by Sir John Bellew (Bedlow) at the Bellew residence (probably in Bellewstown, co. Meath); and the famous harper Crues, retained by the tenth earl of Ormond, Sir Thomas Butler, received 40s, while Butler's own household musicians received 20s. [75] Thus the lion's share of Devereux's rewards for the performing arts was once again directed towards the provision of music.

With Sir John Perrot (1527?–92), we return to the household of another Lord Deputy, though by all accounts an unpromising one for present purposes, given its alleged niggardliness. Perrot was educated at St David's in Wales, and presented at court, first to Henry VIII (his reputed father) and then after Henry's death to Edward VI, who knighted him at his coronation. Perrot's first period of service in Ireland came after the rebellion there of James Fitz Maurice Fitzgerald, the leader of the Desmond Fitzgeralds, in 1568. Elizabeth I had been prevailed upon to establish a presidential government in Munster, and offered the post to Perrot in 1570. He arrived in Dublin in 1571, took his oath before Sir Henry Sidney, then proceeded to Munster, where he waged various campaigns against James Fitz Maurice Fitzgerald. Fitzgerald eventually submitted (albeit temporarily), and accepted a pardon. Perrot returned to England and Wales in July 1573. His next major involvement in Irish affairs, and the period from which the evidence for his household patronage dates, came in 1584 when he was appointed Lord Deputy. Again he undertook extensive campaigns, this time mainly in Ulster. But his relations with certain members of the English administration in Ireland were stormy, and sowed the seeds of his eventual downfall. As previously noted, in February 1588, Sir William Fitzwilliam was appointed to succeed Perrot as Lord Deputy. Perrot surrendered the sword of state to him on 30 June and returned to England. Treason charges had been preferred against him, and he died awaiting sentence as a prisoner in the Tower of London.

A brief note 'discovering the strict and pinching parsimony' of Lord Deputy Perrot's household still survives amongst the Irish State Papers that makes unusual, if gloomy, reading: shabby liveries, scanty commons, and barely adequate 'ffyre or Candle throughout the yeare' all detracted from the wonted dignity of a viceregal lifestyle, 'the like most miserable & strict orders. not beseming his place,' as Perrot's critic primly observed. It is interesting that a document hostile to Perrot should think it worthwhile to publicize these defaults as persuasive grounds for discrediting him.[76] Despite its allegations, Perrot was still observing at least some of the old protocols. A set of his household accounts, which is to be dated to about the time when he received the sword of state on 21 June 1584, declares: 'It hathe bene an olde custome that the Officers herevnder written should have vppon the daye wherin the Lord Deputie receivethe the sworde these fees hereafter followinge; besydes there dynners,' and then it proceeds to head its list with 'Trumpettes' and 'Musicians.' Both these groups of servitors were each to receive 40s.[77] Evidently 'olde custome' was honoured: another set of accounts, dated to about 24 September 1585, lists his six musicians by name and the amount each received.[78] Perrot's household economies had not eaten into the size of his music consort, which was still one of six musicians, as Fitzwilliam's had been before him.[79] Since Perrot also had a harper, Richard Barrett, who does not appear in any household accounts but who is first spoken of in another State Paper document some four years after Perrot's death, it is safe to assume that whatever truth may have been in the accusations of stingy housekeeping, his patronage was originally more extensive and stands now robbed of its detail.[80] But what evidence has survived shows music once more to the fore. In view of some of the considerations discussed earlier, this might have been predicted, and also in view of Perrot's evident disposition, in Wales at any rate: the music room of his Welsh residence at Carew Castle had been generously stocked with books of music and instruments of various sorts, including sackbuts, cornets, flutes, virginals, and an Irish harp.[81]

While no actual household accounts survive which might illustrate in detail the interest taken in drama and the performing arts by the two remaining Lords Deputy with whom we are concerned, Sir William Russell (1558?–1613), first Baron Russell of Thornhaugh, and Sir Charles Blount (1563–1606), first earl of Devonshire and eighth Lord Mountjoy, the evidence of that interest, however brief, is of considerable importance. We may begin with Russell before moving to Blount, the latter Lord Deputy at the time of the death of Elizabeth I, where this section necessarily closes. Russell first came to Ireland in the autumn of 1580, and was garrisoned to the south of Dublin on the borders of co. Wicklow, where his task was to curb the rebellious chieftain Feagh MacHugh O'Byrne. He departed for England in the autumn of 1581, and did not come back to Ireland until 1594, this time returning as Lord Deputy in succession to the ailing Sir William Fitzwilliam. In that meantime Russell had earned a high military reputation for service in the Low Countries, and his viceregal appointment was in part a recognition of his achievements abroad. Evidence of his maintaining a consort of musicians follows soon after his return to Dublin, but other than their activity in Christ Church Cathedral on the eve of All Hallows and at Christmas in 1594, little is known of them.[82] Russell's most pressing military concern now was with the restless province of Ulster, where the ambitions of the powerful Hugh O'Neill, second earl of Tyrone, were fomenting rebellion. By June 1595, Tyrone had been declared a traitor, though he was suing for pardon late in the same year. A truce was then established, which lasted to May 1596, and it is during this period of uneasy calm that the pastimes of the Russell household come briefly into view. By 1597 the Irish situation had worsened drastically, however. Uprisings were now also breaking out in Munster and Leinster, and Russell's commission was revoked. He left Ireland never to return in May of that year.

In 1596 Russell kept New Year's Day in Dublin. His diarist noted that in the evening, 'certen llords and gentlemen presented my Lord with a maske.' As was often their wont, these New Year revels spilled over onto the following day, for here the diarist continues with the comment that 'the LLords and gentlemen who were of the maske, beinge before invited, dyned with my Lord where they ^⌈were⌉ honorably feasted.'[83] The all-male cast of masquers was of the ruling class, appropriately enough, and it is interesting to note how they seem to have monopolized dramatic entertainment on this occasion; the diarist makes no mention of players of any other kind, whether common (that is, professional players) or servants of the household acting for the nonce. An in-house arrangement between social peers seems to have been sufficient unto the day. Moreover, Russell is not known to have patronized any company of players while in Ireland, which is another reason for believing that the diarist's account of what occurred, terse though it is, was comprehensive enough.[84] Presumably the masquers performed either at the Lord Deputy's Kilmainham residence or perhaps more likely, given the social profile of New Year festivities, at Dublin Castle.

The castle had, without question, become a venue for dramatic performances at least by Sir Charles Blount's time, and as was seen in chapter 2, probably very much earlier. Blount was a favourite of Elizabeth I, so much so that he had initially provoked jealousy in another darling of the court, Robert Devereux, twentieth earl of Essex and son of Walter, whose patronage in Ireland of the performing arts was examined above. The enmity between Devereux and Blount led to a duel in which Devereux was worsted, yet he recovered and eventually became one of Blount's closest friends. By the time that Blount was being considered for the Lord Deputyship of Ireland, like Lord Deputy Russell before him he had also covered himself in military glory. Tyrone had inflicted a heavy defeat on the English forces at Blackwater Fort, near Armagh, in August 1598, and news of his success had emboldened further Irish uprisings in Munster and Leinster. A skilled military intervention in Ireland was imperative, and Blount seemed an obvious candidate to take charge of it. Friendship notwithstanding, Devereux intervened to derail Blount's appointment, only to find himself appointed Lord Deputy in Blount's stead in March 1599. The incumbency of Devereux proved a fiasco, however, and by September of the same year he had angered the court after quitting office without official leave. The post was now at once offered to Blount, who after some prevarication accepted it on 21 January 1600. Soon after this Devereux would be charged with treason, convicted, and in 1601 beheaded. In the meantime Blount, now Lord Deputy, remained in Ireland, only narrowly escaping being attainted with Devereux's treason himself, and this by the connivance of the queen, who had personally ordered the suppression of incriminating evidence of his association with the Devereux conspiracy. Henceforth, Blount would be anxious to show himself an even better and more faithful servant of Her Majesty than ever before.

In the light of this history, the performance of *Gorboduc* in Dublin Castle on 7 September 1601, only a few months after the execution of Devereux, is perhaps to be regarded as one of Blount's attempts to rehabilitate himself in the eyes of the establishment, a rehabilitation that would very soon, however, be consummated after his decisive victory at the Battle of Kinsale over the combined Irish forces of Tyrone on 24 December 1601. Though evidence for the *Gorboduc* performance is late, it is doubtless reliable. The eighteenth-century historian of Irish theatre W.R. Chetwood relates that Joseph Ashbury, the Dublin-based actor-manager who succeeded John Ogilby, claimed to have seen a bill for 20s 8d for wax tapers, dated 7 September 1601, 'for the Play of Gorboduc done at the Castle.'[85] Since 7 September was Queen Elizabeth's birthday, it seems likely that the performance was also intended to mark the occasion. Of course, whatever the personal advantage to Blount in being seen to stage *Gorboduc* at this time, it is also true that he had always had a taste for drama, a disposition that he had shared with his less temperate friend Devereux. Together they had attended the Gray's Inn Christmas revels of 1594, when Shakespeare's *Comedy of Errors* received its first known performance.[86] And again, Blount was one of a select group invited to the 'very great Supper' held at Essex House in London on the evening of 14 February 1598 at which two plays were acted and which kept their audience up till one o'clock the following morning.[87] His theatrical appetite did not desert him when he came to Dublin, military commitments notwithstanding. Indeed, sometimes even in the middle of military engagements we can hear his thinking textured with theatrical metaphors.[88] And according to Ashbury again, who had it from John Ogilby, 'Plays had been often acted in the Castle of Dublin when Blount, Lord Mountjoy, was Lord Lieutenant.'[89] Falling when it did in 1601, however, the Dublin *Gorboduc* performance was surely also politically apposite.[90]

Chetwood supposed that gentlemen of the court made up the *Gorboduc* cast, and in this he may have been correct: after all, Russell's New Year's Day masque had been so presented, nor is there any known record of Blount having had with him in Ireland a troupe of players.[91] But one interesting departure (if such it really was) was observed by Blount's personal secretary, Fynes Moryson, whose remarks on sword-dancing were cited earlier. Whatever they felt about troupes of players, members of the sixteenth-century New English administration, both men and women, were fond of their professional fools, as has been seen.[92] Given the strength of the native Irish tradition of professional foolery, and the conceivable political cachet to be had from retaining a fool who was an Irishman, it is perhaps surprising that evidence of an Irish fool in New English employ did not appear sooner in the records than it does. Blount's fool is the earliest. As Moryson put it:

ffor the witts of the Irish, they themselues bragg that Ireland yealdes not a naturall foole, which bragg I haue hard diuers men confirme, neuer any to contradict. My honored lord the late Earle of Deuonshyre, till his dying day kept an Irish man in fooles apparrell, and Commonly called his lordships foole, but wee found him to haue craft of humoring euery man to attayne his owne endes, and to haue nothing of a naturall foole.[93]

Neale Moore was this fool's name, as a document in the Irish State Papers reveals, and he was in Blount's service from at least 1600.[94] Moryson may have been amused by Moore's antics, but he was not fooled as to his motives, and a note of suspicion lingers in his description. Nevertheless, for all the distrust of native Irish performing artists, or the downright (and more typical) antipathy officially professed towards them by New English settlers, some of the latter had been won over, and like Blount, they might be persons who moved in the highest New English echelons.[95] Another way of looking at this, that the appropriation of native Irish performing artists by the New English amounted to cultural booty, will be considered in the case of Sir Richard Boyle, whose career will be examined next. But equally it could be argued that, on the threshold of the seventeenth century, the native tradition was still successfully accommodating itself to the tastes of some of the newcomers. Alive and well in the early modern period was precisely the sort of self-serving versatility that the Gaelic poet had recommended as far back as the fourteenth century.[96]

NEW ENGLISH HOUSEHOLDS OF THE SEVENTEENTH CENTURY

Victory at Kinsale left Blount with what was in effect little more than a tidying up operation to complete before returning to England, with the permission of James I, in May 1603. The routed Tyrone had been pursued into Ulster, and by December 1602 he had found it expedient to throw himself on the queen's mercy and sue for reinstatement. He submitted to the Crown at Mellifont on 30 March 1603. Elizabeth was then in fact already six days dead, and though Blount knew this, he had contrived that it be kept secret until official news of the death, with its accompanying proclamation of the accession of James I, broke in Dublin on 4 April. Neither Blount nor Tyrone, for different sets of reasons, found cause to welcome the accession of the new monarch, though both went through the motions of appropriate display, a celebratory procession on horseback through the streets of Dublin.[97] As it proved, the new king would endorse Blount and recognize Tyrone as a subject and nobleman. Now all that remained for Blount to do was to sedate enthusiasm for Catholicism resurgent in the towns after Elizabeth's death, and then quit Ireland for good.

The opening years of the new reign coincided with a period of relative calm, under the Lord Deputyship of Sir Arthur Chichester from October 1604 to February 1614.[98] Even the most ungovernable of the four Irish provinces, Ulster, had been much subdued following the collapse of united Irish resistance and the subsequent opportunistic incursions of the English army to tighten control there. Munster, the province which had been the site of the clash between the English forces and those of Tyrone, now began to settle down to a period of relative tranquility after its time of war. Here the climate for the pursuit of drama and the performing arts became more temperate than it may formerly have been. By 1639, for example, a set of visitation articles drafted for the diocese of Cloyne presupposed peaceable conditions in the province when it sought to know, amongst other things, whether churches and churchyards were being treated respectfully, and whether there were 'either playes, feasts, banquets, Church-Ales, drinkings, exposing any wares to sale, temporall Courts or Leets, Lay-iuries, Musters, Commisions (other then for causes Eccleasticall) playing at Ball, or any other unseemly actions or misbehaviour' taking place in them.[99] Whole tracts of forfeited Munster land had come up for grabs after

Kinsale, but of all the adventurers who exploited the opportunities for plantation that were to be had, Sir Richard Boyle (1566–1643), from 1620 created first earl of Cork, was the most conspicuous.[100]

Though born in humble circumstances in Canterbury, Boyle showed promise and the means were found to send him to Corpus Christi College, Cambridge, in 1583. After spending some time in London at the Middle Temple and then a short period serving as clerk to Sir Richard Manwood, chief baron of the Exchequer, Boyle came to Ireland in 1588, where he strove to make the acquaintance of influential people. At first things went against him. A rebellion in Munster left him destitute, and he also managed to fall foul of Sir Henry Wallop, treasurer of Ireland. However, he successfully defended himself against Wallop's accusations before Star Chamber, and in the process drew attention to Wallop's own malpractices. Wallop was succeeded at once by Boyle's ally, Sir George Carew, and soon after this through Carew's influence Boyle was appointed clerk of the council of Munster. Carew, who in March 1600 had been elevated to Lord President of Munster, advanced Boyle's interests generally. He chose him to bear the news of the victory at Kinsale to the queen late in December of 1601.

From Sir Walter Raleigh Boyle purchased fertile lands at a bargain price in cos. Cork, Waterford, and Tipperary, and he managed these with great skill. He was knighted in 1603, and in this year also married his second wife (his first had died in childbirth in 1599). Various high offices followed, culminating in his creation on 6 October 1620 as Viscount Dungarvan and first earl of Cork. Though his interests were checked at several turns in the 1630s by the Lord Deputy, Sir Thomas Wentworth, against whom he quietly but strenuously intrigued, he went in due course as a witness to Wentworth's trial in London in 1641, and shed no tears on learning of his execution. Shortly after his return, the 1641 rebellion broke out, and he took up arms against the rebels with his sons. He died on 15 September 1643.

In the midst of a busy career, Boyle made time for substantial patronage of drama and the performing arts. The story of this patronage shifts the focus away from the Dublin Pale, with which the previous section of this chapter has primarily been occupied, towards Munster, bringing especially into view Boyle's principal residence there at Lismore, co. Waterford. The evidence for his patronage is distributed between two different sets of documents: household accounts and his personal diaries. The relevant portions of the accounts begin in 1605 and run to 1607; then a silence of some six years descends before the diaries resume with evidence covering the period between 1613 and 1616. From 1617 to 1641, with gaps in some years, both the accounts and the diaries provide evidence, though the last diary entry of present concern falls on 30 November 1636, after which the accounts take over as the sole source. Thus coverage of the better part of thirty-seven years in the first half of the seventeenth century is afforded of the patronage of this the most influential and successful adventurer of his day, and is coextensive with the ascendancy of his fortune.

It is clear that unlike many English aristocrats of his day, Boyle did not retain any troupe of players, although he certainly patronized and attended dramatic performances, both in Lismore and in Dublin. For example, those occasions when his eldest son, Richard, Viscount Dungarvan, participated in masques, not only in Ireland but also abroad, were carefully recorded by Boyle in his diary. The first masque he noted, on 24 October 1620, cost him £5 given to the children who performed it.[101] Viscount Dungarvan may have been among them (the masque took place only four days after his eighth birthday on 20 October). Certainly, the young viscount appeared in a Christmas masque in 1627, at fifteen years old, and was given £3 by his father to help him purchase necessaries for his part in it.[102] Richard is last heard of at the height of his masking career at the age of twenty-one, now in London and taking part in a 'Royall Maske' of Charles I, as his father proudly noted.[103] This was none other than Thomas Carew's spectacular *Coelum Britannicum*, produced with the aid of Inigo Jones and performed to a packed audience in the Banqueting Hall at Whitehall on 18 February 1634.[104] Of course, the Lismore masques had less resources at their disposal than the royal ones and would doubtless by comparison have seemed provincial, but that is not the most important point: more pertinent is the fact that masques were fashionable for the Boyle household to be putting on; Viscount Dungarvan was being prepared from childhood for his court début, and joining the ranks of those aristocratic English children for whom masking was an approved pastime. (Three of the earl of Bridgwater's children were to appear in that more famous, though equally provincial, masque of *Comus* in Ludlow Castle on 29 September 1634.)[105] On the strength of the diaries and accounts, then, drama generated from within the Boyle household seems largely to have been got up by family members or close family associates on festive occasions. In this it would have resembled the efforts of many other English aristocrats who from the later sixteenth century throughout the British Isles had cultivated the gentle art of masking, now reaching the heights of its sophistication in the early part of the seventeenth century and finding its most glittering manifestations on display at the London court. Such following of courtly fashion is exactly what might have been expected of Boyle, a man eager to cast himself and his heirs in an English aristocratic mould so that, as one critic has aptly put it, he might win social acceptance through conformity.[106] Whatever its other rewards, masking was yet another of the means whereby acceptance through conformity might be realized.

As well as seeing drama produced within the intimate family circle, the Lismore residence, being the seat of so illustrious a gentleman, was likely also to entice visiting troupes of players, especially if the Boyle household supported none of its own. One of the results of the more pacific conditions in Munster after Kinsale seems to have been an increase generally in troupes of players touring the province. The first such troupe known about, the prince's players, came to Lismore in 1616, when they received a payment from Boyle of 22s on 11 February (the eve of Shrovetide in that year, and thus a traditional time of festivity).[107] Given Boyle's disposition, a troupe patronized by no less than the future Charles I was hardly likely to have been turned away. Just before their Lismore visit, and between 1613 and 1615, the prince's players had been visiting Barnstaple, a sheltered port on the north Devon coast which had a vigorous sea trade with the south of Ireland.[108] They also appear in the Barnstaple Receivers' Accounts for the fiscal year 1616–17.[109] There is no mention of them there early in 1616 – necessarily, for they were in Ireland at that time.[110] What they evidently did was to sail from Barnstaple probably to the port of Youghal, co. Cork, in the opening weeks of 1616, and from Youghal a journey to Lismore was not far, a little over twelve miles. They had returned to England by 16 March, when they were paid for an appearance in Dover.[111] It is possible that their Irish tour was prompted by the annual Lenten closure of the London theatres. Sometime between Michaelmas 1616 and Michaelmas 1617, they had arrived back in Barnstaple. From late 1617 to 1618 and in subsequent years, when the prince's players were touring again in the southwest of England, the corporation of Barnstaple began paying them *not* to perform in the town, possibly in deference to the sensibilites and strong local influence there of the puritan earl of Bedford.[112] Despite this discouragement the players continued to visit Barnstaple for at least another four years, perhaps more, even though again on each occasion they were paid to avoid playing in the town. It has been remarked that in these uncongenial circumstances their persistance, and that of other players who were similarly paid to absent themselves from Barnstaple until as late as 1636–7, seems odd.[113] But there is a way in which it could be entirely natural. Barnstaple was a very convenient stopping-off place for a passage to Ireland. It should be noted that, although not this time recording who they were, Boyle paid visiting players on three further occasions (on 8 April 1619, on a day in the week of 29 October to 4 November 1626, and on 18 November 1627).[114] There may have been visits to Lismore that he did not record. For example, as will be seen later from another source, the king's players were on tour in Munster at about this time, and were paid for their attendance on members of Youghal Corporation during the mayoralty of Richard Gough between Michaelmas 1625 and Michaelmas 1626. Youghal, a short distance from Lismore, was also a centre of Boyle interest and investment – indeed, it would be in St Mary's Church in Youghal that Boyle would eventually be interred – and it would have been strange had such a prestigious group of players not sought access to the town's *éminence grise*. If there were more than one potential patron across the Irish Sea ready to welcome them, players would have regarded a voyage as even more worthwhile, especially when they could also no longer hope for much positive encouragement from the sober townsfolk of Barnstaple. Persistent visits by players to Barnstaple might therefore not be an oddity at all; they may be partly accounted for precisely on the grounds that the town gave convenient access to Ireland and the more receptive audiences that might be anticipated there.

Other performers at Lismore – probably visitors and not residents – included puppet players (the first on actual record known in Ireland) on 16 July 1635;[115] jugglers on 24 April 1637;[116] and rope-dancers on 30 March 1638.[117] The trades of puppeteer, juggler, and rope-dancer today all sound very specialist, and while records of performing arts in the British Isles certainly bring specialists in these skills to light,[118] more frequently they were skills exercised by players of more general talents: rope-dancing, for example, had become an extremely popular entertainment at least by the seventeenth century, and was often performed by members of liveried playing troupes.[119] It may therefore be the case that the Lismore visitors of the 1630s were players in the widest sense who were asked to exhibit specific skills on those occasions. The remaining evidence for Boyle's patronage of actors coincides with his periods of residence in Dublin, where he found his own better judgment often in collision with the conspicuous consumption that he also seems to have considered necessary for someone of his social standing. Hence Archie Armstrong, Charles I's fool, was given a princely reward of £5 by Boyle on 2 June 1636, 'for which god forgive me,' Boyle declared in a postscript.[120]

Boyle's Dublin encounter with plays and players will be revisited when the household of his Dublin-based adversary, Sir Thomas Wentworth, is investigated below, but for the moment we may conclude this account of Boyle patronage by observing that by far the most significant outlay that he made on the performing arts was on music and musicians, especially on his own musicians at Lismore. Evidence for his expenditure on music begins as early as 1605,[121] and throughout his career he extended towards musicians that vertical and lateral patronage, doubtless to similar social effect, that was by now so characteristic a practice of members of the English ruling classes. Hence the musicians of Sir Nicholas St Lawrence, Lord Howth, received 2s in Dublin on 13 July 1606; the musicians of Sir Donough O'Brien, fourth earl of Thomond and Lord President of Munster, 2s 6d on 11 June 1617; the musician's (or musicians') boy at the house of Sir Randal Clayton, clerk to the council of Munster, 12d on 10 August in the same year; and the musicians there 2s 6d on 17 March 1623.[122] That affectation of things Irish that Boyle shared with other members of his class who had resolved to set up home in Ireland showed noticeably in his patronage of harpers. Before the seventeenth century – for convenience one might say before the Battle of Kinsale – the English attitude towards harping had been deeply ambivalent. On the one hand, Irish harpers were seen as utterly reprobate while they served native Gaelic interests, but on the other, if once domesticated and brought within the pale of English civility, they might be highly desirable additions to households where, as well as making music, they might stand as living proof to the world of the accommodations that enlightened colonialism was happy to make. By Boyle's day (post-Kinsale), the image of the harper as inciter to Gaelic sedition was largely a thing of the past, but the value of the harper as cultural trophy lingered on. It is therefore not surprising to find Irish harpers retained by others in Boyle's milieu, harpers whom he was quite willing to patronize himself. No less than the wife of James I, Queen Anne of Denmark, retained the Irish harper Donnell dubh O'Cahill, a man with whom Boyle had some commerce, as he also had with Ned Scott, harper to Sir Arthur Chichester and, as Seán Donnelly has shown, probably that same Eamonn Albanach celebrated in Irish in the poetry of Pádraigín Haicéad.[123] In addition to helping to consolidate his position within the New English ascendancy, Boyle's patronage reinforced his cultural ties with the Old English households, as with the Barrys, for example, who were the first to be collected within the sphere of Boyle influence. The blind harper William Barry, harper to Lord David Barry, Viscount Barrymore, was given Boyle's own harp to raise in 1620; in 1621 Boyle had affiliated himself still more intimately with the Barrys through the marriage of his eldest daughter Alice to Viscount Barrymore.[124] And Boyle's benevolence towards harpers might reach even into the remoter and more solidly Gaelic areas of Munster, as in the case of the poet and harper Piaras Feiritéir of Ferriter's Castle, Ballysybil, co. Kerry. Feiritéir had held lands of Boyle, and had depended upon him for protection against the exactions of Boyle's own rent collector.[125]

Household music, so important to the ruling classes in sixteenth-century Ireland, was no less so in the seventeenth, as is seen in epitome in Boyle's household. It is not clear, however, that the harp, despite his having owned one personally and having patronized performers on it elsewhere, was among the instruments regularly heard played by his consort of musicians at Lismore. Rather, viols and lutes are what the records speak of. In 1617 a chest of viols cost Boyle £8 sterling, paid to a Mr Brian (possibly one Randal Brian, a merchant or shipper), who brought them from Minehead in Somerset, another English port which had trading links with Youghal and the south coast of Ireland.[126] And lutes were being used in the household, at least by 1626 if not in fact much earlier.[127] Indeed, what was happening in the Boyle household in this regard typified a wider trend. The importation of instruments for use in aristocratic households seems to have been flourishing throughout Ireland at about this time.[128] The first musician retained by Boyle whose name is recorded was one [William] Stacy, who was paid 40s on 22 July 1616, in the year before the viols were acquired.[129] Their acquisition may mark the beginning of the Lismore consort, as Barra Boydell has suggested, though it is perhaps because of gaps in the evidence that consort members only begin to feature prominently on record from late in 1626.[130] At its height, the Boyle consort comprised six musicians.

In this it would have rivalled the musical consorts of the Lords Deputy themselves, in which by the second half of the sixteenth century six players seems to have been a standard complement.[131] During Boyle's lengthy absences from Lismore between 1628 and 1636, the size of the consort decreased a little, but with one possible and momentary exception, never went below four players.[132] It increased again to six soon after his return in July 1636,[133] though this seems to have been short-lived, for from 5 December in that year, only four regular musicians are spoken of until the time of Boyle's death. The payments during this period to Jack the singing man and to the musician's (or musicians') boy are sporadic and may have been for temporary appointments.[134] Throughout the life of the consort, its members received an annual wage of £5, paid in two moities, due at Lady Day and at Michaelmas. At least some of the musicians also had other employment, and this might help to explain why, unlike the musicians of many other households, Boyle's did not accompany him on his travels away from Lismore.[135]

The core membership of the consort remained stable over several years. This arrangement possibly serves as a paradigm of the membership of consorts which are known to have been maintained in other households yet whose circumstances are much less fully documented than Boyle's. The household of Lord Conway and Kil-lultagh is a case in point, and will be considered later. William Stacy, for example, first heard of in 1616, was a member of the Lismore consort probably until his death about the end of 1634, a period of at least eighteen years. Michael Skryne too, first mentioned by name in Boyle's employ on 30 March 1627, may have entered his service rather earlier: he was already in Youghal in 1618, where he appears in the town's Corporation Book on 2 July as a musician, and with an apprentice, one Edmund Butler, late of King's Lynn in Norfolk.[136] This was around the time that Boyle may have been gathering his Lismore consort together. Skryne and his wife last appear in the household accounts in 1643, the year of Boyle's death.[137] Like many retained musicians elsewhere, all Boyle's consort members were liveried. Five cloaks were bought for them on 30 June 1630, and six on 30 November 1636 made of red cloth.[138] Thus the uniforms of the musicians proclaimed on their sleeve the blazon and interests of the great household that they not only entertained, but also represented to its many visitors and guests, even if not by touring the country or by joining Boyle's entourage when he was away from home. Too ostentatious a dis-play outside Lismore, in any case, may not have been prudent. Its consequences in Dublin, Wentworth's base, for example, could be imagined: Boyle had struck Went-worth as overweening, and six musicians would not have mitigated that impression, seeming to vie with the viceregal household itself.

Visitors called in on the prosperous Munster households for various reasons, and whether on official visits or courtesy calls, they would all have carried away with them a report of the household's nobility and of the hospitality received there. In this they would have behaved rather as the visitors to the Gaelic households surveyed in chapter 1 were wont to behave. Moreover, Anglo-Irish and New English hosts cannot have been insensible to the good report of their guests, whose visits would have been adorned and so made more memorable by performing artists. Part of the unwritten brief of the latter would have been to ensure that visitors and guests went away with the right impression. But these were not always merely passive consumers of the entertainment placed before them. Sometimes they brought contributions of their own to the proceedings, and one such notable case occurred in the household of Boyle's son-in-law, Lord David, Viscount Barrymore (created first earl of Barrymore on 28 February 1628), over Christmas in 1632. This was when a visitor had his *Introduction to the Sword Dance* performed.[139] John Clavell (1601–43), its author, had pursued an extraordinary career. He had been by turns a burglar, brigand, doctor, lawyer, man of letters, and playwright. Having successfully occluded his seamier past, he had now found a warm welcome from Lord David and was also being spoken highly of by Boyle himself. Clavell came to Ireland on at least two occasions.[140] His first arrival may have been in 1631 or 1632, not long therefore before his *Introduction* was presented at Lord David's residence. Clavell embarked for England at Dublin about 27 September 1633, and after a year there he returned for the second time on 14 December 1634. He remained in Ireland until his final departure sometime shortly after 17 June 1637.

Clavell had an uncle living in Munster, Sir William Clavell (1568–1644), who had distinguished himself during the Tyrone rebellion and had acquired property at Carrigrohane, co. Cork. His nephew seems to have come over to Ireland in order to represent him in legal cases. Clavell's first visit was an unhappy one, for he wrote in the manuscript of a play that he had written, *The Sodder'd Citizen*, which he had with him in Ireland, that if he could but get back to England, he would never set foot in Dublin again. But return he did, and into the bargain married Elizabeth Markham, the nine-year-old daughter and sole heiress of a rich Dublin vintner. Clavell was then aged thirty-three. On the 13 November 1635 he was admitted to the bar in Dublin. His name was enrolled in the Black Book of King's Inns, where he is (erroneously) styled 'de Lincolns Inn' in London. Markham, his father-in-law, was well connected, and Clavell seems to have benefited from the introductions to various worthies that he was able to arrange. Clavell had presumably made the acquaintance of Boyle and Lord David during his first Irish visit; since his uncle, Sir William, was a landed gentleman in Munster, it may have been he who provided Clavell with his entrée to the Boyle and Barrymore households. It is not known which Barrymore residence saw the production of the *Introduction to the Sword Dance*, but two seem the chief candidates: either the castle of Shandon, near Cork, or the residence at Castlelyons, in the barony of Barrymore, co. Cork.[141] Since the Castlelyons residence was the Barrys' ancestral home, it may have had the edge over

Shandon as a venue for an occasion which the *Introduction* suggests was a familial, Christmastide gathering. It seems that Lord David's wife, the Countess Alice, was in attendance (the reference in the *Introduction* to 'the countess' is probably to her).

Three aspects of Clavell's *Introduction* seem worth noting in particular. First, in formal terms, it combines the (by now traditional) genres of masking and sword-dancing in an unusual mixture; second, in terms of theatre history, the novelty of this mixture may have been a modish one, yet if so the *Introduction* is the earliest and most developed instance of the fashion yet discovered in the British Isles; and finally, in terms of its immediate historico-cultural significance, it enacted a sexualized presentation of Anglo-Irish politics in which strongly gendered and ethnic identities were fastened onto the respective states of war and peace. The first two of these aspects can be most quickly dealt with, and are moreover related. As has been seen, masking and sword-dancing, independent performing arts, already had a long history in Ireland before 1632. However, the *Introduction* brought both together, weaving them in a complex way. The resulting performance was not merely a dramatic sandwich with a sword-dance filling.[142] Rather, the *Introduction* followed more closely the grammar of the masque, as a short summary of its action will show (and see Appendix IV). It begins with a noise of voices crying 'follow, follow, follow' outside the room in which the performance unfolds, and into which the character Peace enters, agitated and complaining that she is being pursued. She kneels before the countess, suing for protection, while another cry of 'ffollow, follow, follow' is heard without. Her would-be assailants come in and threaten Peace and the ladies in the audience, but are intercepted by Mars. Peace is then given leave by Mars to exit in safety, and he diverts the warlike energy of the band of assailants into a sword dance. Their dance ended, Mars lays his sword down and invites the 'cheife Lady' to dance (probably the spectating countess), and the rest of the band follow suit, presumably approaching other ladies in the room. After the partnered dancing is over, the ladies return to their places, and the band take up their swords again to perform a final dance, a 'warlike maske done with many prety changes.' That ended, Mars leads them out, save the band leader, who before exiting delivers his penitent epilogue, now a convert to love and a subject of the conquering ladies. The interplay of spectators with performers, with its consequent fudging of the distinction between them, which is so characteristic a feature of masque form, is clearly evident here: the performance has designs on the women in the audience whom it has sought to woo into its flirtatious (and political) fiction.[143] Masques were often orientated towards some chief spectator, and in the case of the *Introduction*, that would seem to have been the countess herself. Masque-like too is the *Introduction*'s narrative movement enacting the triumph of order over disorder and, of course, its dancers, who resemble the dancers of order and disorder that inhabit masques and anti-masques elsewhere.[144] It is true that the *Introduction* does not indicate any use of illusionistic scenery of the sort typically associated with court masques of the early-seventeenth century, nor is it played in one of those fictionalised topographies that eventually dissolve into the real time and place of the audience. Yet even in these respects, though in a more subtle sense, it has an affinity with the masque form. While within its own terms geographically placeless, the *Introduction* is played out in a *political* topography contiguous with that inhabited by its audience, as will shortly become clear, just as, by default of a fictionalized topography, the geographical setting of the *Introduction* was none other than the *room* in which it was played and which, as far as we can now tell, was undisguisedly a part of Lord Barrymore's residence. Hence the geographical setting of the *Introduction* was an actual and prime site of Barry family interest and concern, especially if, as would doubtless have been the case, the *Introduction* was played in his residence's hall, the focal point of the household and of family life.

Related to the question of the *Introduction's* formal properties is that of its relation to theatre history. Clavell's *Introduction* is the earliest datable specimen of this mixed form of masque and sword dance whose text survives, though it may have been a form currently in vogue. A few years later, a dramatic prologue comes to light for a sword dance presented at Lathom House, near Ormskirk in Lancashire, a residence of Sir William Stanley, fifteenth earl of Derby, on Ash Wednesday (7 February) 1638. However, it is a perfunctory eight-line affair in comparison with Clavell's much larger offering.[145] It may be imagined that in so long established an Anglo-Irish household as Lord Barrymore's, Clavell could have assumed some familiarity with the native Irish custom of sword-dancing, perhaps to provide his *Introduction* with competent performers but certainly to give its performance added edge in the eyes of its spectators. Who the performers were is not known, but household members seem likely, as was often the way with masques in Ireland, as has been seen. Nor is it known how many sword dancers participated, though five or six would make an appropriate number.[146] Their costumes are the most clearly specified of all the players: 'Cassocks' (military cloaks or long coats), 'Bases' (either plaited cloth skirts appended to the doublet or mailed armour resembling such), 'Helmetts' and 'sowrds drawne.' The remaining players are more readily enumerated. Peace, dressed in a white habit and personified as female, and Mars, accompanied by a page who bears his mailcoat and shield, complete the cast. It is likely that the dance sequences of the performance would have had musical accompaniment, but there is no indication of the forces involved.

The final aspect of the *Introduction* for consideration here is its social and historical valence. The content and elected theatrical dynamic of the *Introduction*, given the peculiar historical circumstances of its performance, would have conspired to endow it with significance far beyond simple entertainment. Understanding this larger significance may also help explain why Clavell won such enthusiastic approval of the Boyle-Barry families. It is clear that Clavell's band of sword dancers, the men whose aggressive energies Mars would constructively redirect, were projected as wild Irish foot soldiers or kern, those perennial disturbers of the peace in (hostile) accounts of Gaelic culture. This is not immediately apparent from their soldierly costumes, despite their relatively elaborate description, but some lines spoken towards the end of the performance by the contrite leader of the band are decisive. He confesses that 'thers noe speare, noe sword, noe skeene, noe darte' – that is, none of the armaments with which he and his band are implicitly associated – that can wound 'like to loue shott from a ladies heart.'[147] The key words here are 'skeene' (whose ultimate etymology is Gaelic) and 'darte.' Both were common collocations in contemporary English descriptions of the Irish kern. And the costume requirement of 'Bases' (mailed armour resembling skirts depending from the doublet) follows suit. As one description of 1548 put it, the Irish were 'armed in mayle with dartes and skaynes after the maner of their countrey.'[148] Thus it is the iconography of the Irish foot soldier that Clavell has invoked in the *Introduction* and fixed upon his sword dancers.[149] The language they use to convey their aggressive intent towards 'that Harlott Peace' is also heavily sexualized: she is a 'Bucksome girle' in whose 'oyly Bowells' they seek to bathe their swords, and by application of a simile which confounds food with rape, she is also rendered a 'Lushious morsell who must bate the sharpnesse of our stomacks.' These Irish kern, then, are passionate and unsocialized. However, once their language and bearing have been demilitarized by Mars's intervention, the sexual charge that remains becomes acceptable; the ladies in the audience, to whom the sexualized threat has also been directed, are finally invited to enter a dance in which they can happily participate since it is now safely shorn of even the make-believe of bodily aggression and has become a game of flirtation and sexual flattery. The masque imposes order on disorder in the wonted way, and this finds expression in the *Introduction* in terms not only of a male and female rapprochement, but also a rapprochement with specific ethnic connotations. The immediate real-life objects of the performance, as earlier noted, were the ladies in the audience. The first of these to be addressed was the countess, probably Alice, wife to Lord Barrymore now for some ten years or more and Sir Richard Boyle's eldest daughter. She it was whom the *Introduction* placed at its ethical centre. It was to her that the character Peace sued as to a deity. Transfigured by Clavell into the role of the protectress of the lady Peace, the (New English) countess became Peace's real-life proxy, as did the other women present whom the (wild Irish) masquers also menaced. In this dialogue between players and audience, not only has the state of peace been feminized but, via the person of the countess, endowed with New English ethnicity. War, conversely, has been made masculine and endowed with an ethnicity resoundingly Irish in the persons of the kern masquers. These ceased behaving as 'Rebellions Route' – that word 'rebellion,' it should be noted, was commonly heard in English discussions of the state of the Irish polity – once Mars had civilized them, but a desirable residue of energy, exoticism, and virility remained with them after rebellion had been purged. In the tradition of Thomas Middleton in an earlier English masque, for Clavell too the Irishman, once 'civilly instructed,' was a paragon of animals.[150] So more than a game, but additionally a covert paradigm of New English colonial relations with both the Anglo-Irish and the 'wild Irish,' Clavell's *Introduction* could not fail to please his hosts.[151] In graciously accepting these blandishments, the Barrys were also accepting Clavell's self-construction as courtier-playwright. Clavell, ever the social shape-shifter, was now appearing in the vein of a Sir William Berkeley or a Sir John Suckling, and doing so to his advantage, as the glowing endorsements of Barry and Boyle testify.

Anyone migrating from Munster north to Ulster during this period would have found himself in a very different geopolitical terrain. After the 'flight of the earls' in 1607, when Tyrone, accompanied by the earl of Tyrconnell and Cú Chonnacht Mág Uidhir, thought it expedient finally to quit Ireland, the province they left behind was now destabilized and even more prone to confiscation and plantation of its land than Munster had ever been. Yet the progress of settlement in Ulster was going far more slowly than the planters had anticipated. The results of the fresh impetus towards urbanization after the earls' departure were in many respects half-hearted.[152] Hence in Ulster relatively few urban centres existed of enough promise to tempt touring performing artists, let alone households with resources sufficient to support resident companies. Even the old established regional capital of Carrick-fergus, co. Antrim, was but a small outpost in comparison with towns like Galway, Limerick, or Cork, its counterparts in the western and southern provinces.[153] Even so, despite the fact that Ulster was a relatively inauspicious province in the main, the few traces of early-seventeenth-century investment in drama and the perform-ing arts that it does yield are of great interest.

The first dramatic enterprise for which evidence survives was not the product of any household in the sense hitherto assumed in this chapter – the residence of a magnate – but it may have been the product of collaboration between several hum-bler ones. It is the case of the aborted performance of *Much Ado about Nothing*, probably Shakespeare's play of that name, at Coleraine, co. Londonderry, sometime before 28 May 1628. It is strange to contemplate that Coleraine, a plantation town only recently developed, would beat Dublin to the first place on record in Ireland for the performance of Shakespeare, even if this performance was called off at the last moment. Closer inspection of the circumstances in which it was to have been put on is most suggestive of the potential for dramatic sponsorship that could exist even in Ulster. Co. Londonderry had first come into being in 1613 and reflects in its name the fact that most of its land, apart from some which had been reserved for the servitor Sir Thomas Phillips, had been made over to the London Companies for development.[154] Phillips had been responsible for overseeing the establishment of the British colony in Coleraine in the early years of the seventeenth century, and it is in a manuscript associated with his administration that the record of *Much Ado* appears:

A coppie of a certificate touching abuses offered to his Maiesties Commissioners Edward Harfleite of Coleraine told me that they had provided themselues to haue entertained ye Commissioners at their coming to Coleraine with a play, the title ∧⌐of⌐ it was. Much adoe about nothing which play he purposed to haue Plaid but that they heard ye Commissioners [..] Tooke a Song that was sung (they are come from seeing ye buildings soe much to hart. [...] by them that they durst not play there play for feare of offending the Commissioners Theis words were spoken by Mr Edward Harfleite vpon Sunday the 25 of May ∧⌐1628⌐. in Mr Walmesleys house of Coleraine I being then present Witnesse my hand this 15° of July 1628

Edward Ellis
Copia vera[155]

It had been intended to perform *Much Ado* as an entertainment on the occasion of a visit to Coleraine of some of the London commissioners. The identity of Edward Harfleet, who seems to have been instrumental in setting up the performance, is not known, but we possibly know a little more about Edward Ellis, the man to whom Harfleet reported the play's cancellation. Ellis may have been that Edward Ellis, provost marshal of Lough Foyle, co. Londonderry, who had been on active service as 'an old soldier in the Low Countries and Ireland' and who was now set-tled in the county.[156] Ellis appears as signatory to a letter to the Lord Deputy Henry Cary, Viscount Falkland, also dated to May 1628 in which the conduct of the agents of the London Companies was held up for censure.[157] Apparently, the Lon-don agents were putting pressure on planters in the county to subscribe to a peti-tion to the king which complained of inadequacies in Sir Thomas Phillips's local management. The planters had refused to comply, however, and were consequently bracing themselves against the agents' recriminations. Some of Ellis's co-signatories to the letter to Viscount Falkland may have been planters like himself: there was, for example, one Robert Stevenson, who may be one of the 'poor planters' of the barony of Loghansholin identified in a petition of c 1622–9; and two others, Francis Barnaby and George Downing, are likely to be the men of the same name who appeared in a Coleraine muster of 20 September 1622.[158] Thus bad blood between the agents and some of the planters may explain why the official arrangements for their reception in May 1628 in Coleraine were soured by some incident intended to cause them offence. Though the meaning of the text quoted above is not entirely clear, it is probable that the song to which the commissioners took exception was some sort of jibe, however mild, aimed at them by persons unknown. Given the circumstances, these persons were probably planters, and not inconceivably, even the putative players themselves.[159] Lest the performance of *Much Ado* in the circumstances further ruffle the commissioners' feathers, Harfleet and his crew decided to abandon it. Harfleet's performance seems to have been so local and Coleraine-centred, and so much a once-off to fête visiting dignitaries, that it may have been produced largely from local means and with local personnel, that is, from the pooled resources of the small householders of Coleraine. Whatever the case, the mooted production is testimony to the planters' awareness of how socially appropriate and useful a play might be for honouring the commissioners' visit. It reveals the planters' notions of how best to mark an occasion, showing how they settled on a play by one of London's foremost playwrights as the most apt offering.[160]

Therefore, unappealing as early-seventeenth-century Ulster may generally have seemed to prospective performers, its inhabitants were not so entirely preoccupied with their planting as to lose all sense of the value of drama and the performing arts. Indeed, perhaps it is to be expected that, precisely because the province was restless with plantation activity, the need to show off smart households, wherever possible, would have been even more urgent than in relatively quieter areas of the country. As has been seen, one of the prime functions of the performing arts in a country so manifestly inhabited by competing ideologies was to articulate and consolidate their host culture, and hence households set up in newly acquired territories might especially hope to benefit from the stabilizing force that cultivation of those arts could exert. Thus a letter which has survived of 9 February 1635, without which we would never have known of the existence of a consort of musicians at the house of Edward Conway (1594–1655), second Lord Viscount Conway and Killultagh, in Lisnagarvy, co. Antrim, should on reflection come as no surprise. This letter is the second piece of evidence extant from the first half of the seventeenth century to demonstrate that the performing arts could hope to function as tokens of cultured normality in the Ulster border-lands.[161] It is worth quoting in full:

Right Honorable

My selfe together with three more of my fellow Musicioners were entertained into your Honors seruice about two yeares since. and therevpon went into Ireland, according your Lordships directions, and euer since haue there remained as your Honors servants, How may it please you since your departure from this Kingdome, two of my fellowes are fallen sicke, whereby wee are like to breake company, and every ˄ᒼManᒾ for himself, And I ffor my [part] selfe humbly intreat your Lordshipp according your direction to mr Rawden, to Lay vs out some plott of land (for our maintenance) here in Kilvltah who desires to liue here, having a charge of a Wife and child, And ffurther May it please your Honor I neither may nor will presume to receiue any Noble Mans entertainment without your Lordships leaue which I humbly craue soe I may not haue [not] wherewith to liue here vnder your Honor behaving my selfe and performing such duties as the rest of your Honors Tennants doe, and withall desiring (if soe please your Honor) to giue directions to mr Rawden (to sett your servant some parsell of land here in Kilvltah that shalbe needfull for him;) as in his discrecion he shall thinke fitte – with s<..>y prayers for your Honors prosperity I Humbly take leaue

Lisnrg: 9° ffebr. 1634   Your Lordship Humble servant
                                     Thomas Richardson[162]

Of course, it must also be said that like Sir Henry Sidney the century before, Conway was already of a disposition to welcome performing artists to his home. While Clarendon's picture of his dissipation may be somewhat overstated – 'a voluptuous man in eating and drinking, and of great licence in all other excesses'[163] – it remains true that Conway was a genial man, interested in performance, and his capacity for enjoyment absorbed music. He was already in residence at Lisnagarvy by December 1629, but seems to have commuted from time to time between here and London.[164] The musician Thomas Richardson, with three others, came to Ireland in Conway's service sometime in 1633, but Conway subsequently left Ireland, some time before 9 February 1635, following which the fortunes of the Lisnagarvy consort took a turn for the worse. Debilitated by the sickness of two of its members, the consort was on the verge of breaking up. Richardson, who had acquired a wife and child, was inclined to settle in Ireland, and wrote to Conway the petition cited above asking him for a parcel of land in his territory of Killultagh. He presumably intended to farm it as one of Conway's tenants, and promised to accept no other noble patronage without Conway's prior consent. It appears that Conway had made provision with his estate manager, Sir George Rawdon, for some such eventuality, since Richardson reminded him of the arrangement. A musician, as ever, needed to be versatile, and not merely within the realm of the performing arts. If Richardson's petition was granted and he was allowed to turn his hand to farming, he would not have ended up doing anything unusual by Irish standards for a member of his profession. Boyle's musicians, it will be recalled, were his tenants too, and the heriot cows that he sometimes made over to them probably went towards swelling their herds. It is interesting to note that Richardson spoke of the possibility of finding other potential noble employers, and from the context it appears that he was thinking of employers in Ireland. There is no question that such existed in the island at large, but perhaps Richardson was thinking even more locally in terms of ones in Ulster, for that was the province in which he had chosen to settle. Thus by the 1620s and 1630s, the performing arts had also started sending down roots in the New English plantation households of Ulster, households both great and small, and though the evidence may be sparse, its nature suggests that far more was happening in these households than surviving records now permit us to know.

With seventeenth-century Munster households well colonized by performance, with Ulster beginning to show a similar inclination, and with Connacht doubtless also following suit (though here the seventeenth-century evidence is scantier even than that from Ulster),[165] the New English households of Leinster, with Dublin at its administrative centre, would be remarkable were they out of step with the rest, or indeed were they not advancing before them and setting trends. It seems that during his incumbency as Lord Deputy, Sir Thomas Wentworth had determined to make Dublin live up to its capital status also in terms of the availability there of drama and the performing arts; his encouragement of Ireland's first public theatre will be explored more fully later in chapter 7. Of present concern are the arrangements that he made within his household. Unlike one of his sixteenth-century viceregal predecessors, Sir John Perrot, Wentworth was not one to skimp on the ostentation of rank. For example, ambitious building projects, such as his lodge at Jigginstown, near Naas, co. Kildare, would have needed matching with correspondingly impressive complements of staff, and he required high standards of all the official residences. It is in Dublin Castle that his household patronage of drama is recorded. He is also known to have patronized a group of 'waite players,' though these, evidently household minstrels, have not come to light on record in Ireland other than twice, in proctors' accounts of Christ Church Cathedral, Dublin.[166] Yet evidently they were vigorous enough to go on tour, for a set of accounts from Coventry dating to 29 November 1637 mentions them receiving 2s 6d, along with a bearward.[167] Wentworth's fool James appears only once, touring in his master's entourage on the Kilkenny progress of August 1637.[168]

The drama recorded at Dublin Castle returns us to the point where this account of the seventeenth-century New English households began, to Sir Richard Boyle. Boyle twice noted in his diary visits to the castle at which plays were acted. Early in 1634 he was in Dublin, staying at the castle with Wentworth. On New Year's Day itself he rewarded various castle personnel, including Wentworth's trumpeters, as well as others, like the Dublin city musicians, who seem to have been drafted in for the occasion.[169] Twelfth Night was marked with gambling and a play acted by Wentworth's gentlemen after dinner.[170] Who the gentlemen were is not told, but in a dramatic context such as this, it is conceivable that one of them was John Ogilby. This Scottish dancing master and impressario, who when he came over to Dublin in Wentworth's service was made a gentleman of his household, was to be instrumental in opening Ireland's first purpose-built theatre in Werburgh Street.[171] The second play at the castle that Boyle recorded, which occurred exactly two years later, demonstrates, as might be expected, that Twelfth Night revels were an established feature of the Wentworth household. Apart from simply servicing the festive season, these revels also provided occasions for the powers that be in the land to congregate within a charmed circle of seasonal jollity where the political tensions between them might be temporarily neutralized, or at least outwardly masked in that civility without which human commerce is apt to miscarry. In January 1634, when Boyle saw his first performance at the castle, faction was an ever-present spectre haunting relations between himself and Wentworth. A power struggle between them had already been played out even before Wentworth's arrival in Ireland.[172] By the time Boyle saw his second castle performance in 1636, even more was at stake. Already in October 1634 he had been summoned before the Court of Castle Chamber in Dublin to answer charges concerning improper acquisition of alienated church temporalities in his home province of Munster. Formal proceedings were not moved against him until March 1635, and these dragged on for more than a year. It appears that he had hit on a plan for currying favour with Wentworth in the matter: he would transfer his interest in the impropriated College of Youghal as a wedding gift to his son Viscount Dungarvan (he of recent masking fame at the court of Charles I); Dungarvan was to marry into the Clifford family, and Wentworth's first wife had been a Clifford. This was the state of play when Boyle saw the Twelfth Night tragedy in the Parliament House of the castle in 1636. At the 1634 performance, Boyle had chosen only to note that the Lord Chancellor, Sir Adam Loftus, was also in attendance. They had been acquainted for many years, for both were admitted into the King's Inns in Dublin together.[173] Now in 1636 he noted in addition the attendance of his son Viscount Dungarvan, and the Lords Digby and Moore.[174] This particular Twelfth Night at the castle must have been a veritable family celebration for Boyle, for both Digby and Moore had Boyle affiliations, either directly through marriage or through the marriage of their kinsmen into the Boyle line.[175] Wentworth had judged the evening well in terms of its guest-list and entertainment. He knew of both Dungarvan's and Digby's theatrical tastes (Digby too had appeared with Dungarvan as one of the masquers in *Coelum Britannicum* in 1634), and had been kept up-to-date on Digby's theatrical comings and goings at the Blackfriars private theatre in London from the gossip of his correspondent, George Garrard.[176] Nevertheless the performance that Wentworth laid on cost them their suppers, presumably on account of its length, and they were cheated of the (by now standard) aristocratic fare of dinner plus drama.[177] But stiffer costs would be incurred by Boyle not a full three months hence, when Wentworth would summon him and threaten him with a public hearing over the matter of his involvement in the impropriated temporalities, with a fine of £30,000 on top.[178] Boyle's diary would make no further mention of convivial New Year visits to Dublin Castle after this.

Boyle did not say who the tragedians of 1636 were. Force of habit might suggest that as in 1634, so now, they were 'his lordships gentle<men>.'[179] If so, an interesting possibility opens up, since by this date John Ogilby had spread his wings beyond the immediate Wentworth household, as the next chapter will show. When Boyle saw the Parliament House tragedy, the public theatre in Werburgh Street had very likely already opened. This theatre, so much the offspring of the Wentworth/ Ogilby collaboration, was from its inception closely responsive to the castle's requirements. The players whom Boyle saw in 1636 may therefore have been members of the company of the new Dublin theatre.

In this web of patronage of drama and the performing arts which drew New English households of the seventeenth century together, Dublin by the mid 1630s could claim to have assumed a central position. Out of the household of one of Ireland's most controversial Lords Deputy had flowed both the resources and political will needed to transform drama into an independent, and as it was hoped, commercially viable public institution. Yet that household retained certain claims on the new institution and used it to accumulate political interest on the capital that had been laid out on its founding. Drama and the performing arts within the Wentworth household, then, had taken a complex turn. The household had spawned an institution requiring a dedicated architectural space and recognition; there may have been a sense in which to enter the Werburgh Street Theatre was to enter vicariously the household of the Lord Deputy himself, or at least to fraternize with its civilized values for the price of a theatre ticket. Outside Dublin, no other place in Ireland would be home to so large an undertaking until well after the Restoration. But further details of the enterprise must wait until the next chapter.

THE GAMES SERVANTS PLAYED

The increasing specialization of Ogilby's role within the Wentworth household, which eventually culminated in the extension of that role outside the household through association with a public playhouse, was a uniquely seventeenth-century, Dublin-based phenomenon. In essence, however, it was a natural evolution of a domestic's role which had precedents across the full ethnic spectrum of households in Ireland, and from the earliest recorded times: household servants bore much of the responsibility for organizing performances as occasion required, and in some cases, it was the performance aspect of their role that came to predominate. This is suggested at its simplest (and earliest) by the exclusiveness of the professional names attached to some of the performing artists of the native Gaelic tradition (the *drúth rig*, for example, the 'king's jester' or 'royal jester,' anchored to a particular patron). Like Ogilby in a later age, many of these early performers also developed a professional existence beyond the immediate household. If any scatter of focus has resulted from distributing the discussion so far under separate ethnic headings, it might be a useful corrective, before passing finally to the evidence for non-aristocratic and institutional patronage, to consider the role of domestics as performers in house-holds. It will become clear that there was a fundamental similarity in how perfor-mances were organized in all the greater households, no matter where in Ireland these were or what their ethnic complexion. The evidence of Old and Middle Irish texts was surveyed in chapter 1. Here will be reviewed three cases from the period with which the bulk of this chapter has been concerned, the sixteenth and seven-teenth centuries. The cases are centripetally focused also in the sense that all are nearly contemporary within roughly twenty-five years, and between them they rep-resent the whole of the country (Munster, Connacht, and Ulster, with Leinster having been represented already, although admittedly as an extraordinary case, in the house-hold of Sir Thomas Wentworth). And they range between the poles of the ethnic spectrum, from native Irish to New English. In sum, they set general inferences about the role of servants as purveyors of performance in households throughout Ireland on a secure basis.

The earliest of the three comes from an Irish household somewhere in Munster, probably in the 1580s. Donnchadh (an tSneachta) Mac Craith (†c 1597), sympathizer with the rebellious earl of Desmond who had caused the English administration so much vexation, maintained a substantial household. Into it he invited on one occa-sion the English Lord President of Munster, whom he showered with hospitality, perhaps by way of détente:

Donatus Macrahus cognomento Niueus Ibernus vir apud populares suos frugalitate & libera- | liberalitate notissimus Momoniarum præfecto Anglo quem hospicio acceperat, non modo lautum, splendidumque conuiuium instruxit, sed etiam domesticos suos choræas, atque ludos exhibere iussit.[180]

[Donnchadh Mac Craith, the 'snowy and wintry' one by name, was a man most renowned amongst his people for frugality and liberality. Not only did he furnish a sumptuous and splendid feast for the English Lord President of Munster, whom he had received in hospi-tality, but he also ordered his household servants to display dances and games/plays.]

The hospitality lavished was finally unavailing, however. Some few days later, the Lord President invited Mac Craith and his retinue to Cork, and subsequently ordered the execution of several of those same servants on the grounds that no honest and frugal man had need of so many, unless he were up to no good – treacherous action in view of the hospitality he had received, which is precisely what the Catholic author of this passage wished us to understand, but predictable, because the English administration had reason to mistrust Mac Craith and fear where his native sympa-thies lay.[181] What is of present interest is the detail that it was the *domestici* of his household that Mac Craith ordered to provide the entertainment of dances and

games/plays. One imagines that these pastimes were already in repertoire, and that
the domestics were therefore not awkwardly put on the spot. It was another group
of domestics, or *famuli* as they were this time called, who, at the latter end of the
period being examined here and in Ulster, presented a whole assortment of Christmastide pastimes. Captain Josias Bodley's visit in 1602 to the house of Sir Richard
Moryson, probably in Downpatrick, co. Down, has already been commented on as
the occasion for a curious hybrid masque, in which outlandishly dressed masquers diced
with the assembled company and then departed. This entertainment had been got up
by *quidam ex Nobilibus Hibernicis* ('various Irish lords').[182] But the lower-class *famuli*
of Moryson's household also contributed one particular *Iocum, siue Gambolium*
('jest or gambol') that impressed Bodley so much that he recorded it in detail:

Alium nunc ex multis monstrabo Iocum, siue Gambolium, quem præsentarunt Nobis
Famuli I Nobis Famuli Domini Morrisoni. Duo Serui sedebant in terram more Mulierum
(sub reuerentia sit dictum) quando chaccant in aprico campo, nisi quod istorum Nates
premebant terram; manus erant simul alligatæ, & ita extensæ, ut genua amplecterentur, &
baculum positum inter flexum brachiorum, & Crura, ita Brachia nullo modo mouere possent;
inter Indices, & pollices utriusque manus bacillum quoddam longitudinis fere vnius pedis
ab anteriore parte acutum tenebant, & isto modo locantur duo illi, alter ex opposito alterius
per distantiam vnius Vlnæ. His ita dispositis incipiunt congredi, & quisque pro se vinctis
pedibus aduersarium subuertere conatur; subuersus enim nunquam se potest recuperare, sed
podicem præbet Sub uersori pungendum cum dicto Bacillo, quod fecit Nos ita ridere per
vnam horam, vt lachrymæ ex oculis nostris distillarent; & Vxor Phillippi Coqui ridebat
etiam, & ipse Lixa, qui fuerunt ambo præsentes. Dixisses, Tonsorem aliquem Chiurgum
fuisse ibi, ad quem omnes monstrabant dentes; ...[183]

[Now I will tell you of another jest or gambol which, amongst many, the domestics of Master Moryson presented for us. Two servants squatted on the ground in the way women do
(reverently let it be said) when they defecate in open field, except that the servants' backsides
pressed upon the ground. Their hands were tied together so that they embraced their knees
between them, and a stick was placed between the bend of their arms and legs so that they
could not move their arms in any way. Between forefinger and thumb of each hand they held
a certain small stick about a foot in length and sharpened at the further end. These two servants are placed in the following way: one faces the other at about an ell's distance. When
these things have been arranged, the two start to approach each other, and tackling with his
feet, each tries to topple his opponent; for once thrown over he can never recover himself,
but he offers his backside to be prodded with the small stick previously mentioned. This
made us laugh for a whole hour so much that the tears streamed from our eyes; and the wife
of Phillip the cook laughed and the kitchen maid too, who were both present. You would
have said that some barber-surgeon were there to whom everyone was showing their teeth.]

The contestants were trussed like oven-ready fowl (see fig. 18), and hopped towards each other for the purpose that Bodley described.[184] There is little doubt but that their *Iocum, siue Gambolium* was an Ulster incarnation of the game that the playwright Henry Medwall incorporated into his interlude *Fulgens and Lucres*, performed in London over a century earlier. There the players referred to it as 'Farte Prycke in Cule.'[185] Its connection with its Ulster relative not only helps to clarify exactly what happened in a boisterous, though obscure, section of Medwall's play, but is of present interest for what it has to reveal about performing arts in the context of an Irish household. First, Medwall's absorption of the game 'Farte Prycke in Cule' into a play resembles the seamless shift in Bodley's narrative from describing the hybrid masque to describing the *Iocum, siue Gambolium*, and thus illustrates yet again the easy commerce in both centuries and countries between the concepts 'play' and 'game.' And second, 'Farte Prycke in Cule' was played by the domestics of the piece, A and B, while Joan, the 'flower of the frying pan,' looked on as umpire. The social tone of their activity – these were games that were played by servants exclusively – is noted once more in Bodley's account. Irish lords had offered their strange masque, and now it was the turn of *famuli* to contribute to the seasonal festivities with a performance appropriate to their class. There is some double-thinking at work here, of course, because even if those of social standing did not directly join in, they joined in the fun; according to Bodley, everyone laughed till their tears flowed, his own included.

The final case locates in the middle of the three, geographically and chronologically, and comes from Galway in 1589. Just as Sir Richard Moryson's New English household had been a meeting place of traditions, it is likely that that of Sir Richard Bingham (1528–99), Lord President of Connacht, was similar, notwithstanding Bingham's famous impatience with things Old English, let alone mere Irish.[186] Old English and Irish factions in the province had gone into rebellion during his presidency because, they maintained, Bingham's conduct towards them had been unjust and ruthless. Five commissioners were despatched to parley with the rebels and enquire into their grievances. They were the Gaelic speaking justice of Connacht Sir Robert Dillon, the Old English reformer and master of the rolls Sir Nicholas White, Sir Thomas Le Strange, and the bishops of Meath and of Kilmore, Thomas Jones and John Garvey. The bishop of Meath was chiefly responsible for penning the account on behalf of the commissioners of the events that befell in Galway between 12 and 27 April 1589, including the one of present concern. On Friday 25 April, the commissioners had assembled in 'the Abbey by the waters side'[187] and were waiting for boats to take them to the rebels who, since they were too afraid of Bingham to risk entering Galway itself, had arranged a rendezvous some short distance from the city. Before the commissioners left, they witnessed the preparations for what subsequently turned into a public satirical impersonation of them by the

18   Reconstruction of 'Farte Prycke in Cule.'

household servants of Bingham and his brother Sir George. This was played out, the commissioners were later informed, not only in the abbey but also in the streets of the city after their embarcation:

There came into the Abbaie twoo of sir Richardes howsehold men thone {'the one'} was his trompeter thothers name is whitwell, and also one of sir George Binghams men, whose name is Ned Baker; Of theis twoo of them were apparelled in womens mantells, and cappes, the third in a blake gowne viz the Trompeter./ I the bishop of meathe sawe them in this attire, and so also did 6. of our servauntes, to passe throughe the Abbaie into the cloister. whervpon I went forthwith vnto the rest of my followers being in the vpper part of the chauncell, and said vnto them, com let vs goo and tarie no longer, for I see they do begin to mocke vs alreadie. And as for certentie wee the bishop of Meithe, Sir Robert Dillon, and sir Thomas Le Strang were that night informed, at our return from the parlie by manie which bothe heard and sawe their vsage of vs, so sone as wee were in boate. they three aforenamed, accompanied with some others, whose names we coulde not learne came into the chauncell of the Abbaie and there challenging to them selfes, the names of her majesties comissioners, One said, I am the bishop of meithe, another said I am the Bishop of kilmore, and another said, I am Sir Robert Dillon, and so of the rest./

He that challenged the name of the bishop of Meithe began on this wise saieng nowe speakes the Bishop of meathe, you are they which have put out theis men into Rebellion against her majestie to spoile the cuntrey. and to hurt the subiectes, howe are you able to answere this? Another of them selves rose vp, and with a lowe curtesie began to saie I thrust your Lordship shalbe better informed./

To the like effect a discant was made of thother .4. comissioners and after this sporte made in scornfull wise, within the Abbaie wee aforenamed were for certentie informed by diuerse that the three first named Actors not contented herewith, in that disguised sort went throughe the streetes of Galwaie, naming them selves the Quenes: comissioners, saieng thus, Rowme for the Quenes: comissioners, I am the Bishop of meathe said one, another said I am the Iustice Dillon, Reverence for the Quenes comissioners. Etcetera./[188]

Although not a play in any traditional sense, this mimetic mockery was on the verge of being precisely that satirical use of drama that the Tudor government had been so sensitive about in Ireland, as much as it had been in England: the Irish parliament of 1560, for example, had legislated against those who sought to detract the Book of Common Prayer in interludes, plays, songs, and rhymes;[189] and only two or three years prior to the Galway charade, and not many miles away in co. Leitrim, the outrage caused by Sir Brian O'Rourke's ritual abuse and degradation of a statue on whose breast he had written the name 'Queen Elizabeth' rumbled on in the State Papers for several years.[190] Now in Galway the state's representatives were being parodied by domestics of the Bingham households, and the gravity of their conduct, in the light of past legislation and recent practice, cannot have been lost on those for whom the bishop of Meath's report was intended.[191] Whether much significance is to be attached to the fact that one of the performers, the impersonator habited in the black gown, was also Bingham's trumpeter, a household musician, is not clear, but the salient point is that those who had taken this performance upon themselves were all servitors in the Bingham households. The implication seems to be that even if they were not set on directly, they were catching and acting out the attitude of their masters. Bingham had made the presidency of Connacht his own bailiwick, and made no secret of his resentment of Dublin interference in how he governed it.[192] A few months later, Bingham wrote to defend himself against the commissioners' report. It is not clear whom he had in mind as the performers of the 'play in the church' that he accused the bishop of Meath of idling his time attending;[193] perhaps this was Bingham's device, sardonic if the bishop's report be credited, for putting a rather different spin on events at the abbey for those who would be reading the report. Certainly, Bingham seems to have latched onto an incipient imputation of frivolity to those who attended plays, frivolity scarsely venial when they were bishops who ought to know better, but quite in character with a bishop content, Bingham claimed, to swear by God's wounds while playing cards.[194] Whether Bingham was glossing the event in the abbey or alluding to another one, it also stands as the single other piece of evidence surviving from outside Dublin, apart from one from Kilkenny, of the use of churches as venues for plays.[195] Household domestics, then, might double as performers. No matter whether a household retained performers on a formal basis, some versatility might be expected of its domestics. Either way, entertainment was likely to be available as occasion required.

INSTITUTIONAL PATRONAGE IN THE SIXTEENTH AND SEVENTEENTH CENTURIES: DUBLIN

Necessarily, a private household's infrastructure was unlike that of those other institutions – guilds, corporations, the church, and so on – that comprised the body politic. While households could often rely on their domestic staff to perform to order, the institutions were obliged to behave somewhat differently. They might, like the households, resort to hiring in performers whenever these came knocking. Alternatively, they might actively seek performers out. The essential point is that lacking infrastructures of the domestic sort, institutions had to make other provisions for performance since they could not rely in quite the same way on in-house arrangements made between their members. It may be true that, rather as households seem to have expected performance from capable domestics as a matter of course, institutions may have expected some of their members to perform from time to time: institutional performance would have had the advantage of marking a member's place in the institution's structure and would thereby have affirmed the integrity of the whole through a celebration of the role of its parts, as has been illustrated in detail in Dublin's case, for example, in chapter 3. Nevertheless, an institution might need to compensate for the special claims it made on its members' time by allocating a formal reward for services rendered, whereas in the household, performance may have been only indirectly remunerated in the form of occasional largesse. Thus, to return to Dublin's example, the corporation may in a sense have resembled a household when it requisitioned performances from its affiliated and dependent institution of the Mayor of the Bullring, whose pageant of the Nine Worthies, as has been seen, was a corporation favourite. But still this was an attenuated version of what households had more immediately to hand, even if there on a more modest scale, for in households, performance may have been regarded as a due towards general domestic well-being, just as much as cooking and cleaning, and part of every servant's unwritten terms of contract. Moreover, within the household it would have been harder to dodge any call for performance, save on the unanswerable grounds of incapacity; by contrast, the Mayor and Sheriffs of the Bullring, though perfectly capable, were occasionally prepared to defy the corporation's demands, as when they refused to perform on May Day in 1599 and were disciplined for non-compliance.[196]

Institutional patronage of performance, the final item on this chapter's agenda, completes the general patronage picture for which evidence survives. Preeminently an urban phenomenon, institutional patronage in Ireland is most clearly shown in Dublin, where extant documentation is densest. It should be stated at the outset that by 'institutional patronage' is meant the sort of patronage exercised by organizations like those cited above, ones whose public face was liable to be even more prominent than that of the households. The institutional needs which performance helped satisfy may have partly overlapped with those of the households, but given the different infrastructure and social function of the institutions, their institutional needs were not precisely coextensive with domestic ones. The concluding investigation will examine the nature and objectives of institutional patronage, as far as sources permit of its reconstruction.

The nearest that Dublin Corporation (or for that matter any other Irish corporation) came to retaining performing artists on a formal basis was in the persons of its civic musicians or waits and certainly these, in the first instance at least, were not players or actors. Nevertheless, subject to availability, players and actors were sometimes patronized, and Dublin has the earliest records of any Irish corporation for doing so. On some occasion between the Michaelmas 1568 and Michaelmas 1569 the Lord Deputy, Sir Henry Sidney, had been invited to the New Hall 'to see the playe.'[197] Some sort of hippocras was served to him to help jolly the evening along (the Treasurer's Book notes that one Nicholas Sedgrave was paid 14s 8d for purchasing the wine and sugar for it). No mention is made of who the players were, but since the corporation retained none of its own, outsiders were probably brought in. Even if the corporation chose not to look very far for them and had required the pageant of the Nine Worthies to be dusted off once again, it imported its players. The possibility that their importation was from an institution so near to hand as was the office of the Bullring might explain why, unlike the wine and sugar, the players entailed no expenses that needed recording in the Treasurer's Book. However, in another set of accounts running between Michaelmas 1588 and Michaelmas 1589 appear the two earliest surviving records of institutional patronage of liveried players in Ireland, and in both cases this patronage extended well beyond the corporation's immediate institutional affinity. One concerns an allocation made to the queen's players and the other to the queen's majesty's players (both titles of the same troupe), as well as to the earl of Essex's players.[198] To be exact, both troupes arrived in Dublin either sometime after 12 October 1588 and before 6 July 1589, or in the height of summer in 1589 between 10 July and 31 August.[199] They were travelling

together during this period, and had sandwiched Dublin into their tour of Lancashire. By now the waters of the Irish Sea were free of the Armada threat and safe to
venture on. Judging by their presence in Lancashire immediately before and after
their Dublin visit, it is likely that both troupes crossed from Chester. They never
returned to Dublin, as far as the Treasurer's Book is concerned, though this was
probably less on account of the size of the sums they received, which were in fact
quite generous, than on account of their being able to make a decent enough living
in England without needing to make a second Irish detour. After all, Dublin was a
little off their beaten track. The first reward of £3 sterling (£4 Irish) 'payed to the
Quenes players coming to this Cittie, as a requittall of there good wylls in showing
there Sporte in this Cittie' sounds as if their performance was a public one.[200] Possibly it contained a preview of the feats of funambulism executed by a cunning
'hongarian' in the troupe that were to hold the citizens of Shrewsbury spellbound
a year later.[201] A second payment of 50s sterling was delivered to them by one
Nicholas Stephens on their departure, as well as a payment of 10s sterling to the
earl of Essex's players for 'making Sporte to the mayor <& al>ldermen.'[202] This performance, by contrast, looks to have been a private bespeak. So it appears that in
1589 the citizens of Dublin may have been treated to a windfall entertainment at
the corporation's expense, a refreshingly adventitious addition to the more predictable round of civic performances, and probably as far as the citizens were concerned one far less encumbered by political freight, obvious or covert. Except, of
course, for the fact that in exercising towards both troupes a patronage resembling
that of the vertical sort so characteristic of the aristocratic households, the corporation was enhancing its position as an institution to be reckoned with, one to hold
up its head beside the powers that be in the land. Any exercise of patronage, of
course, imputes a degree of power and status to the patron.

The nature and objectives of the corporation's patronage of the city music have
already been considered in a previous chapter, so we may pass on to consider the
example set by another Dublin institution, the city trade guilds. On account of the
substantial archival loss sustained by the guild documents in the Four Courts
explosion of 1922, the picture of their performance patronage has been severely
damaged, yet the surviving fragments of evidence suggest that this was managed no
less as a means of securing power and status for the guilds as it was for the corporation. Indeed, in an urban culture in which patronage so frequently expressed the
checks and balances of institutional power, the guilds too might be imagined as
jealously wishing to speak in their own voice and on their own behalf, rather than
merely ventriloquizing the yearly bidding of the corporation to represent themselves in general civic pageantry. The account book of the Tailors guild is probably
representative of what has been lost of other guild documents in this respect. It
shows how the Tailors too hired musicians and players to add a sense of occasion

to special moments in the guild's life, and many of these moments, like many of the events observed by the corporation or by other city guilds, came around with clockwork regularity during the course of the year. Perhaps the most important was the Tailors' annual guild banquet, held at midsummer on the feast of the guild's patron saint, St John the Baptist. This feast was also the swearing-in day of guild officers, so in addition to festivity it saw the transaction of business crucial to the guild's institutional life.[203] Thus, for example, on 24 June 1612, players were given 2s for performing at the time of the banquet.[204] It is not known who these were, but possibly they were members of the guild: just three years before, on 16 January 1609, Sir Robert Jacob had written to Sir John Davys telling him that Christmas-tide in Dublin had gone off with 'dauncing, Masking, and a play by the Taylors of St Patrickes most taylerly acted before the Kinges deputy,' which proves that the Tailors were perfectly capable of putting such performances on and in very high places into the bargain.[205] Music often accompanied occasions of swearing-in, as in 1602 when the guild master took his oath.[206] Other swearings-in, even if of persons less central to the guild's hierarchy, might also be enhanced by music, as when around 16 December 1605, Barnaby Dungan was admitted as a brother, or when Robert Keavan and Edward White were made free bretheren.[207] There were also several ceremonial breakfasts (possibly served on admission to guild membership) that were accompanied by music, and these include the earliest extant reference to the patronage of music that the Tailors' accounts contain: at some time in 1550 there was 'payd to the mynstralis the daye of Richard tauerneres brekeffaste xij d.'[208] Sometimes the Tailors were able to patronize the best musicians that the city had to offer. In 1609 they secured the services of Lord Howth's musicians, but only because William Huggard, chief wait of the city music, had a prior engagement attending on the mayor.[209] In 1610, however, Huggard was hired by the Tailors to perform on one of their guild quarter days (these were other regular occasions on which music and the transaction of guild business might coincide).[210] It is clear, then, that in the early-seventeenth century, patronage of the city music was the guild's first preference, but when that was not possible, Lord Howth's musicians stood in, as again on another occasion in 1610 when Huggard was unavailable, being employed at the circuits.[211] Preferences notwithstanding, no discrimination showed in the fee paid, for both the city waits and Lord Howth's musicians received 3s. The guild also made regular trips to visit property it owned in Baskin, co. Dublin; these were celebrated with music and feasting, as for example on 9 September 1611 when a group of musicians received 5s.[212] An overview of the Tailors' patronage of the performing arts discloses a simple pattern, and it is one which also typifies several of the other patrons examined here: music was the primary, and drama the secondary, choice in performance art for enhancing special occasions. Yet whether the recruitment be of music or drama, it coincided with nodal moments in the institutional life of the guild. Thus the guild empowered itself by rehearsing its structures through means similar to those of other institutions. With them it entered the social colloquy in which music and drama were an agreed language. The guild's hiring of the city musicians was also perhaps the most telling act of appropriation that it made of a key engine of institutional prestige: the Tailors were securing a place for themselves in the scheme of things, and their patronage of the performing arts, especially that revealed in their preferred choice of musicians, was helping them to stake out their claim.[213]

Of the learned, professional institutions that existed in Dublin, only two have left records of performance sponsorship, and they are modest ones at that. It is a little strange that not more is known about what went on in the King's Inns in this respect, especially considering that its more prestigious London counterpart, the Inns of Court, had an imposing reputation for dramatic productions. Since Irish law students were obliged to spend a period training in London, these productions would have been familiar to them.[214] By the seventeenth century, Inns of Court students were involved also in drama on the large scale in the form of masques. Indeed, James Shirley, who was soon after imported to the Werburgh Street Theatre, wrote one of their most lavish for performance in 1634, a couple of weeks before the production of Carew's *Coelum Britannicum*.[215] King's Inns in Dublin had also had at least one playwright on its books who was himself a masque writer, John Clavell, though perhaps it is not coincidental that as an English blow-in who was simply passing through, he was not wholly typical. All that remains recording activity at King's Inns is a note that £2 was 'paid to the players for the grand day,' an occasion that fell sometime in the Hilary Term of 1630.[216] This time the paucity of references is less readily explicable in terms of record loss. Perhaps King's Inns, until only very recently in 1628 a Protestant stronghold that denied Catholics admission, had also been in the grip of that moderating sobriety that was even more palpable in its sister learned institution, Trinity College Dublin, at about the same time.[217] Here, had it not been for the presence of the evangelically minded provost Dr Robert Ussher, and the zealous tradition within the college which he represented, academic drama of the sort that was flourishing in Oxbridge might also have been extensively cultivated. But Trinity College had been staffed with Cambridge men from the more fervent colleges.[218] It is clear nevertheless that a dramatic tradition had once existed, for the first signs of it appear on 23 December 1629 in the college's General Register: 'The senior sophisters exercise dominion over the junior sort this Christmas. A comedy acted by them and a play by ye Batchellours./.'[219] But after Ussher became provost on 4 January 1630, the college's Christmas plays began encountering resistance, as the next reference to them in the General Register, on 29 December 1630, shows: 'It is condescended and agreed that the Batchellours should act their play but not in the Colledge./.'[220] Robert Ware, drawing on his father's manuscript materials, gives a sketch of Ussher's personality which confirms what the entries in the General Register suggest and what one might have suspected of a man of Ussher's cultural formation: 'He was a Serious Man, and noe friend to the Levitie of all Theatricall Gaieties & Representations, as appears by the great difficultie he made of admitting Comedies to be acted in the Colledg dureing his Goverment Tho at last perswaded therevnto by the great Solicitation of Considerable Persons, and at the desire of the Lords Justices who Ruled in his time.'[221] The two Lords Justice importuning for restoration of the college's drama during Ussher's régime were Sir Richard Boyle and Sir Adam Loftus.[222] Whether or not Ussher was a respecter of persons, he would doubtless have respected the Protestant pedigree of these men. Their intervention would have had the effect of endorsing a more general tolerance of drama at the learned institutions, thus indirectly protecting whatever traditions were already in place at their home institution of King's Inns. Perhaps Boyle and Loftus had a liberal humanist eye to the training in self-presentation that plays would provide, and which was thus a useful basis for forensic oratory as well as for general social competence. Perhaps they also had an eye to the very different ethos prevailing in Dublin Castle, where to affect drama would have been to express solidarity with the Crown, and they may have wished to temper the provost accordingly for the sake of amicable relations. For all that the combined pressure is said to have succeeded, no other traces of drama and the performing arts within the college remain on record.

Trinity College, erected in 1592 on the site of the dissolved priory of All Hallows, was to be the centre in which young men could be trained for an evangelical mission to Catholic Ireland and, it might be added, to a substantially recusant city. Just as the Austin canons of the priory and its sister houses had been so active in the promotion of drama during the medieval period and up to the Reformation, so the governing body of Dublin's new Protestant seminary, if the place was to be made a truly upright witness to a city where Catholicism was quietly tolerated and where the state authorities might well have seemed malfeasant and lukewarm in their zeal, must not countenance theatricals, but strive rather to put them down. It is therefore hardly surprising to discover a leaven of anti-theatrical malice at work in the college. There were other worthy citizens outside the college walls who would have been sympathetic. Barnaby Rich, for example, famous excoriator of tobacco, dancing schools, and other social ills, was resident in Dublin early in the seventeenth century, and held the view that not only did theatricals take their toll on the morals of those addicted to them – plays were an effeminate and vicious pastime – but they also resembled the staginess of unreformed religion. This was an old objection, one cunningly negotiated by Bishop Bale in Kilkenny a century earlier. Did not Catholic priests like dressing up and gesticulating at their masses much in the way of stage players? Rich's mouthpiece, conceived, significantly, as 'a young student in Trinity Colledge by Dublin' named Patrick Plain, sums the position up: 'When your priest hath put on his masking apparell, and hath gotten all his trinkets about him, if there were an Irish bag-piper by, that had a deepe Drone, to play and entertayne the time whilst the priest were in his Memento, and had made an ende of all his dumbe showes: what with the musicke of the one, and the gestures of the other, it woulde passe all the Puppet playes in the world.'[223] Self-respecting, virile Protestants, on the other hand, had no business with the likes of these, or with their ways. When Trinity College's anti-theatrical prejudice would have been regarded as exemplary, cherished as it was by the provost and governing body, it is likely that it would have percolated into the state church in which Trinity graduates often found employment. This is precisely what happened. The tenor of the Dublin diocese in this respect is indicated in two sets of visitation articles of the 1630s. Relatively few sets of such articles survive for Ireland. Of those that do, all are from the seventeenth century. Two concern Dublin and fall within the archiepiscopate of Lancelot Bulkeley (from October 1619 until his death in 1650). Bulkeley was known to Ussher and like him 'noe friend to the Levitie of all Theatricall Gaieties & Representations.' In 1634 and 1638, articles including enquiry into whether churches, chapels, and churchyards of the diocese were free from 'playes, feasts, banquets, suppers, churchales, drinkings, exposing any wares to sale, temporal courts or leets, lay-juries, Musters, commissions, (other than for causes Ecclesiastical,) playing at ball, or any other prophane usage' were published,[224] and while it is true that articles were often formulaic in character, the vigilance against theatrical profanity that the Dublin ones might suggest in their instigator is proved in his move against Sir Thomas Wentworth's fledgling theatre in Werburgh Street while Wentworth was briefly away from Ireland, as the next chapter will reveal. Measures taken to avert plague were the pretext, and they were a plausible one when the London theatres had been shut from 12 May 1636 for the same reason. But that it was a pretext, as far as Wentworth was concerned, is clear from his diagnosis of a 'Purity of Zeale' urging the archbishop's actions.

While the volte-face that occurred within the church between the 1530s and 1630s meant that drama could no longer hope for the church's support and patronage, musical performance continued to play an important part in the church's liturgy, especially in those churches where it had a long tradition and where state officials congregated. Hence Dublin had a pool of experienced musicians whose duties were primarily liturgical.[225] However, like the city waits or household musicians (Lord Howth's, for example), these seem often to have been available outside their primary liturgical context.[226] Following the suppression of the choral foundation of St Patrick's Cathedral in 1547, six of its priest vicars and two of its choristers were redeployed in Christ Church Cathedral, a royal grant having been allocated for their maintenance there. In recognition of this arrangement, it became customary for the choir of Christ

Church to sing four times a year in the court of the Exchequer.[227] The first actual proof that this custom was being observed, which dates from 1589, is in the form of payments to choristers for their Exchequer appearances.[228] More than a traditional expression of gratitude, then, the choir's participation in this extra-liturgical ceremony had also become a source of income. Other secular patronage might derive from the guilds whose chapels were housed in city churches and which frequently paid church musicians on guild patronal festivals. Thus the Christ Church choir might hope to benefit again each 22 July from donations of the Barber-Surgeons, whose guild chapel of St Mary Magdalene was in the cathedral,[229] or the 'singing men of St John's' (that is, of the church of St John the Evangelist) from the Tailors on 24 June.[230] The mutual patronage of the city's sacred and secular institutions built bridges over which musicians might cross to perform in either institution. A good example of this is found in the proctors' accounts of Christ Church Cathedral. Mr Richardson, proctor between the Michaelmas 1594 and Michaelmas 1595, entered accounts like the following:

Item to make mery wyth my lords musitians for their paynes in [t] the quere
& helping our vycars: alowid towards the vycars chardges   x s.
…

vppon christemas evenes even at for makyng my lordes deputes [mon]
musitians & our vycars a brekffast
                                                                          vj s.
…

for paper for priking songs & other vses about
…

|fol. [9]|

…

Delyverid to mr bullock in prest vppon hallou even my lordes musitons being
in my chamber
                                                                   ij s. vj d.[231]

And in his accounts between Michaelmas 1595 and Michaelmas 1596 (Christ Church proctors normally served a biennial stint) appear the following entries:

to make mery wyth my lordes musitians with vs.   vj s. viij d.

|fol. [1v]|

…

for the vickers casting their s<ong>es christmas even & wyth my lord deputies
m<u>sitins
                                                                         viij s.
paper for prickyng songe<s> for the quiristers   xviij d.[232]

It is clear from these entries that the joined forces were sometimes performing liturgically, sometimes for pure merriment.[233] Such commerce between sacred and secular is neatly epitomized in the career of Thomas Bateson, organist of Christ Church from 1608 until his death in 1630, but better known for his madrigal compositions.[234] And the snapshot impression of music in Christ Church left by the provost of Trinity College before Ussher took up office, William Bedell, is worth recalling. Bedell was a product of a fervent foundation, Emmanuel College, Cambridge. He came to Dublin in 1627, where between August of that year and his consecration to the bishoprics of Ardagh and Kilmore in September 1629, he would have had first-hand experience of Christ Church liturgy, for he preached there on a regular basis. He regretted the proliferation there of 'organs, sackbutts, cornetts, viols etc. as if it had been at the dedication of Nebuchadnezzar's golden image,' and cathedral accounts prove that his list of musical forces was no exaggeration (viols are the only instruments that the accounts do not directly attest).[235] Such was the musical establishment over which Bateson presided. If a certain worldliness in the conduct of the music of state religion offended the stern, they could not hope for much quarter from the last Lord Deputy before the period under review here drew to an end: Sir Thomas Wentworth, friend of the high-church faction, lover of royalty and of stage plays, would have seemed a discouraging prospect, one whose tastes in this regard were quite beyond reformation.

INSTITUTIONAL PATRONAGE IN THE SIXTEENTH AND SEVENTEENTH CENTURIES:
THE PROVINCES

The sixteenth century is less well served than the seventeenth for detailed, internal evidence of corporate and institutional patronage. Had records survived more extensively, the civic receptions at Clonmel, Cork, Galway, Limerick and Waterford would doubtless all have yielded such evidence, but as it is, they are recorded only externally, through the reactions of those for whom they were organized. It remains to pass on to the seventeenth century, and to return to Munster, the seventeenth-century Kilkenny evidence having already been considered in chapter 5. The corporations in both Cork and Youghal retained civic drummers, though no outlays are recorded for any full-scale band of waits after the Dublin fashion.[236] In Cork as in Dublin, the corporation also took measures to channel the energies of the civic youth constructively, though it is not clear whether or not an officer like Dublin's Mayor of the Bullring was appointed to watch over them and take responsibility for their actions. Some formal measure of civic supervision is hinted at in the 1631 by-law which attempted to restrain 'a very barbarous and uncivil kind of sport upon Easter Tuesdays, May days, Whitson Tuesday, viz., tossing of great balls, and hurling in the open streets with the small ball' at which brawls and even deaths had occurred.[237] Its last clause is noteworthy for the familiarity that it assumes with certain games and pastimes that were, conversely, permitted: 'Provided this bye-law shall not hinder any lawful sports, as to bring home the Summer and Maypole, or other lawful exercises that the young men of the City shall use hereafter, only the hurling upon the streets to be given over.'[238] But responsibility for policing this ultimately fell on the mayor and sheriffs' shoulders, not on any other specially delegated officer. Hence the sort of developed infrastructure that gave corporate patronage greater scope to exercise itself in cities like Dublin, for example, is not recorded. Youghal, though smaller than Cork, has preserved more in the way of internal evidence of its corporate patronage. From external evidence, it seems clear that in the early years of the seventeenth century, its corporation, custodian of civic self-esteem, was wont to hold mayoral banquets, and employed performers to grace these occasions. One such, an annual feast to mark the succession of the new mayor, was unflatteringly preserved in mock heroics by Thomas Scot in *An Irish Banqvet, or the Mayors feast of Youghall*, published in 1616.[239] Apart from its aspersions cast on the banqueters and their fare which was, at best, homely, it included three lines on the performers accompanying the feast: 'The fidling [l] Spheeres made musicke all the while. / And riming [m] Bardes braue meeter did compile / To grace this feast.' The letter glosses are explained in marginal notes, 'l' as 'Two fid- | lers and a- | blind boy | with a bagpipe' and 'm' as 'Their | Poet Chroni- | clers.'[240] One of the interesting things here is the way the patronage of this Old English corporation was bestowed on providing that characteristically Gaelic mix of entertainment, music plus extemporized poetry. But the corporation's patronage could ape that of the local New English magnates too. The king's players had visited Youghal during the mayoralty of Richard Gough between the Michaelmas 1625 and Michaelmas 1626, when they had been paid 5s, presumably for some sort of performance before the aldermen: 'More, paid to the King's Players in company with some of the aldermen … 0 5 0.'[241] Youghal had a tradition of accommodating visiting players well before this. Some five years earlier, one William Durant was made a freeman of Youghal, on various conditions, one of which was to ensure that the windows in the Tholsel be glazed and kept in good repair during his lifetime. He was not to be held responsible, however, if they had been smashed by people wanting to get a better view of any plays that the mayor had licensed for presentation there:

Memorandum that William Durant glasier the xvj[th] daie of ffebruarie Anno Domini 1619 / by vertue of his peticion preferred before that tyme at the last Deere hundred Daie beinge the vij[th] [Daie] of Ianuarie 1619 /, with free consent and good likinge of the Maior Recordor Bayliffs burgesses & Cominaltie of youghall was admitted & graunted to be a freeman at lardge of the Towne & Corporacion of youghall aforesaid Condicionly that he the said William Durant forthwith with all conuenient speed Doe & shall at his one proper Cost and

Chardges glaze all the windowes of the Tollsill house or Court hawle in youghall aforesaid the Towne fyndinge & all owninge Iron barres for the windowes to be sett vpp with the said glasse, And ⌐the said Durant shall⌐ new painte the kinges armes As allsoe to wash ouer the wales there rounde about in the said Court with spanishe white, And after that the said windowes are soe glazed as aforesaid to keepe them henceforward in like manner soe well glassed During his naturall life Except the Maior for the tyme beinge by the givinge leaue to players at anie tyme here after to playe in the same Tollsill & by that meanes. some of those that then come in hither to see the said playe Doe breake & batter the said windowes & glasse There ‸<...> Prouided that the said william Durant shall no<t> at any tyme hereafter Deale in anie kinde of merchandizes with in the said Towne or liberties hereof but in such as belonge and apperteyneth to his trade of a peinter, or glasier

°W Bluytt Mayr°²⁴²

Mayor William Bluytt's decree seems to assume a tradition of letting the Tholsel be used as a theatre for visiting players. However, a by-law of 5 October 1635 was to change all that. Henceforth, any mayor or bailiff giving licenses 'to stages player<s> or to any other of that kind to make vse of the Towne hale of this towne' would be liable for a £10 sterling fine.²⁴³ What had caused the change of heart is unknown: it is more likely to have been a rash of broken windows than any puritanical pressure. But with it two things ended: Youghal's tradition of corporate patronage of drama and the performing arts in the Tholsel, and the evidence, Kilkenny excepted, for provincial institutional patronage in pre-Cromwellian Ireland.

7

Dublin Drama in the Seventeenth Century

THE PRIME MOVERS: SIR THOMAS WENTWORTH AND JOHN OGILBY

All that remains before the final curtain is a return in more detail to that outcropping of theatrical patronage that gave Ireland its first public playhouse. Sir Thomas Wentworth (1593–1641), Lord Deputy from July 1633 until March 1640, apart from during absences in 1636 and 1639–40, was the efficient cause of the Werburgh Street Theatre. His career, and something of his personality, have already been glimpsed in previous chapters. Here it might be added that not only was theatre his personal passion – his correspondant George Garrard regularly chose to regale him with gossip about fashionable productions in London and the provinces, presumably because he knew his tastes in this respect – he also evidently regarded theatre as an indispensable ornament to Ireland's capital.[1] If Dublin were to compare with London, its ruling classes needed access to similar pastimes and pursuits. Thus a playhouse was obligatory, since by the 1630s playgoing and court civilization had become inseparable. The appearance of the queen at a private London playhouse in 1634 (and at various times thereafter) had set new precedents, and at least for some in society, had endorsed theatre's respectability. Not surprisingly, although busy with difficult affairs of state, Wentworth found time to add his weight to the establishment of a playhouse in Dublin. His motives, then, could as much be interpreted as wanting to endow his adoptive city with a basic class amenity as indulging a peculiar viceregal taste or vanity. The building of the Werburgh Street Theatre may therefore also be seen as one in a series of key projects in his general program for Dublin's social upgrading. But it seems that it was left to John Ogilby (1600–76) to see that theatre into being.

It has generally been supposed that the Werburgh Street Theatre opened in the latter half of 1637, but this is probably not so.[2] More likely it opened earlier than this. Stockwell thought that the theatre, so much the offspring of the Wentworth/

Ogilby collaboration, opened after Wentworth had appointed Ogilby, a Scottish dancing master enticed to Dublin from London to serve in the viceregal household, as master of the revels on 28 February 1638.[3] The appointment first appears on record in a retrospective entry in a Patent Roll of 8 May 1661:

> Iohn Ogilby gentleman was heretofore by Instrumente of the hand and seale of Thomas late Earle of Strafford then deputie of our said Kingdome of Ireland bearing date at Dublin the Eight and twentieth day of ffebruary in the yeare of our lord one thousand sixe hundred thirtie and seaven nominated and appointed Master of the Revelles in and through our said Kingdome of Ireland and in pursuance thereof he did at his owne greate costes and charges as wee are informed erect a publick Theater in our Cittie of Dublin ...[4]

The phrase 'in pursuance thereof,' which Stockwell interpreted as meaning that the theatre was built *after* the appointment, is not unambiguous, and could in fact mean the reverse, as Bentley realized.[5] Certainly, the theatre must have been built after Ogilby's arrival in Dublin (and thus after 25 July 1633 when Wentworth took his oath), and before some time in 1638, the year in which *The Royall Master* by James Shirley was published, for its title page announces that it was originally acted in two places in Dublin, 'Before the Right Honorable the Lord Deputie of Ireland, in the Castle,' and also 'in the new Theater.'[6]

But within these limits it is possible to narrow the date further, and to establish the opening of a theatre in Dublin – probably that in Werburgh Street – well before the latter half of 1637. For this there are two pieces of evidence, the first suggestive and the second compelling. The first concerns John Clavell, author of the *Introduction to the Sword Dance* reviewed in the previous chapter. In the same commonplace-book into which he copied his *Introduction*, he also copied a prologue and epilogue to some play destined for performance 'at the New house.'[7] The date and auspices of this prologue and epilogue can be inferred with some confidence. First, since they were written for a play which the prologue advertised as having 'past our English stage,' the production of their accompanying play was evidently taking place not in England but elsewhere. Given Clavell's movements, the production must have occurred somewhere in Ireland. Second, this Irish production was being presented, as the heading to the prologue noted, 'at the New house.' It is likely that this venue was in fact the Werburgh Street Theatre, and for the following reasons. The prologue and epilogue were intended for what had apparently been, in England at any rate, a stage play, and they also envisaged a relatively sophisticated audience attending that play's Irish début. (Sophistication in the Irish audience may be inferred from the refined tone of the prologue and epilogue generally and not only from their ingratiating pitch.) Since the Irish audience that Clavell was wooing was urbane, and since that audience would be gathering in the 'New house,' Dublin's

Werburgh Street Theatre seems the only possible venue: it was the only dedicated playhouse catering to the sort of implied clientele that is known to have existed in pre-Cromwellian Ireland, and it could justly be called 'New' at the time when Clavell was writing (as it also was when Shirley wrote *The Royall Master*). Clavell probably left Dublin for the last time *c* 17 June 1637, yet his 'New house' was presumably already open before he departed. Thus on the face of it, by mid 1637 the Werburgh Street Theatre is likely to have been already open. But a second, and more compelling, piece of evidence for an opening earlier still – though it must be admitted that the Werburgh Street Theatre is not actually so denominated – appears in an unpublished letter of Sir Thomas Wentworth to his old friend Archbishop William Laud on 10 July 1637. Wentworth was describing a contretemps, now amicably settled, between himself and the archbishop of Dublin, Lancelot Bulkeley:

But what long of the Prouost, and what long of a Playhouse lately sett vp and allowed by me / which out of Purity of Zeale ye Primate dureing my being in England had prohibited, least it might, forsooth, haue brought a punishment of ye Plague vpon vs, his Grace is very angry with me and saith yat I neither Care for Church nor Church men where my owne Ends come in question.[8]

The visit to England to which Wentworth here alluded must have been that between early June and late November in 1636. Therefore the theatre, almost certainly Werburgh Street, must have already existed before June 1636.

Perhaps the date may be pushed even further back if we are prepared to believe two eighteenth-century theatre historians whom W.S. Clark disparaged as unreliable witnesses. In *A General History of the Stage*, W.R. Chetwood, the first historian of the Irish stage, as Stockwell called him, dated the establishment of the Werburgh Street Theatre to 1635, 'in the tenth Year of the Reign of King Charles.'[9] Clark dismissed Chetwood, along with another early theatre historian, Thomas Wilkes, for having advanced 'without any specific proofs differing years' for the theatre's opening, and it is undisputably true that Chetwood, like so many others of his vintage, was unperturbed about sourcing his claim.[10] Yet because Chetwood lived in Dublin in the early-eighteenth century, he was well placed to gather authoritative information on early Dublin theatres.[11] Joseph Ashbury, Ogilby's successor in the office of master of the revels, was also still alive in Dublin at this time, and Chetwood may even have received information directly from him.[12] To return to Clark's doubts about Chetwood's credibility: damage to this was caused, he believed, because of a discrepancy between Chetwood's date of 1635 and that advanced by Wilkes – a discrepancy which reflected badly on both of them. But in fact the discrepancy is more apparent than real. Clark said that Wilkes dated the establishment of the theatre to 1634, which is not strictly accurate. What Wilkes said was 'about the year 1634,' thus leaving some small room for manoeuvre around that date.[13] Furthermore Chetwood, alongside his date of 1635, noted very precisely that he had discovered no record of any theatre established in Dublin until the tenth regnal year of Charles I. While 10 Charles I certainly covered part of 1635, its larger part covered 1634, running from 27 March 1634 to 26 March 1635. Therefore, once it is realized that 10 Charles I straddled much of 1634 and the beginning of 1635, the apparently contradictory opinions of Chetwood and Wilkes may be reconciled. In sum, the Werburgh Street Theatre, or at the very least a playhouse somewhere in Dublin, had opened before June 1636; if Chetwood and Wilkes are to be credited – and it seems there are less grounds than previously thought for not crediting them – then that theatre may have opened early in 1635.[14]

John Ogilby, the midwife of Wentworth's wishes for a playhouse, seems to have been born near Edinburgh, but later moved to London to earn a living.[15] John Aubrey, his principal biographer, noted that he had formerly apprenticed himself to a dancing-school master at Gray's Inn Lane, and had lamed himself cutting ambitious capers in the duke of Buckingham's great masque at court.[16] Before his arrival in Dublin, then, Ogilby had been active in London court circles, which is probably where he came to Sir Thomas Wentworth's attention before Wentworth took up his Dublin appointment. Aubrey relates that Ogilby came to Dublin in Wentworth's entourage, and if Aubrey is taken at his word, that must mean July 1633.[17] In any event, Ogilby's arrival cannot have been much later, given the fact that the opening of the Werburgh Street Theatre, in which he had such a large personal stake, very likely took place, as seen, earlier than generally thought.[18] He joined Wentworth's household in two primary capacities, as a teacher and as a dancing instructor to Lady Wentworth and her children, and also as one of the gentlemen riding in Wentworth's troop of guards.[19] Aubrey said nothing about him having come for the express purpose of organizing dramatic and other entertainments at Dublin Castle, though doubtless this was a task which someone of his experience and inclinations might soon assume.[20] Ogilby invested heavily in Wentworth's enterprise. In his later petition to Charles II for confirmation of Wentworth's grant to him on 28 February 1638 of the office of master of the revels in Ireland, he estimated that what with building the theatre and stocking it with actors and musicians imported from England, he had laid out some £2,000 or more, all of which had gone to ruin at the time of the Civil War.[21] His theatre was closed by an act of the Lords Justice William Parsons and John Borlase soon after 22 October 1641,[22] and ended ingloriously with 'a Cowehouse made of ye Stage.'[23] So to summarize this chronology, Ogilby's involvement seems to have run as follows: he came to Dublin with Wentworth in July 1633 or very shortly after; further to discharging the household duties for which he was originally retained, he now took responsibility for delivering and managing a theatre in Werburgh Street, perhaps as early as the beginning of 1635, and almost certainly before June 1636; next he looked to England for actors and musicians, whose recruitment is likely to have begun with the building of the theatre, if not a little before; and finally his theatre, once established, continued until about 22 October 1641.

THE WERBURGH STREET THEATRE

Although its longevity was therefore nothing to boast of – at best it lived for some six years – and although the ambitions that its founders entertained for it would outstrip its performance, the Werburgh Street Theatre was launched with the greatest of expectations. It was built in a fashionable quarter of the city, and not very far from the castle, whose offspring and dependent it was. Where on Werburgh Street it stood cannot now be certainly determined, but it is interesting to note three lots shaded with hatching on John Rocque's *An Exact Survey of the City and Suburbs of Dublin* (1756), one fronting onto the west side of the street and the other two on the east side. Of these latter two lots, one was contiguous with St Werburgh's Church itself, and the other, a little further down the hill, was just behind a terrace of private buildings (see fig. 19). Any of the three might be considered candidates for the site of the theatre-turned-cowhouse, though one of them, that contiguous with the church, may have a small edge on the other two.[24] Each building on these lots was approximately rectangular and of very roughly comparable dimensions.[25] But wherever the theatre was located, it seems likely that its external structure was essentially of rectangular shape (as all the potential sites on Rocque's map suggest), and this would accord with the design of the more prestigious hall playhouses of Caroline London; for befitting its desirable civic location and its viceregal auspices, the Werburgh Street Theatre was hardly likely to be modelled on the demotic, open-air amphitheatres of late Tudor and early Stuart times.[26] In fact Wilkes, alone among the early theatre historians to describe its internal layout, said: 'I have been informed it had a gallery and a pit, but no boxes, except one on the Stage for the then Lord Deputy, the Earl of Strafford, who was Ogilby's patron.'[27] Although Wilkes's information was second-hand, whoever his informant was may have been relating an authentic tradition because his details, though scant, find echoes in Caroline London's hall playhouses. In seeking an English analogue to Wilkes's description, it seems most logical to begin with any theatres that Ogilby may have been personally acquainted with in London before his own 'pritty little Theatre,' as Aubrey styled it, was raised in Dublin.[28]

There is reason to believe that Ogilby's London theatrical connections were with that influential playhouse, the Cockpit, in Drury Lane.[29] This theatre, almost certainly that depicted in a set of Inigo Jones drawings dated to between c 1616 and c 1618, resembled in all essential aspects of internal layout two other major London

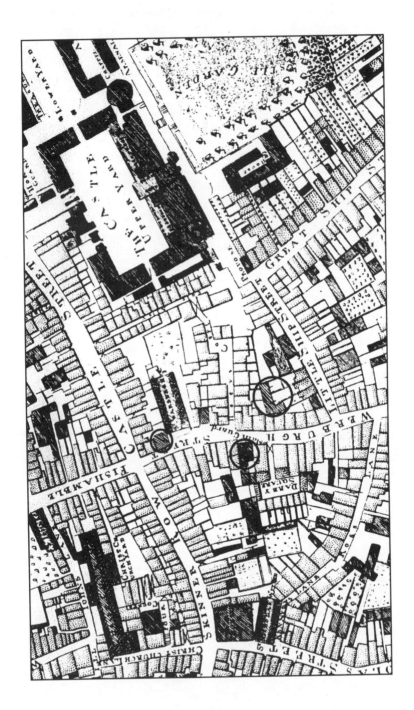

19 John Rocque's map of Dublin, 1756, showing possible sites of the location of the Werburgh Street Theatre.

hall playhouses, Blackfriars and the Salisbury Court: its galleried auditorium was U-shaped; seating also flanked its stage immediately to the left and right; three doors were set in the rear of the stage (one each to the left and to the right, and between these two a larger, central door); and above the doors ran a balcony (see fig. 20).[30] Any notion of the layout of the Werburgh Street Theatre might thus most appropriately take its bearings from that of the Cockpit. When Wilkes's details are compared with those of the Cockpit, they match, as far as they go, save only in incidental respects. For example, Wilkes stated that the Werburgh Street Theatre had a gallery, while the Cockpit had two (it is not known how many Blackfriars had). As for boxes, Wilkes was very clear that a viceregal one existed on the stage at Werburgh Street. This is entirely plausible. It had long been customary to seat chief dignitaries either on the stage or very near it;[31] and anecdotal evidence of a box at Blackfriars in 1632 confirms the arrangement indicated in the Cockpit designs.[32] Again by force of analogy, the Werburgh Street viceregal box may be imagined to have been similar, located sideways on to the stage at either the right or left. Further information on the Werburgh Street Theatre's internal layout is deducible from the staging requirements of plays written for performance there. Of these, theatrically the most demanding was James Shirley's *St. Patrick for Ireland*, yet even this needed nothing more than the resources of a Cockpit-type stage could satisfy. From this play's stage directions and action, it is clear that the Werburgh Street stage had at least two doors for entrances and exits, plus a means of disclosing a scene. (This latter could have been a 'discovery' area revealed by opening the central door to reveal an inner stage.)[33] The stage also had at least one trapdoor.[34] Staging requirements of another known Werburgh Street play, Henry Burnell's *Landgartha*, confirm these features of central door, serving also as 'discovery' area, flanked by doors at either side.[35] The signs are that Ogilby had equipped his theatre building fashionably enough, and it is also clear that he resolved to staff it correspondingly.

JAMES SHIRLEY, THE ACTORS, AND THE REPERTOIRE

In his 1661 petition for recognition of Wentworth's appointment of him as master of the revels in Ireland, Ogilby presumably had no need to mention by name any of the English actors and musicians whom he had recruited for Werburgh Street, still less when they came to Dublin to take up residence. Nor did the petition mention one of the most famous who worked there, James Shirley (1596–1666), a man with a long and successful career in London behind him and well known at court. Shirley's arrival, plausibly estimated by Allan H. Stevenson as late in November 1636, must have seemed like a coup in the early and more hopeful days of Werburgh Street when its enterprise was still young and experience had not yet had occasion to triumph over enthusiasm.[36] It is not known whether Ogilby made the

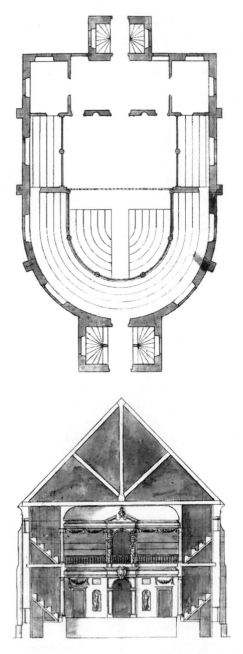

20 Inigo Jones, plan, and section through the stage, of the Cockpit in Drury Lane, London.

first approach, though this seems likely.[37] At any rate Shirley, notwithstanding the prestige he already enjoyed in London's literary and dramatic circles, would have found Dublin an attractive proposition for a host of reasons. Since he was on good terms with Ogilby – their relationship had probably been struck up while Shirley was playwright at the Cockpit before coming to Dublin – he could look forward to cordial relations with his prospective theatre manager. No less importantly, since the plague that had shut the London theatres from 12 May 1636 showed no signs of abating, employment in Dublin must have seemed a viable alternative, especially when many London companies were in danger of going to the wall. Further, in his new Irish base he would have freed himself from the pressure of having to compete with the younger breed of courtier poet-playwrights like Sir William Davenant and Sir Thomas Carew, and from having to curry gilded pastorals which were then so much to the London court's taste.[38] In short, Dublin would have left him more his own man in artistic terms, nor would he need to look over his shoulder at any censoring English master of the revels.[39] In the earliest days of the Werburgh Street Theatre, it is likely that censorship would have been more flexibly exercised than it was in contemporary London. In Dublin, Shirley would have felt less obliged to seek English approval, and indeed, from February 1638 the office of master of the revels in Ireland would be independently vested in his friend Ogilby, which may be another reason for believing that Irish arrangements for licensing plays, such as they were, were made without diligent reference to London. Perhaps the discretion of self-censorship was deemed sufficient, or the playing of plays for which licences had already been obtained, like the plays of John Fletcher for which Shirley wrote prologues for their Dublin performances.[40]

Chetwood provides the only clue as to how the members of the Werburgh Street company may have styled and regarded themselves. On the title-page of his 1750 edition of Shirley's *St. Patrick for Ireland*, he noted that it was 'First Acted By His Majesty's Company of Comedians in the Year 1639.'[41] As in other respects, Chetwood is perhaps to be taken seriously again here, even when he cites no source. On the face of it, his statement sounds credible, and if in fact correct, it would seem that in Dublin, Ogilby and Shirley had felt at liberty to invent themselves as an Irish version of that most eminent of London companies, the king's men. For this it could readily be assumed that they had viceregal endorsement. What with an independent Irish office of master of the revels from 1638, and with the bold appropriation of theatrical status that Chetwood leads us to believe – an appropriation impossible anywhere else in these islands – the official Dublin theatre may have been exploiting an opportunity to set itself up as Ireland's answer to the best in London, claiming primacy in the regulation of theatrical matters, securing a controlling monopoly over playing in the city, and thus conferring even greater institutional prestige upon itself than it had already done by head-hunting Shirley.

When plague forced the London theatres into their long closure from 12 May 1636, Ogilby might expect to have the pick of the talent of the dispossessed play-houses.

Although English players and musicians formed the staple of the company, it is possible that some Werburgh Street Theatre personnel had already been active in Dublin, for the wording of Ogilby's 1661 patent seems to imply that plays were being presented in the city before his theatre opened, and that part of his brief had been to reduce this unlicensed state of affairs to order.[42] Some element of unregulated playing in Dublin in the early years of the century would certainly also accord with Barnaby Rich's description in 1617 of the four roisterers who had nothing better to do for the afternoon than consider whether they should stroll off to watch a play.[43] That, of course, was in the days when play-going was not perceived to be quite as respectable as it was by the 1630s, or at least, 1630s play-going of the élite sort to the hall playhouses, the type that Werburgh Street evidently emulated.[44] If local actors were hired for Werburgh Street, however, Ogilby did not acknowledge it. In fact, of the several persons who must have been needed to supply all his theatre's functions, the names of only three are reasonably secure, with perhaps a fourth, and this despite the best efforts of scholars to add others, including that of the actor Richard Weekes.[45] It may be that John Lyon, the antiquarian transcriber of the supposed 'Weekes' reference, misread his source, but what he actually copied down in his manuscript was not 'Weekes' at all but 'Rookes,' a player of whom no trace has otherwise come to light:

1637 Oct: 29. Lady Fisher ——   N:B: Some Players about this time buryed
                                viz: Armiger — Rookes[46]

Nevertheless, a set of connections can be established between the three or four remaining names that suggests Ogilby's recruitment not only to have had its roots in London, but also depended on a relatively stable theatrical base there (to the extent that 'stable' appropriately describes often fluid exchanges of players and playhouses in Caroline London, even before the protracted plague closure of 1636–7 destabilized previous arrangements). The first name, Armiger, whose obituary notice has just been cited, may have been that Edward Armiger, member of London's Red Bull theatre company, though perhaps only in a travelling capacity.[47] If Armiger died around 29 October 1637, he must have been among the earlier of Werburgh Street's English recruits. The next actor of whom record survives is 'William Cooke ye player,' who is listed in a cess of 20 April 1638 for the parish of St John the Evangelist, where he was resident in Wood Quay.[48] Because Cooke's name does not feature anywhere in the preceding cess of 20 June 1636, it is likely that he was newly ˙rived in the parish. Little is known of him, but since he may be that William Cooke who in 1635 was a member of Prince Charles's (II) players, he is likely to have come into contact with the members of the Red Bull company, for Prince Charles's (II) players were playing in the Red Bull theatre at this time.[49] This contact was in turn likely to have brought Cooke into the orbit of Ogilby and Shirley, given the long-standing relations between the Red Bull and the Cockpit.[50] The signs are, then, that not only was Werburgh Street recruitment London-based, it also progressed in stages, for Cooke may not have come in the first wave. This would accord with the fact that Shirley probably made two trips to England during his Dublin residence, one in the spring of 1637 and probably another the following spring. These trips may have been occasions for recruitment as well as for furthering other business.[51] The third person known to have had a Werburgh Street Theatre connection also appears, like Cooke, in a parish cess, this time of St Werburgh's. Between 25 April 1641 and 10 April 1642, 5s was levied on one 'Mr Perry at the play house.'[52] If, as has been suggested, this Perry was the touring actor William Perry, then he again had a Red Bull connection.[53] The same parish cess yields the last name that may have belonged to a Werburgh Street actor. The record is terse, and were it not for the unusualness of its surname, it would have to be dismissed, because a surname alone would hardly be enough to hang an identity on. Nevertheless, living on the north side of Castle Street, not far opposite the premises of the Dublin publishers of Shirley's plays, was a 'Mr Errington.'[54] In England, and even more so in Dublin, this name is unquestionably rare, and brings with it another suggestive coincidence. Richard Errington, a leader of touring acting companies, had worked on tour with the king's men, Queen Henrietta's men, the king's revels men, and also with the Red Bull.[55] Most resident London companies had affiliated travelling companies who toured under the company's patent, the Red Bull being no exception.[56] Thus of this handful of actors' names in Dublin, all had Red Bull associations, and three, if Errington also be admitted alongside Armiger and Perry, had actually been members of the Red Bull travelling company. The evidence, while modest, is consistent. It seems that when the opportunity of Dublin employment arose, the travelling members of the Red Bull company were the first to seize it.[57]

Decisions about what plays they were to stage at Werburgh Street may have been arrived at collectively, but were doubtless driven by custom and what was thought likely to succeed in the Dublin context. Prologues that Shirley wrote for nine plays produced at Werburgh Street indicate that the repertoire, unsurprisingly, included the contemporary London favourites John Fletcher and Ben Jonson.[58] Naturally, several of Shirley's own plays were produced, as well as at least one by another resident Dublin playwright, Henry Burnell. Written specifically for the Dublin stage, these plays are telling indicators of the sort of theatre that Werburgh Street was intended to be, and thus deserve some careful consideration.

Shirley's output of plays was already substantial before he arrived in Dublin, and it is likely that he drew on them for Werburgh Street. In Ireland this dramatic back-log would have been invaluable, allowing him to provide the city's theatre-going public, proportionally smaller in comparison to London's, with a rapidly changing diet additionally seasoned with tried and trusted Jacobean and Caroline favourites. Three of Shirley's plays were certainly written for initial performance in Dublin: *The Royall Master, The Doubtful Heir, or Rosannia, or Love's Victory* and *St. Patrick for Ireland*.[59] They epitomize not only some of Shirley's familiar dramatic preoccu-pations, but also reveal something of what he hoped his Irish project would achieve. Since they can be shown to have been written in a chronological sequence, they also trace his growing disillusion as gradually it became clear that audiences were not going to live up to expectation, and that the attractions of Art and Wit in Dublin would face stiff competition.[60] The earliest of the three is *The Royall Master*, a play unlikely to have been written to mark the opening of the Werburgh Street Theatre, as previously supposed, but which may have launched Shirley as the theatre's writer in residence.[61] It was composed by 1637, probably by the spring of that year (and cer-tainly before the London theatres had opened again on 2 October after their long plague closure), and it had not yet been staged when Shirley dedicated it to George Fitzgerald, sixteenth earl of Kildare.[62] Its first datable performance took place before Wentworth in Dublin Castle in 1638, on New Year's Day in the evening.[63] Thus the auspices of this early play show how the company was responsive to court needs, just as in London, it was preeminently the king's men who were called to perform before the court: this similarity seems further to underscore the scale of the Werburgh Street Theatre's dramatic ambition and of its company's orientation towards the most prestigious in London for a role model. It must have seemed to the former Red Bull actors that their earlier glories were returning.[64]

The Werburgh Street performance of *The Royall Master*, as opposed to that at the castle, took place either in the latter part of 1637, perhaps a little before the Lord Deputy's New Year bespeak, or very early in 1638.[65] *The Royall Master*, even more conspicuously than *The Doubtful Heir* or *St. Patrick for Ireland*, played to the aristo-cratic gallery, and this at a time when hopes for the success of the Wentworth administration in Ireland were sanguine enough. The whole makes a reassuring pack-age out of the theme of order retrieved, and celebrates a final exposé and excision of the canker of malicious ambition from the body politic. In setting forth the machi-nations of Montalto, the King of Naples's favourite, against the Duke of Florence, suitor to the king's sister Theodosia, Shirley would also have been concocting a familiar mixture of sexual and political intrigue in high places, and salting it with *hominem* observations of the sort that cannot have been lost on Wentworth and ʾle.[66] Content of this sort was perennially interesting to aristocrats, but per- ʾe privately topical, and perhaps suggestive of Shirley's own stance, is the he availed of to comment sceptically on masking, the current craze of

London court culture which he had formerly serviced but from which he had now detached himself by coming to Dublin.[67] This scepticism was put into the mouth of the character Bombo who, not unlike his creator, was likewise a refugee from the court:

> ... Things go not now
> By learning; I have read, 'tis but to bring
> Some pretty impossibilities, for anti-masques,
> A little sense and wit disposed with thrift,
> With here and there monsters to make them laugh:
> For the grand business, to have Mercury,
> Or Venus' dandiprat, to usher in
> Some of the gods, that are good fellows, dancing,
> Or goddesses; and now and then a song,
> To fill a gap:– a thousand crowns, perhaps,
> For him that made it, and there's all the wit![68]

It is tempting to see in these words not only a symptom of topical court-versus-country antagonism,[69] but also in their theatrical particularity a small-time facsimile of Shirley's own position and attitude – distanced, and later in 1638 further disenfranchised when beaten to the poet-laureatship by Sir William Davenant. In such circumstances, Shirley would have been determined to make a go of the Werburgh Street enterprise, and cynicism about the ends and means of masking was a luxury he might permit himself in his new environment.[70]

Next in order of composition, *The Doubtful Heir*, whose Dublin Prologue alludes to Sir Thomas Killigrew's *Claracilla* and Sir John Suckling's *Aglaura*, was probably written in 1638.[71] Once again it rings the changes on aristocratic intrigue and issues of love and honour, but it also introduces a social dimension wanting in the earlier play. In doing this, *The Doubtful Heir* connects with a contemporary class antagonism that would have given it a somewhat wider social topicality than had *The Royall Master*, its predecessor. Dublin tradesmen often found themselves having to chase outstanding debts owed to them by the military and by government officials. From early in Act II of the play, the military and the trades are in dispute over money. The representatives of bourgeois interests, the citizens, are made to look increasingly ridiculous in a subplot, but are finally rehabilitated in Act V once they abandon mercantilism and its attributed parsimony to embrace the soldier's life. Shirley's subplot could hardly have been more socially partisan, nor more calculated to reinforce class prejudice and so define by opposition that slice of Dublin society considered fit for his theatrical ministration: Werburgh Street audiences were doubtless not comprised of (pusillanimous) tradesmen, but did include the (magnanimous) military, and hence by association the state government.[72] *The Doubtful Heir* is the most informative of Shirley's three undisputable Dublin plays about the nature of the audience that in 1638 he saw himself catering for. Lawyers probably constituted another group, as one of Shirley's Dublin Prologues suggests.[73] By 1639, when *St. Patrick for Ireland* is likely to have been performed, his impatience with this audience and its fickleness had already begun, however, to show through.[74] Five of his nine extant Prologues to Werburgh Street productions rail at low audience turn out.[75] One of these, to a play by Fletcher, rehearses that binary topos familiar in discussions of the London theatre scene, that maintained that entertainments were either vulgar or élite, and that a person's choice between them was class-distinctive. However, since (lower-class) pastimes were held responsible by Shirley's Prologue for luring audiences away – 'Were there a Pageant now on foot, or some / Strange Monster from Peru, or Affrick come, / Men would throng to it; any Drum will bring / ... Spectators hither; nay, the Beares invite / Audience, and Bag-pipes can doe more than wit'[76] – it appears that in practice the élite might not be so far removed from the vulgar after all. The alternative attractions that Shirley referred to were historically real in Dublin, where pageants and prodigies, as well as bears and bagpipes, all did the rounds. His details were therefore not simply the jetsam of a conventional polemic against what the well bred should shun on the entertainment scene, but were more likely chosen for their present relevance.[77]

The Prologue to *St. Patrick for Ireland* has moved beyond railing to resignation, though still Shirley confesses himself only too willing to understand what Irish audiences want to see: 'We know not what will take, your pallats are / Various, and many of them sick I feare: / ... We should be very happy, if at last, / We could find out the humour of your taste, / That we might fit, and feast it, so that you / Were constant to your selves, and kept that true.'[78] Now into the third year of his experience of Dublin, he is seen making concessions, and in trying to identify and appeal to his audience's elusive taste, he was prepared to relax the rigorous distinction formerly professed between high and low entertainment. He injected into *St. Patrick for Ireland* scenes and effects more sensational than any in his Dublin plays to date, capitalizing also on current interests in witchcraft.[79] Further, he chose to dramatize an exclusively Irish topic, doubtless in the hope of stiring broader local interest. His treatment of St Patrick too suggests an attempted widening of audience scope, and perhaps acknowledges for the first time an Old English presence in the city as much as the New English one centred on the castle. The saint first enters with all the ceremony of Roman religion, amidst a procession of priests singing in Latin and accompanied by an angel who, bearing a banner and cross, seems like a stray from some ancient Catholic mystery play.[80] Clearly, the religious toleration implicit here would have appealed to any Catholics in the audience.[81] And any soldiers, part of

Werburgh Street's wonted clientele, whom Shirley had been happy to celebrate and cultivate in *The Doubtful Heir* in the person of the Captain,[82] would not have been alienated by the treatment of the soldiers in this play. It is clear that these, mercenaries who delighted in rape and who were prepared to kill members of their family for cash, were not members of the English nation, but were carefully delineated as wild Irish kern.[83] (In terms of theatre history, it seems that the kern was the first stage Irishman to tread the boards in Ireland as well as in England.)[84] In these manoeuvres we may read Shirley's last efforts to temporize with his slippery Irish audience. For all that he tried he presumably did not succeed; the second part of *St. Patrick for Ireland*, promised if the first was well received, was seemingly never written, and in the end Shirley gave up and returned to England in the spring of 1640.

The Werburgh Street Theatre, however, continued for a few more months, and the presence of its last known playwright, the Irishman Henry Burnell, corroborates what Shirley's final attempts to find a winning theatrical formula suggest, that the Werburgh Street Theatre had no longer quite the character it had at its inception. Now no longer simply an outpost of London court culture, it was trying to adapt more flexibly to local Dublin circumstances, however much driven to this adaptation it may primarily have been by financial necessity. At the end of the day actors could not live on high ideals alone. For Burnell personally, however, money seems not to have been a consideration, according to his disclaimer in the Prologue to his play *Landgartha*. In view of his upper-class, Old English family background, this disclaimer seems believable.[85] If he enjoyed the fashionable role of gentleman playwright that anyone of his social standing automatically courted in writing for the stage, that seems not to have been sufficient reason for his writing either. *Landgartha* may have had an agenda more particular than that generally alluded to in its Prologue as the gentle reproof of vice. Burnell openly advised his audience that he purposed 'to invade / Your wills for your owne profit.'[86]

Given the circumstances of the performance, it is possible to conjecture the terms of the invasion of those wills. *Landgartha* was performed in Werburgh Street on St Patrick's Day, 1640, a significant date in that St Patrick's Day always falls in Lent when theatres, by tradition, were closed.[87] In 1640 the opening session of the Dublin parliament of 15 and 16 Charles I had taken place the day before, however, and apparently on this occasion court needs had been allowed to supersede Lenten precedent and austerity.[88] *Landgartha* was played with permission of the master of the revels, John Ogilby, and one imagines that the parliamentary entourage currently in town formed a large part of the play's target audience. Whatever its growing flexibility, the Werburgh Street Theatre was as attentive in 1640 as it had ever been to the interests of Dublin Castle, and the play-going caste that it serviced was still relatively élite. In addition, the central theme of *Landgartha* addressed directly the concerns of one of the bills that had been transmitted to the parliament, the Act for the Repealing of the Statute of Bigamy, and thus anyone attending parliament may have been curious to see how the play chose to resolve the issue.[89] Its plot turns upon the abandonment of Lady Landgartha by her husband, King Reyner of Denmark, for another woman. It stresses Reyner's reprehensibility, and Landgartha's proportional generosity in coming to her bigamous husband's aid, undeserving though he may have been, in a moment of crisis. Thus the play adopted a clear stance on an impending and real political debate, and might even be viewed as an attempt to sway its outcome.

That Burnell was prompted by moral and political, rather than financial, considerations (though it is true that the topicality of bigamy with the target audience can hardly have damaged *Landgartha's* box office returns) seems also likely, given Burnell's niche in Dublin society. Though details of his life are few, he appears to have been that Henry Burnell who married Lady Frances Dillon (†29 May 1640), daughter of Sir James Dillon (†March 1642), first earl of Roscommon, by Eleanor Barnewall, daughter of Sir Christopher Barnewall of Turvey, co. Dublin.[90] Two members of the Barnewall family represented Dublin at the 1640 parliament, so Burnell was moving in circles where the substance of parliamentary debates would soonest register.[91] Part of his extended family is shown in the following chart.

Henry Burnell's extended family

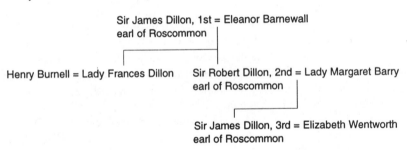

Other Burnell affiliations with the nexus of ruling Old and New English families are apparent here. The first wife of his brother-in-law, Sir Robert Dillon (†27 August 1642), had married Lady Margaret Barry (sister of Lord David, first earl of Barrymore, the patron of John Clavell). Sir Robert's son and successor by Lady Margaret, Sir James Dillon (†8 November 1649), had married into the Wentworth family. Burnell was Sir James's uncle, and Sir James's wife was sister to the Lord Deputy, Sir Thomas Wentworth, host to the 1640 parliament at the castle. That Burnell's play addressed an issue of public concern to these people seems quite clear. Moreover, Wentworth had taken a strong line on bigamy in Ireland in a letter to

Archbishop Laud in 1634, the same year in which the Dublin parliament narrowly voted down a Bill restraining persons from marrying before the death of their spouses.[92] So Burnell's moral and political position in this respect was in direct alignment with the Lord Deputy's.

It was Werburgh Street, then, that gave Burnell, Ireland's first named playwright, his platform. By the time he was writing, Werburgh Street was recognizing the position of people like himself in the social scheme, and their importance to the theatre's survival. Indeed, Burnell's participation in Werburgh Street seems to set the seal on a trend becoming steadily more noticeable during Shirley's incumbency. When an Anglo-Irish playwright finally gained access to the official stage, he used it to display precisely the preoccupations of his social class. Though by all accounts he never went to England, he turned to the example of England's dramatic establishment, in the person of Ben Jonson, for some literary guidance.[93] He also did the fashionably English thing of paying homage to the masque, a form that Shirley was now shunning, by replicating one in Act III. Yet amongst all this courtly Englishness, Burnell's infusion into *Landgartha* of local Irish colour was affectionately handled, and his play's preoccupations directly addressed the concerns of those Old (and New) English ruling classes into whose sphere he had been ever more closely drawn by marriage. *Landgartha* sums up neatly the hybridism that has persistently characterized the drama and the performing arts pursued in these pages. If not merely its publisher's puff, Burnell's play was acted to great applause.[94] Whether or not that was true, the play would undisputably have struck a chord, entertaining its audience and, in treating a tendentious issue, consolidating that audience's sense of selfhood. Werburgh Street was now wholly that audience's hostage once Burnell had secured its stage for the interests of upper-class Anglo-Irish society.

But not for very long. After *Landgartha*, nothing more is heard from Werburgh Street. Shirley had departed. Ogilby went not long after. Wentworth, the theatre's original instigator, faced impeachment and, on 12 May 1641, execution. And on the outbreak of civil strife later that year, the company, assembled at such expense, was finally dispersed.

Epilogue: Revels Ended

With the disbanding of the Werburgh Street Theatre, this survey ends. Its trajectory, broadly characterized at the outset as moving from performance to theatricality, might seem on the face of it to have brought us from one world without the Pale to another, very unlike, within, and to have done so via various provincial detours. Yet just as performance and theatricality have been viewed as shades of the one spectrum that is drama, so it may be none too surprising to notice, on reflection, a certain circularity, that just as we began with Gaelic performers appointed to places in the king's house, so we have ended with actors appointed to serve in a theatre instigated by the king's deputy. To draw attention to this similarlity is not to trivialize the very real, historically and culturally contingent differences that of course distinguished those worlds within and without the Pale, but it does highlight a common ground, a community of function within which drama and performance, no matter what their ethnic origin, would have been commonly intelligible. That common ground came also to be inhabited by the Anglo-Irish, amongst whom conditions were perhaps ripest for the sort of inter-cultural exchange and hybridism that have repeatedly surfaced in this study, most recently indeed in Burnell's case. Interlinking traditions of drama and performance are more richly exemplified everywhere in pre-Cromwellian Ireland than have hitherto been supposed. In many ways their social force and functions were remarkably similar.

While Irish historians have long had some awareness of these traditions, usually their interest in them has tended to remain with one particular ethnic group at the expense of another. The scholarly consequences of partitionist thinking, however, may resemble those of its political counterpart and prove as damaging. And this also holds for those historians of drama and performance whose interests, while paying lip service to the Irish dimension, are fundamentally Anglocentric. One could be forgiven for imagining that for them, Dublin – other places in Ireland barely register – was indeed an outpost of English civilization, its evidence of drama and performance contributing towards an understanding of a general Anglocentric project. In a sense, Dublin's evidence can be plundered for this purpose, but not without, at best, an elision, and at worst, a radical occlusion, of the significance it assumes in its own geopolitical context. But I trust that this survey may not in turn be indictable on similar grounds, that it has dwelt so squarely upon Ireland that the advantages to be gained from attending to the English dimension have grown dim: this would be an unjustifiable eclipse, given the close historical relationship of both islands. For better or for worse, for richer or for poorer, both were handfasted from the twelfth century on, and even before that time, some union between both had been guaranteed by the comings and goings of merchant trade and by the more intellectual and spiritual commerce conducted by the church. Throughout, therefore, I have tried to point up contrasts and comparisons with English practice wherever it has seemed appropriate so to do, but more often than not this has happened in endnotes where some danger of invisibility prevails. So perhaps a couple of their more salient aspects may be rehearsed here. Their rehearsal seems the more necessary because, despite the elected Irish accent of this book, I am very aware that what it says will nevertheless be heard and evaluated in a climate whose prevailing winds of research in the British Isles have blown from the English quadrant of early drama studies. (Scotland and Wales as yet barely signify, and loiter in the wings awaiting their turn.)[95]

England has nothing to match the evidence for early Gaelic performance gathered in chapter 1 of this survey, both in terms of that evidence's quantity and antiquity. Yet it may be that Ireland provides the paradigm for the sort of thing that was to be more widely met with in the British Isles at this date. This being so, even critics with severely Anglocentric concerns cannot afford to leave Ireland out of the question; and those who are already converts to a more holistic approach should find themselves confirmed in their faith once they have considered the Irish evidence. After chapter 1, the remaining chapters have been for the larger part taken up with urban manifestations of drama and performance and with their role within their host communities. In this regard, the chapters contribute towards the clutch of case histories that has grown especially in recent years and that holds out the promise of no less than a transformation of our understanding of the variety and nature of drama and performance before 1642 and the closing of the theatres.[96] At the same time, each Irish case history also insists on its ethnic particularity, and that while each certainly contributes to a general and comparative picture, it remains irreducibly the product of local Irish circumstances. These must be heeded too if the richer significance of each case history is to be appreciated. Consequently, respect for the intrinsic Irishness of the evidence considered in this survey should help us resist the homogenizing and oversimplifying tendency that always haunts general understandings of things. It should, moreover, bring down to earth the lofty view that would maintain that whenever English evidence for some of the sorts of phenomena investigated in this book is more plentiful (as happens, for example, in chapter 5, where the relatively copious English evidence for civic entries of a similar sort puts that from Ireland into the shade), then England's example is somehow essentially more valuable, or demands prior attention. Attention to the Irish evidence offers a salutary reminder that, on the contrary, there was a world elsewhere, and since it was one not utterly divorced from that of England, its neglect proves the more unwarranted. In administering its corrective, the Irish evidence also encourages us to relish dirtying our hands on the grubby idiosyncracies and intractably Irish details of another, though complementary, history. If the general picture cannot cope with these oddities and regional strangenesses (to regard them momentarily from a strictly English point of view), at best it stands compromised by partiality, and at worst, becomes unreliable.

In fine, it is to be hoped that the Irish accent of this survey will have reclaimed a little integrity not only for the history of drama and the performing arts within Ireland, but also within the British Isles generally, and will have increased awareness of how diverse, yet remarkably compatible, were the patterns and purposes of drama and performance in these islands before the leaner years of the Commonwealth.

The Dublin *Visitatio Sepulcri* Play

The introduction to the Dublin *Visitatio Sepulcri* play which follows, based on Egan-Buffet and Fletcher, 'Visitatio Sepulcri,' is arranged under two headings. Under the first, its manuscripts are described in detail. Under the second, the question of the play's date and authorship is considered, and the choice of base text explained and justified.

THE MANUSCRIPTS

Description

M: Dublin, Marsh's Library, MS Z. 4.2.20; parchment; i + 142 + i; 285mm × 190mm (215mm × 130mm).

Collation: 1⁶, 2⁷ (fols 7–13; one added after 4), 3–13⁸, 14¹⁰, 15–16⁸, 17¹⁰, 18⁶ (fols 137–42; wants 2 before 3 and 4 after 6). A modern pencil foliation is added consecutively in the top right-hand corner of each leaf. This is regular, apart from the omission of a folio after fol. 134 (all folio references after fol. 134 follow the actual folio in M rather than the pencilled foliation; hence what is foliated as '135' is in reality fol. 136, and so on). Catchwords appear at the end of each quire. No quire signatures are discernible. The post-medieval binding is of white leather on cardboard. Several folded marginal parchment tabs survive. Initial capital letters are usually written alternately in blue ink or red ink. Major initial capitals are invariably in blue ink, and often flourished in red. There is extensive rubrication throughout the manuscript. There are normally 30 lines of text or 10/11 staves of music per page.

Script: M is copied by at least three hands. The principal scribe, A, copies fols 1–136v;

scribe B copies fols 137–8; scribe C copies fols 138v–40; either a further scribe, D, or a more careful variety of scribe B copies fols 140v–2v. Scribe A writes a Bastard Anglicana script, scribe(s) B and D a variety of Textura Quadrata, and scribe C an Anglicana Formata.[1]

Provenance: Ultimately unknown, but M was owned by the church of St John the Evangelist, Dublin, in the fifteenth century (a declaration of its ownership appears on fol. 142).

Date: As argued below, M must post-date 1352. On palaeographic grounds, the scribes appear to be working *c* 1400 (s. xiv/s. xv).

Contents: Sarum Use, *Processionale*

Blessing of holy water and aspersion	fol. 1–1v
Temporale (including the shorter *Elevatio crucis et hostie* ritual, fols 58v–59, followed by the *Visitatio Sepulcri* play, fols 59–61)	fols 1v–71v
Votive processions and masses	fols 72–3
Litany	fols 73–5
Votive procession and mass	fols 75–6v
Temporale	fols 76v–96v
Proprium Sanctorum	fols 97–120v
Commune Sanctorum	fols 121–3v
Votive processions and masses	fols 123v–30v
Litany	fols 130v–3
Orders of procession for different occasions (reception of a corpse, etc.)	fols 133–4v
Salve Regina (troped)	fols 134v–5
Marian antiphons and hymns	fols 135v–6v
Alternative versicles for a Marian feast, and responds for the feast of St John the Evangelist	fols 137–8v
Abbreviated version of the longer *Elevatio crucis et hostie* ritual	fols 138v–40
Litany	fols 140v–2
Prayer of St Augustine to be said before mass	fol. 142v

R: Oxford, Bodleian Library, MS Rawlinson liturg. D. 4; parchment; i + 190 + i; 280mm × 170mm (180mm × 110mm).

Collation: 1–11⁸, 12⁷ (fols 89–95; wants 1 after 3), 13–17⁸, 18–19¹⁰, 20–1⁸, 22¹⁰, 23⁹ (fols 182–90; the last leaf of the quire serves as a paste-down to the binding). A modern pencil foliation is added consecutively in the top right-hand corner of each folio. Catchwords appear at the end of each quire. No quire signatures are discernible. The binding is medieval, of white leather on bevelled wooden boards, with some modern repair. Traces of two fastening thongs appear on the front and back covers. Several folded marginal parchment tabs survive. Initial capital letters are usually written alternately in blue ink and red ink. Major initial capitals are invariably in blue ink, and often flourished in red. There is extensive rubrication throughout the manuscript. There are 27 lines of text or 9 staves of music per page.

Script: R is copied by one scribe. He writes a variety of Textura Quadrata, and may conceivably be the same scribe as Marsh scribe B (and ?D), though if so his letter forms in R are consistently a little more careful. At any rate, his hand is so similar to Marsh B (and ?D) that his training in the same scriptorium seems plausible.²

Provenance: Ultimately unknown, but R was owned by the church of St John the Evangelist, Dublin, in the fifteenth century (a declaration of its ownership appears on fol. 189v).

Date: As argued below, R must post-date 1352. On palaeographic grounds, the scribe appears to have been working *c* 1400 (s. xiv/s. xv).

Contents: Sarum Use, *Processionale*

Blessing of holy water and aspersion	fols 1–4
Temporale (including the *Depositio crucis et hostie* ritual, fols 68v–70, and the shorter *Elevatio crucis et hostie* ritual, fols 85v–6v)	fols 4–118
Processions for special occasions	fols 118–27v
Longer *Elevatio crucis et hostie* ritual, followed by *Visitatio Sepulcri* play	fols 127v–32
Proprium Sanctorum	fols 132v–58v
Commune Sanctorum	fols 159–62
Votive processions and masses	fols 162v–72v
Litany	fols 172v–5v
Orders of procession for different occasions	fols 175v–6v
Genealogy of Christ according to SS Matthew and Luke	fols 176v–81
Salve Regina (troped)	fols 181–2v
Responds and proses for the feasts of	fols 183–90v

SS Andrew, Nicholas, the Virgin (Purification),
Holy Cross, Catherine, Patrick, Audoen

Date of the manuscripts

It should be said at the outset of this discussion that we have no unequivocal proof that the Dublin *Visitatio* play was ever performed; as is often the case with liturgical plays, no external records survive which mention it having taken place (though see the third point below), nor is there anything in the manuscripts themselves to force this conclusion. Even the spottling of the play's opening in M with wax (on fols 58v–9), presumably from a candle, means no more necessarily than that at some stage the manuscript was open at these pages and that a candle was burning nearby which somehow managed to spill upon them. To go further than this and envisage a choir monk using it either during or in preparation for a play performance might well be to conceive a beguiling fiction.

Nevertheless, it would be taking scepticism too far to insist on the lack of proof positive, and for three good reasons. First, both manuscripts, thoroughly practical books designed to facilitate the liturgy, show clear signs of extensive use through their wear. Second, the elaborate Easter liturgy, in which the *Visitatio* features, was of especial concern to the compilers of the manuscripts. In the Marsh manuscript, the second order for the *Elevatio crucis et hostie* ritual, on fols 138v–40, is copied up, less carefully than the bulk of the text, towards the end of the manuscript and evidently after most of the text had already been completed. Its late insertion implies that even if an afterthought it was one of consequence. This ritual, though an abbreviated version of that appearing on fols 127v–30 of R, was sufficiently important to one of the Marsh scribes to warrant him including it after the manuscript had been largely completed. Had this ritual not been one connected with Easter, the principal feast of the liturgical calendar, then perhaps he would not have troubled to make good its earlier omission. If the fact that he has done so suggests the relative importance that the *Elevatio* portion of the Easter ceremonies held, it may therefore point toward the play (for the play is a natural development of the *Elevatio*) having been performed rather than to the contrary.[3] Third, a unique piece of evidence from 1542 establishes a performance of an Easter drama of the Resurrection, which is precisely the subject of the *Visitatio*, in Christ Church Cathedral, the cathedral immediately adjacent to the church which owned both M and R. Christ Church supplied this church with its clergy.

Both manuscripts declare their place of ownership. In a variety of Textura display script, probably of the second half of the fifteenth century, M states 'Ad ecclesiam Sancti Iohannis ewangeliste pertinet' (fol. 142), while R adds an informative detail, reading 'Iste liber pertinet ecclesie Iohannis Evangeliste' (fol. 189v), written in a regular Secretary hand of the second half of the fifteenth century, followed by the letters 'Dubl' in a later hand, possibly even early sixteenth century. It is clear that both were owned in the fifteenth century by the church of St John the Evangelist, Dublin, and for want of any indication to the contrary it is not impossible that they were intended for that church's use when they were originally manufactured.[4] The date of their original production, which, judging by the variety of scripts they employ, would appear to be *c* 1400, may perhaps be more precisely determined by reference to the content of their *Sanctorale*. Since they both make provision for St Anne's Day, a late liturgical feast expressly ordered for the Dublin diocese by Archbishop John of St Paul at a synod held in Christ Church Cathedral, Dublin, on 21 March 1352, they may be dated after 1352.[5] A *terminus ante quem* for their manufacture is somewhat more difficult to establish since, although certain saints' feasts which were appointed for observance after 1352 are absent, it seems much less reasonable to base a dating argument on the absence than on the presence of some particular feast.[6] The *terminus* is best left to palaeography, and *c* 1400 seems likely in this respect.

The production of the manuscripts sometime between 1352 and *c* 1400, and perhaps for the specific use of the church of St John the Evangelist,[7] locates them largely within the priorates of Stephen de Derby and Robert de Lokynton.[8] Under Derby, the chapter of Augustinian canons at Christ Church Cathedral which served St John's had experienced something of a small renaissance.[9] For example, the high quality of an expensively produced psalter with which Derby's name has become associated, Oxford, Bodleian Library, MS Rawlinson G. 185, testifies to a considerable artistic ferment during his administration;[10] it is tempting to attribute to him the encouragement of the St John's liturgical dramatic tradition,[11] and to regard both M and R as the kind of product that might well follow on in his wake. But whatever the truth of this, it is at least fair to say that in the last years of the fourteenth century the Augustinian canons had access to an Easter liturgy which had been embellished with drama, and in its performance they themselves can reasonably be assumed to have acted.[12]

THE PLAY

Date and authorship

The Dublin *Visitatio Sepulcri* must antedate its manuscripts and post-date the composition of the *Victime paschali* sequence that it incorporates. The latest date of the manuscripts, as was argued, is *c* 1400, and the probable composer of the *Victime paschali*, one Wipo of Burgundy, is known to have died after 1046.[13] Therefore *c* 1046 – *c* 1400 may be regarded as firm *termini*, but this still leaves us with a somewhat unsatisfactorily long period of 350 years within which the play must have been composed. Any further narrowing of the date range is possible only in terms of probability rather than certainty.

Before attempting to narrow the date, it might first be observed that the word 'editor' more accurately describes whoever put the play together (and his identity is unknown) than 'author' for, though exceptionally well controlled, the *Visitatio* is in fact a compilation of various textual and musical layers. Its basic strata appear to be French, with overlays probably of English origin, and their composition needs no rehearsal here.[14] Some critics have considered the play a wholesale import into Dublin from England. Aubrey Gwynn believed so, and Diane Dolan has even proposed Bristol as the place from which it came.[15] But a possibility that should not be ruled out is that the editor of the play was living in Ireland and that he put it together here out of imported parts. This cannot be proved, but it is plausible for, as was earlier noted, nothing forces the conclusion that neither M nor R were of Irish manufacture. If indeed they were, then at least in a minimal sense the play is the result of Irish editorship because, as will be seen, the M and R scribes were editors in as much as they were consciously prepared to adjust what they were copying. Nevertheless, probably neither of these scribes was substantially responsible for editing the play together, though they may have altered details of the redaction here and there. To speak of one principal editor of the Dublin *Visitatio*, effectively its playwright, is another unprovable assumption, but one difficult to resist given the play's high degree of dramatic coherence.[16] He seems either to have been working in England or, just conceivably, in Ireland.

The lines comprising the opening 'Heu' laments of the three Marys (lines 7–8, 11–12, and 14–15 respectively) had already been written by the thirteenth century, since they also appear with only small variations in the *Visitatio Sepulcri* of the so-called Fleury Play Book (MS Orléans 201).[17] Lines 28–9, 31–2, and 34–5 of the Dublin play, where the first Mary announces her intention to anoint the body of Christ, where the second declares that nard prevents flesh decaying, and where the third asks who will move the stone away, are similarly to be found there, and this time their wording is identical.[18] The intervening lines of the Dublin play (lines 17, 19, and 21), more 'Heu' laments though shorter than the first set, had been composed by at least the mid-twelfth century. With the unison declaration of the Marys' intention to hurry to the tomb (lines 24–5), they feature once again in the Fleury Play Book and also, for example, in the Tours *Ludus paschalis*, as well as in the *Visitatio Sepulcri* of the early-fifteeenth-century Barking *Ordinale* manuscript, where their wording corresponds most closely to that of the Dublin play.[19]

The *Quem queritis* dialogue itself (lines 38, 40, and 42–3) is originally of course of early composition, though its working in the Dublin play shows similarities to a *Visitatio Sepulcri* from Rouen whose earliest manuscript witness dates once again to

the thirteenth century.[20] Since much of the dialogue of the Dublin play is therefore
paralleled in texts whose earliest surviving manscript copies are thirteenth-century, the
Dublin play might have largely taken the shape reflected in its two extant manuscripts by the same century, though it could equally have done so at any time between then and the first half of the fourteenth century.[21]

CHOICE OF BASE TEXT

Though the two manuscripts are so similar in content and presentation as to suggest their common origin in one scriptorium, of the two, R is generally the most
carefully copied, and has therefore been selected as a base. The most notable lapse
on M's part is the omission of the first Mary's lines 'Condumentis aromatum' (lines
28–9) and their music. Even the later correcting hand at work in M was not entirely
successful when it attempted to repair the omission. Yet apart from this, there is no
substantive variation whatsoever between the words of the play proper in M and R.
It is in the rubrics that the major variations are to be found. It is interesting to note
in this respect how the much greater variation between rubrics, compared with the
much slighter variation between the two versions of the words of the play proper,
speaks of a distinct scribal attitude. The words of the play matter (obviously, since
they are also determined and stabilized by music) in a way that rubrics do not, and
it appears that when copying the rubrics the scribes allowed themselves a fair amount
of latitude. By and large, the M rubrics tend towards brevity while the R ones are
more expansive, but is this because the M scribe, for one reason or another, abbreviated what was in his exemplar, or did the R scribe amplify? On the other hand, did
the M scribe occasionally amplify and the R scribe occasionally abbreviate? These
questions are complicated by the unknowable degree to which scribal adjustment
of rubrics had already taken place in the M and R exemplar, if, indeed, they both
copied from the same one, which conceivably they did not. It is at least clear that
R did not copy M nor, most probably, did M copy R.[22] Two notable agreements in
error shared by M and R strongly suggest that they both ultimately descend from
the same common archetype (see line 24). However, it is not possible to tell whether,
or precisely how many, intermediaries may lie between it and them, with the result
that a number of stemmata, even if of a basically similar form, are possible to
account for the genetic relationship of both texts.[23] In such circumstances, no stemma
is of any practical use as an aid to textual recension or for representing the textual
superiority of either copy over the other.

Any editor of the Dublin *Visitatio Sepulcri* is thus thrown back on a personal
choice between variants. If he follows one text, emending it only where it is manifestly corrupt (as editors of the words of the play in the past have been inclined to
do), his crediting of this one text with more authority than the other is arbitrary.

While R has been selected here as a base, I have felt freer to choose between its readings and those of M. M has therefore been allowed more or less equal textual authority. Although I have proceeded upon a pragmatic assumption that the archetype would have contained a text freer from error than subsequent copies of it, I am aware that a subsequent copyist might edit the archetype himself, and occasionally even correct its deficiencies, real or imagined, on his own initiative. Indeed the archetype of the Dublin play, as has been noted, was itself not perfect, and as such may have encouraged any scribe so minded to alter it. If it be objected that the resultant edited text represents a version not known for certain ever to have existed, whereas M and R, imperfect though they may be, are given facts, I would suggest that the effort to work towards a more pristine version still seems worthwhile. Moreover, should a reader wish for them, all the facts are available for consideration, since all M and R readings are fully recoverable from the textual apparatus.

Editorial Policy

The editorial policy is essentially the same as that outlined in A Note on Texts, Transcriptions, and Terminology (pp. xiii–xv), that is, principles of transcription are conservative. However, there is one notable exception: emendations have been made in the base text within square brackets. Rejected manuscript readings are indicated in the apparatus at the foot of each page. No attempt has been made to select between musical variants, but M variants are given above those to which they correspond in R in a smaller typeface above the R system (they are not included in the R lineation). Treatment of accidentals requires special mention. Some flat accidentals have been added in a larger, display script at the start of a musical system. In the transcription these have been replaced by the relevant C clefs. Where such replacements occur (line 7, second accidental, lines 42–3, and line 56), the accidental flat signature has been silently inserted, as appropriate, before each affected neum. In some cases, the flat accidental has been moved to a position immediately before the neum (or neum group) that it governs (lines 14, 17, and 25). The 'modern' Gregorian F clef has been used where appropriate.

The Dublin Visitatio Sepulcri *play*

ffinito tercio Responsorio cum suo versu & Gloria patri.
uenient tres persone in superpelliceis & in capis sericis
capitibus uelatis quasi tres marie querentes ihesum singule
portantes pixidem in manibus quasi aromatibus. [quarum]
prima ad ingressum chori uersus sepulcrum precedat per   5
se quasi lamentando dicat.

Heu pi-us pa-stor oc-ci-di-tur quem nul-la cul-pa in-fe - cit

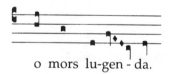

o mors lu-gen - da.

factoque modico interuallo intret secunda
maria consimili modo & dicat.   10

2 sericis] cericis M. 3 ihesum] Christum M. 4 quarum] quasi R. 5 uersus] usque M;
precedat] procedat M. 6 se] *marked for insertion here in M from right margin.* 7 *flat sign*
before nulla *absent in* M. 9 intret] *corrected from* intrent *in* M. 10 consimili] simili M.

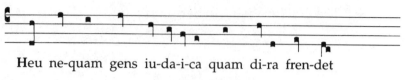

Heu ne-quam gens iu-da-i-ca quam di-ra fren-det

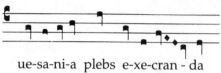

ue-sa-ni-a plebs e-xe-cran - da

deinde tercia maria consimili modo dicat.

Heu ue-rus doc-tor o-bi - jt qui ui-tam func-tis con-tu-lit o

res plan-gen - da.   15

adhuc paululum procedendo prima maria dicat [hoc modo].

Heu mi-se-re cur con-ti-git ui-de - re mor-tem sal-ua-tor-is.

deinde secunda maria dicat.

13 dicat] *omitted* M. 16 hoc modo] *omitted* R. 17 *flat sign within* saluatoris *absent in* M.
18 dicat] *omitted* M.

Heu con-so-la-ci - o no-stra ut quid mor-tem sus-ti-nu - it.

tunc tercia maria.   20

Heu re-demp-ci - o no-stra ut quid ta-li-ter a-ge-re uo-lu - it.

**tunc se coniungant & procedant ad gradum chori
ante altare simul dicentes.**

Iam iam [ec - ce] iam pro-pe-re-mus ad [tu-mu-lum]

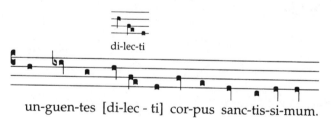

un-guen-tes [di-lec - ti] cor-pus sanc-tis-si-mum.   25

**deinde procedant simul prope sepulcrum & prima
maria dicat per se.**

20 tunc] deinde M. 21 *flat signs absent in* M. 23 simul] omitted M. 24 ecce] esse RM;
tumulum] timulum RM. 25 unguentes] ungentes M; dilecti] delecti R. 26-7 deinde ... se]
omitted M.

Con-du-men-tis a-ro-ma-tum un-ga-mus cor-pus

sanc-tis-si-mum quo pre-ci - o - sa.

tunc secunda maria dicat per se.   30

Nar-di ue-tet com-mix-ti - o ne pu-tre-scat in [tu - mu-lo]

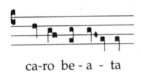

ca-ro be - a - ta

deinde tercia maria dicat per se.

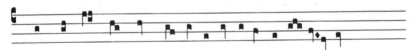

Sed ne-qui-mus hoc pa-tra-re si-ne ad-iu-to - ri - o

quis-nam sa-xum hoc re-uol-uet a mo-nu-men-ti   o-sti-o.   35

28-9 Condumentis ... preciosa] *text and music omitted in* M, *with* Condimentis aromatum
unguentes corpus sanctissimum quo preciosa *added in a later hand at the top of the*
page. 31 tumulo] timulo R. 33 dicat per se] *omitted* M. 35 reuoluet] reuoluit *corrected to*
reuoluet *in right margin of* M.

facto interuallo angelus iuxta sepulcrum [appareat] eis.
& dicat hoc modo.

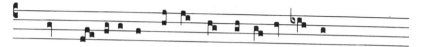

Quem que-ri-tis ad se-pul-crum o cri-sti - co - le.

deinde respondeant tres marie simul dicant.

Ihe-sum na-za-re-num cru-ci-fi-xum o ce-li-co-la.   40

tunc angelus [dicat sic].

Sur-re-xit non est hic si-cut di-xit ue-ni - te et ui-de-te

lo - cum u-bi po-si-tus fu-e-rat.

deinde predicte marie sepulcrum intrent & inclinantes
se & prospicientes undique [intra] sepulcrum. alta   45
uoce quasi [gaudendo] & admirantes & parum a sepulcro
recedentes simul dicant.

36 appareat] appariat M; apparuit R. 39 dicant] omitted M. 40 *flat sign before* crucifixum
also valid at third syllable of celicola, *since all of this music is notated on the one staff.* 41
dicat sic] dicet R. 44 &] *omitted* M. 45 intra] infra R. 46 gaudendo] gaudentes R. 47
simul dicant] dicant simul M.

re-sur-re - xit   al-le-lu-ya

Al-le-lu-ya re-sur-re-xit do-mi-nus al-le-lu-ya re-sur-re - xit

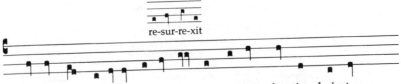

re-sur-re-xit

do-mi-nus ho-di-e re-sur-re - xit po-tens for-tis chris-tus

fi-li-us de-i

50

deinde angelus ad eas [dicens].

Et e-un-tes di-ci-te di-sci-pu-lis e-ius et pe-tro qui-a

sur-re-xit.

**In qua reuertant ad angelum quasi mandatum suum
ad implendum [parate] simul dicentes.**

55

51 dicens] omitted R. 53 *final note of* surrexit, *though omitted in* M, *is heralded by the custos at the end of the staff.* 55 parate] parare R; simul dicentes] dicentes simul M.

E-ya per-ga-mus pro-pe-re man-da-tum hoc per-fi-ce-re.

Interim ueniant ad ingressum chori due persone
nude pedes sub personis apostolorum Iohannis
& Petri indute albis sine paruris cum tunicis.
quarum Iohannes amictus tunica alba. palmam in   60
manu gestans. Petrus uero rubea tunica indutus.
claues in manu ferens. et predicte mulieres de
sepulcro reuertentes & quasi de choro simul
exeuntes. dicat prima maria per se [sequenciam].

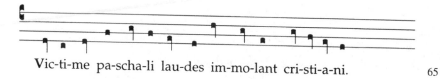

Vic-ti-me pa-scha-li lau-des im-mo-lant cri-sti-a-ni.   65

[secunda maria.]

A-gnus re-de-mit o-ues chri-stus in-no-cens pa-tri

re-con-si-li-a-uit pec-ca-to-res.

56 *the flat signature in M governs the whole line, including the first syllable of* propere; *in* R,
the flat signature is not introduced until just before the second syllable of mandatum, *and
thus governs the remainder of the line, but not the first syllable of* propere. 62 ferens] deferens
M. 64 per se] *omitted* R; sequenciam] sequencia R. 66 secunda maria] *omitted* R.

[tercia maria dicat.]

Mors et ui-ta du-el-lo con-fli-xe-re mi-ran-do dux ui-te   70

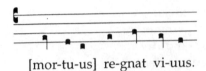

[mor-tu-us] re-gnat vi-uus.

tunc obuiantes eis in medio chori predicti
discipuli interrogantes. simul dicant.

Dic no-bis ma-ri - a quid ui-di-sti in ui-a.

Tunc prima maria [respondeat] quasi monstrando.   75

chri-sti

Se-pul-crum chri-sti ui-uen-tis et glo-ri-am ui-di re-sur-gen-tis.

tunc secunda maria [respondeat similiter quasi] monstrando.

69 tercia maria dicat] *omitted* R. 71 mortuus] mortuis R; mortuis *corrected to* mortuvs *in right margin of* M. 75 respondeat] respondet R. 77 respondeat similiter quasi] respondet similiter R; respondeat quasi M.

An-ge-li-cos te-stes su-da-ri-um & ue-stes.

tunc tercia maria respondeat.

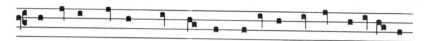

Sur-re-xit chri-stus spes no-stra pre-ce-det uos in ga-li-le - am.   80

et sic precedant simul ad ostium chori. [et] interim
currant duo ad monumentum uerumptamen ille discipulus
quem diligebat ihesus uenit prior ad monumentum iuxta
euangelium. currebant autem duo simul. & ille alius
discipulus precucurrit cicius petro et uenit prior   85
ad monumentum. non tamen introiuit. uidentes discipuli
predicti sepulcrum uacuum. & uerbis marie [credentes]
reuertant se ad chorum dicentes [hoc modo].

Cre-den-dum est ma-gis so-li ma-ri-e ue-ra-ci quam

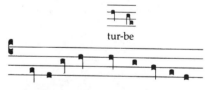

iu-de-o-rum tur-be fal-la-ci.   90

79 tunc] *omitted* M. 81 et ²] *omitted* R. 85 discipulus] discipulis M. 87 predicti] *omitted*
M; credentes] credente R. 88 hoc modo] *omitted* R.

**tunc audita christi resurreccione chorus prosequatur
alta uoce quasi gaudentes & exultantes sic dicentes.**

Sci-mus chri-stum sur-re-xis-se a mor-tu-is ue-re tu no-bis

uic-tor rex mi-se-re - re.

qua finita executor officij incipiat.   95

Te De-um lau-da-mus.

& sic recedant scilicet marie apostoli & angelus.

91 resurreccione] resurrecione M. 92 dicentes] dicant M. 97 & ... angelus] *omitted* M.

Translation

When the third respond has finished, with its verse and the *Gloria Patri*, three people shall come in surplices and silk copes, with their heads covered, as if they are the three Marys seeking Jesus, and each carrying a pyx in the hands as if containing spices. The first of these is to go before to the entry of the choir, towards the Sepulchre. As if lamenting, she is to say:

'Alas! The good shepherd whom no fault tainted is killed. Oh lamentable death!'

After a short interval, let the second Mary enter in exactly the same way and say:

'Alas! Wicked people of the Jews, whom awful madness will crush. Detestable race!'

Afterwards let the third Mary say in exactly the same way:

'Alas! The true teacher who brought life to the dead has died. Oh deplorable event!'

Still proceeding to this place to a small extent, let the first Mary say in the following way:

'Alas! Wretches that we are! Why does it befall that we see the Saviour's death?'

Afterwards let the second Mary say:

'Alas! Our comfort, why did he suffer death?'

Then the third Mary:

'Alas! Our redemption, why did he want to act in such a way?'

Then let them join together and proceed to the step of the choir in front of the altar, saying together:

'Now, now, behold, now let us hurry to the tomb, there anointing the most holy body of the beloved.'

Afterwards let them proceed together near to the Sepulchre, and let the first Mary say:

'Let us anoint the most holy body with condiments of spices which are precious.'

Then let the second Mary say:

'A mixture of spikenard will prevent the blessed flesh from decaying in the tomb.'

Afterwards let the third Mary say:

'But we cannot do this without help. Who will roll back this stone from the entrance of the burial chamber?'

After an interval, let the angel appear to them next to the Sepulchre, and let him say in the following way:

'Whom do you seek at the Sepulchre, O worshippers of Christ?'

Then let the three Marys reply, and let them say together:

'The crucified Jesus of Nazareth, O you of heaven.'

Then let the angel say thus:

'He has risen and is not here, as he told you. Come and see the place where he was laid.'

Afterwards the aforesaid Marys are to enter the Sepulchre, and bowing themselves and looking about on all sides inside the Sepulchre, let them say with a loud voice, as if rejoicing, and wondering, and coming away a little from the Sepulchre:

'Alleluia, the Lord has risen! Alleluia, the Lord has risen today! Christ the Son of God has risen, strong and mighty!'

Afterwards let the angel address them, saying:

'And as you go, tell his disciples and Peter that he has risen.'

Upon which let them turn back to the angel, as if ready to carry out his command, saying together:

'Eia! Let us go quickly to fulfil this command.'

In the meanwhile, two barefooted people are to come to the entry of the choir, in the characters of the apostles John and Peter, vested in unapparelled albs and with tunicles. Of these, John should be clad in a white tunicle, and carrying a palm in his hand. Peter on the other hand should be vested in a red tunicle, and bearing the keys in his hand. And as the aforesaid women return from the Sepulchre and as if exiting together from the choir, let the first Mary say the Sequence:

'Christians offer praises to the Easter Victim.'

The second Mary:

'The Lamb has bought back his sheep. The innocent Christ has reconciled sinners to the Father.'

Let the third Mary say:

'Life and death have struggled together in a great battle; the Lord of life who died, now in life reigns.'

Then the disciples, meeting up with them in the middle of the choir and asking them the following question, are to say together:

'Tell us, Mary, what did you see on your way?'

Then let the first Mary reply, pointing as it were:

'The tomb of the living Christ, and I saw the glory of his rising.'

Then let the second Mary reply similarly, pointing as it were:

'Angels for witnesses, the sudarium and grave-clothes.'

Then let the third Mary reply:

'Christ our hope has risen; he will go before you into Galilee.'

And thus let them go before together to the entry of the choir, and in the meanwhile the two are to run to the tomb. However, that disciple whom Jesus loved comes first to the tomb, according to the gospel: 'They ran together, however, and that other disciple ran before more swiftly than Peter, and came first to the tomb, yet he did not go in.' The aforesaid disciples, when they see the Sepulchre empty and believing the words of Mary, let them turn back to the choir saying in the following way:

'More worthy of belief is a single Mary telling truth than a host of Jews telling lies.'

Then having heard of Christ's Resurrection, let the choir begin with a loud voice, as if rejoicing and exulting, saying thus:

'Truly we know that Christ has risen from the dead; O conquering king, have mercy on us.'

When this is ended, let the conductor of the office begin:

'*Te Deum laudamus.*'

And thus let them return, that is, the Marys, apostles, and angel.

Titvs, or the Palme of Christian Covrage

CUL, Bradshaw Collection, No. 5311, Hib. 7.644.33.
TITVS, | OR THE PALME | OF | CHRISTIAN | COVRAGE: | To be exhibited by
the Schollars of the | Society of IESVS, at Kilken- | ny, *Anno Domini* 1644. | [rule]
THE ARGVMENT.

T*Itus* a noble Gentleman more illustrious for his Christian | courage, then parentage:
was sollicited by the King of | *Bungo,* to desert his Religion by severall, most artificious
in- | fernall plots, all which he sleighted and dashed with his invin- | cible courage,
and generous Christian resolution, whereat the | King amazed, restored him to his
liberty, wife and children, | and granted him the freedome of his Religion, with all
his | lands and possessions of which before he was bereaved as trai- | tor to the Crowne.

This history is compendiously set downe by Father Francis Solier, of | *the Society of IESVS*
in the 18. *booke of his Ecclesiasticall historie* | *of Iaponia, and yeare of our Lord,* 1620.
[rule]
Printed at Waterford by *Thomas Bourke,* M. DC. XLIV.

fol. [1v]

THE PROLOGVE. | Divine love extolleth the *Iaponian's* courage. | *Act* I. *Scene* I. |
IDolatrie stormes at her expulsion out of Ia- | *ponia,* and exciteth hell to revenge. |
Scene 2. | The Emperor of *Iaponia* declareth his affe- | ction towards the Idolls, and
to this end com- | mandeth a solemne sacrifice. | *Scene* 3. | The *Bongo's* receive no
answer from their | gods as they were wont, hence they rage against | the Christians.
Scene 4. | Faith and Fortitude, implore aide of the tri- | umphant Church. *The*
Interlude. | A Countrey Clowne hearing that a procla- | mation was to issue against
the Christians, is | mighty merry, and attempts to robbe a passen- | ger. *Act* 2. *Scene*

I. | THe Emperor commands the edict against | Christians to bee proclaimed. | *Scene* 2. | The edict is promulged. | *Scene* 3. | *Titus* perusing the edict, deliberates, with | death, judgment, hell, heaven and eternitie. | *Scene* 3. | The King of *Bungo* inquireth narrowly af- | ter

fol. [2]

ter the Christians. *Scene* 4. | *Titus* is summoned and biddeth adieu to wife | and children. *Scene* 5. | Idolatrie triumphes before time, and is by | faith repressed. *The Interlude.* | A Souldier fainedly sicke, calleth for the | Doctor, whose purse artificiously he conveyeth | out of his pocket, and hopes by a lad dreaming | to get another. *Act* 3. *Scene* 2. | THe King of *Bungo* endevors first by threats, | then by faire promises to pervert *Titus.* | *Scene* 2. | *Titus* his wife and familie voweth loyaltie to | God before the Crucifix. *Scene* 3. | The militant Church doth comfort them. | *Scene* 4. | S. *Francis Xaverius* appeares & encourageth | them. *Act* 4. *Scene* I. | THe King of *Bungo* menaceth death to | *Titus* his youngest sonne, if the father ab- | jure not his faith. *Scene* 2. | Foure youngmen in vaine seeke to pervert | the lad with the pleasures of the world. | *Scene* 3. | *Martina* the daughter, biddeth adieu, with | mother and brother, assuring them of her con- | stancy. *Scene* 4. | *Simon* the eldest sonne bewaileth for that he is | left

fol. [2v]

left behind. *Scene* 5. | Tidings are brought to *Titus* of his daugh- | ters execution, *Martina* the mother of *Simon* is | summoned. *Scene* 6. | By the King both are sollicited to desert their | faith, *Simon* scourged. | *The Interlude.* | Two souldiers force a lad to discover where | the mothers purse lay hidden by whom they | are deceived. *Act* 5. *Scene* I. | T*Itus* is sent for by the King, in whose view | supposed heads of wife & children are produ- | ced. *Scene* 2. | They are lead from prison before him and a | superficiall command given to kill them in his | presence, if he persists in his constant resolu- | tion. *Scene* 3. | Divine providence declareth Gods care of his | elect, and foretelleth *Titus* his triumph. | *Scene* 4. | The King amazed at this constancie dismis- | seth them, freedome of Religion granted with their lives and estates. | *Epilogue.* | Exhorteth to imitate their couragious Chri- | stian resolution. | *FINIS.*

Sir Henry Sidney's Civic Entry into Waterford

A miscellany of matter largely concerning Ireland is to be found in TCD, MS 581 (E. 3. 18). It includes such items as a copy of Patrick Finglas's *Breviat of the getting of Ireland*, plus chronicles, genealogies, historical tracts, and letters. The items of present concern are a set of descriptions, beginning on fol. 75, of journeys undertaken in Ireland by various New English administrators (Sir Thomas Radcliffe, third earl of Sussex, Sir Henry Sidney, and Sir William Russell). Those relating to Radcliffe were composed by John Butler, Athlone Pursuivant (and probably written in his hand). The others were also probably authored by heralds.

TCD, MS 581 (E. 3. 18); antiquarian collection copied by various scribes in the sixteenth and seventeenth century (including the progresses of Sir Henry Sidney, fols 94–7v, between 14 February 1567 and 22 November 1568, copied by one scribe in the later sixteenth century); Latin (some English); paper; ii + 110 + ii; modern pencil foliation; fol. 94: 310mm × 205mm; no decoration; generally in good condition, though fraying around the edges of some leaves has partially obliterated text; seventeenth-century binding of white leather, on the spine of which is stamped in gold: 'C:E | T:3 | No. 18'; and lengthways beneath this: 'Modus tenendi Parli: &c.'; at the bottom is affixed a label: '581.'

1567
Sir Henry Sidney's Progress   TCD, MS 581 (E. 3. 18)
fol. 94–4v *(25 February)*
...
And one the morowe being twsedaye the xxv daye ffebrwarye he departid ffrome the barrake and wente vnto anothere castell of the said erle of Orrmondes cawlid the grawnowge And ther sartin bwrioses {'burgesses'} of the citie of waterford did attende one the saide Lorde Depwtye withe dyweres bottes {'diverse boats'} and   5

one of the said bootes was verye well trimmid withe cowsshinges {'cushions'}
and ca⌈r⌉petes and cowerid {'covered'} withe afayre pesee of tapsterye and the
same bote was made ffaste to a nothere grete bootte withe oweres and hauing
2 basces {'small cannons'} in the forside the said bootes showthe of {'push out'} at
the departing ffrome the showre {'shore'} thaye rowed vnthe {'unto the'} citye of   10
waterforde where Waterfforde wheare he was verye anscantlye {?'honourably'}
Recewid ffriste with gownes {'guns'} showtes as well of other dyveres shepes
{'ships'} and allso after he had sene the hawene {'haven'} of that place he landed
at the kye {'quay'} of the where the mayore and shreffes and aldermen of the
citie Recewide {'received'} hime verye rewerentlye and the recorder of the citie   15
commauundid mr [white] nicholas [clarke] white mayde anoration vnto the
saide Lorde Depwtie [and] delaring {read declaring} not onlye the good will of
them of the citie towardes the maiesti bwt also vnto the said Lorde Depwtie
and allso the franches vnto them grawntid by dyveres Kinges and prencise
affore time and the lorde Depweti [and allso] afforthe same thanked them of   20
theare gentil[nes] cwrtiesye {'courtesy'} as well towardes the quines maiestie as
vnto hyme particwlare and so entered the saide cetie and withe in the gatte
thare was a payget {'pageant'} and verye properlye in the same verye well
decked whoe wellcomed the said Lorde Depwetie withe a verye good oracione
and in the myde Waye to his logine {'lodging'} thare was another oration alitille   25
Dystante ffrome his logine/ and thws the said mayre beringe the sworde beffor
the Lorde Depwtie and havinge the quenes coott of armes worne afore hyme by
Vlster kinge of armes he was browghte to his logine withe all the said aldermen
of the citie followinge hime vnto his said Logine and theare he thancked the
mayre and the reste of the citieszones ffor thare soo hvmbly recewing [theme]   30
hime promissing them that he wolde consider well of them allso the byshope
of waterfforde in his coppe withe ∧⌈the⌉ canownes and preste of the citie
receuid the saide lorde Depwtie singinge the presescione in ingylshe {read
inglyshe} and so browghte hime singinge to ∧⌈the⌉ chwrche of christechwrche
in waterfford and after sartine prayeres the lorde Depwtye went to his Logine   35
{'lodging'} ...
...

Sir Henry Sidney's Civic Entry into Limerick

1567
Sir Henry Sidney's Progress   TCD, MS 581 (E. 3. 18)
fol. 95v–6 *(26 March)*

...

... and ffrome thence the saide Lorde depwtie depwtie whent vnto Lymmericke and so theare did by the waye a greate compenie of men of Limickericke {*read* Limmericke} mett the said Lorde depwtie ffor that the saide Lorde depwtie was adwartised {'notified'} that the erle of dessmwnte {'Desmond'} hade sente ffor sartin mene to mette hyme bythe waye {'meet him along the way'} and   5
then the men of kilmaloughe wente bake againe and so the Lorde Depwtie wente to the saide citie of Limmericke where he was verye [well] honorabilly reseuide by the maiore & aldermen of the citie of Limmerike and after sartin grete schottes of ordinace {*read* ordinance} and artilerye the saide Lorde depwtie enterid the b⌈a⌉se towne of Limmerike cawllid the Ieris towne {'Irishtown'}   10
and theare a proper lade cawllid barttilmewe white did make anoratione {'an oration'} In the wellcomming of the said [lord] Lorde depwtie and so the Lorde Depwtie enterid the highe towne of Limmerike having as in all othere plaseces {'places'} the sworde borne beffor hime by mr Iackes winkeffilld and the coot of armes of inglande worne as inother plasces by Vlstwre kinge of   15
armes / and the said maiore of Limmerike did beare his maice beffor the said Lorde depwtie and Rid withe the quenes sargginte of armes and beffore the saide Wlstwre kinge of armes and so wente towardes [towardes] the cathedrayll chwrche [of] cawllid owr Laydye chi⌈w⌉rche and by the waye in the highe waye in the streate there was a paygone {'pageant'} declaringe the stat of the   20
saide citie and ∧⌈a⌉ yownge mane cawled stwueffen {'Stephen'} the eldiste sowne and ayre of the said Dominike white Did declare the effecte of that paigion {'pageant'} vnto the said Lorde depwtie Inthe aparell of ∧⌈a⌉ messengar of peace havinge amantell of ascharlite {'scarlet'} abowte hime and a garlande of

baies on his hede / and after he hade delacred {*read* declared} the matter he 25
deliuerid the said oration in writing withe a nother boke of the complayntes
of the citiezenes vnto the said Lorde depwtie whoe gentilie Resewinge the same
gawe thannkes vnto the mayore |fol. 96| and his brotherin ffor theare soe gentilly
reseuige hime In the quenes maisties name and also particwlairye for his own
parte promisinge that he woolde doo his best dewore {'endeavour'} In thare 30
behalffe and soo he wente to the said chewrche {'church'} where the bishope[.] of
Limmerike Recewid hyme in the chwrche yearde with a pressione {'procession'}
in Latine singing and the said bisshope was in his ponticalie {'pontificals'} after
the popes fascion and all the Reste of the priste and clarkes in thear copes and
a crosse bowrne beffor them and so the {*read* they} enterid the said chwrche 35
and [after] ∧⌈the⌉ bishope sange after tentollit {?} prainge ffor the saide Lorde
depwtie …

Notes: l.19 chi⌈w⌉rche] w *is written superscript above* ir.   l.29 reseuige] *for* reseui<n>ge.
l.36 tentollit] *meaning obscure.*

Sir Thomas Wentworth's Civic Entry into Limerick

The letter given below is transcribed from Sir Thomas Wentworth's holograph, sent from Limerick to Lord Conway and Killultagh on 21 August 1637. (A copy exists in SCA, Wentworth Woodhouse Muniments, Strafford Letter Book 10, pp. 44–5.)

London, Public Record Office, SP 63/256 (item 48); copied probably by Sir Thomas Wentworth, 21 August 1637; English; paper; ii + 319 + ii; 282mm × 194mm; modern stamped ink foliation; no decoration; in good condition; modern binding of green half leather, on the spine of which is stamped in gold: 'IRELAND I CHARLES I I VOL.'; above this are affixed respectively the labels: 'SP'; and: '63'; at the bottom of the spine is affixed a label: '256.'

1637
Sir Thomas Wentworth to Lord Conway and Killultagh   PRO, SP 63/256
fol. 133–4 *(21 August)*

My very good Lord.
...
They haue all along to the vttermost of ther skill and breeding giuen me very greate expressions of ther esteem and affection, soe as I beginn allmost to be persuaded, that they here could be content to haue me the minister of his Majestys fauoures towards ˄⌈them as soon [as an other]⌉ as any other.

Oratory hath abundantly magnified it self thorow thes excellent peeces wee haue hearde, one at Casterlaghe, three at Kilkenny, tow very deadly long ones at Clonmell, foure not of the shortest heare at Limmericke:

Architecture and inuention not asleepe, as appeared in ther ark-Triumphalls with ther ornaments and inscriptions; the ingenuose accomodations of ther Cupids, ther Apollo ther antient genij, ther Laurat Poets and such like; here pour la bonne bouche, (as the frenche say) wee saw all the seauen Plannetts in a very spericall and heauenly motion, and hearde eache of them vtter in harmony seuerall verses in our praise, telling vs therby vpon my knowledge, rather what wee ought to be, then what wee were (the common case you will say of all Painters and Orators), and the son the King of Planetts ouer and aboue all the rest, did insteade of his indulgent heate [bening] benignly squirtt of his sweet waters vpon vs forth of a Seringe, my hopes being all the the whilst the instrument was new, and had not been vsed before.

By that time that wee gett backe to Dublin, I trust you will be safely returned to London, for wee heare you meane not to fight this summer noe more then wee doe but for all that, I doubte whether you meet with such intertainment aborde your Triumphe.

well seriously may health and safety be with your goings out and cummings inn from this time forth and for euermore ther is a peece of a sermon for you, and take it for as great a truthe as they in ther pulpetts speake any that I am

Your Lordships
most faithfull humble
seruant./

Limmerick this 21th
of August. 1637.

Wentworth

APPENDIX IV

Introduction to the Sword Dance

The text given below, John Clavell's *Introduction to the Sword Dance*, is transcribed from the unique holograph copy in the Wiltshire Record Office.

Trowbridge, WRO, MS 865/502 (item 2); miscellaneous notebook, including poems, recipes, epitaphs, elegies, and draft letters, copied by John Clavell at various times between *c* 1620–40; English; paper; 45; 295mm × 200mm; modern pencil pagination, odd numbers only, running 1 to 89; text written from pp. 1 to 37 (pp. [38]–39 are blank) and also written from the back, upside down, from pp. [88] to [40]; no decoration; in fair condition, but there is some fading throughout, and p. 89 is detached; six unbound gatherings, sewn together with leather thongs, and in modern pencil on p. 89 is written: 'Clavell | 2d wife Isabel | Fitzgerald d. of | E. of Kildare'; on the front cover is written: '865/502 p. 1'; preserved in a bundle with two other items.

1632
Introduction to the Sword Dance   WRO: 865/502
pp. 13–15 *(25 December)*

An introduction to the Sword daunce at Christmas 1632
At my Lord Barries in Ireland

Noyce without – follow, follow, follow,
Then Enter peace in a white habite et' trembling

PEACE. Ay mee poore feeble peace! for what am I   5
In their sad gripe such is their Tyranny
And emnity so firce, Oh might I fall
Alone my sacrifice to shelter all
That are alike choyce Temper, I should bee

A willing yeilding true Epitomie   10
Of Meekenesse in its puritie! Alas
Their enuy hath noe limite but will passe
As far as violence extends, – Ile try

> Here Peace makes low Congne {'bow'} to the Countesse
> Then knees before her feet and proceeds   15

Here I take shelter this diuinity
will or protect mee or at least it shall
Add one sad sight unto my funerall

> Ther Peace remayn trembling
New noyce without – ffollow, follow, follow,   20
Then Enter the Maskers for the sword dance (as in serch)
Attired in Cassocks, Bases, Helmetts, their sowrds drawne
At last hauing espied Peace sayes the Leader

LEADER. How's this see see, shee hath tane sanctuary,
    giue us that Harlott peace that Bucksome girle   25
    growne mellow with the Iouyce {'juice'} seukd from theis arms
    Th'inheritance of their late able sinewes
    S'hath frozen upp our liuely sparks of valour
    with a cold swett bedewing theis our sourds
    Carired by that infection, but we'lle bathe   30
    Them in her oyly Bowells to regaine
    Their wonted fiery splendour – giue her upp
    That on that Lushious morsell wee may bate
    The sharpnesse of our stomacks – wilt not bee
    Then perish all the faction; feast yee blades   35
    On on to execution

> here they make upp towards the Ladies
> with their swords aduanced, then |

> Enter Mars in fury
> his Coate of Mayle and target {'small shield'} borne by a Page 40
> his sword Aduanced, stepping betweene
> the Ladies and the and the souldiers
> sayes Angerly

MARS. What riote haue wee here? Nay sacralidg?
    Is this a place for Mutiny? or time   45

Rebellions Route: whilst with my fellow Gods
Hauing laide by theis ornaments, wee quaffe
Healths to theis earthly Paragons, inricht
with deuine purenesse and maiestick shapes,
That your dull apprehentions might bee wrought   50
To iudg by patterne thos our heauenly bewties
That thence you might admire fall downe & worshipp
Are theis to bee disturbd:

LEADER. wee persue Peace
        And couett but the exercise of Armes   55

            Then Mars goes gracefully upp
            Takes peace by the hand & sayes

MARS. Peace has deuinity aboute her tis Ioues pleasure
       she bee not thus assalted / till hee bidds /
       Walke of thy single selfe thow art protected   60

                exit peace

            The souldiers cast a threttning countenance
            as shee passes which Mars espijng sayes

Blaspheame not wrech by such another loke
Ile finde imployment for thos blades of yours   65
Obserue and second mee

            Here Mars leades on the sword dance
            into which they all ioyne that finished
            Mars goes upp to the cheife Lady layes his
            Sourd att her feete and takes her out to dance 70
            The rest follow by his example laying poynt
            to hilt, hauing dancd some few dances they
            taking vp their sowrds they daunce their
            warlike maske done with many prety changes
            that done Mars leads them all of {'off'} only the 75
            Leader remaynes and laying downe his sourd
            at his feete sayes

LEADER. Wee are All vanquishd though the rest are gone
         Loaden with guilt and shame here I alone
         Ffor mee and them (o letts not bee denied)   80
         Thus lowe doe pardon craue, and doe subscribe

That thers noe speare, noe sword, noe skeene, noe darte
wounds like to loue shott from a ladies heart

Then suddenly aduancing
his sourd proceeds   85

Thus Ile Maintaine it, whoesoere sayes noe
I likewise mine, as well as bewties foe;

exit

...

Notes: l.22 Cassocks, Bases] 'Cassocks' in this context were either military cloaks or long coats; 'Bases' were either plaited cloth skirts appended to the doublet or mailed armour resembling such. l.30 Carired] This is what the MS apparently reads, though 'Cancred' ('rusted') would make perfect sense, and is probably to be understood here, on the assumption that the -ri- are in fact -cr- badly formed.   l.82 skeene] A 'skeene' (< Irish *scian*) was a knife, and in this context, probably intending one of distinctive Irish manufacture (for further discussion of the appearance of the masquers, see chapter 6, pp. 236–7).

Notes

PROLOGUE

1 *Spenser Poetical Works*, ed. J.C. Smith and E. de Selincourt (Oxford, 1970), p. 475, lines 344–6.

2 See respectively on John Long and Robert Daborne, *DNB*, XXXIV, 106, and XIII, 373–4.

3 The title of the study has tried to strike this balance, for outside specialist theoretical circles, the dominant meaning of 'drama' is the common one given above. See J. Féral, 'Performance and Theatricality: The Subject Demystified,' *Modern Drama* 25 (1982), 170–81; M. de Marinis, *The Semiotics of Performance*, trans. Á. O'Healy (Bloomington and Indianapolis, 1993), pp. 48–51.

4 D. Bergeron, *English Civic Pageantry 1558–1642* (London, 1971), for example, is a touch defensive about discussing his chosen topic as a form of theatre, though latterly, studies have begun taking the legitimacy of such discussion for granted.

5 They probably exported themselves to Anglo-Saxon England and further afield. See A. Breeze, 'Ælfric's *Trup* "Buffoon": Old Irish *Druth* "Buffoon,"' *Notes and Queries* 240 (1995), 155–7 (though Breeze's basic point, that Old English *trup* may be a loan from Old Irish *drúth*, had already been made by A. Bugge, *Vesterlandenes Inflydelse paa Nordboernes og soerlig Nordmaendenes ydre Kultur, Levesæf og Sam Finds Forhold i Vikingetiden* (Christiania, 1905), p. 64). On possible contact between Old Irish and Old Icelandic performers, see T. Gunnell, '"The Rights of the Player": Evidence of *Mimi* and *Histriones* in Early Medieval Scandinavia,' *Comparative Drama* 30 (1996), 1–31.

6 N. Patterson, *Cattle-Lords and Clansmen: The Social Structure of Early Ireland*, 2nd ed. (Notre Dame and London, 1994), p. 14 and following. It may be that the final verdict on the historical reliability of the laws will lie somewhere between the two extremes of doubt and belief, with the balance tilting more in one direction than another, according to the particular law tract under review.

CHAPTER 1

1 P.W. Joyce, *A Social History of Ancient Ireland*, 2 vols (London, 1903)I, 499. He is representative of an opinion already long-standing. Compare J.C. Walker, 'An Historical Essay on the Irish Stage,' *Transactions of the Royal Irish Academy* 2 (1788), 75–90; see p. 77: 'no production in a regular Dramatic form is extant in the Irish language, nor even alluded to by any of our ancient writers. So that if the Stage ever existed in Ireland previous to the middle ages, like the "baseless fabric of a vision" it has melted into air, leaving not a trace behind.' (His later work, *Historical Memoirs of the Irish Bards* [Dublin, 1818], p. 217, had begun to approach the position elaborated in this chapter, however.) The view that native Gaelic culture had no drama, of course, partly depends upon what a particular critic understands by 'drama' (as Joyce's expression 'Drama in the proper sense of the word' implies), and it is likely that his view will be conditioned by the forms of 'drama' prevalent at the time he writes. In the eighteenth and nineteenth century, and for much of the twentieth, drama has normally meant plays of scripted dialogue, staged usually in proscenium arch theatres.

2 C. Fitz-Simon, *The Irish Theatre* (London, 1983), p. 7, says of early Ireland: 'several of those arts which would normally be considered as essential to the self-expression of a comparatively civilized people did not flourish in Ireland – and one of these was theatre.' M. Ó hAodha, *Theatre in Ireland* (Oxford, 1974), pp. xi–xii, begins his book from a similar standpoint; before he wrote there were yet other theatre historians of the same mind. Given such a consensus of opinion, it is not surprising to find it surfacing in more general studies (for example, R. McHugh and M. Harmon, *Short History of Anglo-Irish Literature from its Origins to the Present Day* [Dublin, 1982], p. 143: 'The late development of an indigenous drama in Ireland was due to a number of causes. The Gaelic world had no dramatic tradition'; or more seriously misleading, A.C. Partridge, *Language and Society in Anglo-Irish Literature* [Dublin and Totowa, 1984], p. 194: 'The European Renaissance ... by-passed Ireland, and no interest in drama appeared there until the latter half of the seventeenth century').

3 *EIS*, p. 2. It is interesting to observe Ó hAodha's brief struggle against the confines of his own conception of what constitutes drama when he wrote: 'The shanachie or storyteller had a keen sense of the dramatic but it was by the fireside, not on a stage, that he perfected his craft. It may well be that he favoured a solo performance, a one-man show, preferring to do all the talking himself rather than to share the dialogue with others' (*Theatre in Ireland*, p. xii). His presupposition of what a legitimate 'stage' was seems to have derived from his equation of theatre with the traditional proscenium arch; and no one would deny that *Krapp's Last Tape* is drama simply because it is a monologue. Ó hAodha's radical perception of the immanence of drama in storytelling is finally hamstrung by his deference to later conventions that drama has engendered.

4 M. MacNeill, *The Festival of Lughnasa* (Oxford, 1962), pp. 423–4 and p. 426.

While MacNeill occasionally considers early sources, her chief emphasis is on later material.

5 A. Harrison, *An chrosántacht* (Baile Átha Cliath, 1979); also by him, *The Irish Trickster* (Sheffield, 1989). The *crosáin* were professional jesters and entertainers, whose role will be illustrated further below.

6 This collocation, common in early Irish sources, is edited here from the Old Irish law tract *Uraicecht Becc* (the 'Small Primer'), in its version found in RIA, MS 536 (23 P 12; Book of Ballymote), p. 348, col. a (*CIH*, V, 1617, line 11). See further on this text in note 41 below.

7 The composition of this text, the *Tecosca Cormaic* ('Cormac's Instructions'), has been dated to probably no later than the first half of the ninth century (K. Meyer, ed., *The Instructions of King Cormac Mac Airt*, Todd Lecture Series, volume 15 [Dublin, 1909], p. xi).

8 RIA, MS 132 (23 D 2), p. 8 (Meyer, *Instructions of King Cormac*, p. 10, lines 12–13, and p. 12, lines 16–17). Compare too the role of the *cano* (one of the seven grades into which the early Irish poetic hierarchy was traditionally divided) as outlined in a version of the Old Irish law text *Bretha Nemed* ('Judgments of privileged [or professional] persons'): 'Airfidiud coir com ₍ₐ₎⌐ad⌐ais cach lin i tig megrac [r] mid cuarta soindsce for coimgne co corus coibnes cata cana concana bairdne' ('Correct ... playing of music to every company in the merry house of a mead-hall, eloquence applied to historical lore, proper arrangement [and] harmony are what confer dignity on a *cano* who sings in harmony bardic compositions'; BL, MS Cotton Nero A.vii, fol. 143v; L. Breatnach, ed. *Uraicecht na Ríar*, Early Irish Law Series, volume 2 [Dublin, 1987], pp. 36–7).

9 TCD, MS 1339 (H. 2. 18; Book of Leinster), fol. 15, cols a–b. Another version of this plan appears in the Yellow Book of Lecan (facsimiled by R. Atkinson, ed., *The Yellow Book of Lecan* [Dublin, 1896], p. 418; any variants of interest in this version will be noted in the discussion).

10 *DIL*, **senchaid**. In some contexts, 'storyteller' (a sense to the fore in the word's modern derivative, *seanchaí*) seems as appropriate a translation, and *DIL* notes the link between *senchas* ('old tales,' 'ancient history,' 'tradition'), the province of the *senchaid*, and *scélaigecht* ('storytelling'), the province of the *scélaige* ('storyteller,' 'historian'). A good example is provided in the Annals of Loch Cé under the year 1301, when the death is recorded of Gilla Iosa Mac Fhirbhisigh, an expert in various arts, including *senchas* and *scélaigecht* (W.M. Hennessy, ed. *The Annals of Loch Cé*, 2 vols [London, 1871] I, 524). For links also between *senchas*, *scélaigecht* and musical performance, see note 25 below.

11 The *maccfurmid* (*DIL*, **mac(c)fuirmid**) was second lowest of the seven poetic grades, and specialized in the *sétnad* and *sainemain* metres. He composed satire. The *fochloc* (*DIL*, **fochloc**) was the lowest of the seven poetic grades, and specialized in the *dían* metre. He too composed satire.

12 F. Kelly, 'An Old-Irish Text on Court Procedure,' *Peritia* 5 (1986), 74–106; on pp. 82–3

he notes the existence of seating plans also in the *Tech Midchúarda*, discussed above, and the Old Irish law text *Críth Gablach* ('Branched Purchase'?), composed probably in the opening years of the eighth century (D.A. Binchy, ed. *Críth Gablach* [Dublin, 1941], p. xiv). In fact, the preoccupation with seating arrangements appears in yet other texts (compare too the Old Irish poem *Lanellach Tigi Rich 7 Ruirech* [the 'Full Complement of the Household of a King and an Overking']; M.O Daly, 'Lānellach Tī gi Rich 7 Ruirech,' *Ériu* 19 [1962], 81–6), and was evidently a topos.

13 The rules of *fidchell*, as of most medieval games, are not known; the traditional translation 'chess' is merely a convenience. I have excluded *fidchellaig* from my consideration of entertainers and performing artists. However, on the strong connection between gamblers and itinerant entertainers, see below.

14 By contrast, in the Yellow Book of Lecan plan (Atkinson, *Yellow Book of Lecan*, p. 418), harpers sit with *timpán*-players (the *timpán* was another variety of harp, possibly like a psaltery; *DIL*, **timpán**, sub-sense [b], and A. Bruford, 'Song and Recitation in Early Ireland,' *Celtica* 21 [1990], 61–74; p. 66).

15 Meyer, *Instructions of King Cormac*, p. 46, line 21. Compare also the higher legal status accorded harping in the *Uraicecht Becc* (RIA, MS 536 [23 P 12; Book of Ballymote], p. 347, col. b; *CIH*, V, 1616, lines 31–2): '**Cruit … is e ændan ciuil indsein … dliges sairi**' ('a harp is the one art of music which deserves nobility'; I have omitted the interlinear glosses accompanying this text). F. Kelly, *A Guide to Early Irish Law*, Early Irish Law Series, volume 3 (Dublin, 1988), p. 64, note 195, gives further examples.

16 Though harpers were praised in early sources, by the end of period under review they were increasingly being celebrated by name in poetry. To cite a few, all active in the early years of the seventeenth century, for example, we find: Nicholas dall Pierse (J.H. Pierse, 'Nicholas Dall Pierse of Co. Kerry, Harper,' *Journal of the Kerry Archaeological and Historical Society* 6 [1973], 40–75); Eoghan Ó hAllmhuráin (C. McGrath, 'Two Skilful Musicians,' *Éigse* 7 [1953–5], 84–94); Tadhg Ó Cobhthaigh (E.C. Mac Giolla Eáin, ed., *Dánta Amhráin is Caointe Sheathrúin Céitinn* [Baile Átha Cliath, 1900], pp. 29–31); Conchubhar Mac Conghalaigh (S. Ua Súilleabháin and S. Donnelly, '"Music has Ended": The Death of a Harper,' *Celtica* 22 [1991], 165–75); and Eoghan Ó Eachach, Roiberd óg Carrunn, and Eamonn Albanach (Ned Scott, on whom see further below in chapter 6; M. Ní Cheallacháin, ed., *Filíocht Phádraigín Haicéad* [Baile Átha Cliath, 1962], pp. 13–14, 17, and 19 respectively).

17 BL, MS Egerton 88, fol. 3v, col. a (*CIH*, III, 1268, lines 16–17): 'Cair cia laisin coir milcu. ni annsa. la flaith. cair cia laisin coir oircne. ni annsa. occbriugaid .7 liaigh .7 cruitire .7 rigan.' ('Query: who is entitled to keep a greyhound? Not difficult to tell: a chief. Query: who is entitled to keep a lapdog? Not difficult to tell: a young hospitaller, a doctor, a harper, and a chief's wife.') This tract on livestock and other topics is extant only here. It may belong to the eighth or ninth century. I am grateful to Fergus Kelly for his opinion on its dating.

18 PRO, SP 63/214, fol. 271. (Though Hanmer has headed his text 'How a bullock is to be divided,' he does not seem to have minded that bullocks are not noted for their udders.) This text seems to be an English version of one ultimately Gaelic in origin, and which belonged to the long tradition of discussion of the honorific portions (on which see further below).

19 Richard Stanihurst, if a hostile witness, may nevertheless have had a point when he attributed to Gaelic harpists a fierce jealousy for their art and its dignity. He observed (in *De rebus in Hibernia gestis* [Antwerp, 1584], p. 39): 'Quòd si aures tuas, pulsis filis, peregrinari intelligat, aut si hominis laudem, vlla ex parte, minuas, furere quidam, & tamquam rabiosulus, bacchari videbitur. Nam vt illius cognitionem ore laudes pleniore, non modo petit, verùm etiam exigit.' ('If the harpist realizes that your ears are wandering once he has struck the strings, or if you lessen his praise in the least tittle, he will be seen ranting and raving like a little madman. For he not only asks but also demands that you extol his capabilities fulsomely.')

20 P. Ó Riain, ed., *Cath Almaine* (Dublin, 1978), p. xxvi.

21 Compare Isaiah 5:11–12: 'Woe to those who … tarry late into the evening till wine inflames them! They have lyre and harp, timbrel and flute and wine at their feasts; but they do not regard the deeds of the Lord, or see the work of his hands.' The gravity of biblical censure resonates behind this early Middle Irish passage, and has even conceivably inspired it. Disgusting side effects of feasting were also elaborated by some of the Fathers (compare Ambrose in book 1, chapter 13 of his *De Elia et Ieiunio, Patrologia Latina* 14 [Paris, 1845], col. 715), and these may also have served the Irish compiler as a model.

22 BR, MS 5301–20, pp. 5–6 (J.N. Radner, ed., *Fragmentary Annals of Ireland* [Dublin, 1978], p. 60). The contrast pointed up in this passage between morally pure and impure varieties of feasting is interestingly analogous to the discriminations made in the Old Irish law tract *Córus Béscnai* ('Regulation of Proper Behaviour'), for which see below.

23 TCD, MS 673 (F. 3. 19), p. 234 (D. Murphy, ed., *The Annals of Clonmacnoise* [Dublin, 1896], p. 298). Ó Ceallaigh was lord of the territory of Uí Mhaine in Connacht, a territory running approximately from Clontuskert, co. Roscommon, southwards to the boundary of co. Clare, and from Athlone westwards to Seefin and Athenry in co. Galway. For further discussion of this passage, see chapter 6.

24 R. Thurneysen, *Die irische Helden- und Königsage bis zum siebzehnten Jahrhundert* (Halle, 1921), pp. 65–6. So too did the *timpán*-player. When one poet wanted a horse from his chieftain, Brian Mág Shamradháin (†1298), he claimed: 'Ai briain builidh bindglaraic arightaisich go redi ech uaid dona timpanchaibh ar sgelaidhacht na feni coru ni ar imraidhmid maith dorada rit feni' ('O dear sweet-voiced Brian, generous and princely chieftain, you bestow a horse on the *timpán*-players for reciting Fenian stories. Fitter is the subject of my speech, praise being bestowed on you.'; NLI, MS G 1200 [Book of Magauran], fol. 6, col. a). Horn-blowers and pipers were also capable

of telling stories; these professions are discussed below. For an example of the *scélaige* telling legendary tales as an entertainment art, compare the account of Fis Mac Fochmarc in the late Middle Irish *Tromdámh Guaire* ('Guaire's Burdensome Poetic Band'; ed. M. Joynt, Mediæval and Modern Irish Series, volume 2 [Dublin, 1931], pp. 31–2, lines 1005–26).

25 TCD, MS 1339 (H. 2. 18; Book of Leinster), fol. 101v, col. a (R.I. Best, O. Bergin, M.A. O'Brien, and A. O'Sullivan, eds. *The Book of Leinster formerly Lebar na Núachongbála*, 6 vols [Dublin, 1954–83] III, 542, line 16741). Gilla Mo Dutu úa Casaide was active at Devenish monastery, co. Fermanagh. Just as *senchas* links with *scélaigecht*, as has been seen, so both also link with *seinm* ('instrumental music'); for example, *senchas* consorts with *seinm* in an entry of 1512 in the Annals of the Four Masters (J. O'Donovan, ed., *Annala Rioghachta Eireann. Annals of the Kingdom of Ireland by the Four Masters, from the Earliest Period to the Year 1616*, 7 vols [Dublin, 1851] V, 1312): 'Niall mac cuinn mic aodha buidhe mic briain bhallaigh í neill tighearna trin conghail … fer erccna eolach ar gach nealadhain etir Shenchus, dhan, 7 Sheinm do écc .11. April' ('Niall, son of Con, son of Aodh buidhe, son of Briain Ballagh Ó Néill, Lord of Trian Congail … a man skilled in the sciences, both of *senchas*, poetry, and music, died 11 April').

26 Dublin, Marsh's Library, MS Z.3.1.5 (Codex Kilkenniensis), fol. 107v, col b. On the composition date of the *vita*, see R. Sharpe, *Medieval Irish Saints' Lives: An Introduction to Vitae Sanctorum Hiberniae* (Oxford, 1991), pp. 216 and 370.

27 For instance, the strings on the harp in this picture run in the wrong direction (and see further B. Boydell, 'Music before 1700,' in W. Moody and W.E. Vaughan, eds., *A New History of Ireland IV Eighteenth-Century Ireland 1691–1800* [Oxford, 1986], p. 544). Derricke's commentary too is polemically hostile to native Irish culture (John Derricke, *The Image of Irelande* [London, 1581; *STC* 6734], sig. Fii–iiv; facsimile reprint ed. D.B. Quinn [Belfast, 1985]).

28 Bodl., MS Tanner 444, fol. 5: 'Duo Serui sedebant in terram more Mulierum (sub reuerentia sit dictum) quando chaccant in aprico campo, nisi quod istorum Nates premebant terram' ('Two servants were sitting on the ground in the manner of women [let it be said reverently] when they defecate in open field, apart from the fact that their buttocks were pressing the ground'; 'Bodley's Visit to Lecale, County of Down, A.D. 1602–3,' *Ulster Journal of Archæology* 2 (1854), 73–95; see p. 94). Admittedly, Bodley refers to the hunkering position as a woman's posture.

29 Patterson, *Cattle-Lords*, p. 342, has unhesitatingly interpreted them as performers of *braigitóracht* (on which see further below). P.A. Breatnach, 'Moladh na Féile: Téama i bhFilíocht na Scol,' *Léachtaí Cholm Cille* 24 (1994), 61–76, makes an interesting connection between the Derricke scene and the performance of *crosántacht*, a prose and verse medley in which praise poetry alternated with jesting, often of a scatological kind (see especially ibid., pp. 74–5; on the *crosántacht* genre, see Harrison, *An chrosántacht*

and *Irish Trickster*, passim). Thomas Smyth's 1561 account of the recitation of Irish poetry speaks of the 'Rymer,' who sits by the chief, while his composition is recited by his 'Rakry' or 'Raker' (an anglicized form of *reccaire*, 'reciter'). But the account also mentions that his 'barde which is a kinde of folise fellowe,' accompanies the 'Rakry' too (PRO, SP 63/3, fol. 176v; H.F. Hore, 'Irish Bardism in 1561,' *Ulster Journal of Archaeology* 6 [1858], 165–7; p. 167). Might the bare-bottomed characters in Derricke's picture (see fig. 2) be the 'foolish fellows' noted by Smyth at recitations?

30 Note also the way in which they are associated in one of the Middle Irish poetic *dindshenchas* ('history of notable places,' or literally, 'hill-lore'): 'cornaire, bonnaire ar bríg' ('trumpeter, lusty *buinne*-player'; E. Gwynn, ed., *The Metrical Dindsenchas Part I*, Todd Lecture Series, volume 8 [Dublin, 1903], p. 26, line 171).

31 As, for example, in the Old Irish law text *Críth Gablach*: 'Cu[i]slennaig, cornairi, clesamnaig' (Binchy, *Críth Gablach*, p. 23, line 590). Note also *na pipairedha 7 na clesamnaig 7 na cornaireda 7 na cuislennaig* ('the pipers and the jugglers and the horn-players and the *cuisle*-players') who consort in the quotations from Old Irish law tracts in TCD, MS 1337 (H. 3. 18), p. 874 (*CIH*, III, 1108, lines 23–4).

32 Radner, *Fragmentary Annals*, p. 74.

33 TCD, MS 1339 (H. 2. 18; Book of Leinster), fol. 165v, col. a (E. Gwynn, ed. *The Metrical Dindsenchas Part III*, Todd Lecture Series, volume 10 [Dublin, 1913], p. 18, lines 233–6). The possibility that the poem was composed to commemorate the *aonach* held by Conchobar úa Conchobair in 1079 is explored by Gwynn, ibid., p. 471.

34 TCD, MS 1339 (H. 2. 18; Book of Leinster), fol. 165v, col. a (Gwynn, ibid., p. 20, lines 257–60). In translating *égair* as 'prophane' I have followed Gwynn. It is not clear how these groups would have performed, whether collectively, individually, or both. *DIL* directs us to p. 477 of Gwynn's edition for notes on *fáen-chlíara*. The adjective *fáen* means 'sprawling,' 'prostrate,' 'supine.' It collocates with entertainers elsewhere (compare, for example, the *fuirseoir fáen* in Gwynn, *Metrical Dindsenchas Part I*, p. 26, line 165). The words *fir cengail* are also difficult; they might alternatively be rendered 'men without weapons.'

35 *Drúth*, like the English word 'fool,' is also used to denote madmen or imbeciles, people generally incapable of responsible behaviour (*DIL*, 2 **drúth**, sub-sense II; in this sense it is virtually synonymous with the word *amatán*, '[congenital] fool'). The word *óinmhid*, like *drúth*, can also be used to describe both classes of fool, the professional and the congenital. In the Yellow Book of Lecan plan, *óinmite* ('fools,' presumably of the professional sort) are included as well as the *druith ríg*; they sit in the near-right rank between *deogbaire* ('drink-bearers') and *léigi 7 luamaire* ('physicians and sailors'); Atkinson, *Yellow Book of Lecan*, p. 418. Probably the actions of both classes of fool were sufficiently similar to render the same word apt for both.

36 While a *drúth ríg* suggests a royal or king's jester, some records speak of a *rígdrúth*, a compound admitting three possible interpretations, as Harrison, *Irish Trickster*, p. 27,

has pointed out. Like *drúth ríg*, it could also mean a royal or king's jester, as is the likely meaning in the late Old Irish text *Cath Cinn Abrad* (the 'Battle of Cenn Abrad'), for example (M. O Daly, ed. *Cath Maige Mucrama*, Irish Texts Society 50 [Dublin, 1975], p. 88, lines 715–16), and in addition either a jester who is a king or a jester who is 'king' or master of a jester band.

37 There are a few unusual cases where the word does indeed imply considerable status, as for example in the title *primdruith 7 primollom Condacht* ('chief *drúth* and chief professor of Connacht') given *s.a.* 1067 to one Murchad Úa Carrthaig in the Annals of Tigernach (W. Stokes, 'The Annals of Tigernach. The Fourth Fragment, A.D. 973 – A.D. 1088,' *Revue Celtique* 17 [1896], 337–420; see p. 406). (The *ollam*, a word in later Classical Irish meaning an 'expert in any art or science,' a 'professor,' was a man of high social rank.) However, as *DIL*, 2 **drúth**, subsense I(b) notes, there may be some confusion of the word *drúth* here with *druí* (in later Classical Irish, a 'poet,' 'learned man'; *DIL*, **druí**, subsense [c]). Closeness in spelling, and a certain overlap in meaning, were liable to lead to such confusion.

38 BL, MS Harley 432, fol. 8 (*CIH*, II, 372, lines 31–2).

39 E. MacNeill, 'Ancient Irish Law. The Law of Status or Franchise,' *Proceedings of the Royal Irish Academy* 36 (1923), 265–316; pp. 270–1.

40 TCD, MS 1337 (H. 3. 18), volume 3, p. 16, col. a (*CIH*, II, 585, lines 25–6). The tract has been referred to as the sequel to *Críth Gablach*, but see Kelly, *Early Irish Law*, p. 265. Compare the *Sanas Cormaic* entry, note 62 below.

41 RIA, MS 536 (23 P 12; Book of Ballymote), p. 348, col. a (*CIH*, V, 1617, lines 11–20). Though dated to the late seventh or early eighth century by D.A. Binchy, 'The Date and Provenance of *Uraicecht Becc*,' *Ériu* 18 (1958), 44–54, *Uraicecht Becc* must postdate the composition of the law tract *Bretha Nemed toísech*, on which it draws, and which has been dated to between 721 and 742 (L. Breatnach, 'Law,' in K. McCone and K. Simms, eds., *Progress in Medieval Irish Studies* [Maynooth, 1996], pp. 107–21; see p. 119). The Middle Irish commentary on *Uraicecht Becc*'s canonical text may date to as early as the eleventh century (K. Simms, 'The Brehons of Later Medieval Ireland,' in D. Hogan and W.N. Osborough, eds., *Brehons, Serjeants and Attorneys: Studies in the History of the Irish Legal Profession* [Dublin, 1990], pp. 51–76; see p. 66). *Uraicecht Becc*, another of the *Nemed* group of law texts, may like them have originated in Munster.

42 The meaning of some of this passage is puzzling. The *gillai urraith* (lines 3–4 of translation) were evidently servants of some kind (*DIL*, **gilla**, subsense [d]). Who the *creccairi* were, and what the green *crecad* was (tentatively interpreted as a form of tattooing in *DIL*), are difficult to determine. However, F. Kelly, 'Old Irish *creccaire*, Scottish Gaelic *kreahkir*,' *Ériu* 37 (1986), 185–6, has plausibly suggested that a *creccaire* might have been one of the *fodána* ('lowly professions'), a person who entertained his patron with raucous chatter. I am grateful to Professor Tomás Ó Cathasaigh for help with textual difficulties.

43 RIA, MS 1229 (23 E 25; Lebor na hUidre), p. 92, col. b (R.I. Best and O. Bergin, eds., *Lebor na hUidre* [Dublin and London, 1929], p. 231, lines 7556–9). Though the earliest written account as such (*Lebor na hUidre* dates to sometime before 1106, the year in which its principal scribe died; the story necessarily antedates its copying), it is interesting to note that these Celtic jugglers seem to have had Anglo-Saxon colleagues. A near-contemporary illustration in BL, MS Cotton Tiberius C. vi, fol. 30v, depicts King David surrounded by four lesser figures. Two play horns of different kinds, the third plays a viol-like instrument, and the fourth, the figure in the top left-hand corner of the illustration, is clearly juggling with three knives and three balls (C.R. Dodwell, *The Canterbury School of Illumination 1066–1200* [Cambridge, 1954], plate 10a; for further commentary, see A.J. Fletcher, 'Jugglers Celtic and Anglo-Saxon,' *Theatre Notebook* 44 [1990], 2–10). The twelfth-century H interpolator of *Togail Bruidne Da Derga* in the *Lebor na hUidre* also described the cubicle of the three lesser jugglers named Cless ('Trick'), Clissíne ('Little Trick'), and Clessamun ('Trickster'). Like Tulchinne, they too had shields, balls, and little spears (Best and Bergin, *Lebor na hUidre*, p. 234, lines 7643–5).

44 TCD, MS 1433 (E. 3. 5), part 1, p. 37, col. b (*CIH*, I, 288, lines 11–12).

45 See note 31 above for Old Irish examples of *clesamnaigh* in the company of various musicians.

46 The root of the word *clesamnach* means essentially a 'feat' or 'trick' (*DIL*, **cles**, subsenses (a) and (c); sometimes it may mean the instrument with which the trick was performed, as illustrated in subsense (b)).

47 L.H. Loomis, 'Secular Dramatics in the Royal Palace, Paris, 1378, 1389, and Chaucer's "Tregetoures,"' *Speculum* 33 (1958), 242–55 (reprinted in J. Taylor and A.H. Nelson, eds., *Medieval English Drama* [Chicago and London, 1972], pp. 98–115).

48 Loomis, 'Secular Dramatics' (in Taylor and Nelson, *Medieval English Drama*), p. 100, reproduces the illustration.

49 Rennes, Bibliothèque Municipale, MS 598 (15,489), fol. 67v, col. a (W. Stokes, 'The Gaelic Maundeville,' *Zeitschrift für celtische Philologie* 2 [1899], 1–63 and 226–312; see p. 270). The text was translated into Irish from an English source at Rosbrin, co. Cork, by the Irish chieftain, Fingin O'Mahony (1496). Evidently, *clesaigecht* was thought an appropriate feature of exotic foreign courts. Compare W. Stokes, 'The Gaelic Abridgement of the Book of Ser Marco Polo,' *Zeitschrift für celtische Philologie* 1 (1897), 245–73 and 362–438; see p. 374: 'Seinnter gach fogur 7 gach ceól for bith doibh, co mbi an t-istad uile 'na cairchi ciuil. Doghniad foireann ele cleasaighecht 7 amuinsi doibh.' ('Every tune and melody is played to them, so that the whole court becomes a sound of music. Another set perform tricks and jugglery for them.') This text is also fifteenth-century.

50 And compare S. Ó Suilleabháin, *Irish Wake Amusements* (Cork, 1967; repr 1969), p. 94, for a modern *cleas* whose nature was fully mimetic, the *Cleas an Stóilín* (the 'Stool Trick').

51 BL, MS Additional 18747, fol. 73r–v (S.H. O'Grady, *Silva Gadelica*, 2 vols [London and Edinburgh, 1892] I, 285–6). The earliest version of *Cetharnach Uí Dhomnaill* of which I am aware, however, is preserved in Edinburgh, Advocates' Library, MS 72. 1. 36 (the equivalent passage to that cited above is found on fol. 124r–v). Though the Edinburgh version is less vividly told, and written in *oratio obliqua*, its substance nevertheless agrees with the Additional 18747 version.

52 Compare, for example, the *druith delma aitt* ('fool strange of sound') noted below.

53 D.A. Binchy, 'Bretha Crólige,' *Ériu* 12 (1938), 1–77; p. 48: 'Dlomthair a urcoillte ina otharli(u)g[i]u len. ni l[e]icter fair hi teg druith na dasachtaig … ni fertar cluichi fair hi tig' ('Let there be proclaimed what things are forbidden in regard to him [who is] on his sickbed of pain: there are not admitted to him into the house fools or lunatics. … No games are played in the house'). Although there may be some doubt about whether the *drúith* are professional or congenital, the quotation from the *Di Chethairslicht Athgabála* cited below which bans 'fools and satirists' in similar circumstances suggests the *drúith* intended in the *Bretha Crólige* may well be professional ones. (The composition of *Bretha Crólige* has been dated to the eighth century.)

54 BL, MS Harley 432, fol. 9, col. a (*CIH*, II, 369, line 30): 'na lecter fair i tech druith na cainti' ('fools and satirists are not to be let into the house').

55 TCD, MS 1339 (H. 2. 18; Book of Leinster), fol. 15, col. b (Best, Bergin, O'Brien, and O'Sullivan, *Book of Leinster*, I, 119, line 3758).

56 BR, MS 5301–20, p. 10 (Ó Riain, *Cath Almaine*, p. 9, lines 106–12; the Fergal referred to in the passage was Fergal mac Máele Dúin of the Cenél Eogain, king of Tara). The association of the fool here with a bog (*monaidh*), an inhospitable and liminal place, is interesting. The text known as O'Mulconry's Glossary, which derives its name from one of the Ó Maoilchonaire scribes active in the portion of the Yellow Book of Lecan in which it appears, defines a *grellach* (usually, 'bog,' 'swamp') as an *ech crosain* ('horse of a *crosán*'; TCD, MS 1318 [H. 2. 16; Yellow Book of Lecan], col. 114; W. Stokes, 'O'Mulconry's Glossary,' *Archiv für celtische Lexikographie* 1 [Halle, 1900], 232–324; see p. 264), which seems strange. Conceivably if *ech* here has suffered scribal apocope from an original *echrais* ('resort,' 'meeting place'), the definition would be understandable: perhaps such uncongenial territory was thought an appropriate and typical abode for *crosáin* and their ilk. (The compilation of the glossary is dated by Stokes, 'O'Mulconry's Glossary,' p. 232 to the thirteenth or at latest the fourteenth century.) However, as the *DIL* takes it, *grellach* may be a variant of *grell*, a word also appearing in the glossary where it is defined as an 'animal retroambulans is aire itberar drochech' ('an animal going backwards, that is a bad horse'). In which case, the *crosán* would here be associated with an inferior beast, and that too would be quite in keeping with his low status.

57 Bodl., MS Rawlinson B. 502, fol. 36, col. b (W. Stokes, ed., *The Saltair na Rann* [Oxford, 1883], p. 98, line 6684). This poem was composed *c* 988 (K. Jackson, 'The Historical Grammar of Irish: Some Actualities and Some Desiderata,' in G. Mac Eoin, ed., *Proceedings of the Sixth International Congress of Celtic Studies* [Dublin, 1983],

pp. 1–18; p. 8). However, if *Saltair na Rann* is here anticipating 2 Kings 6:20, Michal's exasperation that David had behaved as 'unus de scurris,' it might be retailing an exegetical commonplace, one found not only in Ireland (the eighth-century compiler of the Reichenau Glossary glossed 'scurris' with 'ioculator,' for example; see P. Corbett, *The Scurra* [Edinburgh, 1986], p. 82).

58 Earlier opinion that held that Gaelic society was innocent of dancing should be jettisoned. To the evidence assembled by M. Ó Sé, 'Notes on Old Irish Dances,' *Journal of the Cork Historical and Archæological Society* 60 (1955), 57–63 and A. Fleischmann, 'The Evidence for Dancing in Ancient Ireland I – Further Evidence,' *Journal of the Cork Historical and Archæological Society* 61 (1956), 58–9 (and notwithstanding the caveats entered by R.A. Breatnach, 'The Evidence for Dancing in Ancient Ireland,' *Journal of the Cork Historical and Archæological Society* 60 [1955], 88–94, 'II – Rejoinder,' *Journal of the Cork Historical and Archæological Society* 61 [1956], 59–60, and 'IV – Rejoinder,' ibid., 65–70) may be added S. Donnelly, 'Dance of Death,' *Ceol na hÉireann* 1 (1993), 74. P. Jovius, *Regionum et insularum atque locorum descriptiones* (Basle, 1578), p. 31, says of Irish women: 'Appellantibus festiuè arrident, & nonnun-quam choreas ad Arpen ducunt … per æreas impa-res chordas argutis digitis pulsant, & modulos alludente uoce comitantur.' ('They laugh merrily at those who call [them], and often lead dances to Arpen (?) … they strike bronze strings of different lengths with their nimble fingers, and accompany the melody with merry voice.') Compare also Philip O'Sullivan Beare in his *Zoilomastix* of *c* 1625, who said that the Irish were *arte saltandi dexterrimi, & agilissimi* ('most dexterous and agile in the art of dancing'; UUL, MS H. 248, fol. 133v).

59 The association may not have been entirely startling, however, given the traditional king/jester liaison. See below. Precisely the same simile was applied to King David in the thirteenth-century Old Norse text *Stjórn*, which translates the Vulgate Old Testament. He was said to have resembled a *trúðr* dancing (C.R. Unger, ed. *Stjórn* [Christiania, 1862], p. 505). Whether any textual dependence connects the Old Irish and Old Norse texts is beyond the scope of the present enquiry.

60 CHL, Book of Lismore, fol. 190v, col. b (M. Joynt, *Tromdámh Guaire*, Mediæval and Modern Irish Series, vol. 2 [Dublin, 1931], p. 27, lines 858–9). That the performers were not specifically *drúith* in the story is immaterial, given the essential interrelation between the entertainer classes now established. Though *crónán* performance must in essence have been some kind of vocal art, *crónán snagach* was evidently more than this, requiring a performance that was also in some way physically energized and demanding.

61 It might be noted that *fuirseoire* appear in the Yellow Book of Lecan version of the seating plan, between the *creacoire* (on the possible meaning of this word, see note 42 above) and the *braigitoire* ('farters') towards the bottom of the near-right rank (Atkinson, *Yellow Book of Lecan*, p. 418).

62 TCD, MS 1318 (H. 2. 16; Yellow Book of Lecan), col. 77 (O.J. Bergin, R.I. Best, K. Meyer, and J.G. O'Keeffe, eds., *Anecdota from Irish Manuscripts*, 5 vols [Halle and Dublin, 1907–13] IV, 95). The *Sanas Cormaic* (usually translated 'Cormac's Glossary')

is attributed to Cormac Úa Cuilennáin (†903), a prince of Cashel and later its bishop. Its core material may be late Old Irish, amplified in the Middle Irish period. (P. Russell, 'The Sounds of Silence: The Growth of Cormac's Glossary,' *Cambridge Medieval and Celtic Studies* 15 [1988], 1–30.) Compare the definition of the *réim* with that given in the *Míadślechta* cited above, note 40.

63 RIA, MS 536 (23 P 12; Book of Ballymote), p. 348, col. a (*CIH*, V, 1617, line 16).

64 TCD, MS 1339 (H. 2. 18; Book of Leinster), fol. 198v (D. Greene, ed., *Fingal Rónáin and Other Stories*, Mediæval and Modern Irish Series, volume 16 [Dublin, 1955], p. 7, lines 153–9).

65 See further E. Poppe, 'A Note on the Jester in *Fingal Rónáin*,' *Studia Hibernica* 27 (1993), 145–54.

66 Etymologically, *drúth* is connected with *drúis* ('lewd behaviour'); Harrison, *Irish Trickster*, p. 26.

67 England had its professional farters too, but unlike the Irish ones, their names seldom declare their avocation (see further on this in chapter 2; Roland *le Fartere*, who entertained Henry II, seems exceptional). Should the idea of an elaborated art of farting sound preposterous, it is worth recalling an undisputable case nearer to our own time. The show-stopping performances of Monsieur Joseph Pujol, a late-nineteenth-century star of the *Moulin Rouge*, were the envy of any box office. Crowds came to hear him perform an elaborate repertoire of sound effects (P. Lennon, 'Prince of Petomane,' *The Guardian* [London, 13 July 1967], p. 5; and see J. Nohain, and F. Caradec, *Le Petomane 1857–1945*, trans. W. Tute [London, 1967]). Records do not relate whether the Gallic finesse of Pujol's repertoire had any medieval Irish equivalent. Even so, his accomplishments at least illustrate what an ambitious *braigetóir* might technically aspire to.

68 RIA, MS 536 (23 P 12; Book of Ballymote), p. 348, col. a (*CIH*, V, 1617, line 17).

69 Sometimes, indeed, *braigetóracht* may have denoted scurrilous buffoonery in general, in which farting in the specialized sense may or may not have been present. (*DIL*, **braigetóracht**, cites the excerpt from *Aislinge Meic Con Glinne* discussed below to illustrate the general sense.) It is interesting to note the association in some texts (as indeed in *Aislinge Meic Con Glinne*) of *cáinte* and *braigetóir*. For example, the Middle Irish poetic *Suidigud Taigi Midchúarda* (the 'Settling of the *Tech Midchúarda*') mentions the *Cuit cáinte 7 braigire. ni léicther ifaill. remur nimda uuall co grinn ni dimda phr[i]aind.* ('The satirist's share and farter's is not neglected. The fat of the shoulder to them pleasantly, not unpleasant to be divided'; TCD, MS 1339 [H. 2. 18; Book of Leinster], fol. 15, col. b; Best, Bergin, O'Brien, and O'Sullivan, *Book of Leinster*, I, 120, lines 3766–9).

70 RIA, MS 1230 (23 P 16; *Leabhar Breac*), p. 215, col. b (K.H. Jackson, ed., *Aislinge Meic Con Glinne* [Dublin, 1990], p. 18, lines 546–50). The story was probably composed in the last quarter of the eleventh century (Jackson, *Aislinge*, p. xxvi), though its earliest manuscript, the *Leabhar Breac*, was copied in the opening years of the fifteenth century.

71 As, for example, the barb: 'Átá ben istír, ní abraim a hainm, / maidid essi a deilm amal chloich a tailm' ('There's a woman in the land, I don't mention her name. Her fart flies from her like a stone from a sling'; K. Meyer, ed., *Bruchstüke der älteren Lyrik Irlands* [Berlin, 1919], p. 34, number 77).

72 Such performance seems implied in the *Aislinge Meic Con Glinne* passage just quoted. J.E. Caerwyn Williams, 'Posidonius's Celtic Parasites,' *Studia Celtica* 14–15 (1979–80), 313–43, notes some extravagantly theatrical performances of satire (see p. 331). Greenland Inuit, for example, apparently treated satire, an instrument of social discipline in their culture, as a public entertainment. Quarrels might be settled by a duel of insults in which the contestants struggled to outface each other with mockery, to the accompaniment of a drum.

73 *DIL*, **mac(c)fuirmid**; the *maccfuirmid* does not appear on the Yellow Book of Lecan plan. On the poetic grades generally, see Breatnach, *Uraicecht na Ríar*, passim.

74 *DIL*, **fochloc**; the *fochloc* appears on the Yellow Book of Lecan plan. On the poetic grades generally, see Breatnach, *Uraicecht na Ríar*, passim.

75 The word *cáinte* does not appear on the Book of Leinster plan. On the Yellow Book of Lecan plan, *cáinti* sit towards the bottom of the near-left rank, next to the *clessamnaig*.

76 Compare also the curiously theatrical liturgy of cursing which features in RIA, MS 536 (23 P 12; Book of Ballymote), p. 294, col. a (W. Stokes, 'The Second Battle of Moytura,' *Revue Celtique* 12 [1891], 52–130; see pp. 119–21). A representative of each of the seven poetic grades was to go before sunrise to a hilltop at the boundary of seven lands. The back of each poet was to be turned to a hawthorn which should also be on the hilltop. The wind had to be blowing from the north. Each poet was to have a slingstone in one hand and in the other a thorn from the hawthorn. Each was to sing his peculiar verse to the slingstone and thorn, then deposit them at the foot of the hawthorn. If the poets were in the wrong, they might expect the earth to swallow them. Alternatively, the same fate would be visited upon the chieftain and members of his household, including his dog. A version of this text in *CIH*, V, 1564, line 27 – 1565, line 19 offers each poet the option of carrying a clay image of the man satirized; their thorns are to be stuck into the image.

77 Compare the description of a *crosán* in one of the Old Irish triads: 'A tri nemtiger croosan rig a oile righ a teighe righe a brond' ('A *crosán* is identified by three things: a stretched mouth, a stretched stomach, a stretched bag [i.e., testicles?]'; cited here from the Old Irish law tract *Bretha Nemed toísech* [the 'First *Bretha Nemed*'] witnessed in BL, MS Cotton Nero A. vii, fol. 144).

78 Compare the verdict delivered on them by the eleventh-century text *Fís Adamnáin* (the 'Vision of Adamnáin'): 'IS iat iarom filet isin phéin sin .i. gataige 7 ethgig 7 æs braith 7 écnaig 7 slataige 7 crechaire 7 brethemain gúbrethaig 7 æs cosnoma mná aupthacha 7 cánti. aithdibergaig 7 fir légind pridchiat eris.' ('These then are they who will be in that torment, that is, thieves and perjurers and treacherous folk and slanderers and robbers and plunderers and false judges and litigious folk, sorceresses and satirists,

inveterate robbers and men of learning who preach heresy'; Best and Bergin, *Lebor na Huidre*, p. 74, lines 2189–92). The *Immacallam in Dá Thuarad* ('Conversation of the Two Sages'), an Old Irish text (J. Carey, 'An Edition of the Pseudo-Historical Prologue to the *Senchas Már*,' *Ériu* 45 [1994], 1–32; see p. 27), observes that among the signs of the last days will be the fact that *fochiura cách cainte do chániud dar a chend* ('everyone will buy a satirist to satirize on his behalf'; W. Stokes, 'The Colloquy of the Two Sages,' *Revue Celtique* 26 [1905], 4–64; p. 40).

79 Kelly, *Early Irish Law*, p. 138. The *cáinte*, lumped together with the *díbergach* ('marauder') in the Old Irish *Bretha Crólige*, was one of those of whom it might be said *is techtta le dia a ndinsed oldas a cumdac* ('it is more fitting in God's sight to repudiate than to protect them'; Binchy, *Bretha Crólige*, p. 40). On the association of the *cáinte* and *díbergach*, see K.R. McCone, 'Werewolves, Cyclopes, *Díberga*, and Fíanna: Juvenile Delinquency in Early Ireland,' *Cambridge Medieval Celtic Studies* 12 (1986), 1–22.

80 For a recent account of praise poetry, its authors and their social function, see P.A. Breatnach, 'The Chief's Poet,' *Proceedings of the Royal Irish Academy* 83 (1983), 37–79.

81 The poem on the *oenach* of Tailtiu discussed below is attributed to him in some manuscripts. His devastating satire is noted in the Annals of Ulster, *s.a.* 1024 (S. Mac Airt and G. Mac Niocaill, eds., *The Annals of Ulster [to A.D. 1131]* [Dublin, 1983], p. 462): 'Cuan H. Lothchan, primeices Erenn, do marbad ... Brenait a n-aen [uair] in luchc ro marb' ('Cúan úa Lothcháin, chief poet of Ireland, was murdered ... The killers became rotten within one hour').

82 Sir Philip Sidney, *An Apology for Poetry or the Defense of Poesy*, ed. G. Shepherd (London, 1965), p. 142, line 26: 'to be rhymed to death, as is said to be done in Ireland'; J.P. Turner, ed., *A Critical Edition of James Shirley's St. Patrick for Ireland* (New York and London, 1979), p. 141, lines 12–13: 'The King's merry Bard; if he have overheard, hee'le save the hangman a labour, and rime me to death.'

83 And indeed to regulate the publishing of satire generally, by no matter whom. The *cáinte* is generally profiled in K.R. McCone, 'A Tale of Two Ditties: Poet and Satirist in Cath Maige Tuired,' in D. Ó Corráin, L. Breatnach, and K.R. McCone, eds., *Sages, Saints and Storytellers: Celtic Studies in Honour of Professor James Carney*, Maynooth Monographs 2 (Maynooth, 1989), pp. 122–43.

84 My emphasis here (and elsewhere in this chapter) tends to isolate the *entertainment* and *performance* aspect of the role under discussion. For example, in other circumstances the *senchaid* is likely to have been called as a solemn witness in property disputes, just as in the case of the *drúth* there is some reason for believing that he might be required to wait at table (see below, and note 157).

85 Compare in this respect the early art of one Vitalis, a *mimus* whose epitaph, composed sometime between the ninth and twelfth centuries, declared: 'Fingebam vultus, habitus, ac verba loquentum / Ut plures uno crederes ore loqui' ('I used to invent the expressions, costumes and words of the people speaking, so that you'd believe several people

to be speaking through the same mouth'). A. Riese and F. Buecheler, eds., *Anthologia Latina sive Poesis Latinae supplementum recens*, 2 vols (Leipzig, 1869–1926) I:2, number 487A.

86 See also P. MacCana, *The Learned Tales of Medieval Ireland* (Dublin, 1984), p. 11.

87 J.H. Delargy, 'The Gaelic Story-Teller, with some Notes on Gaelic Folk Tales,' *Proceedings of the British Academy* 31 (1945), 177–221.

88 Ibid., p. 190 (my italics).

89 Some of the circumstances of his storytelling, its taking place at night, for example, compare with much earlier sources; MacCana, *Learned Tales*, pp. 10–11.

90 The asking of riddles is well illustrated in the case of Dael Duiled, for example, who was a member of the burdensome troupe of poets in the *Tromdámh Guaire* (Joynt, *Tromdámh Guaire*, pp. 27–8, lines 868–900). His skill or 'art' (*ealada*) was to pose (and know the answers to) various conundrums.

91 The three entertainers at an assembly, say the Irish Triads, are 'a *drúth*, a *fuirseóir* and a lap-dog' ('drúth, fuirsire, oirce'); K. Meyer, ed., *The Triads of Ireland*, Todd Lecture Series, volume 13 (Dublin, 1906), p. 32. Meyer dates the Triads to the ninth century. Compare the performance of the *trúðr* Andaðr in the poem *Haraldskvæði*, attributed to Þorbjörn Hornklofi, *c* 900 (B. Einarsson, ed., *Fagrskinna*, *Íslensk Fornrit* 29 [Reykjavík, 1984], p. 64: 'At hundi elskar Andaðr / ok heimsku drýgir / eyrnalausum / ok jǫfur hlægir' ['Andaðr plays with an earless dog and commits foolery and the king laughs']).

92 G. Wickham, *Early English Stages 1300 to 1660*, 2nd edn, 3 vols (London and New York, 1980–1) I, 264–70.

93 I use the word 'minstrel' in a broad sense to signify a professional entertainer, often one who toured.

94 For example, the Annals of Connacht note the death in 1486 of Ruaidrí Mac Diarmata, *congbala cliar 7 cerrbach* ('supporter of minstrel bands and gamblers'; A.M. Freeman, ed., *Annals of Connacht* [Dublin, 1944], p. 588). The association between minstrels and gamblers here, incidentally, suggests that gambling was another aspect of the entertainer's craft. Other sources, discussed further below, confirm this. It might be noted that England too had a tradition of gambling and performance at least from the late-medieval period (see F.M. Powicke and C.R. Cheney, eds., *Councils and Synods with Other Documents Relating to the English Church*, 2 vols [Oxford, 1964] I, 348, for a thirteenth-century set of Norwich statutes in which plays and gambling are associated; also, see the London mumming of 1377 described in note 249 below).

95 The impact of a present-day circus clown seems comparable; here outrageous costume establishes a particular audience relationship and claims attention even before the comic routine begins. Of course, some Gaelic entertainments were played on occasions far from comic in themselves; entertainments at wakes, for example, will be considered below. However, entertainment in such circumstances was less the responsibility of professionals than of the community at large.

96 This phenomenon, or liminality, as social anthropologists have termed it, is classically expounded in A. van Gennep, *Les rites de passage. Étude systématique des rites* (Paris, 1909), and further elaborated by Victor W. Turner, *The Ritual Process: Structure and Anti-structure* (Chicago and London, 1969).

97 Róimid is described as a *rígoinmit* ('royal/king's fool'), but the compound begs comparison with the compound *rígdrúth*, on which see note 36 above.

98 TCD, MS 1339 (H. 2. 18; Book of Leinster), fol. 196, col. a (J. Carmichael Watson, ed. *Mesca Ulad* [Dublin, 1941], pp. 30–1). This tale is generally thought to have been redacted in the late eleventh or early twelfth century.

99 M. Twycross and S. Carpenter, 'Masks in Medieval English Theatre,' *Medieval English Theatre* 3 (1981), 7–44; see pp. 10–12.

100 RIA, MS 1223 (Stowe D iv 2), fol. 51, col. a (A. Harrison, 'Séanadh Saighre,' *Éigse* 20 [1984], 136–48; see p. 142).

101 Though the *crosáin* here are demonic, hence perhaps their blackening, their chant (and probably by extension their appearance) is nevertheless presented as the prototype of all later *crosáin*. See Harrison, 'Séanadh Saighre,' p. 142, where the *crosáin* were *ac cliaraighecht amhail is bés do chrosánaibh ó sin anall* ('chanting over the grave as is the custom of *crosáin* from that time on').

102 *Mesca Ulad* and *Sénadh Saigri* contain the earliest suggestions of face-blackening of which I am aware. Face-blackening has persisted in certain present-day mumming plays (A. Gailey, *Irish Folk Drama* [Cork, 1969], p. 66), and as Gailey, ibid., p. 101, observes, when these mummings were being imported into Ireland, they would not have been entering a culture devoid of comparable folk customs.

103 Again the *Mesca Ulad* account is a particularly early instance in the British Isles of the bell-bearing fool. On the use of bells by fools, see S. Billington, *A Social History of the Fool* (Brighton and New York, 1984), passim. Bells added a dimension of aural strangeness to the general project of otherness which was the fool's performance objective. As noted above, Irish fools also used strange sounds, doubtless to similar liminal effect.

104 Jackson, *Aislinge*, p. 18, lines 545–6: 'gabaid gerrchochall ocus gerrétach imme: girra cach n-úachtarach lais, ocus libru cach n-íchtarach' ('he put on a short hooded garment and short clothes about him: each over-thing that he had was shorter, and each under-thing longer').

105 A. O'Sullivan, 'Verses on Honorific Portions,' in J. Carney and D. Greene, eds. *Celtic Studies: Essays in Memory of Angus Matheson* (London, 1968), pp. 118–23; see p. 120: *A cruachait do crosanaib / ma cennaib coirigtir* ('Its rump to *crosáin*; they are got up with head-dress[?]').

106 Best, Bergin, O'Brien, and O'Sullivan, *Book of Leinster*, V, 1291, lines 38391–415. The incident also connects with an Irish literary topos, the death of the fool in his king's stead. The close association of fool and king manifests itself in other respects.

For example, the *drúth* of Fiachna meic Baetán in the *Mionannála* ('Minor Annals'), *s.a.* 626, who expressed a wish to die in battle with his lord, was promised that his wish would be granted (O'Grady, *Silva Gadelica*, I, 393). And see further below.

107 The *mind* of the fool Da Déra mac Dairbrech in the *Cath Maige Mucrama* (the 'Battle of the Plain of Mucrama'), a text probably of the first half of the ninth century, must have been like this. Here, Da Déra saved the life of his lord, Mac Con mac Luigde, by changing places with him, swapping his *mind* for that of Mac Con (O Daly, *Cath Maige Mucrama*, pp. 40–2, lines 59–74).

108 Cú Chulainn killed the *drúth* of Ailill by mistaking the clothes and golden crown that the *drúth* had put on, though of course here the clothes and crown belonged to Ailill (C. O'Rahilly, ed., *Táin Bó Cúalnge* [Dublin, 1967], p. 67, lines 2461–72). In the Old Irish saga *Táin Bó Fraích*, three *drúith* wear *mind* of silver: 'Bátir tri drúith remib co mindaib argdidib fo díor' ('There were three *drúith* with silver gilt diadems'; W. Meid, ed., *Táin Bó Fraích*, Mediæval and Modern Irish Series, volume 22 [Dublin, 1967], p. 2, lines 35–6).

109 Note particularly the sentence: '**AS** briathar duinn arna crosain nach béra arnétaigini lat uair ní let fein a fuil détach umut' ('"We have [your] word," said the *crosáin*, "that you won't take our clothes with you because what you are wearing is not your own"'; RIA, MS 1134 [23 E 29; Book of Fermoy], p. 171, col. b; A.G. Van Hamel, ed. *Immrama*, Mediæval and Modern Irish Series, volume 10 [Dublin, 1941], p. 101). The tale's composition dates probably to the eleventh century (Van Hamel, *Immrama*, p. 94).

110 RIA, MS 1134 (23 E 29; Book of Fermoy), p. 171, col. b (Van Hamel, *Immrama*, p. 101).

111 Delargy, *Gaelic Story-Teller*, p. 200, observed that such entertainers were at large in Ireland 'for many centuries,' though without citing instances.

112 W. Stokes, 'The Violent Deaths of Goll and Garb,' *Revue Celtique* 14 (1893), 396–449; see p. 412. (Thurneysen, *Helden- und Königsage*, p. 485, estimated a twelfth-century composition for this tale.) The progress also included *senchaide 7 brithemain 7 echlacha 7 obláire 7 forbfhir 7 ónmiti 7 grácberthaig* ('reciters of lore and judges and whores and jugglers and servants and fools and criers'; Stokes, 'Violent Deaths,' p. 414). For an account of the progress, containing harpers, of the fifth-century king of Munster, Oengus Mac Nadfráich, see C. Plummer, ed., *Bethada Náem nÉrenn. Lives of Irish Saints*, 2 vols (Oxford, 1922; repr 1968) II, 102–3.

113 *DIL*, clíar, subsense (b). The troupe of *drúith* who appear in the early-tenth-century *Bethu Phátraic* might be compared (and see further below on this). First they are spoken of as a *cléir aesa ceirdd* (a 'band of men of art'), then as *praecones* ('heralds,' 'criers'), and finally as *druthaib* (*drúith* – 'fools,' 'buffoons'). See K. Mulchrone, ed., *Bethu Phátraic: The Tripartite Life of Patrick* (Dublin and London, 1939), p. 122, lines 2382, 2385, and 2395 respectively. Other instances of itinerant troupes will emege below.

114 Nine members are often mentioned. Compare the *nónbor cáinte* ('nine *cáintí*') who accompanied Glasdámh in the *Bórama* (Best, Bergin, O'Brien, and O'Sullivan, *Book of Leinster*, V, 1291, lines 38391–2); the thrice nine of the *Tromdámh Guaire* discussed above was doubtless one of its burdensome aspects, and compare the twice nine who harrassed St Lasair, discussed below. An example of a troupe hierarchy appears in the *Immram Curaig Ua Corra* cited above, where a *taisech na clere* (a 'leader of the troupe') was evidently in charge.

115 The phrase derives from the *Táin Bó Cualnge* (O'Rahilly, *Táin Bó Cúalnge*, p. 4, line 133).

116 *Seachrán* ('wandering') is a characteristic often attributed to entertainers, and notably to the *crosáin*. Harrison, *Irish Trickster*, p. 77, would also regard the wandering of the kern in *Cetharnach Uí Dhomnaill* as typifying the ubiquitousness frequently associated with the fool/trickster figure.

117 A. Brody, *The English Mummers and their Plays: Traces of Ancient Mystery* (London, 1971), p. 17, note D.

118 TCD, MS 1318 (H. 2. 16; Yellow Book of Lecan), col. 220 (J.G. O'Keeffe, 'Cáin Domnaig,' *Ériu* 2 [1905], 189–214; see p. 208). The language of this text has been dated to the first half of the eighth century (V. Hull, 'Cáin Domnaig,' *Ériu* 20 [1966], 51–177; see pp. 156–8).

119 C. Plummer, ed. *Vitae Sanctorum Hiberniae*, 2 vols (Oxford, 1910) I, cii–ciii.

120 The formula runs as follows: (i) saint encounters jesters; (ii) these threaten satire if their demands are not met; (iii) saint miraculously meets their demands; (iv) disastrous consequences often follow for jesters. There are some variations on this. Sometimes only one jester is involved, and he may not fare too badly. In the late-twelfth-century Life of St Kentigern, the fame of King Rederech of Scotland is said to have spread far and wide: 'Qua de causa a quodam rege Ibernie joculator, officii sui peritus et expeditus, mittitur Cambriam ad predicti Regis curiam, ut videret si veritas fame tam longe lateque diffuse responderet. Admissus aule joculator manu psallebat in tympano et cithara; et letificabat Regem et palatinos ejus, omnibus diebus festivis nativitatis dominice' ('On account of which a jester, prompt and skilled in his office, is sent to Wales to the court of the aforesaid king from a certain king of Ireland, to see if there might be any truth in the reputation that had spread far and wide. Admitted to the hall, the jester made music with his hand on the *timpán* and harp, and he regaled the king and his courtiers all the feast days of the Lord's Nativity'; A.P. Forbes, ed., *Lives of S. Ninian and S. Kentigern* [Edinburgh, 1874], pp. 226–7). The *joculator* (later he is called a *histrio*) demanded a dishful of fresh blackberries as a reward, even though it was the middle of winter. These were produced with St Kentigern's help, and the *joculator/histrio* was chastened: "Amodo non recedam a domo tua, et a servitio tuo; sed ero tibi servus sempiternus, quamdiu vixero." Mansit ergo histrio in aula regis; et arte joculatoria servivit ei diebus plurimis.' ('"From now on I will not leave your house

and service, but I will always be your servant as long as I live." And so the *histrio* stayed in the king's hall and served him with his jester's art for many a day.') In time he renounced his profession and turned to the religious life (Forbes, ibid., p. 227). A vernacular version of a similar motif appears in the Middle Irish *Cath Cairn Chonaill* (the 'Battle of Carn Conaill,' a battle dated by the Annals of the Four Masters *s.a.* 645), and is used to extol the generosity of King Guaire (Best and Bergin, *Lebor na hUidre*, p. 292, lines 9725–30): 'Is é doróni in firt n-amra hi Cluain meic Nóis día rucadsom dia adnocol di. Tánic in drúth dia saigid 7 ro gab algais de im athchuingid fair. Doratsom a laim darsin forbaid immach. 7 ro gab lán a duirnd don ganium 7 ro dibairc i n-uch in druad co nderna bruth óir dé. Conid hé sin enech dedenach Guairi.' ('It is he who performed the marvellous miracle at Clonmacnoise, when he was carried there to his grave. The *drúth* came to him and repeatedly asked a boon of him. [So the dead king] put his hand out over the ground [shroud?], and took a fistful of the sand, and flung it into the *drúth*'s breast, and made a mass of gold from it. So that was Guaire's last deed of generosity.')

121 BR, MS 7672–4 (Codex Salmanticensis), fol. 173v, cols. a–b (W.W. Heist, ed., *Vitae sanctorum Hiberniae e codice olim Salmanticensi nunc Bruxellensi*, Subsidia Hagiographica 28 [Brussels, 1965], p. 296, § 29). The *Codex Salmanticensis*, from which this extract of the *Vita Sancti Flannani* is taken, may have been produced in Clogher, co. Tyrone, and dates to the beginning of the fourteenth century (M. Lapidge and R. Sharpe, *A Bibliography of Celtic-Latin Literature 400–1200* [Dublin, 1985], p. 110, item 382; P. Ó Riain, 'Codex Salmanticensis: A Provenance *inter Anglos* or *inter Hibernos?*', in T. Barnard, D.B. Cróinín and K. Simms, eds. *'A Miracle of Learning': Studies in Manuscripts and Irish Learning, Essays in Honour of William O'Sullivan* [Aldershot, 1998], pp. 91–100). The *vita* itself was composed rather earlier, *c* 1163–7 at Killaloe, on the border of cos. Clare and Tipperary (D. Ó Corráin, 'Foreign Connections and Domestic Politics: Killaloe and the Uí Briain in Twelfth-Century Hagiography,' in D. Whitelock, R. McKitterick, and D. Dumville, eds., *Ireland in Early Medieval Europe* [Cambridge, 1982], pp. 213–31; see p. 216).

122 BR, MS 2324–40, fol. 277 (Plummer, *Bethada*, I, 129): 'Tangattar aos cívil go caoimhgin do chuinge bidh fair, 7 ni raibhe agan érlamh biadh an tan sin. & at bert fríu anadh fris. Ni ro ansat. & ro gabhsat acc imdherccadh an cléirigh. Do rónadh iaramh clocha dona crannaibh civil in éraic imdherccdha an naoimh & mairid affioghracha fós isin tochar allathoir don baile.' ('Minstrels came to Coemgen to ask him for food, and the saint had no food to hand at the time. And he bade them wait for him. And they would not, but began insulting the cleric. Thereupon their wooden instruments were turned into stones in punishment for the insult offered to the saint; and the figures of them still remain on the causeway to the east of the place.') For other versions of the Coemgen story, see Plummer, *Bethada*, I, 131–67.

123 Mulchrone, *Bethu Phátraic*, p. 122, line 2395; a variant in BL, MS Egerton 97 reads

cáintib ('satirists') for druthaib ('fools, buffoons') here (E. Hogan, ed., *The Latin Lives of the Saints,* Todd Lecture Series, volume 5 [Dublin, 1894], p. 55). What often characterizes such groups is their threat of satire; on the church's attitude to satirists, see McCone, 'Two Ditties,' pp. 122–43.

124 L. Bieler, ed., *Four Latin Lives of St. Patrick* (Dublin, 1971), p. 160; Hogan, *Latin Lives,* p. 55, notes the additional text [*cum comitibus suis*] from an unnamed source manuscript.

125 Bieler, *Four Latin Lives,* p. 160: 'Tunc preco ille cum sua familia omnes mortui sunt' ('Then that crier and all his household died').

126 R. Henebry, 'The Life of Columb Cille,' *Zeitschrift für celtische Philologie* 4 (1903), 276–331; see pp. 296–8.

127 BR, MS 7672–4 (Codex Salmanticensis), fol. 89v, col. b (Heist, *Vitae Sanctorum Hiberniae,* p. 117): 'Venientibus aliquando mimis & histrionibus ad sanctum fintanum ut peterent pisces ad comedendum: ... Respondit eis. sicut uerum erat: se non habere quod petebant. Tunc mimus inquit. aqua est propinqua tibi: & si uir sanctus ut diceris esse: facile quod nos petimus a te habebimus. ...' ('*Mimi* and *histriones* once came to St Fintán to ask for fishes to eat. ... He answered them, as was true, that he did not have what they asked for. Then a *mimus* said, "There is water near you, and if you are a holy man as you say, we will easily have from you what we ask."'). Fintán sends his disciples to a well nearby, where they catch a large fish. This resists all efforts to cut it up, but the *mimi* and *histriones* are content: 'Inde mimi dixerunt. Quamuis piscis noster durus est. non tamen a nobis hic derelinquentur. {*read* derelinquetur} & abeuntes suum piscem portabant.' ('Wherefore the *mimi* said, "Although our fish is hard, we won't leave it here." And going away, they carried off their fish.') The *vita* evidently dates to before the late fourteenth century (when the Codex Salmanticensis was copied).

128 BR, MS 4190–200, fols 120v–1. The version published from RIA, MS 236 (Stowe B iv 1) by L. Gwynn, 'The Life of St. Lasair,' *Ériu* 5 (1911), 73–109, is less perfect; see p. 84 for the equivalent text to the above, where the number of visitors is substantially inflated to *náoi náonmar deicsibh 7 daos ealadhna* ('nine enneads of poets and men of learning').

129 Plummer, *Vitae Sanctorum Hiberniae,* I, cii; see also K. Simms, 'Guesting and Feasting in Gaelic Ireland,' *Journal of the Royal Society of Antiquaries of Ireland* 108 (1978), 67–100. Amongst the instructions it gives for interpreting raven cries, a unique Middle Irish tract on *flachairecht* ('raven prognostication') reveals how birds making the sounds 'graacc gracc' and 'grob grob' may disclose that *cáinti* are coming (R.I. Best, 'Prognostications from the Raven and the Wren,' *Ériu* 8 [1916], 120–6; see p. 121).

130 NA, 2/448/1, KB 2/7, p. 36. The record is a transcript of a justiciary roll for 12 June 1315. That the importunity of Gaelic minstrels was a nationwide phenomenon can be supported by a northern Irish case, in contrast to this southern one. Between 1381

and April 1404, a set of synodal statutes were issued for Armagh diocese by Archbishop John Colton. One of them decreed: 'Statutum siue statuta dominorum predecessorum nostrorum Ricardi et dauid contra minos {read mimos} ioculatores poetas timpanistas siue citharedas & precipue contra kernarios ac importunas & improbos donorum petitores quin uerius extortores editum vel edita per omnia renouamus ...' ('We renew in all respects the issued statute or statutes of our predecessors the lords Richard and David against *mimi*, jesters, poets, *timpán*-players or harpers, and especially against kerns and importunate [women] and dishonest seekers, or rather, extorters of gifts'; PRONI, DIO 4/2/3, fol. [151v]). The references to Richard and David are to the Archbishops Richard Fitzralph (†1360) and David Mág Oireachtaigh (†1346) respectively.

131 Cited in H.J. Hore and J. Graves, *The Social State of the Southern and Eastern Counties of Ireland in the Sixteenth Century* (Dublin, 1870), p. 90.

132 NA, 2/447/16, fol. [43] (D.B. Quinn, 'Calendar of the Irish Council Book, 1581–1596,' *Analecta Hibernica* 24 [1967], 93–180; see p. 133). The original, of which only calendared versions now survive, was lost in 1922. It was presented to the Irish Council by Sir Henry Wallop, treasurer at war, on 1 March 1581, as a journal of the daily and ordinary acts of the council and matters of state, and evidently ran between 1581 and 1586. The edict above was issued on 8 November 1582.

133 J.D.A. Ogilvy, '*Mimi, Scurrae, Histriones*: Entertainers of the Early Middle Ages,' *Speculum* 38 (1963), 603–19, demonstrates the likelihood of entertainers active in certain Anglo-Saxon monasteries. Since some of these monasteries had close Irish connections (Lindisfarne, for example), the possibility arises that such activity may have been transmitted to, or have entered from, Ireland. This possibility is strengthened, moreover, in view of the close association in Ireland between the poetic families, some of whose members were entertainers of the kind under consideration, and the church (especially before the twelfth-century ecclesiastical reforms drove a wedge between them), for some of the entertainers of present concern belonged to the lower poetic grades.

134 Bodl., MS Rawlinson B. 512, fol. 42v, col. a (D.A. Binchy, 'The Old-Irish Table of Penitential Commutations,' *Ériu* 19 [1962], 47–62; see p. 58). Compare also L. Bieler, ed., *The Irish Penitentials* (Dublin, 1963), p. 160: 'Haec est poenitentia magi uel uotiui mali si<ue> crudelis, [id est díbergach], uel praeconis uel cohabitatoris uel heretici uel adulteri, id est .vii. anni in pane et aqua' ('This is the penance of a magician or of one devoted to evil or of a cruel person, that is, a *díbergach* ['marauder'], or of a crier or cohabitor or heretic or adulterer, that is, seven years on bread and water'; my insertion in square brackets emends Bieler's reading *iddem ergach* here). In Bieler's view, ibid., p. 9, this text dates to probably no later than the mid-seventh century. The word to note here is *praeco* ('herald,' 'crier'). It appeared in the *Bethu Phátraic* cited above, when it was used of the petulant jester who demanded food from the

saint. On the basis of this and other cases where *praeco* = 'jester,' 'buffoon,' Harrison, *Irish Trickster*, pp. 41–3, suggests that we may be dealing here with a specifically Hiberno-Latin usage of the word.

135 TCD, MS 1316 (H. 2. 15a), volume 4, fol. 29v, col. a (*CIH*, II, 526, lines 15–17). The compiler of the *Córus Béscnai* was discussing three sorts of feast, the *fled deoda* (the 'godly feast'), the *fled doena* (the 'secular feast') and the one of which he disapproves, the *fled domonda* (the 'devil's feast'). This passage is one of the earliest extant Irish vernacular condemnations of entertainers.

136 R. Atkinson, ed., *The Passions and Homilies from the Leabhar Breac: Text, Translation and Glossary*, Todd Lecture Series, volume 2 (Dublin, 1887), p. 233, lines 6872–3. On the date of the homilies, see Jackson, 'Historical Grammar,' pp. 6–7.

137 Warnings against such folk would soon become widely known to clerics, if they were not so already, following the Fourth Lateran Council of 1215: 'Mimis, joculatoribus et histrionibus non intendant' ('Let them give no attention to *mimi, joculatores*, and *histriones*'); E. Friedberg and E.L. Richter, eds., *Corpus Iuris Canonici*, 2nd ed., 2 vols [Leipzig, 1879–81] II, 453). The author of *Aislinge Meic Con Glinne* seems to have been in touch with this clerical tradition.

138 His term for them in the *Speculum perfectionis* (quoted in E.K. Chambers, *The Mediæval Stage*, 2 vols [Oxford, 1903] I, 46).

139 Antimendicant satire made much of the friars' abilities to insinuate themselves into households. Their cultivation of entertainment arts, even if ostensibly for edifying ends, must have made them congenial and sought-after compamy. Note that it was a friar who was the clerical guest at the MacSweeney feast pictured in John Derricke's *Image of Irelande* (see fig. 2).

140 Franciscans in Ireland were evidently diverting secular entertainments to pious ends; for example, Richard Ledrede O.F.M., fourteenth-century bishop of Kilkenny, tried to rob the devil of a few of the best tunes in some of the poems of the Red Book of Ossory. A note in that manuscript (RCB, MS D 11/1/1 [Red Book of Ossory], fol. 70; J.T. Gilbert, ed., *The Manuscripts of the Marquis of Ormonde, the Earl of Fingall, the Corporations of Waterford, Galway, &c.,* Historical Manuscripts Commission, Tenth Report, Part V [London, 1885], p. 242) declares that Ledrede devised his songs *ne guttura eorum & ora deo sanctificata polluantur cantilenis teatralibus turpibus & secularibus* ('lest their throats and mouths made holy for God [i.e., those of his clerics] be polluted with theatrical, base and secular songs').

141 As might be expected, the Dominicans and Franciscans were in the vanguard; J.A. Watt, *The Church in Medieval Ireland* (Dublin, 1972), pp. 60–84.

142 Female performers like the 'she-musician' (*banairfidech*) mentioned in the late-twelfth-century *Acallamh na Senórach* (the 'Conversation of the Ancients'; W. Stokes and E. Windisch, eds., *Irische Texte mit Übersetzungen und Wörterbuch*, fourth series, 2 vols [Leipzig, 1897–1909] I, 200, line 7205) are heard of rather less frequently than their

male equivalents. Moreover, the 'she-musician' here is *Tire Tairrngaise*, 'of the Land of Promise,' a sort of Irish Elysium, and often female musicians in Gaelic tradition prove to be otherworldly. This does not mean, of course, that they never existed in reality, but it may well indicate their comparative rarity, since something quotidian is perhaps less likely to have been considered magical.

143 BL, MS Additional 30512 (Leabhar Uí Mhaoilchonaire), fol. 97, col. a (W. Stokes, 'The Fifteen Tokens of Doomsday,' *Revue Celtique* 28 [1907], 308–26; see p. 318). On its date, see M. Herbert and M. McNamara, eds., *Irish Biblical Apocrypha, Selected Texts in Translation* (Edinburgh, 1989), pp. xxiii–xxiv. A she-satirist is also mentioned briefly in the Old Irish tale of *Longes mac nUslenn* (Best, Bergin, O'Brien and O'Sullivan, *Book of Leinster*, V, 1164, lines 34386–7; the tale has been dated to the late eighth or early ninth century by V. Hull, ed., *Longes mac nUislenn* [New York, 1949], pp. 29–32). The especial reproof reserved for female satirists in the Irish laws is noted by Kelly, *Early Irish Law*, p. 50. It is interesting also to compare the hiring of female lampooners occasionally in medieval England. A female minstrel/lampooner was sent to mock Edward II in 1317 by his nobles (quoted in Chambers, *Mediæval Stage*, I, 44). For a general survey of the satirical aspect of performance in medieval England, see A. Taylor, '"To Pley a Pagyn of þe Devyl": *Turpiloquium* and the *Scurrae* in Early Drama,' *Medieval English Theatre* 11 (1989), 162–74.

144 E. Windisch, 'Ein mittelirisches Kunstgedicht über die Geburt des Königs Aed Sláne. Mit Beiträgen zur irischen Metrik,' *Königl. Sächs. Gesellschaft der Wissenschaften* 36 (1884), 191–243, considered the tale a Middle Irish composition, and since it occurs in a portion of the *Lebor na hUidre* which was copied by the scribe Máel Muire, who died in 1106, the earlier part of the Middle Irish period seems likely.

145 RIA, MS 1229 (23 E 25; Lebor na hUidre), p. 52, col. a (O'Grady, *Silva Gadelica*, I, 82–3).

146 If the *óinseach* ('fool,' 'giddy woman') ever sometimes functioned as a female version of the *drúth*, there is no clear indication of it in the literary sources surveyed by *DIL* (see *DIL*, **óinseach**). However, note that an *óinseach* tradition was strong enough to register in the mind of an antipathetic Englishman, who gave us the first recorded anglicized form of the word in a list of various other classes of reprobate entertainer. A set of *Ordinances for the Government of Ireland*, published in 1534, provided 'that no Yryshe mynstrels, rymours, shannaghes, ne bardes, *unchaghes*, nor messangers, come to desire any goodes of any man dwellinge within the Inglyshrie, uppon peyne of forfayture of all theyr goodes, and theyr bodyes to prison' (*State Papers published under the Authority of His Majersty's Commission. Volume 3. King Henry the Eighth. Part 3.* [London, 1834], p. 215). (The wording of the *Ordinances* seems dependent upon the *Breviat* of Patrick Finglas, on which see below, though the *Breviat* does not in fact mention 'unchaghes.') But it is not clear here that the 'unchaghes' of 1534 were thought to be female.

Notes to pages 35–6

147 Two other treatments exist in medieval Irish sources of the banquet performance of the daughter of Herodias (A.M. Scarre, 'The Beheading of John the Baptist by Mog Ruith,' *Ériu* 4 [1910], 173–81; see pp. 174 and 180; also, K. Müller-Lisowski, 'Texte zur Mog Ruith Sage,' *Zeitschrift für celtische Philologie* 14 [1923], 145–63; see p. 149). Both essentially agree with the details as retailed by the *Leabhar Breac* homilist, and both may be related to the source which he used.

148 RIA, MS 1230 (23 P 16; *Leabhar Breac*), p. 188, col. b (Atkinson, *Passions and Homilies*, p. 66, lines 889–90).

149 Oxford, Corpus Christi College, MS 94, fol. 654 (C. Litton Falkiner, *Illustrations of Irish History and Topography, mainly of the Seventeenth Century* [London, 1904], p. 312). It is not, however, clear whether the women here danced for personal pleasure or to order. Also compare the earlier account of Jovius cited in note 58 above.

150 B. Ó Cuív, ed., *Párliament na mBan* (Dublin, 1970), pp. 52–5. Again, however, it is not clear whether profit or pleasure was their motive.

151 For example, Thomas Smyth wrote in his 1561 tract *Information for Ireland*: 'Ther is a sorte. of women that be calleid. the goyng women they be great blasphemers of. god./ and they rune frome countrye to countrie/ soynge sedicione amongest the people/ they ar comen to all men' (PRO, SP 63/3, fol. 177; Hore, 'Irish Bardism,' p. 167). Edmund Spenser also noted in 1596 the promiscuity of the 'wandering women called Mona Shull' (*A View of the Present State of Ireland*, ed. W.L. Renwick [London, 1934; repr Oxford, 1970], p. 53). A fiant of 20 March 1588 also legislates for the punishment of 'bentules' (< *bean* + *siubhail*?; *The Sixteenth Report of the Deputy Keeper of the Public Records in Ireland* [Dublin, 1882], p. 65). Their association with other performing artists possibly suggests that they served not merely as whores or prostitutes.

152 Harrison's claim, *Irish Trickster*, p. 33, that entertainers would have been expected to be proficient in various performing skills, stands entirely vindicated.

153 Compare an episode in the late Old Irish tale of *Fled Bricrend* ('Bricriu's Feast'): 'Ardopetet iarom a n-æs ciúil ocus airfite, céin both oc taisbenad na flede dóib' ('Then musicians and minstrels played while the feast was being presented to them'; G. Henderson, ed., *Fled Bricrend*, Irish Texts Society 2 [London, 1899], p. 12, lines 29–30). Also compare a similar role for musicians in the fourteenth- or fifteenth-century narrative *Oidheadh Chloinne hUisneach* (the 'Violent Death of the Children of Uisneach'): 'Do comóradh fleadh mhórchaoin mhóradhbhal la Conchobhar mac Fachtna Fháthaigh … Agus ro éirgheadar a lucht ciúil agus oirfididh agus ealadhna do ghabháil a ndréacht agus a nduan agus a ndúchann agus a ngéag ngeinealach agus a gcraobh gcoibhneasa fiadhaibh.' ('A feast, very fine and very splendid, was held by Conchobhar son of Fachtna Fáthach … And their musicians and minstrels and men of arts rose up before them to recite their poems and their songs and their melodies and their genealogies and their branches of kinship'; C. Mac Giolla Léith, ed., *Oidheadh Chloinne hUisneach*, Irish Texts Society 56 [London, 1993], p. 86, lines 1–2 and

6–10). *Oidheadh Chloinne hUisneach* is also of interest for detailing what the musicians and poets performed. Their performance included the recitation of genealogy (the province of *senchas*). As seen earlier, recitation of genealogy was a performance art. Compare too a passage in the *Mionannála s.a.* 626, in which St Comhgall offers Fiachna, son of Deman, a simple choice – either victory in battle (and thus immortalization in bardic recitals at feasts), or the kingdom of heaven. Fiachna chooses the former: 'ocus corob ceol oc fledaib innisin a náir ocus a marbtha a bélaib bard' ('and that the story of their slaughter recited from the mouths of bards may in time coming be for melody at feasts'; O'Grady, *Silva Gadelica,* I, 393).

154 As regards wake performances, note the way in which Geoffrey Keating, in his 1631 work *Trí Bior-ghaoithe an Bháis* ('Three Shafts of Death'), amplified Matthew 9:23. The flute-players playing in the house of Jairus's dead daughter in the gospel narrative are rendered by Keating a little differently (O. Bergin, ed., *Trí Bior-ghaoithe an Bháis,* 2nd ed. [Dublin and London, 1931], p. 273, lines 8717–19): 'Ar dtús, do chuir as an dteach an tsochraide do bhí ann, idir storgánaidhe, oirfideach 7 phíobaire' ('At first, he put from the house the multitude that was there, between trumpet-players, minstrels and pipers'). Perhaps Keating had contemporary wake performers in mind. As regards performers before battle, the entertainer Donnbó was requested in the *Cath Almaine* that he might *déna airfidedh dúin a Doinnbó, fo bith as tú as deach airfididh fail in Eirinn .i. icuisigh, agas icuislendoibh, 7 icruitibh, 7 randaibh, 7 raidsechoibh, 7 rigsgelaibh Eirenn, 7 isin madinsi imbarach do beramne cath do Laignib* ('make minstrelsy for us, Donnbó, because you are the best minstrel in Ireland, that is, in whistling and in piping and in harping and verses and talk and royal stories of Ireland, and tomorrow morning we will give battle to Leinster'; Ó Riain, *Cath Almaine,* p. 5, lines 57–61).

155 A. Poncelet, ed., *Life of Mochulla, Analecta Bolandiniana* 17 (1898), 135–54; see p. 153, lines 5–6. On its composition date, see Ó Corráin, 'Foreign Connections,' pp. 216 and 219 (the *Vita Sancti Flannani,* written between 1163 and 1167 and cited above, was evidently authored by the man also responsible for the life of St Mochulla).

156 D. McCarthy, ed., *Collections on Irish Church History* (Dublin, 1861), p. 144. (This was the third *ordinatio* of the synod.) It is not clear, however, whether the *nebulones* and *joculatores* of the provincial decree were professional, amateur, or both; for other wake performances in which amateur, nonce players were involved, see below.

157 For example, the placing of guests for the feast of Tara described in the Middle Irish prose text *Suidigud Tellaig Temra* (the 'Settling of the Manor of Tara'), mentions *druith 7 deogbairi ic roind 7 ic dáil doib* ('*drúith* and cup-bearers carving and serving for them'), and *araid dano 7 oblóre 7 dorrsaidi oc roind 7 dáil doib* ('charioteers too and jugglers and doorkeepers carving and serving for them'; R.I. Best, 'The Settling of the Manor of Tara,' *Ériu* 4 [1910], 121–67; see p. 124). Also, note that the *Imda na ndeogbaire* (the 'Compartment of the cup-bearers') is described immediately *after* the *Imda na fursiri* (the 'Compartment of the clowns') in the *Togail Bruidne Da Derga.*

The practice in some Anglo-Irish and New English households was comparable, where certain domestic servants would also double as entertainers and impresarios, or vice versa, as occasion required. See further in chapter 6 on this.

158 The so-called Dalway harp, made in 1621, is perhaps one of the most potent expressions of the meeting of performance cultures at the aristocratic level. On its forepillar are carved both the arms of the Fitzgerald family and those of England. With other instances of cultural amalgamation, the harp is discussed further in chapter 6. In the interim, compare, for example, the mixing of tastes in narrative and storytelling that begins to characterize the households of the later medieval Anglo-Irish lords. Translation into Irish of medieval English romances similarly implies a mingling of cultures at the aristocratic level (F.N. Robinson, 'The Irish Lives of Guy of Warwick and Bevis of Hampton,' *Zeitschrift für celtische Philologie* 6 [1907], 9–180, 273–338). MacCana, *Learned Tales*, p. 10, also observes that in the post-Norman period, fashions in storytelling were changing in the noble households due to the availability there of imported narratives. Storytelling itself, of course, was already an established native tradition.

159 D. Comyn and P.S. Dineen, eds., *Foras Feasa ar Éirinn*, Irish Texts Society, vols 4, 8, 9, and 15 (London, 1902–14) I, 62.

160 On Keating's life, see B. Cunningham, 'Seventeenth-Century Interpretations of the Past: The Case of Geoffrey Keating,' *Irish Historical Studies* 25 (1986), 116–28; see pp. 119–20. Although educated on the Continent, Keating spent most of his adult life in Munster. I assume that he was drawing on real, rather than literary, experience here.

161 See Prologue: Insubstantial Pageants.

162 *Geiriadur Prifysgol Cymru: A Dictionary of the Welsh Language* (Cardiff, 1950–), **croessan**; also, for a twelfth-century importation into Wales of Irish harpers, see note 198 below. The possible export of the Irish word *drúth* has been discussed above in the Prologue: Insubstantial Pageants.

163 Thomas Parry, 'Statud Gruffudd ap Cynan,' *The Bulletin of the Board of Celtic Studies* 5 (1929), 25–33; see p. 27. This material first appears in a sixteenth-century copy, but its composition may be late-medieval. I am indebted to Dr J. Rowland for this Welsh reference and for its translation.

164 TCD, MS 574 (E. 3. 20), p. 153 (R. Butler, ed., *The Annals of Ireland by Friar John Clyn and Thady Dowling* [Dublin, 1849], p. 8).

165 A. Saddlemyer, ed., *J.M. Synge: Plays* (Oxford, 1968), p. 122.

166 N. Hawthorne, *The Maypole of Merry Mount*, ed. T.E. Connolly, *Nathaniel Hawthorne: The Scarlet Letter and Selected Tales* (Harmondsworth, 1970), pp. 287–98.

167 That is, when the cleric is consciously 'on duty'; the secular epic *Táin Bó Cualgne* provokes a disclaimer from its copyist in the Book of Leinster, yet he copies it nevertheless. O'Rahilly, *Táin Bó Cúalnge*, p. 136: 'Sed ego qui scripsi hanc historiam aut uerius fabulam fidem in hac historia aut fabula non accommodo. Quaedam enim ibi

sunt praestrigia demonum, quaedam autem figmenta poetica, quaedam similia uero, quaedam non, quaedam ad delectationem stultorum' ('But I who have written this story or rather this fable, give no credence to the various incidents related in it. For some things in it are the deceptions of demons, others poetic figments, some are probable, others improbable; while still others are intended for the delectation of fools').

168 Bergin, Best, Meyer, and O'Keeffe, *Anecdota*, pp. 66–7.

169 This was the *Oenach Carmun*, discussed above. The banqueting of a private household, incidentally, might also sometimes take place out of doors, as in John Derricke's account also discussed above.

170 TCD, MS 842 (F. 3. 16), fol. 199v (G. O'Brien, ed., *Advertisements for Ireland, Journal of the Royal Society of Antiquaries of Ireland*, extra volume [Dublin, 1923], p. 44). O'Brien tentatively suggests (pp. v–viii) that Sir Henry Bourgchier may have authored this tract entitled *Advertisements for Ireland.*

171 *DIL*, **forad** and **fert** respectively; also, C. Doherty, 'The Monastic Town in Early Medieval Ireland,' in H.B. Clarke and A. Simms, eds., *The Comparative History of Urban Origins in Non-Roman Europe: Ireland, Wales, Denmark, Germany, Poland and Russia from the Ninth to the Thirteenth Century* (Oxford, 1985), pp. 45–75; see pp. 51–2, where the role of the *forad* is discussed and compared with the Welsh 'play mounds.'

172 W. Stokes and J. Strachan, eds., *Thesaurus Palæohibernicus*, 2 vols (Cambridge, 1901–3; repr Oxford, 1975) I, 497, lines 38–9.

173 W. Stokes, ed., *Irish Glosses* (Dublin, 1860), p. 137. A gloss on the word *agonetetas* in the *Lorica of Gildas* poem reads: *.i. unde dicitur agonithetas? principes belli .i. nahændachu. Unde dicitur agon? .i. ænach. agon .i. cath l. cuimleng* ('that is, wherefore is it called *agonithetas?* The princes of war, that is, presidents of the *oenach*. Wherefore is it called *agon*, that is, an *oenach?* An *agon*, that is, a contest or conflict').

174 This is true even if they require a spectating audience in only the most minimal sense that players become their own spectators when there is no audience as such.

175 Gwynn, *Metrical Dindsenchas Part III*, p. 14, lines 173–6.

176 E. Gwynn, ed., *The Metrical Dindsenchas Part IV*, Todd Lecture Series, volume 11 (Dublin, 1924), p. 150, lines 45–8.

177 D.A. Binchy, 'The Fair of Tailtiu and the Feast of Tara,' *Ériu* 18 (1958), 113–38; see p. 124. Compare also the word *fert* noted above (note 171), which might denote either a burial tumulus or the raised mound at an *oenach* from which spectators could view the proceedings.

178 Durham, Dean and Chapter Muniments, Misc. Ch. 5822, mb 4; see chapter 2 for further discussion.

179 Another case in point is the association of *crosán* with three *drúith*, with three *oinmhide* a stanza later, and with dispensers and doorkeepers, in *Fégthar tech Finn a nAlmhan* ('Let us look upon the house of Fionn in Almha'): 'TRi drv́ith do bhoí astig thall .

cas is cathmháol is cValann / a tRí cRosáin mín in modh . cles is cinnmear is
cvitmhedh … TRí hoinmhide tighe finn . meall & máol & cnap / gé do bhittís
andeóigh fhían . nochas mhaith ciall na ttrí mac / A thRí dailemhain mhaithe .
drvcht dásacht & daithe / a tRí doirseóir rádh gan ghoid . dRvid & íath is oslaic'
('There were three *drúith* within, Cas and Cathmhaol and Cualann, his three *crosáin*,
a gentle way, Cleas and Cinnmhear and Cuitbheadh … Three fools of Fionn's house,
Meall and Maol and Cnap; although they used to follow the Fiana, the three boys
hadn't much good sense. His three good dispensers, Drúcht, Dásacht, and Daithe.
His three doorkeepers, a guileless saying, Druid and Íath and Oslaic '; Killiney, Fran-
ciscan Library, MS A 20, fol. 12v; G. Murphy, ed., *Duanaire Finn: The Book of the
Lays of Fionn Part I*, Irish Texts Society 7 [Dublin, 1908], p. 27, lines 24–5 and 26–7).
G. Murphy, ed., *Duanaire Finn: The Book of the Lays of Fionn Part III*, Irish Texts
Society 43 (Dublin, 1953), pp. 23–4, dates the poem probably to the late twelfth
century.

180 L. Breatnach, 'Tochmarc Luaine ocus Aided Athairne,' *Celtica* 13 (1980), 1–31; see
p. 16, lines 324–5. He dates the composition of this text to the second half of the
twelfth century.

181 W. Stokes, 'The Destruction of Dind Ríg,' *Zeitschrift für celtische Philologie* 3 (1901),
1–14; see p. 3. The *Orgain Dind Ríg* is dated to the late Old Irish period by Greene,
Fingal Rónáin, p. v.

182 *DIL*, 1 **oenach**, subsense (a).

183 Binchy, 'Fair of Tailtiu,' p. 124: [an *oenach* might feature] 'the holding of games, horse-
racing, and various athletic competitions.' See also W.M. Hennessy, 'The Curragh of
Kildare,' *Proceedings of the Royal Irish Academy* 9 (1867), 343–55; note p. 346. A
Middle Irish narrative in the Book of Leinster seems, however, to distinguish races
from games at the *oenach*: 'Agtair cluicheda 7 ferthair graifni ind Oenuch' ('the *oenach*
games are played and its races run'; Best, Bergin, O'Brien, and O'Sullivan, *Book of
Leinster*, V, 1204, lines 35713–14).

184 BL, MS Stowe 180, fol. 42 (Litton Falkiner, *Illustrations of Irish History*, pp. 361–2).
It should also be recalled that the tract *Advertisements for Ireland* noted above (see
note 170) included funerals amongst those occasions attracting professional performing artists. The dubiousness of wakes was evidently well known: compare the third
ordinatio of David Rothe's provincial synod held in Armagh in 1618 cited above;
further, the Statutes of Tuam in 1631 warned priests to avoid *promiscua convivia, nec
unquam extra parochiam praesumant ad exequias defunctorum, non invitati accedere*
('promiscuous feasts, nor ever should they presume to go to funeral rites uninvited';
McCarthy, *Irish Church History*, p. 493).

185 The fragmentary Old Irish law tract *Mellbretha* ('Sport Judgments') describes various
types of *cluichí*, though much of its meaning is obscure (D.A. Binchy, '*Mellbretha*,'
Celtica 8 [1968], 144–54). One *cluiche* that is clear, however, is juggling (see Binchy,

ibid., p. 149): 'IT e inso ruidilse cluiche ... ardcles conublaib ...' ('These are games with total immunity ... juggling in the air with balls ...').

186 S. Ó Súilleabháin, *Caitheamh Aimsire ar Thórraimh* (Dublin, 1961), pp. 60–83.

187 Ó Súilleabháin, ibid., p. 65.

188 Jane Francesca Wilde, *Ancient Legends, Mystic Charms and Superstitions of Ireland* (London, 1888), p. 122.

189 E. Knott, 'An Irish Seventeenth-Century Translation of the Rule of St. Clare,' *Ériu* 15 (1948), 1–187.

190 Knott, ibid., pp. 110–11.

191 A well-attested meaning at this date; *OED*, **Play** sb., subsense 8.

192 P. Brook, *The Empty Space* (Harmondsworth, 1972), p. 157; on the medieval usage of the words 'play' and 'game,' see V.A. Kolve, *The Play Called Corpus Christi* (London, 1966), pp. 8–32.

193 MacCana, *Learned Tales*, pp. 3–4.

194 Ó Súilleabháin, *Caitheamh Aimsire*, pp. 44–5.

195 E. Barba, ed., *J. Grotowski: Towards a Poor Theatre* (London, 1969), pp. 15–25.

196 A. Gwynn, 'The Origins of the Anglo-Irish Theatre,' *Studies* 38 (1939), 260–74; see p. 270. Evidence for minstrel activity at the London court is extensive; see by C. Bullock-Davies, *Menestrellorum Multitudo: Minstrels at a Royal Feast* (Cardiff, 1978), and *A Register of Royal and Baronial Domestic Minstrels, 1272–1327* (Bury St Edmunds, 1986).

197 E. Knott, *Irish Classical Poetry*, 2nd rev. ed (Cork, 1966), p. 67. The poet Gofraidh Fionn Ó Dálaigh (†1387) wrote this poem for Gerald Fitzgerald, son of Maurice, first earl of Desmond. The Janus-like nature of the late-medieval Irish poet is also noted by J. E. Caerwyn Williams, 'The Court Poet in Medieval Ireland,' *Proceedings of the British Academy* 57 (1971), 85–135; see p. 131 and note 1.

198 Irish harping may already have been known about in Wales before Giraldus. Tradition relates that the prince of north Wales, Gruffud ap Cynan (†1137), had imported into Wales Irish musicians and poets (T. Parry, *A History of Welsh Literature*, trans. H.I. Bell [Oxford, 1955], p. 45, and see the excerpt from Tadeus Dowling's *Annales Hiberniae* cited above).

199 CUL, MS Mm. 5. 30, fol. 24, col. a (Gerald of Wales, *Giraldi Cambrensis Opera Omnia*, ed. J.S. Brewer, J.F. Dimock, and G.F. Warner, Rolls Series 21, 8 vols [London, 1861–91] V, 153). Giraldus also said that Wales strove to emulate Ireland in music. Compare the prominence also accorded to harp and *timpán* in the near-contemporary *Tromdámh Guaire* (Joynt, *Tromdámh Guaire*, pp. 29–31, lines 937–89).

200 *Holinshed's Irish Chronicle*, ed. L. Miller and E. Power, (New York, 1979), p. 113. See also C. Lennon, 'Richard Stanihurst (1547–1618) and Old English Identity,' *Irish Historical Studies* 21 (1978–9), 121–43.

201 Apart from extracts given in Philip O'Sullivan Beare, *Selections from the Zoilomastix of Philip O'Sullivan Beare*, ed. T.J. O'Donnell, Irish Manuscripts Commission (Dublin,

1960), the *Zoilomastix* remains largely unpublished. Composed *c* 1625, it belongs to a tradition of writings which expatriate Irishmen were producing on the Continent in the early seventeenth century (compare in this regard the *Foras Feasa ar Éirinn* of Geoffrey Keating). Their aim was to counteract the negative image which had been foisted on Ireland by unsympathetic writers. O'Sullivan Beare prefaced his account of the excellence of the Irish musical tradition with this attack on Stanihurst: 'Hinc vero Richardus Stanihurstus nec aures, nec tactum videtur habuisse, dum experientia, concordiaque scriptorum fide reclamante, musicos Ibernos vituperauit. Inter coenandum, inquit, adest citharista oculis sæpè captus, {here O'Sullivan Beare continues with a quotation from Stanihurst, *De rebus in Hibernia gestis*, p. 39, about harpers and harping} Citharoedus (crede mihi Stanihurste) vix ullus reperiri potest magis oculis captus, quam tu es mente cæcus: qui si præstitisses historicam fidem, fides numquam ferreas, sed æneas, vel argenteas lyræ, & tympano a musicis nostris aptari, tradidisses.' ('Hence to be sure, with experience and the agreement and assurance of writers contradicting [him], Richard Stanihurst seems to have had neither ears nor feeling while he berated Irish musicians. "At dinner," he said, "the harper, often blind, is present …" Believe me, Stanihurst, it is scarsely possible to find any harper blinder than you are benighted: if you had kept faith with history, you would have related that it is never iron-stringed instruments that are used for harp and *timpán* by our Irish musicians, but bronze or silver ones'; UUL, MS H. 248, fol. 132).

202 A phenomenon not unknown in modern times. See D.I. Kertzer, *Ritual, Politics, and Power* (New Haven and London, 1988), p. 19.

203 A.R. Hart, 'The King's Serjeant at Law in Tudor Ireland, 1485–1603,' in Hogan and Osborough, *Brehons, Serjeants and Attorneys*, pp. 77–100; see p. 81

204 Its full title was *A breviat of the getting of Ireland.* Since a probable textual link exists between the *Breviat* and the 1534 ordinances for the government of Ireland noted above (note 146), its composition probably coincides with or antedates 1534 (W. Grattan-Flood, *A History of Irish Music* [Dublin, Belfast, and Cork, 1905], p. 106, dated it to *c* 1520, but without citing evidence). I have traced four manuscripts of the *Breviat,* but for this particular passage they are all of equal textual authority (a printed version exists in W. Harris, *Hibernica: or, some Antient Pieces relating to Ireland* [Dublin, 1770], p. 98, which was in turn based on his manuscript notes in NLI, MS Collectanea Vol. XVI, p. 25 ff; this latter also has no variants, and may itself have been derived from the TCD manuscript cited above and selected here because it stands relatively early among the extant manuscript copies).

205 TCD, MS 842 (F. 3. 16), fol. 30r–v.

206 PRO, SP 60/4, fol. 91v. Chief Justice Thomas Luttrell was resident in Dublin in the first half of the sixteenth century. His *Booke* expresses similar concerns: 'Item, for that Iryshe beggers, rymors, bordes, comyn wemen, pardoners, pypers, harpers, and suche lyke, have bygyfte money, and ther sustenaunce of the peoplle, and spyeth the countrey

to ther enymyes, and set oute to them ther goodes, wherby they be ofte robbeid; that it be orderid that none shalbe sufferid to come emongest thEnglyshe men, for by ther Iryshe guyftes and minstraunlcye they provokeith the peoplle to an Iryshe order. And, to thentent that every begger shalbe knowen, from whens he comyth, that none be sufferid to begge, but in the paryshe where he dwellyth a serten tyme befoe {*read* before}.' (*State Papers* ... *King Henry the Eighth*, pp. 508–9). There formerly existed an early printed version of this text, from which that in the *State Papers* volume was printed; no early manuscript copy of the *Booke* exists either in PRO or LPL; possibly the printed version, and any early manuscript copy, was destroyed in the Dublin Four Courts fire of 1922. A seventeenth-century manuscript copy exists in BL, MS Additional 4763; see fol. 451v for the relevant passage. The manuscript copy is generally a little inferior to the printed version, and its spelling system less archaic. It records the following variants (the first three of which are superior, however, to the printed text of the relevant passage): bordes] bards; bygyfte] by gift; and ther] & other; and minstraunlcye] *om.*.

207 LPL, MS 627 (Carew Papers), fol. 79 (R. Ó Muireadhaigh, 'Aos Dána na Mumhan 1584,' *Irisleabhar Muighe Nuadhat* [1960], 81–4).

208 Seventy-three is approximate, for the text says *many others* were active in the 'okyll' school; on which see below. Populous with 'Poetes, Cronyclers or Rymers' though the Desmond territories evidently were, they seem to have been exceptional only in that the earl's Gaelic sympathies made them a safer haven than the territories under New English control. A survey of the Tudor and early Jacobean fiants, between 1552 and 1605, yields pardons to many harpers and pipers, for example, from all corners of Ireland. The decade 1550–60 yields two pardons, which rise to four between 1560–70. The decade 1570–80 produces twelve and 1580–90 produces eleven. None is on record for 1590–1600, but 1601–5 produces thirty seven.

209 Compare John Derricke, *Image of Irelande*, sig. Fii (facsimile reprint, ed. Quinn [Belfast, 1985]): 'A Barde and Rimer is all one.' Yet the scribe of the instructions to be observed by the earl of Desmond in LPL, MS 627 (Carew Papers), fol. 80v, three times deleted the word 'rhymer' to substitute respectively 'bard,' 'bard,' and 'poet,' which suggests that he at least perceived differences in meaning (and doubtless he was an Englishman, to judge by his phonetic attempts to render the Irish names that he was listing). Conversely, William Camden, *Britannia*, 6th ed (London, 1607; *STC* 4508), p. 788, equates poets and bards (see the quotation in the main text below). And Edmund Spenser makes no apparent distinction between poets, bards, and rhymers at all in his *View of the Present State of Ireland*. Neither does Barnaby Rich, *A New Description of Ireland* (London, 1610; *STC* 20992), pp. 37–8: 'There are other Septes or professions, namely of Bardes, which are in manner of Poets or Rythmers, which do nothing but fit and compose lies. Then they haue Harpers, and those are so reuerenced among the Irish, that in the time of Rebellion, they will forbeare to hurt

either their persons, or their goods, |p. 38| goods, but are rather inclined to giue them, & are verie bountifull, either to Rymers or Fooles.'

210 John Derricke, for example, who equated bards and rhymers, presented them as performers in his *Image of Irelande*. And some of the surnames of the rhymers in the Desmond inquest of 7 November 1584 betray family descent from the *cáintí* who, as has been seen, were often performers of their satires: 'Gillisa on Canith alias on Cainty {< Ó an Cháinte} of Bordwyn in kenallmeycky Rymor Dormod og on Canty de [eadem] killine ne goilty in kenallmeicky Rymor Moylyn On Canity of lismor in Ibawn Rymor Owen Balluff on Canity Rymor' and 'Donell mac Donogh on Cainty' (LPL, MS 627 [Carew Papers], fols 80v and 81 respectively).

211 See note 29 above. The earliest example of the *reccaire* that *DIL* cites is from the *Tromdámh Guaire*. *DIL* also derives *reccaire* from Anglo-Saxon *reccere*, which suggests an interesting reverse case of exchange in the performing arts, this time from England to Ireland, rather than vice versa, as probably occurred in the case of the *drúth* (see Prologue: Insubstantial Pageants, p. 6 and p. 315, note 5).

212 PRO, SP 63/3, fol. 176 (Hore, 'Irish Bardism,' p. 167). Smyth's 'Rakry' appears to be a reappropriation into English of the Irish word for a reciter, descendants from the original Anglo-Saxon *reccere* having apparently failed to survive into sixteenth-century English.

213 L. McKenna, ed., *Aithdioghluim Dána*, Irish Texts Society 37 and 40, 2 vols (Dublin, 1939–40) I, 347.

214 Ibid., p. 348.

215 C. Giblin, ed., *Irish Franciscan Mission to Scotland 1619–1646* (Dublin, 1964), p. 54.

216 Bodl., MS Rawlinson B. 478, fols 44v-5 (Spenser, *Present State of Ireland*, ed. Renwick, pp. 72–3). My italics. Compare also the account of the Marquis of Clanricarde, pertaining to early-seventeenth-century practice, which notes that the poet would hand over his composition to bards to memorize and perform for him to the accompaniment of harping (*Memoirs of the Right Honourable the Marquis of Clanricarde, Lord Deputy General of Ireland* [London, 1722], p. clxx).

217 LPL, MS 627 (Carew Papers), fol. 81. All were Old English Munster aristocrats, and see further on the Barrys in chapter 6 below.

218 Breatnach, 'Chief's Poet.' For some commentary on the political function of poets and rhymers, see also M. Caball, 'Notes on an Elizabethan Kerry Bardic Family,' *Ériu* 43 (1992), 177–92. Whether the anonymous poet who praised the Old English lord, Sir Thomas Butler, tenth earl of Ormond, was directly patronized by him is unknown, though much praise poetry seems to have been composed with reward in mind (J. Carney, ed., *Poems on the Butlers of Ormond, Cahir, and Dunboyne [A.D. 1400–1650]* [Dublin, 1945], pp. 74–81; see p. 79; the poem was composed in 1588). New English polemic was sceptical about the reasons why the Anglo-Irish retained poets; see, for example, the letter of Robert Crowley to Secretary Thomas Cromwell in PRO, SP 60/4, fol. 91v, cited above.

219 LPL, MS 627 (Carew Papers), fol. 81.

220 LPL, MS 627 (Carew Papers), fol. 80v: 'Dermod odwedy harper Rwshell oge odwedy harper william Roe odwedy harper.' The English sources often reflect what we know from Gaelic ones, namely, that harpers and poets, no less than the personnel of many other professions (brehons, doctors, etc.), tended to run in families. The pervasiveness of harping amongst the Gaelic upper classes is epitomized for the sixteenth century in Meredith Hanmer's observation that households of any substance had one or two harps in them, and that the householders 'always keep a harper to play for them att their meales' (RIA, MS 1135 [24 G 15], p. 21); and for the early seventeenth century, compare the observations of Barnaby Rich, *New Description*, p. 38: 'Euery great man in the Countrey hath his Rymer, his Harper, and his knowne Messenger, to run about the Countrey with Letters,' and of Luke Gernon, *A Discourse of Ireland* (BL, MS Stowe 180, fol. 42; Litton Falkiner, *Illustrations of Irish History*, p. 361): 'They feast together with great iollyty and healths around, towardes the middle of supper, the harper beginns to tune, and singeth Irish rymes of auncient making. If he be a good rymer, he will make one song to the present occasion.'

221 Since it is clear that the roles of *scélaige* ('storyteller,' 'historian') and *senchaid* ('reciter of lore,' 'historian') were overlapping (see note 10 above), they have therefore been treated together here.

222 LPL, MS 603 (Carew Papers), fol. 168 (H.F. Berry, ed., *Statutes and Ordinances, and Acts of the Parliament of Ireland. King John to Henry V* [Dublin, 1907], p. 446). This is the first documented English recognition of *scélaigi* of which I am aware.

223 T.W. Moody, F.X. Martin, and F.J. Byrne, eds., *A New History of Ireland III Early Modern Ireland 1534–1691* (Oxford, 1976), p. 567.

224 PRO, SP 63/3, fol. 176 (Hore, 'Irish Bardism,' p. 166).

225 Camden, *Britannia*, 6th ed, p. 788 (*STC* 4508). The first edition of 1586 does not contain this information. Note also Camden's detail that the various professionals who served the chief might hail from one particular territory or region. Early native sources confirm Camden's accuracy, and show of what antiquity this tradition was. For example, the *Frithfholaid ríg Caisil fria thuatha* (the 'Obligations of Service of the King of Cashel towards his Tribes'), which may have been composed early in the ninth century (M. Gerriets, 'Kingship and Exchange in Pre-Viking Ireland,' *Cambridge Medieval Celtic Studies* 13 [1987], 39–72; see p. 41), notes, amongst other things, from where the king of Cashel got his harpers, *drúith*, and doorkeepers: 'Cruitire o chorco che ... Druith 7 dorsaide o chorco modrad ...' ('Harpers from Corcho Óchae ... *drúith* and doorkeepers from Corcomruad ...'; TCD, MS 1318 [H. 2. 16; Yellow Book of Lecan], col. 339; J. Fraser, P. Grosjean, and J.G. O'Keeffe, eds., *Irish Texts*, 8 vols [London, 1931–3] I, 20–1). F.J. Byrne, *Irish Kings and High Kings* (London, 1973), p. 198, observes the common confusion between *drúth* and *druí*, and suggests reading *druí* here, especially since the tribal name Corcomruad originally meant 'seed

of my druid.' However, the frequent collocation in early Irish texts of *drúith* with doorkeepers, menials, and domestics, as again here, might be thought to weigh against this. A similar sort of list in a text on the customs of Uí Mhaine (a territory from Clontuskert, co. Roscommon, southwards to the boundary of co. Clare, and from Athlone westwards to Seefin and Athenry in present co. Galway), notes the provenance of certain of the retainers of the Ó Ceallaigh family: 'A crvitirechta .i. huí longargain o baile na banabai 7 a chornairechta o lis na cornairega .i. huí sidachain.' ('His harpers [i.e., Ó Ceallaigh's] are the Uí Lonargáin from Ballynabanaba, and his trumpeters are from Lis na Cornaireagha, that is, the Uí Sidheacháin' [RIA, MS 535 (23 P 2; Book of Lecan), fol. 83v, col. a]; J. O'Donovan, ed., *The Tribes and Customs of Hy-Many, commonly called O'Kelly's Country* [Dublin, 1843], p. 92).

226 Edmund Campion in J. Ware, ed., *The Historie of Ireland* (Dublin, 1633; *STC* 25067a), p. 18.

227 *Holinshed's Irish Chronicle*, ed. Miller and Power, p. 114.

228 But recollect that the *cruitire* might operate in the province of the *scélaige*; see above, note 24. And *súantraige*, the harp music that induced sleep, is frequently mentioned in early Irish sources (along with *goltraige* and *gentraige*, the musics that provoked, respectively, tears and laughter). For an account of harp music as soporific, compare the *Cath Muige Rath* (the 'Battle of the Plain of the Fort'), a prose narrative probably of the late Middle Irish period but retailing events held to have occurred *s.a.* 637. Congal Claen, prince of Ulster, is lulled to sleep on the eve of a battle by pipe and *timpán* music (TCD, MS 1318 [H. 2. 16; Yellow Book of Lecan], col. 292; J. O'Donovan, ed., *The Banquet of Dun na nGedh and the Battle of Magh Rath* [Dublin, 1842], p. 168): '7 ro chodail congal iarsin reciuin fhogar na cusleann cfuil 7 re forcad faidhemail fuasaidech fir trvag na téd 7 na timpán ghatadall daigthib 7 dformnadaib eand 7 ingen na súad ga sár sheinm' ('And after this Congal went to sleep on account of the soft sound of the music of the *cuisle* and [the] prophetic, murmuring sound of shadows of strings and *timpán*, which was struck by the tips and sides of the fingers and the fingernails of expert [players] of surpassing melody').

229 The Irish word that *carruage* anglicizes is *cerrbach* ('gambler,' 'card-player'). Later English sources tend to spell it *carrowe*.

230 PRO, SP 63/3, fol. 177 (Hore, 'Irish Bardism,' p. 167).

231 RIA, MS 1219 (Stowe C iii 1), fol. 66v, col. b (Freeman, *Annals of Connacht*, p. 588). And perhaps he had appeared as early as 1351 in the description of the Ó Ceallaigh Christmas feast of that year in the Annals of Clonmacnoise. However, these annals may not be strictly comparable, translated as they were in the seventeenth century by An Dubhaltach Mac Fhirbhisigh from an Irish original now lost (Murphy, *Annals of Clonmacnoise*, p. 298, discussed above, and note 23).

232 PRO, SP 63/9, fols 157 and 162v (fol. 157 appears to contain the draft, made ?17 December 1563, for the fair copy on fol. 162v, made 20 December 1563).

233 Sidney's ordinances were issued 21 July 1576, and are contained in NLI, MS 8065 (item 4), fol. 154 (the carrowes here are spelt 'Carraghers').

234 Hore and Graves, *Social State*, pp. 277–8.

235 *OED*, **Hazarder**.

236 *Holinshed's Irish Chronicle*, ed. Miller and Power, p. 114. Glibs were locks of forehead hair, long enough to fall over the eyes, and a characteristic of Irish male coiffure; a double-entendre might be suspected in the word 'dimissaries,' given what later writers say carrowes were prepared to wager, and in view of the literal inappropriateness here of *dimissories* to gamblers. S.T. Cavanagh, '"The Fatal Destiny of that Land": Elizabethan Views of Ireland,' in B. Bradshaw, A. Hadfield, and W. Maley, eds., *Representing Ireland: Literature and the Origins of Conflict, 1534–1660* (Cambridge, 1993), pp. 116–31, claims (p. 116) that Campion derived his description of carrowes 'from Holinshed' (and presumably hence, although this is not stated, from Stanihurst). But it is more likely that Stanihurst derived his account from Campion (Lennon, 'Old English Identity,' p. 125).

237 The *Discourse for the Reformation of Ireland*, composed 1579–83 (which I note in two manuscripts: Oxford, University College, MS 103, fol. 108v [a slightly superior text] and LPL, MS 621 [Carew Papers], fol. 103); the 1582 *Orders for Connacht* in NA, 2/447/16, fol. [43] (a transcript of an original lost in 1922); Sir John Perrot's notes of 1584 for the reformation of Ireland in LPL, MS 614 (Carew Papers), fol. 260; and his (biolium) letter to the Justices of the Peace, 18 December 1584, in NLI, MS 8013, fol. [2].

238 PRO, SP 63/191, fol. 49; though the bishop's letter is not precisely dated, it is in the same hand that copied the preceding document, dated to 6 July 1596. On *quiddyes* (lines 9, 12, and 15, often spelt 'cuddies' in other documents) and *coyne* and *livery* (line 16), see note 257 below.

239 Compare the notes of Meredith Hanmer in PRO, SP 63/214, fols 231v and 256v: 'The Rimers & carrowes idle losels dic<e ...> play their clothes &c It' his stone an oth<...> be reded vidi mundum coopertum foeno. carner<...> Iesters thefes & partakers, stragglers The Irish geven to enquir after newes. ... Rathes ... |fol. 256v| ... Idle & harkeng after newes Carowes &c & sowers of Ires ˄ᶠwaterford˥ .' (Possibly these notes show the influence of Spenser's *View of the Present State of Ireland*, in which case they were made some time after 1597 and before Hanmer's death in 1604.)

240 Note, for example, the injunctions to Sir John O'Reilly, 28 August 1583, not to 'keep in his house any Bard, Carrogh or Rymer' (NA, 2/447/16, fol. [67]).

241 Oxford, Corpus Christi College, MS 94, fol. 259 (Litton Falkiner, *Illustrations of Irish History*, p. 248).

242 See note 236 above.

243 Barnaby Rich, *New Description*, p. 37. The final recorded notice known to me may be found in LPL, MS 629 (Carew Papers), fol. 31v (a set of acts transmitted

from England for the Irish parliament, against rhymers, gamesters, and the like, in 1611).

244 TCD, MS 786 (D. 3. 16), fol. 146. The passage is worth quoting, both because it includes other Gaelic performers and because none of Lane's work has been published: 'But for that kearne be of a large extent / See by that name what vermine here are ment / [1]Bard [2]Rimer [3]Harper with tale rime and songe / incite the rest like bontefeux {'incendiaries'} to wronge / [4]Horsboy and [5]Carroghe [6]Bastard and the [7]younger brother / to hell and shame they prostitute their mother / whoe giues them all to Idlenes to nourse / that makes them such as Circe could not worse.' The superscript numbers are explained by a marginal note on fol. 146: 'ye xij plagues of Ireland.' Little is known of Lane. He was a captain serving in the army in Ireland, and active c 1600. The earliest reference to him in the State Papers dates to September 1596. He settled in Munster, and was made a freeman of Youghal, co. Cork, on 29 August 1624 (R. Caulfield, ed., *The Council Book of the Corporation of Youghal, from 1610 to 1659, from 1666 to 1687, and from 1690 to 1800* [Guildford, 1878], p. 99). For further details, see A. Ford, 'Reforming the Holy Isle: Parr Lane and the Conversion of the Irish,' in *'A Miracle of Learning': Studies in Manuscripts and Irish Learning. Essays in Honour of William O'Sullivan*, ed. T. Barnard, D. Ó Cróinín, and K. Simms (Aldershot, 1998), pp. 137–63.

245 TCD, MS 842 (F. 3. 16), fol. 199v (O'Brien, *Advertisements for Ireland*, p. 44). This is the final datable reference to them before the close of the period under review of which I am aware. They are mentioned, however, in an unpublished tract on the government of Ireland and the customs of the inhabitants contained in Oxford, Exeter College, MS 154, fol. 59. Though not precisely dated, internal references make it clear that the tract was composed between 1607 and 1625.

246 The broad similiarity of the Rich and Stanihurst accounts of the carrowe possibly suggests Rich's dependence upon Stanihurst. It might be noted, however, that in the passage from Thomas Smyth cited above, carrowes were said to have been maintained 'by the rymers,' which implies their confederation with other performing artists.

247 A. Gailey, 'Straw Costume in Irish Folk Customs,' *Folk Life* 6 (1968), 83–93; compare also his *Irish Folk Drama*, p. 12: 'Disguise consisting of leggings, shirt, cape or coat and tall conical mask rising from shoulder level, all of straw, was widely used in West Ulster and was known elsewhere in Ireland.'

248 Bodl., MS Tanner 444, fol. 4v ('Bodley's Visit to Lecale, County of Down, A.D. 1602–3,' *Ulster Journal of Archaeology* 2 [1854], 73–95; see pp. 92–3).

249 John Stow, *John Stow: A Survey of London*, ed. C.L. Kingsford, 2 vols (Oxford, 1908; repr 1971) I, 96–7. In many respects the circumstances of their pastime, though on a grander scale, bear comparison with those of the pastime in Lecale. On the Sunday before Candlemas in 1377, a troupe of one hundred and thirty Londoners disguised as mummers came by night to Kennington near Lambeth where the young prince was.

They were attended by 'trumpets, sackbuts, cornets, shawms and other minstrels.' They played their dice game, feasted and danced with the prince and his company, drank and took their leave.

250 BL, MS Additional 18991, fol. 11.

251 The pre-existing tradition of associating gamblers and masquers (compare the masquers' dice game before Richard II in note 249) need not inhibit a specifically Irish dimension here in the Lecale performance.

252 'Iam qui vnquam vidit Canem Fuste, vel Lapide percussum currere foras cum Cauda inter Nates pendente, vidisset Mascaros istos domum euntes sine pecunia, sine animo, sine ordine, sine dicere, valete' (Bodl., MS Tanner 444, fol. 4v).

253 And there were sorts apart from those classified in the Old Irish law tract *Córus Béscnai*, quoted above (note 135).

254 PRO, SP 61/2, fol. 36 (the related Munster orders are found in LPL, MS 603, fol. 30, and those for Connacht and Thomond, which are virtually identical, appear there, too, on fol. 25v). A second copy of the Munster orders exists in LPL, MS 611 (Carew Papers), p. 110. It might also be noted that the Irish *joculator/histrio* who reputedly travelled to the court of King Rederech in Scotland, according to the late-twelfth-century Life of St Kentigern, entertained the king and his court over Christmastide (note 120 above). For Gaelic evidence for entertainers at Christmas (and at Easter, another of the times mentioned in the ordinances), see the discussion of the *gairm sgoile* (the 'summons to a bardic assembly') in chapter 6 below.

255 Patterson, *Cattle-Lords*, p. 127.

256 Ecclesiastics also made circuits; Simms, 'Guesting and Feasting,' pp. 74–5.

257 The anglicized terms 'cuddy' (< *cuid oidhche*, 'evening's portion,' 'night supper') and 'coshery' (< *cóisir*, 'banquet,' 'festive party') are common in English sources of the period. For the former, see Bishop Lyon's letter quoted above, and for the latter, good examples are provided by Richard Stanihurst (*Holinshed's Irish Chronicle*, ed. Miller and Power, p. 113) and in 1610 by Rich (*New Description*, p. 39): 'THere is amongst the Irish, a kinde of feasting or banquetting, which they call Coshering, & this is the manner of it; Good company both of men and women being drawne together a feasting, to entertaine the time betweene meales, they haue their Rythmers & their Harpers; the one, to sing, and the other, to play.' The obligations to provide coyn (< *coinnmed*, 'quartering') and livery (accommodation for horses) were also commonly cited.

258 O'Brien, *Advertisements for Ireland*, p. 44.

259 And in relation to the threat of the clown who leaves his shape, compare the observation of D. Handelman, *Models and Mirrors: Towards an Anthropology of Public Events* (Cambridge, 1990), that there may be an affinity 'between the clown type and that sense of power that inheres in the alteration of borders and in the dissolution of mundane realities. So it is not surprising that this type is often perceived as highly dangerous' (p. 248).

CHAPTER 2

1 For the complete text, the Dublin *Visitatio Sepulcri*, see Appendix I (further commentary on the music of the play may be found in M. Egan-Buffet and A.J. Fletcher, 'The Dublin *Visitatio Sepulcri* Play,' *Proceedings of the Royal Irish Academy* 90 [1990], 159–241; Appendix I is based on this article). Subsequent line references to the Dublin *Visitatio* will be to the lineation of Appendix I. The best edition of the fragmentary text, *The Pride of Life*, is N. Davis, ed., *Non-Cycle Plays and Fragments*, EETS, SS 1 (London, 1970), pp. 90–105. The first edition by J. Mills, ed., *Account Roll of the Priory of the Holy Trinity, Dublin, 1337–1346, with the Middle English Moral Play 'The Pride of Life'* (Dublin, 1891), has been reissued with new introductions by J.F. Lydon and A.J. Fletcher (Dublin, 1996).

2 It perhaps takes scepticism too far to insist that they were never performed; circumstantial evidence for the performance of the *Visitatio* at least is excellent (see Egan-Buffet and Fletcher, '*Visitatio Sepulcri*,' p. 162).

3 The two liturgical manuscripts are described in Appendix I. The facsimile of a portion of the play which Mills reproduced as a frontispiece to his edition is now more readily available in Lydon and Fletcher's reissue of Mills, or in Davis, *Non-Cycle Plays*, plate III, and his *Non-Cycle Plays and the Winchester Dialogues*, Leeds Texts and Monographs, Medieval Drama Facsimiles V (Leeds, 1979), p. 23. The account roll was a casualty of the explosion in the Dublin Four Courts during the civil strife of 1922.

4 Appendix I discusses the date of the manuscripts (see pp. 284–5).

5 Appendix I discusses the date and place of the play's composition (see pp. 285–7).

6 Compared with many other liturgical dramas, such detail is unusual. The rubrics of various *Visitatio* plays, including some of those of Dublin, are discussed in C. Mazouer, 'Les indications de mise en scène dans les drames liturgiques de Pâques,' *Cahiers de Civilisation Médiévale* 23 (1980), 361–7.

7 As also does R. The *Elevatio* often accompanied a *Depositio* ritual, as it does in R. On the *Elevatio*, see K. Young, ed. *The Drama of the Medieval Church*, 2 vols (Oxford, 1933) I, 114–22.

8 To argue that the scribe added it merely for the sake of a completer correspondence between his copy and his exemplar seems less likely an explanation than that he included it for the sake of its potential usefulness. Also, the presence of alternative forms of the *Elevatio* perhaps suggests that it was envisaged that this ritual at least would be performed. (The *Elevatio crucis et hostie* ritual, if performed, normally preceded Easter Sunday Matins; Young, *Drama*, I, 114.)

9 These external dimensions are based on those depicted in J. Rocque, *An Exact Survey of the City and Suburbs of Dublin, 1756*, republished by H. Margary (Lympne Castle, 1977).

10 S.C. Hughes, *The Church of S. John the Evangelist, Dublin* (Dublin, 1889), pp. 9–36, discusses the successive rebuildings until the time of Rocque; also H.A. Wheeler and

M.J. Craig, *The Dublin City Churches of the Church of Ireland* (Dublin, 1948), pp. 21–2, note rebuildings and internal dimensions.

11 In both M and R, the *Visitatio* follows on after an *Elevatio* ritual and the first nocturn of Easter matins. Each manuscript contains two orders for the *Elevatio*, a shorter and a longer, and both are quite different in character (the shorter, for example, begins in a fully lit church, while the longer requires all the church lights to be extinguished, apart from the Paschal candle and the lights burning within the Sepulchre). In M it is the shorter one which precedes matins and the play, while in R it is the longer. (The text of the shorter and longer versions, edited from R, are printed in Young, *Drama*, I, 169–72; the longer version is briefly discussed in O.B. Hardison, *Christian Rite and Christian Drama in the Middle Ages* [Baltimore, 1965], pp. 209–10.)

12 The clue to this is found in a rubric: 'eat processio per medium chori cum predicta Cruce de Sepulcro assumpta inter predictos duos sacerdotes ... ad aliquod altare extra chorum ...' ('let the procession go through the middle of the choir with the aforementioned cross taken from the Sepulchre between two priests ... to some altar outside the choir ...'; Young, *Drama*, I, 171).

13 Of these there are several in the course of the Easter liturgy; one is mentioned in the preceding note, for example.

14 Young, *Drama*, I, 169.

15 Young, *Drama*, II, 507–13; a location also within the choir seems to be a typically insular tradition. See also N.C. Brooks, 'The Sepulchrum Christi,' *Journal of English and Germanic Philology* 27 (1928), 147–61, and P. Sheingorn, *The Easter Sepulchre in England* (Kalamazoo, Western Michigan, 1987), pp. 34–5.

16 In the longer *Elevatio* (Young, *Drama*, I, 170), the Sepulchre is censed, its *ostium* opened, and candles lighted from the flame within it.

17 Appendix I, lines 44–5: 'deinde predicte marie sepulcrum intrent & inclinantes se & prospicientes undique [intra] sepulcrum ...' ('Afterwards the aforesaid Marys are to enter the Sepulchre, and bowing themselves and looking about on all sides inside the Sepulchre ...').

18 As seems to have been the case, for example, with the Prüfening Sepulchre (Young, *Drama*, I, 157–61). On English temporary Sepulchres, see H.J. Feasey, *Ancient English Holy Week Ceremonial* (London, 1897), pp. 137–51, and Sheingorn, *Easter Sepulchre*, pp. 33–45.

19 Little is known about the nature of these, whether they were on prickets or set on an altar (if there was one around which the Sepulchre had been set up; see note 21 below). However, that there were more than one is implied in the rubric to the longer *Elevatio*, which requires all church lights to be extinguished *exceptis luminaribus infra Sepulcrum* ('except for the lights inside the Sepulchre'; Young, *Drama*, I, 170).

20 A small coffer may have served the turn. A medieval English one probably used for this purpose still survives in the parish church at Cowthorpe, West Yorkshire; Sheingorn,

Easter Sepulchre, fig. 27. It is of substantially larger dimensions than any Dublin counterpart is likely to have had, however.

21 An altar evidently existed on the north side of the ancient church; H.F. Berry, 'The Merchant Tailors' Guild – that of St John the Baptist, Dublin, 1418–1841,' *Journal of the Royal Society of Antiquaries of Ireland* 48 (1918), 19–64; see p. 52.

22 One might think that since ultimately the bulk of the play's dialogue was imported, so too would have been its rubrics. Indeed, on the face of it this seems probable, for presumably it is broadly correct to say that since it is in the nature of rubrics to be rather general, thus making them adaptable for use in any church whatever its particular layout, they too would have been imported wholesale. However, most of the substantive variation between M and R occurs in the play rubrics, which suggests that the textual transmission of rubrics is far less stable than that of play dialogue proper (to some extent, of course, play dialogue would be stabilized by the music that accompanies it). This state of affairs is typical of the transmission of liturgical drama generally. Consequently, the prospect that M and R rubrics were custom-built in Ireland is perfectly plausible, though the extent to which this may be true is impossible to tell.

23 Appendix I, line 5.

24 Appendix I, line 16.

25 Fletcher Collins, *The Production of Medieval Church Music Drama* (Virginia, 1972), p. 283, suggests three possible entry points for the Marys in the Dublin play, either 'from the sacristy, from some other point or points alongside the choir area, or from three locations at the rear of the church.' I am inclined to discount the first one, since Fletcher Collins appears to understand 'sacristy' here as a room opening into the choir itself, and this would give the Marys comparatively little space to move about as they enter singing their laments. The second one sounds suitably vague but, in the context of a performance within the church of St John the Evangelist, somewhat harder to conceive of than the third possibility, which effectively is the one that I propose here.

26 On the introduction of screens, see C. Platt, *The Parish Churches of Medieval England* (London, 1981), pp. 38 and 155.

27 On figures 4–6, the area comprising chancel and choir has been reckoned to project about a quarter of the way from the east wall down the nave, which in the case of St John's would have been about 16'. This is a pure estimate.

28 Appendix I, line 23.

29 Appendix I, lines 10 and 13.

30 Appendix I, line 16.

31 Egan-Buffet and Fletcher, '*Visitatio Sepulcri*,' p. 204.

32 Appendix I, lines 22–3.

33 Appendix I, lines 36–43. Note that this time the length of the pause is not qualified in the way the first one was (Appendix I, line 9).

34 Appendix I, line 54.

35 Appendix I, line 72. Furthermore, this was the central position that the expression

medius chori, commonly found in liturgical rubrics, normally denoted. On the *medius chori* see F. Ll. Harrison, *Music in Medieval Britain*, 4th ed. (Buren, 1980), p. 52 and passim; for an early-fifteenth-century illustration of singing *in medio chori* see J.W. McKinnon, 'Fifteenth-Century Northern Book Printing and the *A Cappella* Question: An Essay in Iconographic Method,' in S. Boorman, ed. *Studies in Performance of Late Medieval Music* (Cambridge, 1983), pp. 1–17; especially p. 3, note 4 and pl. 1.

36   This seems to be the sense of the rubric at Appendix I, lines 44–7.

37   It is difficult to imagine how the Sepulchre, if it was to accommodate three people, not to mention the possibility of a small altar, could have been much less than this. Also, the amount of physical space which each Mary occupied would have been proportionally increased since each was made bulkier by the wearing of a cope.

38   Appendix I, lines 93–7.

39   The third Mary is not specifically told to enter (Appendix I, line 13), but we are probably meant to understand her rubric as an abbreviation of that previously given to the second Mary (Appendix I, lines 9–10) and essentially similar to it.

40   Appendix I, line 16; this time we must assume rubrical abbreviation for both the second and third Marys (Appendix I, lines 18 and 20), and that the sense of the more explicit rubric for the first Mary carried over to the rest.

41   Appendix I, line 23.

42   This also proves, incidentally, that the rubrics at Appendix I, lines 30 and 33 should be regarded as abbreviated, because the rubric at lines 26–7 has spoken for them all.

43   It is conceivable that the angel opened the Sepulchre for them, but if he did so it is unspecified. One imagines that if he did, he would have done so after he had finished singing his invitation to them. (For an example of the removal of cloth coverings to represent the opening up of the Sepulchre see Young, *Drama*, I, 290.)

44   In some liturgical plays this action was covered by the choir singing the antiphon *Currebant duo* (see Young, *Drama*, I, 309 et passim).

45   Movement and song appear to be coextensive at Appendix I, lines 22–3, for example, and sequential at lines 44–7.

46   Their hands are freer to do so if they have deposited the pyxes they were carrying in the Sepulchre. A clear example of one of the Marys actually pointing *cum digito* towards the Sepulchre is found in a version of the *Visitatio* used in the Sainte-Chapelle, Paris (Young, *Drama*, I, 287).

47   Though if obliged to chose, I would here favour this interpretation. Compare the Fleury *Visitatio*, which has many verbal parallels with Dublin at this point, and which requires the Marys to enter *while singing*: 'procedant tres fratres preparati et vestiti in similitudinem trium Mariarum, pedetemtim et quasi tristes alternantes hos versus cantantes …' ('let three brothers made ready and dressed as the three Maries proceed step by step and as if in sadness singing these verses alternately …'; Young, *Drama*, I, 393). Furthermore, procession while singing is a fundamental characteristic of medieval liturgy; the very existence of the *processional* implies as much.

48 I interpret *inclinantes se* as part of the illusionistic drift of the rubric, in company with *prospicientes undique*. However, it could also be requiring that the Marys reverence the Sepulchre by bowing inside it, in a liturgical fashion.

49 Compare in this respect the earliest *Visitatio* from these islands, in the tenth-century *Regularis Concordia*, which suggests from its instructions to the Marys that they were meant to move as if they were looking for something: 'Dumque tertium percelebratur responsorium residui tres succedant, ... pedetemptim ad similitudinem quaerentium ...' ('And while the third responsory is being sung let the remaining three approach, ... step by step in the likeness of people who are searching ...'; T. Symons, ed., *Regularis Concordia* [London, 1953], pp. 49–50).

50 My assumption here is that *alta uoce* means 'with a loud voice' (J. Stevens, *Words and Music in the Middle Ages* [Cambridge, 1986], pp. 364–6, opts for the translation 'in a high/loud voice' for this collocation).

51 Since the visit to the Sepulchre is commonly depicted in medieval art, it is possible in principle that the scene supplied drama with a fund of potential gestures and attitudes irrecoverable from texts and rubrics alone.

52 Compare R.E. Latham, *Dictionary of Medieval Latin from British Sources* (London, 1975–), **cappa**, subsense 5. When a *cappa* ('cope') is qualified by *serica* ('silk'), as in the Dublin *Visitatio Sepulcri*, it seems to be one of special quality. The word *serica* alone could also be used of a choir cope (R.E. Latham, *Revised Medieval Latin Word List from British and Irish Sources* [Oxford, 1965], p. 434, I **sericum**).

53 Since the rest of their costume comprises liturgical vestments, combined in a nonliturgical way to suggest the play identity of each wearer, it is unlikely that their head coverings would have been non-liturgical when such already existed (as well as the amice, the Augustinian *cucullus* would also have been available for the purpose). Liturgical dramas tend to adapt to their own use liturgical costume (as Mazouer, 'Indications de mise en scène,' p. 364, observed; also, see M.H. Marshall, 'Aesthetic Values of the Liturgical Drama,' reprinted in J. Taylor and A.H. Nelson, eds., *Medieval English Drama* [Chicago and London, 1972], pp. 28–43; p. 37).

54 Perhaps differentiation in this respect was immaterial to the playwright; hence his neglect to specify either one way or another. It may have been that the Marys simply helped themselves to whatever copes were available. (There is at least one Continental example of ad hoc vesting of this kind: a fifteenth-century *Visitatio* from Moosburg required the Marys to be *induti vestibus quibus indui poterunt, ut rubeis casulis vel consimilibus* ['clad in the vestments that they have been able to be clad in, as in red chasubles or the like']; Young, *Drama*, I, 362.) However, the choice of colour in Continental practice, where it is noted, was most usually white, whether the Marys wore copes, dalmatics, or, very occasionally, tunicles, albs, or chasubles. Colour differentiation between them appears to have been rare (though note a fourteenth-century

Fécamp *Visitatio* where one Mary was dressed in a red cope and the other two in white dalmatics; Young, *Drama*, I, 264).

55 T.A. Heslop, 'A Walrus Ivory Pyx and the Visitatio Sepulcri,' *Journal of the Warburg and Courtauld Institute* 44 (1981), 157–60 and pl. 19, argues that the pyx he discusses is probably early-twelfth-century English and depicts scenes from Easter liturgical dramas. If he is correct, may not this same pyx have also been used as a dramatic prop?

56 Young, *Drama*, I, 285; compare also a Padua *Visitatio*, ibid., 294, where angels appear *cum alis et liliis* ('with wings and lillies').

57 A survey of the rubrics of liturgical plays suggests that the alb, even if worn with additional items (stole, amice, etc.), was a relatively stable ingredient of angelic costume.

58 A tunicle, presumably, must be what *tunica* means, and not the 'tunic' as some have translated it (Young, *Drama*, I, 350, and W.L. Smoldon, *The Music of the Medieval Church Dramas* [Oxford, 1980], p. 361). Although Latham, *Word List*, p. 497, **tunica**, only records the sense 'tunicle' in the diminutive form, *tunicula*, it should be noted nonetheless that *tunica* sometimes designates the ecclesiastical tunicle. This sense is clear in a *Visitatio* from Vienne, where a *sacerdos planeta alba, diaconus dalmatica alba, subdiaconus tunica talari alba* ('priest in a white chasuble, a deacon in a white dalmatic, a subdeacon in a white, ankle-length tunicle'; Young, *Drama*, I, 274) take part in a dramatic rendition of the *Victime paschali*. The tunicle was the traditional vestment of the subdeacon. Also, were *tunica* to be interpreted as 'tunic' it would be out of step with the other costumes which are all liturgical.

59 P.H. Barnum, ed., *Dives and Pauper*, EETS, OS 275 (London, 1976), I, part 1, p. 3.

60 Part of the justification for claiming this is the fact that there would probably have been no single *ur*-performance of the play anyway that might notionally be reached through scholarly reconstruction, for if, as seems likely, there were more than one actual performance of the play within the medieval period within St John's, which performance could be said to be any more 'original' than another? Furthermore, any play performed more than once, even if by the same cast in the same place, will not be exactly identical in all respects at each performance.

61 The Dublin *Visitatio* has been revived three times since 1980, most recently in 1994 in the chapel of Trinity College, Dublin (produced by A.J. Fletcher, with musical direction by P. Scott, for the ninth congress of the New Chaucer Society).

62 They are distinguished by their costume and by the iconography of their portable insignia. John also arrives at the Sepulchre first. The word used of their approach to it, *currant*, is emphatically naturalistic and lacking the decorum implied by the word most frequently used for movement in this play, *procedant*. The fact that they run is, of course, traditional, since running also features in some of the Continental liturgical dramas which share this episode.

63 This is particularly noticeable in the way in which naturalistic action has scope to grow

in the interstices, when actors are not preoccupied with singing (for example, when the Marys explore the inside of the tomb, or when the apostles run). But in this play, realistic action seems a means to an end rather than something pursued for its own sake.

64 At the time of the *Visitatio* drama performance (Young, *Drama*, I, 231–2) some artificial lighting (whether by candles, rush lights, or whatever) would have been necessary.

65 W. Hawkes, 'The Liturgy in Dublin, 1200–1500: Manuscript Sources,' *Reportorium Novum* (Dublin Diocesan Record) 2 (1958), 33–67; p. 40.

66 J.L. Robinson, 'On the Ancient Deeds of the Parish of St. John, Dublin,' *Proceedings of the Royal Irish Academy* 33 (1916), 175–224; p. 178.

67 For evidence suggesting renewed artistic interests during de Derby's priorate, see Mills, *Account Roll*, p. xxv. The dates proposed for the composition of the Dublin manuscripts, however (1352 – c 1400, and probably to the latter end of that range; see Appendix I), would tend rather to situate them within the priorate of de Derby's successor, Robert de Lokynton.

68 St Werburgh's Church, for example, maintained an Easter Sepulchre at least from c 1481 to c 1520. Various payments for the Sepulchre, its lights, and wax are recorded in the unpublished medieval churchwardens' accounts. Payments directly relevant to maintenance of an Easter Sepulchre in St Werburgh's may be found in the following documents: RCB, P. 326/27/1/1, fols [1] (22 April 1481–18 April 1484), [2v–3] (4–30 March 1483); P. 326/27/1/2, fols [2v–3] (18 October 1484 – 29 September 1485); P. 326/27/1/4, fol. [8v] (May? 1494 – May? 1496); P. 326/27/1/5, fol. [4v] (1 May 1496 – 1 May 1497); P. 326/27/1/6, fols [8–9] (1 May 1498 – 1 May 1499); P. 326/27/1/8, fol. [7] (1 August 1512 – 9 October 1513); P. 326/27/1/9, fols [3v–4, 7] and P. 326/27/1/10, fol. [1r–v] (both c 1515–20).

69 RCB, C/6/1/26/3, fol. [6v]: 'Item the plaing of the resurrection vj d.'

70 For a summary of the early history of St Patrick's Cathedral, see A. Gwynn and R.N. Hadcock, *Medieval Religious Houses Ireland* (London, 1970; repr Dublin, 1988), pp. 71–5. Though dated, W.M. Mason, *The History and Antiquities of the Collegiate and Cathedral Church of St. Patrick* (Dublin, 1820), is still useful.

71 RCB, C/2/106 (provisional shelfmark), mb. [1] (proctor's accounts from 24 June 1509 to 24 June 1510; Mason, *History*, Appendix, pp. xxviii–xxix).

72 Mayowe appears again in the same set of accounts, where he is paid for his services *in officio Bidelli* ('in the office of bedel'). It is not absolutely clear when he was 'playing' (*ludenti*), whether at Christmas, at the Purification, at both, or at neither. I interpret *ludenti* to mean 'playing' in some dramatic sense; this is the usual connotation of the verb *ludere* in a context like this (A.A. Young, 'Plays and Players: the Latin Terms for Performance,' *Records of Early English Drama Newsletter* 9 [1984], 56–62; see p. 60).

73 RCB, C/2/106 (provisional shelfmark), mb. [1] (proctor's accounts from 24 June 1509 to 24 June 1510; Mason, *History*, Appendix, pp. xxviii–xxix).

74 RCB, C/2/107 (provisional shelfmark), mb. [1] (proctors' accounts for 1555; Mason,

History, Appendix, pp. xxxii-xxxiii). The roll's contents testify to an extensive Catholic refurbishing of the cathedral upon its refounding by Queen Mary.

75 'Threads' seems the best translation for the diminutive, *cordulis*, intensified by its preceding adjective, *paruis*. Some qualitative distinction seems implied between the *cordulae* used for the Holy Spirit, as opposed to the *cordae* of the censing angel.

76 The fact that the strings of the censing angel are noted separately and not as intrinsic to the angel's construction make them sound as if they were *attached* to the angel for some purpose, rather than merely a part of it. Perhaps their purpose was to facilitate its movement. As for the threads employed about the Holy Spirit, if this were a dove, there would be precedents: Lincoln Cathedral, for example, had some sort of Pentecost tableau with a dove (and an angel) on cords (A.H. Nelson, *The Medieval English Stage: Corpus Christi Pageants and Plays* [Chicago and London, 1974], p. 101). Cords frequently animate doves in medieval and Renaissance plays. Compare the dove worked by cords in the Chester play of Noah's Flood (R.M. Lumiansky and D. Mills, eds., *The Chester Mystery Cycle*, EETS, SS 3 and 9 [Oxford, 1974–86] I, 464, Latin sd). A descending dove (presumably mechanical) featured also in John Bale's play of *Johan Baptystes Preachynge* that was staged in Kilkenny in 1553 (John Bale, *The Complete Plays of John Bale*, ed. P. Happé, 2 vols [Cambridge, 1986] II, 48), and see further in chapter 4. For accounts of dramatic props used to embellish the Pentecost liturgy, compare also Young, *Drama*, I, 489–91.

77 For example, in the York Mercers' accounts for their Doomsday pageant wagon (A.F. Johnston and M. Rogerson, eds. *York*, Records of Early English Drama [Toronto, 1979] I, 55–6).

78 The Pentecost play of the York cycle featured an angel (R. Beadle, ed., *The York Plays* [London, 1982], p. 382); Chester's play has two of them (Lumiansky and Mills, *Chester*, I, 388).

79 Not an unheard-of theatrical technique: J.W. Robinson, 'On the Evidence for Puppets in Late Medieval England,' *Theatre Survey* 14 (1973), 112–17. Records of an early-sixteenth-century play on the life of Thomas Becket witness to live actors sharing the stage with a painted mechanical angel, also on a wire (G.E. Dawson, *Records of Plays and Players in Kent, 1450–1642*, Malone Society Collections 7 [Oxford, 1965], p. 192). An early example (twelfth-century) of the mixing of live and mechanical performers is to be found in the *Jeu d'Adam* (W. Noomen, ed., *Le Jeu d'Adam* [Paris, 1971], p. 39, lines 598–600) when a serpent, *artificiose compositus* ('artificially constructed'), rises up next to the trunk of the forbidden tree and Eve turns her ear to it. The 'worm' appearing in Beverley in 1391 (Nelson, *English Stage*, p. 92) may have been of a similar order.

80 By the high and late Middle Ages, what constituted 'liturgical drama' had become a complex matter (compare, for example, the implications of the study by P. Meredith, 'The Bodley Burial and Resurrection: Late English Liturgical Drama?' in A.J. Fletcher and W. Hüsken, eds., *Between Folk and Liturgy*, Ludus 3 [Amsterdam and Atlanta,

1997], pp. 133–55). Some narratives and their modes of presentation, relative to the kernel *Visitatio Sepulcri* plays, were much more diverse and elaborate, and liable to resist containment within the compact category that 'liturgical drama' might suggest. By 'strictly liturgical,' I mean a play that is wholly (or mainly) in Latin, is sung, and is part of the regular liturgy.

81 Young, *Drama*, I, 491.

82 Who the players paid by the cathedral were is unknown. They may even have been commissioned outsiders, people with cathedral connections but not necessarily on its clerical staff, and who in other contexts had acquired experience mounting plays.

83 On the liberty of St Sepulchre, see H. Wood, ed., *Court Book of the Liberty of St. Sepulchre* (Dublin, 1930), pp. viii–ix. The name St Sepulchre refers ultimately to the Holy Sepulchre in Jerusalem, the traditional tomb of Christ, a place whose liberation from the infidel was one of the ostensible reasons for the First Crusade. Devotion to the Holy Sepulchre spread throughout Europe, and especially in those churches where the Sepulchre was honoured, Easter *Quem quaeritis* dramas might be performed.

84 The residence appears to have been known widely as St Sepulchre's. An early reference to it appears in the 1326–7 declaration of the extent of the city boundaries (*CARD*, I, 157).

85 The typology of the seal's depiction compares with that found in some contemporary English analogues. The seal's angel holds what is probably a palm branch (compare, for example, the angel in the de Lisle Psalter illustration of the scene, *c* 1300). There is the suggestion of a wing curving upwards to the left above his head. Opposite him stand the three Marys in a group. Above their heads is suspended a cup-shaped object, probably the lamp within the Sepulchre. Angel and Marys stand behind a rectangular object, which seems hinged, and wider at the left than at the right. This is probably a chest tomb (and if so, of a typical thirteenth-century shape), with lid raised to show the Marys that the body has gone. The scene is framed within a domed structure which represents the Sepulchre. There is a suggestion also of three figures outside the Sepulchre frame and beneath the chest tomb. These probably represent the soldiers appointed to watch over the tomb, but now asleep.

86 Mills, *Account Roll*, p. 185.

87 Davis, *Non-Cycle Plays*, p. lxxxvi.

88 Mills, *Account Roll*, pp. 185–6.

89 A.J. Fletcher, '"Benedictus qui venit in nomine Domini": A Thirteenth-Century Sermon for Advent and the Macaronic Style in England,' *Mediæval Studies* 56 (1994), 217–45; p. 231, note 31.

90 Augustinian prescription for the maintenance of library presses and books was careful (J.W. Clark, *The Observances in Use at the Augustinian Priory of S. Giles and S. Andrew at Barnwell, Cambridgeshire* [Cambridge, 1897], pp. 63–9). For an example of a reverse process, where in the early-fourteenth century part of a play prologue was

copied onto a roll subsequently used for keeping the accounts of a manor belonging to the abbey of Bury St Edmunds, see Davis, *Non-Cycle Plays*, p. cxiv.

91 J. Lydon, *Ireland in the Later Middle Ages* (Dublin, 1973), p. 21, has most recently repeated the suggestion that the play may have been taken from a copy in the possession of some guest at the priory. This scenario invented to account for its presence on the account roll has proved tenacious. It originated with Mills, *Account Roll*, p. xxv, and was perpetuated by St.J.D. Seymour, *Anglo-Irish Literature 1200–1582* (Cambridge, 1929), p. 120, by Gwynn, 'Anglo-Irish Theatre,' p. 262 (where the guest was further conceived as having been an Englishman, hence Gwynn's suggestion that the play was an English import), and then by Clark, *EIS*, p. 9. The guest theory cannot be disproved, of course, but as Davis, *Non-Cycle Plays*, p. xcix, has convincingly suggested, *The Pride of Life* could have been composed in Ireland (and see my argument below). While its authorship is unknown, its author was doubtless clerical: may it have been the composition of an Augustinian canon?

92 Davis, *Non-Cycle Plays*, pp. lxxxv–lxxxvi.

93 Individual parts were sometimes copied, as the Shrewsbury Fragments testify (Davis, *Non-Cycle Plays*, p. xvi) or indeed the part of *Dux Moraud*, copied onto a parchment roll cut from a larger assize roll for Norfolk and Suffolk (Davis, ibid., pp. c–ci).

94 Play manuscripts were not always produced with the needs of the play-producer primarily in mind. Compare, for example, the late-fifteenth-century manuscript of the N-Town plays, which was written by a scribe interested in presenting a text for an ordinary reader as much as for a play producer (A.J. Fletcher, 'The N-Town Plays,' in R. Beadle, ed., *The Cambridge Companion to Medieval English Theatre* [Cambridge, 1994], pp. 163–88).

95 We do not know exactly where in the building the priory accounts would have been kept, but if in library presses, then presumably they ought to have been kept well.

96 Davis, *Non-Cycle Plays*, p. 99, lines 299–302.

97 Mills, *Account Roll*, p. xxvii. The two components of Gailispire seem to be 'Gaili-' or 'Gailis-' + 'spire.'

98 As Davis, *Non-Cycle Plays*, p. xcviii, has implied.

99 L. Price, *The Place-Names of Co. Wicklow*, 7 vols (Dublin, 1945–67)V, 328–9.

100 Price, ibid.. Kilruddery is a townland adjacent to present-day Giltspur. The record of the transaction in the Register of the Abbey of St Thomas, Dublin, says nothing of gilt spurs, however, but rather of an annual rent of two *bisancia* ('bezants'; J.T. Gilbert, ed., *Register of the Abbey of St. Thomas, Dublin*, Rolls Series 91 [London, 1889], p. 150).

101 Price, *Place-Names*, p. 328. Forms with or without -t- evidently coexisted by this date. While phonetic assimilation of the -t- might explain its absence in the forms that do not have it, another explanation, one more economical, is that the forms without -t- witness to an etymon in which no -t- existed in the first place, but into which one was later intruded; see further below.

102 I take it that Gailispire would then be comprised of 'Gailis' (that is, *geil* with genitive inflection) plus 'spire' (derived possibly from *spor*). The -ai- spelling in 'Gaili' / 'Gailis' for a proposed Old Norse etymon with -ei- presents no difficulties if we trust conventional wisdom on the falling together in later Middle English of the ai/ei diphthongs.

103 Gwynn and Hadcock, *Medieval Religious Houses*, pp. 171–3.

104 I am grateful to K.M. Davies of the Royal Irish Academy for helpful discussion on the topography of Kilruddery and Giltspur, and to Howard B. Clarke for advice on the Kilruddery manor house. I have not yet been able to ascertain whether Kilruddery House incorporates the medieval manor house in its core.

105 The nature and extent of the manor buildings are most clearly detailed in an agreement of 1261 (Gilbert, *Abbey of St. Thomas*, p. 177); the Kilruddery property is described as a castle in a deed of 1553 (G.D. Scott, *The Stones of Bray* [Dublin, 1913], p. 88, note 3). This appellation continued into the seventeenth century, as in the grant of Kilruddery Castle to Sir William Brabazon, 14 September 1618 (*Irish Patent Rolls of James I* [Dublin, 1966], p. 447, no. 19).

106 A reference to waiting upon the weather seems intended in line 10 of the play: '<And ter>yith al for þe weder' (Davis, *Non-Cycle Plays*, p. 90).

107 A good example in *The Pride of Life* of a consciously patterned stylistic exaggeration, apt for declamatory purposes in an environment demanding more strenuous voice projection, and where other possible outdoor sounds may have been in competition, is seen in the King of Life's opening rodomontade (Davis, *Non-Cycle Plays*, pp. 93–4, lines 113–26). Only here, in as much of the play as survives, does the playwright employ strenuous alliteration. It is not merely decorative, or even of importance for the lines' metre, but seems a stylistic shorthand for braggadocio, comparable to similar alliterative inflations written locally into the speeches of other medieval dramatic ranters (King Herod of the mystery plays was a famous example). And for other possible evidence of noise in the play, see I. Hengstebeck, 'Wer träumt in *The Pride of Life*?' *Archiv für das Studium der Neueren Sprachen und Literaturen* 208 (1971), 119–22.

108 A wide audience is canvassed in its prologue (Davis, *Non-Cycle Plays*, p. 90, lines 1–8).

109 Although members of the laity may have watched the Dublin *Visitatio Sepulcri*, for the laity was sometimes present at liturgical drama (R. Axton, *European Drama of the Early Middle Ages* [London, 1974], p. 67 and Young, *Drama*, I, 685), most would have found the chanted Latin dialogue inaccessible.

110 Davis, *Non-Cycle Plays*, p. 90, line 9.

111 The King of Life projects roles representing the various estates of society upon the members of his audience, and lords it over them as if he were their monarch. Later the messenger issues to them the King's challenge (Davis, *Non-Cycle Plays*, pp. 104–5, lines 471–502), thus maintaining them in the imaginary role that the King had earlier cast them in. Such audience role-playing also has the advantage of making it receptive to the play's didacticism.

112 Davis, *Non-Cycle Plays*, p. lxxxix, is rightly too cautious to assert that the devils, the Virgin and the soul and body of the King of Life were certainly represented on stage, but as he admits, it is most probable that they were. All extant medieval plays in English which unfold their plot in some sort of prologue proceed to present substantially what the prologue has announced, unless their text has been subsequently corrupted. *The Pride of Life* would be out of kilter with all the rest if it behaved otherwise. Since the plot summary given in *EIS*, p. 9, is slightly garbled, it seems appropriate to give one here. The King of Life, fixed in an absurd belief that he will live forever, is abetted in his opinion by his knights, Strength and Health. Though his Queen, a voice of reason, reminds him that all must die, he defies her, refusing her counsel as uncongenial. While he has withdrawn to sleep, she sends his messenger, Solas, to summon the Bishop to come and preach to him about his inevitable end and of the preparations that he ought to make for the good of his soul in the light of eternity. The Bishop comes, preaches, and is sent packing by the King, who then sends Solas on another errand to announce a challenge to all would-be adversaries, including the King of Death. At this point the text as it survived on the account roll broke off and the remainder of its plot must be reconstructed from the prologue's indications. The King of Death evidently heeded the challenge, came and killed the King of Life's knights and then the King of Life himself. A debate followed between the King of Life's soul and his dead body. The soul was subsequently seized by devils, weighed, but finally interceded for by the Blessed Virgin Mary. The play presumably ended on an optimistic note, since in medieval tradition, her Son unfailingly found such maternal pleas irresistible.

113 The most demanding scene in terms of numbers in the extant portion of the play, where the Bishop preaches to the King of Life on the certainty of death, would have required at least six actors. After the Bishop has been dismissed by the King, he is not heard of again, nor is his return mentioned in the prologue. The knights, Strength and Health, will eventually be liquidated by the King of Death, and there is no apparent need for either the Queen or Solas in the portion of the play that has not survived. Five actors would therefore be freed to fill the roles remaining in the latter part of the play. Although it is not essential to assume doubling, nor is there any obvious proof of it, doubling is an economical solution that would fit the play well. It is commonly documented elsewhere: the *Croxton Play of the Sacrament*, for example, noted that for the twelve roles needed, 'IX may play yt at ease' (Davis, *Non-Cycle Plays*, p. 89). On doubling, see D. Bevington, *From Mankind to Marlowe* (Cambridge, Mass., 1962), esp. pp. 17 and 73.

114 Davis, *Non-Cycle Plays*, p. 99, line 303, and sd after line 306.

115 It is probable that the booth was also situated on a scaffold, for *tentorium* implies one (Latham, *Word List*, p. 480, **tenta** 1). The cognate of *tentorium*, *tentum*, appears several times in the fifteenth-century Cornish *Ordinalia* play manuscript, where it has been interpreted as designating a curtained booth on a scaffold (P. Neuss, 'The Staging of

the Creacion of the World,' *Theatre Notebook* 33 [1979], 119–20 and R. Southern, *The Medieval Theatre in the Round,* 2nd ed. [London, 1975], pp. 229–31). See also A.C. Cawley, M. Jones, P.F. McDonald, and D. Mills, *The Revels History of Drama in English Volume I: Medieval Drama* (London and New York, 1983), p. 17. R. Beadle, 'The East Anglian "Game-Place": A Possibility for Further Research,' *Records of Early English Drama Newsletter* 3 (1978), 2–4, suggests that the 'tentys' / 'tentes' appearing in Yarmouth game-place documents refer to scaffolds (p. 4, note 8), though his view is questioned by D. Galloway, 'Comment: The East Anglian "Game-Place": Some Facts and Fictions,' *Records of Early English Drama Newsletter* 4 (1979), 24–6; pp. 25–6. A reference to some sort of curtained scaffold, into which King Herod withdraws to sleep in the N-Town Passion Play (P. Meredith, ed., *The Passion Play from the N. Town Manuscript* [London and New York], 1990, p. 89, sd, and p. 92, lines 86–9) sounds remarkably similar to *The Pride of Life* booth.

116 Davis, *Non-Cycle Plays,* p. 100, lines 321–2.

117 As, for example, in *The Castle of Perseverance* (*c* 1400–25), an important play in the place-and-scaffold mode. Compare M. Eccles, ed., *The Macro Plays,* EETS, OS 262 (Oxford, 1969), p. 16, sd after line 455, 'Pipe vp musyk'; p. 20, sd after line 574, 'Trumpe vp' (this latter call for music also covers the movement of a group of characters from one locale to another).

118 The manuscript appears to have been deficient at this point. Davis, *Non-Cycle Plays,* p. 104, sd after line 470, following earlier editors, reads: 'Et eat pla<team>' (presumably, 'Let him go through the place'); Southern, *Theatre in the Round,* p. 222, interprets it as 'and he shall go [down] into the place'). The subsequent action of the messenger helps justify the reading 'plateam,' incidentally, since he would have to 'go through the place' to deliver the King of Life's challenge to the audience, which is precisely what he does.

119 On the variations in place-and-scaffold terminology generally, see Southern, *Theatre in the Round,* pp. 219–36; also, Cawley, Jones, McDonald, and Mills, *Revels History,* pp. 14–19. In some performances the shape and size of the *platea* may have been adjustable according to the actors' needs. In *The Pride of Life,* for example, the extra mobility of the standing audience would have given the actors more scope to re-negotiate the *platea* size if required. The speaker of the prologue seems to refer to a ground-level *platea* when he exhorts the audience not to disturb 'oure place' (Davis, *Non-Cycle Plays,* p. 93, line 110). Presumably, therefore, the audience was in a position to disturb the actors' free playing space quite easily.

120 Cawley, Jones, McDonald, and Mills, *Revels History,* p. 221. However, the claim made there that *The Pride of Life,* 'with its large cast and pivotal scene of battle,' is like *The Castle of Perseverance* in having a 'comparable outlay on costumes and effects' goes far beyond both what survives of *The Pride of Life* and what can be inferred about its plot. Doubling, as was noted, would facilitate its performance by as few as six actors.

Bevington, *Mankind to Marlowe*, pp. 49 and 72, has estimated twenty-two actors necessary to play *The Castle of Perseverance* with doubling. Place-and-scaffold production seems to have been extremely common in these islands, and probably commoner than the more famous processional method which posed more complex organizational difficulties (A.H. Nelson, 'Some Configurations of Staging in Medieval English Drama,' in Taylor and Nelson, *Medieval English Drama*, pp. 116–47).

121 Apart from scaffolds for the King of Life and the Bishop, three other locales are possibly suggested in the prologue's plot outline: heaven, hell, and the residence of the King of Death. Heaven and hell were often hosted on scaffolds of their own, as in *The Castle of Perseverance* or the Cornish *Ordinalia*, to name but two. A maximum of five possible scaffolds for *The Pride of Life* would, though solely in this respect, make it comparable to *The Castle of Perseverance*. Production of *The Pride of Life* on a single scaffold, while not strictly impossible, would fit less snugly alongside what is known of the production of other place-and-scaffold plays where a journey through the *platea* connects action between *different* scaffolds.

122 I am grateful to Marion Gunn for drawing this impression. For the costuming of the King of Death, who is depicted on the scaffold throne, we have been guided by a late-fifteenth-century illustration of Atropos watching a tournament (Wickham, *Early English Stages*, I, frontispiece). The size of the available performance budget probably determined whether the play would have been a relatively modest two-scaffold or a lavish five-scaffold affair. The bigger it got, the more expense it would necessarily have incurred. There is no obvious indication of how it was financed. Speculation on this will necessarily follow from whatever assumptions are made about the play's auspices, on which see below.

123 It has recently been spoken of as a 'clerk's play' by I. Lancashire, ed., *Dramatic Texts and Records of Britain: A Chronological Topography to 1558* (Cambridge, 1984), p. xv. However, he is careful not to define too precisely what 'clerks' play,' in the case of *The Pride of Life*, may be taken to mean. The question is complex. On the one hand, the medium of the play's survival implies clerical interest in it, and my discussion will proceed on the assumption of some sort of clerical input in its production. But this may not have been how it was originally produced. See note 124 following.

124 S.J. Kahrl, *Traditions of Medieval English Drama* (London, 1974), p. 102, thought the play's auspices thoroughly secular. He considered it an early example of a play from the repertoire of a professional theatrical troupe. But anything the play suggests about the possible auspices of its production must be balanced against what is suggested by the *context* in which the play survives. Kahrl's view could be right, but in neglecting the context, it is less comprehensive; after all, different interest groups can mount the same play.

125 M. Clark and R. Refaussé, eds., *Directory of Historic Dublin Guilds* (Dublin, 1993), pp. 28–9.

126 On the Tailors guild chapel, see M.V. Ronan, 'Religious Customs of Dublin Medieval Gilds,' *Irish Ecclesiastical Record,* 5th ser 26 (1925), 364–85; see pp. 377–8. Given that *The Pride of Life* copy was written in the first half of the fifteenth century, it could conceivably even be a record of a play which had been taken over and run by the Tailors guild.

127 The Corpus Christi procession is first officially noticed in 1466; see below. The Tailors were evidently gathering experience in open-air presentations, and as an established guild with an organized infrastructure, they would have been the right sort of people to take over the running of a play (compare their later dramatic undertakings discussed in chapter 6).

128 M. Twycross, '"Transvestism" in the Mystery Plays,' *Medieval English Theatre* 5 (1983), 123–80.

129 The likely locations would have been at places accustomed to public displays, such as sites for delivering proclamations. The High Cross, at the junction of High Street and Skinners' Row (see fig. 3), was one such. At this date, the cross marked Dublin's central square. Proclamations were made from it, and on market days, penitents might be exposed as a public spectacle on its highest steps (H.F. Berry, ed., *Register of Wills and Inventories of the Diocese of Dublin* [Dublin, 1898], pp. 25 and 202). One such sixteenth-century spectacle, for example, required a pair of penitents who had been convicted of adultery to sit on the highest steps on market day between 9:00 and 11:00 a.m. dressed in white sheets and holding white rods in each hand (J.T. Gilbert, *A History of the City of Dublin,* 3 vols [Dublin, 1854–9; repr Shannon, 1972] I, 213–16).

130 A correction in the M copy of the *Visitatio* play, fol. 59v, in a hand of the second half of the fifteenth century, suggests that as late as this the play was still of interest.

131 The Hoggen Green Christmastide plays of 1528, discussed in the next chapter, were in part a collaborative venture undertaken by clerical and lay interest groups, and evidently in a tradition similar to that inferred above for *The Pride of Life.*

132 DCA, C1/2/1, fols 56v–7v (*CARD*, I, 239–41).

133 DCA, C1/2/1, fols 56v–7. This first pageant list is written on the first of two bifolia originally appended to complete the Anglo-Norman Laws and Usages of the City of Dublin (*CARD*, I, 224–32). Both pageant lists were later inserted in this spare space at the end of the Laws and Usages. Note the following transcription points: Line 1 christi day a pagent] the upper parts of these words are cropped at the top of the page; 9 avter] *corrected from* auter; 14 <The>] *CARD*, I, 240, reads 'and' here, but elsewhere 'and' is more often written &, and from what can be seen of the remaining ink, 'The' is more likely (hiatus, 11mm); 15 <Goldsm>ythis] *CARD*, I, 240, reads '[Goldsmy]this,' probably correctly (hiatus, 10 mm); 17 hopers] *CARD*, I, 240, reads 'Hoopers,' but although the writing is now virtually illegible, a single -o- spelling is confirmed by the available space (12 mm); 22 An<na>] adoption of this spelling of the name is based

on its spelling in the second list; 23 Conpteours] *CARD*, I, 240, reads 'Courteours,' noting that the manuscript was 'indistinct,' but in fact only the third and fourth letters are a little unclear – perhaps the Conpteours were the city auditors or accountants (the word of nearest resemblance recorded by *OED* is **Countour**); 24 ffisshers þe] these words have been touched up with post-medieval ink, and the þ altered to y.

134 *EIS*, p. 12, interprets the fine, possibly too narrowly, as being imposed for failure to present the pageant.

135 DCA, MR/5/2, mb. 12 (*CARD*, I, 392).

136 DCA, MR/5/2, mb. 6 (*CARD*, I, 324).

137 It is self-evident that capricious variation by any one party cannot be far tolerated if a team enterprise is to be organized; also, it may be that significant alteration of a guild's subject matter was frowned upon, especially in this guild's case where an important pageant, Christ's Passion, was at stake.

138 Seymour, *Anglo-Irish Literature*, pp. 123–4, first put forward the view, tacitly received and endorsed in *EIS*, pp. 11–12, that the pageant list printed in W. Harris, *The History and Antiquities of the City of Dublin* (Dublin, 1766), pp. 147–8, derived from a list formerly in the Chain Book which represents the earliest known form of the Corpus Christi pageant procession. But since Harris's list betrays some misreading and inaccurate paraphrasing of whatever putative original ultimately lay behind it, it must be treated with the greatest caution as a description of something that the Chain Book might be presumed to have once contained. In fact, Harris's list may merely have derived from a transcription of Robert Ware, an earlier antiquarian to whom Harris acknowledges a heavy debt (for his connections with the Ware family, see chapter 3, note 153).

139 Compare Beadle, *York Plays*, p. 31; and M. James, 'Ritual, Drama and Social Body in the Late Medieval English Town,' *Past and Present* 98 (1983), 3–29; see p. 18.

140 The Account Book of the Tailors guild survives in two nineteenth-century transcriptions: DCL, MS 80, and BL, MS Egerton 1765. DCL, MS 80 is demonstrably a copy of BL, MS Egerton 1765, however, and *not* of the lost originals. The original Account Book of the guild of Carpenters, Millers, Masons, and Heliers is DCL, MS 209. The Treasurer's Book is DCA, MR/35.

141 Clark and Refaussé, *Historic Dublin Guilds*, p. 17.

142 Clark and Refaussé, *Historic Dublin Guilds*, passim; on guild organization generally, see also H.F. Westlake, *The Parish Gilds of Medieval England* (London, 1919), and C. Gross, *The Gild Merchant*, 2 vols (Oxford, 1890).

143 There are several indications of Chester immigrants settling in Dublin. See Appendix I, note 4.

144 Hitherto this connection has gone unnoticed; see L.M. Clopper, ed. *Chester*, Records of Early English Drama (Toronto, 1979), pp. li-ii and pp. 234–38 for the Shrove Tuesday ball ceremony, and pp. 23 and 253–4 for the Black Monday celebration. It

may be that Chester has adopted certain Dublin customs here, not vice versa. Though the customs in Chester are more amply described, they are not as early as Dublin's, where the Shrove Tuesday ball bearing, for example, is first recorded as early as 1462 (as opposed to 1540 in Chester; Clopper, ibid., p. li). And in Chester, the origins of the Black Monday customs had been long forgotten by the early seventeenth century.

145 Compare R. Beadle and P. Meredith, *The York Play: A Facsimile of British Library MS Additional 35290 together with a Facsimile of the Ordo Paginarum Section of the A/Y Memorandum Book*, Leeds Texts and Monographs, Medieval Drama Facsimiles VII (Leeds, 1983), fols 252v–5, with fig. 9.

146 The first Dublin list, however, focuses on characters and props while the first York list, though also focusing on characters, seems to mention props only incidentally. It therefore seems that the primary purpose of the first York list was to sketch the narrative events of a pageant.

147 Beadle, *York Plays*, pp. 23–4.

148 Beadle and Meredith, *York Play*, pp. lii–liii.

149 H.F. Berry, 'The Goldsmiths' Company of Dublin,' *Journal of the Royal Society of Antiquaries of Ireland* 31 (1901), 119–33; see p. 127.

150 R.M. Lumiansky and D. Mills, *The Chester Mystery Cycle: Essays and Documents* (Chapel Hill and London, 1983), p. 175.

151 My translation. For the Latin original, see Johnston and Rogerson, *York*, I, 17.

152 However, the wording of the Chain Book list suggests that the angel on the Hoopers' pageant may actually have sung. Nelson, *English Stage*, pp. 40–2, notes the stopping of wagons for partial representation, with brief speeches and the like. This seems to have happened even in places like York, where the plays were played fully in a second procession.

153 For evidence that the Chester Corpus Christi play was presented outside the context of the actual Corpus Christi procession, see Clopper, *Chester*, p. liii.

154 Lumiansky and Mills, *Documents*, p. 169; Clopper, *Chester*, pp. liii–liv.

155 Walker, 'Historical Essay,' p. 83. (The historian J. Walsh, 'Ireland Sixty Years Ago,' *Dublin University Magazine* [1843], p. 657, mentions documentation of 'plays and mysteries' existing 'in the books of the corporation.' It is not clear whether he has overstated the evidence that still survives or whether he saw documents now lost.) The location of St George's Chapel is discussed below.

156 BL, MS Egerton 1765, fols 120 and 121 respectively.

157 On Kilkenny, see chapter 4.

158 That famous dumb show, *The Murder of Gonzago* in *Hamlet*, was, after all, an integral part of its play and was played by players.

159 Such extreme and minimal dramatic forms existed, and were of medieval parentage. D. Mehl, *The Elizabethan Dumb Show* (London, 1965), pp. 13–15, in discussing the

relationship of the dumb show and the emblematic *tableau vivant*, notes how these two modes may shade in and out of each other.

160 For a survey of sixteenth-century drama criticism, see J.W.H. Atkins, *English Literary Criticism: The Renascence* (London, 1947), pp. 216–61.

161 For example Mills, *Account Roll*, p. xxvii, considered plays to be regular events in medieval Dublin.

162 Chambers, *Mediæval Stage*, II, 365.

163 Apart from the fact that fabricated camels were now starting to appear in pageant processions, Dubliners had already been introduced to a camel in the flesh in 1472, when the importation of a live one caused quite a sensation (Freeman, *Annals of Connacht*, p. 561).

164 Only the gospel of Matthew mentions the flight into Egypt, and does not say how the Holy Family travelled. Their apocryphal ass was so well established by this date that it was no doubt mistaken for authentic tradition. Thus it seems unlikely that it would have been exchanged for any other animal, at least not if its purpose was to appear in a play including the flight into Egypt.

165 Strictly, the annunciation to the sheperds preceded the Epiphany. It may be that it is broadly appropriate for this cluster of pageants (part of pageant six, and pageants seven and eight) to follow on after Old Testament pageants. Regarded as a group, they do suggest a step forward in time: we are now watching events associated with Christmastide. However, no strict chronology is observed in the ordering of these events. The same holds true for the Passiontide pageants. It is broadly appropriate that Christ's death follow his birth, but the Passiontide pageants, as will be seen, do not follow each other with strict chronological accuracy.

166 The greater part of the procession, however, in being broadly continuous chronologically, perhaps satisfied a different kind of logic. When holding a procession which for the most part presented episodes from a known narrative, it might have made more sense from a spectator's point of view to see first the most important episodes, then to have them followed with the less distinctive but related ones. Thus less distinctive episodes would be more readily recognized following ones instantly familiar, even if strict chronological continuity was thereby lost.

167 The apostles seem also to have assembled for Creed plays.

168 The word 'tormentor' is a common one in dramatic records for anyone playing the part of a torturer or executioner, usually of Christ, but also sometimes of a martyr saint.

169 On the Nine Worthies, see chapter 3.

170 There is no mention of St George accompanying the dragon (perhaps he was assumed), but even by itself the dragon would have been sufficiently emblematic of the St George guild and hence of Dublin Corporation, appropriately taking pride of place at the

rear of the procession. (This position was frequently reserved for corporation representatives; Nelson, *English Stage*, p. 126.) While from the civic and processional point of view this may have been very appropriate, it was probably immaterial to any possible play cycle.

171 The popularity of particular episodes of sacred history has long been recognized. (An attempt to explain the rationale of their selection is made by Kolve, *Play Called Corpus Christi*, pp. 54–100.)

172 More modest than the cycles of Coventry, Chester, and York, for example, but roughly comparable to a cycle like that of Norwich (for a summary of cycle contents, see Chambers, *Mediæval Stage*, II, 408–26).

173 The Old Free Book list is printed in Davis, *Non-Cycle Plays*, pp. xxix–xxx.

174 J. Dutka, 'Mystery Plays at Norwich: Their Formation and Development,' *Leeds Studies in English*, New Series 10 (1978), 107–20.

175 J. Dutka, 'The Lost Dramatic Cycle of Norwich and the Grocers' Play of the Fall of Man,' *Review of English Studies* 35 (1984), 1–13; pp. 3–6.

176 We may have allowed our expectation of what a typical play cycle should contain to become too rigid, and partly perhaps this may be as a result of Kolve's influential attempt to explain the rationale of cyclic drama (see note 171 above).

177 *CARD*, I, 492; G.L. Barrow, 'The Franchises of Dublin,' *Dublin Historical Record* 36 (1983), 68–80.

178 With the accession of a protestant queen in 1558, religious feeling probably started to turn against Corpus Christi drama again (H.C. Gardiner, *Mysteries' End: An Investigation of the Last Days of the Medieval Religious Stage* [New Haven, 1946]). The Chester cycle, for example, one of the most entrenched, was last performed in 1575 (Lumiansky and Mills, *Documents*, pp. 192–4). The demise of the Dublin Corpus Christi procession may also have had something to do with the decay of St George's Chapel, for which see chapter 3.

179 While individual guilds probably maintained some procession or special observances on the feast of their patron saint, these would have come nowhere near the magnitude of the display on Corpus Christi, or even on St George's Day.

180 In its early days, there was some difficulty about observing the franchise riding regularly, but eventually it became much looked forward to, and did not vanish until the nineteenth century. It is not clear when pageants first entered the franchise procession, but franchise expenses start to feature prominently in guild and corporation documents from *c* 1600. For a fuller account, see further in chapter 3.

181 J. O'Keeffe, *Recollections of the Life of John O'Keeffe, Written by Himself* (London, 1826), p. 43.

182 J.D. Herbert, *Irish Varieties* (London, 1836), p. 71.

183 O'Keeffe, *Recollections*, p. 38, said that he was seated in a front window, and that the procession went by 'close under me.'

184 O'Keeffe, ibid., pp. 39–40.

185 Walsh, 'Ireland Sixty Years Ago,' pp. 655–6.

186 J. Barrington, *Personal Sketches of His Own Times*, 3rd ed, 3 vols (London, 1869) I, 140.

187 Barrington, ibid., I, 141–2.

188 Compare L.J. Morrissey, 'English Pageant-Wagons,' *Eighteenth-Century Studies* 9 (1975–6), 353–74; see p. 360, where a case is made for a basic continuity in form and size between medieval and seventeenth-century London pageant wagons.

189 Barrington, *Personal Sketches*, I, 142.

190 Alternative names, it seems, for Pilate and his wife. See further in chapter 3.

191 Meanings of the word in this period include the carrying out of repairs or decoration (*OED*, s.v. **Trim**).

192 Payments for pageant wagon maintenance are common in dramatic records, as for example in York (Johnston and Rogerson, *York*, I, passim).

193 It is hard to tell whether it may also have been canopied, as were some of the eighteenth-century wagons.

194 The 1498 pageant wagon of Noah's Flood may conceivably have been a wheeled ship; something on these lines paraded in later franchise processions (Walsh, 'Ireland Sixty Years Ago,' p. 656).

195 And compare the dragon-bearers at Walsingham, Lanark, noted by Nelson, *English Stage*, p. 183; he also notes, p. 111, the possiblity that the bearing of a pageant by porters suggests the pageant may not have been of the regular wagon type.

196 For the composition of the Dublin wagons, see chapter 3.

197 This Ommeganck is reproduced and discussed in J. Laver, *Isabella's Triumph* (London, 1947). For a general study of analogous processions, see M. Twycross, 'The Flemish Ommegang and its Pageant Cars,' *Medieval English Theatre* 2 (1980), 15–41 and 80–98.

198 The Dublin pageant wagons would certainly have been smaller than the 12′ × 20′ estimate made for one of the Brussells pageants by R. Hosley, 'Three Kinds of Outdoor Theatre before Shakespeare,' *Theatre Survey* 12 (1971), 1–33; p. 17. The reasons for deducing the size of the Dublin wagons are given in chapter 3.

199 On the construction of the sixteenth-century Dublin dragon, see further in chapter 3.

200 Although small details of the pageant route may have varied over the years, the outline which follows stands.

201 Added credence can be given to Walker's assertion on the grounds that at least by the sixteenth century, the chapel served as a destination for processions, since it is known that the procession on St George's Day normally ended there. The use of the Hoggen Green as a venue for plays is examined in chapter 3.

202 Compare the practice in York, where the pageant wagons assembled on the open area known as Toft Green, just within the city walls and close to the first playing place or station at Holy Trinity Priory (Beadle, *York Plays*, pp. 34–5).

203 The route taken by Corpus Christi processions in other cities in these islands, in those cases where it is known, lay invariably, at least for some of its course, through the city itself.

204 Note that in the eighteenth century, the procession of pageants for the franchise riding moved along Thomas Street (O'Keeffe, *Recollections*, p. 38), though it is not clear whether towards the city or away from it. If Morrissey, 'Pageant-Wagons,' pp. 354–5, is right to claim conservatism for such processional routes, then the eighteenth-century riding through Thomas Street may indeed be a clue to the route of the medieval procession; Thomas Street turned into Newgate Street, which in turn became High Street, one of the streets forming the spine of the medieval city.

205 And compare note 129 above.

206 In Chester, special arrangements were made to have the procession pass before the Pentice, the seat of Chester Corporation (Lumiansky and Mills, *Documents*, pp. 182–3). In Dublin, it might also be noted that the Corpus Christi guild had its chapel in St Michael's Church, also near the High Cross, and thus it would have been most appropriate to lead a procession in this direction.

207 From as early as 1451, the Holy Trinity guild was leasing the upper rooms of the Tholsel. No doubt its guild members would therefore have had access to a good view of the procession. The Tholsel too was a cynosure. For example, a letter of Sir Geoffrey Fenton to Sir Robert Cecil, 26 February 1601, mentions the affixing of a proclamation 'vpon the Tolseale dore for all men to read' (PRO, SP 63/208/Part 1, fol. 148).

208 The incline is still visible today (and see A. Simms, 'Medieval Dublin: A Topographical Analysis,' *Irish Geography* 12 [1979], 25–41, fig. 1, following p. 27).

209 All route distances are derived from Rocque, *An Exact Survey*.

210 As Simms, 'Medieval Dublin,' p. 36, has observed, there was, presumably, some embankment at either side of the gate making the gate necessary.

211 The exact location of the chapel is uncertain. H.B. Clarke, *Dublin c. 840–1540: The Medieval Town in the Modern City*, Ordnance Survey (Dublin, 1978), tentatively locates the chapel here.

212 On wagon propulsion, see P. Butterworth, 'The York Mercers' Pageant Vehicle, 1433–1467: Wheels, Steering, and Control,' *Medieval English Theatre* 1 (1979), 72–81; especially p. 81, note 51.

213 *CARD*, II, 549. Furthermore, the exit of civic processions via the Dame's Gate seems to have been traditional. Compare the report of the 1488 riding of the franchises: 'In þis the seid Mayre and his breþerne toke þer way In þe name of god first owte at the dammys gate' (RCB, C/6/1/2 [White Book of Christ Church], fol. 65; *CARD*, I, 492).

214 However, even where a medieval street width might be ascertainable, it remains impossible to know whether any structural modification to the front of some building may not have projected into the street to some extent, thereby diminishing the street

width from the practical point of view of someone considering leading a procession down it.

215 Even the narrowest width encountered on the third route, according to Rocque, was no less than about 12′ 6″, at the exit point of High Street where it debouched upon the High Cross.

216 *CARD*, II, 557.

217 Derricke, *Image of Irelande* (facsimile reprint, ed. Quinn [Belfast, 1985]), plate X.

218 *CARD*, VI, 222.

219 Ibid. My emphasis.

220 Morrissey, 'Pageant-Waggons,' p. 368 and Twycross, 'Ommegang,' p. 83. There is no way of estimating the approximate length of the medieval Dublin wagons, other than by analogy.

221 A 1476 ordinance from York, for example, puts auditioning onto a formal regular basis (Johnston and Rogerson, *York*, I, 109).

222 Bullock-Davies, *Menestrellorum Multitudo*, pp. 55–60 and 137–8; also her *Register*, pp. 108–9.

223 On Roland, see Bullock-Davies, *Register*, p. 174. As in Ireland, so in England there was a tradition of farting jesters. For example, John of Salisbury attacks such entertainers *quando tumultuantes inferius crebro sonitu aerem foedant, et turpiter inclusum turpius produnt* ('when rumbling below they foul the air with frequent noise, and when what is basely shut in they more basely bring forth'; quoted from T. Warton, *History of English Poetry*, ed. W.C. Hazlitt, 2nd ed., 3 vols [London, 1871] III, 162). The Irish evidence is both more copious and more ancient, however.

224 To some extent these groups would have overlapped, as when liveried entertainers went on tour, for example. In Ireland, the first clear evidence of this dates to the sixteenth century, though the practice is likely to be older. Note the early evidence of Irish *histriones* abroad entertaining in the household of Abbot Walter de Wenlok in a payment made 14 July 1290 (but see note 231 below). B.F. Harvey, ed., *Documents illustrating the Rule of Walter de Wenlok, Abbot of Westminster, 1283–1307*, Camden Society, volume 2 (London, 1965), p. 186: 'Dati ij ystrionibus de Ybernia pridie idus julii iiij s.' ('Given to two minstrels from Ireland on 14 July [1290], four shillings'). A recent general survey of the minstrel class, based chiefly on English evidence, is S.R. Westfall, *Patrons and Performance: Early Tudor Household Revels* (Oxford, 1990), chapter 2.

225 I quote from the earliest source of this tradition that I know, RIA, MS 1135 (24 G 15), p. 295. Though it does not declare it, this manuscript in fact contains Meredith Hanmer's *Chronicle of Ireland* in three parts or 'Books.' The *Chronicle*, written by Hanmer *c* 1591–1604, was compiled here *c* 1610 by one 'J.H.' whose initials appear on p. 5. The *Chronicle* was first published (if from the RIA manuscript, then with editorial adjustment) in Ware, *Historie* (see pp. 133–4 for this excerpt). From Ware's edition this description of Henry's Christmas feast descended to later writers, as for

example W.F. Dawson, *Christmas: Its Origins and Associations* (London, 1902), p. 52, and most recently Fitz-Simon, *Irish Theatre*, p. 9. The masking and mumming which Hanmer mentions would be unusual for the twelfth century. They may be an embroidery, telling us more about what Hanmer expected at such feasts than about what actually happened.

226 The accounts are by Gerald of Wales and Roger of Hoveden. See respectively Gerald of Wales, *Expugnatio Hibernica, the Conquest of Ireland by Giraldus Cambrensis*, ed. A.B. Scott and F.X. Martin (Dublin, 1978), p. 96, lines 27–31, and Roger of Hoveden, *Chronica Magistri Rogeri de Houedene*, ed. W. Stubbs, Rolls Series 51, 4 vols (London, 1868–71) II, 32.

227 J.T. Gilbert, *History of the Viceroys of Ireland; with Notices of the Castle of Dublin and its Chief Occupants in Former Times* (Dublin and London, 1865), p. 220.

228 Compare, for example, some of the minstrel performances at Edward I's spectacular Pentecost feast of 1306 analysed by Bullock-Davies, *Menestrellorum Multitudo, passim*.

229 A.H. Nelson, ed. *Cambridge*, Records of Early English Drama. 2 vols (Toronto, 1989) I, 7 (accounts of King's Hall and of Great St Mary's between 1362 and 1363).

230 See further in chapter 3 on this.

231 Perhaps entertainers were already organized there by the thirteenth century, if this is where the two minstrels mentioned in Abbot Walter de Wenlok's household accounts hailed from (see note 224 above). It seems at least likely that they would have come from some anglicized urban area in Ireland. The entry is also early external evidence of Irish minstrels (or at least, minstrels from Ireland) touring in England.

232 E. Tresham, ed., *Rotulorum patentum et clausorum cancellariae Hiberniae calendarium* (Dublin, 1828), p. 258, cols a–b, item 86 (abbreviations silently expanded).

233 Or at least that they had a hierarchy amongst themselves, perhaps even a guild. Compare the use of the word *marescallus* for the leader of a band of minstrels in a charter of Edward IV of 1469 (Chambers, *Mediæval Stage*, II, 260). The charter sets a group of minstrels over a minstrel fraternity or guild already existing in London.

234 A third possibility is that they were part-timers in households, and free-lancers during the rest of the time.

235 Tresham, *Rotulorum patentum et clausorum*, p. 94 col. b, item 164 (abbreviations silently expanded). The Kilkenny Statute of 1366 that is referred to said (LPL, MS 603 [Carew Papers], fol. 168r–v [Berry, *Statutes and Ordinances*, p. 446]): 'Item que les minstrels Irroies venauntz entre Engleis, espient lez priuetz maners & Comyn des Englises dont grauntz males sovent ad este venz accorde est & defende que nulles ministres {*read* ministrels} Irroies cestascavoir Tympanors fferdanes, Skelaghes, Bablers, Rymors, Clercz ne nullez autres minstrells Irrois veignent entre les Engleis / Et que nul Engleis les resceiue ou don face a eux & que le face & de ceo soit atteint soit pris et imprisone sibien lez Irrois ministreles come les Engleis que les resceiuement {*read* resceiuent} ou donent riens et puis soint reyntes a la volunte de Roy et les instrumentz

de lor ministraeltees forfaitz a nostre seignor le Roy.' ('Item, that the Irish minstrels coming amongst the English, spy out the private and public manners of the English, whereby great evils have often come to pass; it is agreed and forbidden that any Irish minstrels, that is, *timpán* players, poets, *scélaigi*, bablers, rimers, clerics, nor any other Irish minstrels, come amongst the English, and that no English man receive or give them audience; and that whoever is attainted with this be imprisoned, both the Irish minstrels as well as the English who receive them, or those who give them gifts; and then let them be handed over to the king's pleasure and the instruments of their minstrelsy confiscated to our lord the king').

236 Neither 'kerraghers' nor 'skelaghes' are noted in either the *OED* or the *Middle English Dictionary*. Their activities were described in chapter 1.

237 The use of these anglicizations is also a good indicator of the impact of Gaelic culture within the Pale, something which other historical sources confirm. Compare, for example, the Dublin by-law of 1454 to curb residence of the Gaelic Irish in the city and the commission of the same year to ascertain their numbers (*CARD*, I, 280–1); also, the letter from the earl of Kildare to the mayor and bailiffs in 1489 requiring Gaelic Irish vagrants to be expelled from the city (*CARD*, I, 139–40).

238 *OED*, **Bard** sb. 1 and **Crowder** 1 respectively. Usage of 'bard' here may emphasize the importance of an Irish route for this word's way into the English language. 'Crowder' is also ultimately of Celtic origin, though most likely adapted from Welsh *crwth* (the archaic English word 'crowd,' a variety of fiddle, is first recorded in an early-fourteenth-century text from Shropshire, a border county where Welsh influence would have been strong). 'Crowd' would have been well assimilated into English by the time of its use here, although in this context it may have been understood to refer particularly to players of the Irish *cruit* or *timpán*.

239 The first *OED* instance is from 1507, though the word *clairschach* ('harp') itself is recorded from about 1490 (*OED*, **Clairschacher** and **Clairschach** respectively; the source documents for these early citations are of either Northumbrian or Scots, but not Irish, provenance).

240 Ranulf Higden, *Polychronicon Ranulphi Higden Monachi Cestrensis*, ed. C. Babington and J.R. Lumby, Rolls Series 41, 9 vols (London, 1865–86) I, 335. Higden used the *Topographia Hibernica* of Gerald of Wales, from whence this passage derives. What the *timpán* (here, 'tymbre') actually was has been debated. In its earlier stages it may have been a plucked string instrument resembling the harp, and by the later medieval period it may have become a bowed string instrument. A. Fleischmann and R. Gleeson, 'Music in Ancient Munster and Monastic Cork,' *Journal of the Cork Historical and Archæological Society* 70 (1965), 79–98; see p. 83; also Bruford, 'Song and Recitation,' pp. 65–6.

241 As seen in chapter 1, 'rimers,' a word borrowed into English from French, was often commandeered by writers hostile to Gaelic culture.

242 Legislations like the Kilkenny Statute (note 235) or the Dublin measures (note 232) demonstrate cultural mixing. Moreover, mixed marriages would make it inevitable (A. Cosgrove, 'Marriage in Medieval Ireland,' in A. Cosgrove, ed., *Marriage in Ireland* [Dublin, 1985], pp. 25–50; see pp. 34–5).

243 Durham, Dean and Chapter Muniments, Misc. Ch. 5822, mb. 4 (these muniments are currently in the custody of the Archives and Special Collections of Durham University Library). The Constitutions were issued in Lent of 1367 (i.e., between 18 February and 4 April in that year). Similar Constitutions appear outside Ireland in other mid-fourteenth-century episcopal registers; compare, for example, the Constitution issued by Bishop John Trillek of Hereford in 1348 (D.N. Klausner, ed. *Herefordshire Worcestershire*, Records of Early English Drama (Toronto, 1990), pp. 57–8). Line 7 coinquinantur] some text missing after this?

244 The *Crede Mihi* statute dates to the mid-thirteenth century (C.R. Cheney, 'A Group of Related Synodal Statutes of the Thirteenth Century,' in J.A. Watt, J.B. Morrall, and F.X. Martin, eds. *Medieval Studies presented to Aubrey Gwynn s.j.* [Dublin, 1961], pp. 114–32; see pp. 124–5). The hand copying the statute, however, was active between spring 1279 and summer 1283, probably earlier rather than later in that period (G. Hand, 'The Date of the "Crede Mihi,"' *Reportorium Novum* [Dublin Diocesan Record] 3 [1964], 368–70). The church's view of these pastimes was not unnecessarily gloomy; a wrestling contest at Naas in 1305, for example, ended in a bloody brawl (J. Mills, ed., *Calendar of the Justiciary Rolls or Proceedings in the Court of the Justiciar of Ireland preserved in the Public Record Office of Ireland. Edward I. Part 2. XXXIII to XXXV Years* [London, 1914], pp. 127–8).

245 Cawley, Jones, McDonald, and Mills, *Revels History*, pp. 122–32.

246 Compare some modern Ulster Christmas mummers' understandings of why they actually performed reported in H. Glassie, *All Silver and No Brass* (Indiana, 1975), pp. 122–42.

247 R. Potter, *The English Morality Play* (London and Boston, 1975), pp. 14–15; Axton, *European Drama*, pp. 166–8. For a summary of the plot, see note 112 above.

248 Butler, *Annals of Ireland*, p. 35; see also A. Gwynn, 'The Black Death in Ireland,' *Studies* 24 (1935), 25–42.

249 There were further onslaughts throughout the fourteenth and into the fifteenth century (A. Cosgrove, ed., *A New History of Ireland II Medieval Ireland 1169–1534* [Oxford, 1987], pp. 449–50).

250 Davis, *Non-Cycle Plays*, pp. xcix–c.

251 On the narrative episodes of the hero-combat, see A. Helm, *The English Mummers' Play* (Bury St Edmunds, 1981), pp. 27–33; also Brody, *English Mummers*, chapter 3.

252 Possible traces of ancient folk drama in Ireland on the life narrative theme are discussed in MacNeill, *Lughnasa*, pp. 423–4 and p. 426.

253 Beadle, *Cambridge Companion*, p. 240.

254 See J.F. Lydon, 'Richard II's Expeditions to Ireland,' *Journal of the Royal Society of Antiquaries of Ireland* 93 (1963), 135–49, and Cosgrove, *New History of Ireland II*, pp. 391–2 and notes. On Thomas Holland, see *DNB*, IX, 1051–2. I am grateful to Rosamund Allen for drawing my attention to the Holland connection.

255 Clark and Refaussé, *Historic Dublin Guilds*, p. 11, and J.J. Webb, *The Guilds of Dublin* (Dublin, 1929; repr 1960), p. 12.

256 For interesting, if debatable, analysis of the social needs met by performing Corpus Christi drama, see James, 'Social Body.'

257 Cosgrove, *New History of Ireland II*, pp. 533–6.

258 And see further on this question, A.J. Fletcher, 'The Civic Pageantry of Corpus Christi in Fifteenth- and Sixteenth-Century Dublin,' *Irish Economic and Social History* 23 (1996), 73–96.

CHAPTER 3

1 Though the displays focused on here will necessarily be the more theatrical ones, I believe that in some essentials their social function was no different from that of other forms of civic display. Hence they were an aspect, if a uniquely spectacular one, of a general civic project.

2 On 28 October 1510, Henry VIII granted the city an extra £20 per year for forty years out of the fee-farm to help repair the city walls 'which are in many places ruinous, in consequence of the decay of the city by pestilence, invasions of the Irish and desertion of the inhabitants' (*Letters and Papers, Foreign and Domestic, of the Reign of Henry VIII*, 21 vols [London, 1862–1932] I, Part 1, p. 352, no. 632). The buttressing of civic privilege to help cope with the situation had in fact already begun in the late medieval period.

3 *Holinshed's Irish Chronicle*, ed. Miller and Power, p. 48.

4 TCD, MS 591 (E. 3. 28), fols 9, 10, and 13.

5 DCA, Fr/Roll/2, mb. 10 and mb. 11 respectively.

6 Stanihurst, *De rebus in Hibernia gestis*, pp. 30–1: 'Anglice etiam et Hibernice loquuntur, propter cottidiana commercia, quæ cum vicinis Hibernis habent: suos tantum ciues mutua affinitate deuinciunt, & Hibernicos procos, vehementissima animi contentione, repudiant.' ('They speak English and Irish as well, on account of the daily commerce which they have with their Irish neighbours: but the citizens bind themselves together by mutual affinity, and repudiate Irish suitors in the most vehement and wrathful terms.')

7 Stanihurst, ibid., p. 30: 'Anglo-Hiberni, adeo sunt ab antiquis istis Hibernicis dissociati, vt colonorum omnium vltimus, qui in Anglica prouincia habitat, filiam suam vel nobilissimo Hibernicorum principi in matrimonium non daret.' ('To such an extent are the Anglo-Irish removed from those ancient Irish that the last colonist who lived

in the English province would not give his daughter in marriage even to the noblest Irish chieftain.')

8 Stanihurst, ibid., p. 30.

9 Another form of alliance was godparenting. For example in 1566, Sir Henry Sidney stood as godfather to the son of Nicholas Fitzsimon, mayor from 1565–6; the child was named Henry in Sidney's honour (see TCD, MS 591 [E. 3. 28], fol. 28; the day is given there as Thursday, 11 June, an impossible date in 1566, however).

10 DCA, Charter of incorporation, issued at Westminster, 21 April 1548 (summarized in English in *CARD*, I, 35).

11 For a thorough account, see C. Lennon, *The Lords of Dublin in the Age of Reformation* (Dublin, 1989).

12 Normally of someone who had formerly served as city bailiff, or after 1548, when their title was changed by the charter of incorporation, as city sheriff.

13 Lennon, *Lords of Dublin*, p. 53, suggests the 'numbers' may have been temporarily defunct.

14 Ibid.

15 Ibid.

16 *CARD*, II, 97.

17 Black Monday was so named in commemoration of an early-thirteenth-century massacre of Dubliners by marauding Irish. The citizens had gone for their recreation on Easter Monday to Cullenswood, some two miles south of the city, when they were surprised (for Stanihurst's account, see *Holinshed's Irish Chronicle*, ed. Miller and Power, p. 43). Black Monday ceremonies were also observed in Chester, but the reason for them had been forgotten by the early seventeenth century. Given the connections between Dublin and Chester, it is conceivable that Dublin provided Chester with its tradition (and see also note 72 below on the Shrove Tuesday ball bearing ceremony).

18 *CARD*, II, 30–1.

19 G.L. Barrow, 'Riding the Franchises,' *Dublin Historical Record* 33 (1980), 135–8.

20 *CARD*, II, 188: 'for want of ryding and perambulating the same, the citties rights are lycke to be extinguished.' Anxieties about lapses in the riding were aired again 20 May 1603 and 18 July 1606 (DCA, MR/5/10, mbs 52 and 70 respectively).

21 Compare the sense of alarm in the 1584 wording (note 20 above). This was a time of civic insecurity. See further below.

22 The 1584 order (note 20 above) required the franchises to be ridden by the mayor henceforth every second year. It also acknowledged and made some provision for the costs incurred.

23 *CARD*, I, 324.

24 Compare how the *Dublin Chronicle* often sets Dublin in a European context, as for example when the 1430s coronation of Henry VI in Paris, 'the Chif Cittie in all ffraunce,' is recorded (TCD, MS 591 [E. 3. 28], fol. 2).

25 Citizens from Bristol and Chester formed an important caucus in early Dublin; more-

over, after 1573 on days of civic ceremonial, the corporation legislated for hoods and gowns to be worn by members of the council, to bring the city into line (and solidarity) with the practice of London (*CARD*, II, 230; compare also the 1570 edict, *CARD*, II, 60–1, that the city waits should resemble those employed in English cities). Chester was home to a St George play, incidentally, already by 1431 (Clopper, *Chester*, p. 8).

26 A sense of an *Anglo-Irish* identity, defined now in reaction to the New English governmental presence, as well as in traditional reaction to the native Gaels, may be clearly traced by the late sixteenth century. See further below.

27 Thus, for example, the Mariners (and other related maritime guilds) played Noah's Ark, and the Goldsmiths the Three Magi.

28 *Hollinshed's Irish Chronicle*, ed. Miller and Power, p. 43.

29 TCD, MS 591 (E. 3. 28), fol. 26v: 'Item the xx of Iune Sir Nicholoas [vnreue] arold l. Iustes had [a power to pawe] send vnto Master maior beinge Corpescies Crestie [Day] ys ewen {'the eve of Corpus Christi Day'} that he shuld send his offyceres to all constabeles to giv warneinge that no arthyffyeares {'artificers,' 'tradesmen'} shold {i.e., 'should keep'} the Daye as holie daye.' Another, more satisfactory, record of the ban appears in the building accounts of Peter Lewis, proctor of Christ Church (TCD, MS 575 [E. 3. 21], fol. 38v; R. Gillespie, ed., *The Proctor's Accounts of Peter Lewis, 1564–5* [Dublin, 1995], p. 86): 'Note that this presend day sir Nicolas arnold Lord Ivstes send to mr fyane then meyre of dublin be the consayll of my Lord primat adam loftes & my lorde of Myethe hywghe brady ij of the Quenys hey {'high'} commyssyoners send to all the parayshe churche in dublin that they schuld nat kepe corpus christi day hally day but that ewry {'every'} man & womane schuld worke as they dyde ewry other worken day in the wycke A pone A great penallytie & dyspleassure of throubull Tady hellyer wroght in sklattyng of the churche this thursday & with hym iij workemen in his taske.'

30 *CARD*, II, 54.

31 *Hollinshed's Irish Chronicle*, ed. Miller and Power, p. 325; Clark and Refaussé, *Historic Dublin Guilds*, p. 44.

32 TCD, MS 591 (E. 3. 28), fol. 14v: 'Anno domini Mo Vo xlij xxxiiijto henrie occtauie walter Tyrrell Maiore Thomas ffane and Iohn spenfeld baillifis this yer Sir antony sellenger Deputie with the the kinges conyssiall held a parlament at Dublin and ther came to it the Irle of wormond the erle of Desmond the lord Barie makegillpatricke obrenens sonnes makcart mor with mane Irishe lordes and one carpus Christie Daye they rode about with the pro$_\wedge$⌐ce⌐ssion in the parlement Robes and the ix Wortheis was [ply] played and the maiore bare the masse befor the Deputie on horse bake corpus / Cristie Daye the xvjth Daye of Iune Dominicall letter on b the prime on ther and the sondaie after [p] in sainete patrickes churche kinge henrie was proclamed king of Irlond and the next sondaye after the {*read* they} had tormentes {*read* tornamentes} on horsback and after had Roninge at the ringe with speres on horse bake ....' (The regnal year is wrongly given as 34 Henry VIII [22 April 1542 – 21 April 1543]. It should be

33 Henry VIII.) The 1541 parliament ran from 13 June to 20/23 July. The Nine Worthies pageant, often the responsibility of the Mayor of the Bullring, proved serviceable: it appeared not only in 1541, but in 1554 (when it is spoken of as an old institution; see note 106 below), and is last on extant record in 1561 (Harris, *History*, p. 312), when the Worthies were acted after a mayoral dinner in honour of Sir Thomas Radcliffe, third earl of Sussex, Lord Lieutenant of Ireland.

33 Close links between the Corpus Christi guild (and indeed between the various religious guilds of Dublin) and the corporation would no doubt have helped safeguard it against Reformation changes.

34 RCB, C/6/1/26/13, fols 28–9.

35 LPL, MS 623 (Book of Howth), fol. 83.

36 PRO, SP 63/214, fol. 19v. These are Meredith Hanmer's notes referring to a hanging on the Hoggen Green in connection with the Dublin coronation of the pretender Lambert Simnel in 1487.

37 The 'Hogges Butt' is first recorded in 1468 (*CARD*, I, 329).

38 TCD, MS 591 (E. 3. 28), fol. 22r-v.

39 However, the Hoggen Green possibility cannot be insisted on. The Dame's Gate, which faced the Hoggen Green, is in fact known to have round towers to either side of it, but such towers are not clear from the Derricke woodcut.

40 Its civic importance as a rallying site continued into the seventeenth century; a large assembly was convened at the Hoggen Butts in 1613, when the mayor nominated the city recorder and an alderman (C.W. Russell and J.P. Prendergast, eds., *Calendar of the State Papers, relating to Ireland, of the Reign of James I. 1611–1614* [London, 1877], p. 441). By 1621 it was also home to an 'inrayled bowling place' (*CARD*, III, 133), and was evidently a common for civic recreation. On the general ceremonial importance of Dublin's eastern suburb, in which the Hoggen Green was located, see H.B. Clarke, '"Urbs et suburbium": Beyond the Walls of Medieval Dublin,' in C. Manning, ed., *Dublin and beyond the Pale: Studies in Honour of Patrick Healy* (Dublin, 1998), pp. 43–56.

41 TCD, MS 543/2/14, mb. 1 dorse. This *Dublin Chronicle* entry is much obscured by rubbing, and though the regnal year is unclear, it can be confirmed by comparison of surrounding legible entries. Harbard must have been mayor in 1505–6. Other versions of the entry (in TCD, MS 591 [E. 3. 28], fol. 7v and BL, MS Additional 4791, fol. 135v) substantially agree with the text above. Perhaps this Hoggen Green play was performed under the auspices of the Corpus Christi guild. However, a play on the Passion was also presented in 1528 on the Hoggen Green under monastic auspices (see below), possibly even on Corpus Christi, though the date is not specified. While the Passion was clearly an important episode for dramatization in Dublin, the 'play of the passion on Palm Sunday in 1538 at St John's well at Kilmainham' is in fact a chimera (C. Lennon, 'The Chantries in the Irish Reformation: the Case of St Anne's Guild, Dublin, 1550–1630,'

in R.V. Comerford, M. Cullen, J.R. Hill, and C. Lennon, eds., *Religion, Conflict and Coexistence in Ireland* [Dublin, 1990], pp. 6–25; see p. 11). The alleged source of this Passion play simply complains that the stations were still being rehearsed and pardons dispensed at Kilmainham under the auspices of the Hospital of St John of Jerusalem (*State Papers … King Henry the Eighth*, pp. 1–2). There is no mention of any Passion play.

42 TCD, MS 543/2/14, mb. 2 dorse. Three other versions of this entry exist, but their substantive variants are not of material interest to the discussion (TCD, MS 591 [E. 3. 28], fol. 10v; BL, MS Additional 4791, fol. 137; and Bodl., MS Rawlinson B. 484, fol. 33v). This reference to a St Laurence play (feast day 10 August) is the earliest known, unequivocal reference to a miracle play in Ireland. Although Dublin knew another St Laurence (Laurence O'Toole, or in Irish, Lorcán Ua Tuathail, feast day 14 November), it is far more likely that the ancient St Laurence, whose graphic martyrdom over a griddle had elsewhere lent itself to extensive dramatic treatment (S.K. Wright, 'Is the Ashmole Fragment a Remnant of a Saint's Play?' *Neophilologus* 75 [1991], 139–49), was the man intended here.

43 It is interesting to compare the liaison between chronicle and civic pageantry later embodied for London in the person of Thomas Middleton (J. Knowles, 'The Spectacle of the Realm: Civic Consciousness, Rhetoric and Ritual in Early Modern London,' in J.R. Mulryne and M. Shewring, eds., *Theatre and Government under the Early Stuarts* [Cambridge, 1993], pp. 157–89; see p. 161).

44 Armagh, Public Library, *The History and Antiquties of Dublin*, no shelfmark, p. 140. Line 10 Passion] *corrected from* passion. This manuscript history of Dublin was prepared by Robert Ware in 1678, largely from papers of his father, the antiquarian Sir James Ware. Judging by the style of the entry, its ultimate source may have been some expanded version of the *Dublin Chronicle*, now lost. The reference to 'Thomas fitz Gerrald Earl of Kildare, Lord Lieutenant of Ireland' having attended the plays needs clarification. The text is categorical that Thomas Fitzgerald was the person invited. Harris, *History*, p. 144 (followed by *EIS*, p. 15), believed this to be erroneous, since at Christmastide in 1528, Piers Butler, earl of Ossory, was Lord Deputy; no Thomas Fitzgerald held such state office then (Butler was Lord Deputy from 14 October 1528 to 4 September 1529). Thus Harris (and Clark, *EIS*) asserted that it was Ossory who saw the plays. But before adopting the radical solution of dispatching the name Thomas Fitzgerald, an alternative explanation for the apparent confusion should be considered. One of two possible Thomas Fitzgeralds may be intended here: one was the brother of the ninth earl of Kildare, Sir Gerald Fitzgerald, and the other was Sir Gerald's son, his successor as tenth earl. Although Thomas Fitzgerald the brother had no state office by Christmastide 1528, he had served briefly as Lord Justice from 15 May (and see S.G. Ellis, *Tudor Ireland: Crown, Community and the Conflict of Culture, 1470–1603* [London and New York, 1985], pp. 118–19). Perhaps this might correspond to

the 'Lord Lieutenant' of the 1528 entry. However, he never became earl of Kildare, which title the chronicle entry also clearly identifies. Thomas Fitzgerald the son, on the other hand, familiarly known as Silken Thomas, did become earl in 1534. If the chronicle entry were *recalling* Silken Thomas retrospectively, it might well have described him as earl, even though in 1528 he had not yet become so.

45 Eight plays are mentioned in the description of the event. If one were presented daily, beginning on Christmas day, then the last would fall on New Year's Day.

46 Ceres had already been treated in the fifteenth-century mumming at Eltham by John Lydgate (*The Minor Poems of John Lydgate*, ed. H. N. MacCracken, EETS, os 192 [London, 1934], pp. 672–4).

47 For the destination of the Corpus Christi procession at St George's Chapel, we have only the (undocumented) assertion of Walker, 'Historical Essay,' p. 83. For possible processional routes, see chapter 2.

48 *Holinshed's Irish Chronicle*, ed. Miller and Power, p. 43.

49 *CARD*, I, 445–7. Cusack (20 September 1564) would at that date have had a recent and automatic association with the guild chapel. He had been mayor of Dublin twice, first in 1552–3 and then in 1563–4; by tradition, he would have become warden of the guild of St George following his mayoral year, and thus in 1553–4, just one year before the civic assembly ordered him to build and erect the chapel, he would have been familiar with the guild's business. That familiarity, plus sufficient wealth, is likely to have suggested him as the candidate to undertake a rebuilding. But see the following note.

50 DCA, MR/35, p. 196, associates Cusack with the civic oven; this is noted in a set of accounts running from the Michaelmasses of 1563 to 1564, but the oven had evidently been built before then, perhaps in fact in 1555. In an assembly held 19 July in that year, the Assembly Rolls record Cusack's discharge from the earlier mandate to build and erect the chapel (see the previous note), and mention that he had not observed his earlier mandate, but had used chapel fabric for a 'wourk' (the civic oven?) of benefit to the citizens (*CARD*, I, 447).

51 DCA, MR/35, p. 139.

52 DCA, MR/35, p. 195; any shadow of doubt about the possible meaning of this entry is dispelled by a reference to 'St Georges being wast' in a note in the accounts of Henry Browne, alderman and executor to the late Robert Goldyng, presented on 8 November 1565 (DCA, MR/35, p. 199). This note also mentions the city bakehouse (the oven spoken of in Stanihurst and elsewhere).

53 *CARD*, II, 36–7.

54 *Holinshed's Irish Chronicle*, ed. Miller and Power, p. 49.

55 *EIS*, p. 13, erroneously dated the list to 1564.

56 BL, MS Additional 4791, fol. 149r–v.

57 My summary of the guild's history is dependent on Clark and Refaussé, *Historic Dublin Guilds*, pp. 35–7.

58 The guild, founded at the request of the mayor and council, received its charter on 27 June 1426. It is not to be confused with Dublin's military guild of St George (which had in any case been suppressed by 1494; Clark and Refaussé, *Historic Dublin Guilds*, pp. 41–2). Nevertheless, its former existence testifies to an awareness among the English administration of the importance of St George ceremonial.

59 This was the guild's custom; see the reference under 1577 in *CARD*, II, 119.

60 *Holinshed's Irish Chronicle*, ed. Miller and Power, p. 49: the mayor and his brethren, with the pageants, went annually to the chapel, 'there to offer' ('offer' in the liturgical sense of the word; *OED*, **Offer**, senses 1. and 1.b.).

61 Johnston and Rogerson, *York*, I, 318–19, and see E. White, '"Bryngyng Forth of Saynt George": The St. George Celebrations in York,' *Medieval English Theatre* 3 (1981), 114–21. The York St George play is first recorded in 1554. St George was paid 3s 4d, a procession was made, and a sermon commissioned for the occasion: the Dublin event invites comparison in each respect. For a survey of St George pageantry in the British Isles, see C. Davidson, 'The Middle English Saint Play and its Iconography,' in C. Davidson, ed., *The Saint Play in Medieval Europe*, Early Drama, Art, and Music Monograph Series 8 (Kalamazoo, 1986), pp. 31–122; see pp. 60–9.

62 On all these, see Clark and Refaussé, *Historic Dublin Guilds*.

63 From 1403, the mayor of Dublin had been granted the right to have a sword borne before him, putting him on a par in this regard with the mayor of London. C. Blair and I. Delamer, 'The Dublin Civic Swords,' *Proceedings of the Royal Irish Academy* 88 (1988), 87–142; they stress the powerful symbolic overtones of bearing swords, and suggest that the mayoral sword was a proxy for the royal sword of state, symbolic of the fact that the mayor acted in lieu of the monarch (pp. 88 and 93).

64 TCD, MS 591 (E. 3. 28), fol. 9.

65 TCD, MS 591 (E. 3. 28), fol. 14.

66 TCD, MS 591 (E. 3. 28), fol. 22v. Mayor William Sarsfield was knighted in Christ Church by Sir Henry Sidney on Sunday, 17 November 1566, for having taken part in a campaign against the O'Reillys.

67 PRO, SP 60/6, fol. 13.

68 For example, St George's Chapel was required to be 'well hanged & apparelled to every purpose with cushins .... russhes & other neccessaries belonging for said St Georges day' in the pre-1548 prescription for St George's Day celebrations, and the choir of Christ Church for that feast in 1578 was hung with blue broadcloth embossed with the arms of the Order of the Garter 'all gorgiusly wrought in metall' (see respectively BL, MS Additional 4791, fol. 149v and TCD, MS 772 [E. 4. 11], fol. 18). Note too the beautifying of the place in which an oration was made to greet Sir Robert Devereux, twentieth earl of Essex, on his arrival in Dublin (DCA, MR/35, p. 578; the accounts relating this date between the Michaelmasses of 1598 and 1599; the welcome probably occurred *c* 15 April 1599, when Devereux was sworn in as Lord Deputy).

69 As on 28 January 1547, when the corporation paid for two hogsheads of Gascon wine spent at the High Cross for the triumph of the coronation of Edward VI, or on 7 April 1603, when a hogshead of wine was set in the streets at the triumph of the proclamation of James I as king of England (DCA, MR/35, pp. 57 and 635 respectively).

70 *CARD*, II, 30; this is the 1563 admonition to the Butchers and Fishmongers.

71 See, for example, *CARD*, II, 19, for the 1561 legislation that sheriffs for the year should take their place 'after and behind all the aldermen,' that is, in the position of greater honour, 'in like manner as is used in the cittie of London'; also ibid., 230, for the 1589 legislation that on station days, guild masters should ensure that guild members, other than those entitled to wear corporation livery, should be appropriately attired, so that the 'showe in the stacion may be the more semly.'

72 The details of the ball bearing ceremony are vague, but it also took place in the context of a procession. It is first recorded in 1462 (*CARD*, I, 312). Evidently, those who had married during the year would process (or possibly ride on horseback) along some unknown route carrying a ball. Some newly-weds had tried to avoid the payment of a fine to the city treasury which accompanied the ceremony by marrying on Shrove Tuesday itself (see *CARD*, II, 78, for the 1572–3 legislation to curb this practice).

73 *CARD*, I, 395.

74 *CARD*, I, 249; this record is from the Chain Book. Stanton's wardenship of the Newgate jail is confirmed by the account of his activity in Holinshed; see below.

75 *CARD*, I, 397.

76 *Holinshed's Irish Chronicle*, ed. Miller and Power, pp. 273–4.

77 *CARD*, I, 398.

78 *CARD*, I, 400. Stanton was serjeant and water bailiff in 1537, serjeant only in 1539, and serjeant and water bailiff in both 1540 and 1541; *CARD*, I, 402, 405, and 408–9 respectively.

79 *CARD*, I, 410.

80 *CARD*, I, 411.

81 *CARD*, I, 415, 417, 419, 422, 423, 426, and 429.

82 *CARD*, I, 434.

83 *CARD*, I, 437; this is recorded as having been paid in DCA, MR/35, p. 122 (accounts presented 5 November 1555). Since this is the last recorded reference to Stanton in the Treasurer's Book, he may have died soon after.

84 DCA, MR/35, p. 122 (accounts presented 5 November 1555). Richard Stanton's annuity referred to above is also noted as having been paid in these accounts.

85 DCA, MR/35, p. 168 (accounts presented in 1560).

86 M.J. McEnery, ed., 'Calendar of Christ Church Deeds 1174–1684,' in *The Twenty-third Report of the Deputy Keeper of the Public Records in Ireland* (Dublin, 1891), p. 149, no. 1245. (His surname is spelt Springan here.) The leased property was in a lane leading to the 'Poll Myll.'

87 DCA, MR/35, p. 157 (accounts of the late Mayor John Spensfield).

88 DCA, MR/35, p. 174.

89 DCA, MR/35, p. 179. Rochford was appointed city auditor in 1557 and sheriff in 1558 (*CARD*, I, 465 and 474 respectively).

90 McEnery, 'Christ Church Deeds,' p. 159, no. 1294 and p. 160, no. 1295 respectively. Deed no. 1294, for the Oxmantown property, levies a 9s rent, heriots when due, two watch hens at Christmas, and all chief rents, with covenants for distress, re-entry, and repairs. Deed no. 1295, for the messuage and garden, levies a 10s rent, with covenants for re-entry and repairs.

91 See the *Dublin Chronicle* in TCD, MS 591 (E. 3. 28), fol. 26.

92 DCA, MR/35, p. 229; the accounts run between the Michaelmasses of 1567 and 1568.

93 *CARD*, I, 400–37.

94 DCA, MR/35, p. 79.

95 *CARD*, II, 5.

96 Robinson, 'Ancient Deeds,' p. 212.

97 *Pace EIS*, p. 12, the Triumph of the Peace referred to in MR/35, p. 46, is *not* explicitly connected with the proclamation of Henry VIII as king of Ireland in 1541. It appears in a set of accounts running between 29 September 1545 and 4 November 1546.

98 DCA, MR/35, p. 225: 'Payed to George Springham for playinge the pagent of Sainct George per warrantum iij <s>'; although this might be thought to mean that Springham simply played some part in the pageant, not necessarily the role of St George himself, doubt is dispelled by the amount he was paid for playing. The fact that he received 3s (the rest of the payment is obscured in the defective right margin of the manuscript) corresponds, and were the manuscript intact would probably correspond exactly, to the 3s 4d stipulated as the payment for St George in the Chain Book.

99 BL, MS Egerton 1765, fol. 120 (accounts from 25 July 1554 to 5 July 1555); the 1556 record (fol. 121) occurred at Corpus Christi (4 June in that year), and while Casse is only paid for playing, and his role is not specified, the amount he received, 2s, corresponds exactly to the amount he received for playing Pilate in 1554–5.

100 *Holinshed's Irish Chronicle*, ed. Miller and Power, p. 43. The Mayor of the Bullring often appears in civic documents in the context of expenditures on gunpowder (presumably for military drills, ceremonial or otherwise). For example, note was made 25 April 1589 of the powder barrels 'borrowed for making sporte vppon maye daye & other tymes wherin the mayor of bulring vseth sporte' (DCA, MR/5/9, mb. 50 [*CARD*, II, 223]; the same word, 'sporte,' was that used of the public performance, discussed below and in chapter 6, of the queen's majesty's players and the earl of Essex players in Dublin in the same year). The Mayor of the Bullring is also often mentioned as a prosecutor of bawds and investigator of alehouses (for example, DCA, MR/5/6, mb. 3 [*CARD*, I, 439], an edict of 26 October 1554 and MR/5/7, mb. 1 dorse [*CARD*,

II, 38–9], an edict of 18 May 1565). This function lingered on into the seventeenth century (compare Rich, *A New Description*, p. 73: 'but I wil here leaue my women Tauerne-Keepers to Maister Maior of the Bull-Ringe to looke vnto'). The Mayor of the Bullring might perhaps be characterized as a public master of the revels. On 22 May 1559, Sir Henry Sidney gave the Mayor of the Bullring 12d to help him with his forthcoming Corpus Christi pastime (25 May in that year; KAO, U1475 027/3, fol. [4]), and on 20 January 1604, the Mayor of the Bullring complained of the expenses he incurred in solemnizing the coronation of James I (DCA, MR/5/10, mb. 55; *CARD*, II, 416): 'Whear Christofor Cosgrowe nowe maior of ye bullringe, shewed by his peticion yat he was at great chardges for ye credditt of this Cittie in solempnizinge ye kinges ma<ies>ties coronacion: he therfore humblie praied in respect therof to be remittid of an old debte claymed by the Cittie vppon his father Thomas Cosgrowe alderman dysceased. & to haue a Concordatum for paiement of a barraile of powder borrowed by him for that purpose, & the Cittie hauinge a good regard of his forwardnes in yat office. It is therfore agreed by the aucthorytie afforesaid that he shalbe remittid of that debte, & shall haue a Concordatum for the powder as he required./.'

101 'The felicity of the city inheres in its citizens' obedience.' The city motto is first known to appear in this form in the 1607 grant of arms; I am grateful to the city archivist, Mary Clark, for this information.

102 DCA, C1/2/1, fol. 57 (*CARD*, I, 240): 'þe maire of þe bulring & bachelers of þe same þe ix worthies ridyng worshupfully with ther followers acordyng peyn. xl s.'; see chapter 2 for discussion. The Nine Worthies traditionally comprised three pagans (Hector of Troy [or Jason], Alexander of Macedon, and Julius Caesar; three Jews [Joshua, David and Judas Maccabaeus]; and three Christians [Charlemagne, King Arthur, and Godfrey of Boulogne]; J.L. Nevinson, 'A Show of the Nine Worthies,' *Shakespeare Quarterly* 14 [1963], 103–7).

103 BL, MS Additional 33991 (a compilation of Sir James Ware). A notice in a seventeenth-century list of the manuscript's contents on fol. 2v attests the former presence of verses on the Nine Worthies.

104 Lancashire, *Dramatic Texts and Records*, passim.

105 DCA, MR/35, p. 715: 'More he is to be chardged with soe mvche receauid of Edward Goughe maior of ye boulringe for a barraile of gvnn powder for the mvster at Maij 1607:. vj li. xiij s. iiij d.'

106 DCA, MR/5/6, mb. 3 dorse (*CARD*, I, 440): 'Hit is alsoo ordeyned by this said assemblee that the maior of bolring fro hensforthe shall haue no suche Money as was paied by the citizens nowe of late for setting forthe the ix worthies / But the mair of bolring fro hensforthe to haue according thauncient custume. And that the same pagentes be not neclectid by the Mairs of bolring herafter one payne of xli sterling ˄[to the cittie] And it is further ordeyned that thos yong men of the cittie that shalbe chosyn by the maior of bolring for tyme being to play any parte of the said ix worthies

& they or eny of them <r>efusing hit forfait vj s viij d sterling to the said Mayr of bolring.' 6s 8d was also the fine imposed by a by-law of 16 July 1557 on any youth in dereliction of the Mayor of the Bullring's orders. DCA, MR/5/6, mb. 6 (*CARD*, I, 465): 'It is also ordeyned that euery baccheler being a yongeman of this Cittie that shall herafter refuse to waite vpon the Maior or Shiryfs of the bulring by nyght or daie for thexecucion & administracion of their charge without iust cause to be allowid by the Maior of this Cittie & his bretherne shall forfait for every default vj s viij d to the Tresorie of the Cittie / And thother halfe to the maior & Shiryfs of the bulring.'

107 DCA, MR/5/6, mb. 6 (*CARD*, I, 464–5). That the corporation needed to be vigilant that the Mayor of the Bullring and his officers did as instructed is also evident from a sanction imposed on 18 May 1599 in the Friday Book (DCA, MR/17, fol. 52v; H.F. Berry, 'Minute Book of the Corporation of Dublin, known as the "Friday Book," 1567–1611,' *Proceedings of the Royal Irish Academy* 30 [1912–13], 477–514; see p. 496): 'Where by the Auncyent Custome & vsadge of this Cittie the Mayor & Sheryves of bulring should be at Chardge in making a semly shoe {'show'} by muster & other wayes vppon Maye daye, And the Mayor & shryves of the bulring at this present [being] for good respects being tollerated withall this last Maye daye, & [were] comaunded by mr Mayor & Aldermen [the] to make the said shoe vppon Assencion daye, They lytle pondering there dutie, [but] ⌈did⌉ in Contemptuous maner [did] not perform the same, It is therfore resolved. in a meeting this daye that the Mayor & shryves of the bulring shalbe Caullid vppon before mr Mayor & Ceyttd {'cited'} for there Contempt aforsaid, and that they shall not be deliuered tyll they putt in sufficient pawnes or enter in bond, (at mr Mayor Choyse, that they shall perform such farther order other by fyne or ponishment as shalbe Inflyctid vppon them by the Mayor Sheryves comons & Cittezes in the next assebly/ {*read* assembly}.'

108 TCD, MS 591 (E. 3. 28), fol. 14v (see note 32).

109 TCD, MS 591 (E. 3. 28), fol. 18v: 'in this yer the ix worthes was plaid and the maior gawe {'gave'} them a goodlie Dener and iiij trompeteres mony for ther paines that is to saye xx s sterling and found them horsses.' The opening of this entry in the manu- script specifies 1557, followed by the regnal year 3–4 Philip and Mary, which was in fact 25 July 1556 – 5 July 1557. Probably the mayoralty of John Challyner (between the Michaelmasses of 1556 and 1557) was intended. In which case, reconciling the mayoral year with the regnal year, the performance would have occurred some time between 29 September 1556 and 5 July 1557.

110 For example compare DCA, MR/35, p. 93 (accounts for one year ending 10 November 1551): 'Item to the Shirif ffitz Symon for a banket gyven by the Cittie to the Lord Deputie in the Tolsell vijli. ijs.' Several similar entries appear in the Treasurer's Book.

111 On the associations of brass instruments, see R. Rastall, '"Alle Hefne Makyth Melody,"' in P. Neuss, ed. *Aspects of Early English Drama* (Cambridge and Totowa, 1983), pp. 1–12; see p. 4.

112 They continued until well into the next century. The last on record falling within the terms of this study was on 5 June 1632, when the mayor of Dublin gave a banquet for Sir Richard Boyle, Sir Adam Loftus, and George Fitzgerald, sixteenth earl of Kildare (CHL, Lismore Papers, Volume 26, p. 296): 'This day the L Chancellor, thearle of kildare, and my selfe were royally feasted by the Maior of dublin in their Courthouse with a plentefull bancquet, and then all 3 made freemen, and I gaue the Cytty mvsicons xx s sterling.'

113 *Holinshed's Irish Chronicle*, ed. Miller and Power, p. 42: 'not onely their officers so farre excell in hospitalitie, but also the greater parte of the ciuitie is generally addicted to such ordinarie and standing houses.'

114 On the choir schools of the two Dublin cathedrals, see W.H. Grindle, *Irish Cathedral Music* (Belfast, 1989), pp. 7–8. (The earliest extant depiction of a minstrel group in Dublin is carved on a capital, *c* 1200, in the north aisle of Christ Church Cathedral; R. Stalley, 'The Medieval Sculpture of Christ Church Cathedral, Dublin,' *Archaeologia* 106 [1979], 107–22; see plate 10.) On the retained musicians of the aristocratic households, see chapter 6.

115 PRO, SP 63/180, fol. 23v; two warrants dated respectively 27 November 1594 and 3 February 1595 were issued for their payment. The 'Courte' in which they sang was the court of the Exchequer (and see further on this in chapter 6). On 29 September 1609, the choristers of Christ Church were paid for singing in the Exchequer at the end of every term for a whole year, ending at Michaelmas, according to their wonted custom (PRO, SP 63/230, fol. 208v). This is probably the tradition to which the 1594–5 payments belonged. The first recorded appearance of the practice may be on 9 August 1589 (PRO, SP 63/146, fol. 41v; two warrants for the payment of the singing men of Christ Church had been signed on 17 May and 17 June respectively in that year). The admission of Walter Kennedy in January 1584 is recorded in DCA, MR/5/9, mb. 27 (*CARD*, II, 185). Kennedy was organist of Christ Church in the early 1590s.

116 On 17 January 1567 the city musicians were given liberty, subject to mayoral licence, to serve the earl of Kildare (DCA, MR/5/7, mb. 12; *CARD*, II, 46–7); the Tailors resorted to hiring the musicians of Christopher St Lawrence, Lord Howth, in 1609 and again in 1610 when William Huggard and his fellow musicians (on whom see below) had been unavailable (BL, MS Egerton 1765, fols 132v and 133v respectively); the corporation paid the Lord Deputy's musicians 'for a play' some time between the Michaelmasses of 1583 and 1584 (DCA, MR/35, p. 375).

117 B. Boydell, 'Dublin City Musicians in the Late Middle Ages and Renaissance, to 1660,' *Dublin Historical Record* 34 (1981), 42–53; see p. 42; also, J. Southworth, *The English Medieval Minstrel* (Woodbridge, 1989), pp. 118–32.

118 DCA, MR/5/2, mb. 4 (*CARD*, I, 320).

119 DCA, MR/5/1, mb. 8 (*CARD*, I, 291).

120 DCA, G1/1, mb. 32, col. b (P. Connolly, ed., *The Dublin Guild Merchant Roll, c. 1190–*

1265 (Dublin, 1992), p. 85). (It is unlikely, incidentally, that 'pipere' could have meant 'plumber'; *OED* cites only two cases of the word 'piper' meaning 'plumber,' and both are later and from the Dublin Assembly Rolls. In fact, however, nothing in the context supports the *OED* sense. On the contrary, a late-sixteenth- [or early-seventeenth-] century annotator has noted opposite one of the items cited by the *OED*: 'Citty Musitians.') A William the piper, with his wife, Alice, also appeared in a lost Christ Church deed of *c* 1260, when he received intramural land with buildings in the parish of St Werburgh (*Twenty-third Report of the Deputy Keeper*, p. 83); he may have been the same man.

121 Boydell, 'Dublin City Musicians,' p. 42; though Boydell is right in finding no early documentary references to instruments serving to summon Dublin citizens (p. 43), the thirteenth-century seal of the city of Dublin, whose matrix is still held by the corporation, clearly depicts watchmen sounding horns on the walls of the embattled city. The later practice of having the city trumpeter also look after the city clock (first on record from 29 September 1586; DCA, MR/35, p. 394), may hearken back to the traditional waits' role as setters of the watch.

122 DCA, MR/5/2, mb. 6 dorse (*CARD*, I, 326).

123 DCA, MR/5/7, mb. 15 dorse (*CARD*, II, 60–1); an edict of 17 July 1618 (*CARD*, III, 96) specified the three days as Sundays, Tuesdays, and Thursdays (i.e., nearly every other day each week). This hebdomadal circuit no doubt served to rouse citizens to their labours and to set the watch.

124 The 4d levied on halls and 2d levied on shops suggests that the trade guild members, those who substantially comprised the ninety-six, also shared in the waits' maintenance.

125 The first mention of the waits' liveries proper (as opposed to the liveries of the cere-monial musicians, trumpeter and drummer) occurs in a set of accounts running between the Michaelmasses of 1567 and 1568 (DCA, MR/35, pp. 223 and 231). Further such livery payments are not very frequent until the early-seventeenth century, though there are small gaps between 1596 and 1605 inclusive, and 1612 and 1617 inclusive. The 1618 livery payment to William Huggard and his associates mentions that they were being rewarded for services 'in tyme of necessytie when none others would then attend' (DCA, MR/5/11, mb. 57; *CARD*, III, 96–7). Perhaps this explains the gaps noted earlier. There are only two more livery payments after this, one in 1620 and the other in 1636, but it can be safely assumed that there were no breaks in the waits' service in between whiles.

126 DCA, MR/5/7, mb. 15 dorse (*CARD*, II, 60–1), and MR/5/10, mb. 32 (*CARD*, II, 336).

127 *CARD*, III, 120.

128 That Lawless and his fellows were not principally retained civic waits seems likely not from the use of the word *mimi* to describe them, since waits sometimes were so called (Southworth, *English Medieval Minstrel*, p. 125), but from the context in which their

complaint was framed (see chapter 2). They were general entertainers and music-makers whose territory was being poached.

129 DCA, MR/35, pp. 77, 79, and 83 record payments respectively 'to Patricke Cawyll fydler' for wages due at Easter and Michaelmas 1549 and 'to bulloke & Patricke ffydler' for wages due at Michaelmas in the same year, while a payment on p. 84 refers to them both as 'Mynstrals' who were being paid wages for half a year ending at Easter 1550 (Bullock's profession as 'taboret' is noted on p. 87). The fact that they were being retained for long lengths of time suggests they too may have been waits.

130 Boydell, 'Dublin City Musicians,' p. 46.

131 DCA, MR/35, p. 223. It is not clear whether Quycke, who was probably also a wait, is to be counted as well; if he is, then a total of five waits seems likely.

132 On 17 January 1567 it was decreed that Quycke should serve the mayor in the field as drummer whenever necessary (DCA, MR/5/7, mb. 12; *CARD*, II, 46–7). See further on Quycke and his consort in chapter 6.

133 DCA, MR/35, p. 46. Boydell, 'Dublin City Musicians,' did not have the benefit of this manuscript (the Treasurer's Book) when he wrote. The Book establishes a longer tradition of civic musicians than has hitherto been supposed.

134 Hautboys '& other Instrvmentes' are mentioned in the commission to Edward Gore and his fellow musicians on 16 July 1591 (DCA, MR/5/9, mb. 61; *CARD*, II, 247–8). Singing boys are first recorded in January 1584 as being required to accompany the mayor on station days and other occasions, but at that time they were organized by the clerk Walter Kennedy, not himself a wait (see note 115). Maintenance of singing boys had become the waits' responsibility at least by 17 January 1620 (DCA, MR/5/11, mb. 66 (*CARD*, III, 117–18), the source of the quotation above), and are stipulated again on 14 October 1636 (DCA, MR/5/12, mb. 61; *CARD*, III, 324).

135 See Southworth, *English Medieval Minstrel*, p. 126.

136 Indoor trumpets, as for example in Christ Church Cathdral on ceremonial occasions like the receiving of the sword of state by the Lord Deputy, marked special events, and were in any case not necessarily the trumpets of waits but of household or military musicians. This may have been the case, for example, on 26 May 1556, when Sir Thomas Radcliffe, Lord Fitzwalter, received the sword of state, and after administration of his oath 'the trumpetts sounded and drummes beate' (LPL, MS 621 [Carew Papers], fol. 15; a version of this account is also found in TCD, MS 581 [E. 3. 18], fol. 75). However, it is true that waits might assist music in church. See further in chapter 6 for the liturgical employment of secular musicians.

137 Robinson, 'Guy of Warwick,' p. 52.

138 Choice of text may imply an anglicized taste; and the native Irish were entertained to such music in English cities, as when the Gaelic chieftain O'Brennan was entertained with the Lord Deputy in the Tholsel to the music of minstrels (DCA, MR/35, p. 21; accounts running from *c* 10 November 1541 to 10 November 1542): 'Item to the

Mynstrallis in the Tolsell ther beyng my lord Deputie. Obrenen with dyuers oþer strangers iij s. iiij d.' The O'Brennan in question may have been the father of the men who had ridden in their parliamentary robes in the Dublin Corpus Christi procession of 16 June 1541 (TCD, MS 591 [E. 3. 28], fol. 14v; see note 32 above).

139 J. Mills, ed., *Calendar of the Justiciary Rolls or Proceedings in the Court of the Justiciar of Ireland preserved in the Public Record Office of Ireland. XXIII to XXXI Years of Edward I.* (Dublin, 1905), p. 107. One Symon le Harpur features amongst the earliest of Dublin's recorded harpers, in the Roll of the Dublin Guild Merchant of *c* 1192–1200 (DCA, G1/1, mb. 7, col. b; Connolly, *Dublin Guild Merchant Roll*, p. 24): '.Symon le Harpur llllllllll Sol.'

140 On 3 April 1558, Donald O'Lalor of Dublin, harper, was pardoned for the murder of Boolaghe McKegan of Dublin, harper (*The Ninth Report of the Deputy Keeper of the Public Records in Ireland* [Dublin, 1877], p. 80). It may be of interest to note that these two men had Gaelic, not English, names. Perhaps they were some of those disenfranchised musicians who had long been entering Dublin from outside to ply their trade, often to the annoyance of civic musicians and waits who, from at least 1436, sought to corner the musical market and its remunerations for themselves.

141 Mills, *Account Roll*, p. 19. Immediately before this payment is another to 'Johanni Faytour Waffrer' also for 3d; waferers often appear in minstrel contexts elsewhere (Bullock-Davies, *Menestrellorum Multitudo*, pp. 44–50).

142 James Hanwood, harper, was admitted to the city franchises by special grace on 11 May 1487; DCA, Fr/Roll/2, mb. 17 (Franchise Roll of the City of Dublin).

143 Compare the situation in Chester, where also by the late sixteenth century the profession of wait was to some extent an hereditary one (D. Mills, 'Music and Musicians in Chester: A Summary Account,' *Medieval English Theatre* 17 [1995], 58–75; see p. 63).

144 DCA, MR/5/10, mb. 32 (*CARD*, II, 336). The conditions were these: not to leave the city without the mayor's licence and then not for longer than eight days; to adhere to the accustomed course for their watch; and to be diligent in attendance on the mayor on station days and at his pleasure.

145 DCA, MR/5/9, mb. 63 (*CARD*, II, 250). The terms of the waits' payments specified here, of a quarterly levy of 9d sterling on every alderman, 6d sterling on each of the forty-eight and some sum (presumably less than 6d sterling, but the document is defective) on each of the ninety-six, are probably those referred to in the legislation admitting Huggard on 12 October 1599. It is not known whether any waits from Gore's band were subsequently absorbed into Huggard's, but there may in any event have been a musical tradition in the Gore family, since a John Gore, musician, is recorded between 24 March 1610 and 23 March 1611 as having been admitted to the franchises (DCA, Fr/Reg/1, p. 136).

146 DCA, MR/5/10, mb. 56 (*CARD*, II, 415); the fine was subsequently remitted (*CARD*, II, 417).

147 DCA, MR/5/12, mb. 36 (*CARD*, III, 266).
148 In a deposition which he made in the case of one John Heathcote, *c* 1636, his age is given as about forty-nine years (Bodl., MS Carte 176, fol. 11); he must therefore have been admitted to the franchises in his mid or late teens.
149 A parson's cess for 10 May 1643 in the vestry book of the church of St John the Evangelist records 'Iohn Huggard Musitian' in Fishamble Street with three 'inmates': Robert Sparke (styled 'gentleman'), Peter Mallady, and Henry Withers (RCB, P. 328/5/1, p. 230). A later cess of 1646 (RCB, P. 328/5/1, p. 260) makes it clear that John was still living there, and specifies on the east side of the street, though only in the 10 May 1643 record is there any mention of him as a musician. John was in Fishamble Street (with a tenant) at least as early as 1626 (RCB, P. 328/5/1, p. 62), and apparently continuously from that time since he reappears in subsequent cesses. He is not in the 1622 cess (RCB, P. 328/5/1, p. 28 ff), and the next one is that for 1626, so he presumably arrived in the street between 1622–6. Though last heard of in official civic documents on 12 October 1638 (BL, MS Additional 11687, fol. 8; a Tholsel Court complaint brought by Huggard against the button maker David Chadsey), he probably retained the post of city wait either until his death in 1654 (*CARD*, IV, 68) or until not long before.
150 It is just conceivable that the Huggard sons were musicians elsewhere, not waits. John's son, another William, broke with the immediate family tradition by becoming a goldsmith; he was admitted to the franchises on 17 April 1640 (DCA, MR/5/12, mb. 78 dorse; *CARD*, III, 371).
151 A musical monopoly is first evidenced in 1436, though those musicians were not explicitly called waits. In the sixteenth century, the monopoly was endorsed on 22 October 1591, and again in the seventeenth century, on 17 July 1618 (*CARD*, II, 250 and III, 96 respectively). The repetition of the terms of a monopoly is a witness to the activity of alternative musicians in Dublin at this time.
152 This was the incentive to travel that presumably explained the repeated injunctions on the waits not to absent themselves but to attend the mayor; compare the 24 October 1466 injunction, for example, and on 12 October 1599, William Huggard was required not to absent himself without mayoral permission and in any case for no longer than eight days at a time (*CARD*, II, 336).
153 Harris, *History*, p. 292; on Fitzsimon, see Lennon, *Lords of Dublin*, passim. It may have been part of the ceremonial role of the city recorder to give orations on such occasions. Harris probably had access to a version of the *Dublin Chronicle*, from which he derived this item. (Compare his record of Fitzsimon's oration with that in the version of the *Dublin Chronicle* in BL, MS Additional 4791, fol. 138; here, the corresponding passage, though not nearly as elaborate as the Harris account, like it also incorrectly cites 1530 for the Lord Deputyship of Sir William Skeffington. Skeffington was in fact appointed Lord Deputy on 30 July 1534.) It is traditionally thought that Harris

inherited Sir James Ware's papers from having married his granddaughter, but of this there is no real evidence (C. McNeill, 'Harris: Collectanea de Rebus Hibernicis,' *Analecta Hibernica* 6 (Dublin, 1934), 248–450; see p. 248), even though Harris did consult the Armagh Public Library manuscript of Robert Ware's *The History and Antiquties of Dublin*, which includes memoranda by Sir James, for his *History and Antiquities of the City of Dublin*, published five years after his death in 1761.

154 There were two St Mary's Abbeys, one of Arroasian nuns near the Hoggen Green, the other (and larger), of Cistercian monks, on the north side of the city. Which of the two was intended here is unknown, but that on the north side would have been nearest to where the Lord Deputy landed.

155 TCD, MS 591 (E. 3. 28), fol. 22r–v; it is not known whether orations were delivered on this occasion. Compare also the 26 October 1568 reception in the city suburbs by the mayor and aldermen of Sir Henry Sidney, Lord Deputy, and the Lords Justice (TCD, MS 581 [E. 3. 18], fol. 97). Though where exactly this reception occurred is not known, nor whether orations were delivered, an impressive advance party of six hundred horse and citizens, plus the two sheriffs, went out to meet them.

156 DCA, MR/35, pp. 563, 572–3, and 578. The reception probably occurred *c* 15 April 1599, when Devereux took the oath as Lord Deputy. Sir Thomas Butler, tenth earl of Ormond, was received on the same occasion.

157 The victory at the siege of Kinsale was won on 24 December 1601; the Dublin entry dates to shortly after that time.

158 Compare the Limerick case of 1567 discussed in chapter 5.

159 *Holinshed's Irish Chronicle*, ed. Miller and Power, pp. 101–2; see Lennon, *Lords of Dublin*, p. 143, on Fitzsimon's possible identification with the same Michael Fitzsimon who was eventually executed in 1591 after the Baltinglass rebellion.

160 N. Sanders, R. Southern, T.W. Craik, and L. Potter, *The Revels History of Drama in English Volume II 1500–1576* (London and New York, 1980), pp. 210–15.

161 The first grammar school master paid by the corporation of whom I am aware, a Mr Cusack, appears in a set of accounts for 1563 (DCA, MR/35, p. 189). He may well have been the same Patrick Cusack whom Richard Stanihurst mentioned (Lennon, *Lords of Dublin*, pp. 138–9). On the school and its personnel generally, see Lennon, ibid.

162 His appointment is noted in 1583 (Lennon, ibid., p. 139); he occurs in other records, including the Dublin Assembly Rolls, as late as 1588 (*CARD*, II, 181). The payment for the Black Monday interlude occurs in a set of accounts running between the Michaelmasses of 1582 and 1583 in the Treasurer's Book (DCA, MR/35, p. 364): 'More payed to david duke scole master for his paynes in playeng an enterlute vppon blackmonday; per warrantum dicti maioris & aldermannorum xxvj s. viij d.'

163 CHL, Lismore Papers, Volume 25, p. 258: 'Geven the Children vli for their Mask.' (The reference, in the diary of Sir Richard Boyle, is discussed further in chapter 6;

children were also being trained for the Kilkenny Corpus Christi play at least by 1631; see further on this in chapter 4.)

164 E.K. Chambers, *The Elizabethan Stage*, 4 vols (Oxford, 1923) II, 24–7; also H.N. Hillebrand, *The Child Actors* (Urbana, Illinois, 1926).

165 On the interlude, see N. Davis, 'The Meaning of the Word "Interlude": A Discussion,' *Medieval English Theatre* 6 (1984), 5–15. Though the interlude was not inevitably an indoor performance, as Davis notes, he also notes that 'the private hall grew in importance as a customary venue [for interludes] during the sixteenth century' (ibid., p. 13).

166 DCA, MR/35, p. 427. This item and its dating is discussed further below in chapter 6.

167 If only in the sense that he may have actually authored the interlude, as the orators authored their welcoming speeches.

168 William Shakespeare, *A Midsummer Night's Dream*, ed. H.F. Brooks (Bristol and Bungay, 1979), p. 108.

169 DCL, MS 209, p. 153: 'Item more payt for tymyr {'timber'} to the Gamayll ix d.' I take the 'Gamayll' (also spelt 'Gaymaylle' in the 1559 record of it; DCL, MS 209, p. 33) to have been the camel. The only oddity is the spelling with initial 'g' for initial 'c.' However, a phonetic shift from a voiceless to a voiced consonant here is not a difficult matter in what must also have been a relatively exotic word.

170 DCL, MS 209, p. 153: 'Item more payt for the workmanschype [to my selfe] to Nycholus hoyll & phylype Iwnor mete drynke & wagys when they was dresyng the gamayl xx d.'

171 DCL, MS 209, p. 33: 'Item paied agrotte {'a groat'} sterling for dressynge of the Gaymaylle that is to say ij d. sterling in nayles & ij d. sterling in hopes/.'

172 DCA, MR/35, p. 169: 'Item to the hooper for mending the dragon & Lynen cloth & nails to the same x s. iiij d. Item for peanting the same xij s.'

173 Twycross, 'Flemish Ommegang,' p. 83, has accurately inferred the basic construction of the Dublin camel without the benefit of the guild records. One porter is likely in the dragon's case, as a payment in accounts running from 29 September 1545 to 4 November 1546 suggests (DCA, MR/35, p. 51): 'Item to Iohn Ogan for bering of the Dragon the daye of the Tryumphe of the peax iij s.' Compare the dragon of Norwich, which had a single bearer (D. Galloway, ed., *Norwich 1540–1642*, Records of Early English Drama [Toronto, 1984], p. lxv), and see fig. 12.

174 Compare the Kilkenny Marys discussed in chapter 4, who regularly received pairs of gloves for their performances.

175 In the 25 July 1554 to 5 July 1555 accounts, and in the 1569 accounts; see respectively BL, MS Egerton 1765, fol. 121: 'payed for paynting the emperorrs hed xviii d.' and fol. 123: 'payd to the payntor for paynten of the hed for thempror [& for the crowen] xviiii d. st.'

176 Twycross and Carpenter, 'Masks,' pp. 18–19, examine the possible meanings of 'head' in similar contexts. References to painting heads are common enough in similar accounts;

compare the painting of St Thomas's 'head' in a set of Kentish pageant accounts of 1504 (Chambers, *Mediæval Stage*, II, 345).

177 P. Meredith, 'Stage Directions and the Editing of Early English Drama,' in A.F. Johnston, ed., *Editing Early Drama: Special Problems and New Directions* (New York, 1987), pp. 65–94; see pp. 81–5.

178 DCA, MR/5/6, mb. 9 dorse (*CARD*, I, 476): 'Sainct Georgis harnes as the saie {?'as they say'} with the cutler & fladge {?'flag'} for fott men whit & Reade & ijstandardes for horsemen.'

179 DCA, MR/35, p. 225, quoted in note 98 above, and see the references concerning Sir Nicholas Arnold's ban quoted in note 29 above. Though the corporation was still deferential to the order of precedence in the Corpus Christi lists as late as 21 January 1569, this is absolutely the last known reference to the feast in civic documents (DCA, MR/5/7, mb. 13; *CARD*, II, 54): 'It is agreed for eschuing contrauersie that maye ryse on Shroftuysday in bearing balles that euery occupacion to keape ordre in ryding with their ballis as they are appointed to go with their pageauntes yn Corpus christi daye / by the chayne boke / Saving to euery man the auncyent preemynence of byrthe and mariadge.'

180 This rift was caused by various grievances between city and state, including, for example, the new get-tough policies adopted by the state from about 1577 against recusancy (M.V. Ronan, *The Reformation in Ireland under Elizabeth 1558–1580 [from Original Sources]* [London and New York, 1930], pp. 525–52; R. Dudley Edwards, *Church and State in Tudor Ireland* [Dublin and Cork, 1935], pp. 206–21 and 247–61). The approach of the English administration to recusancy had been relatively temperate, until after Sir Henry Sidney's departure in 1571.

181 Another ceremonial testimony to diverging bailiwicks may be seen in the fact that Christ Church Cathedral, hitherto a focus of civic and governmental public display and collaboration, was receiving fewer aldermanic burials after about 1560 (Lennon, *Lords of Dublin*, p. 144), and in 1596, the corporation's station day observances were officially shifted to St Audoen's Church, now much in favour with the corporation (*CARD*, II, 298).

182 TCD, MS 772 (E. 4. 11), fol. 18.

183 KAO, U1475 034, fols [30v] and [31] respectively. Though the accounts run between these dates, the feast in question here probably fell in 1569.

184 BL, MS Additional 12562, fol. 5.

185 The 1578 display is the first on record of such pageantry in the city organized by the English administration, as opposed to the corporation.

186 Some observance of St George's Day on the part also of the English administration may have already been traditional. An early-sixteenth-century example appears 12 December 1515, when the men of Westmeath were ordered to muster on the hill of Tara on St George's Day (PRO, SP 60/1, fol. 26v). It was doubtless also symbolically appropriate

that the Lord Deputy, Leonard, Lord Grey, chose this day for his hosting against the O'Connors of co. Offaly in 1536 (though rain washed his expedition out; TCD, MS 591 [E. 3. 28], fol. 13). For early-seventeenth-century instances of the administration's continuing awareness of the significance of St George, see the letter of 24 April 1600 from Sir Oliver Lambert to Lord Deputy Mountjoy (E.G. Atkinson, ed., *Calendar of the State Papers relating to Ireland of the Reign of Elizabeth, 1600, March-October, preserved in the Public Record Office* [London, 1903], p. 120), and in 1606, note a report of how the sick earl of Ormond, Sir Thomas Butler, had his robes laid out on his bed to honour St George's feast (PRO, SP 63/218, fol. 163v).

187 F. Moryson, *An Itinerary VVritten by Fynes Moryson Gent. First in the Latine Tongue, and then translated by him into English* (London, 1617; STC 18205), Part II, p. 99.

CHAPTER 4

1 *Holinshed's Irish Chronicle*, ed. Miller and Power, p. 58; W. Camden, *Britannia* (London, 1586; STC 4503), p. 504.

2 Moody, Martin, and Byrne, *New History of Ireland III*, p. 87.

3 On Kilkenny recusancy, see further below. A sixteenth-century epitome of the town's religious persuasion is found in the fact that when Archbishop Dermot O'Hurley was in prison there in 1583, leading citizens received communion from him (W.G. Neely, *Kilkenny: An Urban History, 1391–1843* [Belfast, 1989], p. 47).

4 This was the family of Sir Richard Shee (Neely, *Kilkenny*, p. 74). For Shee connections with the plays, see table 1 below.

5 The town was well established before the Anglo-Normans arrived. Its Anglo-Norman phase was ushered in by the first lord of Leinster (Cosgrove, *New History of Ireland II*, p. 166).

6 S. Barry, 'The Architecture of the Cathedral,' in A. Empey, ed., *A Worthy Foundation: The Cathedral Church of St Canice Kilkenny, 1285–1985* (Mount Rath, Port Laoise, 1985), pp. 25–48; see pp. 25–6. The landmarks noted in this discussion are shown in fig. 15.

7 J.C. Erck, ed., *A Repertory of the Inrolments on the Patent Rolls of Chancery, in Ireland; commencing with the Reign of King James I*, 2 vols (Dublin, 1846–52) II, 633. The sovereign (from 1609, mayor) began his office from the following Michaelmas.

8 On the composition of Kilkenny Corporation at this date, see Neely, *Kilkenny*, p. 28. The distribution of merchant and artisanal professions between the greater and lesser twelve respectively seems broadly comparable to the arrangements pertaining in Dublin; see chapter 3.

9 LPL, MS 603 (Carew Papers), fol. 168 (Berry, *Statutes and Ordinances*, p. 446). The fact that the first three types of minstrel are referred to by anglicized forms of Gaelic words (their Classical Irish forms, nominative singular, would be respectively *timpánach*,

fer dána and *scélaige*) possibly betrays the measure of their success in attracting English audiences.

10 As might be expected, the Dominicans and Franciscans were in the vanguard; the Dominicans had established a Kilkenny house in 1225 (the Black Abbey, see fig. 15) and the Franciscans a house between 1232 and 1240 (St Francis's Abbey, see fig. 15). The other two main mendicant orders never got a foothold (Watt, *Church in Medieval Ireland*, pp. 60–84).

11 RCB, D 11/1/1 (Red Book of Ossory), fol. 70; Gilbert, *Manuscripts of the Marquis of Ormonde*, p. 242. Recent work by Joan Rimmer on the Latin songs is suggesting that many of them were based on dance measures, and may have been devised with dancing specifically in mind. I am obliged to her for private information on this. It is also not certain how many of the songs were actually composed by Ledrede himself; A.G. Rigg, 'The Red Book of Ossory,' *Medium Ævum* 46 (1977), 269–78, has shown that some of them were certainly the work of the earlier Franciscan poet Walter of Wimborne; see also his 'Walter of Wimborne, O.F.M.: An Anglo-Latin Poet of the Thirteenth Century,' *Mediæval Studies* 33 [1971], 371–8.)

12 On the role of the friars in promoting drama, see D.L. Jeffrey, 'Franciscan Spirituality and the Rise of Early English Drama,' *Mosaic* 8 (1975), 17–46.

13 If, as an unpublished, early-fifteenth-century Franciscan sermon put it, 'good mynstralcye' was one of the four things needful when offering a friend hospitality (Bodl., MS Lat. th. d. 1, fol. 173), the visit of a king would seem to demand at least as much. On Richard's two Kilkenny visits, see Lydon, 'Richard II's Expeditions.' It is not until the early seventeenth century, however, that records survive of the earls of Ormond retaining minstrels (P. Watters, 'Notes of Entries in the Corporation Records, Kilkenny, relative to a Visit of Lord Viscount Wentworth to Kilkenny in the year 1637,' *Journal of the Royal Society of Antiquaries of Ireland* 16 [1883–4], 242–9; see p. 243). Butler patronage is discussed further in chapter 6.

14 Before he travelled to Ireland with Henry IV's son, Thomas, William Dodmore had already served as harper to Richard II, though whether he had accompanied the king on his Irish visits in 1395 and 1399 is not clear (PRO, C. 66/379, mb. 7; Westminster Patent Roll entry of 29 July 1408): 'Willielmus Dodmore alias dictus Willielmus Blyndharpour qui in obsequio Regis in comitiua carissimi filij Regis Thome de lancastre Senescalli Anglie & locumtenentis Regis in terra sua hibernie super salua custodia eiusdem terre moratur habet litteras Regis de proteccione ...' ('William Dodmore, alias the said William Blyndharpour, who remains in the service of the king in the company of the king's most dear son Thomas of Lancaster, seneschal of England and deputy of the king in his land of Ireland, has in addition to the safe custody of that land the king's letters of protection ...').

15 The economic security of Kilkenny during Elizabeth I's reign is noted by E. Curtis, ed., *Calendar of Ormond Deeds*, 6 vols (Dublin, 1932–43) VI, iii–iv.

16 East Anglian dramatic traditions are surveyed by J.C. Coldewey, 'The Non-cycle Plays and the East Anglian Tradition,' in Beadle, *Cambridge Companion*, pp. 189–210, and see also G. McMurray Gibson, *The Theater of Devotion: East Anglian Drama and Society in the Late Middle Ages* (Chicago and London, 1989); for the dramatic records of the university, see Nelson, *Cambridge*.

17 A. Stewart, '"Ydolatricall Sodometrye": John Bale's Allegory,' *Medieval English Theatre* 15 (1993), 3–20; see p. 6 and note 9.

18 Their chronology is discussed in *Complete Plays of John Bale*, ed. Happé, I, 2–11.

19 J. Bale, *The Vocacyon of Johan Bale to the bishoprick of Ossorie in Ireland* (Wesel, 1553; *STC* 1307), fol. 24r–v.

20 Bale, *Vocacyon*, fol. 32. (Both the summer sermon, on the ploughman, and the winter one, on the good shepherd, were on themes appropriate enough: respectively *Exivit qui seminat seminare* and *Ego sum pastor bonus*.)

21 Bale, *Vocacyon*, fol. 21v.

22 Bale, *Vocacyon*, fol. 22v.

23 BL, MS Additional 4796, fol. 34v. This quotation is taken from a fragment of what may have been David Rothe's *Hierographia Hiberniae*, a work composed *c* 1615 but whose greater part has been lost. The fragment in this manuscript is preserved thanks to the compiling activity of Sir James Ware. The quotation is from a section headed *De Ossoriensi Dioecesi*.

24 Bale, *Vocacyon*, fol. 24r–v (*Complete Plays of John Bale*, ed. Happé, I, 6–7).

25 Bale, *Vocacyon*, fol. 30v. Reformers from Tyndale on applied the language of theatricality to Roman liturgy (J. Barish, *The Antitheatrical Prejudice* [Berkeley and London, 1981], pp. 160–5). Bale was keeping up the tradition.

26 His use of the animated dove for Christ's baptism may be a case in point. If K. Walls, 'The Dove on a Cord in the Chester Cycle's Noah's Flood,' *Theatre Notebook* 47 (1993), 42–7, has correctly analysed how such a descent may have been contrived in the Chester play of Noah's Flood (she suggests the descent of a dove-shaped pyx), then Bale may again have been turning a staging device with strongly Catholic overtones to his own use.

27 One of his qualms may show in his offering the option of singing the Advent O-Antiphons in English rather than in Latin – a concession, perhaps, towards reformed sensibility.

28 Three sections in *Johan Baptystes Preachynge* (*Complete Plays of John Bale*, ed. Happé, II, 38–42, lines 36–188; 42–5, lines 189–337; and 45–8, lines 338–457) and four in *The Temptacyon of Our Lorde* (ed. Happé, ibid., 54–7, lines 36–182; 57–9, lines 183–266; 59–61, lines 267–350; and 61–2, lines 351–98).

29 *Complete Plays of John Bale*, ed. Happé, II, 49, lines 490–1.

30 Compare too the clothing of Sodomy in Bale's *Three Laws* 'lyke a monke of all sectes' (*Complete Plays of John Bale*, ed. Happé, II, 121). This device became a topos of Protestant polemical drama; compare the use made of it by Christopher Marlowe in

The Tragical History of Dr Faustus, when Faustus conjures Mephistophilis to return in the shape of a Franciscan friar, since 'that holy shape becomes a devil best' (*The Complete Works of Christopher Marlowe*, ed. R. Gill [Oxford, 1987–] II, 10, lines 23–6). Gill, p. xxvii, observes that in these lines Marlowe 'affirms his Protestant sympathies'; it might be truer to say that he has simply connected with an antimendicant topos, already present in his source, but to which he has given sharper edge.

31 *Complete Plays of John Bale*, ed. Happé, II, 61, line 337.

32 *Complete Plays of John Bale*, ed. Happé, I, 22, suggests they were household servants, but there is no evident support for this in the case of the Kilkenny production. See further below, and note 38.

33 J.G.A. Prim, 'Olden Popular Pastimes in Kilkenny,' *Journal of the Royal Society of Antiquaries of Ireland* 2 (1852–3), 319–35; see p. 324. And on 13 October 1609, future Lords of Bullring were voted a salary of £6 13s 4d (ibid.).

34 Ibid., p. 323.

35 Ibid. On the greater and lesser twelve, see above and note 8.

36 KCA, CR/J22 (9).

37 The Christmas holidays were another. Bulls were provided by the butchers (Prim, 'Olden Popular Pastimes,' p. 324).

38 Bale, *Vocacyon*, fol. 28v. Note Bale's choice of terms. He called the personnel who performed his Kilkenny production 'yonge men,' and it was the 'yonge men' who sang their songs of thanksgiving at his rescue. These were evidently not household servants.

39 Grindle, *Irish Cathedral Music*, pp. 5 and 22. In Bale's day the cathedral had four vicars choral and four stipendiaries in its musical establishment; Bale's successor added to this foundation a further four choristers.

40 A John Lawless, organ maker, is mentioned in a Kilkenny indenture of 1476 (P. Watters, 'Original Documents connected with Kilkenny,' *Journal of the Royal Society of Antiquaries of Ireland* 12 [1872–3], 532–43; see p. 543). St Mary's in Kilkenny, the church most strongly identified with the town's Protestant enclave (see below), retained an organ clerk, so Bale would probably not have been embarrassed for an organist either.

41 Such public architectural features were often incorporated into play or pageant stages (Wickham, *Early English Stages*, I, 55–8), and quite possibly the Kilkenny Market Cross was similarly used.

42 *Complete Plays of John Bale*, ed. Happé, II, 18, line 493.

43 According to Rocque's scale, the width of High Street at the same place is 65′, a measurement corresponding virtually exactly with my own measurement of the street.

44 Compare in this regard the Chester play of Noah's Flood and the 1555 Pentecost pageant in St Patrick's Cathedral, Dublin, both discussed in chapter 2.

45 *Complete Plays of John Bale*, ed. Happé, II, 58, line 202.

46 The current whereabouts of the original picture from which this engraving was made (the original is reproduced in W. Carrigan, *The History and Antiquities of the Diocese of*

Ossory, 4 vols [Dublin, 1905] III, facing p. 59) have not been traced, though the engraving does it justice. Five steps are also shown on another engraving of the Market Cross reproduced in Walker, 'Historical Essay,' p. 90.

47 Bale, *Vocacyon*, fol. 31. The Rob Davie mentioned in this passage was, as Bale explains elsewhere (*Vocacyon*, fol. 22), a special drink with aqua vitae. (Here a printer's error has probably confounded K and R which in black letter font look much alike.)

48 P. Moran, 'The Bishops of Ossory from the Anglo-Norman Invasion to the Present Day,' *Transactions of the Ossory Archæological Society* 2 (1882), 199–306. A letter by the protestant bishop of Ossory, John Horsfall, written 8 June 1604 to the Lord Deputy and council of Ireland, complained how his clergy were Romish, and listed notable catholic priests currently operating in his diocese (Ibid., pp. 263–4).

49 J.C. Beckett, 'The Confederation of Kilkenny Reviewed,' in M. Roberts, ed., *Historical Studies II* (London, 1959), pp. 29–41; also, Moody, Martin, and Byrne, *New History of Ireland III*, pp. 298–302.

50 Prim, 'Olden Popular Pastimes,' p. 323.

51 P. Watters, 'Notes of Particulars extracted from the Kilkenny Corporation Records relating to the Miracle Plays as performed there from the year 1580 to the year 1639,' *Journal of the Royal Society of Antiquaries of Ireland* 16 (1883–4), 238–42; see p. 241.

52 I have searched all the obvious Dublin and Kilkenny archives, with the exception of a few uncatalogued and inaccessible holdings in NLI, NA, and DCA. These holdings necessarily remain uncharted territory until such time as they are made available for inspection.

53 KCA, CR/1/D (Liber Primus Kilkenniensis), fol. 51v (C. McNeill, ed., *Liber Primus Kilkenniensis* [Dublin, 1931], p. 113).

54 Erck, *Repertory*, I, 642.

55 Neely, *Kilkenny*, p. 79.

56 A by-law of 5 January 1567 called for streets to be cleaned on Corpus Christi, the feasts of St Canice (11 October) and of St Patrick (17 March), Christmas, and Easter (J. Ainsworth, 'Corporation Book of the Irishtown of Kilkenny 1537–1628,' *Analecta Hibernica* 28 [1978], 1–78; see p. 29).

57 Paris, Bibliothèque Mazarine, MS 1869, p. 620 (John Lynch, *De Historia Ecclesiae Hiberniae*). This incident may offer further indirect evidence that Corpus Christi play production was concentrated in the Hightown, not in the Irishtown where St Canice's Cathedral stands. John Lynch (*c* 1600–*c* 1674) wrote the *De Historia Ecclesiae Hiberniae* in 1672. The Bibliothèque Mazarine manuscript formerly belonged to the Oratoire de Saint-Magloire, whose superior, Fr. Louis Abel de Sainte-Marthe, had urged Lynch to undertake the work. The Paris manuscript, evidently in the hand of a French scribe, may have been copied from Lynch's holograph. It is quoted here since it served as exemplar for the other extant manuscript copies of *De Historia Ecclesiae Hiberniae*.

58 Early evidence for Kilkenny guilds appears, for example, in the *Liber Primus*, where a

controversy between the guilds of Glovers and Shoemakers is mentioned in 1514 (McNeill, *Liber Primus*, p. 135), but there is no early evidence whatsoever for any participation by the guilds in the organization of civic pageantry of the sort that was seen in Dublin. A list of 1604 gives the seven trades of the Irishtown as follows: Shoemakers, Glovers, Weavers, Cotners, Carpenters, Smiths, and Tailors (Ainsworth, 'Corporation Book,' p. 53). Hightown records are even more scattered, but guilds after 1656 include also Merchant Tailors, Cordwainers, Hammermen, and Bakers (Neely, *Kilkenny*, pp. 67–8). By the seventeenth century, it appears that guilds may have been entering extravagantly into the spirit of things on Corpus Christi, for a memorandum in the Red Book of Kilkenny Corporation (on which manuscript, see note 72 below) for 23 January 1628, legislated as follows: 'The masters of companies usually running in debt on account of the feasts they annually gave the freemen on Corpus Christi day, and being ruined thereby, the said feasts are abolished' (J.G.A. Prim, 'Ancient Civic Enactments for Restraining Gossiping and Feasting,' *Jornal of the Royal Society of Antiquaries of Ireland* 1 [1849–51], 436–41; see p. 439). Nevertheless, it is still not clear that they were officially and corporately involved in the civic drama by this date.

59 Many members of the prominent Kilkenny families were merchants, as, for example, Nicholas Langton (see table 1 below). He was one of the townsmen sent to London to negotiate the 1609 charter which raised Kilkenny to city status.

60 A solitary record of a St George procession in Kilkenny, a great cavalcade when the lords rode in their appointed places, is recorded for 1594 (C. Vallancey, ed., *Collectanea de Rebus Hibernicis*, 6 vols [Dublin, 1770–1804] II, 391). Interestingly, this occurs not long after a possible time of sensitivity in the town towards Corpus Christi in 1591, discussed above.

61 The published sources of these names are Watters, 'Notes of Particulars'; and Prim, 'Olden Popular Pastimes'; the unpublished sources are: NLI, MSS 3302 and 11048 (item 2), and KCA, CR/J11, CR/J13, CR/J15, and CR/K13.

62 All these families were of Anglo-Norman origin, apart from the family of Shee, which was Irish. A couplet naming the chief families – 'Archdekin, Archer, Cowley, Langton, Ley / Knaresborough, Lawless, Raggett, Rothe and Shee' – was well known in Kilkenny and circulating there already by the eighteenth century.

63 J.G.A. Prim, 'The Corporation Insignia and Olden Civic State of Kilkenny,' *Journal of the Royal Society of Antiquaries of Ireland* 11 (1870), 280–305; also McNeill, *Liber Primus*, p. 18. The church had been founded at least before 1206, when exequies were held there on the death of Theobald Butler, first chief butler of Ireland.

64 Curtis, *Ormond Deeds*, VI, 112–13 (he also appears as a witness pp. 10, 38, and 73). Also, a William Kelly was deprived as vicar of Kilbeacon 16 September 1583 (J.B. Leslie, *Ossory Clergy and Parishes* [Enniskillen, 1933], p. 284).

65 Moran, 'Bishops of Ossory,' p. 264, and table 1 below. A John Murphy also appears to have been a witness to a document of 6 April 1601, but the nature of his profession

there is withheld (Curtis, *Ormond Deeds*, VI, 114; see also the document p. 181). A William Lawless is named in Horsfall's list, but the play involvement of another William Lawless in 1637 (table 1 below) looks rather late to suggest that he was the same person.

66 Curtis, *Ormond Deeds*, VI, 42.

67 Watters, 'Notes of Particulars,' p. 238.

68 *OED*, **Clerk**, subsense 6.

69 KCA, CR/J10, obverse. Krininge signs in acknowledgment of receipt of payment on 23 December 1583.

70 Prim, 'Olden Popular Pastimes,' p. 328.

71 W. Healy, *History and Antiquities of Kilkenny (County and City)* (Kilkenny, 1893), pp. 171–2.

72 Ironically enough, the antiquarians may themselves be to blame for misplacing some of the documents. A forlorn appeal went out in the mid-nineteenth century for corporation documents which had been removed in the eighteenth and nineteenth centuries and never returned: 'and I trust that any other gentleman in whose family such documents may have been handed down from ancestors who were members of the old corporation, will, upon reading this enquiry concerning them, afford all possible information on the subject' (J.G.A. Prim, 'Missing Records. No. II. Muniments of the Corporation of Kilkenny,' *Journal of the Royal Society of Antiquaries of Ireland* 1 [1849–51], 427–32; see p. 431). The appeal produced no results. Indeed, only very recently has anything serious been done to conserve the archives, and within living memory, archival material was kept at the Tholsel in random and dishevelled heaps. A major loss from our point of view was the Red Book of Kilkenny Corporation, already missing by the mid-nineteenth century, whose entries began in Elizabeth I's reign. A mid-eighteenth-century summary of its contents, made by the Kilkenny alderman, William Colles, was available to Prim, and from it he printed extracts in 'Olden Popular Pastimes.' I have not succeeded in tracing the Colles summary. I am obliged to Peter Farrelly, former town clerk of Kilkenny, for helpful discussion, and to Donal O'Brien, the present town clerk, for allowing me access to the corporation archive.

73 The discovery of additional relevant corporation documents (KCA, CR/J4, CR/J11, CR/J13, CR/J15 and CR/K13), proves that Watters, 'Notes of Particulars,' pp. 238–42, was selective, not exhaustive. Bearing this in mind, we may conclude that possibly the plays, and certainly the civic celebrations which were their context, may have been an annual event by the 1580s. It is also interesting to note that in his 1603 petition, given below, William Courcy spoke in terms implying annual play performances.

74 *OED*, **Set forth**, subsense (c).

75 Ainsworth, 'Corporation Book,' pp. 23, 25, 27, 33, 36, 38–9, 44, and 45–6. As well as portreeve in 1566, his posts for the Irishtown corporation between these years included those of proctor, auditor, and constable.

76 See respectively Curtis, *Ormond Deeds*, VI, 44 and NLI, MS 2510, p. 42. Greyfriars was St Francis's Abbey (see fig. 15).

77 Curtis, *Ormond Deeds*, VI, 42; also note a John Kennedy who was presented 3 November 1559 to the vicarage of St Mary, Templegate, in Ossory (Leslie, *Ossory Clergy*, p. 218).

78 However, it is unlikely that the 1584 Courcy was also one and the same person, unless he were a *child* then.

79 KCA, CR/K13, obverse and dorse. The addition on the dorse is probably in the hand of George Shee.

80 Another theoretical possibility, that the comedy of the Resurrection was a play for another occasion than Corpus Christi, has very little to recommend it, given the Corpus Christi emphasis of Courcy's complaint and the fact that the Resurrection was sometimes spoken of as being presented on Corpus Christi.

81 See note 65 above.

82 Ainsworth, 'Corporation Book,' p. 68; a John Lawless, burgess, who is probably the same person, features in a document of 5 July 1626, (pp. 75–6).

83 Compare also the case of John Lawless in table 1 above, for example, who performed in various years.

84 Note the annual stipend voted in 1631 to William 'Consey' for instructing the children for the Corpus Christi play in table 1. What the children did, exactly, is not clear, but it seems likely that they performed. Note also Mary Rothe's breakfast for the 'Young Men' who acted in the Corpus Christi play in 1637 in table 1.

85 Watters, 'Notes of Particulars,' p. 241, for both warrants, that ordering payment and that acknowledging payment.

86 There is no direct evidence that William Courcy was a setter forth again, but the fact that Mary Rothe is spoken of in another warrant, one acknowledging payment, as being William Courcy's wife (Watters, 'Notes of Particulars,' p. 241) suggests that responsibility for production aspects of plays may have run within a family, if this was in fact the same William 'Consey' (a transcription or printing error for 'Corsey'?) who was voted an annual stipend in 1631. A William Courcy also submitted the petition of 1603; once again, if this is the same man, or even if it is the father of the (1631?) and 1637 William Courcy, it similarly suggests a long-standing family involvement with play production. Necessarily, the William Courcy who was paid for acting in 1584, unless he were a child at the time, could not be the William 'Consey' of 1631, and in view of this I have given him a separate entry in table 1. He could conceivably be, however, the William Courcy of the 1603 petition.

87 Sometimes the payee would also sign the warrant to acknowledge receipt of payment (Watters, 'Notes of Particulars,' p. 238, where James Krininge acknowledged his receipt; also similarly Adam Shee in table 1 above). NLI, MS D 3302, which is a chance survival of a quire from an otherwise lost Kilkenny Corporation account ledger, shows John Mooney (Kilkenny town bailiff in 1600) in action, entering the note of his dis-

bursement into his ledger after being presented with a warrant (fols 3v–4): 'Item an other warrant from the said Soveraigne and chamberlaines dated the xvij th of Iune 1600 to pay Symon Archer ten shillings st for playing a Conqueror his parte on mydsomer eaue x s. sterling |fol. 4| Item an other warrant from mr Soveragne and the chamberlaines dated the xvij th of Iune to deliver Phillip Lawles and his brother Iohn for playing two conquerours partes the som of twenty and one shilling sterling. xxj s. sterling.' The warrant which originally ordered Mooney's payment, no longer traceable, was evidently that available to Watters, 'Notes of Particulars,' p. 239.

88 Prim, 'Olden Popular Pastimes,' pp. 327–8; it should be noted that Prim (or his source, the Colles transcription) transcribed as 'Morries' what I believe was originally a reference to the *Marys*, and assumed this amounted to a reference to a morris dance (J. Fry and A.J. Fletcher, 'The Kilkenny Morries, 1610,' *Folk Music Journal* 6 [1993], 381–3).

89 J. Hogan, 'The Three Tholsels of Kilkenny,' *Journal of the Royal Society of Antiquaries of Ireland* 15 (1879–82), 236–52; he noted, p. 243, an inquisition 21 August 1619 taken in 'le new Tholsel.' This new building at least antedated 1603, however, as William Courcy's petition of that year, given above, makes clear.

90 My view of the staging differs radically from that of *EIS*, pp. 23–4, which has moved quite beyond the evidence.

91 Prim, 'Olden Popular Pastimes,' p. 328.

92 Compare, for example, the forty-one year lease taken out in 1608 on a shop under the new Tholsel by Piers Archer Fitz Richard (NLI, MS 2510, p. 32).

93 Prim, 'Olden Popular Pastimes,' p. 327 (my emphasis).

94 The High Street town houses were owned mainly by those merchant families who also dominated the corporation. Some of these mansions (those of the Archers, Langtons, Rothes, and Shees) still survive in the city to greater or lesser extents.

95 The Butter Slip runs between High Street and modern St Kieran's Street (this street was known c 1600 as Low Lane, and by the time of Rocque's map in 1758 as Back Lane). It was probably in existence before c 1600 and already in Bale's day. In 1602, the corporation allowed Nicholas Langton (possibly the same man who subscribed to a payment to John Kennedy on 20 June 1603 in table 1 above) to build a town house in the High Street on the south side of the Market Cross, provided he leave open the public access between the High Street and Low Lane. The Butter Slip conforms exactly to the measurements laid down in the corporation's agreement with Langton. Langton's house was not built until 1609 (J.G.A. Prim, 'Memorials of the Family of Langton, of Kilkenny,' *Journal of the Royal Society of Antiquaries of Ireland* 8 [1864], 59–108).

96 Though not quite identical, the phrase 'to go in stations,' recorded in *OED*, **Station** sb., subsense 24, from the mid-fifteenth century, is sufficiently close to the Kilkenny usage to invite comparison. *OED* gives its meaning as 'to perform the prescribed acts of devotion in succession at certain holy places, or at the Stations of the Cross.' Kilkenny usage would seem to mean something like 'to perform the prescribed acts ...

in succession at certain ... places.' Compare also with the Kilkenny event the reference to 'stations' made by the character Poeta in the play of the *Conversion of St Paul* (D.C. Baker, J.L. Murphy and L.B. Hall, Jr., eds., *The Late Medieval Religious Plays of Bodleian MSS Digby 133 and e Museo 160*, EETS, OS 283 [Oxford, 1982], p. 6, line 155). See further on the staging of the *Conversion* below and note 102.

97 Watters, 'Notes of Particulars,' p. 238.

98 Watters, 'Notes of Entries,' p. 247.

99 Butler, *Annals of Ireland*, p. xxxiv, notes an order of 9 February 1609 in the transcription of the Red Book that 'the market cross and Croker's cross be for ever repaired and kept in repair by the company of masons, in such manner as the mayor shall direct.'

100 Watters, 'Notes of Particulars,' p. 239.

101 Whatever happened at a station might at least be related to the play in terms of its subject matter. Those who 'went in stations' were characters like Christ, St Michael, and the devil. These characters also featured in the play, though it may not necessarily have been the same person who performed the same part in play and station. In fact, Thomas Langton's chit to Robert Archer cited above may imply a clear distinction between the devil that played in the Resurrection and 'the other Devill ... that went in Stacions.'

102 Baker, Murphy, and Hall, Jr., *Late Medieval Religious Plays*, pp. xxv–xxx.

103 See table 1 above.

104 Moran, 'Bishops of Ossory,' p. 262.

105 This is the usual order in other places in the British Isles, wherever it can be determined. For example, Beverley, Coventry, Chester, and Newcastle-upon-Tyne all had processions before plays (Nelson, *Medieval English Stage*, pp. 91, 142, 155, and 205–6 respectively).

106 Perhaps the 'going in stations' was also part of what the documents refer to as the Corpus Christi 'riding.' If there was any conservatism about processional routes in Kilkenny (such as has been argued in the case of London, for example, by Morrissey, 'English Pageant-Wagons'), then enough evidence survives of the processional routes taken by Viscount Wentworth in 1637 and by Archbishop Rinuccini in 1645 in their civic entries from which to conjecture something of the Corpus Christi route (and see further in chapter 5). However, these speculations cannot be aired here.

107 Watters, 'Notes of Particulars,' p. 238.

108 Apart from a few notable exceptions, most of the corporation payment warrants are prospective, not retrospective, and indicate that people were paid just before the feast (see table 1 above).

109 For example, the Resurrection was played in St Mary's on Midsummer in 1588, and it was also played, this time presumably in the High Street, on Corpus Christi in 1590. (It is most unlikely that two different Resurrection plays were presented.) See

Watters, 'Notes of Particulars,' p. 239. Since the Midsummer and Corpus Christi plays appear to have been similiar, if not basically identical, then even if Krininge's payment on 9 June 1585 was in fact for a Midsummer play, it is immaterial to my argument.

110 But it must be confessed that this argues from silence, and moreover, Midsummer could include a 'riding'; see Watters, 'Notes of Particulars,' p. 238 (the payment ordered by Arthur Shee to David Savage).

111 Watters, ibid., p. 238.

112 The question of whether Krininge and Busher were between them 'setting forth' the same play on the same day or were 'setting forth' the same play on separate occasions has been broached above. Note, incidentally, that both Krininge and Busher must have been *literate* (and in Krininge's case, we know his profession).

113 Watters, 'Notes of Particulars,' p. 239 (in Thomas Archer's payments ordered on 1 and 25 June 1588 respectively).

114 Ibid. The 'pereles' were possibly *parrels* (*OED*, **Parrel** sb.), bands of rope, of chain, or of iron (though how they may have been used in the construction of the Sepulchre is unknown), or *parrels* (*MED*, **ap(p)areil** n.), furnishings, trappings, or ornaments.

115 Were the preposition 'in' being used loosely here, it might conceivably mean that the play was put on in the churchyard, but on balance, it looks as if 'in' should be taken at face value to mean that the play was indeed put on *inside* the church. Compare the use of a church to host a play in Galway in November 1589 discussed in chapter 6, and the practice also existed commonly enough in sixteenth-century England (M. Aston, 'Segregation in Church,' in D. Wood, ed., *Women in the Church*, Studies in Church History 27 [Oxford, 1990], 237–94; see p. 248; A.F. Johnston, '"What Revels Are in Hand?": Dramatic Activities Sponsored by the Parishes of the Thames Valley,' in A.F. Johnston and W. Hüsken, ed., *English Parish Drama*, Ludus 1 [Amsterdam and Atlanta, 1996]; see p. 100).

116 Seymour, *Anglo-Irish Literature*, p. 131, reconstructed a 'Kilkenny cycle' of five plays: a play of Christ's Temptation, of his Crucifixion, of the three Marys, of the Resurrection, and of the Last Judgment. But his (apparent) inclusion of the subject matter of one of two Bale plays, *The Temptacyon of Our Lorde*, is unwarranted, and the presence of St Michael and assorted devils, which has presumably suggested to him the Last Judgment, fits more nearly a play of the Harrowing of Hell.

117 In this compare English practice, where 'the most common kind of Biblical play ... was some form of Easter play' (Johnston, 'Revels,' in Johnston and Hüsken, *English Parish Drama*, p. 99).

118 M. Stokes, 'The Instruments of the Passion,' *Journal of the Royal Society of Antiquaries of Ireland* 28 (1898), 137–40, finds an iconographic preoccupation with the Arma Christi to be characteristic of cos. Kilkenny, Carlow, and southeast co. Kildare at this date.

119 Watters, 'Notes of Particulars,' p. 239; the date here is misprinted: for '1598' read 1593.

120 Ibid., p. 241.

121 The musicians of the Corpus Christi play were also paid this year (ibid., p. 241). This is the first and only direct reference to musical accompaniment in the plays (though as was seen, James Krininge in the 1580s was by profession an organ clerk).

122 In various warrants in Watters, ibid., pp. 240–2; these men also acted similar roles at Midsummer.

123 The only explicit evidence of part doubling comes from the Nine Worthies pageant. A 'Conqueror' seems to be the general term for a Worthy. Sometimes the Worthies are named, as Godfrey and Hector here; Julius Caesar and Joshua are also mentioned in a 1602 warrant (Watters, ibid., pp. 239–40). The Kilkenny Worthies appear to have conformed to the standard list (see chapter 3, note 102).

124 NLI, MS 16085, p. 113 (the notebook of Edmund Sexton of Limerick, c 1590–1630). But it is possible that Sexton had seen a Nine Worthies pageant at some time or other; civic pageantry was certainly staged on an impressive scale in Limerick in the sixteenth and seventeenth centuries, as will be seen in chapter 5.

125 F. Finegan, 'Jesuits in Kilkenny,' *Jesuit Year Book* (1971), 9–23.

126 The history covers the years 1641–50 (and 1655–62).

127 Dublin, Leeson Street, Jesuit Archives, 'Missio Societatis Jesu in Hibernia ab initio ad usque annum salutis 1655 …,' no shelfmark, p. 58 (this is a nineteenth-century antiquarian transcription of an original manuscript, not yet located, in Rome, Archivum Romanum Societatis Iesu).

128 CUL, Bradshaw Collection, No. 5311, Hib. 7.644.33 (a bifolium, printed in Waterford in 1644; see Appendix II). It is clear that drama was still continuing to be of great importance to Kilkenny's civic life in the 1640s. Compare the statement of the anonymous author of the *Aphorismical Discovery of Treasonable Faction* that 'representations of comedies and stage playes, with mightie content' were frequently found there (see J.T. Gilbert, ed. *A Contemporary History of Affairs in Ireland from 1641 to 1652*, 4 vols [Dublin, 1879–80] I, Part 1, p. 46). And note that the polemical, pro-Catholic and nationalist play by Henry Burkhead, *A Tragedy of Cola's Furie, OR, Lirenda's Miserie*, was published in Kilkenny in 1646 (though whether it was actually performed there is unknown; see P. Coughlan, '"Enter Revenge": Henry Burkhead and *Cola's Furie*,' *Theatre Research International* 15 [1990], 1–17).

129 F. Solier, *Histoire Ecclesiastiqve des Isles et Royavmes dv Iapon* (Paris, 1627). The play is an imaginative reworking of the events described in book 9, chapters 9 and 12.

130 Solier, *Histoire Ecclesiastiqve*, p. 622. The only name shared by play and *Histoire* is Bungo. The play is populated too by theatrical abstractions, like Idolatry, the Church Triumphant, Divine Providence, and the like, none of which has any place in the *Histoire*.

131 Moody, Martin, and Byrne, *New History of Ireland*, III, p. 298.

CHAPTER 5

1 Christopher Marlowe, *The Complete Works of Christopher Marlowe*, ed. R. Gill, 2nd ed., 2 vols (Cambridge, 1981) I, 102.

2 The best general study is still Bergeron, *English Civic Pageantry*.

3 If delivery of an oration be used as the minimum criterion for deeming an Irish civic entry dramatic, then evidence is in fact available for dramatic entries laid on for five Lords Deputy. In chronological order these were: (i) of Sir Henry Sidney into Waterford in 1567; into Limerick in 1567 and 1576; into Dublin in 1568; into Kilkenny in 1575; and into Cork in 1576; (ii) of Sir William Russell into Galway in 1595; (iii) of Sir Robert Devereux into Clonmel, Kilkenny, and Limerick in 1599; (iv) of Sir Charles Blount into Waterford in 1603; and (v) of Sir Thomas Wentworth into Carlow, Clonmel, Kilkenny, and Limerick in 1637. The sources of all these entries will be more fully discussed in my forthcoming volume on the Irish dramatic records. The two most colourful sources, for the entries of Sir Henry Sidney (Dublin, 1568) and Sir Thomas Wentworth (Limerick, 1637), have been selected for discussion below.

4 TCD, MS 581 (E. 3. 18), fol. 97.

5 N.P. Canny, *The Elizabethan Conquest of Ireland: A Pattern Established 1565–76* (Trowbridge, 1976), p. 56.

6 Compare the identification also implicit in Sidney's description of his reception in Kilkenny in a letter to the Privy Council of 15 December 1575 (PRO, SP 63/54, fol. 52): 'At this towne lykewise the Earle of Ormound, feasted, and entreated me veary honorablie, and accompanied me to this cittie veary curteouslye, where I was received with all shewes and tokens, of gladnes, and pompe, aswell vpon the water, as the land; presented with the best commoditie they had,: which ceremonie of their thankefulnes, and good wills, *as true pledges of their obedience to her Mmajestie and governor*, I could not passe over in vnthankefull scylence' (my italics). Compare too a similar pitch in the Waterford oration of 3 May 1603 delivered to Sir Charles Blount (PRO, SP 63/215, fol. 124v–5): 'At the crosse ther was an oration in Latin, *magnifyeng the King, honouring my Lords person*; remembring his sevices {*read* services}, in suppressing the rebellion, declaring ther auncient and vntainted fidelity to the Kinges of England; iustifyeng and excusing ther disorderly courses, that what they had done, was only for ther consciences, and the publick professing of ther religion, in which they were borne, which they had receaved from ther ancestors, and which they wold leave vnto ther children. My Lord with a short speech commended ther faith and duty to the King; of himself he spake nothing, but thanked them for their welcome; and for ther excuse it was not the eloquence of the greatest Oratour, but the grace and mercy of the King of England | England, that must excuse them ...' (my italics).

7 Possibly near Tholsel Lane? See fig. 17.

8 PRO, SP 63/55, fol. 57v (letter of Sir Henry Sidney to the Privy Council).

9 PRO, SP 63/54, fol. 52 (letter of Sir Henry Sidney to the Privy Council, 15 December 1575). Thomas Churchyard could conceivably have had a hand in this, since he was in Kilkenny at about this time (see chapter 6, note 19).

10 John Dymmok, author of *A Tretice of Ireland*, poured scorn on Limerick orations delivered when the Lord Deputy Sir Robert Devereux visited there sometime between 10 May and 9 September 1599: 'he was enterteyned with two englesh orations, in which I know not which was more to be discommended, wordes, composition or orators, all of them having their particuler excellencies in barbarisme, harshnes, and rusticall both pronounce & action' (BL, MS Harley 1291, fol. 29; *A Treatice of Ireland, by John Dymmok*, in *Tracts relating to Ireland, printed for the Irish Archæological Society*, ed. R. Butler, 2 vols [Dublin, 1841–3] II, 35). Kilkenny and Clonmel had done better, in Dymmok's view, receiving Devereux 'with as much ioye of the cytizens as could be expressed, either by lyvely orations or by sylent strowinge of the streetes with greene hearbes & rushes' (ibid., fol. 28; Butler, *Treatice*, II, 33).

11 Bergeron, *Civic Pageantry*, passim. Such arches appear in the sixteenth century, but by the seventeenth are ubiquitous.

12 Aurelian Townsend, *Aurelian Townshend's Poems and Masks*, ed. E.K. Chambers (Oxford, 1912), p. 90. *Tempe Restord*, words by Aurelian Townshend and stage design by Inigo Jones, was presented to the king at Whitehall on 14 February (Shrove Tuesday) 1631.

13 Bergeron, *Civic Pageantry*, p. 105.

14 J. Ferrar, *The History of Limerick* (Limerick, 1787), p. 114: 'Wise Strafford's earl, the viceroy of the nation, / On his progress hither comes for recreation; / His grandeur solemnized, like never heard, / The city's chief young men are his life guard, / Bunratty to and from in city barge he's rowed, / A silver gilded cup on them bestowed / Worth three score pounds; was treated at Lax weir, / At his departure knighted master mayor.' The manuscript source of this, a rhyming chronicle of Limerick to 1680, is now lost. Details recorded here can be fleshed out by reference to James White, *The Annals of the City and Diocess of Limerick*, p. 60 (manuscript in possession of the Roman Catholic bishop of Limerick): Wentworth stayed nine days; fifty young men of Limerick formed his guard of honour; he knighted Dominic White at his departure from St John's Gate; and as a parting gift he gave a silver gilt cup worth £60 to the corporation. (His presence at Bunratty is confirmed by his letter of 25 August 1637 from there; SCA, Wentworth Woodhouse Muniments, Strafford Letter Book 10, pp. 43–4.)

15 Watters, 'Note of Entries,' pp. 242–9. (M.M. Phelan, 'Sir Thomas Wentworth's Visit to Kilkenny August 1637,' *Journal of the Butler Society* 2 [1981–2], 190–2, maintains that the original documentation of the visit is still held by Kilkenny Corporation. This is not in fact so.)

16 E. Cooper, ed., *The Life of Thomas Wentworth, Earl of Strafford and Lord-Lieutenant of Ireland*, 2 vols (London, 1874) II, 41. Wentworth in his letter to Lord Conway and Killultagh also spoke of three Kilkenny orations (see Appendix IIIc).

17 Watters, 'Note of Entries,' p. 247. This suggests two performers, but more are indicated in Kyvan's acknowledgment of receipt of payment 'for my own and the rest of my felowes paines' (ibid.). A Peter Fitzgerald was also paid for writing orations and verses, ibid., p. 246.

18 R.P. Mahaffy, ed. *Calendar of State Papers relating to Ireland, of the Reign of Charles I. 1633–1647. Preserved in the Public Record Office* (London, 1901), pp. 164–5 (letter of George Rawdon to Lord Conway and Killultagh).

19 His pages and harbinger were in Kilkenny 10 August; he wrote to his wife from Clonmel 13 August (Cooper, *Thomas Wentworth*, II, 39), and from Kilkenny 16 August, as noted above, but also to the duke of Lennox on 16 August from Clonmel (SCA, Wentworth Woodhouse Muniments, Strafford Letter Book 10, pp. 43–4).

20 *Letters and Dispatches of the Earl of Strafforde*, ed. W. Knowler, 2 vols (London, 1739), II, 95–8; letter from Bunratty 25 August 1637 (SCA, Wentworth Woodhouse Muniments, Strafford Letter Book 10, pp. 47–8).

21 Letter from Naas, co. Kildare, 12 September 1637 (SCA, Wentworth Woodhouse Muniments, Strafford Letter Book 10, p. 49). It is likely that Wentworth stayed at the earl of Thomond's house while in Bunratty.

22 Watters, 'Note of Entries,' p. 243. Here the warrant for their payment of 10s is said to have been dated 20 August 1637. This may be a misprint, however, for 10 August; first, a date on 20 August would be out of sequence in a set of accounts otherwise presented almost entirely chronologically; and second, another chit authorized payment to the earl of Ormond's musicians for the same sum, 10s, on 10 August (Watters, 'Note of Entries,' p. 246).

23 Watters, 'Note of Entries,' pp. 243–4. The painting and decorating was chiefly the responsibility of one William Fludd.

24 Watters, 'Note of Entries,' pp. 247–8. John Connell, who erected the stages, was also responsible for a stage at St John's Street, probably part of the 'Pageant made at Ss. John's bridge uppon my Lord Deputie his departure out of this Citty after his return from Munster' (Watters, 'Note of Entries,' p. 248), that William Fludd the painter also had a hand in.

25 Watters, 'Note of Entries,' pp. 244–5.

26 Explosive sometimes quite literally: for example, fireworks were used for Wentworth's Kilkenny reception (Watters, 'Note of Entries,' p. 245).

27 Compare, for example, the bridge location of the first pageant in a series devised to welcome Katharine of Aragon to London in 1501 (*The Receyt of the Ladie Kateryne*, ed. G.L. Kipling, EETS, os 296 [Oxford, 1990], pp. 12–13).

28 Why else was one Peter Fitzgerald paid for making fair copies of the orations that Wentworth heard unless they were for presentation? Books and orations handed to visitors, the palpable traces of words uttered, might compromise the accepter. Also, the force of the civic proclamation made by pageantry is witnessed in the fact that

sometimes Lords Deputy felt obliged to resist by public modification or contradiction what they were being told.

29 Watters, 'Notes of Particulars,' p. 243.

30 G. Kipling, 'Triumphal Drama: Form in English Civic Pageantry,' *Renaissance Drama*, new series 8 (1977), 37–56; see pp. 44 and 53.

31 BL, MS Additional 12562, fol. 5v: 'There was two Orations made: one in Englishe: the other in Latten, one perswading to Clemencye, the other incitinge to rigour. Then {*read* They *or* Then they} called the traitor inimici insteade of Rebelles, for which my lord reprehended them, declaringe there error: the vndeserued name of Ennime to any traitor and the difference of them boothe.' For another example of resistance to the civic position statement, compare that offered by Mary Queen of Scots during her coronation triumph. When presented with that Protestant icon, the Bible in English, she handled it perfunctorily and evidently with some displeasure (Kipling, 'Triumphal Drama,' pp. 54–5).

32 Compare Bergeron, *Civic Pageantry*, p. 14, who notes that the monarch was made very much a *part of the action*, a theme resumed by Kipling, 'Triumphal Drama.'

33 Compare S. Anglo, *Spectacle, Pageantry, and Early Tudor Policy* (Oxford, 1969), p. 357.

34 On the capacity of public ritual to achieve solidarity without consensus, see Kertzer, *Ritual, Politics, and Power*, pp. 67–9.

CHAPTER 6

1 Seventeenth-century Anon., *Tuar guil, a cholaim, do cheol* (S. Ó Tuama and T. Kinsella, ed., *An Duanaire 1600–1900: Poems of the Dispossessed* [Mountrath, 1981], p. 22, lines 17–18).

2 The principles of this circumspection have been outlined in the Prologue: Insubstantial Pageants, and shown in application in chapter 1.

3 To references passim in chapter 1 may be added the case of the personnel maintained in the encampment of Ruaidhrí Mac Diarmada in 1561. In this year Ruaidhrí was harrying in co. Roscommon, and of his encampment the annalist said: 'ni roibhe a nerenn forlongport inar lía eich .7 éidedh feoil .7 fíon aos civil .7 oirfidigh .7 ealadhna galloglaech .7 giomanaigh .7 albanaigh iná an forlongport sin mic diarmada' ('there was not in Ireland a camp in which horses and armour, meat and wine, musicians, minstrels, and men of science, gallowglasses, mercenaries, and Albanachs, were more numerous than that camp of Mac Diarmada'; TCD, MS 1293 (H. 1. 19), fol. 132 (Hennessy, *Annals of Loch Cé*, II, 380).

4 TCD, MS 1293 (H. 1. 19), fol. 112 (Hennessy, *Annals of Loch Cé*, II, 204). This is part of the obituary notice of Maghnus, son of Brian Mac Donnchadha, who was buried at Loch Key, co. Roscommon, in 1504. In the same annals, fol. 126 (Hennessy, *Annals of Loch Cé*, II, 516), *s.a.* 1636 (New Style, 1637) and again in co. Roscommon, it was

noted in the obituary of Brian óg Mac Dermot that *asse as mo ro tiodlaic et ro toirbir do ollamnaib .7 deigsib et daois ealadna do cuirib ... do vaislib do oirfidib et do adbail senoiribh ...* ('it was he who presented and dispensed most to professors and to poets and to men of art ... to nobles, to minstrels and to great elders'). To prove that such patronage was widespread throughout Ireland, and not merely a local practice, compare also the obituary notice in 1520 for Maurice Fitz Thomas Fitz James Fitzgerald, ninth earl of Desmond. He was surrounded with so many *dollamhnaibh. déigsibh. & dfilidhibh. deisrectoibh .7 dobhloraib* ('professors, authors and poets, orphans and jugglers/jesters'; RIA, MS 756 (23 E 26), p. 290; S.H. O'Grady, ed., *Caithréim Thoirdhealbhaigh*, Irish Texts Society 26 and 27 [London, 1929] I, p. 170), that, says the text, he could have fought a battle with them.

5 'Fedh amairc ón mv́r amach . ré fáoidhibh cheóil na cathrach / gé bheith mé ar villinn gach fir . ní clvinim é mvn amsin' ('When just in sight of the rampart even were I at the shoulder of any man I could not hear him because of the strains of music from the citadel'; Clonalis, co. Roscommon, Book of the O'Connor Don, fol. 149; Tadhg dall Ó hUiginn, *The Bardic Poems of Tadhg Dall Ó Huiginn (1550–1591)*, ed. E. Knott, Irish Texts Society 22 and 23 [London, 1922–6] I, 51, lines 33–6; Knott's translation, ibid., II, 35, stanza 9, given above). The poem was composed in 1577 (ibid., II, 222). The Creeve was west of the river Bann, near Coleraine, co. Londonderry. Toirdhealbhach Luineach Ó Néill (1567–95) was cousin to the second earl of Tyrone. His successor, Hugh, fled Ireland in 1607 (see below). Similarly, another Ulster household, the residence of Domhnall Mac Suibhne Fánad at Rathmullan Castle, co. Donegal, was said by the same poet to be incomparable, better even than the legendary castle of Allen in Ulster: 'Lía daitheirach áosa ciúil do lucht sgaoilti sgéal taidhiúir. do mnaibh rísluaigh móir menmnaigh. ag síoruaim óir illd⌈e⌉albhaigh' ('More numerous the variety of its musicians, its reciters of soothing tales, more numerous the royal host of light-hearted women, ever weaving diverse gilt broideries'; RIA, MS 475 (24 P 25; Leabhar Chlainne Suibhne), p. 149 (*Tadhg Dall Ó Huiginn*, ed. Knott, I, 196, lines 37–40; Knott's translation, ibid., II, 131, stanza 10, adapted and given above). This poem was composed between c 1570 and 1587, the year in which Sir John Perrot lured Mac Suibhne Fánad to his ship. And a final example, again from Ulster, was the household in Enniskillen Castle, co. Fermanagh, said to have been well supplied with poets and musicians in a poem which Ó hUiginn composed c 1570–89 (*Tadhg Dall Ó Huiginn*, ed. Knott, I, 75, lines 57–60 and 76, lines 85–8).

6 RIA, MS 998 (23 F 21), p. 6 (Carney, *Poems on the Butlers*, p. 24). The poem, dedicated to Theobald Butler of Cahir, must antedate 1596, the year of his death.

7 NLI, MS G 1200 (Book of Magauran), fol. 3v, col. a (L. McKenna, ed., *The Book of Magauran* [Dublin, 1947], p. 26, lines 387–90; his translation, ibid., p. 299, stanza 23, is given above).

8 NLI, MS G 1200 (Book of Magauran), fol. 8v, col. a (McKenna, *Book of Magauran*, p. 86, lines 132–5; his translation, ibid., p. 323, stanza 28, is adapted above).

9 As has been pointed out by J.F. Lydon, 'The Branganstown Massacre, 1329,' *County Louth Archaeological and Historical Journal* 19 (1977–80), 5–16.

10 TCD, MS 574 (E. 3. 20), p. 380 (Butler, *Annals of Ireland*, p. 20). Line 7, the (*blank*) is approximately 30mm. Compare the entry in the Annals of Ulster (TCD, MS 1282 (H. 1. 8), fol. 69, col. b (W.M. Hennessy and B. Mac Carthy, eds., *Annals of Ulster*, 4 vols [Dublin, 1887–1901] II, 444): 'IN cæch mac cerbaill .i. mælruanaigh æn raga timpanach erenn 7 alban 7 in domain uile 7 ni derbthair a leitheid do thecht riamh o thus domain risin eladhain sin a marbadh fein 7 derbrathair maith eile do ar in lathair. cetna' ('The blind Mac Cearbhaill, namely, Maelruanaigh, the choicest *timpán*-player of Ireland and Scotland, and of all the whole world – and it is not verified that an equal to him in that art ever came from the beginning of the world – was killed, as was another good brother of his on the same spot').

11 See chapter 1, note 23.

12 E. Knott, 'Filidh Éireann go hAointeach: William Ó Ceallaigh's Christmas Feast to the Poets of Ireland, A.D. 1351,' *Ériu* 5 (1911), 50–69 (see pp. 50–1; the castle of Gallach, Castle Blakeney, co. Galway, and the castle of Gáille on Loch Ree have been suggested as possible locations). Ó Ceallaigh was lord of the Gaelic lordship of Uí Mhaine, a territory which ran from Clontuskert, co. Roscommon, southwards to the boundary of co. Clare, and from Athlone westwards to Seefin and Athenry in present-day co. Galway.

13 See further Simms, 'Guesting and Feasting,' p. 91.

14 Knott, 'William Ó Ceallaigh's Christmas Feast,' p. 58, lines 81–92.

15 BL, MS Additional 4799, fol. 56 (J. O'Donovan, 'The Annals of Ireland, from the Year 1443 to 1468, translated from the Irish by Dudley Firbisse, or, as he is more usually called, Duald Mac Firbis, for Sir James Ware, in the Year 1666,' in *The Miscellany of the Irish Archaeological Society* 1 [Dublin, 1846], pp. 198–302; see pp. 227–8). The annals were translated in 1666 in Castle Street, Dublin, by An Dubhaltach Mac Fhirbhisigh (†1670) for Sir James Ware, in Sir James's house, from a lost Irish original.

16 The last example noted by Simms, 'Guesting and Feasting,' p. 91, dates to 1549, though the practice evidently continued till a generation later. The 1577 poem of Tadhg dall Ó hUiginn, for example, tells of the Christmas hospitality to poets of Toirdhealbhach Luineach Ó Néill (see note 5 above), and his 1595 obituary notice in the Annals of the Four Masters (O'Donovan, *Annals of the Kingdom of Ireland*, VI, 1984) mentions his many Christmastide invitations to poets.

17 BL, MS Additional 29614, fol. 46v (Carney, *Poems on the Butlers*, p. 79). Carney (p. 137) dates the poem to *c* 1588 on internal evidence.

18 Freeman, ed., *Annals of Connacht*, p. 434 (Donnelly, 'Dance,' p. 74). The entry of John Butler into the dancing school is noted in household accounts of 30 October, 3 and

30 November 1630 (see respectively NLI, MS 2549, fol. 6v: 'paide for mr Iohns entrance in the daunching Scoole ye 30: of 8tober: 1630 00–10–06'; fol. 12v: 'to mr Iohn the same day at his goeing to the daunching scoole 00–01–00'; and fol. 24: 'to mr Iohn Butler to pay the daunching master the last of Nouember 00–05–00.' The vogue for dancing schools, and their affiliation with dramatic pastimes, is attacked by that early-seventeenth-century Dublin resident Barnaby Rich, in *Faultes Faults, and Nothing Else but Faultes* (London, 1606; *STC* 20983), fols. 8v–9: 'But whom have we here, one, two, three, foure fiue? One, two, three, foure, fiue, and nothing else but, one, two, three, foure, fiue? O ho, I vnderstand him now, this is one of the Skipping Arte, that is newly come from the Dauncing Schoole; ... he hath some smacke of iudgement in vawting {'vaulting'}, tumbling, and in dauncing with the Iebie {'hobby'} horse. And he will speake of Playes, Players, and who be the best Actors, and lightly he is acquainted with her that keepes the best Brothell-house.'

19 Churchyard went to Ireland after serving in Scotland with Sir William Drury, the latter also going there as President of Munster in 1576. Churchyard arrived probably in late July or August 1575. Sir Henry Sidney had been reappointed Lord Deputy on 4 August, and it is possible that Churchyard travelled in his entourage; see further on the Sidney-Churchyard connection in J.A.B. Somerset, ed., *Shropshire*, 2 vols, Records of Early English Drama (Toronto, 1994) I, 220, and II, 664–5. Sidney had been campaigning in Ulster from late September, but soon after had travelled down to Munster, where he spent Christmas of 1575 in Cork (PRO, SP 63/55, fol. 55v). Since the epistle is addressed to Sidney in Cork, and evidently after a campaign, its composition seems to fit a date around Christmas 1575 or early New Year 1576. Its *terminus ante quem* is 1579, the year of its publication (see note 20 following).

20 T. Churchyard, *A generall rehearsall of warres* (London, 1579; *STC* 5235), sig. Dd .iij. verso.

21 PRO, SP 65/9, fol. 55v (household accounts of Sir Walter Devereux, from 6 May to 28 September 1575): 'Crues my lord of Ormondes harper xl s ... Therle of Ormondes musicions xx s ...' Payments to the Ormond musicians appear in Sir Henry Sidney's household accounts, on which see below. Crues is also mentioned in a letter of Sir Henry Wallop to Sir Francis Walsingham of 20 August 1583, in which 'blynde Crewse the harper' is noted as having delivered letters to Wallop (PRO, SP 63/104, fol. 52). His fame was taken up by Richard Stanihurst (*De rebus in Hibernia gestis*, p. 39): 'Viuit, hac nostra ætate, Crusus, ad lyram, post hominum memoriam quàm maximè insignis. is ab illo incondito strepitu, qui incontentis, secumque discordantibus fidibus fit, plurimùm abhorret: contraque eo modorum ordine, sonorum compositione, musicum obseruat concentum, quo auditorum aures mirabiliter ferit, vt eum citius solum quam summum citharistam iudicares.' ('In our time lives Crues, since the memory of man the most distinguished on the harp. He exceedingly abhors that uncouth noise which makes harps tuneless and discordant. On the contrary, he practises concerted music

with that order of modes and composition of sounds by which he strikes the ears of his listeners wonderfully, so that you would judge him the only, rather than the greatest, harper'), and by Philip O'Sullivan Beare in his *Zoilomastix* (UUL, MS H. 248, fol. 133–3v): 'Illi lyram summis digitis, tympanum plectris pulsant: & utroque instrumentis iuxta vnanime bene sentientium iudicium ita excellunt, ut non vnus apud eos Crusus, sed quam plurimi nu- nu-|numerosa harmoniæ dulcedine audientium animos mirificè permulceant.' ('They strike the harp with their finger tips, the *timpán* with plectrums. And on both instruments, in the unanimous opinion of those who well understand, they excel so much that you would not reckon one Crues to be among them, but many who wonderfully delight the minds of listeners with the rhythmical sweetness of harmony').

22 Note the earl of Ormond's musicians who played for Wentworth, as discussed above in chapter 5. These were probably members of his household. Also, the 1630 Desmond inventory of the chattels of Kilkenny Castle included a harp in the gallery (NLI, MS 2552, fol. 9).

23 NLI, MS 2549; see respectively fol. 5, where the trumpeters are those of the 'Lord Deputy'; fol. 5v, where the 'Musitioners' were those of the Lords Justice (at this date, Adam, Viscount Loftus, and Richard Boyle, first earl of Cork, whose musical establishment is discussed further below); fols. 6v and 21, where the drummers were respectively at Gowran and Carlow; fol. 7; fol. 12v; and fols. 21v and 31v, where the harpers were respectively at 'Rathvill' (probably the barony of Rathvilly, co. Carlow), and 'Ballycommen,' probably in the same region but unidentified.

24 NLI, MS 2549, fol. 17. While it seems reasonable to assume that Kilkenny Castle was the play's venue, it must be conceded that the payment is not explicit.

25 Another possibility, though the least likely, is that they were household domestics, people who often participated in household revels. The use of the word 'actors' to describe them would seem a little out of place were this so, however.

26 The Dalway harp fragments are preserved in the National Museum of Ireland.

27 Pierse, 'Nicholas Dall Pierse,' pp. 66–7; also, E. O'Curry, *On the Manners and Customs of the Ancient Irish*, ed. W.K. Sullivan, 3 vols (Dubin, 1873) III, 292. The arms of Sir John are impaled with those of his wife, Ellen Barry, whom he had married in 1611. Ellen was a daughter of David Barry, Viscount Buttevant, and sister to Lord David Barry, Viscount Barrymore, who retained a harper of his own. This Lord David married the eldest daughter of Sir Richard Boyle (see further below).

28 J. Morrin, ed., *Calendar of the Patent and Close Rolls of Chancery in Ireland of the Reigns of Henry VIII., Edward VI., Mary, and Elizabeth*, 2 vols (Dublin, 1861) I, 69. The original was doubtless destroyed in 1922. Cappervarget no longer exists, but Rathangan is a town and parish in the barony of Offaly East, co. Kildare, as well as the name of a demesne in the same barony.

29 Ellis, *Tudor Ireland*, p. 93, attributes the success of the ninth earl to an ambiguity of

416 Notes to pages 213-16

stance, 'intelligible in different ways to both English and Gaelic.' Another harper pardoned in Kildare in 1602 (*The Eighteenth Report of the Deputy Keeper of the Public Records in Ireland* [Dublin, 1886], p. 89), one 'Owny McKyernane,' as the fiant styles him, may have been a relative, and if so, he is testimony to the longevity of the Gaelic tradition of harping descending in families.

30 They were named as James Delahyde and a certain Hayward (*Hollinshed's Irish Chronicle*, ed. Miller and Power, p. 279). A popular, late-fifteenth- or early-sixteenth-century song-motet on this text by the Franco-Netherlandish composer Johannis Prioris is extant. If this was the music that Delahyde and Hayward sang, the chapel repertoire in Maynooth had a cosmopolitan and fashionable cast. Evidently the Fitzgeralds, like a few other English aristocrats, were emulating the London court, whose Chapel Royal had won international fame. (Compare the musical establishment maintained by Henry Algernon Percy [†1527]; T. Percy, ed., *The Regulations and Establishment of the Household of Henry Algernon Percy, the Fifth Earl of Northumberland, at his Castles of Wresill and Lekinfield in Yorkshire* [London, 1770], pp. 43–4.)

31 J.M. Wasson, ed. *Devon*, Records of Early English Drama (Toronto, 1986), p. 230.

32 On Sidney's policies in Ireland, see Canny, *Elizabethan Conquest*, passim.

33 The chronology of his Irish residence may be summarized in four phases as follows: (i) May 1556–August 1559 (with a brief absence from April to June in 1557); (ii) October 1565–October 1567; (iii) October 1568–March 1571; and (iv) September 1575–September 1578.

34 LPL, MS 623 (Book of Howth), fol. 127.

35 However, there are four modern Loughlinstowns, two in co. Dublin, one in co. Meath, and one in co. Kildare. Which was intended is unknown.

36 KAO, U1475 028/19, fol. [1v] (household accounts of September in either 1556, 1557, or 1558). The Lord Delvin spoken of here was Richard Nugent, Baron Delvin (†1559). He had distinguished himself fighting against the rebel Irish, especially in the campaigns of 1557. He is buried in the church at Castletown-Delvin, co. Westmeath.

37 The sixteenth-century Gaelic poetic anthology, NLI, MS G 992, was passed down in the Delvin family (Moody, Martin, and Byrne, *New History of Ireland III*, 522); note that Richard Nugent, Baron Delvin (that is, the grandfather of Richard whom Sir Henry Sidney met) had married a daughter of Thomas Fitzgerald, second son of Gerald Fitzgerald, earl of Kildare.

38 Limerick was large enough to sustain waits, and was certainly no stranger to civic ceremonial of the sort that would have required them (see chapter 5). Sir Henry Sidney cultivated through patronage people performing on behalf of corporations; for example, on 22 May 1559, he made a payment of 12d to the Dublin Mayor of the Bullring 'to helpe him in his pastime vpon corpus christi Day' (KAO, U1475 027/3, fol. [4]; Corpus Christi that year fell on 25 May). Compare too Sir William Fitzwilliam's

reward to the Dublin waits attending on New Year's Day 1592, noted below, and similarly in the seventeenth century Sir Richard Boyle's rewards.

39 KAO, U1475 021, fol. [10] (household accounts from 1557 to 1558). By this date Radcliffe also had a troupe of players (Wasson, *Devon*, p. 231 and A. Douglas and P. Greenfield, eds. *Cumberland/Westmorland/Gloucestershire*, Records of Early English Drama [Toronto, 1986], p. 305, for payments made to the troupe in 1544–5 and 1574–5 respectively). I have not detected its presence in Ireland.

40 KAO, U1475 028/44, single sheet (household accounts for 4 April in either 1558 or 1559). There is also some evidence that the women in charge of the households may have taken some responsibility for supervising the domestic music.

41 KAO, U1475 028/44, single sheet (household accounts for 4 April in either 1558 or 1559). Lord Slane at this date was James Fleming (†1573). Like Baron Delvin, Lord Slane had also been active in the military defence of the Pale. He held many commissions in co. Meath and the Pale from 1554. He assisted in the hosting against the Scots in 1556. His principal residence was in Slane, co. Meath.

42 Oxford, Corpus Christi College, MS 94, fols. 662–3 (Litton Falkiner, *Illustrations of Irish History*, pp. 322–3). This is Moryson's *Itinerary*. It is possible that the sword players associated their sword performance with a masque (compare Lord Barry's Christmas sword dance in 1632, discussed below). Note too the bone plate, which originally had some connection with the Desmond Fitzgeralds of Munster and which dates probably to the earlier part of the seventeenth century, upon which is an engraving of what are apparently five sword or withy dancers (H.F. McClintock, 'Engraved Bone Plate in the National Museum Dublin,' *Journal of the Royal Society of Antiquaries of Ireland* 63 [1933], 29–37).

43 T. Pettitt, 'English Folk Drama in the Eighteenth Century: A Defense of the *Revesby Sword Play*,' *Comparative Drama* 15 (1981), 3–29; the play may have been presented by the lord's tenants at the manor house for the lord's household (ibid., p. 6). Also on sword dances, see Chambers, *Mediæval Stage*, II, 270–6, Appendix J, and C.J. Sharp, *The Sword Dances of Northern England, together with the Horn Dance of Abbots Bromley* (London, 1911–13).

44 Compare *OED*, **Matachin**, for late-sixteenth-century English examples which make clear the frequent connection between the matachin sword dance and masking. For the masque text, see Appendix IV.

45 KAO, U1475 018, fol. 22 (household accounts from 5 April 1556 to 29 September 1559).

46 KAO, U1475 031, fol. 23 (household accounts from 31 August 1566 to 30 September 1568); and fol. 68 (household accounts from 31 December 1566 to 1 January 1569). However, note that Sidney left Ireland between October 1567 and October 1568, and so depending on exactly when these payments fell (which is not clear), they may have been for activity in England, *not* Ireland.

47 W. Wager, *The longer thou liuest, the more foole thou art* (London, [1569]; *STC* 24935), sig. A iii.

48 KAO, U1475 A50/10, fol. [4v] (household accounts from January to February 1576): 'Item for Sheyntton iij yerdes of motley to make his Cote viij s. vj d.'

49 In the third phase of Sidney's residence, October 1568 to March 1571, in KAO, U1475 034, fol. [29v] (household accounts from 29 September 1568 to 29 September 1570): 'Will' ffoole Also paid by this Accomptunt at diuerse and sondry tymes this yere for Showes {'shoes'} & other Weares for him ix s. ij d.'; and in the fourth phase, September 1575 to September 1578, in KAO, U1475 A50/10, fol. [4v]: 'Item for Sheyntton iij yerdes of motley to make his Cote viij s. vj d.' Sheyntton was evidently reimported when Sir Henry Sidney left Ireland for the last time, since Sidney was still retaining his fool 'Shington' (as he now appears) in the last year of his life (Somerset, *Shropshire*, I, 88 and II, 645).

50 The identity of the four minstrels who were paid by Sir Henry Sidney's wife, Lady Mary, on 2 April 1557, is a mystery, in KAO, U1475 025/1, fol. [99] (household accounts from 19 July 1556 to 1 January 1558): 'In rewarde to iiijor mynstrells by my Lads comaundement xij d.'

51 DCA, MR/5/7, mb. 12: 'It is agreed that the Musicians of this Cittie shall haue an officer to levie tharrerages {'the arrears'} of ther stipend / and to call in the same henceforth from tyme to tyme or to take pawnes for it / Also that they shall haue suche libertie to aunswere the Earle of Kildare as mr Maior of this Cittie for tyme being shall see to be meet and not without his licence. It is also graunted that Thomas Quycke shalbe henceforth free from cesses and chardges soo that he shall serue in person as a drommer whensomeuer the Maior of this Cittie shall goo into the fielde if the said Thomas be therunto required having reasonable stipend for his seruice' (*CARD*, II, 46–7; a decree of the Assembly held on 12 January 1567). See also DCA, MR/35, p. 223, for a payment to Thomas Quycke for four waits' liveries, granted in the year ended Michaelmas 1568.

52 KAO, U1475 031, fol. 69v (household accounts from 31 December 1566 to 1 January 1569): 'Quick & his men Mynstrelles at ij tymes lxxv s.'

53 KAO, U1475 031, fol. 69v (household accounts from 31 December 1566 to 1 January 1569): 'Mr Geraldes Mvsicions x s. Welche harwood xxx s. Mr Iustice mynstrelles x s.'

54 KAO, U1475 031, fol. 62v (household accounts from 31 May 1567 to 1 January 1568): 'Singing boyes at Drogheda' (it is not known under whose auspices these performed); KAO, U1475 031, fol. 23 (household accounts from 31 August 1566 to 30 September 1568): 'Musicion boyes by Iohn Thomas lxx s. ix d.' (here the singing boys sound as if they had secular auspices, and they were expensive; perhaps they were involved in a relatively elaborate performance?); KAO, U1475 034, fol. [71v] (household accounts from 29 September 1569 to 29 September 1570): 'The Singing men at Tradath. {Drogheda} xxxj s.' (it is not known under whose auspices these performed,

but 'singing men' is a normal collocation for singers whose primary employment was liturgical; perhaps the singing boys mentioned earlier were part of the same establishment?); KAO, U1475 034, fol. [46v] (household accounts from 29 September 1570 to 29 September 1571): 'Quirestors in christes churche reward – x s.'

55 KAO, U1475 034, fol. [16v] (household accounts from 29 September 1568 to 29 September 1570).

56 How ancient this habit was is perhaps to be seen, for example, in a civic *tripudium* performed at the arrival in Dublin of Godred II, *c* 1157, in the *Cronica Regum Mannie et Insularum* (BL, MS Cotton Julius A. vii, fol. 36v–7: 'Anno . ṁ . c̄ . x̄l . iiii. cepit regnare godredus & xxx.^ta tribus annis regnauit. ... Tertio anno regni sui miserunt propter illum dublinienses ut regnaret super se. Qui collecta nauium multitudine & copioso exercitu dubliniam uenit & gratanter a ciuibus cum magno tripudio susceptus est.' ('Godred [II] began to reign in the year 1144 and he reigned for thirty years. ... In the third year of his reign the people of Dublin sent to him to rule over them. He came to Dublin with a great number of ships gathered together and a large army, and was willingly received by the citizens with a great dance/jubilation.')

57 KAO, U1475 031, fol. 69v (household accounts from 31 December 1566 to 1 January 1569): 'To a Barward {'bearward'} xx s.'; KAO, U1475 031, fol. 62v (household accounts from 31 May 1567 to 1 January 1568): 'he that Danced there {i.e., at Carrickfergus, co. Antrim} with Thobby horse v s.'; KAO, U1475 034, fol. [71v] (household accounts from 29 September 1569 to 29 September 1570): 'The lord of Misrule at Tradath {Drogheda} x s.' This Carrickfergus hobby-horse antedates the earliest known Irish hobby-horse (E.C. Cawte, *Ritual Animal Disguise* [Cambridge, 1978], p. 82) by over two hundred years. The reward to the hobby-horse dancer may have been a response to his *quête*. The activity of the Drogheda lord of misrule, the first documented reference to this Christmas revels master in Ireland, must date to the Christmastide of 1569.

58 On Fitzwilliam and his Irish policies, see C. Brady, *The Chief Governors: The Rise and Fall of Reform Government in Tudor Ireland 1536–1588* (Cambridge, 1994), pp. 299–300.

59 The exception is NRO, MS Fitzwilliam Irish 55. Though the documents span the better part of twenty years, all were prepared by the same household steward, Alexander Westlake.

60 Found respectively in NRO, Fitzwilliam Irish 55, fol. [39] (household accounts of 13 May 1575): 'In [p] Reward the xiij^th of Maye to the Maye game xvj d.'; Fitzwilliam Irish 30, mb. [12] (household accounts of 1 May 1590): 'to the singing boies of Christchurche on May day x s., To a shomakers boye and a piper ij s.'; Fitzwilliam Irish 31, mb. [7 dorse] (household accounts of May 1591): 'Gyven at Grangorman in rewarde by your L in Maye laste xx s. To the Nurse there vj s. viij d. To the Musitions there vj s. viij d. To a poore souldier there xij d. To my Lo of houthes man and boy that brought

a hauke to your L. xij s.'; and Fitzwilliam Irish 45, mb. [3 dorse] (household accounts from 12 May to 8 June 1594): 'To the musitions at Sir william Sarsfeldes iij s. iiij d. To the mayor of the maye game there vj s.'

61 For example, KAO, A56/2, a set of accounts running between Easter 1574 and Michaelmas 1575 which include, fol. [2], payments of 12d for 'the Syngers on maye day' and of 3s 'to them yat plaied Robin hood' (the Robin Hood play or game is not dated, but may belong to the May observances).

62 NRO, Fitzwilliam Irish 31, mb. [7] (household accounts from 5 April to 2 October 1591): 'To the L. Chancellors ffoole at ij° seueral tymes ij s.'; Fitzwilliam Irish 32, mb. [5] (household accounts 20 December 1591): 'To ye Lo chaunccellor his foole ij s. in all by bill signed by your L. the xxth of december 1591'; Fitzwilliam Irish 33, mb. [5 dorse] (household accounts from 26 December 1591 to 22 January 1592): 'Also to Iohn the Lo Chancellors foole ij s.'

63 NRO, Fitzwilliam Irish 30, mb. [12] (household accounts from 19 April 1590 to 4 April 1591): 'for the Cariedge of Mistris Annes virginalles to kyllmaynham and back againe to dublin, xij d.' The mistress Anne referred to was probably Fitzwilliam's wife. Note also the virginal repairs detailed in NRO, Fitzwilliam Irish 31, mb. [12] (household accounts from 5 April to 2 October 1591): 'for a newe frame for a paire of virginalles iij s. iiij d. for mending the frame of an other paire xij d.' Compare Lady Mary Sidney's musical activities noted above.

64 NRO, Fitzwilliam Irish 31, mb. [7] (household accounts from 5 April to 2 October 1591): 'To Plunckett your llordshipes harper in rewarde x s.' mb. [11 dorse]: 'Also paid by the said accomptante for leather, Cotton and threed bought by william higges to make Cases for your llordships ij harpes as by bill of the xviijth of September 1591 signed by my ladye appeareth xx s .xj d.'; and mb. [12]: 'V ll' of wier for the harpe ij s. and for drawinge of the said wier xviij d.'

65 Also, note the payment to Sir Robert Sidney's harper by the time of Fitzwilliam's second period in office as Lord Deputy (NRO, Fitzwilliam Irish 31, mb. [13 dorse] (household accounts from 5 April to 2 October 1591): 'To the harper Sir Robert Sydneys man x s.'

66 NRO, Fitzwilliam Irish 55, fols [4], [7v], [11] and [14v], record payments of £5 to the musicians at the end of each quarter in 1574.

67 See the discussion on this in chapter 3 above; six musicians seems to have been the regular size of viceregal consorts (compare Sir John Perrot's discussed below).

68 NRO, Fitzwilliam Irish 31, mb. [7] (household accounts from 5 April to 2 October 1591): 'to the waytes of Tradath {Drogheda} the xvjth of Aprell v s. and to a Tabor and Pype there ij s.'; NRO, Fitzwilliam Irish 33, mb. [5 dorse] (household accounts from 26 December 1591 to 22 January 1592): 'to the waytes of Dublin on Newyers day vj s. viij d. ... To a boy that song a Carroll att the Mayors house when your L. dyned ther v s.' (The Dublin waits whom Fitzwilliam patronized in 1592 were the band led by Edward Gore, discussed in chapter 3 above.) New Year's Day was also honoured by

Fitzwilliam in 1575, when trumpeters and musicians received £2 13s. 4d. (NRO, Fitzwilliam Irish 55, fol. [28v] [household accounts of 1 January 1575]: 'To the trompeters and mvsyssians liij s. iiij d.').

69 See respectively NRO, Fitzwilliam Irish 55, fol. [50v] (household accounts from 10 to 16 October 1575): 'to the musysions at Sir christofer barnwell iij s. iiij d.'; NRO, Fitzwilliam Irish 42, mb. [6 dorse] (household accounts from 3 October to 27 November 1591): 'To the Lo: of Slane his Musitions x s. to his Lps Cooke x s. To the lo: of Slanes servantes xxx s. To your llps owne harper x s.'; and NRO, Fitzwilliam Irish 45, mb. [3 dorse] (household accounts from 12 May to 8 June 1594): 'To the musitions at Sir william Sarsfeldes iij s. iiij d. To the mayor of the maye game there vj s.' Sir Christopher Barnwell, noted by Holinshed as being 'wholy addicted to grauitie' though also 'a great householder' (*Hollinshed's Irish Chronicle*, ed. Miller and Power, p. 93), was sheriff of Dublin in 1560; he died on either 5 or 7 August 1575, shortly after Sir Henry Sidney's last reappointment as Lord Deputy. On Lord Slane see note 41 above. Sir William Sarsfield (†27 November 1616), of Lucan, co. Dublin, was knighted on 16 November 1566 by Sir Henry Sidney for having rescued Sidney's wife, Lady Mary, from the Irish.

70 PRO, SP 65/9, fol. 55v (household accounts from 6 May to 28 September 1575): 'your Lordes musicions C s.'

71 Douglas and Greenfield, *Cumberland/Westmorland/Gloucestershire*, p. 305.

72 It was also traditional, of course, for patrons' players to travel, though perhaps this is a sign of how relatively more expendable they were from the household personnel.

73 PRO, SP 65/9, fol. 33v (household accounts from 3 April to 4 June 1575). But another possibility might be that they were boys of the Devereux household.

74 PRO, SP 65/9, fol. 42v (household accounts from 4 June to 13 October 1575).

75 PRO, SP 65/9, fol. 55v (household accounts from 6 May to 28 September 1575). And see note 21 above on the harper Crues.

76 PRO, SP 63/119, fol. 13; the complaint is dated 4 September 1585. It is clear evidence of the existence of strong ideas about what was thought appropriate in a Lord Deputy's household.

77 Bodl., MS Add. C. 39, fol. 13v. 40s divided by 6 = 6s 8d, which seems a probable reward for each performer. Hence there may have been six in the consort.

78 PRO, SP 63/119, fol. 116: James Davies received £13 6s 8d; James Nowere and Edward Gower, £6 13s 4d each; and Edward Mylls, Robert Trewman, and John Bradshaw, £5 each.

79 Note that Sir Anthony St Leger's consort seems to have been of four, though perhaps this is not fully representative, since the consort was on tour. See above.

80 PRO, SP 63/186, fol. 27 (a letter of Sir Henry Wallop and Sir Robert Gardener to Burghley, 10 January 1596): 'And one Barrett sometime Sir Iohn Perrottes harper a man of noe desart ... is by practize departed, and as is Creddeblie enformed gon to the Rebelles in vlster.' The Barrett in question was one of the sons of the baron of Ennis,

co. Mayo. I am grateful to Seán Donnelly for drawing my attention to this reference.

81 G. Dyfnallt Owen, *Elizabethan Wales: The Social Scene* (Cardiff, 1962), pp. 38–9.

82 RCB, C/6/1/26/3 (item 6), fols [9] and [2v] respectively (accounts of Mr Richardson, 29 September 1594 to 29 September 1595). See further below on the associations of the Lord Deputy's music with Christ Church Cathedral.

83 LPL, MS 612 (Carew Papers), fol. 44v. Masking was a familiar pastime in the Russell entourage. About one month before, on 1 December 1595 in Galway, the same diarist recorded, 'This night the Noblemen and Captens presented my Lord with a maske' (fol. 43).

84 Players were certainly retained by both his grandfather and father. The players of the former are noticed between 1543 and 1554 in Cambridge (Nelson, *Cambridge*, I, 130) and the players of the latter between 9 and 15 July 1564 in Newcastle upon Tyne (J.J. Anderson, ed. *Newcastle upon Tyne*, Records of Early English Drama [Toronto, 1982], p. 38).

85 W.R. Chetwood, *A General History of the Stage* (Dublin, 1749), p. 50. (The early theatrical career of John Ogilby, dancing master and impressario, is reviewed in chapter 7 below.) Chetwood was resident in Dublin and worked in its theatres at the beginning of the eighteenth century.

86 The circumstances of the performance are discussed in William Shakespeare, *The Comedy of Errors*, ed. R.A. Foakes (London, 1962), pp. 115–17.

87 A. Collins, ed., *Letters and Memorials of State*, 2 vols (London, 1746) II, 91 (a letter of Rowland White to Sir Robert Sidney). The audience included the Ladies Leicester, Northumberland, Bedford, Essex, and Rich, and the Lords Essex, Rutland, and Mountjoy. Play plus lavish dinner, already seen here in the late sixteenth century, was to become a standard way for the influential to make a splash by the early seventeenth century (P. Edwards, G.E. Bentley, K. McLuskie, and L. Potter, *The Revels History of Drama in English, Volume 4 1613–1660* [London and New York, 1981], p. 25).

88 LPL, MS 615 (Carew Papers), fol. 31v: 'I haue played the lord of misrule in theas parts this christmas' (in a letter of 1 January 1601 to Sir George Carew concerning Blount's campaigning in 'Monasterewen,' written 'from the campe amongst the rocks and the woods in thies diuells countrye').

89 Chetwood, *General History*, p. 50. Blount also enjoyed reading playbooks for recreation, according to Fynes Moryson, *An Itinerary*, Part II, p. 47 (*STC* 18205). Compare the taste of Roger Boyle, first earl of Orrery, who in a letter written home to his father Sir Richard Boyle *c* 1638 mentions his having read 'Playbooks Comical and Tragedicall' in Ireland (K.M. Lynch, *Roger Boyle, First Earl of Orrery* [Tennessee, 1965], p. 19).

90 The play always seems to have carried a political charge whenever performed; F.P. Wilson, *The English Drama 1485–1585*, ed. G.K. Hunter (Oxford, 1969), p. 135.

91 His father, James Blount, sixth Lord Mountjoy, is recorded as having patronized a

troupe: 'Des Lord Moundtÿadt Spilleüten' ('Lord Mountjoy's Players') were rewarded with 2s on 30 May 1569 (Douglas and Greenfield, *Cumberland/Westmorland/
Gloucestershire*, p. 126). In fact, his father's troupe was among the most active in Elizabethan England.

92 For a fool retained by a woman, see KAO, U1475 A50/10, fol. [4v] (household
accounts for January and February 1576): 'Item for my Ladie Haringhtons foole for
Ierkin gastons {'breeches'} and Cap vj yerdes of motley xvij s.' Lady Harrington was
Lucy, sister of Sir Henry Sidney.

93 Oxford, Corpus Christi College, MS 94, fol. 657 (Litton Falkiner, *Illustrations*, p. 315).

94 PRO, SP 63/207/Part 4, fol. 293v, mentions 'one Neale Moore an Irishe ffoole' in
the context of a letter sent by Onie MacRory O'Moore on 16 August 1600 to
Blount, while being besieged by Blount in co. Laois, that Blount forwarded to Neale
Moore to reply to. I am grateful to Seán Donnelly for drawing my attention to this
reference.

95 Various Lords Deputy issued proclamations against Gaelic performing artists, calling
them sowers of sedition, as noted in chapter 1. But in spite of this, they were insinu-
ating themselves; compare Perrot's 1584 injunctions, on the one hand, and on the
other, his retaining of Barrett as a harper.

96 See chapter 1, p. 46 and note 197.

97 Moryson, *An Itinerary*, Part II, pp. 283–4. F.M. Jones, *Mountjoy 1563–1606: The
Last Elizabethan Deputy* (Dublin and London, 1958), p. 163.

98 Nothing is known of drama within Chichester's household save one item, a play performance by the Tailors of Dublin at Christmastide in 1608. This is mentioned in a
letter of Sir Robert Jacob of 16 January 1609 to Sir John Davys (note 205 below).
The detail is of interest for showing the continued dramatic activity of the Tailors, as
well as the extension of Dublin Castle's patronage in this regard towards the members
of a trade guild.

99 *Articles to be Inquired of by the Chvrch-Wardens and Questmen of every Parish, in the
ordinary Visitation of the Right Reverend Father in God George by divine Providence Lord
Bishop of Cloyne* (Dublin, 1639; *STC* 14265.7), sig. A3. In contrast to England, Ireland has preserved relatively few sets of episcopal visitation articles from this period.

100 On the Munster plantations, see D.B. Quinn, 'The Munster Plantation: Problems
and Opportunities,' *Journal of the Cork Historical Society* 21 (1966), 19–40, and M.
McCarthy Morrogh, *The Plantation of Munster* (Oxford, 1986).

101 CHL, Lismore Papers, Volume 25, p. 258 (A.B. Grosart, ed., *The Lismore Papers [First
Series], viz. Autobiographical Notes, Remembrances and Diaries of Sir Richard Boyle,
First and 'Great' Earl of Cork*, 5 vols [London, 1886] I, 262): 'Geven the Children v li.
for their Mask. wherof I paid them out of my own purse iiij li. xvij s., & gaue order
to Mr walley to ad iij s. to make vp the 5 li.' (John Walley, mentioned in several of
the accounts, was the household steward of Lismore.)

424 Notes to pages 229–30

102 NLI, MS 6897, fol. [85v] (household accounts of 24 December 1627): 'Deliuered the same day to my Lo Viscount to help. his Lordship with necessaries for his parte of the Maske iij li.'

103 CHL, Lismore Papers, Volume 27, p. 16 (Grosart, *Lismore Papers*, IV, 23): 'This daie Captain Gerrard ffookes acquainted me that the daye after my son Dongarvan had wayted [to] on his Majesty in his Royall Maske, and had been an actor therin, Captain ffookes delivered him six hundreth powndes in gold, vppon my sons bill of exchandge, chardging me with the repayment therof the xxv^th of Maye next ...' This entry is dated 12 April 1634, and the masque took place 18 February 1634. The event seems to have taken a while to register with Boyle.

104 Lord Dungarvan is named in the list of masquers (Thomas Carew, *The Poems of Thomas Carew with his Masque Coelum Britannicum*, ed. R. Dunlap [Oxford, 1949; corrected reprt, 1957], p. 185, line 1148). A letter of George Garrard to Sir Thomas Wentworth (*Letters and Dispatches of the Earl of Strafforde*, ed. W. Knowler, 2 vols [London, 1739] I, 207), makes clear that *Coelum Britannicum* played to a packed audience (tickets were issued). The production was splendid, as Queen Henrietta Maria remarked: 'Pour les habits, elle n'avoit vue de si brave' ('As for the costumes, she had not seen any as fine'; *The Dramatic Records of Sir Henry Herbert, Master of the Revels, 1623–1673*, ed. J.Q. Adams, [New Haven, Conn., 1917], p. 55). For nineteen designs for the production, see P. Simpson and C.F. Bell, eds., *Designs by Inigo Jones for Masques and Plays at Court* (Oxford, 1924), pp. 83–8; a masquer's costume such as Dungarvan would have worn is shown on p. 86.

105 Somerset, *Shropshire*, II, 396.

106 N.P. Canny, *The Upstart Earl: A Study of the Social and Mental World of Richard Boyle, First Earl of Cork, 1566–1643* (Cambridge, 1982), p. 73.

107 CHL, Lismore Papers, Volume 25, p. 115 (Grosart, *Lismore Papers*, I, 100): 'given the princes plaiers xxij s.'

108 As payments in the Barnstaple Receivers' Accounts prove; Wasson, *Devon*, p. 49.

109 Wasson, *Devon*, p 49. (The fiscal year ran from Michaelmas to Michaelmas.)

110 *SPC*, p. 410, omits their Irish visit.

111 *SPC*, p. 410. It seems likely that Dover was the port to which they returned from Ireland.

112 Wasson, *Devon*, pp. 49–50. On the question of payments for non-performance, see the case history studied by J. Coldewey, 'Carnival's End: Puritan Ideology and the Decline of English Provincial Theatre,' in M. Twycross, ed., *Festive Drama* (Cambridge, 1996), pp. 279–86.

113 Wasson, *Devon*, p. xiii. For records of other players paid for not playing (their affiliation is not noted), see pp. 50–1.

114 CHL, Lismore Papers, Volume 25, p. 219 (Grosart, *Lismore Papers*, I, 245): 'Receaved for Barck money of the tanner of yoghall iij li., wherof I gaue the Players 22 s.'; NLI,

MS 6897, fol. [11] (household accounts from 29 October to 4 November 1626): 'Geven by your Lordships direccion to the Players .this last weeke xxij s.'; NLI, MS 6897, fol. [79] (household accounts of 18 November 1627): 'Geven the same day to the Players by your Lordship xx s.'

115 NLI, MS 6898, fol. [248v] (household accounts 16 July 1635): 'Given .i6°. by your Lordships direccon {*read* direccion}. to the poppit players. x s.' However, a puppet play in Dublin, possibly in the summer of 1611, is alluded to in Barnaby Rich, *A Catholicke Conference Betvveene Syr Tady Mac. Mareall a popish priest of VVaterforde, and Patricke Plaine, a young student in Trinity Colledge by Dublin in Ireland* (London, 1612; STC 20981), fol. 21v, sig. [F 3v]:

> 'Pa. I will neuer deny it Syr Tady, I confesse I haue seene a Masse.
>
> Ta. Then you haue not liued altogether so irreligiously, but that you haue once seene a Masse, but tell mee truely, howe did you like it?
>
> Pa. O passing well, I neuer sawe a thing that better pleased me, but once:
>
> Ta. And what was that one thing, that you say pleased you better?
>
> Pa. It was a Puppet play, that was playd at Dubline, but nowe this last summer.'

116 NLI, MS 6899, fol. [49v] (household accounts 24 April 1637): '24 Given by Thomas Badnedge by your Lordships direccon {*read* direccion}. to some Iuglers. v s.'

117 NLI, MS 6899, fol. [107] (household accounts 30 March 1638): '30. Given by your Lordship to the Rope=dauncers x s.'

118 Compare, for example, the puppet players of Elizabeth I mentioned in a set of Corporation Chamberlains' Accounts of 1581–2, whose avocation sounds specific (Douglas and Greenfield, *Cumberland/Westmorland/Gloucestershire*, p. 308), or the company which had a royal license specifically to perform rope-dancing 'and other feates of activity' in Norwich on 17 June 1616 (Galloway, *Norwich 1540–1642*, p. 147).

119 Though various rope-dancers are collected in the pages of the Records of Early English Drama volumes published to date, a particularly vivid description of assorted feats of funambulism by a 'hongarian' and members of the queen's majesty's players in Shrewsbury on 24 July 1590 is given in Somerset, *Shropshire*, I, 247. And as will be seen below, the queen's majesty's players were in Dublin not long before, with the earl of Essex's players, where they made 'Sporte to the mayor <& a>ldermen' (DCA, MR/35, p. 431). Rope-dancing may have been a constituent of their 'Sporte.' The persistence in Ireland of rope-dancing into the Commonwealth period is attested as late as *c* 1657 in Londonderry. The Quaker preacher, William Edmundson (1627–1712), successfully lured a crowd away from some stage players and rope-dancers: 'The next Day I came to Londonderry; it was Market-Day, and there were Stage-players and Rope-Dancers in the Market-Place, and Abundance of People gather'd ... {The players prevail on the mayor to have Edmundson imprisoned, but he continues preaching from his cell} ... I thrust my Arm out at the Window, and wav'd it, till some of them espying, came near, and others followed apace; so that presently I had most of the People from

the Stage-Players, which vexed them much: then they got the Mayor to cause the Gaoler to keep me close; so he bolted me, and lock'd my Leg to a Place where he used to fasten Condemned Persons.... As I sat in a heavenly Exercise, I heard the People shout and say, The Man had broke his Back. It was the Man Dancing on a Rope, which broke, or gave way, so that he fell on the Pavement, and was sore hurt.' (*A Journal of the Life, Travels, Sufferings, and Labour of Love in the Work of the Ministry, of that Worthy Elder and Faithful Servant of Jesus Christ, William Edmundson, who departed this Life, the Thirty First of the Sixth Month, 1712.* [London, 1715], pp. 37–8).

120 CHL, Lismore Papers, Volume 27, p. 155 (Grosart, *Lismore Papers*, IV, 191). Archie was evidently on leave from his royal master at the time.

121 CHL, Lismore Papers, Volume 1 (item 136), fol. 285v (household accounts of 10 June 1605; a payment by Mistress Ann of 9d 'that she gaue to Musitions'). The musical patronage of Boyle has been extensively surveyed by B. Boydell, 'The Earl of Cork's Musicians: A Study in the Patronage of Music in Early Seventeenth Century Anglo-Irish Society,' *Records of Early English Drama Newsletter* 18 (1993), 1–15.

122 See respectively CHL, Lismore Papers, Volume 2 (item 20), fol. 31v (household accounts of 13 July 1606); CHL, Lismore Papers, Volume 8 (item 55), single sheet, obverse (household accounts of 11 June 1617); CHL, Lismore Papers, Volume 8 (item 107), single sheet, obverse (household accounts of 10 August 1617); and CHL, Lismore Papers, Volume 14 (item 1), bifolium, fol. [1] (household accounts of 17 March 1623).

123 S. Donnelly, 'A Cork Harper at the Stuart Court: Daniel Duff O'Cahill, the Queen's Harper,' *Journal of the Cork Historical and Archæological Society*, forthcoming. O'Cahill is mentioned in several places in Boyle's diaries between 1613 and 1616 (CHL, Lismore Papers, Volume 25, pp. 33, 55, 82, 114, 131, 132, and 136; see respectively Grosart, *Lismore Papers*, I, 20, 36, 65, 100, 119, 120, and 124). He was acquiring land from Lord Barrymore (see Donnelly, 'Cork Harper.') Ned Scott is mentioned once, on 21 July 1621, being given 40s to carry messages to Chichester (CHL, Lismore Papers, Volume 25, p. 279; Grosart, *Lismore Papers*, II, 20). (The harper's common function as messenger, a role often mentioned in sixteenth- and seventeenth-century documents, was evidently continuing: compare, for example, the letter of Sir Conyers Clifford to the Lord Deputy and Council, 9 August 1597, in PRO, SP 63/200, fol. 232v: 'that night a Harper that I had sent vnto Orwarks, came vnto me, and assured me your Lordship was gonn and bydd me be assured, for he had seen a lettre sent from your honor vnto me which thenemy had intercepted, and told me parte of the contentes.') It is not absolutely clear which Arthur Chichester was intended: either it was Sir Arthur Chichester (1563–1625, created Baron Chichester of Belfast in 1613), twice sworn in as Lord Deputy of Ireland (in 1605 and in 1614); or it was his nephew, Sir Arthur Chichester (1606–75, created first earl of Donegall in 1647), who inherited his uncle's estates in Belfast and Carrickfergus.

124 Canny, *Upstart Earl*, pp. 47–8, traces the tightening control of Boyle over Barrymore's interests.

125 Canny, *Upstart Earl*, p. 127.

126 Boydell, 'Earl of Cork's Musicians,' p. 13, note 27.

127 NLI, MS 6897, fol. [17] (household accounts of 5 December 1626): 'Paid the same day for stringes for the Vyalles. and Lute bought by ffrances Iones. v s.'

128 For example, Boyle's associate, Sir Donough O'Brien, fourth earl of Thomond and from 1615–24 Lord President of Munster, had been intended to receive a fiddle and two pairs of virginals in a shipment of goods that had been impounded in 1604 at the Isle of Wight (J.C. Appleby, ed., *A Calendar of Material relating to Ireland from the High Court of Admiralty Examinations 1536–1641* [Dublin, 1992], pp. 107–8). I am grateful to Seán Donnelly for directing me to this reference. That O'Brien retained a consort of musicians is clear from a payment to them in the accounts of Sir Richard Boyle, prepared by Abraham Bates, steward of the household, on 11 June 1617: 'giuen to my Lo: Presidentes Musiciantes ij s. vj d.' (CHL, Lismore Papers, Volume 8 [item 55], single sheet).

129 CHL, Lismore Papers, Volume 25, p. 131 (Grosart, *Lismore Papers*, I, 119): 'given Stacie my mvsicon {*read* mvsicion} xl s.' (the 'x' is badly formed, however, and may conceivably be 'c'; Grosart, *Lismore Papers*, I, 119).

130 Boydell, 'Earl of Cork's Musicians,' p. 5.

131 Six in Perrot's, which may have been a traditional number (and see note 67 above).

132 Only three players were paid on 14 May 1638, NLI, MS 6899, fol. [118] (household accounts of 14 May 1638): 'Paid to 3 Musitions [for] and to Iohn ffoster for their Wages due at our Lady 1638: ix li. x s.' but this may have been a temporary anomaly, for there were four musicians shortly before, NLI, MS 6899, fol. [89] (household accounts of 14 December 1637): 'Paid to the 4. Musitions, and to Iohn ffoster for half a yeares Wages due at Michaelmas. 1637 xij li.' and again shortly after, CHL, Lismore Papers, Volume 19 (item 105), a booklet, fol. [5] (household accounts of 5 November 1638): 'Paid to 4. Musitians and to John ffoster for wages due at Michaelmas 1638 xij. li.'

133 Six livery cloaks were purchased and tailored on 30 November 1636, NLI, MS 6899, fol. [24v] (household accounts of 30 November 1636): '30. Paid to Willm Page for 21 yards dimidium of broadcloth to make six Clokes for your Musitions, and 2 suites for your Lordships footmen. at 9 s. per yard. ix li. xiij s. vj d.'; and CHL, Lismore Papers, Volume 27, p. [174] (Grosart, *Lismore Papers*, IV, 214): 'Cleered all accompts with [Tho] ⌃⌐William⌐ Page the Clothier of Kilmckee for the red cloathe to make 6 clokes for my six Musicons {*read* Musicions} and sutes for my 2 footmen, and paid him xxj li. ix s. vj d.'

134 NLI, MS 6899, fol. [25v] (household accounts of 5 December 1636): 'Paid to Vallentyne Wayman which he laid forth for Clothes for the Musition Jack. xx s.';

NLI, MS 6899, fol. [29v] (household accounts of 20 December 1636): '20. Given yo Iacke the singing Musition to make vp his liuery Cloke ix. s.'; NLI, MS 6899, fol. [45v] (household accounts of 6 April 1637): 'Given by your Lordship to the Musition boy dischardged v s.'

135 Boydell, 'Earl of Cork's Musicians,' p. 5. One possible exception to this appears in a payment in the household accounts of Sir Walter Butler, 6 May 1630 (NLI, MS 2549, fo. 5v): 'M' to the Lo: Iustices theire Musitioners thusday the 6 of May 00 – 05 – 00.' The Lords Justices at this date were Sir Richard Boyle and Sir Adam Loftus, and the payment may have been made in Dublin. However, this need not necessarily imply that the musicians were those of Boyle's household, alongside those of Loftus. Perhaps he engaged musicians other than his household ones when away from home. Boyle's household musicians also rented houses from him, and appear regularly in his rentals. Since some also kept cattle, and were involved in the Boyle household in non-musical capacities, it seems likely that they were indeed relatively rooted to the area (Boydell, 'Earl of Cork's Musicians,' p. 7).

136 CAI, U 138, p. 272 (Caulfield, *Council Book of the Corporation of Youghal*, p. 203): 'Memorandum that Edmond Butler late of Kinges Lynn in the County of Norffolk yeoman hath putt him self apprentice to Michaell Skryne Musicion for vij yeres from the last daie of August Anno domini 1615/.' (Though the entry is dated 2 July 1618, its internal date reference to 31 August 1615 probably means that Skryne was in Youghal already some three years earlier.)

137 NLI, MS 6900, fol. [65] (household accounts of 12 August 1643): 'Geven by your Lordships direccon {*read* direccion} to Michael Skrene and his Wife x s.' Of the five named musicians paid on 2 May 1629, [William] Stacy, [William] Knowles, Valentine [Wayman], [Michael] Skryne and Francis Jones (NLI, MS 6897, fol. [170] (household accounts of 2 May 1629), four, with the exception only of William Stacy, were still being retained in the last notice of them as musicians, 24 November 1641, NLI, MS 6900, fol. [13v] (household accounts of 24 November 1641). These men were probably the core members, even when the group was at its smallest. Who the sixth musician was is less clear, but it was possibly one John Miles, who is noted in two musical contexts on 30 March and 14 November 1627 (see respectively CHL, Lismore Papers, Volume 26, p. 96 (Grosart, *Lismore Papers*, II, 211): 'I gaue to 3 of my mvsicons {*read* mvsicions} 3 english Cowes that I had for Herriotts, one to Michaell Skryne, another to An swetes husband ffrances, the third vnto vallentyne of which I had 2 from Silvester my Carpenters widdo and I gaue to Iohn Miles 50 s., that was due for olde Iohn Crokfordes herriott, paid him in money'; and NLI, MS 6897, fol. [78] (household accounts of 14 November 1627): 'Paid the same day to 5. Musitions for their Wages due at Michaelmas last, Iohn Myles being paid before xij li. x s.').

138 CHL, Lismore Papers, Volume 26, p. 220 (Grosart, *Lismore Papers*, III, 41): 'Paid for ffive Clokes for my Mvsicons {*read* Mvsicions} by Henry Staynes viij li.'; and NLI,

MS 6899, fol. [24v] (household accounts of 30 November 1636): 'Paid to Willm Page for 21 yards dimidium of broadcloth to make six Clokes for your Musitions, and 2 suites for your Lordships footmen. at 9 s. per yard. ix li. xiij s. vj d.'

139 WRO, 865/502, pp. 13–15 (see Appendix IV).

140 J.H.P. Pafford, 'John Clavell (1601–43), Burglar, Highwayman, Poet, Dramatist, Doctor, Lawyer,' *Notes and Queries for Somerset and Dorset* 32 (1986), 549–62. My account of Clavell's movements depends on that given here, but Pafford's account of the *Introduction* itself is not entirely secure.

141 In 1634, Lord David was depending on his father-in-law's assistance in helping refurbish the family seat at Castlelyons (Canny, *Upstart Earl*, p. 48).

142 As, for example, was the Shetland sword dance first recorded in the eighteenth century (Chambers, *Mediæval Stage*, II, 270–6, Appendix J). This sword dance was evidently older, but precisely how much is not known. In 'Mummers of County Wexford' (*The Daily Chronicle* [London], 2 March 1929 and repr in *The Irish Book Lover* 17 [1929], 59–61), Fred Heneghan printed excerpts of a sword dance which he maintained was derived from a seventeenth-century manuscript of a Wexford mummers' play on the Seven Champions of Christendom, and which, he also claimed, had been performed in Wexford in 1490. However, the text Heneghan printed corresponds quite closely to that of the Shetland sword dance printed by Chambers, and since Heneghan gave no shelfmark reference for the purported manuscript, his claims are unverifiable.

143 Note the fudging of the boundary between audience and actors which has been stressed as a masque feature by S. Orgel, *The Jonsonian Masque* (Cambridge, Mass., 1965), pp. 6–7; H. Cooper, 'Location and Meaning in Masque, Morality and Royal Entertainment,' in D. Lindley, ed., *The Court Masque* (Manchester, 1984), pp. 135–48.

144 Though in respect of its ritualized violence, the sword-dancing of the *Introduction* might be thought most nearly to resemble the dancing of the anti-masque, it was evidently no hobbling or grotesque antic, but an impressive feat of skill.

145 D. George, ed. *Lancashire*, Records of Early English Drama (Toronto, 1991), p. 184. Perhaps the sword dance originally had rather more dialogue than is now recorded?

146 Five sword or withy dancers appear on the early-seventeenth-century Fitzgerald bone plate (McClintock, 'Bone Plate'). The Shetland sword dance had six (Chambers, *Mediæval Stage*, II, 270–6, Appendix J).

147 Appendix IV, lines 85–6.

148 *OED*, **Skene**. Compare the famous 1594 picture of Captain Thomas Lee, by Marcus Gheeraerts the Younger, in which Lee is depicted holding a javelin in his right hand, one of the kern's accoutrements (K. Hearn, ed., *Dynasties: Painting in Tudor and Jacobean England 1530–1630* [London, 1995], p. 177; other kern similarities are discussed there). Whatever the complex political meaning of the painting, recent suggestions that Lee's costume also resembles masking costume (for example, H. Morgan,

'Tom Lee: The Posing Peacemaker,' in Bradshaw, Hadfield, and Maley, *Representing Ireland*, pp. 132–65; p. 142) beg comparison with Clavell's kern masquers.

149 Irish kerns had entered the English dramatic tradition by the sixteenth century (J.O. Bartley, *Teague, Shenkin and Sawney, being an Historical Study of the Earliest Irish, Welsh and Scottish Characters in English Plays* [Cork, 1954], pp. 9–10), but Clavell's are the first of their kind known on Irish soil.

150 The 'civilly instructed Irishman' is extolled in Orpheus's speech of welcome in Middleton's masque *The Triumphs of Love and Antiquity*, presented on 29 October 1619 on the occasion of Sir William Cockayne taking his oath as Lord Mayor of London (Thomas Middleton, *The Works of Thomas Middleton*, ed. A.H. Bullen, 8 vols [London, 1885–6] VII, 321).

151 It would be interesting to know who played Mars, a man of the kerns' nation but at the same time a civilized leader who combined the best of both worlds. If the player was the Anglo-Irish Lord Barrymore, a man of the middle nation, the role would have seemed particularly à propos. After all, royals too could enter a comparable masking relationship, as when in Aurelian Townshend's contemporary *Albion's Triumph* (1632), the military Albanactus (Charles I) is on a quest for Alba (Henrietta Maria). Her love finally tempers Albanactus's conquering power (Aurelian Townsend, *The Poems and Masques of Aurelian Townshend*, ed. C.C. Brown [Reading, 1983], p. 84).

152 A. Sheehan, 'Irish Towns in a Period of Change, 1558–1625,' in C. Brady and R. Gillespie, eds., *Natives and Newcomers: Essays on the Making of Irish Colonial Society 1534–1641* (Dublin, 1986), pp. 93–119; see p. 115.

153 Ibid., p. 97.

154 T.W. Moody, 'Sir Thomas Phillips of Limavady, Servitor,' *Irish Historical Studies* 1 (1938–9), 251–72; also by him, *The Londonderry Plantation 1609–41* (Belfast, 1939). For the distribution of the Ulster plantation lands generally at this date, see Cosgrove, *New History of Ireland II*, 198, Map 5.

155 PRONI, T. 510/2, p. 145 (*Londonderry and the London Companies 1609–1629, being a Survey and Other Documents submitted to King Charles I by Sir Thomas Phillips* [Belfast, 1928], pp. 119–20).

156 C.W. Russell and J.P. Prendergast, eds., *Calendar of the State Papers relating to Ireland, of the Reign of James I. 1615–1625* (London, 1880), p. 551. This document is a list of Irish soldiers, describing their services and qualifications, dated after 1 December and before the end of 1624.

157 *London Companies*, pp. 116–17.

158 *London Companies*, pp. 132, 52, and 54 respectively.

159 It is hard to see how any of the songs in *Much Ado* might have caused further offence, unless it be Balthasar's song on the faithlessness of men (*Much Ado*, Act II, scene III). But if so, the commissioners must have been touchy indeed. Perhaps more likely they had been the butt of some lampoon.

160 Accounts of the play's stage history have not recognized that this 1628 *Much Ado* is the second record of the play, cancellation notwithstanding, after the first in 1613 (*Much Ado About Nothing*, ed. F.H. Mares [Cambridge, 1988], p. 10). Through their choice the planters also showed themselves aware of what was currently popular in London theatrical circles, and thus likely to please their guests. On the play's popularity, see Mares, *Much Ado*, p. 10.

161 Lisnagarvy is in the barony of Massereene Upper, co. Antrim. Its nearest settlement of appreciable size was Belfast, some ten miles to the north east.

162 PRO, SP 63/255, fol. 34.

163 Cited from *The Complete Peerage*, ed. Vicary Gibbs, et al., 12 vols (London, 1910–59) III, 401.

164 The first letter from his father to him at Lisnagarvy in the State Papers dates to 10 December 1629; another, dated 7 April 1630, mentions a deer park gracing the Lisnagarvy house – a luxury feature. The last such letter is dated 11 November 1630. Sir Thomas Wentworth's letter of 21 August 1637 describing the Limerick triumphs (Appendix IIIc) envisaged Lord Conway and Killultagh visiting London in that year.

165 The shipment of instruments is all there is to go on, and that was to an Old English household. Record loss is doubtless responsible once again. However, traces of a tradition in Connacht already in the sixteenth century appear in the activity within the New English household of Sir Richard Bingham, examined below.

166 RCB, C/6/1/26/3 (item 26), fol. [2v] (accounts of William Carvile, 29 September 1637 to 29 September 1638): 'Item to the Lord deputies Musicke 6–13–4'; and RCB, C/6/1/26/3 (item 27), fol. [7] (accounts of Henry Dilson, April to 29 September 1638 and December 1638 to 14 April 1639): 'Item to the musicioners 6–13–4.' Though the musicians are not named as the Lord Deputy's in the latter payment, the sum paid to them is identical.

167 R. Ingram, ed. *Coventry*, Records of Early English Drama (Toronto, 1981), p. 440. Wentworth at this date was still in Dublin.

168 Watters, 'Notes of Particulars,' p. 245. On the progress, see chapter 5.

169 CHL, Lismore Papers, Volume 27, p. 1 (Grosart, *Lismore Papers*, IV, 5–6). It is not absolutely clear that Boyle's reward of the Dublin waits happened in the context of a castle occasion, but this seems the likeliest explanation.

170 CHL, Lismore Papers, Volume 27, p. 1 (Grosart, *Lismore Papers*, IV, 5–6). *EIS*, p. 26, erroneously dated the occasion to 2 January 1634.

171 Ogilby came to Dublin some time between 1633 and 1636, but probably earlier rather than later in that time. John Aubrey says Ogilby rode in Wentworth's troop of guards, as one of his gentlemen (Bodl., MS Aubrey 8, fol. 45; John Aubrey, *'Brief Lives,' chiefly of Contemporaries, set down by John Aubrey between the Years 1669 and 1696*, ed. A. Clark, 2 vols [Oxford, 1898] II, 101: 'he went into Ireland with the Lord Strafford Deputy ... and taught his Lady and children to Dance yat was his

Place ... – and rode in his Troupe of Guards as one of my Lords Gentlemen ...'). See further on Ogilby and the Werburgh Street Theatre in chapter 7.

172 H.F. Kearney, *Strafford in Ireland 1633–41* (Cambridge, 1989), p. 40. Boyle and the New English faction were opposing the allied interests of Wentworth, Mountnorris, and the Old English.

173 In 1610 (C. Kenny, *King's Inns and the Kingdom of Ireland The Irish 'Inn of Court' 1541–1800* [Dublin, 1992], p. 89).

174 Lord Digby was Robert Digby, Baron Digby of Geashill; Lord Moore was Sir Charles Moore, Viscount Moore of Drogheda, on whom see further in the following note.

175 Digby's first wife was Sarah, Boyle's second daughter by his second wife, Catherine. Digby had married her in 1626. Before her marriage Sarah had also been the widow of Lord Moore's brother, Sir Thomas Moore (†1623). Digby's connections with the Boyle household were lifelong; he died in the Boyle Dublin residence, Cork House, in 1642.

176 In a letter of 19 May 1635, George Garrard informed Wentworth of the quarrel that had broken out at the Blackfriars Theatre between Digby and one Will Crofts (*Letters and Dispatches*, ed. Knowler, I, 426).

177 A fashionable formula in aristocratic circles (Edwards, Bentley, McLuskie, and Potter, *Revels History of Drama in English Volume IV*, p. 25), and one that had long appealed to Lord Digby. He organized 'a great supper and a play' at Whitehall as early as December 1618 (John Chamberlain, ed., *The Letters of John Chamberlain*, ed. N.E. McClure, Memoirs of the American Philosophical Society 12, 2 vols [Philadelphia, 1939] II, 193).

178 See Kearney, *Strafford in Ireland*, on the circumstances; a compromise was reached, but the affair still cost Boyle a £15,000 settlement.

179 CHL, Lismore Papers, Volume 27, p. 1 (Grosart, *Lismore Papers*, IV, 5–6).

180 P. O'Sullivan Beare, *Historiæ Catholicæ Iberniæ Compendium* (Lisbon, 1621), fols 106v–7.

181 Mac Craith was pardoned twice, and had been complicit with the Desmond rebellion of 1582–3. The author, Philip O'Sullivan Beare, wanted to point up the English treachery, of course, and he used an infringement of the code of hospitality, a hospitality made more generous precisely because of its inclusion of *choræas atque ludos*, as the means to do so.

182 Bodl., MS Tanner 444, fol. 4v ('Bodley's Visit,' p. 92).

183 Bodl., MS Tanner 444, fols 4v–5 ('Bodley's Visit,' p. 94; a version of this text in the early-seventeenth-century transcript in BL, MS Additional 4784, fols 93v–4v, has the following two superior readings: line 5 ita Brachia] ita vt Brachia; line 8 pro se vinctis] per se iunctis). Bodley evidently had a taste for drama and the performing arts. A friend of his, Thomas Bellot, testifies to Bodley's musical leanings in a letter to Sir Michael Hickes of 16 January 1612 (BL, MS Lansdowne 92, fol. 143: 'Sir I am not vnmyndfull of you for an Irishe harp, and [to] to that end a sennight {'seven night,'

'week'} past I entreated Sir Iosias Bodleighe my awncient acquaintance that if he cold vnderstand of anye suche that were excellent (beinge skilfull also himeself in Musick) that he wold make me knowe it, to which he awnswered that if he cold heare of a speciall good one, he wold bestowe and send it youe fro himeself').

184 Compare the Ulster name 'Skiver (i.e., Skewer) the Goose' given to this game, which survived as late as the nineteenth century and was played at harvest time, Hallowe'en, and Christmas. I am grateful to Meg Twycross for drawing fig. 18.

185 G. Wickham, ed., *English Moral Interludes* (London and Totowa, 1976), p. 71, lines 1165–6. See also P. Meredith, '"Farte Prycke in Cule" and Cock Fighting,' *Medieval English Theatre* 6 (1984), 30–9, and A.J. Fletcher, '"Farte Prycke in Cule": A Late-Elizabethan Analogue from Ireland,' *Medieval English Theatre* 8 (1986), 134–9.

186 On Bingham and the Connacht presidency, see B. Cunningham, 'The Composition of Connacht in the Lordships of Clanricard and Thomond 1577–1641,' *Irish Historical Studies* 24 (1984–5), 1–14; and her 'Natives and Newcomers in Mayo, 1560–1603,' in R. Gillespie and G. Moran, eds. *'A Various Country': Essays in Mayo History 1500–1900* (Westport, 1987), pp. 24–43.

187 The description seems to fit best the friary of St Francis (at this date being referred to as St Francis's Abbey, as on Sir John Perrot's map of Galway of 1583). The abbey formerly stood on a small island just outside the north gate of the city. Its location is shown clearly on the 1651 map of Galway (J. Hardiman, *The History of the Town and County of the Town of Galway, from the Earliest Period to the Present Time* [Dublin, 1820], opposite p. 30).

188 PRO, SP 63/144, fols 88v–9.

189 Edict of the Irish Parliament, 12 January 1560 (*In this volume are contained all the statutes made in Ireland* [London, 1572; *STC* 14129], fol. 135, sig. [Liv]): 'And it is ordeined & enacted by thaucthoritie abouesaid, yat if any person or persons whatsoeuer after ye sayde feast of S. Ihon Baptist shall in any enterludes, playes, songs, rimes or by other open words, declare or speake any thing in derogacion deprauing or despising of the same boke or of any thing therin conteined or any part thereof, yat then euery such person being thereof lawfully conuicted in forme abouesaid, shal forfait to ye Queene our soueraign Lady her heirs & successors for the first offence an C. marks, …' (penalties of 400 marks, and of confiscation of property plus life imprisonment, follow for second and third offences respectively).

190 The clearest account of Sir Brian O'Rourke's treasonable profanation is found in a letter from the Lord Deputy, Sir William Fitzwilliam, to Sir William Cecil, 9 April 1589 (PRO, SP 63/143, fol. 23r–v): 'OrRoorck, about two. or. 3. yeres since, hauing found in a churche or in some other place an ymage of a tall woman writ vpon the brest thereof Quene Elizabeth: which done he presentlie fell with such spightfull & trayterous speaches to rayle at it & otherwise so filthelie to vse it, as I protest vnto your Lo: I abhorre to remember & canne by no meanes frame my pen to write;

During which tyme, his barbarous Gallowglassis standing by played their partes as fast,, who with their Gallyglasse axes striking the ymage one while on the head, an other while on the face and sometymes stabbing it in the bodie, never ceasid vntill with hackling & mangling they ^⌈had⌉ vtterlie defacid it; And being neuertheles not contentid herewith, they, the more to manyfest the mallice of their trayterous hartes fastnid an halter about the neck of the ymage & tying it to a horsse tayle dragged it a long vpon the ground, and so beating it with their axes & reyling most dispightfully at it, they endid fynished their trayterous pagent: ...' Note too John Ball's declaration of April (or later) 1590, which suggests that the statue was turned into a sort of pageant on wheels (PRO, SP 63/151, fol. 259): 'I was sent in to ororkes contre ther [the] to receve her majesties composyssyon and in the tyme of my beinge ther at mc glannans [hovse] tovne standinge vpon a grene I sawe the pictar of a woman carved in a blocke standinge vpon whelles of small tymbar I asked the in habetend {'inhabitants'} of the tovne what It was thaye tolde me it was mad for a callyaghe {< caillech, 'old woman'} I asked what she was thaye told me on {'one'} that denyed a carpenter of myllke I de manded wher she did dwell thay sayd in the far syde of the water by the tovne ther wase a loghe {'lough'} I thovght thay ment in the far syde therof & so sayd no more of that.' The incident occurred in 1586 or 1587, and was still receiving substantial notice in the State Papers as late as 1593.

191 Bingham did the state the service of crushing Sir Brian O'Rourke's rebellion in co. Leitrim in 1591; O'Rourke was captured and sent for execution in England.

192 Cunningham, 'Natives and Newcomers,' p. 28 and 'Composition of Connacht,' p. 3, emphasizes the autonomy enjoyed by the Connacht presidents, Bingham in particular.

193 PRO, SP 63/148, fol. 118v (November, 1589).

194 PRO, SP 63/148, fol. 112v.

195 For the play in St Mary's, Kilkenny, see chapter 4.

196 They were brought to book by the aldermen at a meeting of the standing committee of the corporation on 18 May (DCA, MR/17 [Friday Book of Dublin Corporation], fol. 52v; Berry, 'Minute Book,' p. 496): 'Where by the Auncyent Custome & vsadge of this Cittie the Mayor & Sheryves of bulring should be at Chardge in making a semly shoe {'show'} by muster & other wayes vppon Maye daye, And the Mayor & shryves of the bulring at this present [being] for good respects being tollerated withall this last Maye daye, & [were] comaunded by mr Mayor & Aldermen [the] to make the said shoe vppon Assencion daye, They lytle pondering there dutie, [but] ⌈did⌉ in Contemptuous maner [did] not perform the same, It is therfore resoved {read resolved}. in a meeting this daye that the Mayor & shryves of the bulring shalbe Caullid {the reading of this word uncertain} vppon before mr Mayor & Ceyttd for there Contempt aforsaid, and that they shall not be deliuered tyll they putt in sufficient pawnes or enter in bond, (at mr Mayor Choyse, that they shall perform such farther order other

by fyne or ponishment as shalbe Inflyctid vppon them by the Mayor Sheryves comons
& Cittezes {*read* Cittezens} in the next assebly {*read* assembly}.'
197 DCA, MR/35, p. 240.
198 DCA, MR/35, p. 427 and p. 431.
199 George, *Lancashire*, pp. 180–2.
200 DCA, MR/35, p. 427.
201 Somerset, *Shropshire*, I, 247. This was in July. A little earlier, on 22 April, the queen's
players were performing in Norwich (again the earl of Essex's players seem to have
been with them) with a 'Turke' (a change of nationality for the 'hongarian'?) who
similarly 'wente vponn Roppes' (Galloway, *Norwich*, p. 96).
202 DCA, MR/35, p. 431.
203 Clark and Refaussé, *Historic Dublin Guilds*, p. 28.
204 BL, MS Egerton 1765, fol. 134. This is the first reference to players (as such) in the
accounts.
205 Huntington Library, HA 15057, single sheet. Jacob's reference to 'the Taylors of
St Patrickes' is probably indicative of the fact that the Tailors Hall, which had been
built in Back Lane in 1583, was not far from the cathedral. Hence it is more likely
that they were the Tailors of St Patrick's in the sense that their base was nearby, rather
than in the sense that they were cathedral employees. Given their craft, the costumes
they wore were doubtless impressive.
206 BL, MS Egerton 1765, fol. 131v. This was presumably on 24 June in that year, though
not all swearings-in necessarily occurred on that day.
207 BL, MS Egerton 1765, fol. 131v. On both occasions the musicians received 3s 9d.
208 BL, MS Egerton 1765, fol. 119.
209 BL, MS Egerton 1765, fol. 132v.
210 BL, MS Egerton 1765, fol. 133v. On the Tailors' quarter days, see Webb, *Guilds of
Dublin*, p. 89. BL, MS Egerton 1765, fol. 132v, records a payment of 3s to the musicians for performing on the quarter day after Christmas 1608. Whose musicians they
were is not stated, but they may have been the city waits.
211 BL, MS Egerton 1765, fol. 133v. The preference for the city music continued until
the close of the period under review. In 1637, 2s were paid 'to the Cittie musicke'
(BL, MS Egerton 1765, fol. 139v). This is the last time the waits appear in the Tailors'
accounts before 1642.
212 BL, MS Egerton 1765, fol. 134.
213 The fact that the Tailors preferred to patronize the city musicians may express not
just the guild's musical tastes, but also, and perhaps more significantly, its awareness
of the ties that still linked it to civic authority as represented by the corporation.
214 From its inception in 1542, King's Inns law students were obliged to spend a period
of residence in London. From 1628, this period was stipulated as five years (Kenny,

King's Inns, pp. 40–8 and p. 99). For dramatic activities of the legal profession at the London Inns, see O. Horner, 'Christmas at the Inns of Court,' in Twycross, *Festive Drama*, pp. 41–53.

215 Shirley's masque *The Triumph of Peace* was presented by the Inns of Court at court on 2 February 1634.

216 Dublin, King's Inns, MS 38 (Black Book of King's Inns), fol. 27v. The 'grand day' probably fell at Christmas, or early in New Year (compare Horner, 'Inns of Court,' pp. 42–5).

217 Kenny, *King's Inns*, pp. 70–98.

218 R.B. McDowell and D.A. Webb, *Trinity College Dublin 1592–1952: An Academic History* (Cambridge, 1982), pp. 4, 7, and 8–9. Nelson, *Cambridge*, II, 708–9, notes how drama was checked at the colleges where puritanism was strong. By contrast, the high church and royalist colleges there continued to perform plays.

219 TCD, Mun/V/5/I, p. 26.

220 TCD, Mun/V/5/I, p. 34.

221 Armagh Public Library, MS 'The History and Antiquties of Dublin,' no shelfmark, p. 265.

222 Both were appointed in 1629 and held office until 1633 (Kenny, *King's Inns*, pp. 102–3).

223 Rich, *A Catholicke Conference*, fol. 21v, sig. [F 3v].

224 *Constitutions of the Synod of Dublin* (Dublin, 1634; *STC* 14264), p. 50. The *Articles to be inqvired of by the Church-wardens and Questmen of every Parish in the Lord Primates Visitation Metropoliticall* (Dublin, 1638; *STC* 14265.9) (Visitation Articles of Archbishop Lancelot Bulkeley) contain a closely corresponding article (sig. A3). The wording of the article on the profanation of holy ground in the visitation articles of George Synge, bishop of Cloyne (see note 99) is identical to that in Bulkeley's articles.

225 On the choral foundations of the two Dublin cathedrals in the Middle Ages, see Grindle, *Irish Cathedral Music*, chapter 1.

226 And compare a case across the Irish Sea, the contract issued to a church musician of Chester in 1518. The contract, in stipulating that he should not abandon his post for private (secular) service, suggests that such practices may have been common (see Mills, 'Music and Musicians,' p. 59).

227 P. LeHuray, *Music and the Reformation in England 1549–1660* (London, 1967; corrected repr, Cambridge, 1978), pp. 14–15.

228 PRO, SP 63/146, fol. 41v (two warrants dated 17 May and 17 June 1589): 'Singing menn of Christchurch By two warrantes signed by the barrons, thone dated xvij° maij 1589 sterling xiij s. iiij d. [et] ⌐& thother⌐ xvij° Iunij 1589. sterling xiij s. iiij d. xxvj s. viij d.'; PRO, SP 63/180, fol. 23v (two warrants dated 27 November 1594 and 3 February 1595): 'The singingmen of christechurch By ij Warrauntes of the Barons of her majesties Exchequer datis xxvij° Novembris et 3mo ffebruarij 1594 for theire fee or reward for singing in the said Courte after theire wonted manner xxvj s. viij d.'; PRO, SP 63/230, fol. 208v (payment for one year ended Michaelmas 1609): 'Choristers

of Christchurch Paid to them for singing in theschecquer at thend of euerie Tearme ad Liij s. iiij d. per annum for one whole yeare end at michaelmas 1609.'

229 TCD, MS 1447 (item 6), fol. 44 (22 July 1577): 'Payed ∧⌈for⌉ a pottell of seeke A mary mavdlyne day at nyght when I was [chossin] made mr to the chanclere and company of crystchorch xij .[d] sterling'; fol. 37v (21 July 1582): 'Item A mary mawdline ewne {'eve'} to the company of crystchorche ij s. vj d. sterling to the querysters the same nyght vj d. sterling'; fol. 39v (22 July 1584): 'to the clergy bellis & curistors iij s. iiij d. sterling.'

230 BL, MS Egerton 1765, fol. 132v (1608): 'It more paid to the singing men of S[t]. Johns Churche iii s.'; fol. 136 (24 June 1622): 'Item paid to the singinge men which songe on St: Johns daie at seruice in the Churche vi s.'; fol. 136 (unspecified date in 1624): 'Item paid to the Choristers vi s.'; fol. 137 (unspecified date in 1628): 'Item paid for Singing men of St. Johns Church vi s. vi d.' The Tailors guild chapel was in St John's. Very likely the church's singers were drafted from Christ Church nearby.

231 RCB, C/6/1/26/3 (item 6), fols [2v] and [9] (accounts of Mr Richardson, 29 September 1594 to 29 September 1595).

232 RCB, C/6/1/26/3 (item 7), fol. [1] (accounts of Mr Richardson, 29 September 1595 to 29 September 1596). The music making occurred on Christmas Eve, 1595.

233 The accounts of the proctor William Carvile from the Michaelmas of 1637 to Michaelmas 1638 note a payment to the Lord Deputy's music of £6 13s 4d (see note 166 above). The accounts of the proctor Henry Dilson for April to 29 September 1638 and December 1638 to 14 April 1639 also note a payment of the same amount 'to the musicioners' (RCB, C/6/1/26/3 [item 27], fol. [7]), who were possibly again those of the Lord Deputy.

234 Bateson's first collection of madrigals was issued in 1604, while he was serving in Chester Cathedral, and his second in 1618. For musical forces other than organ in Christ Church Cathedral, cornets are mentioned in the proctor's accounts of John Bradley (RCB, C/6/1/26/3 [item 16], fol. [4]; between the Michaelmas 1629 and Michaelmas 1630): 'To them that plaid on the Cornettes 0 – 2 – 6'); in the proctor's accounts of William Carvile (RCB, C/6/1/26/3 [item 26], fol. [2v]; between the Michaelmas 1637 and Michaelmas 1638) is found: 'for making a seate for the sacke-but 0 – 1 – 0'; and annual provision was made 18 June 1638 for £12 to pay two sackbuts and two cornets to serve in Christ Church Cathedral every Sunday (RCB, C/6/1/7/2, fol. 31v). An unusual item, a violin, is mentioned in the proctor's accounts of William Carvile (RCB, C/6/1/26/3 [item 25], fol. [2v]; between the Michaelmas 1636 and Michaelmas 1637).

235 LeHuray, *Music and the Reformation*, p. 128. See the previous note for cathedral accounts mentioning instruments.

236 Cork between 1611 and 1637 records payments to one, sometimes two, civic drummers (R. Caulfield, ed., *The Council Book of Cork* [Guildford, 1876], passim). One of these, James Kurtane or Curtaine, served for the best part of twenty years, from 1611

to 1630 (Caulfield, *Council Book*, pp. 28 and 151). Youghal's drummer is on record from 8 January 1618, where he was already a town drummer of long standing (CAI, U 138, p. 122): 'Cornelas Lorgan of the Towne of youghall aforesaid Brogmaker hath of longe continewance of tyme hearetofore binn allowed drummer of the said Towne.'

237 Caulfield, *Council Book*, p. 157.

238 Caulfield, *Council Book*, p. 157. Significant traces remain of the pastimes elsewhere in urban Irish sub-cultures, especially of May games. For example, Galway had a game, first noted *s.a.* 1619 or 1620 (TCD, MS 886 [I. 4. 11], fol. 29; P. Walsh, 'An Account of the Town of Galway,' *Journal of the Galway Archæological and Historical Society* 44 [1992], 47–118; see p. 70) held on May Day, 'being an vsual day for a game for ye youths and tradesmen of the town.' And maypoles were put up in and around Dublin from at least the sixteenth century (PRO, SP 63/202/Part 1, fol. 243, a letter complaining of the enormities of Captain Thomas Lee): 'Arte o toole, was taken by Lea notwithstanding his protection, and within vij miles from dublin there bounde him to a may pole, and (the soldiors refusing to be ye actors of so barbarous a crueltye dangerous to them selfes) at his comandment and for rewarde of Artes horsse and weapons, a base man of Leas with [both] his thombes did thruste oute both his eyes./.' By the seventeenth century, Dublin evidence is substantial. Compare DCA, MR/5/11, mb. 41 dorse (*CARD*, III, 61–2, a by-law of 20 October 1615): 'It is further ordered and agreed by the said aucthorytie that howsoeuer {'whosoever'} herafter shall take downe any May poles sett vppe within this Citty or subvrbes to their owne private vses shall forfeite tenn shillinges sterling to this Cittie for which the thresurer for the tyme being shall bring an accion of debte against the offender. and that the said maypoles shalbe within three monnethes after they are sett vppe / taken downe and converted by the mr of woorkes to this Citty vse./' And again BL, MS Egerton 1765, fol. 138 (29 June 1631): 'Imprimis paid for a warrant against the Jorneymen and prentizes for bringinge of a May Pole on St. Peeters Day ii s.'

239 As part of his collection, Thomas Scot, *Certaine Pieces of this Age Parabolizd* (London, 1616; *STC* 21870). See *An Irish Banqvet*, page facing sig. M3v.

240 *An Irish Banqvet*, sig. M3v.

241 Omitted from *SPC*, p. 391. Quoted in Grosart, *Lismore Papers*, I, xix. Though the accounts of Richard Gough still survive in CAI, F (i), they are now extremely fragmentary, and the entry originally read by Grosart is no longer extant. This record may have been of a performance before the civic authorities, already in England a standard preliminary to the public playing of visiting companies. Compare Douglas and Greenfield, *Cumberland/Westmorland/Gloucestershire*, pp. 362–3; compare also the Dublin performance before the aldermen noted in chapter 3. It is likely that the Youghal performance in fact took place in the latter part of 1625. Their visit may have been motivated by the plague that had kept London theatres closed that year until about

the last week of November (Edwards, Bentley, McLuskie, and Potter, *Revels History of Drama in English Volume IV*, p. 71).

242 CAI, U 138, p. 140 (a memorandum of 16 February 1620; Caulfield, *Council Book of the Corporation of Youghal*, pp. 64–5). The text indicated by <...> comprises just over three lines, originally copied at the bottom of the page, but then deleted and expunged, and now hard to read. This expunged text was subsequently written out again lengthways in the left margin, beginning with the next word, 'Prouided ...' As in many an English town already in the seventeenth century, so now in Ireland, local authorities often took responsibility for licensing performances of visiting companies (*SPC*, pp. 38–9).

243 CAI, U 138, p. 439 (a by-law of 5 October 1635; Caulfield, *Council Book of the Corporation of Youghal*, p. 188).

CHAPTER 7

1 Garrard fed Wentworth's theatrical interest in many letters (for example, *Letters and Dispatches*, ed. Knowler, I, 510 [comedies in Cambridge]; II, 56 [a reference to actors starting up at once after the plague closure of 1636]; and passim).

2 *EIS*, p. 30; A.H. Stevenson, 'James Shirley and the Actors at the First Irish Theater,' *Modern Philology* 40 (1942–3), 147–60; see p. 151; and A. Wertheim, 'The Presentation of James Shirley's "St. Patrick for Ireland" at the First Irish Playhouse,' *Notes and Queries*, 212 (1967), 212–15; see p. 212. *JCS*, II, 518, gives 1635 as the year of opening (presumably following the eighteenth-century theatre historians noted below), but IV, 949–50 and V, 1140, prefer 1637.

3 La Tourette Stockwell, *Dublin Theatres and Theatre Customs (1637–1820)* (Kingsport, Tenn., 1938), p. 2. Having confused Old and New Style dating, she supposed that the appointment was made on 28 February 1637. Similarly Stevenson, 'First Irish Theater,' p. 151, concluded that according to Ogilby's petition (see following note), the theatre must have been built 'after February 1636/7,' and erroneous dating was compounded by his belief in Stockwell's indefensible theory that Ogilby's office *preceded* his appointment (see further below).

4 PRO, C. 66/2995, mb. 38 (*EIS*, p. 181). The question of appointment before building or building before appointment is also not resolved by the other pertinent document here, the petition of John Ogilby, 8 May 1661, in PRO, SP 63/345, fol. 61 (*EIS*, p. 180).

5 *JCS*, IV, 949. In fact, Bentley's alternative was correct, as can be proved from the earlier dating of the opening of the Werburgh Street Theatre (argued below). Thus Ogilby's grant of the office of master of the revels in Ireland was retrospective on the opening of the theatre.

6 J. Shirley, *The Royall Master* (London, 1638; *STC* 22454), sig. [A1].

7 WRO, 865/502, p. 86.

8 SCA, Wentworth Woodhouse Muniments, Strafford Letter Book 7, p. 39 (C.V. Wedgwood, *Thomas Wentworth, First Earl of Strafford 1593–1641: A Revaluation* [London, 1961], p. 260, note 7). (The provost whom Wentworth mentioned was Robert Ussher's successor, William Chappell, a more moderate religionist and Archbishop Laud's appointee. He was elected 24 August 1634.)

9 Chetwood, *General History*, p. 51. Stockwell, *Dublin Theatres*, p. 1.

10 *EIS*, p. 31, note 2.

11 J.C. Greene and G.L.H. Clark, *The Dublin Stage, 1720–1745* (Bethlehem, PA, London, and Toronto, 1993), p. 11.

12 It was Chetwood, for example, who related the story about a bill for the purchase of candles for the play of *Gorboduc* done at Dublin Castle in 1601 (see chapter 6). The story was said to have come from Ashbury, who had it from Ogilby, though Chetwood does not in fact claim to have heard it from Ashbury personally. Given the dates of both men and their residence in Dublin, however, this would have been possible.

13 T. Wilkes, *A General View of the Stage* (London, 1759), p. 306.

14 It may not be coincidental that it was at this time that the Irish parliament of 26 January to 21 March (prorogued to 24 March) 1635 legislated against unlicensed popular players (see the text cited in note 74 below). Perhaps the state was lending its aid to the newly instituted state-dependent theatre.

15 *JCS*, IV, 948–50, summarises Ogilby's biography and its sources.

16 Bodl., MS Aubrey 7, fol. 20 and MS Aubrey 8, fol. 44 ('*Brief Lives,*' ed. Clark, II, 100).

17 Bodl., MS Aubrey 8, fol. 45 ('*Brief Lives,*' ed. Clark, II, 101): he 'went into Ireland with the Lord Strafford Deputy.' *EIS*, p. 27, says that Wentworth secured Ogilby 'sometime between 1633 and 1636.'

18 *EIS*, p. 27, says that Wentworth imported Ogilby 'to take charge of dramatic and other entertainment' at Dublin Castle. But this is not strictly what Aubrey said; see further below.

19 Bodl., MS Aubrey 8, fols 44v–5 ('*Brief Lives,*' ed. Clark, II, 101).

20 *EIS*, p. 27, is far too categorical.

21 PRO, SP 63/345, fol. 61 (*EIS*, p. 180).

22 Chetwood, *General History*, p. 52. Probably not simply on account of the Puritan pressure that Gilbert, *City of Dublin*, I, 41 and S.C. Hughes, *The Pre-Victorian Drama in Dublin* (Dublin, 1904), p. 2 spoke of, though it is certainly true that Parsons is known to have had Puritan sympathies. The state of emergency in the wake of the general revolt that broke out in Ireland on 22 October 1641 must, as Chetwood noted, have been a consideration. Public meeting-places were customarily closed whenever there was danger of riotous assembly (M. Butler, 'Two Playgoers, and the Closing of the London Theatres, 1642,' *Theatre Research International* 9 [1984], 93–9).

23 Bodl., MS Aubrey 7, fol. 20v ('*Brief Lives,*' ed. Clark, II, 103 note).

24 Rocque, *An Exact Survey*. *EIS*, p. 29, opts for a location corresponding to that indicated within the westerly circle on fig. 19, nearly opposite the entrance to Hoey's Court. The advantage of this location is that it has a street frontage, apt (though not essential) for a public theatre, while the easterly lot at the bottom of the street was behind a terrace. However, the advantage of street frontage was also enjoyed by the lot contiguous with St Werburgh's Church. Had Clark read Rocque's key to the various types of hatching on the map, he would have seen that the darker hatching on the westerly lot indicated a public building, while the lighter on the easterly ones indicated *stables or warehouses*. The latter would more closely accord with the cowhouse function recorded by Aubrey.

25 The westerly building was *c* 30′ × *c* 80′. The easterly one by the church was (slightly under) 30′ × (slightly over) 30′. For some reason Rocque has not clearly defined its east wall; perhaps the building was originally longer (and therefore more pronouncedly rectangular) than on Rocque it appears to have been. The other easterly building down the hill was *c* 20′ × *c* 60′ (a little narrow for a playhouse, however). Compare the dimensions of the following London hall theatres (figures supplied from J. Orrell, *The Human Stage: English Theatre Design, 1567–1640* [Cambridge, 1988], p. 190): Cockpit 40′ × 55′ (external dimensions excluding stair turrets); Blackfriars 46′ × 66′ (internal dimensions); and Salisbury Court 40′ (internal width, length not known).

26 On the distinction between hall playhouse and open-air amphitheatre companies, see *SPC*, p. 139.

27 Wilkes, *A General View of the Stage*, p. 306. *EIS*, p. 30, departs from Wilkes, without warrant, in describing the provision of theatre boxes. Wilkes is categorical about there being only one, reserved for the Lord Deputy, and on the stage itself.

28 Bodl., MS Aubrey 7, fol. 20 (*'Brief Lives,'* ed. Clark, II, 101, note e).

29 *JCS*, II, 517–18.

30 On the dating of the drawings, see J. Orrell, *The Theatre of Inigo Jones and John Webb* (Cambridge, 1985), pp. 42–3. The essential internal similarity of the Cockpit, Blackfriars, and the Salisbury Court is established in Orrell, *Human Stage*, pp. 186–203.

31 Compare the arrangements made in King's College Chapel, Cambridge, for Elizabeth I to see a play in 1564 (A.H. Nelson, *Early Cambridge Theatres: College, University and Town Stages, 1464–1720* [Cambridge, 1994], p. 11, fig. 5; see also, pp. 41 and 109).

32 Orrell, *Human Stage*, p. 191.

33 On the large central door of Blackfriars being used to open up on a 'discovery' space, see Orrell, *Human Stage*, p. 192.

34 Shirley, *St. Patrick for Ireland*, p. 131, where a sd requires 'An altar discovered'; pp. 133 and 146, where sds make clear that at least two doors were on stage; and p. 246, where a sd calls for the magician Archimagus to sink into the ground. Bentley rightly points to the sparseness of evidence for innovations like the use of a scenic stage at Werburgh Street (*JCS*, IV, 51).

35 H. Burnell, *Landgartha* (Dublin, 1641; Wing 5751) sig. [Cv] (sd indicating a 'discovery'

area); sigs. D and [I 4v] (sds respectively for an entry and an exit 'in the middle'); sigs. F 3 and [H 4] (two [flanking] doors).

36 A.H. Stevenson, 'Shirley's Years in Ireland,' *Review of English Studies* 20 (1944), 19–28.

37 Whether Wentworth and Ogilby personally recruited Shirley in London between June and November 1636 will probably never be known (Stevenson, 'Shirley's Years in Ireland,' p. 20), but whatever form the initial approach took, it would have seemed more appealing to Shirley because the new Dublin theatre was then already open, not merely a projection.

38 *SPC*, p. 150 and pp. 154–6.

39 Sir Henry Herbert had reproved him, and the queen's men, for offensive topicality early in the 1630s (*Sir Henry Herbert*, ed. Adams, p. 19). On the extent of the master of the revels' authority, which is not likely to have extended to Ireland, see R. Dutton, 'Ben Jonson and the Master of the Revels,' in Mulryne and Shewring, *Theatre and Government*, pp. 57–86.

40 Shirley wrote two known prologues for John Fletcher's plays in Dublin (J. Shirley, *Narcissus, or, The Self-Lover* [London, 1646; Wing 3480], pp. 35–6 and 42–3; W. Gifford and A. Dyce, eds. *The Dramatic Works and Poems of James Shirley*, 6 vols [London, 1833; repr New York, 1966] VI, 490 and 493–4).

41 Stevenson, 'First Irish Theater,' p. 159 and note 65.

42 The patent of 8 May 1661 suggests as much (PRO, C. 66/2995, mb. 38 obverse; *EIS*, p. 181): 'Whereas Iohn Ogilby gentleman was heretofore by Instrumente of the hand and seale of Thomas late Earle of Strafford then deputie of our said Kingdome of Ireland bearing date at Dublin the Eight and twentieth day of ffebruary in the yeare of our lord one thousand six hundred thirtie and seaven nominated and appointed Master of the Revelles in and through our said Kingdome of Ireland and in pursuance thereof he did at his owne greate costes and charges as wee are informed erect a publick Theater in our Cittie of Dublin *and did effectually reduce the publick presentacions of tragedies and comedies to the proper and harmeles use whereby those recreacions formerly obnoxious were made inoffensive to such of our subjectes and other strangers voluntarily resorting thereunto*' (my italics).

43 B. Rich, *The Irish Hvbbvb or, The English Hve and Crie* (London, 1617; *STC* 20989), p. 37. See also the 1635 edict cited below, note 77.

44 *SPC*, p. 146.

45 Stevenson, 'First Irish Theater,' pp. 155–7, also suggests Thomas Jordan, but *pace* Stevenson, the name Jordan is *not* a rare name in Dublin registers at this date. Stevenson's suggestion that the former Cockpit players William Allen, Michael Bowyer, Hugh Clark, and William Robins may have come to Dublin (pp. 149–50) is plausible, but wanting proof, and I have not encountered them in any of the unpublished Dublin documents I have examined.

46 NLI, MS 104, fol. [11], misread in *EIS*, pp. 30–1, note 6. This document, containing amongst other things excerpts from the Vestry Book of St Werburgh's Church, was

made by Lyon evidently before 1754, when the original was lost in a fire. If, however, 'Rookes' is Lyon's mistranscription, and if the original did in fact read Weekes, then that would certainly be credible, since like Armiger, Weekes too was a Red Bull member (*SPC*, p. 448). But since all this is speculation, Weekes's name must now be dropped from the list of known Werburgh Street actors.

47 *JCS*, II, 350; *SPC*, pp. 441–2 and 448. Both omit this Irish reference.

48 RCB, P. 328/5/1, p. 188. This is a Vestry Book of St John the Evangelist. Cooke's levy was 4s.

49 *JCS*, II, 413. *SPC*, p. 138, table 2; also p. 442.

50 *SPC*, pp. 123–31, p. 442 and passim, on relations between the Red Bull and the Cockpit.

51 Allen, 'Shirley's Years in Ireland,' p. 24. Trips taken in the spring probably coincided with the traditional Lenten closure of the theatre, which Werburgh Street doubtless also observed. But see below.

52 RCB, P. 326/27/3/28, fol. [3v]. This is a set of St Werburgh's Poor Relief levies.

53 On Perry, see *SPC*, p. 392, note 63 (though Perry's possible Dublin career goes unnoticed).

54 RCB, P. 326/27/3/28, fol. [6]. The cess notes a 'Mr Crooke & Mr Serger stacioners {*read* stacioners}' resident on the south side of Castle Street (fol. [4v]). See A. H. Stevenson, 'Shirley's Publishers: The Partnership of Crooke and Cooke,' *The Library*, 4th Series, 25 (1944–5), 140–61 (the Werburgh's cess reference is not noticed).

55 *JCS*, II, 431–2; *SPC*, pp. 391, 433, 436 and 448. His last known recorded appearance was at Coventry on 22 April 1636. In less than a month hence plague would close the London theatres. If the Dublin Errington and the actor are indeed one and the same, he presumably came to Ireland after that date.

56 *SPC*, pp. 38–41 and p. 438.

57 I have not noticed other known touring members of the Red Bull, Nicholas Hanson, Richard Weekes, John Kirke, Hugh Tatterdell, David Feeris, Robert Hint, and George Williams (*SPC*, p. 448), in unpublished Dublin documents that I have read.

58 Three-quarters of the plays selected for court performance between 1613 and 1625 had been by Fletcher, Shakespeare, and Jonson, in that descending order of priority (Edwards, Bentley, McLuskie, and Potter, *Revels History of Drama in English Volume IV*, p. 80). Shakespeare is not reported in Werburgh Street. Perhaps record loss may be held accountable. Shirley's adaptation of at least one play by Thomas Middleton, *No Wit, No Help like a Woman's*, was played in Werburgh Street, as Shirley's Prologue to it testifies (Shirley, *Narcissus*, pp. 40–1). To the Werburgh Street repertoire gathered by A. Harbage, *Annals of English Drama 975–1700*, rev. S. Schoenbaum (London, 1964), pp. 136–41, should be added: Ben Jonson, *The Alchemist*; possibly Henry Burnell's first play, alluded to in the Prologue of *Landgartha* (see below) but now lost; two John Fletcher plays (their identity is conjectured by Stevenson, 'Shirley's Publishers,' pp. 150–1); and possibly Shirley's *The Opportunity*.

59 Circumstantial evidence is strong for Werburgh Street production of four others: *The Constant Maid, The Gentleman of Venice, The Opportunity,* and *The Politician* (see *JCS,* V, 1095–6, 1112–14, 1134–7 and 1137–9 respectively).

60 Art and Wit, repeated concepts in his Prologues to plays performed in Ireland, allow no simple interpretation. They might perhaps be understood as the civilizing and aesthetic presentation of concerns germane to good theatre. Audiences welcoming them would show proof of refinement. These concepts, hallmarks of theatre of a particular social brand, were in general circulation. Compare Sir William Davenant's characterization of the London Blackfriars as a playhouse where 'Art, or Witt' might be expected, as opposed to the 'shewes, Dancing, and Buckler fights' on display at the Globe (W. Davenant, *News from Plymouth* [1635], Prologue, in *The Works of Sr William D'avenant Kt Consisting of Those which were formerly Printed, and Those which he design'd for the Press* [London, 1673; Wing 320]).

61 The suggestion that *The Royall Master* was written to mark the opening of Werburgh Street is very doubtful (Stevenson, 'First Irish Theater,' p. 147, n. 3; *JCS,* V, 1140).

62 J. Shirley, *The Royall Master* (London and Dublin, 1638; *STC* 22454 and 22454a), sig. A2r–v. The dedication page is also published in Gifford and Dyce, *Dramatic Works,* IV, 103.

63 *STC* 22454, sig. [A1]. Both the London and Dublin imprints of *The Royall Master* were published in 1638.

64 Though the Red Bull company had been called to perform at court early in the Jacobean era, invitations ceased after 1617 (*SPC,* p. 127).

65 It was 'Acted in the new Theater in Dublin' (*STC* 22454, sig. [A1]), probably after 9 August 1637 (Jonson's death is alluded to in one of the dedicatory verses), and either very shortly before its castle production or very shortly after it and before publication in 1638 (it was entered in the Stationers' Register 13 March 1638 [*JCS,* V, 1140]).

66 For example, cynical maxims like Montalto's that officers of state are affected more for their office than for their person (Gifford and Dyce, *Dramatic Works,* IV, 169) chime well with Wentworth's own taste in irony repeatedly revealed in his letters. For a useful study of Shirley's dramatic preoccupations, see T.G. Fitzgibbon, 'Purpose and Theme in the Drama of James Shirley,' (PhD thesis, University College, Cork, 1982).

67 Most recently serviced obliquely, however, because his notoriously expensive masque *The Triumph of Peace,* an Inns of Court commission, implicitly presumed to offer the king advice (M. Butler, 'Politics and the Masque: *The Triumph of Peace,*' *The Seventeenth Century* 2 [1987], 117–41).

68 Gifford and Dyce, *Dramatic Works,* IV, 121–2.

69 On this antagonism, see S. Adams, 'Early Stuart Politics: Revisionism and after,' in Mulryne and Shewring, *Theatre and Government,* pp. 29–56; see pp. 37 and 40.

70 *The Triumph of Peace* was not peopled by such mythical figures as Bombo sneers at; conversely, the same could not be said of Carew's *Coelum Britannicum,* to which repre-

sentatives of the Inns of Court were invited and which was performed only five days after *The Triumph of Peace*. Here Mercury, if not 'Venus's dandiprat,' had by contrast a large role to play.

71 *JCS*, V, 1105–6.

72 Compare the Prologue to a lost play called *The General*, which again implies the presence of the military (Gifford and Dyce, *Dramatic Works*, VI, 495–6). In *The Doubtful Heir*, the military is even further valorized (though not surprisingly, in a more muted way) by being beneficially offset against courtly decadence: an old soldier says 'musk and civet / Have too long stiffled us; there's no recovery / Without the smell of gunpowder' (Gifford and Dyce, *Dramatic Works*, IV, 282).

73 To the Middleton play (Gifford and Dyce, *Dramatic Works*, VI, 492–3).

74 On the play's date, see Turner's edition, *St. Patrick for Ireland*, p. 38, and Chetwood, cited in Stevenson, 'First Irish Theater,' p. 159 and note 65.

75 Shirley, *Narcissus*, pp. 38–9, 40–1, 42–3, 44–5 and 47–8 (Gifford and Dyce, *Dramatic Works*, VI, 491–2, 492–3, 493–4, 494–5 and 495–6). Also, note the Prologue to the play of Thomas Middleton, where Shirley mentions that he has been in Dublin for two years; this establishes the date by which disillusion had already set in.

76 Shirley, *Narcissus*, p. 43 (Gifford and Dyce, *Dramatic Works*, VI, 494). Both Stockwell, *Dublin Theatres*, p. 7 and P. Kavanagh, *The Irish Theatre* (Tralee, 1946), p. 20, interpreted this Prologue to mean that it was the Werburgh Street Theatre company itself that put on these alternative displays, of which Shirley did not approve. But this interpretation is without foundation. Rather, on the significance of the Prologue, see the note following.

77 Public pageants, as already seen, were strongly associated with the trades and the interests of the city government. For bears (and bulls), see the corporation edict of 28 April 1620 (DCA, MR/5/11, mb. 67 dorse; *CARD*, III, 123–4): 'fforasmuch as Certaine the Commons Complained to this Assemblie against diuers new vaine Customes lately growing in this Cittie and vsed by forriners and strandgers As Bull baytinges Beare baytinges and other vnciuell and vnlawful games and excercises allureing vnto them from all partes of the Cittie other mens prentizes and seruantes who thereby fall into much vice and idlenes to ye decaie and Impouerishing of theire Masters and other the Cittizens, Wherefore and for the Auoyding of such vncivell plaies and excercises, It is enacted and ordained by the said Aucthoritie that ye Maior for the time being shall from time to time restraine the Common passadge of Beares and Bulles through the Cittie or any parte thereof, to draw prentizes or other seruantes to ye bayting of them, and likewise by aduise of mr Recorder or other Counsell of this Cittie, ₐ⌈punish⌉ all such offendors formerlie Complained of by fines and Imprisonment as he shall thinke fitt./'; and the Irish parliament of 1635 (26 January to 21 March, prorogued to 24 March) legislated against: 'all idle persons going about in any Countrey either begging, or using any subtile craft or vnlawfull games or playes … all Fencers, Beare-wards,

Common players of Enter-ludes, & Minstrels wandring abroad, all Juglers, and wandring persons' (*A Collection of all the Statutes now in Use in the Kingdom of Ireland* [Dublin, 1678; Wing 356], pp. 456–7). On bagpipers, compare chapter 6 and note 223.

78 Turner, *St. Patrick for Ireland*, p. 82, lines 1–2 and 5–7.

79 Compare the contemporary London interest in witchcraft on stage. Though this had always been popular, interest in it was currently being reinvigorated (*SPC*, pp. 146–7).

80 Turner, *St. Patrick for Ireland*, p. 97, sd.

81 But then, theatre at this date was hardly a friend of sectarian Protestant zeal. There is also a possibility that Shirley may himself have been a Catholic (*JCS*, V, 1067–8; though some doubt has been cast on this by W.D. Wolf, 'Some New Facts and Conclusions about James Shirley: Residence and Religion,' *Notes and Queries* 226 [1982], 133–4). Perhaps more than arguing Shirley's Catholic credal allegiance, the play's 'Catholic' tone, centring on St Patrick, may rather have signalled approval for Laudian high-church liturgy. A public parade of such approval would not have offended Wentworth, Laud's friend. Moreover, St Patrick's recent laundering as a respectable Protestant by Archbishop James Ussher in *A Discourse of the Religion Anciently Professed by the Irish and British* of 1623 would have made him ripe for such treatment (and see further J. McCafferty, 'St Patrick for the Church of Ireland: James Ussher's *Discourse*,' *Bullán* 3 [1997–8], 87–101). If this explanation of the play's 'Catholic' tone is correct, however, it is hard to imagine that Ussher would have rejoiced over the brand of Protestantism that St Patrick had been made to purvey.

82 Compare the eulogy on the soldier's life in *The Gentleman of Venice*, Act III, sc. ii (Gifford and Dyce, *Dramatic Works*, V, 40). The Dublin imprint of this play is circumstantial evidence for its Dublin performance.

83 Note not only the second soldier's reference to the typically Irish practice of coshering (Turner, *St. Patrick for Ireland*, p. 216, line 7), but also his statement that he will not return to the scene of his assault, and that if he does, 'let me be glib'd' (p. 223, line 92). Turner has explained this as a corruption of 'libbed' ('castrated'), but it could equally include the sense to be docked of one's glib, that characteristic Irish forelock.

84 What Bartley, *Teague, Shenkin and Sawney*, pp. 9–10 has found for England holds true for Ireland: compare John Clavell's *Introduction to the Sword Dance* (discussed in chapter 6 and printed in Appendix IV).

85 Burnell, *Landgartha*, sig. [A4v]: 'this … he made / To please you, not for Money.'

86 Ibid.

87 Ibid., sig. [A1] and sig. [Kv].

88 This is not to imply that *Landgartha* was a court bespeak (for there is no evidence of that), simply that a new play opening at Werburgh Street at such a busy time in the city would have seemed opportune to all interested parties, actors and audiences alike. As was traditional, the parliament was held at Dublin Castle.

89 This Act was the first in the series constituting the Third Transmission to the Dublin

parliament opening 16 March 1640 (*The Journals of the House of Commons of the Kingdom of Ireland*, 19 vols [Dublin, 1796–1800] I, 127, col. b). The bill did not receive its first reading until the Dublin parliament of 16 Charles I, however, on 27 October 1640 (I, 160, col. a).

90 *DNB*, VII, 386; Gilbert, *City of Dublin*, I, 296–7. His marriage is noted in Dublin, Genealogical Office, MS 72, p. 55 and MS 172, p. 78. It is probable that Burnell (and possibly Shirley) was Catholic; this may also indicate the tolerant ethos of the Werburgh Street Theatre.

91 *Journals of the House of Commons*, I, 129, col. b.

92 *Journals of the House of Commons*, I, 66, col. a (first reading of bill, 23 July 1634) and I, 81, col. a (voting down of bill, 17 November 1634). Wentworth wrote to Laud 31 January 1634 (Knowler, *Letters and Dispatches*, I, 188) expressing concern that the relatively clandestine nature of marriages contracted by some people in private houses meant that any man thus married, who had a mind to repudiate his wife and offspring, had no public witnesses to gainsay him.

93 And he showed it in a prominent place: his Amazonian Prologue is reminiscent of Jonson's armed Prologue to *Poetaster* (as Kavanagh, *Irish Theatre*, p. 41, noted; G.A. Wilkes, ed., *The Complete Plays of Ben Jonson*, 4 vols [Oxford, 1981–2] II, 127).

94 Burnell, *Landgartha*, sig. [A 1].

95 Volumes on Scotland (ed. J.J. McGavin) and Wales (ed. David N. Klausner) are being prepared under the auspices of the Records of Early English Drama project and are much looked forward to for they will help greatly to make good the deficit. The most recent volume in that series, Rosalind C. Hays and C.E. McGee/Sally Joyce and Evelyn Newlyn, eds., *Dorset/Cornwall* (Toronto, 1999), is extremely helpful. Useful recent work on Cornwall has also been done by B. Murdoch, *Cornish Literature* (Cambridge, 1993).

96 This advance has notably been thanks to the Records of Early English Drama project, whose volumes have become the backbone of any serious study of early drama and performance in the British Isles.

APPENDIXES

1 My terminology follows M.B. Parkes, *English Cursive Book Hands 1250–1500* (Oxford, 1969; repr with minor revisions, London, 1979). For Marsh scribe A, compare Parkes, *Book Hands*, pls 7 and 8; for scribe(s) B (and ?D), pl. 22 (ii); for scribe C, pls 5 (i) and (ii).

2 Compare Parkes, *Book Hands*, pl. 22 (ii); in the hierarchy of scripts, Textura is the most careful and formal.

3 To argue that the scribe added it merely for the sake of a more complete correspondence between his copy and his exemplar seems less likely an explanation than that he included it for the sake of its potential usefulness. Also, the presence of alternative forms of the

Elevatio perhaps suggests that it was envisaged that this ritual at least would be performed. (The *Elevatio crucis et hostie* ritual, if performed, normally preceded Easter Sunday Matins; Young, *Drama*, I, 114.)

4 Another possibility, that both manuscripts had migrated to St John's from Christ Church Cathedral, will be canvassed below. Gwynn, 'Anglo-Irish Theatre,' pp. 260–1, believed that both manuscripts were imported from England. I think this unlikely. W. Hawkes, 'Liturgy,' pp. 41 and 46, notes the appearance of St Werburgh in both processionals, which he evidently attributes to the presence of a considerable number of Chester settlers in late-medieval Dublin (the cult of St Werburgh was particularly strong in Chester and, as Hawkes notes, p. 46, her appearance in Sarum lists is uncommon). He observes that she features again in a third extant medieval manuscript known to have belonged to St John's, Dublin, an antiphonary of the fifteenth century (TCD, MS 79 [B. 1. 4]), and also in the so-called Clondalkin Breviary (TCD, MS 78 [B. 1. 3]). Though he assumes settlers in Dublin from Chester, his contention can soon be supported by historical evidence. Work on the written dialect of medieval Hiberno-English has stressed the importance in it of a northwest Midlands linguistic stratum (south Lancashire and Cheshire). See A. McIntosh and M.L. Samuels, 'Prolegomena to a Study of Medieval Anglo-Irish,' *Medium Ævum* 37 (1968), 1–11, esp. p. 8. Evidently sufficient numbers were coming from these parts of England to affect the complexion of written Hiberno-English. There are also various documented points of historical contact between Ireland and Cheshire. When, for example, Richard II came personally to intervene in Irish affairs in 1395, he brought with him a large troop of Cheshire archers. Chester was also, of course, a port with important trading links with Dublin. At least by the sixteenth century, Dublin was thought to contain a substantial Chester enclave. Richard Stanihurst speaks in the sixteenth century of the church of St Werburgh in Dublin and the activity in the city of people from Chester (Gilbert, *City of Dublin*, I, 27–30). With respect to the question of whether or not both manuscripts were made in Dublin, I would also draw attention to the group of responds and proses for the feasts of SS Andrew, Nicholas, the Virgin (feast of the Purification), the Holy Cross, Catherine, Patrick, and Audoen, which concludes R. It is intriguing to note that each of these (excepting the Holy Cross) has a church dedicated to him or her in Dublin and not far from the site of St John's. Furthermore, T. Bailey, *The Processions of Sarum and the Western Church* (Toronto, 1971), p. 7, observes that added to the *Sanctorale* in M are processions for SS Patrick, Columba, and Stephen; although the first two are widely known Irish saints, the *circumstances* of their addition surely sustain the inference that M is of Irish manufacture.

5 A. Gwynn, 'Provincial and Diocesan Decrees of the Diocese of Dublin during the Anglo-Norman Period,' *Archivium Hibernicum* 11 (1944), 31–117; see p. 85: 'statuimus et ordinamus quod festum sancte Anne memorate in feria proxima post festum sancti Jacobi apostoli … in singulis ecclesiis diocesis et provincie predictarum sub duplici

festo singulis annis diebus suis solempniter celebrentur' ('we decree and ordain that the feast of St Anne commemorated on the next feria after the feast of St James the Apostle … should be solemnly celebrated as a double feast on their days each year in all churches of the aforesaid diocese and province'). Of course, as R.W. Pfaff, *New Liturgical Feasts in Later Medieval England* (Oxford, 1970), pp. 2–5, has noted, observance of a feast may precede its official ratification. If the exemplars behind M and R were imported from England, and if they included St Anne's feast in their calendar, then the date of M and R is more likely to be after 1383 (the feast was ordered by Urban VI in order to popularize the marriage of Richard II with Anne of Bohemia; Pfaff, *New Liturgical Feasts*, p. 2).

6 For example, since no mention of St Winifred is made anywhere in either of the manuscripts, it might appear that they ought to be dated before 1415, or even indeed before 1398 (in 1415 Henry Chichele, archbishop of Canterbury, raised the rank of her feast throughout his province, though it had already been established in the province of Canterbury by Roger Walden, archbishop during the exile of Thomas Arundel, in 1398; on this see D. Wilkins, ed., *Concilia Magnae Britanniae et Hiberniae ab Anno MCCCL ad Annum MDXLV*, 4 vols [London, 1737] III, 376–7 and 234–6 respectively). The same might be said also on account of the omission of any mention of St David, whose feast was similarly established for the Canterbury province in 1398. Cumulatively, such omissions may be significant, but it still seems safer to argue from who is included rather than from who is left out.

7 As mentioned earlier, there is no obvious evidence to the contrary. However, the possibility also occurs to me that both M and R may have been originally manufactured for use in Christ Church Cathedral. By the late fifteenth century, for reasons now obscure, both could have passed into St John's custody and use, since it was a parish church that the cathedral was obliged to serve.

8 Hawkes, 'Liturgy,' p. 55; de Derby was succeeded by de Lokynton. The date of de Lokynton's death is given as 9 August 1397 in BL, MS Additional 4787, fol. 319 (a seventeenth-century antiquarian compilation by Sir James Ware).

9 Archbishop Luke of Dublin, *c* 1230, had decreed that the Augustinian canons should serve in person at the church of St John the Evangelist, and not assign its cure to any deputy. On the flourishing of the chapter under de Derby see Mills, *Account Roll*, p. xxv.

10 O. Pächt, 'A Giottesque Episode in English Medieval Art,' *Journal of the Warburg and Courtauld Institute* 6 (1943), 51–70.

11 It is possible that liturgical drama was being acted elsewhere in Dublin at an earlier date. Dolan, *La drame liturgique de Pâques en Normandie et en Angleterre au moyen âge* (Paris, 1975), p. 114, reasonably speculates that Christ Church Cathedral may have been the first to incorporate liturgical drama in its ritual.

12 Possibly a boy sang the angel's part, since there was a strong tradition for this (see, for example, Young, *Drama*, I, 240–1), and the tessitura of the angel's line is perceptibly

higher than that of the other singers. Moreover, trained boy singers were probably available in the nearby cathedral of Christ Church (when the statutes of the new foundation of Christ Church in 1539 provided for boy choristers, they were putting on a formal basis an existing tradition; Harrison, *Music in Medieval Britain*, pp. 44 and 437–9). But this need not necessarily have been so.

13 F.L. Cross and E.A. Livingstone, eds., *The Oxford Dictionary of the Christian Church*, 3rd ed (Oxford, 1997), p. 1755.

14 Dolan, *La drame liturgique de Pâques*, pp. 157–72.

15 Ibid., pp. 167–71.

16 A quality noted by Young, *Drama*, I, 350; even the one small incongruity he notices has been deemed justifiable by W.L. Smoldon, *The Music of the Medieval Church Dramas* (Oxford, 1980), p. 361, note 3. Smoldon (p. 361) also assumes one man to have been largely responsible for putting the play together. If the play were not the product of one principal editor, but rather the result of gradual, piecemeal revision, it is harder to imagine such coherence being achieved.

17 Compare Young, *Drama*, I, 393. Dolan, *Drame Liturgique de Pâques*, p. 158, compares the Dublin and Fleury texts (the word *obiit* has been left out of her seventh line of the Dublin text). My line numbers here and subsequently refer specifically to the text lines of the edition of Appendix I.

18 Compare Young, *Drama*, I, 394.

19 See respectively Young, *Drama*, I, 666; I, 441; and I, 382 for these plays (the Barking play may have been introduced by Abbess Katherine of Sutton, between 1363 and 1376). The Tours and Fleury versions have the order 'Heu! misera (misera] misere *Fleury*) … Heu! redempcio … Heu! consolacio,' while the Barking version, closer to Dublin, has the order 'Heu! misere … Heu! consolacio … Heu! redempcio.' Compare lines 17, 19, and 21 of the Dublin play below. A version of these lines is in fact to be found even earlier, in the twelfth century (Young, *Drama*, I, 269–70). The lines 'Iam, iam, ecce' of Dublin (lines 24–5) are also found in a few places, as for example in the *Ludus paschalis* of the *Carmina Burana* manuscript and the Shrewsbury Fragments (see Young, *Drama*, I, 436, and II, 517, respectively), but again it will be noted that their earliest appearance is in manuscripts of the thirteenth century.

20 The earliest appearance of the *Quem queritis* dialogue in these islands is in the tenth-century *Regularis Concordia* (Symons, *Regularis Concordia*, pp. 49–50). The earliest witness to the Rouen *Visitatio* is Paris, Bibliothèque Nationale, MS Lat. 904 (*c* 1200; Dolan, *Drame liturgique de Pâques*, p. 83). The connections between it and the Dublin play are lines 42–3 ('uenite et uidete … positus fuerat') and lines 52–3 ('Et euntes … surrexit'). Compare Young, *Drama*, I, 660, for the Rouen text in MS Lat. 904.

21 The line unique to the Dublin play, unaccounted for elsewhere, is line 56. Its music is also unique. Susan Rankin, 'The Music of the Medieval Liturgical Drama in France and in England,' PhD thesis, 2 vols (Cambridge, 1982) I, 292, observes that thirteenth-

century ceremonies can be distinguished by their introduction of new metrical material. This is the case here.

22 R could not have copied from M since then it too would have omitted the words of the first Mary (lines 28–9), and the words added by the later correcting hand are in any case a little corrupt. M cannot have copied R, unless we assume a high degree of editorial intervention on the part of the M scribe, not only in shortening (generally) the rubrics but also occasionally in rewording them (for example, lines 47 and 55). This is not strictly impossible, but taken together amounts to an improbably tall order.

23 The simplest stemma would be:

Other possible stemmata would be mere variations on this basic model.

Bibliography

The bibliography is divided into two parts, I (primary sources, itself in two sections: (i) manuscript sources; and (ii) printed sources), and II, secondary works. In I(i) are listed alphabetically by repository all manuscripts cited in this study, while I(ii) also includes in its list of printed sources modern editions of some of the manuscripts cited in I(i). In a few cases, manuscript shelfmarks are followed by their old shelfmarks in parentheses, since in many secondary works the old shelfmark is still customarily used. (The names by which a few famous manuscripts are more familiarly known may also be included in parentheses.) Apart from primary sources and secondary works cited repeatedly and referred to in the Notes by abbreviation or acronym (for whose bibliographical details see separately under Abbreviations, pp. xi–xii), references in the notes, after their first appearance, are usually shortened to the author's/ editor's surname plus short title.

I(i)

Armagh, Armagh Public Library
The History and Antiquties of Dublin, no shelfmark

Belfast, Public Record Office of Northern Ireland
DIO 4/2/3
T. 510/2

Brussels, Bibliothèque royale Albert Ier
2324–40
4190–200
5301–20
7672–4 (Codex Salmanticensis)

Cambridge, University Library
Mm. 5. 30

Chatsworth House Library, Derbyshire
Book of Lismore
Lismore Papers, Volume 1 (item 136)
Lismore Papers, Volume 2 (item 20)
Lismore Papers, Volume 8 (item 55)
Lismore Papers, Volume 8 (item 107)
Lismore Papers, Volume 14 (item 1)
Lismore Papers, Volume 19 (item 105)
Lismore Papers, Volume 25
Lismore Papers, Volume 26
Lismore Papers, Volume 27

Clonalis, co. Roscommon
Book of the O'Connor Don

Cork, Cork Archives Institute
F (i)
U 138

Dublin, Dublin City Archives
C1/2/1
Fr/Reg/1
Fr/Reg/2
Fr/Roll/2
G1/1
MR/5/1
MR/5/2
MR/5/6
MR/5/7
MR/5/9
MR/5/10
MR/5/11
MR/5/12
MR/17
MR/35
Charter of incorporation, issued at Westminster, 21 April 1548

Dublin, Dublin City Library
80
209

Dublin, Genealogical Office
72
172

Dublin, King's Inns Library
38 (Black Book of King's Inns)

Dublin, Leeson Street, Jesuit Archives
'Missio Societatis Jesu in Hibernia ab initio ad usque annum 1655 ...' no shelfmark.

Dublin, Marsh's Library
Z.3.1.5 (Codex Kilkenniensis)
Z.4.2.20

Dublin, National Archives
2/447/16
2/448/1, KB 2/7

Dublin, National Library of Ireland
104
2510
2549
2552
3302
6897
6898
6899
6900
8013
8065 (item 4)
11048 (item 2)
16085
D 3302
G 992
G 1200 (Book of Magauran)
Collectanea Vol XVI

Dublin, Representative Church Body Library
C/2/106 (St Patrick's Cathedral, Proctor's Accounts, 1509–10, provisional shelfmark)
C/2/107 (St Patrick's Cathedral, Proctor's Accounts, 1555, provisional shelfmark)

C/6/1/2 (White Book of Christ Church)
C/6/1/7/2
C/6/1/26/3 (item 26)
C/6/1/26/3 (item 27)
C/6/1/26/13
D 11/1/1 (Red Book of Ossory)
P. 326/27/1/1
P. 326/27/1/2
P. 326/27/1/4
P. 326/27/1/5
P. 326/27/1/6
P. 326/27/1/8
P. 326/27/1/9
P. 326/27/1/10
P. 326/27/3/28
P. 328/5/1

Dublin, Royal Irish Academy
132 (23 D 2)
236 (Stowe B iv 1)
475 (24 P 25; *Leabhar Chlainne Suibhne*)
535 (23 P 2; Book of Lecan)
536 (23 P 12; Book of Ballymote)
756 (23 E 26)
998 (23 F 21)
1134 (23 E 29; Book of Fermoy)
1135 (24 G 15)
1219 (Stowe C iii 1)
1223 (Stowe D iv 2)
1229 (23 E 25; Lebor na hUidre)
1230 (23 P 16; *Leabhar Breac*)

Dublin, Trinity College
78 (B. 1. 3)
79 (B. 1. 4)
543/2/14
574 (E. 3. 20)
575 (E. 3. 21)
581 (E. 3. 18)
591 (E. 3. 28)
673 (F. 3. 19)

772 (E. 4. 11)
786 (D. 3. 16)
842 (F. 3. 16)
886 (I. 4. 11)
1282 (H. 1. 8)
1293 (H. 1. 19)
1316 (H. 2. 15a)
1318 (H. 2. 16; Yellow Book of Lecan)
1337 (H. 3. 18)
1339 (H. 2. 18; Book of Leinster)
1433 (E. 3. 5)
1447 (item 6)
Mun/V/5/I

Durham, Dean and Chapter Muniments
Misc. Ch. 5822

Edinburgh, Advocates' Library
72. 1. 36

Huntington Library, Huntington, CA
HA 15057

Kilkenny, Kilkenny Corporation Archives
CR/1/D (*Liber Primus Kilkenniensis*)
CR/J4
CR/J10
CR/J11
CR/J13
CR/J15
CR/J22 (9)
CR/K13

Killiney, co. Dublin, Franciscan Library
A 20

London, British Library
Additional 4763
Additional 4784
Additional 4791
Additional 4796

Additional 4799
Additional 11687
Additional 12562
Additional 18747
Additional 18991
Additional 29614
Additional 30512 (*Leabhar Uí Mhaoilchonaire*)
Additional 33991
Cotton Julius A. vii
Cotton Nero A. vii
Cotton Tiberius C. vi
Egerton 88
Egerton 97
Egerton 1765
Harley 432
Harley 1291
Lansdowne 92
Stowe 180

London, Lambeth Palace Library
603 (Carew Papers)
611 (Carew Papers)
612 (Carew Papers)
614 (Carew Papers)
615 (Carew Papers)
621 (Carew Papers)
623 (Book of Howth)
627 (Carew Papers)
629 (Carew Papers)

London, Public Record Office
SP 60/1
SP 60/4
SP 60/6
SP 61/2
SP 63/3
SP 63/9
SP 63/54
SP 63/55
SP 63/104

SP 63/119
SP 63/143
SP 63/144
SP 63/146
SP 63/148
SP 63/151
SP 63/180
SP 63/186
SP 63/191
SP 63/200
SP 63/202/Part 1
SP 63/207/Part 4
SP 63/208/Part 1
SP 63/214
SP 63/215
SP 63/218
SP 63/230
SP 63/255
SP 63/256
SP 63/345
SP 65/9
C. 66/379
C. 66/2995

Maidstone, Kent Archives Office
U1475 A50/10
U1475 A56/2
U1475 018
U1475 021
U1475 025/1
U1475 027/3
U1475 028/19
U1475 028/44
U1475 031
U1475 034

Northampton, Northamptonshire Record Office
Fitzwilliam Irish 30
Fitzwilliam Irish 31
Fitzwilliam Irish 32

460   Bibliography

Fitzwilliam Irish 33
Fitzwilliam Irish 42
Fitzwilliam Irish 45
Fitzwilliam Irish 55

Orléans, Bibliothèque de la Ville
201

Oxford, Bodleian Library
Add. C. 39
Aubrey 7
Aubrey 8
Carte 176
Lat. th. d. 1
Rawlinson B. 478
Rawlinson B. 484
Rawlinson B. 502
Rawlinson B. 512
Rawlinson G. 185
Rawlinson liturg. D. 4
Tanner 444

Oxford, Corpus Christi College
94

Oxford, Exeter College
154

Oxford, University College
103

Paris, Bibliothèque Mazarine
1869

Paris, Bibliothèque nationale
Lat. 904

Rennes, Bibliothèque municipale
598 (15489)

Sheffield, Sheffield City Archives
Wentworth Woodhouse Muniments, Strafford Letter Book 7
Wentworth Woodhouse Muniments, Strafford Letter Book 10

Trowbridge, Wiltshire Record Office
865/502

Uppsala, University Library
H. 248

I (ii)

Ainsworth, J. 'Corporation Book of the Irishtown of Kilkenny 1537–1628.' *Analecta Hibernica* 28 (1978), 1–78.
Ambrose of Milan. *De Elia et Ieiunio.* Patrologia Latina 14. Paris, 1845.
Aphorismical Discovery of Treasonable Faction. In *A Contemporary History of Affairs in Ireland from 1641 to 1652,* ed. J.T. Gilbert.
Appleby, C.J., ed. *A Calendar of Material Relating to Ireland from the High Court of Admiralty Examinations 1536–1641.* Dublin, 1992.
Articles to be inqvired of by the Church-wardens and Questmen of every Parish in the Lord Primates Visitation Metropoliticall. Dublin, 1638; *STC* 14265.9.
Articles to be Inquired of by the Chvrch-Wardens and Questmen of every Parish, in the ordinary Visitation of the Right Reverend Father in God George by divine Providence Lord Bishop of Cloyne. Dublin, 1639; *STC* 14265.7.
Atkinson, E.G., ed. *Calendar of the State Papers relating to Ireland, of the Reign of Elizabeth, 1600, March–October, preserved in the Public Record Office.* London, 1903.
Atkinson, R., ed. *The Passions and Homilies from the Leabhar Breac: Text, Translation and Glossary.* Todd Lecture Series. Volume 2. Dublin, 1887.
– *The Yellow Book of Lecan.* Dublin, 1896.
Aubrey, John. *'Brief Lives,' chiefly of Contemporaries, set down by John Aubrey between the Years 1669 and 1696.* Ed. A. Clark. 2 vols. Oxford, 1898.
Baker, D.C., J.L. Murphy, and L.B. Hall, Jr., eds. *The Late Medieval Religious Plays of Bodleian MSS Digby 133 and e Museo 160.* EETS, os 283. Oxford, 1982.
Bale, John. *The Vocacyon of Johan Bale to the bishoprick of Ossorie in Ireland.* Wesel, 1553; *STC* 1307.
– *The Complete Plays of John Bale.* Ed. P. Happé. 2 vols. Cambridge, 1986.
Barnum, P.H., ed. *Dives and Pauper.* EETS os 275 and 280. London, 1976–80.
Barrington, Jonah. *Personal Sketches of His Own Times.* 3rd ed. 3 vols. London, 1869.
Beadle, R., ed. *The York Plays.* London, 1982.

Beadle, R., and P. Meredith, eds. *The York Play: A Facsimile of British Library Additional 35290 together with a Facsimile of the Ordo Paginarum Section of the A/Y Memorandum Book*. Leeds Texts and Monographs. Medieval Drama Facsimiles VII. Leeds, 1983.

Bergin, O.J., R.I. Best, K. Meyer, and J.G. O'Keeffe, eds. *Anecdota from Irish Manuscripts*. 5 vols. Halle and Dublin, 1907–13.

Berry, H.F. 'Minute Book of the Corporation of Dublin, known as the "Friday Book," 1567–1611.' *Proceedings of the Royal Irish Academy* 30 (1912–13), 477–514.

Berry, H.F., ed. *Statutes and Ordinances, and Acts of Parliament of Ireland. King John to Henry V.* Dublin, 1907.

Best, R.I. 'The Settling of the Manor of Tara.' *Ériu* 4 (1910), 121–67.

– 'Prognostications from the Raven and the Wren.' *Ériu* 8 (1916), 120–6.

Best, R.I., and O. Bergin, eds. *Lebor na hUidre*. Dublin and London, 1929.

Best, R.I., O. Bergin, M.A. O'Brien, and A. O'Sullivan, eds. *The Book of Leinster formerly Lebar na Núachongbála*. 6 vols. Dublin, 1954–83.

Bieler, L., ed. *The Irish Penitentials*. Dublin, 1963.

– *Four Latin Lives of St. Patrick*. Dublin, 1971.

Binchy, D.A. 'Bretha Crólige.' *Ériu* 12 (1938), 1–77.

– 'The Old-Irish Table of Penitential Commutations.' *Ériu* 19 (1962), 47–62.

– '*Mellbretha*.' *Celtica* 8 (1968), 144–54.

Binchy, D.A., ed. *Críth Gablach*. Dublin, 1941.

'Bodley's Visit to Lecale, County of Down, A.D. 1602–3.' *Ulster Journal of Archaeology* 2 (1854), 73–95.

Breatnach, L., ed. *Uraicecht na Ríar*. Early Irish Law Series. Volume 2. Dublin, 1987.

Burnell, Henry. *Landgartha*. Dublin, 1641; Wing 5751.

Butler, R., ed. *The Annals of Ireland by Friar John Clyn and Thady Dowling*. Dublin, 1849.

Camden, William. *Britannia*. 1st ed. London, 1586; *STC* 4503.

– *Britannia*. 6th ed. London, 1607; *STC* 4508.

Carew, Thomas. *The Poems of Thomas Carew with his Masque Coelum Britannicum*. Ed. R. Dunlap. Oxford, 1949; corrected repr. 1957.

Carey, J. 'An Edition of the Pseudo-Historical Prologue to the *Senchas Már*.' *Ériu* 45 (1994), 1–32.

Carmichael Watson, J., ed. *Mesca Ulad*. Dublin, 1941.

Carney, J., ed. *Poems on the Butlers of Ormond, Cahir, and Dunboyne (A.D. 1400–1650)*. Dublin, 1945.

Caulfield, R., ed. *The Council Book of Cork*. Guildford, 1876.

– *The Council Book of the Corporation of Youghal, from 1610 to 1659, from 1666 to 1687, and from 1690 to 1800*. Guildford, 1878.

Chamberlain, John. *The Letters of John Chamberlain*. Ed. N.E. McClure. Memoirs of the American Philosophical Society 12. 2 vols. Philadelphia, 1939.

Churchyard, Thomas. *A generall rehearsall of warres*. London, 1579; *STC* 5235.

Clark, J.W. *The Observances in Use at the Augustinian Priory of S. Giles and S. Andrew at Barnwell, Cambridgeshire.* Cambridge, 1897.

Clopper, L.M., ed. *Chester.* Records of Early English Drama. Toronto, 1979.

A Collection of all the Statutes now in Use in the Kingdom of Ireland. Dublin, 1678; Wing 356.

Collins, A., ed. *Letters and Memorials of State.* 2 vols. London, 1746.

Comyn, D., and P.S. Dineen, eds. *Foras Feasa ar Éirinn,* by Geoffrey Keating. Irish Texts Society 4, 8, 9, and 15. London, 1902–14.

Connolly, P., ed. *The Dublin Guild Merchant Roll, c. 1190–1265.* Dublin, 1992.

Constitutions of the Synod of Dublin. Dublin, 1634; STC 14264.

Davenant, William. *The Works of Sr William D'avenant Kt Consisting of Those which were formerly Printed, and Those which he design'd for the Press.* London, 1673; Wing 320.

Davis, N., ed. *Non-Cycle Plays and Fragments.* EETS, ss 1. London, 1970.

– *Non-Cycle Plays and the Winchester Dialogues.* Leeds Texts and Monographs. Medieval Drama Facsimiles V. Leeds, 1979.

Dawson, G.E. *Records of Plays and Players in Kent, 1450–1642.* Malone Society Collections 7. Oxford, 1965.

Derricke, John. *The Image of Irelande.* London, 1581; STC 6734. Facsimile reprint by D.B. Quinn. Belfast, 1985.

Douglas, Audrey, and Peter Greenfield, eds. *Cumberland/Westmorland/Gloucestershire.* Records of Early English Drama. Toronto, 1986.

Dymmok, John. *A Treatice of Ireland, by John Dymmok.* In *Tracts Relating to Ireland, printed for the Irish Archaeological Society,* ed. R. Butler. 2 vols. Dublin, 1841–3.

Eccles, M., ed. *The Macro Plays.* EETS, os 262. Oxford, 1969.

Edmundson, W. *A Journal of the Life, Travels, Sufferings, and Labour of Love in the Work of the Ministry, of that Worthy Elder and Faithful Servant of Jesus Christ, William Edmundson, who departed this Life, the thirty First of the Sixth Month, 1712.* London, 1715.

The Eighteenth Report of the Deputy Keeper of the Public Records in Ireland. Dublin, 1886.

Einarsson, B., ed. *Fagrskinna. Íslensk Fornrit* 29. Reykjavík, 1984.

Erck, J.C., ed. *A Repertory of the Inrolments on the Patent Rolls of Chancery, in Ireland; commencing with the Reign of King James I.* 2 vols. Dublin, 1846–52.

Fraser, J., P. Grosjean, and J.G. O'Keeffe, eds. *Irish Texts.* 8 vols. London, 1931–3.

Freeman, A.M., ed. *Annals of Connacht.* Dublin, 1944.

Friedberg, E., and E.L. Richter, eds. *Corpus Iuris Canonici.* 2nd ed. 2 vols. Leipzig, 1879–81.

Galloway, D., ed. *Norwich 1540–1642.* Records of Early English Drama. Toronto, 1984.

George, D., ed. *Lancashire.* Records of Early English Drama. Toronto, 1991.

Gerald of Wales. *Giraldi Cambrensis Opera Omnia.* Ed. J.S. Brewer, J.F. Dimock, and G.F. Warner. Rolls Series 21. 8 vols. London, 1861–91.

– *Expugnatio Hibernica, the Conquest of Ireland by Giraldus Cambrensis.* Ed. A.B. Scott and F.X. Martin. Dublin, 1978.

Giblin, C., ed. *Irish Franciscan Mission to Scotland 1619–1646.* Dublin, 1964.

Gifford, W., and A. Dyce, eds. *The Dramatic Works and Poems of James Shirley.* 6 vols. London, 1833; repr. New York, 1966.

Gilbert, J.T., ed. *A Contemporary History of Affairs in Ireland from 1641 to 1652.* 4 vols. Dublin, 1879–80.

– *The Manuscripts of the Marquis of Ormond, the Earl of Fingall, the Corporations of Waterford, Galway, &.* The Historical Manuscripts Commission, Tenth Report, Appendix, Part V. London, 1885.

– *Register of the Abbey of St. Thomas, Dublin.* Rolls Series 91. London, 1889.

Gillespie, R., ed. *The Proctor's Accounts of Peter Lewis, 1564–5.* Dublin, 1995.

Greene, D., ed. *Fingal Rónáin and Other Stories.* Mediaeval and Modern Irish Series. Volume 16. Dublin, 1955.

Grosart, A.B., ed. *The Lismore Papers (First Series), viz. Autobiographical Notes, Remembrances and Diaries of Sir Richard Boyle, First and 'Great' Earl of Cork.* 5 vols. London, 1886.

Gwynn, A. 'Provincial and Diocesan Decrees of the Diocese of Dublin during the Anglo-Norman Period.' *Archivium Hibernicum* 11 (1944), 31–117.

Gwynn, E., ed. *The Metrical Dindsenchas Part I.* Todd Lecture Series. Volume 8. Dublin, 1903.

– *The Metrical Dindsenchas Part III.* Todd Lecture Series. Volume 10. Dublin, 1913.

– *The Metrical Dindsenchas Part IV.* Todd Lecture Series. Volume 11. Dublin, 1924.

Harris, W. *Hibernica: or, some Antient Pieces relating to Ireland.* Dublin, 1770.

– *The History and Antiquities of the City of Dublin.* Dublin, 1776.

Harrison, A. 'Séanadh Saighre.' *Éigse* 20 (1984), 136–48.

Harvey, B.F., ed. *Documents illustrating the Rule of Walter de Wenlok, Abbot of Westminster, 1283–1307.* Camden Society, 4th ser. Volume 2. London, 1965.

Hawthorne, Nathaniel. *Nathaniel Hawthorne: The Scarlet Letter and Selected Tales.* Ed. T.E. Connolly. Harmondsworth, 1970.

Hays, Rosalind, and C.E. McGee/Sally Joyce and Evelyn Newlyn, eds. *Dorset/Cornwall.* Records of Early English Drama. Toronto, 1999.

Heist, W.W., ed. *Vitae sanctorum Hiberniae e codice olim Salmanticensi nunc Bruxellensi.* Subsidia Hagiographica 28. Brussels, 1965.

Henderson, G., ed. *Fled Bricrend.* Irish Texts Society 2. London, 1899.

Henebry, R. 'The Life of Columb Cille.' *Zeitschrift für celtische Philologie* 4 (1903), 276–331.

Hennessy, W.M., ed. *The Annals of Loch Cé.* 2 vols. London, 1871.

Hennessy, W.M., and B. Mac Carthy, eds. *Annals of Ulster.* 4 vols. Dublin, 1887–1901.

Herbert, Henry. *The Dramatic Records of Sir Henry Herbert, Master of the Revels, 1623–1673.* Ed. J.Q. Adams. New Haven, CT, 1917.

Herbert, J.D. *Irish Varieties.* London, 1836.

Higden, Ranulf. *Polychronicon Ranulphi Higden Monachi Cestrensis.* Ed. C. Babington and J.R. Lumby. Rolls Series 41. 9 vols. London, 1865–86.

Hogan, E., ed. *The Latin Lives of the Saints.* Todd Lecture Series. Volume 5. Dublin, 1894.

Holinshed, Raphael. *Holinshed's Irish Chronicle.* Ed. L. Miller and E. Power. New York, 1979.

Hore, H.F. 'Irish Bardism in 1561.' *Ulster Journal of Archaeology* 6 (1858), 165–7.

Hore, H.F., and J. Graves. *The Social State of the Southern and Eastern Counties of Ireland in the Sixteenth Century.* Dublin, 1870.

Hull, V. *Longes mac nUislenn.* New York, 1949.

Hull, V., ed. 'Cáin Domnaig.' *Ériu* 20 (1966), 51–177.

Ingram, R., ed. *Coventry.* Records of Early English Drama. Toronto 1981.

In this volume are contained all the statutes made in Ireland. London, 1572; *STC* 14129.

Irish Patent Rolls of James I. Dublin, 1966.

Jackson, K.H., ed. *Aislinge Meic Con Glinne.* Dublin, 1990.

Johnston, A.F., and M. Rogerson, eds. *York.* 2 vols. Records of Early English Drama. Toronto, 1979.

Jonson, Ben. *The Complete Plays of Ben Jonson.* Ed. G.A. Wilkes. 4 vols. Oxford, 1981–2.

The Journals of the House of Commons in the Kingdom of Ireland. 19 vols. Dublin, 1796–1800.

Jovius, P. *Regionum et insularum atque locorum descriptiones.* Basle, 1578.

Joynt, M., ed. *Tromdámh Guaire.* Mediaeval and Modern Irish Series. Volume 2. Dublin, 1931.

Keating, Geoffrey. *Trí Bior-ghaoithe an Bháis.* Ed. O. Bergin. 2nd ed. Dublin and London, 1931.

Klausner, D.N., ed. *Herefordshire/Worcestershire.* Records of Early English Drama. Toronto, 1990.

Knott, E. 'Filidh Éireann go hAointeach: William Ó Ceallaigh's Christmas Feast to the Poets of Ireland, A.D. 1351.' *Ériu* 5 (1911), 50–69.

– 'An Irish Seventeenth-Century Translation of the Rule of St. Clare.' *Ériu* 15 (1948), 1–187.

– *Irish Classical Poetry.* 2nd rev. ed. Cork, 1966.

Letters and Dispatches of the Earl of Strafforde. Ed. W. Knowler. 2 vols. London, 1739.

Letters and Papers, Foreign and Domestic, of the Reign of Henry VIII. 21 vols. London, 1862–1932.

Litton Falkiner, C. *Illustrations of Irish History and Topography, mainly of the Seventeenth Century.* London, 1904.

Londonderry and the London Companies 1609–1629, being a Survey and Other Documents submitted to King Charles I by Sir Thomas Phillips. Belfast, 1928.

Lumiansky, R.M., and D. Mills, eds. *The Chester Mystery Cycle.* EETS, ss 3 and 9. Oxford, 1974–86.

Lydgate, John. *The Minor Poems of John Lydgate.* Ed. H.N. MacCracken. EETS, os 192. London, 1934.

Mac Airt, S., and G. Mac Niocaill, eds. *The Annals of Ulster (to A.D. 1131).* Dublin, 1983.

McCarthy, D., ed. *Collections on Irish Church History.* Dublin, 1861.

McEnery, M.J., ed. 'Calendar of Christ Church Deeds 1174–1684.' In *The Twenty-third Report of the Deputy Keeper of the Public Records in Ireland.* Dublin, 1891, 75–152.

Mac Giolla Eáin, ed. *Dánta Amhráin is Caointe Sheathrúin Céitinn,* by Geoffrey Keating. Baile Átha Cliath, 1900.

Mac Giolla Læith, C., ed. *Oidheadh Chloinne hUisneach.* Irish Texts Society 56. London, 1993.

McKenna, L., ed. *Aithdioghluim Dána.* Irish Texts Society 37 and 40. Dublin, 1939–40.

– *The Book of Magauran.* Dublin, 1947.

McNeill, C., ed. *Liber Primus Kilkenniensis.* Dublin, 1931.

MacNeill, E. 'Ancient Irish Law. The Law of Status or Franchise.' *Proceedings of the Royal Irish Academy* 36 (1923), 265–316.

Mahaffy, R.P., ed. *Calendar of the State Papers relating to Ireland, of the Reign of Charles I. 1633–1647. Preserved in the Public Record Office.* London, 1901.

Marlowe, Christopher. *The Complete Works of Christopher Marlowe.* 2 vols. Ed. F. Bowers. 2nd ed. Cambridge, 1981.

– *The Complete Works of Christopher Marlowe.* Ed. R. Gill. Oxford, 1987–.

Memoirs of the Right Honourable the Marquis of Clanricarde, Lord Deputy General of Ireland. London, 1722.

Meid, W., ed. *Táin Bó Fraích.* Mediaeval and Modern Irish Series. Volume 22. Dublin, 1967.

Meredith, P., ed. *The Passion Play from the N. Town Manuscript.* London and New York, 1990.

Meyer, K., ed. *The Triads of Ireland.* Todd Lecture Series. Volume 13. Dublin, 1906.

– *The Instructions of King Cormac Mac Airt.* Todd Lecture Series. Volume 15. Dublin, 1909.

– *Bruchstüke der älteren Lyrik Irlands.* Berlin, 1919.

Middleton, Thomas. *The Works of Thomas Middleton.* Ed. A.H. Bullen. 8 vols. London, 1885–6.

Mills, J., ed. *Account Roll of the Priory of the Holy Trinity, Dublin, 1337–1346, with the Middle English Moral Play 'The Pride of Life.'* Dublin, 1891.

– *Calendar of the Justiciary Rolls or Proceedings in the Court of the Justiciar of Ireland preserved in the Public Record Office of Ireland. XXIII to XXXI Years of Edward I.* Dublin, 1905.

– *Calendar of the Justiciary Rolls or Proceedings in the Court of the Justiciar of Ireland preserved in the Public Record Office of Ireland. Edward I. Part 2. XXXIII to XXXV Years.* London, 1914.

– *Account Roll of the Priory of the Holy Trinity, Dublin, 1337–1346, with the Middle English Moral Play 'The Pride of Life.'* With new introductions by J.F. Lydon and A.J. Fletcher. Dublin, 1996.

Moryson, Fynes. *An Itinerary VVritten by Fynes Moryson Gent. First in the Latine Tongue, and then translated by him into English.* London, 1617; *STC* 18205.

Mulchrone, K., ed. *Bethu Phátraic: The Tripartite Life of Patrick.* Dublin and London, 1939.

Müller-Lisowski, K. 'Texte zur Mog Ruith Sage.' *Zeitschrift für celtische Philologie* 14 (1923), 145–63.

Murphy, D., ed. *The Annals of Clonmacnoise*. Dublin, 1896.

Murphy, G., ed. *Duanaire Finn: The Book of the Lays of Fionn Part I*. Irish Texts Society 7. Dublin, 1908.

– *Duanaire Finn: The Book of the Lays of Fionn Part III*. Irish Texts Society 43. Dublin, 1953.

Nelson, A.H., ed. *Cambridge*. 2 vols. Records of Early English Drama. Toronto, 1989.

Ní Cheallacháin, M., ed. *Filíocht Phádraigín Haicéad*, by Pádraigín Haicéad. Baile Átha Cliath, 1962.

The Ninth Report of the Deputy Keeper of the Public Records in Ireland. Dublin, 1877.

Noomen, W., ed. *Le Jeu d'Adam*. Paris, 1971.

O'Brien, G., ed. *Advertisements for Ireland*. Journal of the Royal Society of Antiquaries of Ireland. Extra volume. Dublin, 1923.

Ó Cuív, B., ed. *Párliament na mBan*. Dublin, 1970.

O'Daly, M. 'Lánellach Tigi Rich 7 Ruirech.' *Ériu* 19 (1962), 81–6.

O'Daly, M., ed. *Cath Maige Mucrama*. Irish Texts Society 50. Dublin. 1975.

O'Donovan, J., ed. *The Banquet of Dun na nGedh and the Battle of Magh Rath*. Dublin, 1842.

– *The Tribes and Customs of Hy-Many, commonly called O'Kelly's Country*. Dublin, 1843.

– 'The Annals of Ireland, from the Year 1443 to 1468, translated from the Irish by Dudley Firbisse, or, as he is more usually called, Duald Mac Firbis, for Sir James Ware, in the Year 1666.' In *The Miscellany of the Irish Archaeological Society* 1 (Dublin, 1846), 198–302.

– *Annala Rioghachta Eireann. Annals of the Kingdom of Ireland by the Four Masters, from the Earliest Period to the Year 1616*. 7 vols. Dublin, 1851.

O'Grady, S.H. *Silva Gadelica*. 2 vols. London and Edinburgh, 1892.

O'Grady, S.H., ed. *Caithréim Thoirdhealbhaigh*. Irish Texts Society 26 and 27. London, 1929.

Ó hUiginn, Tadhg dall. *The Bardic Poems of Tadhg Dall Ó Huiginn (1550–1591)*. Ed. E. Knott. Irish Texts Society 22 and 23. London, 1922–6.

O'Keeffe, J.G. 'Cáin Domnaig.' *Ériu* 2 (1905), 189–214.

O'Keeffe, John. *Recollections of the Life of John O'Keeffe, Written by Himself*. London, 1826.

Ó Muireadhaigh, R. 'Aos Dána na Mumhan 1584.' *Irisleabhar Muighe Nuadhat* (1960), 81–4.

O'Rahilly, C., ed. *Táin Bó Cúalnge*. Dublin, 1967.

Ó Riain, P., ed. *Cath Almaine*. Dublin, 1978.

O'Sullivan, A. 'Verses on Honorific Portions.' In *Celtic Studies*, ed. Carney and Greene (1968), 118–23.

O'Sullivan Beare, Philip. *Historiae Catholicae Iberniae Compendium*. Lisbon, 1621.

– *Selections from the Zoilomastix of Philip O'Sullivan Beare*. Ed. T.J. O'Donnell. Irish Manuscripts Commission. Dublin, 1960.

Ó Tuama, S., and T. Kinsella, eds. *An Duanaire 1600–1900: Poems of the Dispossessed.* Mountrath, 1981.

Parry, Thomas. 'Statud Gruffudd ap Cynan.' *The Bulletin of the Board of Celtic Studies* 5 (1929), 25–33.

Percy, T., ed. *The Regulations and Establishment of the Household of Henry Algernon Percy, the Fifth Earl of Northumberland, at his Castles of Wresill and Lekinfield in Yorkshire.* London, 1770.

Plummer, C., ed. *Vitae Sanctorum Hiberniae.* 2 vols. Oxford, 1910.

– *Bethada Náem nÉrenn. Lives of Irish Saints.* 2 vols. Oxford, 1922; repr. 1968.

Poncelet, A., ed. *Life of Mochulla. Analecta Bolandiniana* 17 (1898), 135–54.

Powicke, F.M., and C.R. Cheney, eds. *Councils and Synods with Other Documents Relating to the English Church.* 2 vols. Oxford, 1964.

Prim, J.G.A. 'Ancient Civic Enactments for Restraining Gossiping and Feasting.' *Journal of the Royal Society of Antiquaries of Ireland* (formerly *Transactions of the Kilkenny Archaeological Society*) 1 (1849–51), 436–41.

– 'Olden Popular Pastimes in Kilkenny.' *Journal of the Royal Society of Antiquaries of Ireland* (formerly *Transactions of the Kilkenny Archaeological Society*) 2 (1852–3), 319–35.

– 'The Corporation Insignia and Olden Civic State of Kilkenny.' *Journal of the Royal Society of Antiquaries of Ireland* (formerly *The Journal of the Royal Historical and Archaeological Association of Ireland*) 11 (1870), 280–305.

Quinn, D.B. 'Calendar of the Irish Council Book, 1581–1596.' *Analecta Hibernica* 24 (1967), 93–180.

Radner, J.N., ed. *Fragmentary Annals of Ireland.* Dublin, 1978.

The Receyt of the Ladie Kateryne. Ed. G.L. Kipling. EETS, os 296. Oxford, 1990.

Rich, Barnaby. *Faultes Faults, and Nothing Else but Faultes.* London, 1606; *STC* 20983.

– *A New Description of Ireland.* London, 1610; *STC* 20992.

– *A Catholicke Conference Betvveene Syr Tady Mac. Mareall a popish priest of VVaterforde, and Patricke Plaine, a young student in Trinity Colledge by Dublin in Ireland.* London, 1612; *STC* 20981.

– *The Irish Hvbbvb or, The English Hve and Crie.* London, 1617; *STC* 20989.

Riese, A., and F. Buecheler, eds. *Anthologia Latina sive Poesis Latinae supplementum recens.* 2 vols. Leipzig, 1869–1926.

Robinson, F.N. 'The Irish Lives of Guy of Warwick and Bevis of Hampton.' *Zeitschrift für celtische Philologie* 6 (1907), 9–180 and 273–338.

Rocque, J. *An Exact Survey of the City and Suburbs of Dublin, 1756.* Repr. by H. Margary. Lympne Castle, 1977.

Roger of Hoveden. *Chronica Magistri Rogeri de Houedene.* Ed. W. Stubbs. Rolls Series 51. 4 vols. London, 1868–71.

Russell, C.W., and J.P. Prendergast, eds. *Calendar of the State Papers, relating to Ireland, of the Reign of James I. 1611–1614.* London, 1877.

– *Calendar of the State Papers, relating to Ireland, of the Reign of James I. 1615–1625*. London, 1880.

Saddlemyer, A., ed. *J.M. Synge: Plays*, by John Millington Synge. Oxford, 1968.

Scarre, A.M. 'The Beheading of John the Baptist by Mog Ruith.' *Ériu* 4 (1910), 173–81.

Scot, Thomas. *Certaine pieces of this Age paraboliz'd*. London, 1616; *STC* 21870.

Shakespeare, William. *The Comedy of Errors*. Ed. R.A. Foakes. London, 1962.

– *A Midsummer Night's Dream*. Ed. H.F. Brooks. Bristol and Bungay, 1979.

– *Much Ado About Nothing*. Ed. F.H. Mares. Cambridge, 1988.

Shirley, James. *The Royall Master*. London, 1638; *STC* 22454.

– *The Royall Master*. London and Dublin, 1638; *STC* 22454 and 22454a.

– *Narcissus, or, The Self-Lover*. London, 1646; Wing 3480.

Sidney, Philip. *An Apology for Poetry or the Defense of Poesy*. Ed. G. Shepherd. London, 1965.

The Sixteenth Report of the Deputy Keeper of the Public Records in Ireland. Dublin, 1882.

Solier, F. *Histoire Ecclesiastique des Isles et Royavmes dv Iapon*. Paris, 1627.

Somerset, J.A.B., ed. *Shropshire*. 2 vols. Records of Early English Drama. Toronto, 1994.

Spenser, Edmund. *A View of the Present State of Ireland*. Ed. W.L. Renwick. London, 1934; repr. Oxford, 1970.

– *Spenser Poetical Works*. Ed. J.C. Smith and E. de Selincourt. Oxford, 1970.

Stanihurst, Richard. *De rebus in Hibernia gestis*. Antwerp, 1584.

State Papers published under the Authority of His Majesty's Commission. Volume 3. King Henry the Eighth. Part 3. London, 1834.

Stokes, W. 'The Second Battle of Moytura.' *Revue Celtique* 12 (1891), 52–130.

– 'The Violent Deaths of Goll and Garb.' *Revue Celtique* 14 (1893), 396–449.

– 'The Annals of Tigernach. The Fourth Fragment, A.D. 973–A.D. 1088.' *Revue Celtique* 17 (1896), 337–420.

– 'The Gaelic Abridgement of the Book of Ser Marco Polo.' *Zeitschrift für celtische Philologie* 1 (1897), 245–73 and 362–438.

– 'The Gaelic Maundeville.' *Zeitschrift für celtische Philologie* 2 (1899), 1–63 and 226–312.

– 'O'Mulconry's Glossary.' *Archiv für celtische Lexikographie* 1 (1900), 232–324.

– 'The Destruction of Dind Ríg.' *Zeitschrift für celtische Philologie* 3 (1901), 1–14.

– 'The Colloquy of the Two Sages.' *Revue Celtique* 26 (1905), 4–64.

– 'The Fifteen Tokens of Doomsday.' *Revue Celtique* 28 (1907), 308–26.

Stokes, W., ed. *Irish Glosses*. Dublin, 1860.

– *The Saltair na Rann*. Oxford, 1883.

Stokes, W., and J. Strachan, eds. *Thesaurus Palaeohibernicus*. 2 vols. Cambridge, 1901–3; repr. Oxford, 1975.

Stokes, W., and E. Windisch, eds. *Irische Texte mit Übersetzungen und Wörterbuch*. 4th ser. 2 vols. Leipzig, 1897–1909.

Stow, John. *John Stow: A Survey of London*. Ed. C.L. Kingsford. 2 vols. Oxford, 1908; repr. 1971.

Symons, T., ed. *Regularis Concordia*. London, 1953.

Titvs, or the Palme of Christian Covrage. Waterford, 1644; Wing 1314.

Townshend, Aurelian. *Aurelian Townshend's Poems and Masks*. Ed. E.K. Chambers. Oxford, 1912.

– *The Poems and Masques of Aurelian Townshend*. Ed. C.C. Brown. Reading, 1983.

Tresham, E., ed. *Rotulorum patentum et clausorum cancellariae Hiberniae calendarium*. Dublin, 1828.

Turner, J.P., ed. *A Critical Edition of James Shirley's St. Patrick for Ireland*. New York and London, 1979.

The Twenty-third Report of the Deputy Keeper of the Public Records in Ireland. Dublin, 1891.

Ua Súilleabháin, S., and S. Donnelly. '"Music has Ended": The Death of a Harper.' *Celtica* 22 (1991), 165–75.

Unger, C.R., ed. *Stjórn*. Christiania, 1862.

Vallancey, C., ed. *Collectanea de Rebus Hibernicis*. 6 vols. Dublin, 1770–1804.

Van Hamel, A.G., ed. *Immrama*. Mediaeval and Modern Irish Series. Volume 10. Dublin, 1941.

Wager, William. *The longer thou liuest, the more foole thou art*. London, [1569]; *STC* 24935.

Ware, J., ed. *The Historie of Ireland*. Dublin, 1633; *STC* 25067a.

Wasson, J.M., ed. *Devon*. Records of Early English Drama. Toronto, 1987.

Watters, P. 'Original Documents connected with Kilkenny.' *Journal of the Royal Society of Antiquaries of Ireland* (formerly *The Journal of the Royal Historical and Archaeological Association of Ireland*) 12 (1872–3), 532–43.

– 'Note of Entries in the Corporation Records, Kilkenny, relative to a Visit of Lord Viscount Wentworth to Kilkenny in the year 1637.' *Journal of the Royal Society of Antiquaries of Ireland* (formerly *The Journal of the Royal Historical and Archaeological Association of Ireland*) 16 (1883–4), 242–9.

– 'Notes of Particulars extracted from the Kilkenny Corporation Records relating to the Miracle Plays as performed there from the year 1580 to the year 1639.' *Journal of the Royal Society of Antiquaries of Ireland* (formerly *The Journal of the Royal Historical and Archaeological Association of Ireland*) 16 (1883–4), 238–42.

Wickham, G., ed. *English Moral Interludes*. London and Totowa, 1976.

Wilde, Jane Francesca (Speranza). *Ancient Legends, Mystic Charms and Superstitions of Ireland*. London, 1888.

Wilkes, T. *A General View of the Stage*. London, 1759.

Wilkins, D., ed. *Concilia Magnae Britanniae et Hiberniae ab Anno MCCCL ad Annum MDXLV*. 4 vols. London, 1737.

Wood, H., ed. *Court Book of the Liberty of St. Sepulchre*. Dublin, 1930.

Young, K., ed. *The Drama of the Medieval Church*. 2 vols. Oxford, 1933.

II

Adams, S. 'Early Stuart Politics: Revisionism and after.' In Mulryne and Shewring, *Theatre and Government*, 29–56.

Anglo, S. *Spectacle, Pageantry, and Early Tudor Policy.* Oxford, 1969.

Aston, M. 'Segregation in Church.' In Wood, *Women in the Church*, 237–94.

Atkins, J.W.H. *English Literary Criticism: The Renascence.* London, 1947.

Axton, R. *European Drama of the Early Middle Ages.* London, 1974.

Bailey, T. *The Processions of Sarum and the Western Church.* Toronto, 1971.

Barba, E., ed. *J. Grotowski: Towards a Poor Theatre.* London, 1969.

Barish, J. *The Antitheatrical Prejudice.* Berkeley and London, 1981.

Barnard, T., D. Ó Cróinín, and K. Simms, eds. *'A Miracle of Learning': Studies in Manuscripts and Irish Learning. Essays in Honour of William O'Sullivan.* Aldershot, 1998.

Barrow, G.L. 'Riding the Franchises.' *Dublin Historical Record* 33 (1980), 135–8.

– 'The Franchises of Dublin.' *Dublin Historical Record* 36 (1983), 68–80.

Barry, S. 'The Architecture of the Cathedral.' In Empey, *A Worthy Foundation*, 25–48.

Bartley, J.O. *Teague, Shenkin and Sawney, being an Historical Study of the Earliest Irish, Welsh and Scottish Characters in English Plays.* Cork, 1954.

Beadle, R., 'The East Anglian "Game-Place": A Possibility for Further Research.' *Records of Early English Drama Newsletter* 3 (1978), 2–4.

Beadle, R. ed. *The Cambridge Companion to Medieval Theatre.* Cambridge, 1994.

Beckett, J.C. 'The Confederation of Kilkenny Reviewed.' In Roberts, *Historical Studies II*, 29–41.

Bergeron, D. *English Civic Pageantry 1558–1642.* London, 1971.

Berry, H.F. 'The Goldsmiths' Company of Dublin.' *Journal of the Royal Society of Antiquaries of Ireland* 31 (1901), 119–33.

– 'The Merchant Tailors' Guild – that of St John the Baptist, Dublin, 1418–1841.' *Journal of the Royal Society of Antiquaries of Ireland* 48 (1918), 19–64.

– ed. *Register of Wills and Inventories of the Diocese of Dublin.* Dublin, 1898.

Bevington, D. *From Mankind to Marlowe.* Cambridge, MA, 1962.

Billington, S. *A Social History of the Fool.* Brighton and New York, 1984.

Binchy, D.A. 'The Date and Provenance of *Uraicecht Becc*.' *Ériu* 18 (1958), 44–54.

– 'The Fair of Tailtiu and the Feast of Tara.' *Ériu* 18 (1958), 113–38.

Blair, C., and I. Delamer, 'The Dublin Civic Swords.' *Proceedings of the Royal Irish Academy* 88 (1988), 87–142.

Boorman, S., ed. *Studies in Performance of Late Medieval Music.* Cambridge, 1983.

Boydell, B. 'Dublin City Musicians in the late Middle Ages and Renaissance, to 1660.' *Dublin Historical Record* 34 (1981), 42–53.

– 'The Earl of Cork's Musicians: A Study in the Patronage of Music in Early Seventeenth Century Anglo-Irish Society.' *Records of Early English Drama Newsletter* 18 (1993), 1–15.

Bradshaw, B., A. Hadfield, and W. Maley, eds. *Representing Ireland: Literature and the Origins of Conflict, 1534–1660.* Cambridge, 1993.

Brady, C. *The Chief Governors: The Rise and Fall of Reform Government in Tudor Ireland 1536–1588.* Cambridge, 1994.

Brady, C., and R. Gillespie, eds. *Natives and Newcomers: Essays on the Making of Irish Colonial Society 1534–1641.* Dublin, 1986.

Breatnach, L. 'Tochmarc Luaine ocus Aided Athairne.' *Celtica* 13 (1980), 1–31.

– 'Law.' In McCone and Simms, *Progress in Medieval Irish Studies*, 107–21.

Breatnach, P.A. 'The Chief's Poet.' *Proceedings of the Royal Irish Academy* 83 (1983), 37–79.

– 'Moladh na Féile: Téama i bhFilíocht na Scol.' *Léachtaí Cholm Cille* 24 (1994), 61–76.

Breatnach, R.A. 'The Evidence for Dancing in Ancient Ireland.' *Journal of the Cork Historical and Archaeological Society* 60 (1955), 88–94.

– 'II – Rejoinder.' *Journal of the Cork Historical and Archaeological Society* 61 (1956), 59–60.

– 'IV – Rejoinder.' *Journal of the Cork Historical and Archaeological Society* 61 (1956), 65–70.

Breeze, A. 'Ælfric's *Trup* "Buffoon": Old Irish *Druth* "Buffoon".' *Notes and Queries* 240 (1995), 155–7.

Brody, A. *The English Mummers and Their Plays: Traces of Ancient Mystery.* London, 1971.

Brook, P. *The Empty Space.* Harmondsworth, 1972.

Brooks, N.C. 'The Sepulchrum Christi.' *Journal of English and Germanic Philology* 27 (1928), 147–61.

Bruford, A. 'Song and Recitation in Early Ireland.' *Celtica* 21 (1990), 61–74.

Bugge, A. *Vesterlandenes Inflydelse paa Nordboernes og soerlig Nordmaendenes ydre Kultur, Levesæf og Sam Finds Forhold i Vikingetiden.* Christiania, 1905.

Bullock-Davies, C. *Menestrellorum Multitudo: Minstrels at a Royal Feast.* Cardiff, 1978.

– *A Register of Royal and Baronial Domestic Minstrels, 1272–1327.* Bury St Edmunds, 1986.

Butler, M. 'Two Playgoers, and the Closing of the London Theatres, 1642.' *Theatre Research International* 9 (1984), 93–9.

– 'Politics and the Masque: *The Triumph of Peace*.' *The Seventeenth Century* 2 (1987), 117–41.

Butterworth, P. 'The York Mercers' Pageant Vehicle, 1433–1467: Wheels, Steering, and Control.' *Medieval English Theatre* 1 (1979), 72–81.

Byrne, F.J. *Irish Kings and High Kings.* London, 1973.

Caball, M. 'Notes on an Elizabethan Kerry Bardic Family.' *Ériu* 43 (1992), 177–92.

Caerwyn Williams, J.E. 'The Court Poet in Medieval Ireland.' *Proceedings of the British Academy* 57 (1971), 85–135.

– 'Posidonius's Celtic Parasites.' *Studia Celtica* 14–15 (1979–80), 313–43.

Calendar of the Patent and Close Rolls of Chancery in Ireland of the Reigns of Henry VIII. Edward VI. Mary, and Elizabeth. Ed. J. Morrin. 2 vols. Dublin, 1861.

Canny, N.P. *The Elizabethan Conquest of Ireland: A Pattern Established 1565–76.* Trowbridge, 1976.

– *The Upstart Earl: A Study of the Social and Mental World of Richard Boyle, First Earl of Cork, 1566–1643.* Cambridge, 1982.

Carney, J., and D. Greene, eds. *Celtic Studies: Essays in Memory of Angus Matheson.* London, 1968.

Carrigan, W. *The History and Antiquities of the Diocese of Ossory.* 4 vols. Dublin, 1905.

Cavanagh, S.T. '"The Fatal Destiny of that Land": Elizabethan Views of Ireland.' In Bradshaw, Hadfield, and Maley, *Representing Ireland,* 116–31.

Cawley, A.C., M. Jones, P.F. McDonald, and D. Mills, eds. *The Revels History of Drama in English Volume I: Medieval Drama.* London and New York, 1983.

Cawte, E.C. *Ritual Animal Disguise.* Cambridge, 1978.

Chambers, E.K. *The Mediæval Stage.* 2 vols. Oxford, 1903.

– *The Elizabethan Stage.* 4 vols. Oxford, 1923.

Cheney, C.R. 'A Group of Related Synodal Statutes of the Thirteenth Century.' In Watt, Morrall, and Martin, *Medieval Studies,* 114–32.

Chetwood, W.R. *A General History of the Stage.* Dublin, 1749.

Clark, M., and R. Refaussé, eds. *Directory of Historic Dublin Guilds.* Dublin, 1993.

Clarke, H.B. *Dublin c. 840–1540: The Medieval Town in the Modern City.* Ordnance Survey. Dublin, 1978.

– '"Urbs et suburbium": Beyond the Walls of Medieval Dublin.' In Manning, *Dublin and beyond the Pale,* 43–56.

Clarke, H.B., and A. Simms, eds. *The Comparative History of Urban Origins in Non-Roman Europe: Ireland, Wales, Denmark, Germany, Poland and Russia from the Ninth to the Thirteenth Century.* Oxford, 1985.

Coldewey, J. 'Carnival's End: Puritan Ideology and the Decline of English Provincial Theatre.' In Twycross, *Festive Drama,* 279–86.

– 'The Non-cycle Plays and the East Anglian Tradition.' In Beadle, *The Cambridge Companion to Medieval Theatre,* 189–210.

Collins, Fletcher. *The Production of Medieval Church Music Drama.* Virginia, 1972.

Comerford, R.V., M. Cullen, J.R. Hill, and C. Lennon, eds. *Religion, Conflict and Coexistence in Ireland.* Dublin, 1990.

The Complete Peerage. Vicary Gibbs, et al. 12 vols. London, 1910–59.

Cooper, E., ed. *The Life of Thomas Wentworth, Earl of Strafford and Lord-Lieutenant of Ireland.* 2 vols. London, 1874.

Cooper, H. 'Location and Meaning in Masque, Morality and Royal Entertainment.' In Lindley, *The Court Masque,* 135–48.

Corbett, P. *The Scurra.* Edinburgh, 1986.

Cosgrove, A. 'Marriage in Medieval Ireland.' In Cosgrove, *Marriage in Ireland,* 25–50.

– ed. *Marriage in Ireland.* Dublin, 1985.

– ed. *A New History of Ireland II Medieval Ireland 1169–1534.* Oxford, 1987.

Coughlan, P. '"Enter Revenge": Henry Burkhead and *Cola's Furie.*' *Theatre Research International* 15 (1990), 1–17.

Cross, F.L., and E.A. Livingstone, eds. *The Oxford Dictionary of the Christian Church.* 3rd ed. Oxford, 1997.

Cunningham, B. 'The Composition of Connacht in the Lordships of Clanricard and Thomond 1577–1641.' *Irish Historical Studies* 24 (1984–5), 1–14.

– 'Seventeenth-Century Interpretations of the Past: The Case of Geoffrey Keating.' *Irish Historical Studies* 25 (1986), 116–28.

– 'Natives and Newcomers in Mayo, 1560–1603.' In Gillespie and Moran, '*A Various Country,*' 24–43.

Curtis, E., ed. *Calendar of Ormond Deeds,* 6 vols. Dublin, 1932–43.

Davidson, C. 'The Middle English Saint Play and Its Iconography.' In Davidson, *The Saint Play in Medieval Europe,* 31–122.

Davidson, C., ed. *The Saint Play in Medieval Europe.* Early Drama, Art, and Music Monograph Series 8. Kalamazoo, 1986.

Davis, N. 'The Meaning of the Word "Interlude": A Discussion.' *Medieval English Theatre* 6 (1984), 5–15.

Dawson, W.F. *Christmas: Its Origins and Associations.* London, 1902.

Delargy, J.H. 'The Gaelic Story-Teller, with Some Notes on Gaelic Folk Tales.' *Proceedings of the British Academy* 31 (1945), 177–221.

Dodwell, C.R. *The Canterbury School of Illumination 1066–1200.* Cambridge, 1954.

Doherty, C. 'The Monastic Town in Early Medieval Ireland.' In Clarke and Simms, *The Comparative History of Urban Origins,* 45–75.

Dolan, D. *La drame liturgique de Pâques en Normandie et en Angleterre au moyen âge.* Paris, 1975.

Donnelly, S. 'Dance of Death.' *Ceol na hÉireann* 1 (1993), 74.

– 'A Cork Harper at the Stuart Court: Daniel Duff O'Cahill, the Queen's Harper.' *Journal of the Cork Historical and Archæological Society,* forthcoming.

Dudley Edwards, R. *Church and State in Tudor Ireland.* Dublin and Cork, 1935.

Dutka, J. 'Mystery Plays at Norwich: Their Formation and Development.' *Leeds Studies in English,* new ser 10 (1978), 107–20.

– 'The Lost Dramatic Cycle of Norwich and the Grocers' Play of the Fall of Man.' *Review of English Studies* 35 (1984), 1–13.

Dutton, R. 'Ben Jonson and the Master of the Revels.' In Mulryne and Shewring, *Theatre and Government,* 57–86.

Edwards, P., G.E. Bentley, K. McLuskie, and L. Potter, eds. *The Revels History of Drama in English, Volume 4 1613–1660.* London and New York, 1981.

Egan-Buffet, M., and A.J. Fletcher. 'The Dublin *Visitatio Sepulcri* Play.' *Proceedings of the Royal Irish Academy* 90 (1990), 159–241.

Ellis, S.G. *Tudor Ireland Crown, Community and the Conflict of Culture, 1470–1603.* London and New York, 1985.

Empey, A., ed. *A Worthy Foundation: The Cathedral Church of St Canice Kilkenny, 1285–1985.* Mount Rath, Port Laoise, 1985.

Feasey, H.J. *Ancient English Holy Week Ceremonial.* London, 1897.

Féral, J. 'Performance and Theatricality: The Subject Demystified.' *Modern Drama* 25 (1982), 170–81.

Ferrar, J. *The History of Limerick.* Limerick, 1787.

Finegan, F. 'Jesuits in Kilkenny.' *Jesuit Year Book* (1971), 9–23.

Fitzgibbon, T.G. 'Purpose and Theme in the Drama of James Shirley.' PhD thesis, University College, Cork, 1982.

Fitz-Simon, C. *The Irish Theatre.* London, 1983.

Fleischmann, A. 'The Evidence for Dancing in Ancient Ireland I – Further Evidence.' *Journal of the Cork Historical and Archaeological Society* 61 (1956), 58–9.

Fleischmann, A., and R. Gleeson. 'Music in Ancient Munster and Monastic Cork.' *Journal of the Cork Historical and Archaeological Society* 70 (1965), 79–98.

Fletcher, A.J. '"Farte Prycke in Cule": A Late-Elizabethan Analogue from Ireland.' *Medieval English Theatre* 8 (1986), 134–9.

– 'Jugglers Celtic and Anglo-Saxon.' *Theatre Notebook* 44 (1990), 2–10.

– 'The N-Town Plays.' In Beadle, *The Cambridge Companion to Medieval Theatre*, 163–88.

– '"Benedictus qui venit in nomine Domini": A Thirteenth-Century Sermon for Advent and the Macaronic Style in England.' *Mediæval Studies* 56 (1994), 217–45.

– 'The Civic Pageantry of Corpus Christi in Fifteenth- and Sixteenth-Century Dublin.' *Irish Economic and Social History* 23 (1996), 73–96.

Fletcher, A.J., and W. Hüsken, eds. *Between Folk and Liturgy.* Ludus 3. Amsterdam and Atlanta, 1997.

Forbes, A.P., ed. *Lives of S. Ninian and S. Kentigern.* Edinburgh, 1874.

Ford, A. 'Reforming the Holy Isle: Parr Lane and the Conversion of the Irish.' In Barnard, Ó Cróinín, and Simms, '*A Miracle of Learning,*' 137–63.

Fry, J., and A.J. Fletcher, 'The Kilkenny Morries, 1610.' *Folk Music Journal* 6 (1993), 381–3.

Gailey, A. 'Straw Costume in Irish Folk Customs.' *Folk Life* 6 (1968), 83–93.

– *Irish Folk Drama.* Cork, 1969.

Galloway, D. 'Comment: The East Anglian "Game-Place": Some Facts and Fictions.' *Records of Early English Drama Newsletter* 4 (1979), 24–6.

Gardiner, H.C. *Mysteries' End: An Investigation of the Last Days of the Medieval Religious Stage.* New Haven, 1946.

Geiriadur Prifysgol Cymru: A Dictionary of the Welsh Language. Cardiff, 1950–.

van Gennep, A. *Les rites de passage. Étude systématique des rites.* Paris, 1909.

Gerriets, M. 'Kingship and Exchange in Pre-Viking Ireland.' *Cambridge Medieval Celtic Studies* 13 (1987), 39–72.

Gibson, G. McMurray. *The Theater of Devotion: East Anglian Drama and Society in the Late Middle Ages.* Chicago and London, 1989.

Gilbert, J.T. *Historical Manuscripts Commission*. 10th Report. London, 1885–7.
– *A History of the City of Dublin*. 3 vols. Dublin, 1854–9; repr Shannon, 1972.
– *History of the Viceroys of Ireland; with Notices of the Castle of Dublin and its Chief Occupants in Former Times*. Dublin and London, 1865.
Gillespie, R., and G. Moran, eds. *'A Various Country': Essays in Mayo History 1500–1900*. Westport, 1987.
Glassie, H. *All Silver and No Brass*. Indiana, 1975.
Grattan-Flood, W. *A History of Irish Music*. Dublin, Belfast, and Cork, 1905.
Greene, J.C., and G.L.H. Clark, *The Dublin Stage, 1720–1745*. Bethlehem, PA, London, and Toronto, 1993.
Grindle, W.H. *Irish Cathedral Music*. Belfast, 1989.
Gross, C. *The Gild Merchant*. 2 vols. Oxford, 1890.
Gunnell, T. '"The Rights of the Player": Evidence of *Mimi* and *Histriones* in Early Medieval Scandinavia.' *Comparative Drama* 30 (1996), 1–31.
Gwynn, A. 'The Black Death in Ireland.' *Studies* 24 (1935), 25–42.
– 'The Origins of the Anglo-Irish Theatre.' *Studies* 38 (1939), 260–74.
Gwynn, A., and R.N. Hadcock. *Medieval Religious Houses: Ireland*. London, 1970; repr. Dublin, 1988.
Gwynn, L. 'The Life of St. Lasair.' *Ériu* 5 (1911), 73–109.
Hand, G. 'The Date of the "Crede Mihi."' *Reportorium Novum* (Dublin Diocesan Record) 3 (1964), 368–70.
Handelman, D. *Models and Mirrors: Towards an Anthropology of Public Events*. Cambridge, 1990.
Harbage, A. *Annals of English Drama 975–1700*. Rev. S. Schoenbaum. London, 1964.
Hardiman, J. *The History of the Town and County of the Town of Galway, from the Earliest Period to the Present Time*. Dublin, 1820.
Hardison, O.B. *Christian Rite and Christian Drama in the Middle Ages*. Baltimore, 1965.
Harrison, A. *An chrosántacht*. Baile Átha Cliath, 1979.
– *The Irish Trickster*. Sheffield, 1989.
Harrison, F.Ll. *Music in Medieval Britain*. 4th ed. Buren, 1980.
Hart, A.R. 'The King's Serjeant at Law in Tudor Ireland, 1485–1603.' In Hogan and Osborough, *Brehons, Serjeants and Attorneys*, 77–100.
Hawkes, W. 'The Liturgy in Dublin, 1200–1500: Manuscript Sources.' *Reportorium Novum* (Dublin Diocesan Record) 2 (1958), 33–67.
Healy, W. *History and Antiquities of Kilkenny (County and City)*. Kilkenny, 1893.
Hearn, K., ed. *Dynasties: Painting in Tudor and Jacobean England 1530–1630*. London, 1995.
Helm, A. *The English Mummers' Play*. Bury St Edmunds, 1981.
Heneghan, F. 'Mummers of County Wexford.' *The Daily Chronicle*. London, 2 March 1929, repr. in *The Irish Book Lover* 17 (1929), 59–61.

Hengstebeck, I. 'Wer träumt in *The Pride of Life?' Archiv für das Studium der Neueren Sprachen und Literaturen* 208 (1971), 119–22.

Hennessy, W.M. 'The Curragh of Kildare.' *Proceedings of the Royal Irish Academy* 9 (1867), 343–55.

Herbert, M., and M. McNamara, eds. *Irish Biblical Apocrypha, Selected Texts in Translation.* Edinburgh, 1989.

Heslop, T.A. 'A Walrus Ivory Pyx and the Visitatio Sepulcri.' *Journal of the Warburg and Courtauld Institute* 44 (1981), 157–60.

Hillebrand, H.N. *The Child Actors.* Urbana, IL, 1926.

Hogan, D., and W.N. Osborough, eds. *Brehons, Serjeants and Attorneys: Studies in the History of the Irish Legal Profession.* Dublin, 1990.

Hogan, J. 'The Three Tholsels of Kilkenny.' *Journal of the Royal Society of Antiquaries of Ireland* 15 (1879–82), 236–52.

Horner, O. 'Christmas at the Inns of Court.' In Twycross, *Festive Drama*, 41–53.

Hosley, R. 'Three Kinds of Outdoor Theatre before Shakespeare.' *Theatre Survey* 12 (1971), 1–33.

Hughes, S.C. *The Church of S. John the Evangelist, Dublin.* Dublin, 1889.

– *The Pre-Victorian Drama in Dublin.* Dublin, 1904.

Jackson, K.H. 'The Historical Grammar of Irish: Some Actualities and Some Desiderata.' In Mac Eoin, *Proceedings*, 1–18.

James, M. 'Ritual, Drama and Social Body in the Late Medieval English Town.' *Past and Present* 98 (1983), 3–29.

Jeffrey, D.L. 'Franciscan Spirituality and the Rise of Early English Drama.' *Mosaic* 8 (1975), 17–46.

Johnston, A.F. '"What Revels Are in Hand?": Dramatic Activities Sponsored by the Parishes of the Thames Valley.' In Johnston and Hüsken, *English Parish Drama*, 95–104.

Johnston, A.F., ed. *Editing Early Drama: Special Problems and New Directions.* New York, 1987.

Johnston, A.F., and W. Hüsken, eds. *English Parish Drama.* Ludus 1. Amsterdam and Atlanta, 1996.

Jones, F.M. *Mountjoy 1563–1606: The Last Elizabethan Deputy.* Dublin and London, 1958.

Joyce, P.W. *A Social History of Ancient Ireland.* 2 vols. London, 1903.

Kahrl, S.J. *Traditions of Medieval English Drama.* London, 1974.

Kavanagh, P. *The Irish Theatre.* Tralee, 1946.

Kearney, H.F. *Strafford in Ireland 1633–41.* Cambridge, 1989.

Kelly, F. 'Old Irish *creccaire*, Scottish Gaelic *kreahkir*.' *Ériu* 37 (1986), 185–6.

– 'An Old-Irish Text on Court Procedure.' *Peritia* 5 (1986), 74–106.

– *A Guide to Early Irish Law.* Early Irish Law Series. Volume 3. Dublin, 1988.

Kenny, C. *King's Inns and the Kingdom of Ireland: The Irish 'Inn of Court' 1541–1800.* Dublin, 1992.

Kertzer, D.I. *Ritual, Politics, and Power.* New Haven and London, 1988.

Kipling, G. 'Triumphal Drama: Form in English Civic Pageantry.' *Renaissance Drama,* new ser 8 (1977), 37–56.

Knowles, J. 'The Spectacle of the Realm: Civic Consciousness, Rhetoric and Ritual in Early Modern London.' In Mulryne and Shewring, *Theatre and Government,* 157–89.

Kolve, V.A. *The Play Called Corpus Christi.* London, 1966.

Lancashire, I., ed. *Dramatic Texts and Records of Britain: A Chronological Topography to 1558.* Cambridge, 1984.

Lapidge, M., and R. Sharpe. *A Bibliography of Celtic-Latin Literature 400–1200.* Dublin, 1985.

Latham, R.E. *Revised Medieval Latin Word List from British and Irish Sources.* Oxford, 1965.

– *Dictionary of Medieval Latin from British Sources.* London, 1975– .

Laver, J. *Isabella's Triumph.* London, 1947.

LeHuray, P. *Music and the Reformation in England 1549–1660.* London, 1967; corrected repr. Cambridge, 1978.

Lennon, C. 'Richard Stanihurst (1547–1618) and Old English Identity.' *Irish Historical Studies* 21 (1978–9), 121–43.

– *The Lords of Dublin in the Age of Reformation.* Dublin, 1989.

– 'The Chantries in the Irish Reformation: The Case of St Anne's Guild, Dublin, 1550–1630.' In Comerford, Cullen, Hill, and Lennon, *Religion, Conflict and Coexistence,* 6–25.

Lennon, P. 'Prince of Petomane.' *The Guardian.* London, 13 July 1967, p. 5.

Leslie, J.B. *Ossory Clergy and Parishes.* Enniskillen, 1933.

Lindley, D., ed. *The Court Masque.* Manchester, 1984.

Loomis, L.H. 'Secular Dramatics in the Royal Palace, Paris, 1378, 1389, and Chaucer's "Tregetoures."' *Speculum* 33 (1958), 242–55; repr. in Taylor and Nelson, *Medieval English Drama,* 98–115.

Lumiansky, R.M., and D. Mills. *The Chester Mystery Cycle: Essays and Documents.* Chapel Hill and London, 1983.

Lydon, J.F. 'Richard II's Expeditions to Ireland.' *Journal of the Royal Society of Antiquaries of Ireland* 93 (1963), 135–49.

– *Ireland in the Later Middle Ages.* Dublin, 1973.

– 'The Branganstown Massacre, 1329.' *County Louth Archaeological and Historical Journal* 19 (1977–80), 5–16.

Lynch, K.M. *Roger Boyle, First Earl of Orrery.* Tennessee, 1965.

MacCana, P. *The Learned Tales of Medieval Ireland.* Dublin, 1984.

McCafferty, J. 'St Patrick for the Church of Ireland: James Ussher's *Discourse.*' *Bullán* 3 (1997–8), 87–101.

McCarthy Morrogh, M. *The Plantation of Munster.* Oxford, 1986.

McClintock, H.F. 'Engraved Bone Plate in the National Museum Dublin.' *Journal of the Royal Society of Antiquaries of Ireland* 63 (1933), 29–37.

McCone, K.R. 'Werewolves, Cyclopes, *Díberga*, and Fíanna: Juvenile Delinquency in Early Ireland.' *Cambridge Medieval Celtic Studies* 12 (1986), 1–22.

– 'A Tale of Two Ditties: Poet and Satirist in Cath Maige Tuired.' In Ó Corráin, Breatnach, and McCone, *Sages, Saints and Storytellers*, 122–43.

McCone, K.R., and K. Simms, eds. *Progress in Medieval Irish Studies.* Maynooth, 1996.

McDowell, R.B., and D.A. Webb. *Trinity College Dublin 1592–1952: An Academic History.* Cambridge, 1982.

Mac Eoin, G., ed. *Proceedings of the Sixth International Congress of Celtic Studies.* Dublin, 1983.

McGrath, C. 'Two Skilful Musicians.' *Éigse* 7 (1953–5), 84–94.

McHugh, R., and M. Harmon. *Short History of Anglo-Irish Literature from its Origins to the Present Day.* Dublin, 1982.

McIntosh, A., and M.L. Samuels. 'Prolegomena to a Study of Medieval Anglo-Irish.' *Medium Ævum* 37 (1968), 1–11.

McKinnon, J.W. 'Fifteenth-Century Northern Book Printing and the *A Cappella* Question: An Essay in Iconographic Method.' In Boorman, *Studies in Performance*, 1–17.

McNeill, C. 'Harris: Collectanea de Rebus Hibernicis.' *Analecta Hibernica* 6 (1934), 248–450.

MacNeill, M. *The Festival of Lughnasa.* Oxford, 1962.

Manning, C., ed. *Dublin and beyond the Pale: Studies in Honour of Patrick Healy.* Bray, 1998.

de Marinis, M. *The Semiotics of Performance.* Trans. Á. O'Healy. Bloomington and Indianapolis, 1993.

Marshall, M.H. 'Aesthetic Values of the Liturgical Drama.' Repr. in Taylor and Nelson, *Medieval English Drama*, 28–43.

Mason, W.M. *The History and Antiquities of the Collegiate and Cathedral Church of St. Patrick.* Dublin, 1820.

Mazouer, C. 'Les indications de mise en scène dans les drames liturgiques de Pâques.' *Cahiers de Civilisation Médiévale* 23 (1980), 361–7.

Mehl, D. *The Elizabethan Dumb Show.* London, 1965.

Meredith, P. '"Farte Prycke in Cule" and Cock Fighting.' *Medieval English Theatre* 6 (1984), 30–9.

– 'Stage Directions and the Editing of Early English Drama.' In Johnston, *Editing Early Drama*, 65–94.

– 'The Bodley Burial and Resurrection: Late English Liturgical Drama?' In Fletcher and Hüsken, *Between Folk and Liturgy*, 133–55.

Middle English Dictionary. Ed. Hans Kurath and Sherman H. Kuhn, et al. Ann Arbor, 1952–.

Mills, D. 'Music and Musicians in Chester: A Summary Account.' *Medieval English Theatre* 17 (1995), 58–75.

Moody, T.W. 'Sir Thomas Phillips of Limavady, Servitor.' *Irish Historical Studies* 1 (1938–9), 251–72.

– *The Londonderry Plantation 1609–41*. Belfast, 1939.

Moody, T.W., F.X. Martin, and F.J. Byrne, eds. *A New History of Ireland III Early Modern Ireland 1534–1691*. Oxford, 1976.

Moody, T.W., and W.E. Vaughan, eds. *A New History of Ireland IV, Eighteenth-Century Ireland 1691–1800*. Oxford, 1986.

Moran, P. 'The Bishops of Ossory from the Anglo-Norman Invasion to the Present Day.' *Transactions of the Ossory Archæological Society* 2 (1882), 199–306.

Morgan, H. 'Tom Lee: The Posing Peacemaker.' In Bradshaw, Hadfield, and Maley, *Representing Ireland*, 132–65.

Morrissey, L.J. 'English Pageant-Wagons.' *Eighteenth-Century Studies* 9 (1975–6), 353–74.

Mulryne, J.R., and M. Shewring, eds. *Theatre and Government under the Early Stuarts*. Cambridge, 1993.

Murdoch, B. *Cornish Literature*. Cambridge, 1993.

Neely, W.G. *Kilkenny: An Urban History, 1391–1843*. Belfast, 1989.

Nelson, A.H. 'Some Configurations of Staging in Medieval English Drama.' In Taylor and Nelson, *Medieval English Drama*, 116–47.

– *The Medieval English Stage: Corpus Christi Pageants and Plays*. Chicago and London, 1974.

– *Early Cambridge Theatres: College, University and Town Stages, 1464–1720*. Cambridge, 1994.

Neuss, P. 'The Staging of the Creacion of the World.' *Theatre Notebook* 33 (1979), 119–20.

Neuss, P., ed. *Aspects of Early English Drama*. Cambridge and Totowa, 1983.

Nevinson, J.L. 'A Show of the Nine Worthies.' *Shakespeare Quarterly* 14 (1963), 103–7.

Nohain, J., and F. Caradec. *Le Petomane 1857–1945*. Trans. W. Tute. London, 1967.

Ó Corráin, D. 'Foreign Connections and Domestic Politics: Killaloe and the Uí Briain in Twelfth-Century Hagiography.' In Whitelock, McKitterick, and Dumville, *Ireland in Early Medieval Europe*, 213–31.

Ó Corráin, D., L. Breatnach, and K.R. McCone, eds. *Sages, Saints and Storytellers: Celtic Studies in Honour of Professor James Carney*. Maynooth Monographs 2. Maynooth, 1989.

O'Curry, E. *On the Manners and Customs of the Ancient Irish*. Ed. W.K. Sullivan. 3 vols. Dublin, 1873.

Ogilvy, J.D.A. '*Mimi, Scurrae, Histriones*: Entertainers of the Early Middle Ages.' *Speculum* 38 (1963), 603–19.

Ó hAodha, M. *Theatre in Ireland*. Oxford, 1974.

Orgel, S. *The Jonsonian Masque*. Cambridge, MA, 1965.

Ó Riain, P. 'Codex Salmanticensis: A Provenance *inter Anglos* or *inter Hibernos*?' In Barnard, Ó Cróinín, and Simms, '*A Miracle of Learning*,' 91–100.

Orrell, J. *The Theatre of Inigo Jones and John Webb*. Cambridge, 1985.

– *The Human Stage: English Theatre Design, 1567–1640*. Cambridge, 1988.

Ó Sé, M. 'Notes on Old Irish Dances.' *Journal of the Cork Historical and Archæological Society* 60 (1955), 57–63.

Ó Súilleabháin, S. *Caitheamh Aimsire ar Thórraimh*. Dublin, 1961.

– *Irish Wake Amusements.* Cork, 1967; repr. 1969.

Owen, G. Dyfnallt. *Elizabethan Wales: The Social Scene.* Cardiff, 1962.

Pächt, O. 'A Giottesque Episode in English Medieval Art.' *Journal of the Warburg and Courtauld Institute* 6 (1943), 51–70.

Pafford, J.H.P. 'John Clavell (1601–43), Burglar, Highwayman, Poet, Dramatist, Doctor, Lawyer.' *Notes and Queries for Somerset and Dorset* 32 (1986), 549–62.

Parkes, M.B. *English Cursive Book Hands 1250–1500.* Oxford, 1969; repr. with minor revisions, London, 1979.

Parry, T. *A History of Welsh Literature.* Trans. H.I. Bell. Oxford, 1955.

Partridge, A.C. *Language and Society in Anglo-Irish Literature.* Dublin and Totowa, 1984.

Patterson, N. *Cattle-Lords and Clansmen: The Social Structure of Early Ireland.* 2nd ed. Notre Dame and London, 1994.

Pettitt, T. 'English Folk Drama in the Eighteenth Century: A Defense of the *Revesby Sword Play.*' *Comparative Drama* 15 (1981), 3–29.

Pfaff, R.W. *New Liturgical Feasts in Later Medieval England.* Oxford, 1970.

Phelan, M.M. 'Sir Thomas Wentworth's Visit to Kilkenny August 1637.' *Journal of the Butler Society* 2 (1981–2), 190–2.

Pierse, J.H. 'Nicholas Dall Pierse of Co. Kerry, Harper.' *Journal of the Kerry Archæological and Historical Society* 6 (1973), 40–75.

Platt, C. *The Parish Churches of Medieval England.* London, 1981.

Poppe, E. 'A Note on the Jester in *Fingal Rónáin.*' *Studia Hibernica* 27 (1993), 145–54.

Potter, R. *The English Morality Play.* London and Boston, 1975.

Price, L. *The Place-Names of Co. Wicklow.* 7 vols. Dublin, 1945–67.

Prim, J.G.A. 'Missing Records. No. II. Muniments of the Corporation of Kilkenny.' *Journal of the Royal Society of Antiquaries of Ireland* (formerly *Transactions of the Kilkenny Archaeological Society*) 1 (1849–51), 427–32.

– 'Memorials of the Family of Langton, of Kilkenny.' *Journal of the Royal Society of Antiquaries of Ireland* (formerly *The Journal of the Kilkenny and South-East of Ireland Archæological Society*) 8 (1864), 59–108.

Quinn, D.B. 'The Munster Plantation: Problems and Opportunities.' *Journal of the Cork Historical Society* 21 (1966), 19–40.

Rankin, S. 'The Music of the Medieval Liturgical Drama in France and in England.' PhD thesis, 2 vols, Cambridge, 1982.

Rastall, R. '"Alle Hefne Makyth Melody."' In Neuss, *Aspects of Early English Drama,* 1–12.

Rigg, A.G. 'The Red Book of Ossory.' *Medium Ævum* 46 (1977), 269–78.

– 'Walter of Wimborne, O.F.M.: An Anglo-Latin Poet of the Thirteenth Century.' *Mediæval Studies* 33 (1971), 371–8.

Roberts, M., ed. *Historical Studies II.* London, 1959.

Robinson, J.L. 'On the Ancient Deeds of the Parish of St. John, Dublin.' *Proceedings of the Royal Irish Academy* 33 (1916), 175–224.

Robinson, J.W. 'On the Evidence for Puppets in Late Medieval England.' *Theatre Survey* 14 (1973), 112–17.

Ronan, M.V. 'Religious Customs of Dublin Medieval Gilds.' *Irish Ecclesiastical Record*, 5th ser 26 (1925), 364–85.

– *The Reformation in Ireland under Elizabeth 1558–1580 (from Original Sources)*. London and New York, 1930.

Russell, P. 'The Sounds of Silence: The Growth of Cormac's Glossary.' *Cambridge Medieval and Celtic Studies* 15 (1988), 1–30.

Sanders, N., R. Southern, T.W. Craik, and L. Potter, eds. *The Revels History of Drama in English Volume II 1500–1576*. London and New York, 1980.

Scott, G.D. *The Stones of Bray*. Dublin, 1913.

Seymour, St.J.D. *Anglo-Irish Literature 1200–1582*. Cambridge, 1929.

Sharp, C.J. *The Sword Dances of Northern England, together with the Horn Dance of Abbots Bromley*. London, 1911–13.

Sharpe, R. *Medieval Irish Saints' Lives: An Introduction to Vitae Sanctorum Hiberniae*. Oxford, 1991.

Sheehan, A. 'Irish Towns in a Period of Change, 1558–1625.' In Brady and Gillespie, *Natives and Newcomers*, 93–119.

Sheingorn, P. *The Easter Sepulchre in England*. Kalamazoo, MI, 1987.

Simms, A. 'Medieval Dublin: A Topographical Analysis.' *Irish Geography* 12 (1979), 25–41.

Simms, K. 'Guesting and Feasting in Gaelic Ireland.' *Journal of the Royal Society of Antiquaries of Ireland* 108 (1978), 67–100.

– 'The Brehons of Later Medieval Ireland.' In Hogan and Osborough, *Brehons, Serjeants and Attorneys*, 51–76.

Simpson, P., and C.F. Bell, eds. *Designs by Inigo Jones for Masques and Plays at Court*. Oxford, 1924.

Smoldon, W.L. *The Music of the Medieval Church Dramas*. Oxford, 1980.

Southern, R. *The Medieval Theatre in the Round*. 2nd ed. London, 1975.

Southworth, J. *The English Medieval Minstrel*. Woodbridge, 1989.

Stalley, R. 'The Medieval Sculpture of Christ Church Cathedral, Dublin.' *Archaeologia* 106 (1979), 107–22.

Stevens, J. *Words and Music in the Middle Ages*. Cambridge, 1986.

Stevenson, A.H. 'James Shirley and the Actors at the First Irish Theater.' *Modern Philology* 40 (1942–3), 147–60.

– 'Shirley's Years in Ireland.' *Review of English Studies* 20 (1944), 19–28.

– 'Shirley's Publishers: The Partnership of Crooke and Cooke.' *The Library*, 4th ser, 25 (1944–5), 140–61.

Stewart, A. '"Ydolatricall Sodometrye": John Bale's Allegory.' *Medieval English Theatre* 15 (1993), 3–20.

Stockwell, La Tourette. *Dublin Theatres and Theatre Customs (1637–1820)*. Kingsport, TN, 1938.

Stokes, M. 'The Instruments of the Passion.' *Journal of the Royal Society of Antiquaries of Ireland* 28 (1898), 137–40.

Taylor, A. '"To Pley a Pagyn of þe Devyl": *Turpiloquium* and the *Scurrae* in Early Drama.' *Medieval English Theatre* 11 (1989), 162–74.

Taylor, J., and A.H. Nelson, eds. *Medieval English Drama*. Chicago and London, 1972.

Thurneysen, R. *Die irische Helden- und Königsage bis zum siebzehnten Jahrhundert*. Halle, 1921.

Turner, V.W. *The Ritual Process: Structure and Anti-structure*. Chicago and London, 1969.

Twycross, M. 'The Flemish Ommegang and Its Pageant Cars.' *Medieval English Theatre* 2 (1980), 15–41 and 80–98.

– '"Transvestism" in the Mystery Plays.' *Medieval English Theatre* 5 (1983), 123–80.

Twycross, M., ed. *Festive Drama*. Cambridge, 1996.

Twycross M., and S. Carpenter. 'Masks in Medieval English Theatre.' *Medieval English Theatre* 3 (1981), 7–44.

Walker, J.C. 'An Historical Essay on the Irish Stage.' *Transactions of the Royal Irish Academy* 2 (1788), 75–90.

– *Historical Memoirs of the Irish Bards*. Dublin, 1818.

Walls, K. 'The Dove on a Cord in the Chester Cycle's Noah's Flood.' *Theatre Notebook* 47 (1993), 42–7.

Walsh, J. 'Ireland Sixty Years Ago.' *Dublin University Magazine* (1843), 655–8.

Walsh, P. 'An Account of the Town of Galway.' *Journal of the Galway Archæological and Historical Society* 44 (1992), 47–118.

Warton, T. *History of English Poetry*. Ed. W.C. Hazlitt. 2nd ed. 3 vols. London, 1871.

Watt, J.A. *The Church in Medieval Ireland*. Dublin, 1972.

Watt, J.A., J.B. Morrall, and F.X. Martin, eds. *Medieval Studies presented to Aubrey Gwynn s.j.* Dublin, 1961.

Webb, J.J. *The Guilds of Dublin*. Dublin, 1929; repr. 1970.

Wedgwood, C.V. *Thomas Wentworth, First Earl of Strafford: 1593–1641. A Revaluation*. London, 1961.

Wertheim, A. 'The Presentation of James Shirley's "St. Patrick for Ireland" at the First Irish Playhouse.' *Notes and Queries* 212 (1967), 212–15.

Westfall, S.R. *Patrons and Performance: Early Tudor Household Revels*. Oxford, 1990.

Westlake, H.F. *The Parish Gilds of Medieval England*. London, 1919.

Wheeler, H.A., and M.J. Craig. *The Dublin City Churches of the Church of Ireland*. Dublin, 1948.

White, E. '"Bryngyng Forth of Saynt George": The St. George Celebrations in York.' *Medieval English Theatre* 3 (1981), 114–21.

Whitelock, D. R. McKitterick, and D. Dumville, eds. *Ireland in Early Medieval Europe*. Cambridge, 1982.

Wickham, G. *Early English Stages 1300 to 1660*, 2nd ed. 3 vols. London and New York, 1980–1.

Wilson, F.P. *The English Drama 1485–1585*. Ed. G.K. Hunter. Oxford, 1969.

Windisch, E. 'Ein mittelirisches Kunstgedicht über die Geburt des Königs Aed Sláne. Mit Beiträgen zur irischen Metrik.' *Königl. Sächs. Gesellschaft der Wissenschaften* 36 (1884), 191–243.

Wolf, W.D. 'Some New Facts and Conclusions about James Shirley: Residence and Religion.' *Notes and Queries* 226 (1982), 133–4.

Wood, D., ed. *Women in the Church*. Studies in Church History 27. Oxford, 1990.

Wright, S.K. 'Is the Ashmole Fragment a Remnant of a Saint's Play?' *Neophilologus* 75 (1991), 139–49.

Young, A.A. 'Plays and Players: The Latin Terms for Performance.' *Records of Early English Drama Newsletter* 9 (1984), 56–62.

Index

Cetharnach Uí Dhomnaill, 20, 30, 324n51,
332n116
Chadsey, David, 392n149
Chain Book, of Dublin Corporation, 91,
93–4, 97–9, 101, 103, 130, 132–3,
137, 146, 157, 367n138, 384n74,
385n98, 395n179
Challyner, John, 387n109
Chambers, E.K., 98–9
Chapel Royal, 416n30
Chappell, William, 263, 440n8
Charles I, king of England, 195, 202,
229–31, 243, 263–4, 308, 409n12,
424n103, 426n120, 430n151, 444n67,
447n89
Charles II, king of England, 264
Charles V, king of France, 20
charter of incorporation of 1548. *See under*
Dublin
Chaucer, Geoffrey, 80, 82; *The Miller's
Tale,* 80
Cheshire, 448n4
Chester, 95–7, 125, 128, 158, 252, 359nn76,
78, 367n143, 368nn144, 153, 370nn172,
178, 372n206, 378n17, 379n25,
391n143, 398n26, 399n44, 405n105,
436n226, 448n4. *See also* Noah's Flood,
Chester play of; *and under* Corpus
Christi
Chester Cathedral, 437n234
Chetwood, W.R., 225–6, 263–4, 269,
422n85, 440nn12, 22; *A General History
of the Stage,* 263
Chichele, Henry, archbishop of Canterbury,
449n6
Chichester, Sir Arthur, 227, 232, 400n48,
423n98, 426n123
Chichester, Sir Arthur, first earl of Donegall,
426n123
children, appearing in masques and plays,

156, 178, 181, 187, 393–4n163, 403n84,
423n101
Christ Church Cathedral, Dublin, 62–4,
68, 75, 77–8, 80, 82, 90, 108, 133–4,
141, 143, 149, 159, 197, 218–19, 224,
242, 256–8, 284–5, 379n29, 383nn66,
68, 388nn114–15, 389n120, 390n136,
395n181, 419nn54, 60, 422n82,
436nn225, 228, 437nn228–30, 234–5,
448n4, 449nn7, 11, 450n12; prior of,
136, 152. *See also* de Derby, Stephen;
de Lokynton, Robert; *and under* Augustinian canons
Christ Church Cathedral, Waterford, 305
Christ Church meadow, Dublin, 96, 107
Christ Church Place, Dublin, 107
Christmas plays, at Trinity College, Dublin.
See under Trinity College, Dublin
Christmas revels, at Gray's Inn, London,
226
Christmastide plays of 1528, Dublin. *See
under* Hoggen Green, Dublin
Chronicle of Ireland. See under Hanmer,
Meredith
chroniclers. *See senchaid*
*Chronicles of England, Scotlande, and Irelande.
See under* Holinshed, Raphael
church dramas, in Dublin, 62–80
churches, as venues for plays, 249–50. *See
also* church dramas, in Dublin
Churchyard, Thomas, 211, 409n9, 414n19
Cirencester, 123
city musicians. *See* waits and city musicians
civic charter, of Kilkenny, 176
civic entries, 7–8, 197–205, 280, 304–9,
405n106, 408n3
cladiri, 12
Clanricarde, marquis of, 346n216
Claracilla. See under Killigrew, Sir Thomas
clarions. *See* trumpets and trumpeters